FINANCIAL
ACCOUNTING
A · N · D
REPORTING

FINANCIAL ACCOUNTING

A · N · D

REPORTING

First Canadian Edition

BRYAN J. AUSTIN
University of Regina

MARK E. HASKINS
University of Virginia

KENNETH R. FERRIS
Thunderbird, American School of International Management

ROBERT J. SACK
University of Virginia

BRANDT R. ALLEN
University of Virginia

Represented in Canada by:
McGraw-Hill Ryerson Limited

IRWIN

Toronto ■ Chicago ■ New York ■ Auckland ■ Bogotá ■ Boston ■ Buenos Aires
Caracas ■ Lisbon ■ London ■ Madrid ■ Mexico ■ Milan ■ New Delhi
San Juan ■ Singapore ■ Sydney ■ Tokyo

McGraw-Hill

A Division of The McGraw·Hill Companies

FINANCIAL ACCOUNTING AND REPORTING

1 2 3 4 5 6 7 8 9 0 VH VH 9 0 9 8 7 6

ISBN 0-256-18993-5

Publisher: *Roderick T. Banister*
Developmental editor: *Sabira H. Charlesworth*
Project supervisor: *Karen J. Nelson*
Production supervisor: *Pat Frederickson*
Cover designer: *Michael Warrell*
Prepress buyer: *Jon Christopher*
Compositor: *Shepard Poorman Communications Corp.*
Typeface: *10.5/12 Times Roman*
Printer: *Von Hoffmann Press, Inc.*

Library of Congress Catalog number 96-60970

http://www.mhcollege.com

To Judy, Jennifer, Barbara and Michelle

PREFACE

STATEMENT OF PURPOSE

An article titled "18,000,000 Books Nobody Reads" cited corporate annual reports as very low in interest, clarity, and understandability. This text's primary objective is to confront this problem by developing future managers' financial-statement literacy and to do so in a way that is firmly grounded in the issues of modern business concerns. The literacy objective incorporates the abilities to (1) understand the nature of business transactions, (2) identify relevant economic events for reporting, (3) determine the most appropriate financial measures for those events, and (4) analyze the effects of those events on firm performance and financial condition. To this end, an underlying theme of the text is that accounting is not divorced from the world it describes or from the behaviours it measures and influences.

Philosophically, we believe that an introductory accounting text does not need to explore every nuance of accounting practice and thought. Rather, the most important and predominant contemporary and classical accounting conventions are our foci. In this regard, the goal is to expose and discuss the underlying rationales of those practices and evaluate their effectiveness in providing useful information for decision making. Foremost among the practices investigated are those that purport to portray corporate financial position, operating results, cash flows, manager performance, and financial strength.

Even though the rule orientation of accounting practice cannot be ignored, both the classroom and the boardroom are appropriate places for questioning and debating those rules and conventions. Such scrutiny is crucial because it is important for students to develop an understanding of the management choices that must be made regarding what information to report, how best to report it, when to do so, and where controls are needed to assure reliable and relevant reporting. A critical aspect of these choices, dealt with in this text, is a concern for (1) the characteristics of information that make it most useful for decision making; (2) the characteristics of decision makers that also influence the usefulness of information; and (3) the subsequent behaviour of managers, subordinates, and external constituencies that can be expected as a result of implementing certain reporting choices.

There are two reasons for our management/user approach. First, it allows us to deal comprehensively with a complex topic. Second, it helps the student retain a focus on concepts and ideas, rather than on procedures. This approach requires considerable discipline on the part of the student, to mentally delegate his or her time to an understanding of business issues and a mastery of the basic financial reporting concepts without becoming too preoccupied with accounting mechanics. Thus, this text is designed primarily for those courses and student groups where the focus is on a balance between the understanding and use of accounting information and its preparation. Provided with a backdrop of contemporary management and financial concerns, students will see that accounting is a significant part of the world it purports to portray, and that it is not an end in itself. On the contrary, students are provided the perspective that accounting information is a critical instrument in presenting a corporation's financial picture to important external constituencies. The raising of issues and concerns springing from this orientation facilitates a focus on substance and also frames the student's learning because they have the comfort of a more familiar general business context for thinking about the accounting issue at hand.

KEY FEATURES

Real world based.

The authors view accounting as an integral part of management decision making and financial analysis. Thus, accounting is not an end but a means to achieving relevant and reliable insights about business conditions, results, and opportunities. The book repeatedly grounds the discussion of accounting issues and methods in contexts of management decision making, financial analysis, management judgments and estimates, behavioural consequences, and/or the political arena, whichever context is most germane. Such an approach poses accounting as a vital, dynamic phenomenon rather than a sterile, procedural set of mechanics. To this end, the text contains several excerpts from annual reports that serve to highlight the realities of the issue at hand and to exemplify the fact that the financial reporting issues presented are pertinent to the day-to-day information concerns faced by real-world managers, lenders, investors, and financial-statement users in general.

Holistic business approach.

The book's managerial orientation frequently leverages the discussion of a particular topic via linkages with strategic and other functional area concerns typically encountered by managers. For example, receivables issues involve credit and collection policies in addition to the accounting issues.

Opportunities for student involvement.

The end-of-chapter materials provide opportunities for a well-rounded student experience. Discussion questions provide issues for thought and debate where "solutions" are well reasoned, integrated views as opposed to looking up the chapter paragraph that provides the answer. Problems are structured to provide ample opportunities for polishing one's procedural skills as well as for developing a feel for the differences in results when different methods, assumptions, and/or judgments are invoked. The cases provided real-world settings for exploring the usefulness of accounting information to decision makers who have different perspectives and purposes, come from different environments, and value different outcomes.

Group work and communication skills.

Many of the cases lend themselves to group assignments and/or classroom presentation and write-up. Instructors are presented with materials that provide degrees of freedom in this regard.

Key concepts and terms.

The language involved in financial reporting encompasses many new terms. Each time a key term is used in the text, it appears in bold type and is defined in the margin. In addition, a listing of key terms appears at the end of each chapter and an extensive glossary appears at the end of the text.

ORGANIZATION

This text consists of four major parts and is organized not unlike other texts in its basic sequencing. Do not, however, conclude that it is just like other texts. As has already been pointed out, the orientation taken toward topics, the emphasis placed on certain facets of the topics, and the integration within a larger context make this text distinctive.

Part I Overview of Accounting and Financial Statements

These introductory chapters provide the background for the entire text. In particular, the first chapter's presentation of the Maple Leaf Gardens, Limited annual report sets the financial reporting agenda and "creates the need to know." During its discussion, students realize that accounting quickly transcends the necessary but mundane concerns of a green-eye-shaded bookkeeper to encompass those of key managers interested in knowing, among other things, what has been achieved, identifying what remains to be done, monitoring and motivating people better, and efficiently, effectively, and inexpensively raising capital from external sources.

Using familiar business contexts, a variety of basic skills are developed in the Part I chapters. Paramount among the skills developed are (1) familiarity with the language of accounting; (2) an understanding of some of the fundamental concepts of accounting (e.g., accrual vs. cash, matching, historical costs, materiality) and of the process by which accounting standards are set; (3) preparation of balance sheets, income statements and the statement of changes in financial position; and (4) the double-entry method of recording transactions.

The objectives of these chapters are for students to become comfortable defining a user's information needs, report the most pertinent information in the most useful way, and interpret the story reflected by the information. The identification of the key assumptions underlying the information being reported, and consideration of the alternative interpretations is examined. Establishing such a process at a text's outset is important because students must continually consider such an array of issues in order to appreciate and understand the evolutionary nature of contemporary accounting practice.

Part II Measuring and Reporting Assets

The three chapters in this section of the text commence the introduction in detail to the financial statements elements. All three chapters draw heavily on the concepts, language, and concerns raised in Part I. Moreover, all three chapters integrate the Maple Leaf Gardens annual report presented in Chapter 1 into their discussions as well as utilizing other corporate annual report examples. Part II continues the emphasis placed on financial statement analysis introduced in Part I.

An explicit premise running through these three chapters is that management has a great deal of influence over the results presented. That is, the financial statements are discussed in such a way as to highlight the fact that they are a part of management's thinking as they make decisions throughout the years. We believe such an orientation is not only valid, but also ascribes a great deal of vitality to the statements because they are not merely a sterile codification process of numerous transactions whose total implications and results are not known until year-end.

The chapters in this part are centered on the theme of measuring, reporting, interpreting, and using financial information pertaining to assets. It is in these chapters that students really begin to see clearly and powerfully that accounting simply describes events and circumstances, and those descriptions are a joint product of certain official guidelines, and, more importantly, of the assumptions, actions, and judgments of managers. These chapters consider the financial reporting issues surrounding some of the daily and strategic concerns of managing assets. Moreover, they explore the tension between reporting the "most favourable" versus the "most realistic" picture.

As an example, the text and some of the end-of-chapter materials pertaining to temporary investments bring to light the issues of (1) distinguishing the relative merits of reporting historical costs versus current market values, and (2) dealing with the prescriptive nature of CICA Handbook rules. Both issues underlie much of financial reporting. In particular, the first issue is often viewed by the uninformed as a shortcoming of financial reporting. We believe students should be sensitive to the pros and cons of reporting costs and current values and should be able to identify situations where one of the other may be more appropriate. In regard to the second issue, students become acutely aware of the volatility that is possible in reported earnings if how things are to be reported is simply left to the discretion of management. They thus realize a need for constraining the discretion available to managers in reporting their companies' financial position and results of operations. This is not to say that the need for management judgments and the consequences of such decisions become less important; on the contrary, a thorough knowledge of official guidelines (constraints) is merely an important prerequisite to identifying viable reporting options, structuring business transactions compatibly with the most desirable ways of reporting them, and factoring into one's decisions the information needs of their interested constituencies.

Part III Measuring and Reporting Liabilities and Equity

The chapters in this part are centered on the theme of measuring, reporting, interpreting, and using financial information pertaining to liabilities and shareholders' equity.

Besides grounding an accounting issue in the context of a business decision or a user's information needs, the chapters also leverage students' understanding of other topics to help in their learning of particular financial reporting topics that may be new to them. For example, anticipating the potentially overwhelming nature of the bonds, mortgages, leases, pensions, and deferred income tax topics, the text builds on a thread common to all these topics and familiar to most management students at this point in their education--the present value of a stream of future cash flows. As each of these topics is introduced via this touchstone, the awesomeness of dealing with the technical aspects of their financial reporting requirements fades. In fact, for most students, the literacy threshold for these topics, which at the outset seemed unachievable, becomes reachable with the use of the present value perspective building block already familiar and mastered by most.

Part IV Understanding Financial Reports

This final section of the book provides students with some classical financial analysis tools and then challenges them to use those tools in conjunction with what they have learned about financial reporting to create a corporate "story" based on a company's annual report. The desire is for students to bring together financial reporting disclosures, managerial concerns, and user perspectives in such a way as to be able to fully flesh out (1) a corporate picture of financial strengths/weaknesses, and (2) an awareness of the extent to which reported results could have been different if other legitimate judgments, estimates, and methods had been invoked. In this same vein, students are introduced to the notion of "quality of earnings" and provided an orientation to some ways of thinking about the quality of a company's earnings. Emphasis is placed on the cash flow analysis using the statement of changes in financial position. Alternative accounting policies are summarized in Part IV.

SUPPLEMENTS

The *Study Guide* enables students to review text material and to test their understanding. The guide includes a summary of each chapter's highlights, and an abundance of questions and problems.

The *Solutions Manual* includes worked out solutions to the text's questions, problems, and cases. The *Solutions Transparencies* are acetate transparencies of solutions to selected problems and cases. They are presented in a large boldface type, for ease of viewing from a distance.

ACKNOWLEDGMENTS

The text in its present form would not have been possible without the contributions of the following faculty reviewers, who provided criticism and constructive suggestions:

Robert Schenk
Bishop's University

Dr. Ronald A. Davidson
Simon Fraser University

Gerald Cook
University of New Brunswick — Fredericton

Joan E.D. Conrod
Dalhousie University

Murray W. Hilton
University of Manitoba

Morton Nelson
Wilfrid Laurier University

Dr. Pamela Ritchie
University of New Brunswick — Fredericton

Don Lockwood
University of British Columbia

Darrell Herauf
Carleton University

Ray F. Carroll
Dalhousie University

Stuart Jones
University of Calgary

Catherine Seguin
University of Toronto

Leo Gallant
St. Francis Xavier University

Charlotte Heywood
Wilfrid Laurier University

Judy Cumby
Memorial University of Newfoundland

Jan Thatcher
Lakehead University

NOTE TO THE STUDENT

This text was created to provide you with a high-quality educational resource. As a publisher specializing in college texts for business and economics, our goal is to provide you with learning materials that will serve you well in your studies and throughout your career.

The educational process involves learning, retention, and the application of concepts and principles. You can accelerate your learning efforts by utilizing the features found in this text:

Key concepts and terms are located after the summary at the end of each chapter. The new concepts and terms are referenced with appropriate page numbers. These terms appear in colour when they are first mentioned in the text. A glossary of Key terms appears at the end of the text.

Comprehensive review problem with solution. Each chapter contains a comprehensive problem that will ask you to solve a problem associated with the chapter material. Solutions to these problems are presented at the end of the text.

Review and discussion questions foster a conceptual approach. Many are laid out in point/counterpoint structure and address ethical issues. Located at the end of the chapter, review and discussion questions employ several concepts at a time and expose you to the integration of several topics in a problem material environment.

Problems. A wide variety of assignment problems are included in each chapter. Instructors may select from a number of problems using either the user or preparer perspective.

Cases. Each chapter incorporates case problems designed to suit the individual chapter material.

In addition to the learning features presented in the text, you may wish to consider using the Study Guide. The Study Guide is designed to help you better your performance in the course. This supplement highlights key points in the text and provides you with assistance in mastering basic concepts. For each chapter, the guide includes the main focus and objectives, review of key ideas, and true/false, multiple choice, and matching questions. Solutions for all questions are included in the study guide. Check your local bookstore or ask the bookstore manager to place an order for you today.

We at Irwin/McGraw-Hill Ryerson Limited sincerely hope that this text will assist you in reaching your goals both now and in the future.

McGraw-Hill Ryerson Limited
College Division
300 Water Street
Whitby, Ontario L1N 9B6

CONTENTS

CHAPTER
3

Operating Activities: The Income Statement
and the Statement of Changes in Financial
Position 98

CHAPTER
4

The Accounting Process and Financial
Statement Analysis 150

**CHAPTER
5**

**Accrual Basis of Accounting: Revenue
Recognition 214**

**PART
II**

**CHAPTER
6**

**Cash, Temporary Investments, and
Receivables 272**

**CHAPTER
7**

Inventories and Cost of Goods Sold 328

CHAPTER
10

Leases, Pensions, and Deferred Income Taxes 486

CHAPTER
11

Accounting for Equity 521

------------------ **PART** ------------------
IV

Understanding Financial Reports 565

——

CHAPTER
12

**Analyzing and Interpreting Financial
Statements 566**

——

PART I

Overview of Accounting and Financial Statements

An Introduction to Accounting: The Language, Financial Reporting, and Generally Accepted Accounting Principles

Outline

Objectives

After completing this chapter, you will be able to:
1. Distinguish between preparers and users of financial reports.
2. Discuss management's and the auditor's responsibility in the financial reporting process.
3. Identify and discuss the basic financial statements.
4. Describe different accounting entities.
5. Describe generally accepted accounting principles.
6. Explain the flexibility of generally accepted accounting principles.
7. Discuss the role of ethics in accounting.

1.1 WHAT IS ACCOUNTING?

Accounting as a Language

Most people have preconceived ideas about accounting. Many associate accounting with the different forms of business organizations. However, accounting is used by all organizations, large or small, profit or non-profit. One formal definition of *accounting* is: Accounting is the *art* of recording, summarizing, and analyzing financial information about an economic unit. A simpler definition of *accounting* describes accounting as a *language*. This language is used to communicate the financial position of an organization. The financial statement is the vehicle used to communicate the language of accounting. Similar to other languages, accounting follows certain conventions and applies certain concepts. Users of financial statements must understand the language of accounting to better understand the story conveyed by an organization's financial statements. The primary objective of this book is to help you understand those concepts and conventions, and consequently become literate and conversant in the language of accounting and develop a sound understanding of financial reports.

stakeholder
A stakeholder is any party that has an interest in the financial operations of the organization.

Organizations use accounting to communicate with interested stakeholders *both* inside and outside a company. A **stakeholder** is any party that has an interest in the financial operations of the organization. Within a company, managers use accounting to communicate the organization's results to those senior managers who have overall responsibility and to those line managers who have day-to-day operational responsibilities. This internal accounting communication serves two principal purposes. First, it describes the effectiveness with which the various levels of management exercise their custodianship or **stewardship** of the company's resources. Those responsible for overseeing the company want to know whether management deserves increased operating autonomy or requires more intense, critical scrutiny. More directly, incentive compensation schemes are often based on the stewardship results included in internal management reports — for example, should operating management be rewarded or reprimanded for this period's reported results? Second, accounting reports help management in making decisions that influence the enterprise's future operations. These decisions often focus on such questions as: Should the company increase its investment in plant and equipment? Should the company raise the price on its products? Should it try to reduce the cost of production? To answer these questions, and others, managers need relevant, reliable, and timely accounting information.

stewardship
The management and supervision of enterprise resources.

Organizations must also communicate financial results to stakeholders outside the organization. For example, managers need to communicate with current or potential investors, creditors, customers, suppliers, labour unions, consumer groups, and with municipal, provincial, and federal government agencies, such as the Revenue Canada Taxation. Again, accounting is the language by which these communications are made possible. These outside parties use accounting reports to evaluate the stewardship of top-level management and to make decisions about the company. These decisions often focus on such questions as: Should investors buy shares in the company or invest their resources in another company? Should creditors extend loans to the organization? Should an existing loan be called? If an investor decides to invest or a creditor decides to extend a loan, what price is appropriate for the shares, and what interest rate should be charged on the loan? How does the risk of an investment in this company compare with the risks involved in other available investment alternatives? Should labour negotiators push for increased employee benefits or agree to salary reductions? Accounting information serves a critical role in the deliberations of these external parties.

E X H I B I T 1 . 1

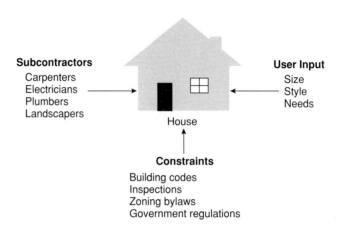

No language created has ever claimed perfect communication effectiveness. Although accounting has wide acceptance as *the* financial communication media, everyone who is involved with it acknowledges its limitations. In the following chapters, we will focus on the ways accounting is used, and also identify the areas in which accounting conventions remain inadequate. The notion of accounting as a language to be used as a communications vehicle and the importance of the issues that language endeavours to address raise important questions for managers. Every manager has the obligation to do the most effective job possible communicating the results of his or her business responsibility so that the most advantageous decisions can be made. To make that communication effective, managers must know how to make the best use of the available accounting conventions and, when necessary, develop supplemental communications. Managers often have a personal stake in the decisions that will be made regarding their company. That vested interest has the potential for a conflict of interest. All managers have an ethical obligation to use accounting in a way that describes objectively and fairly the results of their enterprises — regardless of the effect that communication may have on their personal well-being.

As previously mentioned, accounting should be considered more of an art than an absolute science. Individuals who have not studied accounting sometimes consider accounting a very precise science. They view financial reports as if they were prepared by a supreme being and therefore are not subject to question. The profession of accounting may be compared to that of architecture. The design of a building involves many specific requirements for structural soundness, but at the same time, most buildings have a significant artistic component. An architect carefully and artistically designs structures to meet the needs and desires of his or her clients. The architect coordinates the activities of several subcontractors or builders: carpenters, plumbers, electricians, and landscapers. The architect must design the structure within certain constraints: building codes, inspections, zoning bylaws, and government regulations. (See Exhibit 1.1.)

The role of the accountant is quite similar to that of an architect designing a building. The accountant must also coordinate the activities of different "subcontractors"

EXHIBIT 1.2

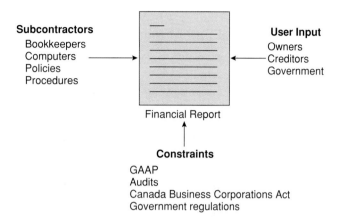

Accountant/Designer

Subcontractors
Bookkeepers
Computers
Policies
Procedures

Financial Report

User Input
Owners
Creditors
Government

Constraints
GAAP
Audits
Canada Business Corporations Act
Government regulations

of financial reports: bookkeepers, computer specialists, and company policies and procedures. The accountant must take into consideration the needs or objectives of the users of the financial report. Like the architect, the accountant must operate within certain constraints: generally accepted accounting principles (GAAP), audits, the Canada Business Corporations Act, and government regulations. (See Exhibit 1.2.) **Generally accepted accounting principles** are general and specific principles and concepts that provide guidelines for the preparation of financial statements.

A major objective of any introductory financial accounting course is to make students aware of the subjectivity and assumptions associated with financial reporting. Accounting is not an objective discipline with strict, hard-and-fast rules. Students should start to view accounting as less objective and scientific, and more of a *flexible* design function within sets of constraints and objectives from a variety of parties.

Preparers and Users

The definition of *accounting* used previously was: Accounting is the *art* of recording, summarizing, and analyzing financial information about an economic unit. The accountant must be knowledgeable in all of these functions. The recording and summarizing activities are actually preparer or bookkeeping functions. As an architect oversees the activities and functions of plumbers and carpenters, the accountant must be familiar with the activities of bookkeepers or preparers. Managers, investors, creditors, and other users of financial reports are concerned with the analyzing function of accounting. A basic understanding of accounting requires a sound understanding of both the preparer's and user's perspective of accounting and financial reporting. Traditionally most accounting textbooks have emphasized the preparer/bookkeeper perspective. Unfortunately the preparer's perspective may lead to misconceptions about the discipline of accounting. Accounting is more than simply recording and summarizing financial information. The preparing or bookkeeping aspect of accounting is really only the starting process in communicating financial information about an economic unit. A sound understanding of the preparation function is beneficial to an overall

generally accepted accounting principles (GAAP) Those methods identified by authoritative bodies as being acceptable for use in the preparation of external accounting reports.

understanding of accounting. Chapter 4 examines the accounting process — the steps involved in the preparation of financial reports. However, the overall focus of this textbook is to examine accounting from the user's perspective, to provide a greater understanding of the language of accounting.

Financial and Managerial Accounting

For intracompany communications, managers usually establish accounting rules and conventions to be used solely in the company's *internal* reporting system. As a consequence, the reports produced by the internal reporting system can be tailored to the specific informational needs of a variety of different managers. For example, a production manager might need accounting information about the number and cost of units in production, and a sales manager might need information focusing on the selling price and quantities available for sale. Thus, the internal reporting system may produce a diverse set of accounting reports, each prepared to satisfy a particular informational need of an internal user. The rules and conventions that guide the internal reporting system can be designed by the managers themselves to suit their specific informational needs. This internal reporting system is commonly called **managerial accounting.**

managerial accounting
The accounting rules and conventions used in the preparation of internal accounting reports.

Although internal accounting reports may vary between companies, *external* accounting reports are more standardized. Because a dispersed audience with very different backgrounds read external accounting reports, it is obviously more efficient if all reporting organizations follow a somewhat uniform approach in preparing their external financial reports. Although some unique "dialects" are used in highly specialized industries, by and large, external financial reporting adheres to a common body of communication practices mutually accepted and established by the financial community. The rules and conventions that guide the public communication of financial results are referred to as *generally accepted accounting principles* or *GAAP,* and the process is commonly called **financial accounting.**

financial accounting
The accounting rules and conventions used in preparing external accounting reports.

1.2 FINANCIAL REPORTING

In spite of the very important role that GAAP play in the accounting communication process, GAAP alone report nothing — they are simply the media by which a company's financial activities can be measured and reported to the various interested constituencies. See Exhibit 1.3 for a diagram illustrating the process of preparing a

E X H I B I T   1 . 3

The Financial Reporting Process

Management's Responsibilities

Design, implement, and maintain	Determine how GAAP are to be applied	Review & sign off
Internal Control System	**Financial Reporting System**	**Financial Statements**
Test effectiveness (GAAS)	Evaluate application of GAAP	Express a professional opinion

Independent Auditor's Activities

EXHIBIT 1.4

Main Components of the Annual Report

1. Management's discussion and analysis.
2. Management's responsibility for financial reporting.
3. Auditors' report.
4. Financial statements.
5. Notes to financial statements.

---

internal control system
A system to assure that all transactions and all necessary judgments have been recognized and that they are classified and correctly described in the accounting records.

financial reporting system
A system to sort all of the transactions and judgments into similar or related groupings.

generally accepted auditing standards (GAAS)
Those auditing practices and procedures established by the CICA that are used to evaluate a company's accounting system and financial results.

management's discussion and analysis
The section of the annual report that includes an overview of the company's operations and financial position for the most recent accounting period.

company's financial statements. The process of preparing the financial statements flows left to right, through the centre of the diagram, subject to the control of management and the influence of the independent auditor.

Financial statements are nothing more than the summary of an organization's transactions and a wide variety of financial judgments made by management. Those transactions and judgments are subject to the organization's **internal control system,** which assures that all transactions and all necessary judgments have been recognized and that they are classified and correctly described in the accounting records. The **financial reporting system** sorts all of the transactions and judgments into similar or related groupings and then aggregates that input so that the summarized financial statements can be prepared. Moving through the centre of the diagram, the summarization of that data and its presentation in the financial statements follow the requirements of GAAP.

As suggested by the top portion of the diagram, the design and maintenance of an internal control system and the preparation of financial statements are the direct responsibilities of management. Management is responsible for maintaining a system of internal control that ensures that all transactions are recognized, all judgments are made, and the raw data are summarized and presented fairly. Management establishes the system and has internal auditors and other systems monitor its performance. External auditors evaluate the system of internal control and the financial reporting system. GAAS or **generally accepted auditing standards** provide the procedures and standards to be adhered to when completing the audit. At the culmination of the process, management evaluates the resulting financial statements to be sure that the end result makes good economic sense.

The focus of this text is the understanding of financial statements from a user's perspective. To facilitate the understanding of financial statements, the annual reports of publicly held companies contain many pages of discussion and comments on the financial statements. Many annual reports are 40 to 50 pages in length, with the financial statements comprising only 4 or 5 pages. The main components of a typical annual report are listed in Exhibit 1.4 and discussed in the remainder of this section.

Management's Discussion and Analysis

The **management's discussion and analysis** section of the annual report includes an overview of the company's operations and financial position for the most recent accounting period. Any special or unusual circumstances or events that may have impacted the financial statements are described. Comments on general economic conditions and the impact on the organization may be discussed. In this section of the annual report management presents information on the organization's different divisions, departments, product lines, and its domestic and international operations. Information is frequently presented in graphical format to facilitate the understanding of the financial information.

Management's Responsibility for Financial Reporting

Annual reports normally include a report from management and the board of directors that acknowledges its responsibilities for the fairness of the financial statements, and which asserts its discharge of those responsibilities. The management report for Imperial Oil Limited is shown below:

The accompanying consolidated financial statements and all information in this annual report are the responsibility of management. The financial statements have been prepared by management in accordance with generally accepted Canadian accounting principles and include certain estimates that reflect management's best judgments. Financial information contained throughout this annual report is consistent with these financial statements.

Management has developed and maintains an extensive system of internal control that provides reasonable assurance that all transactions are accurately recorded, that the financial statements realistically report the company's operating and financial results, and that the company's assets are safeguarded. The company's internal audit department reviews and evaluates the adequacy of and compliance with the company's internal controls. As well, it is the policy of this company to maintain the highest standard of ethics in all its activities.

Imperial's board of directors has approved the information contained in the financial statements. The board fulfils its responsibility regarding the financial statements mainly through its audit committee.

Price Waterhouse, an independent firm of chartered accountants, was appointed by a vote of shareholders at the company's last annual meeting to examine the consolidated financial statements and provide an independent professional opinion.

Corporate management has an obligation to make a full and fair disclosure of a company's financial affairs, and management uses the basic financial statements, supplemented with footnotes, to discharge that responsibility. The management report is a public acknowledgment of this responsibility by management; it is an assertion that the company's system of internal control is adequate and a pledge by top management that the presented data are fair, free from bias, and reliable.

Auditors' Report

Although management is responsible for preparing the financial statements and ensuring their overall fairness, the independent external auditor is responsible for testing the underlying accounting data and expressing an opinion as to the fairness of the resulting financial statements. For a number of reasons, management might have a vested interest in the financial picture that the statements portray, and because of the potential for a serious conflict of interest, the financial community has determined that it is useful to have an independent opinion as to the fairness of those statements. Many organizations engage an **independent auditor** to review the financial statements for fairness and consistency with GAAP.

independent auditor
A professionally trained individual whose responsibilities include the objective review of a company's financial statements.

An auditor's examination of a set of financial statements (typically referred to as an *audit*) is conducted according to generally accepted auditing standards (GAAS). These standards require the auditor to test the way the system processes routine transactions, to consider the appropriateness of the accounting methods used in individually material transactions, and to evaluate the application of GAAP in the company's financial statements. Because an audit relies on test samples of the company's transactions and financial statement accounts, an auditor is typically not held responsible for immaterial errors in the financial statements or for small frauds. But most courts have said that an auditor is responsible for finding *material* misstatements, whether they result from accounting errors or from management fraud.

auditor's report
A report by an independent auditor summarizing his or her findings with regard to the company's financial statements.

Based on their examination, independent auditors issue a report presenting an opinion as to the fairness of the financial statements prepared by management. The most important element of the **auditors' report** is the auditors' opinion. If all goes well, the auditor expresses the opinion that the financial statements *do* present fairly the company's financial condition and results of operations in accordance with generally accepted accounting principles. Obviously, the financial community expects to see such a positive opinion (referred to as an **unqualified opinion**) in every company's financial statements. Occasionally, an auditor finds it necessary to issue an opinion indicating that some portions of the financial statement do *not* fairly present the company's financial condition and results of operations in accordance with GAAP for one reason or another (referred to as a **qualified opinion**). However, the power of the public's expectations is typically so great that most managers work diligently to avoid a financial reporting dispute with their independent auditors. The auditors' report of Imperial Oil Limited is shown below:

To the Shareholders of Imperial Oil Limited

We have audited the consolidated statements of earnings and of cash flows of Imperial Oil Limited for each of the three years in the period ended December 31, 1995, and the consolidated balance sheets as at December 31, 1994 and 1993. These financial statements are the responsibility of the company's management. Our responsibility is to express an opinion on these financial statements based on our audits.

We conducted our audits in accordance with generally accepted auditing standards. Those standards require that we plan and perform an audit to obtain reasonable assurance that the financial statements are free of material misstatement. An audit includes examining, on a test basis, evidence supporting the amounts and disclosures in the financial statements. An audit also includes assessing the accounting principles used and significant estimates made by management, as well as evaluating the overall financial statement presentation.

In our opinion, these consolidated financial statements present fairly, in all material respects, the results of operations and cash flows of the company for each of the three years in the period ended December 31, 1995, and its financial position as at December 31, 1995, and 1994, in accordance with generally accepted accounting principles in Canada.

The auditors' report of Price Waterhouse, independent public accountants, follows the standard, three-paragraph approach recommended by the accounting profession and that the financial community has come to expect. The first paragraph of the report is a statement of the scope of the audit examination and a brief statement differentiating management's responsibilities for the financial statements from those of the independent auditor. The second paragraph states whether or not the audit was performed in accordance with generally accepted auditing standards. It also briefly explains what an audit entails and emphasizes the auditors' role in investigating possible material misstatements of the financial statements. The third paragraph is a statement of opinion as to whether the company's financial condition and results of operations have been reported "fairly, in all material respects . . . in conformity with generally accepted accounting principles." The opinion expressed by Imperial Oil's independent public accountant is the standard "clean" or unqualified opinion.

Financial Statements

"Financial statements of profit oriented enterprises normally include a balance sheet, income statement, statement of retained earnings and the statement of changes in financial position. Financial statements of non-profit organizations normally include a balance sheet and other statements that are similar to those of profit oriented enterprises except that the titles and format of the individual statements may be different according to the nature of the organization" (CICA Handbook 1000.04). The annual report may also contain schedules and additional supplemental financial information for the past 5 to 10 years. This longer term financial data is provided to assist the user with trend analysis. The next section provides examples of these statements and a discussion of their elements.

unqualified opinion When an auditor expresses the opinion that the financial statements do present fairly the company's financial condition and results of operations in accordance with generally accepted accounting principles.

qualified opinion An opinion issued by an independent auditor indicating that the financial statements of a company are fairly presented on a consistent basis and use generally accepted accounting principles, but for which some concern or exception has been noted.

Notes to Financial Statements

notes to financial statements
Notes to the financial statements are explanations and supporting schedules to which the financial statements are cross-referenced.

investing activities
The acquiring long-lived, noncurrent assets.

financing activities
The activity of funding the organization by issuing long-term liabilities or equity.

operating activities
The day to day functions of the organization, of earning revenue and incurring expenses.

balance sheet
An accounting statement describing, as of a specific date, the assets, liabilities, and equity of an enterprise.

income statement
An accounting statement describing the revenues earned and expenses incurred by an enterprise for a given period.

statement of changes in financial position
An accounting statement describing the sources and uses of cash flows for an enterprise for a given period.

"**Notes to the financial statements** and supporting schedules to which the financial statements are cross-referenced are an integral part of such statements" (CICA Handbook 1000.04). All notes should be thoroughly examined by the user. The preparation of financial statements involves several decisions, estimates, and assumptions. The notes to the financial statements describe the accounting procedures and policies selected by management in the preparation of the financial statements. In most cases the footnote section of the annual report is longer and more detailed than the formal financial statements. The footnote section typically provides additional financial information in the form of schedules and summaries. Section 1.9 presents the annual report of Maple Leaf Gardens, Limited, including its notes to financial statements.

1.3 FINANCIAL STATEMENTS

Investing, Financing, and Operating Activities

Organizations are involved in three basic economic activities: investing, financing, and operating. **Investing** is the activity of acquiring long-lived, non-current assets such as property, plant, and equipment. **Financing** is the activity of funding the organization by issuing long-term debt or other non-current liabilities or equity funding received from the owners of the organization. When an organization is created, a number of financing and investing activities are necessary to get it up and running. Once the organization is established, it may commence operating activities. **Operating** activities involve the day-to-day functions of the organization. For example, if the organization is a fast food restaurant, the primary activities may be selling burgers and fries. In accounting terms, operating activities involve earning revenues and incurring the related expenses. As many operating activities may not require the immediate exchange of cash, operating activities also involve receivables and payables and other current assets and liabilities. The results of investing and financing activities are displayed on the **balance sheet.** Operating activities for the period are summarized on the operating statement or **income statement. The statement of changes in financial position** or cash flow statement discloses the impact on cash as a result of all three activities: investing, financing, and operating. The relationships among the economic activities of the organization and the financial statements are summarized in Exhibit 1.5.

Elements of Financial Statements

The elements of financial statements are the most common items portrayed in financial reports. The elements may be placed in two categories: those that describe the economic resources, obligations, and equity at a particular point in time, and those that describe the *changes* in economic resources, obligations, and equity over a particular time period.

The balance sheet describes the financial position of the organization at a specific point in time. It is sometimes described as a "snapshot" of the organization. The three main components of the balance sheet are assets, liabilities, and equity.

"**Assets** are the economic resources controlled by an entity as a result of past transactions or events from which *future* economic benefits may be obtained" (CICA Handbook 1000.29). Examples of assets are cash, accounts receivable, investments, land, buildings, equipment, vehicles, natural resources like gold mines or oil wells, and intangible items like trademarks, patents, and copyrights.

Relationships among Economic Activities and
Financial Statements

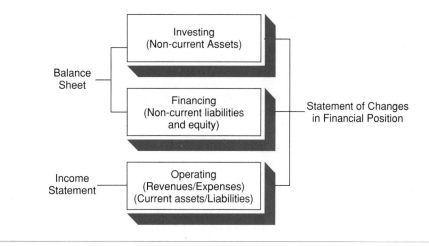

assets
Tangible and intangible resources of an enterprise that are expected to provide it future economic benefits.

liabilities
The dollar value of an enterprise's obligations to repay monies loaned to it, to pay for goods or services received by it.

equity
A claim against the assets of a company by the owners.

"**Liabilities** are obligations of an entity arising from past transactions or events, the settlement of which may result in the transfer or use of assets, provision of services, or other yielding of economic benefits in the future" (CICA Handbook 1000.32). Examples of liabilities are accounts payable, taxes payable, mortgages, and bonds payable.

"**Equity** is the ownership interest in the assets of a profit oriented enterprise after deducting its liabilities" (CICA Handbook 1000.35). Equity or net assets is a residual of assets less liabilities. Equity comprises two elements: the capital that has been contributed by the owners and the capital that has been earned by the organization. Assets, liabilities, and equity are disclosed on the balance sheet.

The balance sheet summarizes the results of investing and financing activities at the end of the period. A balance sheet is illustrated below:

CANUCK COMPANY
Balance Sheet
At December 31

Assets		Liabilities	
Current assets:		Current liabilities:	
Cash	$ 5,000	Accounts payable	$ 8,000
Accounts receivable	9,000	Wages payable	5,000
Inventory	16,000	Income taxes payable	4,000
Total current assets	$30,000	Total current liabilities	$17,000
Capital assets:		Long-term liabilities:	
Equipment	$20,000	Loan payable	10,000
Accumulated amortization	(2,000)	Total liabilities	$27,000
	$18,000	**Shareholders' equity**	
		Share capital	$15,000
		Retained earnings*	6,000
		Total equity	$21,000
Total assets	$48,000		$48,000

*Net income of 7,000 less dividends of 1,000.

contributed capital
The sum of the share capital accounts.

retained earnings
Those earnings of an enterprise that have been retained in the enterprise.

revenues
The inflow of assets, the reduction in liabilities, or both, from transactions involving an enterprise's principal business activity (e.g., sales of products or services).

expense
An outflow of assets, an increase in liabilities, or both, from transactions involving an enterprise's principal business activity (e.g., sales of products or services).

gain
An increase in asset values, unrelated to the principal revenue-producing activity of a business.

loss
The excess of expenses over revenues for a single transaction. Losses are decreases in equity/net assets from peripheral or incidental transactions.

net income
The difference between the aggregate revenues and aggregate expenses of an enterprise for a given accounting period.

Equity comprises two distinct elements: **contributed capital** and **retained earnings.** Contributed capital represents the resources contributed by the owners of the organization. Retained earnings is the cumulative net income/loss of the organization net of any distribution of resources to the owners. The total owners' equity is displayed on the end of period balance sheet. The income statement describes the results of the organization's operating activities for a given time period: month, quarter of year, or year. The two main components of the income statement are revenues and expenses. "**Revenues** are increases in economic resources, either by way of inflows or enhancements of assets or reductions of liabilities, resulting from the ordinary activities of an entity. Revenues of entities normally arise from the sale of goods, the rendering of services or the use by others of entity resources yielding rent, interest, royalties or dividends" (CICA Handbook 1000.37). "**Expenses** are decreases in economic resources, either by way of outflows or reductions of assets or incurrences of liabilities, resulting from the revenue generating or service providing activities" (CICA Handbook 1000.38).

"**Gains** are increases in equity/net assets from peripheral or incidental transactions and events affecting an entity" (CICA Handbook 1000.39). "**Losses** are decreases in equity/net assets from peripheral or incidental transactions and events affecting an entity" (CICA Handbook 1000.40). The disposal of long-term assets typically results in the recognition of a gain or loss on disposal. Revenues, expenses, gains, and losses are disclosed on the income statement.

The income statement summarizes the operating activities for the period. An income statement is illustrated below:

CANUCK COMPANY
Income Statement
For the Period Ending December 31

Sales		$98,000
Cost of sales		53,000
Gross profit		$45,000
Rent expense	$ 6,000	
Wage expense	19,000	
Utility expense	5,000	
Interest expense	1,000	
Amortization expense	2,000	33,000
Income before taxes		$12,000
Income tax expense		5,000
Net income		$ 7,000

If revenues exceed expenses, a **net income** has been earned by the organization. If expenses exceed revenues, a **net loss** has been incurred. The term *net income/loss* is appropriate for profit-oriented organizations. Non-profit organizations commonly use the term **excess of revenues over expenses** in lieu of net income. The net income of the organization is transferred to the equity section of the balance sheet.

The statement of changes in financial position describes the changes in cash for a given time period: month, quarter of year, or year. Increases and decreases in cash result from investing, financing, and operating activities. Investing relates to the acquisition and disposal of non-current assets. Financing involves non-current liabilities and owners' equity. Operating activities include the net income/loss and current assets and liabilities. A statement of changes in financial position is shown below:

net loss
A net loss is incurred when aggregate expenses exceed aggregate revenues.

excess of revenues over expenses
Non-profit organizations commonly use the terminology excess of revenues over expenses in lieu of net income.

CANUCK COMPANY
Statement of Changes in Financial Position
For the Period Ending December 31

Operating activities:		
Net income	$ 7,000	
Items not involving cash:		
Amortization	2,000	
Change in working capital items:		
Accounts payable	8,000	
Accounts receivable	(9,000)	
Inventory	(16,000)	
Wages payable	5,000	
Income taxes payable	4,000	$ 1,000
Investing activities:		
Equipment purchase		(20,000)
Financing activities:		
Long-term loan	$10,000	
Share capital issued	15,000	
Dividends paid	(1,000)	24,000
Increase in cash		$ 5,000
Cash — January 1		0
Cash — December 31		$ 5,000

The ending cash balance is also disclosed on the balance sheet as an asset. Financial reports are the vehicle used to communicate the language of accounting. Each of the financial statements will be examined in detail in later chapters.

historical cost concept
An accounting concept that stipulates that all economic transactions should be recorded using the dollar value incurred at the time of the transaction.

fair value basis
Fair value basis may be the replacement cost, net realizable value or present value.

accrual basis of accounting
An accounting measurement system that records the financial effects of transactions when a business transaction occurs without regard to the timing of the cash effects of the transaction.

Recognition and Measurement Criteria

"Recognition is the process of including an item in the financial statements of an entity" (CICA Handbook 1000.41). Recognition consists of two elements: an amount and a description (e.g., equipment of $20,000, or sales of $98,000). "Measurement is the process of determining the amount at which an item is recognized in the financial statements. Financial statements are prepared primarily using the **historical cost** basis of measurement whereby transactions and events are recognized in financial statements at the amount of cash or cash equivalents paid or received or the fair value ascribed to them when they took place" (CICA Handbook 1000.53).

Historical cost can objectively be verified by supporting documentation like a sales invoice or cancelled cheque. The equipment disclosed on the Canuck Company balance sheet is recorded at its historical cost of $20,000. Historical cost is the most frequently used measurement method. **Fair value basis** may be the replacement cost, net realizable value, or present value. Replacement cost is the amount needed to currently acquire an *equivalent* asset. Net realizable value is the amount received from selling an asset, less any disposal costs. Present value is the discounted amount of future cash flows expected from an asset or required to settle a liability. The fair value or market value basis of measurement is *subjective.* Some resources, such as Canuck Company's inventory, may have a replacement cost or fair value that is easily determinable. For other assets the determination of a market value may be very difficult. Therefore, the use of fair values occurs infrequently. The historical cost measurement method is used for most resources.

The **accrual basis of accounting** gives recognition to revenues and expenses in the period in which the transactions or events *occurred,* regardless of whether there has been a receipt or payment of cash or its equivalent. The sales figure of $98,000 for Canuck Company represents the dollar value of goods and services provided during the period. Some of these services would have been paid for in the current period; others will be paid for in subsequent periods. Similarly, the expenses of Canuck Company of $33,000 represent goods and services received and used during the period. As with sales, some of these services will have been paid for; others will be unpaid at the end of the period. Independent of cash flow, the accrual basis recognizes revenues and expenses. The accrual basis of accounting is strongly recommended for almost all organizations.

cash basis of accounting
An accounting measurement system that records the financial effects of business transactions when the underlying event has a cash effect.

The **cash basis of accounting** gives recognition *only* to revenues and expenses in the period in which cash has been paid or received. In today's society, the large majority of economic events are *not* conducted on a cash basis. Most economic events involve an exchange of goods or services in one period followed by an exchange of cash in a *subsequent* period. Therefore, the cash basis of accounting is *not* recommended for most organizations. The cash and accrual methods are covered in detail in Chapter 3.

1.4 ACCOUNTING ENTITIES

The definition of *accounting* mentioned earlier in this chapter made reference to reporting financial information for an *economic unit*. The term *economic unit* has been used to emphasize that *all* organizations, profit or non-profit, large or small, generate financial information. Although these organizations may be different in many ways, from an accounting perspective all organizations have several similarities. They all maintain bank accounts; they pay their employees salaries; and they provide goods and services to their customers or a specific client group. It may be argued that accounting *is* accounting, whether dealing with large corporate firms or small non-profits. We use a variety of different economic units throughout this text to illustrate different accounting concepts. It is recognized that many accounting differences exist among the wide variety of economic organizations found in modern society. However, many similarities *do* exist as well and we will compare and contrast these whenever possible. The illustration in Exhibit 1.6 displays the different economic units.

Proprietorships and Partnerships

proprietorship
A business enterprise owned by one person.

A **proprietorship** is simply a one-person business organization. Many small businesses are established as sole proprietorships. No special legal requirements are necessary for proprietorships. As a result, proprietorships are a common form of business entity. For legal purposes the individual owner and the business entity are viewed as one and the same. Should either the individual or the proprietorship encounter financial difficulties, assets of either may be legally attacked.

partnership
A business enterprise jointly owned by two or more persons.

A **partnership** is similar to a proprietorship except there are two or more owners. As with proprietorships, for legal purposes the individual partners and the business entity are viewed as one and the same. Therefore, the partners' personal assets may be legally attacked to resolve any financial problems encountered with the partnership. As with proprietorships, no special legal requirements are necessary to form a partnership. Partnerships are a common form of business entity. Accounting and legal firms are frequently established as partnerships. All partnerships should have a partnership agreement, preferably in writing. The partnership agreement should specify the basis

EXHIBIT 1.6

Economic Units and Accounting Entities

```
┌──────────────┐  ┌──────────────┐  ┌──────────────┐  ┌──────────────┐
│Proprietorships│  │ Partnerships │  │ Corporations │  │ Consolidated │
│              │  │              │  │              │  │corporate groups│
└──────────────┘  └──────────────┘  └──────────────┘  └──────────────┘

                    ┌──────────────────┐
                    │  Economic Unit   │
                    │------------------│
                    │ Accounting Entity│
                    └──────────────────┘

              ┌──────────────┐    ┌──────────────┐
              │  Non-profit  │    │  Government  │
              │organizations │    │    bodies    │
              └──────────────┘    └──────────────┘
```

on which the partners will be sharing profits and losses, and other financial matters related to the operating of the partnership. The partnership form of ownership is contrasted with the corporate form in Chapter 11, "Accounting for Equity."

Corporations and Consolidated Corporate Groups

corporation
A business enterprise owned by one or more owners, called shareholders, that has a legal identity separate and distinct from that of its owners.

consolidated corporate group
Business combinations that are created when one corporation gains control over another corporation.

non-profit organizations
Non-profit organizations include organizations as small as a church group, to the very large government units like the federal government of Canada.

Corporations are recognized as a *separate legal entity* distinct from its shareholders or owners. Legally, corporations may be established under either provincial or federal legislation. Corporations incorporating federally incorporate under the Canada Business Corporation Act, 1975. Some corporations prefer to incorporate provincially, although there is no significant difference between provincial and federal incorporation since most provincial incorporation acts are modelled after the Canada Business Corporation Act. The number of corporations in Canada is not large in comparison to the number of proprietorships and partnerships. However, corporations do comprise a significant portion of Canada's economic wealth.

Consolidated corporate groups or business combinations are created when one corporation gains control over another corporation. Business combinations allow organizations to diversify and expand their operations. Most large corporations are actually a combination of several companies combined for economic purposes. Consolidated corporate groups have a significant impact on the Canadian economy. The Hudson's Bay Company, through its retail divisions the Bay and Zellers, accounts for nearly 40 percent of Canadian department store sales. Many consolidated corporate groups operate worldwide. Moore Corporation Limited is a global corporation operating in 58 countries. They have more than 100 manufacturing facilities and 22,000 employees worldwide.

Non-Profit Organizations and Government Bodies

Accounting for **non-profit organizations** covers a very broad spectrum, from the small non-profit organizations like a church group, to the very large government units like the federal government of Canada. To simplify the classification, non-profits may be broken down into two broad groups: government bodies and other non-profits. For example, other non-profit organizations include organizations such as the Canadian Cancer Society, the Girl Guides, and amateur sport and cultural organizations.

government bodies include municipal, provincial and federal governments, including all their related sub units and departments.

Government bodies include municipal, provincial, and federal governments, including all their related subunits and departments. In addition to government bodies like the city of Lethbridge or the province of Ontario, government bodies include crown corporations, such as Canada Post, Canadian National Railways, or Sask Power. The government unit is the most distinct and unique of the different accounting entities described in this section. While the other entities have many similarities, government entities are quite different and encompass concepts and procedures covered in advanced financial accounting courses.

1.5 THE STANDARD-SETTING PROCESS

International Accounting Standards

The internationalization of economies has added another dimension to the accounting communications required of most organizations. If, for example, a company has debt or equity securities traded on the public exchanges of other countries, it will probably be required to prepare financial reports according to the GAAP and tax rules of those countries. Each major country has developed its own approach to creating financial accounting standards. As a consequence, although there is some uniformity, significant differences in these standards also exist worldwide. Participants in the international markets, however, have become impatient with those reporting differences and argue that they create impediments to the flow of capital between countries; the capital market regulators (e.g., the SEC in the United States) in the leading countries have also mandated that these reporting differences be reconciled. The task of harmonizing international accounting standards is very difficult and continues at a slow pace.

Standard Setting in the United States

The Financial Accounting Standards Board (FASB) was established in the United States in 1973. Board members are selected for their expertise in financial accounting and reporting without regard to their previous affiliations. The accounting standards issued by the FASB are accepted by the Securities and Exchange Commission (SEC) and the courts as meeting GAAP requirements for reports of companies with publicly traded securities. The American Institute of Certified Public Accountants (AICPA) has also resolved that the standards issued by the board are to represent GAAP for the general purpose, publicly distributed financial statements of privately held companies as well.

The pronouncements of the FASB influence GAAP in Canada. The Canadian approach tends to allow the professional accountant to use professional judgment to analyze the situation and make the appropriate decision for each particular situation.

The Accounting Profession in Canada

The Accounting profession in Canada consists of three national professional accounting bodies: the Canadian Institute of Chartered Accountants (CICA), the Society of Management Accountants of Canada (SMAC), and the Certified General Accountants

Association of Canada (CGAC). The professional accounting bodies are active participants in setting accounting standards in Canada. The professional bodies make significant contributions to accounting research and accounting education. Much of the accounting education in Canada takes place within the postsecondary institutions in the country. However, many accounting students continue their education by enrolling in one of the professional accounting programs.

Standard Setting in Canada

The Canadian Institute of Chartered Accountants (CICA) has the primary responsibility for the development of accounting standards in Canada. The CICA has established the Accounting Standards Board (ASB), comprised of members from the accounting professions and the financial community. The board normally consists of 13 voting members with a broad range of backgrounds and experience, including public accounting, industry, commerce and finance, and postsecondary education. In addition, consideration is given to persons in other occupations such as government service, law, and economics. The board reviews matters of accounting theory and practice, and with the written approval of at least two-thirds of its voting members, makes recommendations it considers to be of benefit to the public, including users, preparers, and auditors of financial information.

The ASB periodically commissions accounting research studies. The research studies are reviewed by the ASB and if the issue is significant, the research study is circulated widely for additional input and comments in the form of an exposure draft. After a specified time period the comments on the exposure draft are reviewed. The review may result in a reexposure draft and a repeated process. Ultimately, after due process, with the approval of the ASB the accounting proposals in the exposure draft may be added to the CICA Handbook.

CICA Handbook

CICA handbook
The CICA Handbook provides recommendations for the accounting of specific financial statement items.

The **CICA Handbook** provides recommendations for the accounting of specific financial statement items. The process by which accounting recommendations are added to the CICA Handbook is a function of the standard-setting process. The handbook is not a static document, as each year there are revisions and additions of accounting policies and procedures.

GAAP provide a number of alternative acceptable approaches to deal with particular financial reporting issues. The footnotes to the financial statements are typically used to describe the policies selected when the choice from those alternatives is important to a company's financial presentation and to a reader's understanding of the company's financial health. For example, the Ford Motor Company of Canada describes its accounting policies in a footnote as follows: " . . . The following is a summary of certain significant accounting policies followed in preparation of the consolidated financial statements. The policies conform to generally accepted accounting principles and have been applied on a consistent basis." The note goes on to describe the methods used for accounting for inventories, warranty costs, income taxes, fixed assets, and other significant policies. Such a footnote is an important element of an organization's annual report.

This flexibility in GAAP is sometimes frustrating to students because it means that there may be more than one acceptable answer to a question. But that flexibility is important to the working of the system. It provides an exciting challenge for managers

E X H I B I T 1 . 7

Generally Accepted Accounting Principles

Objectives of financial reporting	Useful, meaningful information for investing and credit decisions Information on future cash flows
Qualitative characteristics of accounting information	Understandability, relevance, reliability, comparability
Elements of financial statements	Assets, liabilities, equity/net assets Revenues, expenses, gains, losses
Recognition and measurement criteria	Asset/liability measurement — historical cost, fair value basis Revenue/expense recognition — cash basis, accrual method
Assumptions	Entity concept, periodic concept, going concern
Principles	Unit of measure, matching, consistency, disclosure
Constraints	Materiality, conservatism, industry practices, cost/benefit
Specific accounting policies, procedures, and rules	CICA Handbook

to make the best use of the potential power of the accounting language in communicating the essence of the business they have created.

Generally accepted accounting principles is the term used to describe the basis on which financial statements are normally prepared. Generally accepted accounting principles encompass not only specific rules, practices, and procedures relating to particular circumstances but also broad principles and conventions of general application. Exhibit 1.7, which summarizes GAAP, is provided to facilitate the learning of these important concepts.

1.6 GENERALLY ACCEPTED ACCOUNTING PRINCIPLES (GAAP)

All companies that have publicly traded debt or equity securities must issue financial statements prepared in accordance with generally accepted accounting principles (GAAP). As well, non-profit organizations and companies that are not publicly traded commonly issue their financial statements in accordance with GAAP. We say that financial statements "must" be prepared in accordance with GAAP because the requirement is both legal and pragmatic. The financial community has come to expect GAAP-based statements as the standard form of financial communication and is generally unwilling to invest the time and effort to understand a unique accounting language proposed by any one organization. The requirement is also a legal one — the courts have determined that companies with publicly traded securities must issue GAAP-based financial statements in order to comply with the financial statement–filing requirements of the provincial securities laws and the Canada Business Corporation Act.

EXHIBIT 1.8

Objectives of Financial Reporting

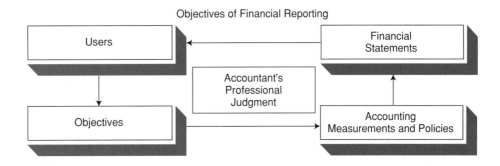

Objectives of Financial Reporting

Objectives of Financial Reporting

"The objective of financial statements is to communicate information that is useful to investors, members, contributors, creditors and other users ("users") in making their resource allocation decisions and/or assessing management's stewardship" (CICA Handbook 1000.15).

The objective of financial reporting may be viewed from a macro- or microperspective. From a broad, macroperspective the objective of financial reporting is to provide useful, meaningful information for investing and credit decisions, and information on future cash flows. The microperspective views the objective of financial reporting from the perspective of a particular user of the financial information. The objectives of financial reporting depend on who the users are. Users include owners or investors, lending agencies/creditors, directors, managers, employees/unions, government agencies, customers, and suppliers. The objectives of the users may include stewardship, cash flow prediction, and/or performance measurement. Exhibit 1.8 outlines a user's perspective of financial reporting and the influence particular users have on the financial reporting process.

The left side of the exhibit illustrates that an organization may have a number of different users of financial information with a variety of different uses or objectives. The right side of the exhibit illustrates that a number of different accounting measurements and policies are available when preparing financial reports. When issuing financial statements, the accountant must use professional judgment to select the accounting measurements and policies that are appropriate for the particular users and their related objectives.

professional judgement
The decision process to be used by the accountant to select the most appropriate alternative accounting approach to solve financial reporting issues.

Professional Judgment

Professional judgment relates to the decision process used by the accountant to select the most appropriate alternative accounting approach to solve financial reporting issues. The judgment process should have the following characteristics:

■ Be based on experience.
■ Be based on an understanding of relevant accounting standards.

- Involve consultation with other professionals as a means of broadening the sphere of experience.
- Be based on an understanding of the consequences the judgment has on the users of financial information.
- Be considerate of the objectives of financial reporting and the qualitative criteria of the financial information.

Qualitative Characteristics

qualitative characteristics
The attributes of information provided in financial statements that make that information useful to users.

"**Qualitative characteristics** define and describe the attributes of information provided in financial statements that make that information useful to users. The four principal qualitative characteristics are understandability, relevance, reliability and comparability" (CICA Handbook 1000.18). Sometimes conflicts between the criteria may exist. For example, conflicts develop when comparing the relevance of current costs to the reliability of historical costs. In such circumstances the accountant should use professional judgment to select the measurement method deemed most appropriate. A brief description of the qualitative characteristics follows.

understandability
The concept of understandability assumes information provided in financial statements must be capable of being understood by users.

The concept of **understandability** assumes information provided in financial statements is capable of being understood by users. "For the information provided in the financial statements to be useful, it must be capable of being understood by users. Users are assumed to have a reasonable understanding of business and economic activity and accounting, together with a willingness to study the information with reasonable diligence" (CICA Handbook 1000.19).

relevance concept
An accounting concept used to select which accounting information should be presented in a company's financial statements.

The principle of **relevance** states: "For the information in the financial statements to be useful, it must be relevant to the decisions made by the users. Information is relevant by its nature when it can influence the decisions of the users by helping them evaluate the financial impact of past, present or future transactions and events or confirm, or correct previous evaluations. Relevance is achieved through information that has predictive value or feedback value and by its timeliness" (CICA Handbook 1000.20).

reliability concept
An accounting concept that stipulates that accounting reports, must be reliable to be useful to financial statement users.

"For information provided in the financial statements to be useful, it must be reliable. Information is reliable when it is in agreement with the actual underlying transactions and events, the agreement is capable of independent verification and the information is reasonably free from error and bias. **Reliability** is achieved through representational faithfulness (substance over form), verifiability and neutrality (free from bias)" (CICA Handbook 1000.21). Reliability is also referred to as *objectivity. Objectivity* refers to information that can be objectively verified by reference to a specific document.

comparability
Comparability is a characteristic of the relationship between two pieces of information rather than of a particular piece of information by itself.

"**Comparability** is a characteristic of the relationship between two pieces of information rather than of a particular piece of information by itself. It enables users to identify similarities in and differences between information provided by two sets of financial statements. Comparability is important when comparing the financial statements of two different entities and when comparing the financial statements of the same entity over two periods or at two different points in time" (CICA Handbook 1000.22). It is generally thought information is more valuable when it can be compared to similar information. Therefore, financial statements should always be issued on a comparative basis (e.g., this year's financial data compared to last year's, as illustrated in the annual report of Maple Leaf Gardens, Limited, in Section 1.9).

Assumptions, Principles, and Constraints

The following is a brief description of the assumptions, principles, and constraints involved in the development of useful, meaningful financial statements. The concepts presented here will be reinforced throughout the later chapters with additional discussion and illustrations.

Financial statements include or encompass only the activities of a particular entity and any other entities that it controls. For example, typical published corporate financial statements include the legal parent company and all of the subsidiary companies it controls, but the statements do not include the activities of its diverse shareholders or its suppliers or customers. This convention is known as the **entity concept.**

entity concept
An accounting convention that views a corporate enterprise as separate and distinct from its owners.

The financial success or failure of any organization will not be known precisely until the end of the life of the organization. Users of financial information, shareholders or creditors, do not wish to wait until the organization is ending its economic life. The **periodic concept** assumes users need financial information for decision-making purposes on a periodic basis. Accounting reports are for *short time* periods, usually one year or less. The periodic concept requires the accruing of revenues and expenses and the allocating of costs to the appropriate time periods. The shorter the time period, the more difficult the allocation process becomes. The periodic concept requires the use of accrual basis of accounting. Many organizations select the calendar year as their time period for financial reporting. Other annual periods may be equally acceptable. Most organizations also prepare quarterly or monthly financial statements.

periodic concept
The periodic concept assumes users need financial information for decision making purposes on a periodic basis. The periodic concept requires the accruing of revenues and expenses and the allocating of costs to the appropriate time periods.

The **going concern concept** assumes the entity will not be liquidated, but will continue to pursue its objectives. "Financial statements are prepared on the assumption the entity is a going concern, meaning it will continue in operation for the foreseeable future and will be able to realize assets and discharge liabilities in the normal course of operations" (CICA Handbook 1000.58). The going concern concept assumes that an organization will, for example, sell merchandise inventory, collect accounts receivable, make payments on liabilities, or use assets in a normal fashion. The going concern assumption is an important concept in accounting that influences the valuation of the financial statements elements. If it is determined the organization is no longer a going concern, the financial statement elements should be valued on a liquidation basis. The annual report of Denison Mines, Limited, includes a note on the going concern concept:

going-concern concept
An accounting concept that assumes that the enterprise will continue its operations for the foreseeable future.

> The consolidated financial statements have been prepared on the basis of accounting policies applicable to a going concern. Accordingly, they do not give effect to adjustments that would be necessary should the Company not be able to continue as a going concern or be required to realize its assets and liquidate its liabilities in other than the ordinary course of business.

unit of measure
In Canada the unit of measure is the Canadian dollar.

In Canada the **unit of measure** is the Canadian dollar. Therefore, the economic activities of the organization are presented on the financial report in Canadian dollars. The use of money allows dissimilar items to be presented in financial statements on a comparative basis. It is assumed the monetary unit is a *stable* measuring unit, which does not increase or decrease in value or purchasing power. Unfortunately, currencies over time do *not* remain stable, and typically decrease in purchasing power over time. The result is financial reports being prepared with mixed measuring units. That is, financial statements are prepared using this year's dollars and with last year's dollars, and possibly some elements are measured in terms of 1980 or 1960 dollars. The dilemma of mixed dollar accounting has not been resolved by accountants. Many research studies have been completed, but the dilemma remains.

The **matching principle** states that expenses that are linked to revenue in a cause and effect relationship are normally matched with the revenue in the accounting period in which the revenue is recognized. In some instances expenses cause revenues to be earned. For example, most businesses incur advertising expenses. Management anticipates the advertising expense will cause customers to purchase the business's products, allowing revenue to be earned. On the other hand, earning revenue causes some expenses to be incurred. Revenues earned will cause income taxes, commissions, bonuses, and other expenses to be incurred. The challenge in financial reporting is to ensure all revenues and expenses are *matched* in the same accounting period. The matching principle is an important accounting principle that will be thoroughly examined and illustrated in later chapters.

The **consistency principle** requires organizations to use the same accounting concepts and policies from period to period. To enhance comparability an entity should use the same set of accounting principles from one accounting period to the next. However, situations may arise when a change is deemed appropriate and a means of improving financial reporting. When a change in accounting policy is deemed appropriate, disclosure of the change and the impact the change has on the financial statements is necessary to maintain comparability. Such changes are applied retroactively and the particulars of the change are disclosed in a note to the financial statements.

The **disclosure principle** states financial statements must disclose all of the relevant information about the economic affairs of the entity. The objective of the disclosure principle is to provide users of financial statements with sufficient information to make rational investment and credit decisions. Disclosure also implies providing understandable, comparable, timely information. It often requires the use of notes, schedules, and other supplementary presentations to complement the financial statements. Organizations should disclose their significant accounting policies in a note to the financial statements. An example of the disclosure principle is shown in a note from Canada's Sports Hall of Fame annual report.

> Economic dependence
> A major portion of the operations of the Sports Hall of Fame is funded by Federal Government grants and by the Board of Governors of Exhibition Place. The contributions from the Board of Governors of Exhibition Place consist of a cash grant of $129,500 and an amount equivalent to the cost of maintenance to the building of $9,678. In addition, the premises are provided at a nominal charge of $1 under a lease which is automatically renewed on an annual basis.

The **materiality principle** states "an item of information, or an aggregate of items, is material if it is probable that its omission or misstatement would influence or change a decision. Materiality is a matter of professional judgment in the particular circumstance" (CICA Handbook 1000.17). An item that is material in one instance may be immaterial in another. For example, $100,000 to a small business is very significant, but to a large international corporate group it is relatively insignificant. The principle of materiality does not mean that immaterial items should not be included in the financial report. The materiality principle means *strict adherence* to the related accounting policy is not required for immaterial items.

The **conservatism principle** states "when uncertainty exists, estimates of a conservative nature attempt to ensure that assets, revenues and gains are not overstated and, conversely, that liabilities, expenses and losses are not understated. However, conservatism does not encompass the deliberate understatement of assets, revenues and gains

---

matching principle
An accounting concept that stipulates that when revenues are reported, the expenses incurred to generate those revenues should be reported in the same accounting period.

consistency principle
An accounting concept that stipulates that an enterprise should, when possible, use the same set of GAAP from one accounting period to the next.

Disclosure principle
Must disclose all of the relevant information about the economic affairs of the entity to provide users of financial statements, sufficient information to make rational investment and credit decisions.

materiality principle
An accounting concept stipulates that only those transactions that might influence the decisions of a reasonable person should be disclosed in detail in the financial statements; all other information may be presented in summary format.

conservatism principle
An accounting concept that stipulates that when there is a choice between two approaches to record an economic event, the one that produces the least favourable yet realistic effect on net income or assets should be adopted.

or the deliberate overstatement of liabilities, expenses and losses" (CICA Handbook 1000.21). It is generally believed the users of financial reports are better served with information that *understates* income and assets than reports that overstate income and assets. Similarly, it is generally thought users' decisions are less hindered by the *overstatement* of liabilities and expenses than understatement. The conservatism principle states when two acceptable accounting policies are available, the policy providing the lowest income or asset value, or the highest liability or expense value, should be used. Accounting for investments illustrates the conservatism principle. The Arthritis Society included the following note in its annual report:

> Investments are recorded at cost. Should the market value of investments become lower than cost and this decline in value is considered to be other than temporary, the investments are written down to market value.

Accountants must be careful to ensure financial statements are not prepared in an ultraconservative format, keeping in mind the basic concept of providing users with useful, meaningful financial information.

industry practices
The concept that exceptions to general accounting principles and practices may be made in the financial statements of specialized industries, assuming such departure from GAAP provides more useful, meaningful information to the users.

The concept of **industry practices** states selective exceptions to general accounting principles and practices may be made in the financial statements of specialized industries, assuming such departure from GAAP provides *more* useful, meaningful information to the users. Specialized industries like banking, insurance, or utilities, because of their unique economic activities, have their own set of accounting practices and policies specific to their particular industry. Some industries are also subject to regulatory controls, regulated pricing policies, and restricted reporting practices. The Consumers' Gas Company, Ltd., included the following footnote in its annual report:

> The Company follows generally accepted accounting principles which are modified for certain accounting practices in its utility operations. Such modifications occur when the regulatory agencies exercise their statutory authority and render specific accounting and other rate making decisions, which generally involve the timing of revenue and expense recognition. In addition to defining certain accounting requirements, the regulatory agencies have jurisdiction over a number of other principal matters which include the rates to be charged for the sale and transportation of gas, approval for major construction and operations.

Even in specialized industries many accounting policies will be commonplace. Therefore, *exceptions* to generally accepted accounting principles should be made with *much caution*.

cost/benefit
The benefits expected to arise from providing information in the financial statements should exceed the cost of doing so.

The concept of **cost/benefit** states "the benefits expected to arise from providing information in the financial statements should exceed the cost of doing so. The nature and amount of benefits and costs is substantially a judgment process" (CICA Handbook 1000.16). Costs would involve data collection and preparation, and possibly the cost of providing too much information to competitors. Benefits would be the improved decision making of financial statements users.

1.7 GAAP ARE FLEXIBLE

Generally accepted accounting principles are flexible. That is not to say GAAP can be manipulated to meet the needs of the organization. However, users of financial information should be aware of the number of different accounting policies and procedures that are recognized as being generally accepted and used in practice. Exhibit 1.7 summarized the different broad and specific concepts known as GAAP. This exhibit may create the impression that GAAP are very rigid and fall nicely into specific groups or categories. The opposite is true — GAAP are *not* fixed or certain, and financial reports are not precise and exact. Users of financial information should realize a number of decisions, estimates, and predictions must be made to present useful, meaningful financial reports. It was previously mentioned that notes to the financial statements should be considered an integral part of the financial report. Most annual reports include as their first note a description of the accounting policies and procedures in use by the organization for the financial statements presented. Such is the case with the annual report of Maple Leaf Gardens, Limited, presented in Section 1.9 of this chapter.

Before we leave this introduction to GAAP, one final observation is in order: GAAP-based accounting is not so categorical and as rule oriented as it might seem on the surface. You should be beginning to realize that GAAP are *flexible*. It is true that some basic conventions and rules have been established through common usage or pronouncement and must be accepted as they are; however, as with any language, the application of GAAP provides for a surprising amount of latitude in the preparation of financial statements. That flexibility arises as a result of three factors. First, for some transactions, widely diverse accounting approaches had become entrenched as alternative GAAP long before the current standard-setting process was established, and so those *equally acceptable alternative* approaches remain in the "language." Second, the financial community continues to develop creative new business transactions, and until new standards are established (the standard-setting process can take a long time) diverse accounting approaches to those creative transactions will become accepted in practice. And, third, business transactions are complex and unique, and very often managers face a real challenge as they try to apply a broadly written, generalized financial reporting standard to their particular business events.

At this point, students may find the different accounting alternatives overwhelming. Complete understanding of the concepts and policies presented in this chapter should not be expected. The purpose of the chapter is to provide an overview of accounting and to illustrate the flexibility and decision-making process involved in the selection of appropriate accounting policies. These concepts will be examined in greater depth in later chapters. Two Flexibility of GAAP cases are presented to illustrate the assumptions and estimates that managers must make during the decision-making process of selecting alternative accounting policies and compiling information for the annual reports.

Flexibility of GAAP: Case 1

Tom, Dick, and Marry started a small business at the start of the current year. One of their first investments was to acquire a delivery van for $27,000 to be used for business purposes. During their weekly management meeting a discussion on the proper accounting for the van took place. Tom felt that since the van was paid for in cash and used all year, it should be recorded as an item used for $27,000. Dick argues that since the firm plans to use the van for at least three years, the cost should be allocated evenly over each year or at a rate of $9,000 per year. Marry says she is more optimistic and believes the van will last for at least five years, averaging a cost of only $5,400 per year. Another point of conversation was the fact that similar vans now cost $29,000. How should the van be accounted for? Provide comments on the different accounting treatments discussed above.

The accounting for a capital asset like the delivery van in Case 1 requires a number of decisions and estimates to be made by management. Capital assets should be recorded at their historical cost, in this case $27,000. The more recent price of $29,000 is not considered reliable, due to its subjectivity, and is not used. Tom argued that since the van had been paid for in cash, the total value of $27,000 should be written off. There are two important accounting concepts involved here. First, whether the van has been paid for in full or is financed over several years is not relevant. How the van is financed does not influence whether the van can be used or not. Second, the van will be used for more than one accounting period and its cost should be allocated over that same period and not all written off in its first year of operations. The key decision or estimate management must make is for how many accounting periods are they going to use the van — three, five, or possibly some other number? In addition, the van should still have some value after it has been used by the organization. This residual value must also be estimated. If the managers were to decide they will use the van for four years, after which it could be sold for $7,000, the cost to be allocated to each of the four years would be $5,000 ($27,000 − $7,000 = 20,000/4 years = $5,000).

Flexibility of GAAP: Case 2

Grey Enterprises, Limited, has been in operation for several years. An analysis of its accounting records reveals the following information about two different assets. The company has purchased merchandise inventory during the year. Most of the merchandise purchased during the year has been sold. However, a total of $37,000 of inventory remains on hand at the end of the accounting period. An examination reveals $6,000 of the inventory, which is either seriously damaged or obsolete. The second asset is the land on which the Grey Enterprises office resides. The accounting records indicate the land has a recorded value of $37,000. Last week, identical property across the street sold for $51,000. How should these assets be valued on Grey Enterprises Limited's financial statements?

Case 2 deals with the concept of measuring asset values, and the underlying constraint of the principle of conservatism. Grey Enterprises has two different assets — one has increased in value and one has decreased. Generally accepted accounting principles require assets to be valued at their historical cost. Therefore, even though there is an indication the value of the land may have increased, no increase in value should be recognized. The land is not measured at its fair market value because there is no strong objective evidence to support the market value. Such objectivity would only be available if the land were actually sold and an objective market value determined by the sales transaction. As well, if the increase in value of the land were to be recognized, a gain would need to be recognized, but since an economic event has not transpired, no gain should be realized. However, the inventory should be written down to a more realistic value. The inventory is currently overvalued in the financial records of Grey Enterprises and the principle of conservatism requires when an asset is overvalued its value should be reduced to a more realistic figure. The underlying principle in determining the value of both assets is that of conservatism. It is generally thought users are better served if asset values are understated rather than overstated. Therefore, the land value is not increased. Similarly, conservatism requires assets to not be overvalued and thus the value of the inventory should be reduced.

The preceding cases have discussed some of the basic principles of accounting. These concepts will become clearer as they are further discussed and illustrated throughout the text. It may be inappropriate to describe generally accepted accounting principles as flexible, but they are definitely not rigid. The user of financial statements should realize a high degree of *subjectivity* exists with the selection of accounting policies and procedures. To determine which accounting policies are appropriate in different circumstances requires management to use their professional judgment in the selection process, taking into consideration the impact the different alternatives may have on the financial statements, and any potential impact on the decisions of the financial statement users.

1.8 ETHICS IN ACCOUNTING

Ethics deals with determining what is right or wrong, good or bad. Society and individuals are faced with making morally correct decisions. Some behaviour is unlawful, while other actions, although within the law, are widely recognized as unethical behaviour. Individuals are faced with ethical decisions every day. The media is constantly scrutinizing public figures for their proper or unethical actions. How does ethics relate to management and specifically accounting?

Individuals develop their own standards of moral and ethical behaviour. The accounting profession plays a vital role in the generation and dissemination of financial information. To provide standards of acceptable behaviour the professional accounting bodies in Canada provide their memberships with guidelines for professional conduct. The Institute of Chartered Accountants, the Certified General Accountants Association, and the Society of Management Accountants have rules of professional conduct.

As discussed in the previous sections in this chapter, accountants are provided with a wide range of generally accepted accounting principles. The flexibility of GAAP provides many alternative accounting policies and procedures for financial reporting purposes. The decisions made by accountants selecting appropriate accounting policies affect the decisions of the users of financial reports. Therefore, on a daily basis accountants are faced with ethical considerations. Consider the ethical implications in the following example.

The accountant at Quality Manufacturing, Ltd., is in the process of completing the annual financial statements for the company. The company completed a reasonably successful year of operations, but not as successful as the board of directors expected. During the year, a new factory was constructed at a cost of $6,000,000. The new factory was financed on a short-term basis, and the company must arrange for long-term financing in the new year by issuing share capital or by obtaining a long-term loan. The company anticipated that the factory would operate at full capacity and produce high-quality products generating additional profits for the company. Production has been below optimum capacity and revenues from new products have been slow in developing. Industry practice is to allocate costs of manufacturing facilities over a relatively short period of five years. Historically the industry has experienced rapid and significant technological changes, causing major improvements to manufacturing facilities to be required every few years. At a meeting this morning, the president recommended the cost of the new factory be allocated over a 15-year period. The president was very frank about his rationale for suggesting the longer allocation period. His objective is for the company to disclose a high net income on its financial statement. A higher net income would please the board of directors, and facilitate the required long-term financing.

Estimating the useful life of long-term assets is one of the decisions faced by management and accountants. In this example, if the cost of the factory is allocated over five years, the annual cost would be $1,200,000 ($6,000,000/5 years). If the longer period of 15 years is selected, the annual cost would be only $400,000

($6,000,000/15 years). If the longer allocation period suggested by the president is used, net income for the period would increase by $800,000 ($1,200,000 – $400,000). What should the accountant do? As an ethical matter, the accountant should not be influenced by the fact one method presents a more favourable result over another. Therefore, it appears the president's suggestion is unreasonable. What if an allocation period of only 10 years is used? Would this be unethical? What about a period of six or seven years? Ethical decisions are personal decisions and ones that cannot always be made easily.

The preceding example is not uncommon. Accountants are faced with such decisions on an ongoing basis. The decision among alternative accounting policies may influence the financial decisions of users. Accountants must carefully consider the economic and ethical consequences of their decisions. As different accounting policies are discussed throughout the text, ethics in accounting cases are presented for discussion.

1.9 MAPLE LEAF GARDENS, LIMITED: AN ILLUSTRATION

The typical corporate annual report contains more than the basic financial statements and the related text. In some cases, portions of the annual report may be used for public relations, highlighting particular social or financial accomplishments of the company. Most companies devote considerable effort to the annual report, and it serves a multitude of purposes. Most of the information in corporate annual reports is interesting, telling us something about the company and its management and providing a context within which we can evaluate the company's financial health and prospects.

To focus our discussion and to illustrate the rules and conventions used in accounting, we will often refer to examples from *actual* financial statements. We have elected to use the annual report of Maple Leaf Gardens, Limited, as a central example.

Overall, the annual report contains an enormous quantity of financial information about the organization and its operations. Take a few moments to familiarize yourself with the general content of the annual financial report of Maple Leaf Gardens, Limited, presented in the following pages.

MAPLE LEAF GARDENS, LIMITED ANNUAL REPORT

MANAGEMENT'S DISCUSSION AND ANALYSIS

INTRODUCTION

The following comments and analysis on the current financial condition, results from operations and future prospects should be read in conjunction with the financial statements, the notes thereto and other information presented in the Corporation's annual report to shareholders and annual information form.

GENERAL

The Corporation is in the entertainment business in Canada through its ownership and operation of the Toronto Maple Leaf Hockey Club (the "Maple Leafs") and the arena facilities at 60 Carlton Street, Toronto, Ontario. It derives all of its operating income from these assets. Its revenues are derived primarily from four sources: (1) admission fees from Maple Leafs games, (2) broadcast, promotional and advertising rights, (3) building use fees and related revenues from other than Leafs games and (4) merchandising and food & beverage concession sales.

During 1994, the Corporation changed its year end to June 30 of each year from May 31. Consequently, the 1994 financial year consists of thirteen months. The change was effected so as to have a year end which incorporates a full hockey season, including playoffs. The new year end is also consistent with the year end of the National Hockey League ("N.H.L." or "League") and most of its member clubs.

OPERATING RESULTS
Analysis of Total Revenues

	1994 (13 months)	1993 (12 months)	$ Change	% Change
Ticket Sales (excluding playoffs)	$ 23,938,969	$ 20,617,953	$ 3,321,016	16.11%
Broadcast, Promotional & Advertising	15,387,659	14,283,924	1,103,735	7.73%
Private Boxes	6,307,187	5,599,727	707,460	12.63%
Food & Beverage	3,255,566	2,322,018	933,548	40.20%
Souvenirs	2,524,846	1,563,679	961,167	61.47%
Attractions	2,251,429	1,789,820	461,609	25.79%
Other	596,113	415,318	180,795	43.53%
Playoff Revenues	8,431,405	8,851,831	(420,426)	(4.75%)
Revenue from Operations	62,693,174	55,444,270	7,248,904	13.07%
Investment and Other Income	850,022	754,089	95,933	12.72%
Total Revenues	$ 63,543,196	$ 56,198,359	$ 7,344,837	13.07%

The increase in ticket sales during the regular season and pre-season over last year results from an overall average ticket price increase of 15.8%.

The net increase in Broadcast, Promotional & Advertising rights results from (a) increased revenues from Promotional & Advertising rights, including new advertising signage in Maple Leaf Gardens, in ice advertising and increased fees from existing contracts and (b) a decrease of approximately $180,000 in Broadcast revenues resulting from a decrease in the revenues from the N.H.L.'s U.S. transborder agreement.

The increase in private box revenues is mainly attributable to the change in year end and an increase in private box prices.

The increase in Food & Beverage sales results primarily from regular season alcoholic beverage sales increases of approximately $764,000 due to an entire season of sales. Alcoholic beverage sales started on January 30, 1993. The remainder of the Food & Beverages sales increase results from increased license fees from catering services.

Souvenir sales experienced another year of significant growth. The team's performance and improved product mix continues to drive sales, particularly through LeafSport, the retail merchandising outlet of the Corporation.

4

MAPLE LEAF GARDENS, LIMITED ANNUAL REPORT

Attraction revenues consist of building use fees, souvenir commission sales income, food and beverage sales, and other miscellaneous revenues in connection with other events and attractions. The revenues have increased due to an increase in the number of well attended live concerts and attractions for which tickets are sold, where the Corporation receives a licence fee based upon a percentage of net gate receipts.

In 1994, the Maple Leafs played nine home playoff games generating total additional revenues of $8,431,405, versus 11 home games and revenues of $8,851,831 in 1993. These revenues consist mainly of ticket sale revenues but also include other related revenue sources such as private box nightly rentals, food and beverage sales and souvenir sales.

Broadcast Rights

The Corporation derives significant revenues from broadcast rights to N.H.L. hockey games. In general, these consist of the right to broadcast regular season games of the Maple Leafs in the Toronto area, the right to block the broadcast of other N.H.L. games in the Toronto area on nights when the Maple Leafs are playing at home, and the right to sell a package of regular season home games in other markets besides Toronto (subject to the local rights of the other teams and subject to N.H.L. national television package rights).

The Corporation's revenues from broadcasting are derived from (a) an agreement between the Molson Breweries of Canada Limited ("Molson") whereby the Corporation granted to Molson all its broadcasting rights ("Molson Agreement") and (b) the Corporation's rights under N.H.L. broadcast agreements. These revenues amounted to $6,386,155 in 1994 and $6,602,482 in 1993. The Molson Agreement expires at the end of the 1994-95 season. See "Future Operations".

Subject to the local rights in respect to the Maple Leafs noted above, the N.H.L. controls the rights to broadcast two nights of hockey on a national basis, in both French and English, per market, per week by virtue of the 1988 Modified Member Club Agreement ("MMCA"). Pursuant to the MMCA, the N.H.L. has a new agreement with Molson for national network rights in Canada. This agreement expires at the end of the 1997-98 season and will result in additional revenues of approximately $500,000 in the 1994-95 season.

By virtue of the MMCA, the N.H.L. also has the rights to sell a national package of games to conventional cable broadcasters in the United States. In 1993, the N.H.L. entered into an agreement with ESPN, a U.S. cable service serving close to 61.5 million homes. The ESPN agreement is important for the exposure of the N.H.L. but does not constitute a material portion of the overall broadcasting revenues of the Corporation.

1975-1981
Darryl Sittler

Jim Thompson

Sid Smith

Ted Kennedy

Bob Davidson

Syl Apps

Red Horner

Charlie Conacher

Hap Day

Analysis of Operating Expenses
(including depreciation and amortization)

	1994 (13 months)	1993 (12 months)	$ Change	% Change
Hockey Operations	$ 34,482,261	$ 27,130,986	$ 7,351,275	27.10%
Building	7,664,524	7,160,666	503,858	7.04%
Finance & Administration	3,508,480	3,340,347	168,133	5.03%
Food & Beverage	2,472,603	2,318,908	153,695	6.63%
Souvenirs	1,803,384	1,363,177	440,207	32.29%
Marketing & Private Boxes	1,263,035	955,276	307,759	32.22%
Playoff Costs	4,624,355	4,979,373	(355,018)	(7.13%)
Total Operating Expenses	$ 55,818,642	$ 47,248,733	$ 8,569,909	18.14%

5

MAPLE LEAF GARDENS, LIMITED ANNUAL REPORT

**1969-1975
Dave Keon**

Doug Gilmour

Wendel Clark

Rob Ramage

Rick Vaive

Darryl Sittler

Dave Keon

George Armstrong

The increase in Hockey operation expenses is primarily due to an increase in players' remuneration, excluding playoff bonuses and awards, of $5,067,300. This includes contract buyouts of $1,840,935, ($983,877 in 1993).

Building costs and Finance & Administration expenses increased as a result of the change in year end.

Food & Beverage costs increased as a result of sales increases, an entire season of alcoholic beverage sales and because of increased labour costs associated with a newly unionized workforce.

The increase in Souvenir costs results primarily from an increase in the cost of souvenir sales of $539,418 due to the 61.5% increase in souvenir sales.

The increase in Marketing & Private Boxes costs is attributable to increases in employee remuneration and third party commission expenses.

Playoff costs consist of employee remuneration, cost of Food & Beverage sales, League assessments and other building and direct costs incurred as a result of the 1994 playoffs. The main components of these expenses were N.H.L. playoff assessments of $1,840,823 ($2,109,540 in 1993), employee remuneration of $1,521,466 ($1,313,696 in 1993) and playoff travel costs of $593,090 ($647,405 in 1993).

NATIONAL HOCKEY LEAGUE

The Corporation is one of 26 members of the N.H.L., an unincorporated not-for-profit association.

All of the expansion fees from the 1993 N.H.L. expansion in Orange County, California and South Florida have been received by the League and have been distributed to the member clubs except for a $5 million (U.S.) broadcast claim reserve. The Corporation recorded before income taxes $3,112,931 (Cdn) in 1994 and $525,333 (Cdn) in 1993 as its share of these payments. The tax treatment of such payments to the Corporation is at issue. See note 9(b) to the 1994 financial statements. Although the Board of Governors of the N.H.L. has stated, in principle, an intention to further expand so as to become a league of 28 teams by the year 2000, that possibility is uncertain at the present time.

In February 1994, the Ontario Court of Appeal released a decision dismissing an appeal by the N.H.L., the N.H.L. Pension Society, its member clubs (including the Maple Leafs) and others of a decision of the Ontario Court of Justice dated October 22, 1992. The Ontario Court of Justice had ruled in favour of certain retired N.H.L.

players in respect of a reallocation of certain pension funds to such players. The order is against all of the N.H.L. member clubs on a joint and several basis and includes all legal fees.

As a result of the Court of Appeal's decision, the Corporation has recorded as a prior period adjustment its estimated liability of $2,800,000 less an income tax reduction of $200,000. This estimate is subject to calculations and determinations ordered pursuant to the Court of Justice's decision. The N.H.L. sought a leave to appeal to the Supreme Court of Canada the decision of the Court of Appeal. Subsequent to the Corporation's period end the Supreme Court of Canada denied such leave.

LIQUIDITY AND CASH FLOW

The Corporation continues to be debt free and has available bank lines of credit in the amount of $10 million. As the Corporation has income in U.S. dollars sufficient to meet its travelling and other expenses incurred in the U.S., it does not utilize financial instruments such as foreign exchange hedges and interest rate swap agreements.

As a member of the N.H.L., the Corporation is required to participate in League sponsored operations and it participates in League generated revenues, however in all other respects the Corporation is autonomous in managing its own affairs and in generating revenues and controlling costs. Historically, cash from operations has been sufficient to fund capital expenditures, deferred charges on player signings, and regular dividend payments. This is expected to continue largely as a result of management's ability to control such costs as well as salaries.

During the year, cash and interest bearing deposits have decreased to $10,188,543 from $12,086,374 mainly as a result of a decrease in cash from operations, resulting from the balance of accounts payable and accrued liabilities being less at June 30, 1994 than at May 31, 1993.

The change in year end to June 30, 1994 contributed to a reported net decrease in cash and interest bearing deposits caused by a net cash outflow of $9,481,593 in June 1994. This net cash outflow results mainly from the payment of approximately $6,500,000 in ticket refunds for unplayed playoff games.

MAPLE LEAF GARDENS, LIMITED ANNUAL REPORT

FUTURE OPERATIONS

Collective Bargaining Agreement ("CBA")

The CBA between the N.H.L. and the N.H.L. Players' Association ("NHLPA") expired in September 1993. Currently, the N.H.L. and the Toronto Maple Leafs face the possibility of an indefinite postponement of the start of the 1994-95 season as a result of the lack of a Collective Agreement with the NHLPA. If such postponement occurs it could have a negative impact on the earnings of the Corporation. The Corporation believes the players will continue to demand increased salaries in future negotiations. However, the effect of players' remuneration costs on future profitability is uncertain.

The 1994 - 95 Season

The Corporation has announced ticket price increases for the 1994-95 season averaging approximately 12%. Past ticket price increases have not led to a decrease in ticket sales and this trend is expected to continue. During the 1994 fiscal period, the Corporation was host to 127 events (123 in 1993) including 54 Maple Leafs games (56 in 1993). In 1994, other than the Maple Leafs games, no single event or series constituted a material portion of the revenue of the Corporation. The booking of events cannot be predicted until it becomes clear that a group or attraction will be undertaking a tour. The number of groups on tour has remained low over the last four years as compared to the late eighties, and the Corporation continues to face competition for events primarily from two other major southern Ontario event facilities. It is not known whether bookings will improve when economic conditions improve.

In the event that the Maple Leafs compete in post season play for the Stanley Cup, this will have a positive effect on profitability. The extent of profitability will be determined primarily by the number of games played and the total gate receipts, and compensation arrangements between clubs and with players. However, at this time it is not possible to quantify the effect on the Corporation of these variables. The Corporation does not receive any additional revenue from broadcasting for participating in the Stanley Cup playoffs.

Acquisition of Control by MLG Ventures Limited ("MLG Ventures") and Proposed Privatization by Amalgamation

MLG Ventures recently acquired approximately 91% of the shares of the Corporation and has sought to amalgamate the Corporation with its wholly owned subsidary. This would have resulted in the amalgamated Corporation becoming a private corporation. In this connection, the Public Trustee for the Province of Ontario in August, 1994 commenced an action against the Corporation and others. An injunction was obtained preventing the amalgamation pending the outcome of the action, which will proceed on its merits. See note 9(c) to the 1994 financial statements. The day to day operations of the Corporation are not being affected by this litigation.

Broadcast and Related Agreements

The Molson Agreement expires at the end of the 1994-95 season and provides that the parties shall commence negotiations on September 1, 1994 for a new agreement. The Agreement provides for the Corporation and Molson holding exclusive negotiations from September 1, 1994 to December 31, 1994 for a new agreement.

If no agreement is reached by December 31, 1994, the Molson Agreement provides, among other things, that the Corporation will advise Molson of what the Corporation is willing to accept for broadcast rights, and if Molson is not willing to purchase such rights on that basis, the Corporation will be free to sell such rights to any third party on terms at least equal to that proposed to Molson.

Agreements between Molson and the Corporation for promotional and related rights also expire at the end of the 1994-95 season and are also subject to the same renegotiation terms as the Molson Agreement. The revenues from such promotional and related rights agreements have averaged approximately $2,200,000 per year over the past three years.

Purchase of Adjacent Property

The Corporation has entered into an agreement to purchase a commercial building adjacent to Maple Leaf Gardens for approximately $1,000,000. The Corporation's intention is to relocate staff from Maple Leaf Gardens into the commercial building. This will facilitate the expansion of revenue producing concession areas in Maple Leaf Gardens. This will also complement the Corporation's effort to maximize revenue, to improve the Maple Leaf Hockey Club and maintain Maple Leaf Gardens as a premier sports and entertainment facility.

1957-1969
George Armstrong

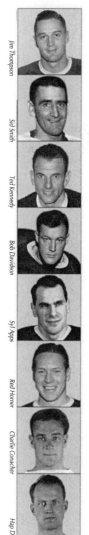

Jim Thompson

Sid Smith

Ted Kennedy

Bob Davidson

Syl Apps

Red Horner

Charlie Conacher

Hap Day

7

MAPLE LEAF GARDENS, LIMITED ANNUAL REPORT

MANAGEMENT STATEMENT ON FINANCIAL REPORTING

The management of Maple Leaf Gardens, Limited is responsible for the preparation, presentation and integrity of the financial statements contained on pages 9 through 14 of this Annual Report and of financial information, discussion and analysis consistent therewith, presented on other pages. The accounting principles which form the basis of the financial statements and the more significant accounting policies applied are described in Note 1 on page 12. Where appropriate and necessary, professional judgments and estimates have been made by management in preparing the financial statements.

In order to meet its responsibility, management maintains accounting systems and related internal controls designed to provide reasonable assurance that assets are safeguarded and that transactions and events are properly recorded and reported.

Ultimate responsibility for financial reporting to shareholders rests with the Board of Directors. The Audit Committee of the Board, a majority of

whom are outside directors, meets quarterly with management and with external auditors to review accounting principles and procedures. External auditors have unlimited access to the Audit Committee. The Audit Committee recommends to the Board of Directors the accounting firm to be named in the resolution to appoint auditors at each annual meeting of shareholders. The Audit Committee reviews financial statements and the other contents of the Annual Report with management and the external auditors and reports to the directors prior to their approval for publication.

KPMG Peat Marwick Thorne, independent auditors appointed by the shareholders, express an opinion on the fair presentation of the financial statements. They meet regularly with both the Audit Committee and the management to discuss matters arising from their audit, which includes a review of accounting records and internal controls. The Auditors' Report to the Shareholders appears on this page.

Cliff Fletcher
President and Chief Operating Officer

J. Donald Crump
Secretary-Treasurer

AUDITORS' REPORT TO THE SHAREHOLDERS

We have audited the balance sheets of Maple Leaf Gardens, Limited as at June 30, 1994 and May 31, 1993 and the statements of income, retained earnings and changes in cash flow for the thirteen months ended June 30, 1994 and the year ended May 31, 1993. These financial statements are the responsibility of the Corporation's management. Our responsibility is to express an opinion on these financial statements based on our audits.

We conducted our audits in accordance with generally accepted auditing standards. Those standards require that we plan and perform an audit to obtain reasonable assurance whether the financial statements are free of material misstatement. An audit includes examining,

on a test basis, evidence supporting the amounts and disclosures in the financial statements. An audit also includes assessing the accounting principles used and significant estimates made by management, as well as evaluating the overall financial statement presentation.

In our opinion, these financial statements present fairly, in all material respects, the financial position of the Corporation as at June 30, 1994 and May 31, 1993 and the results of its operations and the changes in its financial position for the thirteen months ended June 30, 1994 and the year ended May 31, 1993 in accordance with generally accepted accounting principles.

KPMG Peat Marwick Thorne
Chartered Accountants

Toronto, Canada
August 5, 1994

MAPLE LEAF GARDENS, LIMITED ANNUAL REPORT

BALANCE SHEETS

June 30, 1994 and May 31, 1993

	1994	1993
		(as restated - note 3)
ASSETS		
Current assets:		
Cash and interest-bearing deposits	$ 10,188,543	$ 12,086,374
Accounts receivable	1,734,925	3,135,671
Prepaid expenses and other assets	981,915	511,338
	12,905,383	15,733,383
Fixed assets (note 4)	14,129,736	13,510,803
Deferred charges	782,600	632,644
Deferred income taxes	2,405,900	1,459,120
Franchises:		
National Hockey League	100,001	100,001
	$ 30,323,620	$ 31,435,951
LIABILITIES AND SHAREHOLDERS' EQUITY		
Current liabilities:		
Accounts payable and accrued liabilities	$ 7,036,834	$ 12,315,755
Deferred compensation payable within		
one year (note 5)	246,718	87,616
Income and other taxes payable	110,148	330,163
Deferred income	1,045,337	1,608,055
	8,439,037	14,341,589
Deferred compensation payable (note 5)	3,786,959	2,248,783
Shareholders' equity:		
Capital stock (note 6):		
Authorized:		
4,999,500 (1993 - 5,000,000) common shares		
Issued:		
3,677,400 (1993 - 3,677,900) common shares	36,774	36,779
Retained earnings	18,060,850	14,808,800
	18,097,624	14,845,579
Commitments and contingencies (note 9)		
	$ 30,323,620	$ 31,435,951

See accompanying notes to financial statements.

On behalf of the Board of Directors,

Steve A. Stavro
Director

J. Donald Crump
Director

1955-1956
Sid Smith

 Jim Thompson

 Sid Smith

 Ted Kennedy

 Bob Davidson

 Syl Apps

 Red Horner

 Charlie Conacher

Hap Day

MAPLE LEAF GARDENS, LIMITED ANNUAL REPORT

**1948-1955
Ted Kennedy**

Doug Gilmour

Wendel Clark

Rob Ramage

Rick Vaive

Darryl Sittler

Dave Keon

George Armstrong

STATEMENTS OF INCOME

Thirteen months ended June 30, 1994 and year ended May 31, 1993

	1994	1993
Revenue from operations	$ 62,693,174	$ 55,444,270
Investment and other income	850,022	754,089
	63,543,196	56,198,359
Operating expenses other than the undernoted	53,175,423	44,320,930
Operating income before the following	10,367,773	11,877,429
Depreciation	1,097,556	957,841
Amortization	1,545,663	1,969,962
Operating income	7,724,554	8,949,626
N.H.L. expansion fees (note 7)	3,112,931	525,333
Income before income taxes	10,837,485	9,474,959
Income taxes (note 8):		
Current	5,573,000	5,212,000
Deferred reduction	(946,780)	(990,140)
	4,626,220	4,221,860
Net income	$ 6,211,265	$ 5,253,099
Earnings per share	$ 1.69	$ 1.43

See accompanying notes to financial statements.

STATEMENTS OF RETAINED EARNINGS

Thirteen months ended June 30, 1994 and year ended May 31, 1993

	1994	1993
Retained earnings, beginning of period:		
As previously reported	$ 17,408,800	$ 15,098,021
Prior period adjustment (note 3)	(2,600,000)	(2,600,000)
As restated	14,808,800	12,498,021
Net income	6,211,265	5,253,099
	21,020,065	17,751,120
Dividends - $0.80 per share	2,942,320	2,942,320
Excess of amounts paid over paid-up capital on redemption of common shares (note 6)	16,895	
Retained earnings, end of period	$ 18,060,850	$ 14,808,800

See accompanying notes to financial statements.

10

MAPLE LEAF GARDENS, LIMITED ANNUAL REPORT

STATEMENTS OF CHANGES IN CASH FLOW

Thirteen months ended June 30, 1994 and year ended May 31, 1993

	1994	1993
CASH PROVIDED BY (USED FOR):		
(a) Operations	$ 2,776,219	$ 11,557,677
(b) Investments	(3,412,108)	(2,685,606)
(c) Financing	1,680,378	1,534,508
Dividends	(2,942,320)	(2,942,320)
Increase (decrease) during the period	(1,897,831)	7,464,259
Cash and interest-bearing deposits, beginning of period	12,086,374	4,622,115
Cash and interest-bearing deposits, end of period	$ 10,188,543	$ 12,086,374
(a) Operating activities:		
Net income	$ 6,211,265	$ 5,253,099
Items not involving cash from operations:		
Depreciation and amortization	2,643,219	2,927,803
Deferred income tax reduction	(946,780)	(990,140)
	7,907,704	7,190,762
Other non-cash working capital items	(5,131,485)	4,366,915
	$ 2,776,219	$ 11,557,677
(b) Investment activities:		
Purchase of fixed assets	$ (1,716,489)	$ (1,483,428)
Increase in deferred charges	(1,695,619)	(1,202,178)
	$ (3,412,108)	$ (2,685,606)
(c) Financing activities:		
Increase in deferred compensation payable	$ 1,697,278	$ 1,534,508
Redemption of common shares	(16,900)	
	$ 1,680,378	$ 1,534,508
Other non-cash working capital items:		
Decrease (increase) in accounts receivable	$ 1,400,746	$ (1,538,229)
Increase in prepaid expenses and other assets	(470,577)	(55,084)
Increase (decrease) in accounts payable and accrued liabilities	(5,278,921)	6,550,952
Decrease in income and other taxes payable	(220,015)	(819,150)
Increase (decrease) in deferred income	(562,718)	228,426
	$ (5,131,485)	$ 4,366,915

See accompanying notes to financial statements.

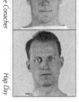

11

MAPLE LEAF GARDENS, LIMITED ANNUAL REPORT

NOTES TO FINANCIAL STATEMENTS

Thirteen months ended June 30, 1994 and year ended May 31, 1993

1943-1945
Bob Davidson

Doug Gilmour

Wendel Clark

Rob Ramage

Rick Vaive

Darryl Sittler

Dave Keon

George Armstrong

1. SIGNIFICANT ACCOUNTING POLICIES:

These financial statements have been prepared by management in accordance with accounting principles generally accepted in Canada. The significant policies are as follows:

(a) Segmented reporting:

The Corporation's directors have determined that the dominant industry segment of the Corporation is its operation in the entertainment industry in Canada.

(b) Fixed assets:

Land, building and equipment are stated at cost. Depreciation is provided on a diminishing balance basis, over the fixed assets estimated useful life, using rates of 5% per annum for buildings and 20% and 30% per annum for equipment.

(c) Deferred charges:

The Corporation has entered into employment contracts with certain of its employees which provide for substantial initial cash payments. These cash payments are reflected on the balance sheet as deferred charges and are being amortized on a straight-line basis over the life of the employment contracts. Any unamortized balance relating to a terminated contract is written off in the period of termination.

(d) Foreign exchange:

Deferred compensation payable denominated in United States dollars is translated into Canadian dollars at the period end rate of exchange. Exchange gains or losses on translating this deferred compensation payable are deferred and amortized on a straight-line basis over the remaining life of the obligation. All other exchange gains or losses are included in income.

(e) Franchises:

The National Hockey League ("N.H.L.") franchise represents the costs of purchase of the predecessor hockey club which upon reorganization eventually became the Toronto Maple Leaf Hockey Club and a member of the N.H.L. The franchise rights are recorded as an intangible asset.

(f) Income taxes:

The Corporation records income tax expense on the tax allocation basis. The tax effect of claiming amounts for income tax purposes different from those recorded in the accounts is included in the statement of income and recorded in the balance sheet as deferred income taxes. Timing differences consist principally of book depreciation in excess of tax depreciation, the deferral of certain costs for accounting purposes which costs are expensed for tax purposes, and deferred compensation payable which is not deductible for tax purposes until paid.

(g) Deferred income:

Deferred income represents payments received in advance for events and services which have not yet been performed. These amounts will be recorded in income as earned.

(h) Revenue:

Included in revenue from operations are:

(i) the gross revenues for those attractions for which the Corporation is the promoter;

(ii) the Corporation's share of the gross revenues for those attractions for which the Corporation is a co-promoter; and

(iii) a minimum licence fee or percentage of the gate (whichever is greater) in those cases where the Corporation licences the use of its facility.

2. CHANGE OF YEAR END:

During the period, the Corporation changed its fiscal year end to June 30. Previously, the fiscal year ended on May 31. As a result, the statements of income, retained earnings and changes in cash flow for the current fiscal period are for thirteen months ended June 30, 1994. The comparative figures are for the year ended May 31, 1993.

3. PRIOR PERIOD ADJUSTMENT:

On February 17, 1994, the Ontario Court of Appeal released its decision dismissing an appeal by the N.H.L., the N.H.L. Pension Society, its member clubs and others of a decision of the Ontario Court of Justice dated October 22, 1992. The Ontario Court of Justice had found in favour of certain retired N.H.L. players in respect of a reallocation of certain pension funds to such players.

As a result of the Court of Appeal's decision, the Corporation has recorded a prior period adjustment to reflect the estimated liability of $2,800,000 less an income tax reduction of $200,000. A payment of $456,346 towards this liability was made during fiscal 1994.

On July 28, 1994, the N.H.L.'s application for leave to appeal the decision of the Ontario Court of Appeal to the Supreme Court of Canada was denied.

MAPLE LEAF GARDENS, LIMITED ANNUAL REPORT

4. FIXED ASSETS:

	Cost	Accumulated depreciation	1994 Net book value	1993 Net book value
Land	$ 358,811	$ –	$ 358,811	$ 358,811
Building	18,622,562	6,785,576	11,836,986	11,037,258
Equipment	6,452,000	4,596,579	1,855,421	1,615,565
Construction-in-progress	78,518	–	78,518	499,169
	$ 25,511,891	$ 11,382,155	$ 14,129,736	$ 13,510,803

5. DEFERRED COMPENSATION PAYABLE:

The Corporation has entered into contracts with certain employees, which provide for certain compensation payments to be deferred until a future date. The amount equal to the present value of these future payments is included in operating expenses in the period in which the compensation is earned.

The present value of future payments due in each of the next five years and thereafter under these contracts is as follows:

Year ending June 30:	
1995	$ 246,718
1996	308,952
1997	1,036,618
1998	156,887
1999	241,418
Thereafter	2,043,084
	$ 4,033,677

Interest expense recorded in connection with this deferred compensation payable balance amounted to $125,886 (1993 - $115,870). This interest expense has been recorded in the statement of income as a reduction of investment and other income.

6. CAPITAL STOCK:

During fiscal 1994, the Corporation redeemed 500 common shares for total proceeds of $16,900 and reduced the authorized capital stock by 500 common shares.

7. N.H.L. EXPANSION FEES:

In 1993, the N.H.L. granted conditional franchises for Orange County, California and South Florida. Those franchises were granted on a conditional basis as both the N.H.L. and the potential members were obligated to meet certain conditions. The fee established for these individual franchises was $50 million (U.S.), including a non-refundable deposit of $5 million (U.S.). $25 million (U.S.) of the Orange County,

California franchise fee was paid to the Los Angeles Kings in exchange for sharing their territorial rights in southern California. The N.H.L. is withholding a further $5 million (U.S.) in reserve for a claim for broadcast rights infringement filed by the Tampa Bay Lightning. The remaining $70 million (U.S.), less certain legal and direct charges, was shared equally amongst the 24 member clubs. The Corporation's share amounted to $3,112,931 (Cdn.) before income taxes and was received and recorded as income during fiscal 1994.

In 1993, the Corporation received and recorded as income its share of the initial deposits amounting to $525,333 (Cdn.).

8. INCOME TAXES:

Income tax expense differs from the amount which would be obtained by applying the combined Federal/Provincial statutory income tax rate to the respective period's income before income taxes. The difference results from the following items:

	1994	1993
Statutory income tax rate	**44.3%**	44.3%
Increase (decrease) in tax rate resulting from:		
Non-taxable portion of N.H.L. expansion fees	**(2.4)**	(0.6)
Non-deductible expenses	**0.8**	0.8
Effective income tax rate	**42.7%**	44.5%

9. COMMITMENTS AND CONTINGENCIES:

(a) There are a number of actions in Canada and the United States against the N.H.L. and its member clubs for damages and costs allegedly sustained by plaintiffs. While these actions are being defended, it is not possible, in the opinion of the N.H.L.'s solicitors, to predict the outcome or the extent of any liability should any of the actions ultimately be successful.

1940-1943 Syl Apps

Jim Thompson

Sid Smith

Ted Kennedy

Bob Davidson

Syl Apps

Red Horner

Charlie Conacher

Hap Day

13

MAPLE LEAF GARDENS, LIMITED ANNUAL REPORT

No provision has been made in the accounts for any legal awards which may be incurred as a result of the above actions. Any amounts awarded against the Corporation as a result of the actions will be recorded as a prior period adjustment in the period of such award.

(b) In discussions with another N.H.L. member club, Revenue Canada has indicated it intends to challenge the tax filing position adopted by the Corporation and fellow Canadian member clubs on expansion fees received in the period from 1991 to 1994. The Corporation intends to oppose this proposed reassessment and believes it has very strong defenses on this matter. Should Revenue Canada reassess in the manner they are proposing and should this reassessment be upheld, the exposure to the Corporation at present, including interest, would be approximately $1,125,000. Any amounts awarded against the Corporation as a result of this proposed reassessment will be recorded as a prior period adjustment in the period of such award.

(c) On August 4, 1994, the Public Trustee for the Province of Ontario commenced an action against the Corporation and others in the Ontario Court of Justice, General Division ("Court") seeking amongst other things that the Court:

(i) require the Corporation to pay to the Estate of Harold E. Ballard (the "Estate") its share of undistributed profits of the Corporation from April 11, 1990 to date;

(ii) not allow the amalgamation of the Corporation with any other corporation;

(iii) declare that the affairs of the Corporation have been carried on in an oppressive and unfair manner to the prejudice of security holders, including the Estate and beneficiaries of the Estate;

(iv) set aside the acquisition of the shares of the Corporation by MLG Ventures Limited directly or indirectly through the acquisition of the shares of Harold E. Ballard Limited and cause the return to the Estate of its direct and indirect interest in the Corporation.

An injunction in connection with this action was obtained from the Ontario Court of Justice enjoining the Corporation and others from taking any steps to amalgamate the Corporation with a wholly owned subsidiary of MLG Ventures Limited, pending the outcome of the action, which will proceed on its merits.

The statement of claim of the Public Trustee makes no claim for damages. The claims by the Public Trustee against the Corporation are vague and lack particulars and demand has been made by the Corporation for further particulars. Based upon the information currently available, legal counsel for the Corporation is of the opinion that there is no merit in these claims.

However, if any amounts are found payable by the Corporation they would be accounted for as a prior period adjustment in the year the amounts are determined to be payable.

(d) At June 30, 1994, the Corporation has planned capital expenditures, including the purchase of a building, for the 1995 fiscal year of approximately $2,000,000.

(e) The Corporation has an employment agreement with its chief operating officer which expires on June 30, 1996. This agreement provides the employee with the right to terminate the agreement if a change in control as defined occurs or his responsibilities are altered in a meaningful fashion. The agreement also provides for severance arrangements if the employee is terminated without cause. Should the agreement be terminated after June 30, 1994, this employee will receive his annual remuneration until June 30, 1996 as severance.

10. RELATED PARTY TRANSACTIONS:

(a) The Molson Companies Limited beneficially owned approximately 19.9% of the common shares of the Corporation until April 2, 1994, at which time it disposed of these shares. These shares were acquired under an option agreement, were held in trust and were subject to cross-ownership rules of the N.H.L. As a result of the disposal of these shares, the Molson Companies Limited is no longer considered to be a related party. During fiscal 1994, up until the date of disposal of the common shares, the Corporation earned revenue on the sale of television and radio rights to N.H.L. hockey, promotional and other advertising activities in the amount of approximately $6,726,000 (1993 - $7,987,000) from the Molson Companies Limited.

(b) During 1993, the Corporation entered into a license agreement with J.J. Muggs Inc., a company owned by one of the Corporation's Directors, to provide food and beverage catering services for the arena private boxes. This agreement provides for a license fee to be payable to the Corporation based on a percentage of sales. The total license fee for 1994 earned by the Corporation was $343,171 (1993 - $197,659).

(c) The Corporation paid J.J. Muggs Inc. $243,416 (1993 - $173,998) for other catering services supplied during fiscal 1994.

11. COLLECTIVE BARGAINING AGREEMENT:

Currently the N.H.L. and the Corporation face the possibility of an interruption of the 1994-95 hockey season as a result of the lack of a Collective Agreement with the National Hockey League Players' Association. If such an interruption occurs, it could have a negative impact on the earnings of the Corporation.

14

1.10 SUMMARY

Accounting is a language. Financial statements are used to communicate the language of accounting. Financial statements convey information about the financial health and performance of organizations to various internal and external users, such as managers, creditors, lenders, shareholders, public interest groups, employees, and various governmental agencies.

Management is responsible for implementing and maintaining a system of internal control and a financial reporting system that produce meaningful, reliable financial statements. Independent auditors are used to test the effectiveness of the internal control system and adherence to GAAP and to express a professional opinion on the financial statements.

Financial reports reveal the financing, investing, and operating activities of the organization. These activities are disclosed in three basic financial statements: the balance sheet, the income statement, and the statement of changes in financial position.

Financial statements are prepared for specific entities. Such entities may include proprietorships, partnerships, corporations, consolidated corporate groups, non-profit organizations, or government bodies.

A sophisticated standard-setting process exists for the development of generally accepted accounting principles. The development of GAAP involves the use of professional judgment, and the consideration of the objectives of financial reporting. GAAP are *flexible*. They encompass not only specific rules, practices, and procedures relating to particular circumstances but also broad principles and conventions of general application. Because of the flexibility of GAAP, accountants are faced with many ethical questions concerning the selection of accounting policies and the disclosure of meaningful financial statements.

The focus of this text is on financial accounting and the generally accepted accounting principles used in accounting reports. Our goal is to help you become financial statement literate and conversant in the language of accounting.

1.11 KEY CONCEPTS AND TERMS

The list of new concepts and terms in this first chapter may appear overwhelming. You should consider these terms to be a vocabulary list for your new language of accounting. You will see many of these terms again in later chapters as these basic concepts are reinforced. Take time to see if you understand the terms listed below. If you do not remember a specific concept, review the appropriate discussion in the chapter. Page numbers have been provided as a reference.

Accrual basis of accounting (p. 13)
Assets (p. 11)
Auditors' report (p. 8)
Balance sheet (p. 10)
Cash basis of accounting (p. 14)
CICA Handbook (p. 17)
Comparability (p. 20)
Conservatism principle (p. 22)
Consistency principle (p. 22)
Consolidated corporate groups (p. 15)
Contributed capital (p. 12)
Corporations (p. 15)
Cost/benefit (p. 23)
Disclosure principle (p. 22)
Entity concept (p. 20)
Equity (p. 11)
Excess of revenues over expenses (p. 12)

Expenses (p. 12)
Fair value basis (p. 13)
Financial accounting (p. 6)
Financial reporting system (p. 7)
Financing activities (p. 10)
Gains/losses (p. 12)
Generally accepted accounting principles
    (GAAP) (p. 5)
Generally accepted auditing standards
    (GAAS) (p. 7)
Going concern concept (p. 21)
Government bodies (p. 16)
Historical cost (p. 13)
Income statement (p. 10)
Independent auditor (p. 8)
Industry practices (p. 23)
Internal control system (p. 7)

Investing activities (p. 10)
Liability (p. 11)
Management's discussion and
   analysis (p. 7)
Managerial accounting (p. 6)
Matching principle (p. 21)
Materiality principle (p. 22)
Net income/loss (p. 12)
Non-profit organizations (p. 15)
Notes to financial statements (p. 10)
Operating activities (p. 10)
Partnerships (p. 14)
Periodic concept (p. 21)
Professional judgement (p. 19)

Proprietorships (p. 14)
Qualified opinion (p. 9)
Qualitative characteristics (p. 19)
Relevance (p. 20)
Reliability (p. 20)
Retained earnings (p. 12)
Revenues (p. 12)
Stakeholder (p. 3)
Statement of changes in financial
   position (p. 10)
Stewardship (p. 3)
Understandability (p. 20)
Unit of measure (p. 21)
Unqualified opinion (p. 9)

1.12 COMPREHENSIVE REVIEW QUESTION

R1.1 Financial statement elements. Analyze the Maple Leaf Gardens, Limited, financial statements and identify the following financial statement elements, indicating the amount and the financial statement on which they can be found:

Prepaid expenses   _____
Purchase of fixed assets   _____
Revenue from operations   _____
Accounts payable   _____
Operating expenses   _____
Financing activities   _____
N.H.L. expansion fees   _____
Investment and other income   _____
Increase in accounts receivable   _____
Income before income taxes   _____

1.13 REVIEW AND DISCUSSION QUESTIONS

Q1.1 Describe three different economic units and provide an example of each.

Q1.2 Describe the two distinct elements of equity.

Q1.3 Distinguish between financial and managerial accounting.

Q1.4 Describe the role professional judgment has in financial reporting.

Q1.5 Describe the qualitative characteristics of accounting information.

Q1.6 Compare the accrual and cash basis of accounting.

Q1.7 Describe the process by which accounting policies and measurements become part of the CICA Handbook.

Q1.8 Briefly describe the cost/benefit constraint of accounting information.

Q1.9 Describe and provide examples of the accounting concepts of materiality, consistency, and matching.

Q1.10 Describe the economic activities of investing, financing, and operating. Provide an example of each.

Q1.11 Describe the three different paragraphs that comprise the auditors' report.

Q1.12 One definition of *accounting* describes accounting as an art. Using the information from Chapter 1, write a brief report to support this idea.

Q1.13 Distinguish between preparers and users of financial statements.

Q1.14 Distinguish among proprietorships, partnerships, corporations, and non-profit organizations.

Q1.15 Identify five different users of accounting information and discuss briefly the kinds of decisions they must make and the kinds of accounting information they should have in making those decisions.

Assume that the Maple Leaf Gardens, Limited, financial statements are typical of the statements provided by Canadian companies to their public shareholders. Do those statements meet the information needs you outlined above? To the extent that they do not, why might that be so? Where might your users go to find the information needed?

Q1.16 You are the chief accounting officer of a major manufacturing company. Identify and describe five principal differences that might exist between your company's managerial accounting reports and its financial accounting reports. Why might these differences exist?

Q1.17 Assume that it is the early 1930s and the Depression is a very painful reality for everyone. The financial reporting systems in our country have been allocated part of the blame for the financial collapse, and new answers are being sought for old questions. A number of different voices are arguing for different positions. Some believe that we ought to have a government-mandated financial reporting system to which every company that wants to sell shares to the public must adhere. Others who believe that the marketplace will reward those companies that provide useful information and will penalize those that do not, argue that we should have no standardized financial reporting requirement. They argue that each company should be allowed to devise its own report to shareholders. In the middle ground are those who argue for some standardization of financial reports disseminated to the public but at the same time insist that the standardized format be developed by private sector initiative.

a. Outline the advantages and disadvantages of each of the above three alternatives from the standpoint of the financial community as a whole.

b. Assume that each of the three alternatives is offered in legislation. Which alternative would you vote for and why?

Q1.18 In your own words, explain what is meant by an *internal control system*. You may find it helpful to express your explanation in the context of a hypothetical company, for example, a rapidly growing manufacturer of electronic components

Q1.19 It has been suggested that we change the rules that now require all publicly held companies to issue quarterly reports. One suggestion is that we follow the practice of some other countries and require only semi-annual reports. Outline the advantages and disadvantages of that proposal from as many different perspectives as you think might be relevant.

Q1.20 Based on your reading of the report of Maple Leaf Gardens management and the report from the independent auditor, describe in your own words the responsibilities of management and of the auditors for the preparation of the Maple Leaf Gardens financial statements. How are they similar? How are they different? The division of responsibilities has evolved over time. Why might it have evolved as it did?

Q1.21 In footnote 1(*b*) of its financial statements, Maple Leaf Gardens describes its policies with regard to fixed assets. What other approach could management have taken with regard to the amortization of these assets? How might Maple Leaf Gardens' financial statements have been different if an alternative approach had been adopted?

Q1.22 Based on your reading of the Maple Leaf Gardens' financial statements, identify five measures of performance that you believe to be important and explain why you selected these five. Also identify five measures of Maple Leaf Gardens' performance that you believe might be relevant in making a decision whether to buy Maple Leaf Gardens' shares but are not available to you from these financial statements. Why might those measures not be reported in a public financial statement?

Q1.23 Tomorrow night you will have dinner with a friend who is now a successful professional accountant. Based on your understanding of financial statements, identify the 10 most important questions about accounting and the financial reporting process that you would like to ask your friend. (Try to make these questions as complete as possible. At the conclusion of this course, go back and see how many of these questions you can answer.)

Q1.24 Review the financial statements of Maple Leaf Gardens, Limited, and identify an example of each of the elements of the financial statement.

Q1.25 Three different professional accounting bodies exist in Canada. Identify these organizations and the related professional accounting designations they offer. The student accounting organization at your school and/or your academic counsellor should be able to provide you with this information.

Q1.26 Generally accepted accounting principles are said to be flexible. Provide an example of this flexibility.

Q1.27 Distinguish between cost and value, and explain how these two ideas are used in preparing financial statements for the annual report to shareholders.

Q1.28 You are the sole owner of a company whose accounting records reflect an equity of $275,000. Assuming that you are ready to retire, would you agree to sell your business for $275,000? Why or why not? If you decide to accept an offer of more than $275,000, what value do you think the purchaser would use in his or her subsequent financial reports for the net assets purchased from you? Why? Assume that you rejected a firm offer of more than $275,000 and decided to wait for a better offer. What value should you use in your subsequent financial statements? Why?

Q1.29 Does the issuing of an unqualified opinion in an auditors' report indicate the financial statements are free of errors and misrepresentations?

Q1.30 Included in many financial statements are long-lived assets like land, buildings, and equipment. These assets may have been purchased several years ago and have a current value significantly higher than their original purchase price. For financial statement purposes, should such assets be valued at their original cost or their current values? Which values are the most relevant? Which values are the most reliable?

Q1.31 Review the list of key concepts and terms at the end of the chapter. If you have difficulty with a specific concept, refer to the page number provided to gain a better understanding of the concept. Make a list of terms you do not thoroughly understand. When you have finished Chapter 2, refer back to this list to see if your understanding has improved. Repeat this process again after you finish each chapter.

1.14 PROBLEMS

P1.1 Financial statement elements. Analyze the Maple Leaf Gardens, Limited, financial statements and identify the following financial statement elements, indicating the amount and the financial statement on which they can be found:

Total assets _____

Depreciation _____

Total equity _____

Total current assets _____

Net income _____

Capital stock issued _____

Total current liabilities _____

Earnings per share _____

Increase (decrease) in cash _____

Total investment activities _____

P1.2 Financial statement elements. Analyze the Maple Leaf Gardens, Limited, financial statements and identify the following financial statement elements, indicating the amount and the financial statement on which they can be found:

Amortization _____

Accounts receivable _____

Retained earnings _____

Operating activities _____

Dividends _____

Capital stock authorized _____

Prior period adjustment _____

Operating income _____

Other non-cash working capital items _____

Income and other taxes payable _____

P1.3 Financial statement errors. Jamie Sanderson owns a small repair shop, which has been in operation for some time. The following statements summarize the shop's operations for January 1996:

SANDERSON REPAIR DEPOT
Income Statement
For the month ending January 31, 1996

Revenues:		
Repair fees earned	$17,000	
Accounts payable	3,700	
Accounts receivable	16,300	$37,000
Operating expenses:		
Rent expense	$ 6,300	
Miscellaneous expense	700	
Supplies on hand	9,800	16,800
Net income		$20,200

SANDERSON REPAIR DEPOT
Balance Sheet
At January 31, 1996

Assets		Owner's Equity	
Cash	$ 7,500	Jamie Sanderson capital, January 1	$19,600
Supplies used	1,100		
Salaries expense	4,800		
Mortgage payable	6,200		
Total assets	$19,600	Total owner's equity	$19,600

Required:

Prepare a corrected income statement and balance sheet for January.

P1.4 Flexibility of GAAP. Pat and Gerry have completed their first year of operations and are in the process of preparing their first annual balance sheet. The accounting records indicate accounts receivable of $20,500 owing from customers and temporary investments purchased at a cost of $11,000. The two partners are trying to measure the value of these two assets for financial statement purposes. Pat comments that she thinks accounts receivable are overvalued, "I think we were a little careless granting credit to new customers during our first few months, and then we made matters worse by not working diligently on collecting our outstanding accounts. I would estimate we will probably collect only $19,000 from our accounts receivable." Gerry agrees with Pat's observation on their accounting for accounts receivable, but adds "At least, we were lucky with our temporary investments. I see in the financial pages our investments have a current market value of $12,000." Discuss how the two assets should be valued for financial statement purposes.

P1.5 Account identification. Identify each of the following accounts as either assets, liabilities, or equity:

a. Accounts Payable.

b. Prepaid Insurance.

c. Cash.

d. Share Capital.

e. Supplies Inventory.

f. Rent Payable.

g. Land and Building.

h. Advance Deposit by Customer.

i. Loan Payable.

j. Accounts Receivable.

k. Retained Earnings.

l. Warranty Liability.

m. Temporary Investments.

n. Receivables from Employees.

P1.6 Flexibility of GAAP. Dorthee's Furniture Sales, Ltd., sells fine furniture to the community of Monarchville. During the first week of January, an oak table was sold for $660.00. Prior to the sale, the company had only four oak tables on hand. Since all the tables were identical, it is not known specifically which one was sold. To complicate matters, the tables were purchased at different points in time, at different costs. One table was purchased at a cost of $400.00, another table was purchased for $420.00, another for $375.00, and the fourth table cost $460.00. For accounting purposes, what is the cost of the table which has been sold, what is the profit on the sale, and what is the cost of the tables remaining on hand?

P1.7 Balance sheet preparation. Presented below in alphabetical order are the balance sheet accounts of the J. W. Wong Enterprises, Ltd., as of December 31, 1996:

Accounts payable	$ 3,000
Accounts receivable	2,200
Buildings	12,000
Cash	1,700
Equipment	9,000
Income taxes payable	2,100
Inventory — merchandise	2,700
Land	7,000
Long-term loan payable	8,000
Share capital	10,000
Temporary investments	1,400
Patent	8,000
Retained earnings	?
Salaries payable	900

Required:

Prepare the December 31, 1996, balance sheet of the J. W. Wong Enterprises Ltd.

P1.8 Balance sheet preparation. Presented below is a partially completed balance sheet for Beshara Limited, at December 31, 1996, together with comparative data for the year ended December 31, 1995. From the statement of changes in financial position for the year ended December 31, 1996, you determine that:

Net income for the year ended December 31, 1996, was $26.

Dividends paid during the year ended December 31, 1996, were $8.

Cash increased $8 during the year ended December 31, 1996.

The cost of new equipment acquired during 1996 was $15; no equipment was disposed of.

There were no transactions affecting the land account during 1996, but it is estimated that the fair market value of the land at December 31, 1996, is $42.

Complete the following balance sheet at December 31, 1996.

BESHARA LIMITED
Balance Sheets
December 31, 1996, and 1995

Assets	1996	1995	Liabilities	1996	1995
Current assets:			Current liabilities:		
Cash	$____	$ 30	Note payable	$ 49	$ 40
Accounts receivable	126	120	Accounts payable	123	110
Inventory	241	230			
			Total current liabilities	$____	$150
Total current assets	$____	$380			
			Long-term debt	$____	$ 80
Capital assets:			Total liabilities	$____	$230
Land	$____	25	**Shareholders' Equity**		
Equipment	____	375			
			Share capital	$200	$200
Less: Accumulated			Retained earnings	$____	190
amortization	(180)	(160)			
			Total Shareholders' Equity	$____	$390
Total Capital assets	$____	$240			
			Total Liabilities and		
Total Assets	$____	$620	Shareholders' Equity	$____	$620

Investing and Financing Activities: The Balance Sheet and the Statement of Changes in Financial Position

--------------- **Objectives** ---------------

After completing this chapter, you will be able to:
1. Describe different types of investing and financing activities.
2. Record accounting transactions for investing and financing activities using the preparer concepts: balance sheet equation, debits and credits, and general journal entries.
3. Define assets, liabilities, and equity.
4. Prepare a balance sheet and a statement of changes in financial position resulting from investing and financing activities.
5. Analyze the financial strength of an organization.

Economic Activities

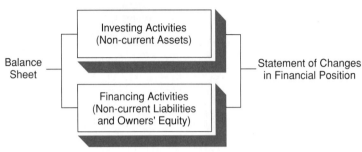

2.1 INVESTING AND FINANCING ACTIVITIES

As described in Chapter 1, investing and financing are two activities carried out by organizations, particularly during the start-up phase of their lives. Investing is the activity of acquiring long-lived, non-current assets such as property, plant, and equipment. Financing is the activity of funding the organization by issuing long-term debt or other non-current liabilities or equity funding received from the owners of the organization. As illustrated in Exhibit 2.1, the results of an organization's investing and financing activities are disclosed on the balance sheet and the statement of changes in financial position (cash flow statement). The balance sheet displays the cumulative effect of the activities at a particular point in time (e.g., December 31). The statement of changes in financial position displays the specific events *during* the period (e.g., for the year ended December 31). The statement of changes in financial position indicates the sources and uses of cash during the period.

Investing Activities

Investing activities involve the acquisition and disposal of non-current assets. Cash is used to purchase non-current assets like equipment or machinery. In addition, such non-current assets are a source of cash when they are sold.

Financing Activities

There are two types of financing activities: those involving non-current liabilities and those involving owners' equity. Cash may be provided by obtaining a long-term liability like a mortgage, and then later, cash is used to make payments on the mortgage. Similarly, cash may be provided and used from equity transactions. The owners provide cash to the company, and then subsequently the company may disburse cash back to the owners.

2.2 PREPARER CONCEPTS AND TECHNIQUES

The preparation of financial statements for most organizations is a time-consuming, and often tedious, task. A large majority of users of financial reports have no real interest in how the financial statements are actually prepared. However, an understanding of some of the basic preparation concepts and procedures will assist the financial statement user in gaining a better understanding of the language of accounting and in using financial reports. This section provides an illustration of the basic concepts and the process followed in recording economic events/transactions.

Balance Sheet Equation

balance sheet equation
The accounting equation is the basis of double entry accounting. The balance sheet equation states: assets = liabilities + equity.

The **balance sheet equation** may be used to illustrate investing and financing activities. The balance sheet or accounting equation may be used to conceptually record economic activities for *any* organization, large or small, profit or non-profit. The accounting equation is the basis of what is commonly called "double-entry accounting." For *any* economic event, at least two activities occur. Such activities, called *transactions,* commonly involve an exchange of goods and services. The balance sheet equation states:

$$\text{Assets} = \text{Liabilities} + \text{Equity}$$

Assets are the economic resources of the organization that possess future economic benefits. Liabilities are the obligations of the organization requiring the yielding of economic benefits in the future. Equity is the ownership interest in the residual of assets less liabilities. The accounting equation is used to record the transactions of the organization. When recording economic events for an organization, the accounting equation is typically associated with the process of breaking the transaction into debits and credits.

Debits and Credits

account
(T-account) An accounting information file usually associated with the general ledger.

Manual accounting systems use accounts that are physically divided into a left-hand side and a right-hand side. **Accounts** represent the place where the financial effects of a company's economic events and transactions are accumulated. For reasons that are now lost in time, the left-hand side of accounts is referred to as the *debit side* and the right-hand side is referred to as the *credit side.* The words *debit* and *credit* are, unfortunately, used in a variety of ways in the business world, for example, credit memo or debit memo. When they are used in an accounting record-keeping context, *debit* and *credit* are simply shorthand ways to refer to the parts of an accounting entry that affects the *left-hand (**debit**)* side of an account and the *right-hand (**credit**)* side of an account, respectively. (Incidentally, when those terms are written, the shorthand is often carried further — debit is usually abbreviated Dr. and credit is usually abbreviated Cr.)

debit
An entry on the left side of an account; debits increase asset and expense accounts but decrease liability, shareholders' equity, and revenue accounts.

Account	
Debit	Credit

credit
An entry on the right side of an account; credits increase liability, shareholders' equity, and revenue accounts but decrease asset and expense accounts.

The use of the terms *debit* and *credit* gained wide acceptance during the period when manual accounting systems were in place. They continue to be widely used in accounting discussions today — even in these days of computerized systems when accounts do not have a right- or left-hand side but are simply a collection of electronic impulses.

We have explained that debits are recorded on the left-hand side of an account and credits on the right-hand side of an account. But what does this really mean? Is a debit an increase or decrease in an account? The answer is it depends on the type of account. An increase in an asset is a debit. Therefore, it follows that a decrease to an asset must be a credit. When moving to the opposite side of the accounting equation, the opposite rule applies. Credits are increases in liabilities and equity, with debits being decreases. The balance sheet equation and the debit and credit rules are shown below:

ASSETS	=	LIABILITIES	+	EQUITY
Debits increase assets		Debits decrease liabilities		Debits decrease equity
Credits decrease assets		Credits increase liabilities		Credits increase equity

Custom has determined that, at least in Canada, balance sheets are prepared with assets on the left-hand side of the balance sheet and the liabilities and owners' equity on the right-hand side. From that convention, it followed that an increase to an asset account was entered on the left-hand side of the asset T-account, whereas increases in liabilities and equity were entered on the right-hand side of the T-accounts. From that custom, it followed further that an increase to an asset was a debit entry (entered on the left), whereas a decrease to an asset was a credit entry (entered on the right). Of course, an increase to a liability or an equity account was a credit entry, and decreases to liabilities and equity accounts were debit entries. The use of debits and credits reinforces the concept of double-entry accounting. For any economic event, at least two activities occur. These two or more activities *must* result in total debits for the event equal to total credits for the event. The logic of maintaining accounts — that is, the use of debits and credits — can be readily seen in the following illustration:

Assets		=	Liabilities		+	Equity	
Debit	Credit		Debit	Credit		Debit	Credit
Increase	*Decrease*		*Decrease*	*Increase*		*Decrease*	*Increase*

The words *debit* and *credit* continue to be used in the same way even in companies in which the accounting system is computerized — the debit entry means an increase in an asset or a decrease in a liability or owners' equity account, and so forth. The day may come when an increase in an asset account is referred to simply as an *increase* and a decrease in a liability account is referred to simply as a *decrease*. Until that day comes, however, it is easier for accountants and managers to adopt existing conventions and refer to those entries as *debits* and *credits*.

We will now examine a number of transactions to illustrate investing and financing activities using the balance sheet equation and debits and credits. For each individual transaction debits *must* equal credits. Ted, a young entrepreneur, has decided to start his own delivery business. Before Ted commenced operations, he completed a number of financing and investing transactions for Ted's Trucking. These transactions are summarized below:

Transactions	Cash	Land	Building	Truck	Loan	Mortgage	Capital
		Assets			=	**Liabilities** + **Equity**	
1. Ted deposits $20,000 in the business bank account.	Dr. 20,000						Cr. 20,000
2. Purchase of land for $5,000 cash.	Cr. (5,000)	Dr. 5,000					
3. Acquired a $40,000 mortgage and purchased a building.			Dr. 40,000			Cr. 40,000	
4. Obtained a $10,000 loan and purchased a truck.				Dr. 10,000	Cr. 10,000		
5. Sold one-fifth of the land for $1,000 cash.	Dr. 1,000	Cr. (1,000)					
6. Cash payment of $2,000 on the mortgage.	Cr. (2,000)					Dr. (2,000)	
7. Ted withdrew $1,000 cash from the business.	Cr. (1,000)						Dr. (1,000)
Account totals	Dr. 13,000	Dr. 4,000	Dr. 40,000	Dr. 10,000	Cr. 10,000	Cr. 38,000	Cr. 19,000
	Total debits = 67,000				Total credits = 67,000		

For each of the above individual transactions debits equal credits. Therefore, when the transactions are summarized, total debits must equal total credits ($67,000).

General Journal Entries

All accounting systems, whether manual or computerized, first require the financial information to be entered in the accounting records. The previous section illustrated the accounting equation and debits and credits as a means of recording transactions. Most organizations use some form of specialized journals to first document their economic activities. A common method of teaching accounting transactions is to use the general journal format. This format will be used throughout the remaining chapters to facilitate the understanding of accounting concepts and principles. The seven transactions for Ted's Trucking are illustrated in general journal format:

Transaction 1. The asset Cash increases by $20,000. An increase in an asset is recorded as a debit. An increase in Ted's capital of $20,000 is recorded as a credit entry.

```
1.  Dr. Cash . . . . . . . . . . . . . . . . . . . . . . . . . . . . . . . . . . . . 20,000
        Cr. Capital, Ted . . . . . . . . . . . . . . . . . . . . . . . . . . . . . .      20,000
        Ted contributes cash to his new business entity.
```

Transaction 2. The asset Land is debited to record the $5,000 increase in assets. The offsetting credit entry to the asset Cash records the decrease in assets of $5,000.

```
2.  Dr. Land . . . . . . . . . . . . . . . . . . . . . . . . . . . . . . . . . . . .  5,000
        Cr. Cash . . . . . . . . . . . . . . . . . . . . . . . . . . . . . . . . . . .       5,000
        Purchase of land for cash.
```

Transaction 3. The asset Building is debited to recognize the increase in assets of $40,000, offset by a credit entry to record the increase in the liability Mortgage Payable.

```
3.  Dr. Building . . . . . . . . . . . . . . . . . . . . . . . . . . . . . . . . . 40,000
        Cr. Mortgage Payable . . . . . . . . . . . . . . . . . . . . . . . . . . .      40,000
        Acquired a mortgage and purchased a building.
```

Transaction 4. The asset Truck is debited to recognize the increase in assets of $10,000, offset by a credit entry to the liability Loan Payable, to recognize the increase in liabilities.

```
4.  Dr. Truck  . . . . . . . . . . . . . . . . . . . . . . . . . . . . . . . . . . . 10,000
        Cr. Loan Payable . . . . . . . . . . . . . . . . . . . . . . . . . . . . .      10,000
        Obtained a loan and purchased a truck.
```

Transaction 5. The asset Cash increases by $1,000, offset by a decrease in the asset Land of $1,000. The Cash account is debited to recognize the increase in assets. The credit entry is to the Land account to recognize the decrease in assets.

```
5.  Dr. Cash . . . . . . . . . . . . . . . . . . . . . . . . . . . . . . . . . . . .  1,000
        Cr. Land . . . . . . . . . . . . . . . . . . . . . . . . . . . . . . . . . . .       1,000
        Sold one-fifth of the land for $1,000 cash.
```

Transaction 6. The asset Cash decreases by $2,000, offset by a decrease in the liability Mortgage Payable of $2,000. The liability Mortgage Payable is debited to recognize the decrease in liabilities. The credit entry is to the Cash account to recognize the decrease in assets.

```
6.  Dr. Mortgage Payable . . . . . . . . . . . . . . . . . . . . . . . . . . . . .  2,000
         Cr. Cash . . . . . . . . . . . . . . . . . . . . . . . . . . . . . . . . . . . . .          2,000
    Made a $2,000 cash payment on the mortgage.
```

Transaction 7. The asset Cash decreases by $1,000, offset by an decrease in equity of $1,000. The Drawings account is debited to recognize the decrease in equity. The credit entry is to the Cash account to recognize the decrease in assets.

```
7.  Dr. Drawings, Ted  . . . . . . . . . . . . . . . . . . . . . . . . . . . . . .  1,000
         Cr. Cash . . . . . . . . . . . . . . . . . . . . . . . . . . . . . . . . . . . . .          1,000
    Ted withdraws $1,000 cash from the business.
```

The first seven transactions described the financing and investing activities for Ted, and the related impact on assets, liabilities, and equity. Users of financial statements are not particularly interested in individual transactions, but only the overall effect of these events. Therefore, the transactions are summarized and disclosed in a balance sheet and a statement of changes in financial position. The balance sheet is simply the bottom line of the accounting equation, previously used to record the transactions. The balance sheet for Ted's Trucking at January 31 appears below:

TED'S TRUCKING
Balance Sheet
At December 31

Assets		Liabilities	
Cash	$13,000	Loan payable	$10,000
Land	4,000	Mortgage payable	38,000
Building	40,000		$48,000
Truck	10,000	**Equity**	
	$67,000	Capital, Ted	19,000
			$67,000

The above balance sheet may appear to be very formal and therefore to reflect an accurate financial position for Ted's trucking at January 31. However, users of financial statements should not be fooled by general appearances. Many users will detect several items that have *not* been disclosed in the financial statement. These include interest owing on the mortgage and loan. As well, no amortization has been recorded on the building and truck. Such items have been omitted at this stage to focus on the key elements of the balance sheet. These concepts are discussed at length in later chapters.

When an organization purchases *and* finances an asset, it may be typically treated as a single economic event and recorded in the accounting records as such. For example, when Ted acquired the building, the asset Building increased by $40,000, offset by an increase in the liability Mortgage Payable:

$$\text{ASSETS} \quad = \quad \text{LIABILITIES} \quad + \quad \text{EQUITY}$$
$$\underline{\text{Building}} \qquad \underline{\text{Mortgage payable}}$$
$$\text{Dr. } 40{,}000 \quad = \quad \text{Cr. } 40{,}000$$

To provide the most meaningful information to the users of the statement of changes in financial position such transactions should be treated as *two* economic events, disclosing *both* the investing activity and the financing activity. Therefore, in the Ted's Trucking example the building transaction is more appropriately reflected as follows:

ASSETS		=	LIABILITIES	+	EQUITY
Cash	Building		Mortgage payable		
Dr. 40,000		=	Cr. 40,000		
Cr. (40,000)	Dr. 40,000				

These activities are disclosed in the statement of changes in financial position as a *source* of cash of $40,000 under financing activities and as a *use* of cash of $40,000 under investing activities. The purchase and financing of Ted's truck should also be treated as two distinct economic events: as a financing source of $10,000, offset by a $10,000 investing activity.

Return to the accounting equation used to record the transactions for Ted's Trucking, and examine the entries in the Cash account. An analysis of the *changes* in Ted's Cash account during the period divides the activities into investing and financing activities and summarizes them in a statement of changes in financial position:

TED'S TRUCKING
Statement of Changes in Financial Position
For the Month Ending January 31

Investing activities:		
Land purchase	$ (5,000)	
Building purchase	(40,000)	
Truck purchase	(10,000)	
Land sale	1,000	
Cash (used) for investing		$(54,000)
Financing activities:		
Ted's contributed capital	$ 20,000	
Mortgage payable	40,000	
Loan payable	10,000	
Payment on mortgage	(2,000)	
Ted's withdrawals	(1,000)	
Cash provided from financing		67,000
Increase in cash		$ 13,000
Cash — January 1		–0–
Cash — January 31		$ 13,000

The statement of changes in financial position explains the change in cash from the beginning to the end of the accounting period. The final section of the statement discloses the beginning cash balance of $0 and the end-of-period balance of $13,000. The $13,000 also appears on the end-of-period balance sheet as an asset. This relationship between the balance sheet and the statement of changes in financial position is portrayed in Exhibit 2.2.

The Ted's Trucking example has been used to illustrate the development and presentation of the balance sheet and the statement of changes in financial position. These two statements are the focus of Chapter 2. The balance of the chapter explains concepts and terms that will facilitate your understanding of these two important statements.

To provide a basis for discussion, we will frequently refer to the comparable balance sheets of Maple Leaf Gardens, Limited. The statements detail the year-end balances for each of Maple Leaf Gardens' principal asset accounts, as well as the principal creditor and owner claims on those assets.

We have said that a balance sheet presents a picture of a company's financial status at a given point in time. Theoretically, a balance sheet could be prepared as of any day

EXHIBIT 2.2

The Relationship between the Statement of Changes in
Financial Position and Consecutive Balance Sheets

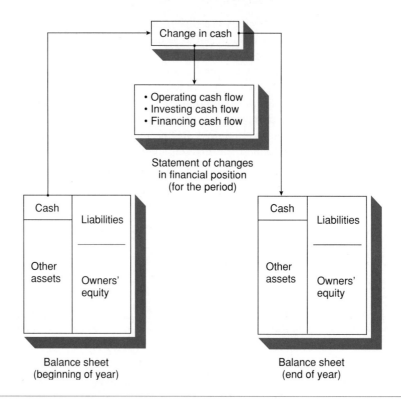

Balance sheet
(beginning of year)

Balance sheet
(end of year)

of the year. For example, for Ted's Trucking, a balance sheet *could have* been prepared after *each* transaction. Most companies monitor individual elements of their balance sheet on a daily or weekly basis, but normally the complete financial picture is analyzed only as of a month-end, quarter-end, or year-end. Most companies use a calendar year for their accounting reports, but they are not required to do so. In fact, it is often more logical to use a different 12-month period, referred to as a **fiscal year,** ending after a business peak. Many retail companies, for example, use a fiscal year that ends in February or March because December and January are significant trade periods. Maple Leaf Gardens uses a fiscal year ending on the last day of June.

fiscal year
Any continuous
12-month period,
usually beginning
after a natural
business peak.

2.3 RECOGNITION, MEASUREMENT, AND CLASSIFICATION

The recognition, measurement, and classification of asset, liability, and equity accounts on the balance sheet, reflects a diverse set of GAAP subject to a variety of management estimates, judgments, and preferences. In Chapters 6 to 12, we will discuss these issues at length; however, for the moment, let us simply overview the core set of concepts and conventions.

Recognition is the process of determining when to *include* an item in the financial statement of an entity. *Measurement* is the process of determining the *amount* at which

E X H I B I T   2 . 3

Balance Sheet Concepts

Recognition*	Measurement†	Classification
Assets		
Future economic benefit obtained, reasonable assurance as to amount	Historical cost Replacement cost Net realizable value Present value cash flows	Current assets Long-term investments Capital assets
Liabilities		
Obligation incurred, reasonable assurance as to amount	Cash value Present value cash flows	Current liabilities Long-term liabilities
Equity		
Contributed capital — when received	Residual value	Owner's equity Partners' equity Shareholders' equity
Earned capital — when assets/liabilities recognized		Members' equity Surplus

*CICA Handbook 1000.41–.46.

†CICA Handbook 1000.53, .54.

an item is to be included in the financial statements. *Classification* is the process of placing different financial statement items into meaningful *categories*. Exhibit 2.3 summarizes the recognition, measurement, and classification of balance sheet elements.

As defined in Chapter 1, the balance sheet is an accounting report that summarizes the assets a company owned, the liabilities it owed, and the owners' investment — their original investment and that portion of prior years' earnings that have been left with the company. The balance sheet may be thought of as a photograph of the financial condition of a company. The balance sheet, like a photograph, depicts the assets and the equities of a company as of a particular date. To appreciate fully the photograph's colour, texture, and tone — that is, to understand the complete image in that picture — the financial statement user must understand the specific elements that compose the balance sheet and how these elements are related. That understanding is the focus of this chapter.

Assets

The recognition of assets is dependent on two criteria. First, the organization must obtain future economic benefit. Second, there must be assurance as to the amount of the benefit. As noted in Chapter 1, the fundamental system used to prepare financial statements is the accrual basis of accounting. Under the accrual method, the financial effects of a transaction are recognized when it *occurs* without regard to the timing of its cash effects. Thus, the amounts due from customers for product sales that have not yet been paid for (i.e., accounts and notes receivable) should be recognized as assets. As well, the amounts owed for purchases of inventories or other assets (i.e., accounts and notes payable) should be reported as liabilities on the balance sheet. Thus, whether or not cash has been received or paid is *irrelevant*. Assets are recognized on the balance sheet when a company takes possession of or receives title to an asset, and liabilities are recorded when it has incurred an obligation.

The measurement of the value to be assigned to an asset is typically its acquisition cost, which is assumed to be the fair market value at the time of acquisition. For accounting purposes, **acquisition cost** encompasses more than just the invoice price of an asset. All costs incurred in bringing an asset to its intended, usable condition are considered to be part of its cost. Thus, transportation costs, installation costs, or legal fees associated with the asset are a part of its cost in addition to the purchase price.

acquisition cost
Acquisition cost is defined as all costs incurred in bringing an asset to its intended, usable condition.

The value of most assets fluctuates over time. In some cases, as with land, the value may increase, whereas with other assets, such as an automobile, the value will probably decrease. Under the historical cost concept, however, the original acquisition cost of an asset is preserved on the balance sheet. There are a number of reasons for this rigidly observed convention. Most importantly, original cost values represent *objective* evidence as to the value of an asset. Experience has demonstrated that it is often quite difficult and expensive to obtain similarly objective estimates of market values. Management has generally been reluctant to estimate market values for assets, because such estimates have so often proven to be wrong and the management involved has lost credibility. Interestingly, users have also been reluctant to give much credence to estimated values and so there has been only marginal demand for that information. As a result, GAAP-based financial statements recognize value changes only when they are validated by a sale in an arm's-length transaction to a third party.

What is true for increases in an asset's value, however, is not the case if the value of an asset *declines* over time. In such a case, the diminishment in value should be recognized in the financial statements in one of several ways. Consider, for example, current assets. Because current assets are considered to be available for use in current operations and for the repayment of current liabilities, an attempt is made to value these assets at their **net realizable value.** For example, when it is determined that an account receivable is not expected to be collected, an estimate of the uncollectible amount is determined and deducted from the receivable balance. As a consequence, only the net realizable value (i.e., the net collectible value) of the receivables is included in the total current asset balance. Similar valuation practices are also followed for other current assets like temporary investments and inventory.

net realizable value
The amount of funds expected to be received upon the sale or liquidation of an asset.

In the case of non-current assets, the downward revaluation process may occur in several forms. In general, if the value of any asset becomes permanently impaired such that the future revenue-producing capacity of the asset is materially diminished, the value of the asset should be written down. If an organization held shares in another company and the value of the shares decreases, and the decline in value was deemed to be permanent, the value of the investment would be written down. The value of some assets, however, declines over time due to their use in operations. Property, plant, and equipment, for example, are consumed (or used up) in the process of producing goods and services for sale by a company. This kind of value diminishment is recognized under the matching concept. Each period a portion of the original cost of property, plant, and equipment is removed from the balance sheet and allocated to the income statement as amortization expense.

replacement cost
The cost to reproduce or repurchase a given asset (e.g., a unit of inventory).

In the large majority of cases assets are valued at either historical cost or net realizable value. Other bases of measurement are also used, but only in limited circumstances. "**Replacement cost** is the amount that would be needed currently to reacquire an equivalent asset" (CICA Handbook 1000.54). Replacement cost can only be used with any degree of reliability if a viable market exists for the asset in question. Most inventory items have such a market. Therefore, replacement cost may be used to value inventory, should the replacement cost fall below the historical cost (conservatism principle). **Present value,** which is "the discounted amount of future cash flows expected to be received from an asset or to settle a liability" (CICA Handbook 1000.54), is also used on a limited basis. *Present value* refers to today's value of receiving (or paying) a given sum of money. For example, if we are able to deposit $1.00 in a bank today and interest is compounded annually at 10 percent, the value of our deposit will be $1.10 at the end of one year. The value to be received at the end of one year is known as the *future value.* To understand the concept of present value, it is a simple matter to consider merely the *reverse (or inverse)* of the concept of future value. For example, if we are to receive $1.10 in one year, and if interest is calculated at 10 percent annually, what is the value of that payment today? To determine the present value of receiving $1.10 in one year, it is a matter of reversing the concept of future value; thus, the present value of receiving $1.10 in one year at 10 percent interest is $1.00. Present value techniques may be used to estimate the cost of pension benefits. Present value concepts are covered in detail in a later chapter.

The measurement of asset values are based on the assumption of the going concern concept — that is, the organization is going to be in operation long enough in the foreseeable future to realize its assets in the normal course of operations. In other words, the organization is going to continue in operations long enough to collect its receivables, sell its inventory, and use its non-current assets and other resources.

To summarize, then, assets are initially recorded at their historical or acquisition cost. When such values decline due to market externalities or to internal use, the asset values are typically reduced to their net realizable value. When such values increase, with few exceptions, *no* recognition is given in the financial statements. Thus, it may be said that asset values are rarely overstated (conservatism principle), but may indeed be understated relative to their current fair market value.

The classification of assets and liabilities is based on the urgency of converting assets to cash or the urgency of making cash payments on liabilities. The balance sheet classification is intended to inform the user of the relative liquidity of the assets and the liabilities that require the earliest payment. *Liquidity* is the ability of the organization to pay its short-term obligations as they become due. A basic distinction is made between commitments that are due within 12 months and those due in more than 12 months. Thus, the balance sheet is split into current/non-current segments with the dividing line being the operating cycle or a 12-month period, whichever is longer. Exhibit 2.4 displays this basic classification.

Assets and liabilities also have the characteristic of being either monetary or nonmonetary. **Monetary items** are balance sheet items that have a cash value fixed by contract. Monetary assets include cash, temporary investments, and receivables. Monetary liabilities are obligations that must be paid in cash. **Non-monetary items** do not have a fixed cash value. Non-monetary assets include inventory, including intangibles. Non-monetary liabilities would include deposits received for season tickets, where an

present value
The value today of a future stream of cash flows calculated by discounting the cash flows at a given rate of interest.

monetary assets
Resources of an enterprise, whose principal characteristic is monetary denomination.

nonmonetary assets
Those resources of an enterprise, whose principal characteristic is other than its monetary denomination or value.

E X H I B I T 2 . 4

Balance Sheet Classification

Current assets	Current liabilities
Non-current assets	Noncurrent liabilities
	Equity

obligation exists to provide a good or service at a future date. Section 2.4 looks at the specific classification of assets.

Liabilities

The recognition of liabilities occurs when an obligation has been incurred and there is reasonable assurance as to the amount of the liability. As with the recognition of assets, the recognition of liabilities is directly related to the accrual basis of accounting. That is, when inventory or other assets are purchased, typically a cash payment is not made until a later period. However, under accrual accounting the purchase and the related liability (payable) should be recognized during the current period.

The measurement of liabilities on the balance sheet is substantially less complex than the valuation of assets. Theoretically, all liabilities are valued at the present value of the future cash outflows (or other equivalent asset flows) required to satisfy the obligation. The present value of a liability is determined by discounting the required future cash outflows using a given rate of interest called the *discount rate*. In a word, the discounting process recognizes the time value of money and the fact that a dollar due tomorrow is less costly than a dollar due today.

Although present value is the fundamental valuation approach used for all liabilities, as a practical matter it is rarely used to value short-term liabilities. By definition, short-term liabilities are expected to be satisfied or paid in the coming year, and there is little difference between the maturity value of a short-term liability and its present value. Thus, current liabilities are normally reported on the balance sheet at their maturity value or the amount of cash required to satisfy the obligation at its maturity or due date. Long-term liabilities are usually stated at their present values because they carry an (unrecorded) interest obligation. So long as the required interest on an obligation is equal to the market rate of interest on the date when the debt is incurred, the debt can be considered to be stated at its present value. The present value of a liability is determined only once — when the obligation is initially incurred. Section 2.5 looks at the specific classification of liabilities.

Equity

Equity is recognized when contributed capital has been received or when capital has been earned. The earning process is directly related to the accrual basis of accounting, and is the result of the recognition process for assets and liabilities. Although the measurement of assets and liabilities may be defined or explained with reference to specific valuation concepts or methods, the valuation of shareholders' or owners' equity is generally not. The valuation of owners' equity on the balance sheet is not an independent process but is the residual valuation that results from subtracting the liabilities from the assets. Share capital is valued at the amount of assets received in exchange for the shares. **Dividends** are the distribution of resources to the shareholders of a corporation. **Withdrawals** are the distribution of resources to the owners of a proprietorship or partnership. Dividends and withdrawals are the exact opposite of capital contributed by owners. Dividends and withdrawals decrease equity. The reported value of retained earnings — the residual earnings after dividends have been paid — depends on the revenues and expenses reflected in the income statement. As you will learn in Chapter 3, every revenue and expense decision impacts an asset or a liability. Therefore the residual of those asset-liability/revenue-expense accounting decisions comes to rest in retained earnings. Section 2.6 looks at the specific classification of equity items.

dividend
A distribution of the earned income of an enterprise to its owners.

withdrawals
Withdrawals are the distribution of resources to the owners of a proprietorship or partnership.

2.4 ASSETS

Assets are the resources that an organization owns or controls, and that it expects will provide *future* economic benefit to the organization. Assets are the resources that can be used to generate revenue for the organization. Maple Leaf Gardens, Limited, had $30,323,620 in assets as of June 30, 1994. Maple Leaf Gardens' principal asset categories are: current assets; property, plant, and equipment; and intangible assets.

Current Assets

current asset
Those resources of an enterprise, whose consumption or use is expected to occur within the current operating cycle.

"**Current assets** should include those assets ordinarily realizable within one year from the date of the balance sheet or within the normal operating cycle, where that is longer than a year" (CICA Handbook 1510.01). These assets include cash, accounts receivable, inventory, prepaid expenses, and other miscellaneous current assets. The order of presentation of the current assets is intended to inform the reader of the relative liquidity of the assets. (Remember that *liquidity* refers to the likelihood or ability of a company to satisfy its short-term obligations.) Thus, the most liquid current asset is cash, whereas the least liquid is prepaid expenses. This presentation format of most to least liquid is also followed for the asset category as a whole. The most liquid assets, that is, current assets, are listed first with the least liquid assets, that is, intangible assets, listed last. Within the current asset category, Maple Leaf Gardens discloses three different accounts: Cash, Accounts Receivable, and Prepaid Expenses.

MAPLE LEAF GARDENS, LIMITED

	1994	1993
Current assets:		
Cash and equivalents	$10,188,543	$12,086,374
Accounts receivable	1,734,925	3,135,671
Prepaid expenses	981,915	511,338
	$12,905,383	$15,733,383

cash
A current asset representing the amount of money on hand or in the bank.

The item **cash** of $10,188,543 refers to funds held in corporate bank accounts, cash on hand at various company locations, and cash invested in short-term financial instruments, such as certificates of deposit.

accounts receivable
Amounts due to a company from customers who purchased goods or services on credit.

Accounts receivable of $1,734,925 represents the amounts owed to Maple Leaf Gardens by its customers who purchased the company's goods and services on credit but had not, as of June 30, 1994, paid for those purchases. Accounts receivable are also frequently called *trade receivables* and usually represent sales whose payments are expected in 30, 60, or 90 days after the customer has received the goods and been billed for them. **Notes receivable,** on the other hand, represent amounts owing on credit sales whose payments are usually not expected within 90 days and because of the large amount of money involved, a formal contractual agreement to pay, that is, a "note" is prepared. Under GAAP, sales involving accounts or notes receivable are recognized as revenues earned in the period in which the goods or services are exchanged. The asset received in exchange for the goods delivered is a promise to be paid, and, thus, a receivable is recorded by the selling company.

notes receivable
Amounts due from customers who purchased goods or services on credit; the obligation is evidenced by a legal document called a note.

The final item in the current assets section of the balance sheet of Maple Leaf Gardens, Limited, is prepaid expenses of $981,915. These assets involve expenditures for the prepayment of such items as rent, insurance, or taxes. Some contractual ar-

prepaid expenses
A current asset that represents prior expenditures and whose consumption is expected to occur in the next accounting period.

rangements (e.g., rent and insurance) often require payment in advance. **Prepaid expenses** represent past cash outflows for which the company expects to receive some future benefit. Following the matching principle, which we discussed in Chapter 1, that prepayment will be removed from the asset account and charged to an expense account over time as the future benefits are realized.

Other examples of current assets *not* included in the Maple Leaf Gardens, Limited, statements include items like temporary investments, merchandise inventory, and supplies inventory.

The classification of investments under the current asset category can become somewhat confusing because of the number of different terminologies used for investments. The terms *marketable securities*, *temporary investments*, and *short-term investments* are frequently used interchangeably. Investments of a *very* short term (three months or less) are frequently classified *with* cash, as cash equivalents. Investments to be held for longer than three months, but less than one year are classified under current assets as **temporary investments** (CICA Handbook terminology). This practice is followed by a number of Canadian companies and is illustrated in the notes from their annual reports:

temporary investments
Short-term investments in the shares or bonds of other corporations.

Northern Telecom Limited

Cash equivalents:
All highly liquid investments with original maturities of three months or less are classified as cash and equivalents.

Interprovincial Pipe Line System, Inc.

Cash and short term investments:
Cash includes short term deposits, which are highly marketable securities with a maturity of three months or less when purchased. Short term investments, which are marketable securities with a maturity of more than three months when purchased, are valued at the lower of cost and market.

Although a portion of Maple Leaf Gardens' assets are clearly identified as current, by inference the remaining assets are considered non-current. Because of the delineation between current and non-current assets (and liabilities), Maple Leaf Gardens' balance sheet is said to be a **classified balance sheet.** That distinction, however, is not required in all cases, and when no distinction between current and non-current assets (or liabilities) exists, the balance sheet is considered to be an unclassified balance sheet. The decision to present a classified balance sheet or an unclassified balance sheet is usually tied to the company's operating cycle. If the company's operating cycle — that is, the period of time between the beginning production of a product and collecting the proceeds from the sale of a finished product — is less than one year, a classified balance sheet is prepared. An unclassified balance sheet is often used by companies whose operating cycle is longer than one year (e.g., a winery, a timber company, a real estate development company).

classified balance sheet
A balance sheet that delineates the assets and liabilities as current and noncurrent.

Long-Term Investments

noncurrent assets
The long-lived resources of an enterprise, whose consumption or use is not expected to be completed within the current operating cycle.

Long-term investments is the first asset in the general group of assets called *non-current assets*. Non-current assets also include capital assets such as property, plant, and equipment and intangible assets. **Non-current assets** are a company's long-lived resources whose use will take place over *more* than one year or one accounting period. These assets are frequently segmented into tangible and intangible assets.

E X H I B I T   2 . 5

Classification of Investments

Cash and equivalents	Held for 3 months or less
Temporary investments	Held for longer than 3 months, but less than 12 months
Long-term investments	Held for longer than 1 year

tangible asset
Those resources of an enterprise, that possess physical characteristics or have a physical presence.

Tangible assets, like property, plant, and equipment, possess identifiable physical characteristics, whereas intangible assets, like goodwill, do not. Nonetheless, both tangible and intangible assets possess revenue-producing characteristics that make them valuable to a company over future periods.

long-term investments
Investments in other companies' shares or bonds that will be held for longer than twelve months.

Long-term investments involve investments in other companies' shares or bonds that will be held for longer than 12 months. In most cases the purpose of the long-term investment is to gain a degree of control over another entity. For example, a retail company may wish to gain control over a wholesale company to guarantee a steady supply of inventory. Other companies acquire long-term investments to diversify their operations. In contrast, short-term investments are merely the investment of excess cash for the purposes of earning a return over the short term (12 months or less). Exhibit 2.5 summarizes the classification of short-term and long-term investments.

Capital Assets

capital assets
Long-lived assets include property, plant and equipment; intangible properties; and natural resources.

Capital assets are long-lived assets necessary to conduct an organization's basic operations. "Capital assets, comprising property, plant and equipment and intangible properties, are identifiable assets that meet all of the following criteria: (a) are held for use in the production or supply of goods and services, for rental to others, for administrative purposes or for the development, construction, maintenance or repair of other capital assets; (b) have been acquired, constructed or developed with the intention of being used on a continuing basis; and (c) are not intended for sale in the ordinary course of business." (CICA Handbook 3060.04)

fixed assets
The terminology often used in practice for capital assets.

Maple Leaf Gardens has capital assets or fixed assets of $14,129,736. **Fixed assets** is a term frequently used in practice to describe capital assets. Note 4 to the Maple Leaf Gardens' statement provides a schedule indicating the company has included land, building, equipment, and construction in progress in its fixed asset category. A company's fixed assets are an integral part of its basic operations, but they differ from inventory in two important respects. First, property, plant, and equipment are not owned for the purpose of being sold to customers. Second, these assets are expected to benefit the organization's operations for many years. Because of the extended productive life of these assets, the company's cost of capital assets is allocated over the assets' expected useful lives rather than totally expensed in the year of acquisition.

amortization
A systematic allocation process that allocates the acquisition cost of a long-lived asset over the estimated productive life of the asset.

The process of allocating a capital asset's cost over various years is called **amortization** and is based on the historical cost concept discussed previously. When an asset is amortized, a portion of its original cost is charged to expense, and the other side of the entry increases a contra asset account. Many financial statement users want to know the original cost of the capital assets; hence, the annual amortization charge is

contra account
An account that is subtracted from a related account; for example, accumulated amortization.

accumulated amortization
A contra asset account that represents the portion of the original cost of an asset that has been allocated to prior accounting periods.

not deducted from the asset account directly but rather is accumulated in a **contra asset account.** The contra asset account, called **Accumulated Amortization,** is presented on the asset side of the balance sheet as a *negative* amount or deduction. The balance in the Accumulated Amortization contra asset account, as reported on the balance sheet, includes *not only* the current period's charge to expense but also that portion of the asset's cost that has been allocated (i.e., expensed) in prior accounting periods. The Accumulated Amortization account balance is deducted from the capital asset account balance in reporting the *net* capital assets in the balance sheet. The original cost of an asset less the balance in the Accumulated Amortization account is called the *net book value* or *carrying value* of the asset. A review of Maple Leaf Gardens' footnote 4 reveals that the acquisition cost of its property, plant, and equipment was $25,511,891 as of June 30, 1994, and the accumulated amortization as of that date was $11,382,155. Only the net book value of these assets (i.e., $14,129,736) is included in the company's assets on the balance sheet.

MAPLE LEAF GARDENS, LIMITED

	Cost	Accumulated Amortization	1994 Net Book Value	1993 Net Book Value
Fixed Assets				
Land	$ 358,811	—	$ 358,811	$ 358,811
Building	18,622,562	$ 6,785,576	11,836,986	11,037,258
Equipment	6,452,000	4,596,579	1,855,421	1,615,565
Construction in progress	78,518	—	78,518	499,169
	$25,511,891	$11,382,155	$14,129,736	$13,510,803

We will have more to say about the accounting for capital assets and about the process of amortization in Chapter 8. At this point, however, it is perhaps helpful to emphasize that accounting for amortization is intended only as a process to allocate the cost of the asset to future periods. From an economic standpoint, capital assets lose and gain value over time as a result of a wide variety of factors. As we noted in our discussion of the historic cost concept, GAAP accounting is based on original costs and thus does not deal with day-to-day, year-to-year changes in market values. Hence, the financial statements do not reflect the impact that economic effects such as new technologies or increased market demand might have on the values of a company's capital assets. Again, amortization is simply the process of *allocating the original cost* of an asset over the future periods expected to benefit from that earlier investment.

intangible assets
Those resources of an enterprise, that lack an identifiable physical presence.

goodwill
An intangible asset representing the excess of the purchase price of acquired net assets over their fair market value.

Another non-current asset category is intangible assets. **Intangible assets** include assets that typically lack physical substance, but have future value due to the rights they possess. "Intangible properties are capital assets that lack physical substance. Examples of intangible properties include brand names, copyrights, franchises, licenses, patents, software, subscription lists, and trademarks" (CICA Handbook 1000.35,36). In many cases the cost of the intangible is the legal cost of obtaining the right to use a particular product or process. In the context of accounting, **goodwill** does not refer to a company's favourable or positive consumer image. Instead, goodwill indicates that an organization has previously acquired one or more other companies for a purchase price in excess of the fair market value of the acquired company's identifiable net assets (i.e., its total assets minus total liabilities). The acquisition of many long-term investments results in a substantial amount of goodwill by paying a premium for the acquisition of well-established successful companies. Maple Leaf Gardens, Limited, has only one intangible asset, that being a franchise in the National Hockey League. Note 1(*e*) of the Maple Leaf Gardens statement describes this asset. Like property, plant, and equipment, the cost of goodwill and other intangible assets is normally allocated over the expected useful life of these assets. The process of allocating the cost of an intangible asset over its useful life is called *amortization*.

The final non-current asset category is natural resources. Natural resources include such assets as mining properties and oil and gas properties. "Mining properties are capital assets represented by the capitalized costs of acquired mineral rights and the costs associated with exploration for and development of mineral reserves. Oil and gas properties are capital assets represented by the capitalized costs of acquired oil and gas rights and the costs associated with exploration for and development of oil, gas and related reserves" (CICA Handbook 3060.08,11). **Depletion** is the term frequently used for the amortization or cost allocation of a natural resource.

depletion
Depletion is a term used to refer to the amortization or cost allocation of natural resources.

2.5 LIABILITIES

As defined in Chapter 1, the liabilities of a company are the dollar measures of its obligations to repay money loaned to it, to pay for goods or services it has received, or to fulfill commitments it has made. In essence, a company's liabilities represent claims on its assets. As with assets, it is convenient to aggregate liabilities into current and non-current categories, which delineate the expected repayment period for the liability. Thus, "**current liabilities** should include amounts payable within one year from the date of the balance sheet or within the normal operating cycle, where this is longer than a year" (CICA Handbook 1510.03). A non-current liability is one that will be paid at some future point in time beyond the next operating cycle or year. Maple Leaf Gardens' balance sheet shows that the company has two principal liability categories: current liabilities and long-term liabilities.

current liability
An obligation of an enterprise whose settlement requires the use of current assets or the creation of other current liabilities.

Current Liabilities

Within the current liabilities category, Maple Leaf Gardens discloses four different accounts: Accounts Payable, Deferred Compensation Payable, Income Taxes Payable, and Deferred Income. The basis for the sequencing of these accounts is not as clear-cut as it is on the asset side of the balance sheet. The sequencing within the current liability section of the balance sheet is primarily intended to reflect the priority standing of the various creditors. The priority ranking, however, is tempered by the expected order of repayment of the various liabilities (i.e., current liabilities followed by long-term debt, accounts payable followed by taxes payable). The disclosure of these accounts on Maple Leaf Gardens' balance sheet appears as follows.

MAPLE LEAF GARDENS, LIMITED

	1994	1993
Current Liabilities		
Accounts payable	$7,036,834	$12,315,755
Deferred compensation payable	246,718	87,616
Income and other taxes payable	110,148	330,163
Deferred income	1,045,337	1,608,055
	$8,439,037	$14,341,589

accounts payable
Amounts owed to
suppliers for
merchandise
purchased on credit
but not yet paid for;
normally classified as
a current liability.

Accounts payable or trade payables represent the amounts owed to various suppliers for goods and services purchased on credit but not yet paid. The common business practice of giving a purchaser 30 days to pay results in an account receivable for the seller/supplier and an account payable for the buyer/user.

Deferred compensation payable represents compensation to be paid to employees at a future date. Certain employees have employment contracts that call for the deferred payment of their compensation. These employees have performed services for the company during the fiscal year and the company has, therefore, recognized the salary expense of the employee in the current period, even though actual payment of the compensation is not due until a subsequent period. Deferred compensation to be paid within the next 12 months is classified as a current liability. Compensation payable over a longer period of time is classified as a long-term liability. The accounting for deferred compensation is an example of the use of the accrual basis of accounting. Additional information on the deferred compensation payable of Maple Leaf Gardens, Limited, is disclosed in note 5 to their financial statements.

The item income taxes payable represents Maple Leaf Gardens' estimate of the income taxes that will be owed to federal, provincial, municipal, and other authorities when the tax returns for the period are completed. Under accrual accounting, the balance sheet must reflect all obligations owed as of the date of the statement, even if the exact amounts due are not immediately determinable. Thus, the preparation of the 1994 balance sheet may require that some liabilities be estimated.

The final current liability of Maple Leaf Gardens, Limited, is deferred income. Note 1(*g*) states deferred income represents payments received in advance for events and services that have not yet been performed. Such items would include season tickets or concert tickets that have been sold in advance of the event. The cash for such tickets has been received, but the actual event is scheduled for after Maple Leaf Gardens' fiscal year-end of June 30.

Current liabilities *not* included in the Maple Leaf Gardens, Limited, statements may include items like short-term borrowings, current maturities of long-term debt, and trade notes payable. Short-term borrowings refer to cash loans that are usually due in 90 to 180 days. Current maturities of long-term debt, on the other hand, represent the portion of long-term bank loans or other borrowings that are due to be paid within the next operating cycle or year. As an example, the principal portion of a 20-year mortgage that is due to be paid in the next 12 months is classified in the current liabilities section of the balance sheet. Trade notes represent amounts owed to suppliers for goods or services purchased on credit. Other current liabilities represent those miscellaneous obligations of the company, which individually are immaterial in amount and thus are aggregated. Examples of this might include various accrued expenses such as wages owed for work done or utilities payable for electricity already used.

Long-Term Liabilities

Maple Leaf Gardens' non-current or long-term liabilities fall into only one principal category: deferred compensation payable. This long-term liability is similar to the current liability deferred compensation payable, except the payments are not due within the current year but over an extended period of time. A schedule of the deferred compensation payable of Maple Leaf Gardens, Limited, is disclosed in note 5 to their financial statements.

MAPLE LEAF GARDENS, LIMITED

	1994	1993
Long-Term Liabilities		
Deferred compensation payable	$3,786,959	$2,248,783

long-term debt
(long-term liabilities)
The obligations of a
company payable
after more than one
year.

Long-term liabilities *not* included in the Maple Leaf Gardens, Limited, statements may include items like long-term debt, other liabilities, and deferred income taxes. The **long-term debt** includes amounts borrowed from financial institutions, various bonds sold in Canada and other countries, and certain types of long-term lease obligations. A bond is a financial instrument carrying a specified rate of interest (the coupon rate) and a specified repayment date (the maturity date), which is normally sold to investors as a way to raise funds for a company. Lease obligations refer to non-cancellable lease arrangements involving the use of various leased assets, such as machinery and equipment.

**deferred income
taxes**
The portion of a
company's income
tax expense not
currently payable,
and that is postponed
because of
differences in the
accounting policies
adopted for financial
statement purposes
versus those policies
used for tax
reporting purposes.

Other liabilities is an aggregation of miscellaneous long-term liabilities and various accounts having a credit balance. Finally, **deferred income taxes** refers to income taxes that are not currently being paid but will be paid at some future date. The topic of deferred income taxes is covered in detail in a later chapter.

2.6 EQUITY

Equity refers to the owners' or shareholders' investment in a company, or a members' interest in a non-profit organization. As noted earlier, equity is comprised of two distinct elements: contributed capital or the shareholders' purchase of shares from the company and earned capital, the company's retention of a portion of its earnings. The actual classification and terminology for equity varies depending on the accounting entity. "Equity is the ownership interest in the assets of a profit oriented enterprise after deducting its liabilities. While equity of a profit oriented enterprise in total is a residual, it includes specific categories of items, for example, types of share capital, contributed surplus and retained earnings. In the case of a non-profit organization, net assets, sometimes referred to as equity or fund balances, is the residual interest in its assets after deducting its liabilities. Net assets may include specific categories of items that may be either restricted or unrestricted as to their use." (CICA Handbook 1000.35,.36)

Contributed Capital

share capital
A certificate
representing an
ownership interest in
an enterprise.

When a company sells shares, the proceeds are reflected in the **Share Capital** account. The discussion of the entity concept in Chapter 1 pointed out that the financial statements reflect *only* the transactions of the entity and not the personal transactions of the owners. Therefore, the financial statements reflect purchases of shares by the shareholders directly from the company as well as sales of shares back to the company. However, the company's financial statements do *not* reflect purchases and sales of shares *between* shareholders and other outsiders.

A company's charter of incorporation specifies, among other things, the maximum number of shares of share capital that can be issued; these are often referred to as the

authorized shares
The total number of share capital that are authorized to be sold under a company's charter of incorporation.

issued shares
The number of shares of share capital sold to shareholders less any shares repurchased and retired.

authorized shares. When authorized shares are sold to investors, they become **issued shares.** The shareholders' equity of Maple Leaf Gardens indicates that of the 4,999,500 authorized shares, 3,677,400 shares have been issued for $36,774.

Earned Capital

The second principal form of shareholders' equity is the earned capital or retained earnings. The retained earnings of a company represent the historical, cumulative portion of net income that has been retained in the company to support on-going operations and has not been paid out to shareholders as dividends. The concept of net income will be examined in Chapter 3. The shareholders' equity of Maple Leaf Gardens reveals retained earnings of $18,060,850, as of June 30, 1994.

MAPLE LEAF GARDENS, LIMITED

	1994	1993
Shareholders' Equity		
Share capital:		
Authorized: 4,999,500 (1993 — 5,000,000)		
Issued: 3,677,400 (1993 — 3,677,900)	$ 36,774	$ 36,779
Retained earnings	18,060,850	14,808,800
	$18,097,624	$14,845,579

It is worth repeating that equity simply is the difference between the company's assets stated at their book values and the company's liabilities stated at their book values. Equity would be a measure of the fair value of a company only if the book value of the assets and the liabilities were also equal to their market values — a coincidence that rarely happens. Therefore, the equity number must be understood to be no more (or less) than a balancing number, the result of the accounting process and the maintenance of the accounting equation: Assets = Liabilities + Equity.

2.7 ANALYZING FINANCIAL STATEMENTS

General Approach/Techniques

As we observed in Chapter 1, accounting is a language, a communication device, and, therefore, not an end in itself. Thus, the presentation of accounting information in a format such as the balance sheet is merely the beginning of the communication process. The recipient of the balance sheet and the other financial statements must use the presented financial data to draw inferences and conclusions about the financial status of an organization.

We now focus on the question of how to analyze, evaluate, and interpret financial statement data. The subject of financial statement analysis is very extensive and is often covered in a single textbook. An advanced level of analysis is beyond the scope of this book. However, as the focus of this book is on the user of financial reports, some basic approaches to financial statement analysis are presented herein.

An underlying rule of financial statement analysis is that of comparison. A value by itself has little significance. For example, what significance does the value 187 have? If 187 is your weight it may or may not be significant depending on your height, age, and

EXHIBIT 2.6

Financial Statement Analysis Techniques

Analyzing absolute amounts
Trend analysis
Common-size statements
Ratio analysis

other characteristics. If 187 was your weight, you would have some basis of comparisons already established: your current weight, your weight last year, the weight of other people you know, and so on. The accounting principle of comparability supports this idea. In the section on qualitative criteria in Chapter 1, we learned comparability is a characteristic of the relationship between two pieces of information rather than of a particular piece of information by itself. It is an important concept when comparing two different entities or the same entity over different time periods. It is generally thought information is more valuable when it can be compared to similar information. Therefore, financial statements should always be issued on a comparable basis. For example, this year's financial report should be compared to last year's.

A variety of analysis techniques and approaches are available to the financial statement user. We will discuss some of the different approaches to provide you with a basic understanding of financial statement analysis. Fundamental financial statement analysis includes the four techniques listed in Exhibit 2.6. When interpreting and analyzing financial reports, in most cases it will be necessary to use all of the techniques (and probably several others). The individual techniques should *not* be considered to provide all the answers to the understanding of financial statements.

Analyzing Absolute Amounts

The analysis of financial statements can occur at various levels of sophistication. At the most fundamental level, as a first step, the financial statement user can review and identify the absolute amount of important account balances. For example, it may be important to note the absolute level of cash on hand. If the level of cash on hand is sufficient to meet a company's most urgent needs (e.g., to pay employee salaries and replenish sold inventory), it is unlikely that the company will need to borrow money in the current period. In most cases, however, merely identifying the absolute level of various account balances does not provide sufficient information to analyze fully a company's financial position. The absolute level of inventory on hand, for example, informs us only that a company does have some inventory on hand to begin operations in the next period; the absolute level does not tell us, however, whether the available inventory will be sufficient to sustain sales or whether the company will need to purchase or manufacture additional units, and, if so, how soon. To address these more sophisticated questions, it is often useful to construct ratios of various related account balances.

trend analysis
The analysis of ratios or absolute balances over one or more accounting periods to identify the direction or trend of a company's financial health.

Trend Analysis

Trend analysis involves the comparison of financial data over time. For example, key figures like total revenues, total assets, and net income for the past 5 or 10 years may be presented in a series and analyzed to determine if any trends exist in the organization's finances or operations. Many publicly held companies include 5- or 10-year summaries in their annual reports for this purpose. Frequently such financial information is presented in graphical format to facilitate its analysis and interpretation. A portion of the Hudson Bay Company's Comparative Financial Summary is presented below:

HUDSON BAY COMPANY
Comparative Financial Summary
(in millions of dollars)

	1993	1992	1991	1990	1989	1988	1987
Assets employed	$2,897	$2,637	$2,588	$2,401	$2,198	$2,231	$2,388
Debt	$1,200	$1,239	$1,335	$1,243	$1,147	$1,441	$1,549
Debt-to-equity ratio	0.7:1	0.9:1	1.1:1	1.1:1	1.1:1	1.8:1	1.8:1

The trend analysis clearly indicates the firm's assets employed have increased and its debts have decreased over the time period.

Common-Size Statements

common-size financial statements Financial statements in which the dollar amounts are expressed as a percentage of some common statement item.

Trend analysis is also often aided by the use of **common-size financial statements,** in which all amounts are expressed as a percentage of some base financial statement item. For example, a common-size balance sheet might express all asset accounts as a percentage of total assets and all equity accounts as a percentage of total equities. Trend analysis of common-size statements permits the analyst to determine, for example, how the relative composition of total assets or total equities is changing over time.

When preparing common-size financial statements, three financial statement numbers — total assets, total equities, and net sales — may be converted to a base of 100 percent. Each item within the assets and equities on the balance sheet, or each item on the income statement, is then expressed as a percentage of the base number. Since for any given set of financial statements the base numbers represent 100 percent, the restated financial statements are called *common-size statements*.

To illustrate common-size financial statements, Exhibit 2.7 presents Maple Leaf Gardens' common-size balance sheets for 1994 and 1993. Note that the common-size statements permit both a within-period analysis (e.g., in 1994, current assets were 42.6 percentage of total assets) and across-period trend analysis (e.g., current assets as a percentage of total assets decreased from 50.1 percent in 1993 to 42.6 percent in 1994).

Ratio Analysis

ratio analysis Ratio analysis is a common financial statement analysis technique which compares financial statement elements on a ratio basis.

Ratio analysis is frequently used to gain a more complete understanding of a company's financial condition. Ratios may be investigated both within a given accounting period and across a number of accounting periods. When ratios (or absolute amounts) are compared across time periods, particular trends in a company's financial condition or operations may be identified. Not surprisingly, this type of across-period analysis is called *trend analysis*. To facilitate the analysis of financial trends, most companies provide accounting data for at least the current period and the prior period. Moreover, some companies provide summary financial data for as many as 10 years in the annual report.

In addition to comparing a company's performance from one year to the next, it is also instructive to compare the financial results of a given company with those of other

EXHIBIT 2.7

MAPLE LEAF GARDENS, LIMITED
Balance sheet
At June 30, 1993, and 1994

	1994	Common-Size Percentage	1993	Common-Size Percentage
Current assets:				
Cash and equivalent	$10,188,543	33.6	$12,086,374	38.5
Accounts receivable	1,734,925	5.7	3,135,671	10.0
Prepaid expenses	981,915	3.3	511,338	1.6
Total current assets	$12,905,383	42.6	$15,733,383	50.1
Fixed assets	14,129,736	46.6	13,510,803	43.0
Deferred charges	782,600	2.6	632,644	2.0
Deferred income tax	2,405,900	7.9	1,459,120	4.6
Franchises: N.H.L.	100,001	.3	100,001	.3
Total assets	$30,323,620	100.0	$31,435,951	100.0
Current liabilities:				
Accounts payable	$ 7,036,834	23.2	$12,315,755	39.2
Deferred compensation	246,718	.8	87,616	.3
Income taxes payable	110,148	.4	330,163	1.0
Deferred income	1,045,337	3.4	1,608,055	5.1
Total current liabilities	8,439,037	27.8	14,341,589	45.6
Deferred compensation payable	3,786,959	12.5	2,248,783	7.2
Shareholders' equity:				
Capital stock:				
Authorized: 4,999,500 (1993 —				
5,000,000) common shares				
Issued: 3,677,400 (1993 —				
3,677,900) common shares	36,774	.1	36,779	.1
Retained earnings	18,060,850	59.6	14,808,800	47.1
Total liabilities and equity	$30,323,620	100.0	$31,435,951	100.0

companies within the same industry or with industry averages. For example, by comparing the financial results of Maple Leaf Gardens with those of other companies in the entertainment business, an investor may be able to identify which firm presents the best investment opportunity within the industry. Similarly, investor service firms provide industry data to permit comparisons of one company against the average of similar companies within a given industry. Use of such data may enable an investor to determine whether a company is outperforming or underperforming the average for that industry. Exhibit 2.8 provides a small sample of the comparative key business ratios available from Dun & Bradstreet Canada.

It is important to again emphasize the significance of comparative data when performing financial analysis. Whether the user is analyzing absolute amounts, ratios, or trends, it is crucial to compare the data to similar data within or outside the organization.

CICA Research Report on Financial Ratios

The Canadian Institute of Chartered Accountants has issued a research report entitled "Using Ratios and Graphics in Financial Reporting." The research study provides an interesting look at many of the problems and difficulties of financial statement analy-

EXHIBIT 2.8

Ratio Guides

Industry	Current Ratio	Total Debt to Equity
Women's clothing	1.5	206.4%
Gas/service stations	1.2	277.6
Farm machinery	1.4	290.0
Gold mining	3.1	47.9
Truck transport	0.9	264.1

Source: Dun & Bradstreet Canada.

EXHIBIT 2.9

Financial Statement Analysis

Financial Strength		Management Performance	
Liquidity	Solvency	Profitability	Asset Management

sis. The CICA study is mentioned herein, as it provides an excellent framework for analysis. The framework for financial statement analysis recommended by the CICA research study has been modified to be more relevant for an introductory-level discussion of the topic. A basic framework of financial statement analysis is summarized in Exhibit 2.9.

Different forms of financial analysis are typically utilized to gain an understanding of a organization's financial strength and/or its management performance. Depending on the individual users and their objectives, different analysis approaches may be appropriate. Creditors may focus on **financial strength** to evaluate the organization's ability to meet its financial obligations. Owners of the organization may be more interested in the performance of management and the profitability of the firm. The analysis of an organization's financial strength is covered in the next section, Analyzing the Balance Sheet. **Management performance** involves profitability and asset management. *Profitability* refers to a company's overall income-generating ability, and *asset management effectiveness* refers to the ability of a company's managers to utilize its assets effectively to produce a return for the company's creditors and owners. Most profitability ratios are based on income statement accounts; consequently, this topic and asset management is to be deferred until Chapter 3.

2.8 ANALYZING THE BALANCE SHEET

The balance sheet is a good source of information regarding an organization's financial strength. Financial strength may be viewed from a short-term or long-term perspective. **Liquidity** refers to the likelihood or ability of a company to satisfy its short-term obligations; **solvency** refers to a company's ability to satisfy its long-term obligations. Exhibit 2.10 summarizes some widely accepted indicators of an organization's liquidity and solvency.

financial strength
Financial strength is the organization's ability to meet its financial obligations.

management performance
Management performance involves profitability and asset management.

liquidity
The short-term debt repayment ability of a company.

solvency
The long-term debt repayment ability of a company.

EXHIBIT 2.10

Ratio Analysis Indicators of Financial Strength

Liquidity	Solvency
Quick ratio	Total debt-to-equity ratio
Current ratio	Long-term debt-to-invested capital ratio

Liquidity

Liquidity is frequently evaluated on the basis of four indicators:

1. The amount of cash on hand.
2. The level of working capital.
3. The current ratio.
4. The quick ratio.

The amount of cash and cash equivalents on hand is a precise indication of the level of highly liquid resources available for a company's debt repayment or other operating needs. Cash on hand is very measurable and therefore quite certain, but it is also a very conservative measure of liquidity. Only in the most extreme circumstances would a company have to pay all of its bills using only its cash on hand.

working capital
A measure of liquidity calculated as total current assets minus total current liabilities.

A somewhat more general indicator of liquidity that is broader in scope is the level of working capital. **Working capital** is current assets minus current liabilities. Thus working capital is a measure of the net current assets that would be available to support a company's continuing operations if all of its current assets could be converted to cash at their balance sheet values and the proceeds used to satisfy its current liabilities. The equation is as follows:

$$\text{Working capital} = \text{Current assets} - \text{Current liabilities}$$

current ratio
A measure of liquidity calculated as current assets divided by current liabilities.

A ratio based on the concept of working capital is the **current ratio,** which is calculated by dividing current assets by current liabilities:

$$\text{Current ratio} = \frac{\text{Current assets}}{\text{Current liabilities}}$$

Both working capital and the current ratio are "coverage" indicators; the former indicates the extent to which current assets cover current liabilities in an absolute sense, and the latter indicates the extent of coverage in a relative sense. A high current ratio (i.e., a substantial amount of working capital) indicates good liquidity, suggesting that a company's currently maturing obligations are likely to be paid on time. A ratio that is too high, however, may indicate an unproductive use of resources and suggest that current assets might be used more effectively by investing them in other resources.

quick ratio
A measure of liquidity calculated as quick assets divided by current liabilities.

Another measure of liquidity is the quick ratio, which is calculated as follows:

$$\text{Quick ratio} = \frac{\text{Cash} + \text{Temporary investments} + \text{Accounts receivable}}{\text{Current liabilities}}$$

quick assets
Highly liquid, short-term assets such as cash, cash equivalents, short-term investments, and receivables.

The **quick ratio** examines only the liability coverage provided by the quick assets. **Quick assets** are highly liquid current assets such as cash, cash equivalents, temporary investments, and receivables, that is, cash or assets that can be quickly converted to cash. Temporary investments may be easily sold and quickly converted to cash. Accounts and notes receivables are considered to be quick assets because they can usually be converted to cash quickly by being sold to a factor. A *factor* is a financial institution that buys receivables from other companies at a discount (i.e., at a price *less* than the amount to be collected) and earns a profit when the receivables are collected. Other current assets like inventory take a longer period of time to be converted to cash and are *excluded* from quick assets.

To illustrate these liquidity measures, let us consider Maple Leaf Gardens' balance sheet for 1994. The balance sheet reveals that, as of June 30, 1994, Maple Leaf Gardens had cash and cash equivalents of $10,188,543 on hand, working capital of $4,466,346, a current ratio of 1.53, and a quick ratio of 1.41. The current and quick ratios reveal that for every dollar of current liabilities, Maple Leaf Gardens held $1.53 of current assets and $1.41 of quick assets. To determine whether these measures indicate high, low, or average liquidity, one *should* compare them to existing industry averages, to those of a competitor, and to the results of prior years. Since Maple Leaf Gardens' balance sheet contains comparative data for 1993, a trend analysis can be easily undertaken. A comparison indicates that Maple Leaf Gardens' liquidity in 1994 improved significantly from that in 1993. Although the level of cash and cash equivalents actually decreased by about $2 million, the level of working capital increased by more than $3 million. The increase in working capital is also depicted in the increase in both the current and quick ratios.

MAPLE LEAF GARDENS, LIMITED

	1994	1993
Liquidity		
Cash and equivalents	$10,188,543	$12,086,374
Working capital	$ 4,466,346	$ 1,391,794
Current ratio	1.53:1	1.10:1
Quick ratio	1.41:1	1.06:1

Solvency

Solvency refers to a company's long-term debt repayment ability and may be evaluated on the basis of a number of different techniques. We have selected two common ratios to illustrate the analysis of a firm's solvency:

1. The total debt-to-equity ratio.
2. The long-term debt-to-invested capital ratio.

The concept of solvency and the thrust of these debt-level ratios suggest a negative connotation, as though debt is to be avoided and reduced whenever possible. Debt is not always bad; in fact, it is sometimes healthy. A more positive way to describe a company's debt level is to say that the shareholders' equity is leveraged; in effect, a leveraged company supplements its owners' funds with funds from other sources to "lever up" the return to the owners. The ratios that follow describe a company's debt exposure, but they should be looked at from two perspectives. Creditors obviously want to maximize their protection, but shareholders look for the best balance of debt and equity to ensure the highest return with the least risk. These ratios measure the relative amount of long-term debt outstanding.

total debt to equity ratio
The total debt to equity ratio is a measure of the extent to which a company's assets are financed by creditors as compared to the amount financed by owners.

The **total debt-to-equity ratio** is a measure of the extent to which a company's assets are financed by creditors as compared to the amount financed by owners. This ratio provides a measure of the extent to which an organization relies on borrowed funds to finance its operations. The total debt to equity ratio is calculated as follows:

$$\text{Total debt-to-equity ratio} = \frac{\text{Total debt}}{\text{Equity}}$$

In general, the lower this ratio, the higher the proportion of long-term financing provided by the owners and the more solvent a company is thought to be. Alternatively, the higher this ratio, the more leveraged a company is and the less solvent it is thought to be. In general, creditors like a lower debt-to-equity ratio because they have a prior claim on a company's assets and prefer to have a larger equity cushion beneath them.

long-term debt to invested capital ratio
The long-term debt to invested capital ratio measures the relative composition of a company's long-term capital structure.

The **long-term debt-to-invested capital ratio** measures the relative composition of a company's long-term capital structure, or capitalization. *Invested capital* refers to the *total* of long-term debt and shareholders' equity. The ratio measures the portion of total capital provided by long-term debt. A high ratio may indicate a difficulty in meeting interest payments during periods of low earnings. However, this ratio varies significantly from industry to industry and a careful *comparable* analysis should be used with it. The long-term debt-to-invested capital ratio is calculated as follows:

$$\text{Long-term debt-to-invested capital ratio} = \frac{\text{Long-term debt}}{\text{Invested capital}}$$

In general, the lower the ratio, the more solvent a company is thought to be. The higher the ratio, the less solvent and the more highly leveraged a company is considered to be. As compared to 1993, Maple Leaf Gardens' solvency in 1994 improved significantly. The ratio of total debt to equity declined from 1.12 times to only .68 times in 1994. (Stated alternatively, the level of debt as a percentage of equity declined from 112 percent to 68 percent.) The long-term debt-to-invested capital ratio increased from .13 in 1993 to .17 in 1994. However, the portion of the business financed by long-term debt is still very low.

MAPLE LEAF GARDENS, LIMITED

	1994	1993
Solvency		
Total debt-to-equity ratio	.68:1	1.12:1
Long-term debt-to-invested capital ratio	.17:1	.13:1

The analysis of financial statements will continue in the remaining chapters.

2.9 SUMMARY

Organizations are involved in investing and financing activities. The language of accounting, using the balance sheet equation, summarizes these activities in two financial statements: the balance sheet and the statement of changes in financial position. The balance sheet, prepared to communicate a company's financial status and condition, summarizes the assets a company owned, the liabilities it owed, and the accumulated funds that its owners have invested in or left with the company to cover its operating needs. The statement of changes in financial position examines an organization's sources and uses of cash during the period.

An understanding of recognition, measurement, and classification of financial statement elements is important to the understanding of financial statements. Recognition is the process of determining when to include an item in the financial statement of an entity. Measurement is the process of determining the amount at which an item is to be included in the financial statements. Classification is the process of placing different financial statement items into meaningful categories.

Balance sheet entries are generally classified on a current/non-current basis. Major asset categories include current assets, long-term investments, and capital assets including intangible assets. Liabilities are classified as either current or non-current. Equity is typically classified as contributed or earned. However, the terminologies vary considerably depending on the accounting entity.

Financial statement analysis is a complex issue. An analysis focussing on financial strength and management performance provides a framework for comparisons. The balance sheet may be used to investigate a company's financial strength, or liquidity and solvency. By itself, the balance sheet reveals very little about the profitability of a company's operations. The development of a complete understanding of a company's financial situation requires considerations beyond the balance sheet and the statement of changes in financial position. The analysis of management performance, operating activities, and the income statement are the focus of the next chapter.

2.10 KEY CONCEPTS AND TERMS

Accounts (p. 49)
Accounts receivable (p. 59)
Accounts payable (p. 64)
Accumulated Amortization (p. 62)
Acquisition cost (p. 56)
Amortization (p. 61)
Authorized shares (p. 66)
Balance sheet equation (p. 49)
Capital assets (p. 61)
Cash (p. 59)
Classified balance sheet (p. 60)
Common-size financial
    statements (p. 68)
Contra asset account (p. 62)
Credit (p. 49)
Current assets (p. 59)
Current liabilities (p. 63)
Current ratio (p. 71)
Debit (p. 49)
Deferred income taxes (p. 65)
Depletion (p. 63)
Dividends (p. 58)
Financial strength (p. 70)
Fiscal year (p. 54)
Fixed asset (p. 61)
Goodwill (p. 62)
Intangible assets (p. 62)

Issued shares (p. 66)
Liquidity (p. 70)
Long-term debt (p. 65)
Long-term debt-to-invested capital
    ratio (p. 73)
Long-term investments (p. 61)
Management performance (p. 70)
Monetary items (p. 57)
Net realizable value (p. 56)
Non-current assets (p. 60)
Non-monetary items (p. 57)
Notes receivable (p. 59)
Prepaid expenses (p. 60)
Present value (p. 57)
Quick assets (p. 71)
Quick ratio (p. 71)
Ratio analysis (p. 68)
Replacement cost (p. 56)
Share Capital (p. 65)
Solvency (p. 70)
Tangible assets (p. 60)
Temporary investments (p. 60)
Total debt-to-equity ratio (p. 73)
Trend analysis (p. 67)
Withdrawals (p. 58)
Working capital (p. 71)

2.11 COMPREHENSIVE REVIEW QUESTIONS

R2.1 Analysis of financial strength. Shown below are the balance sheets for Coca-Cola Beverages, Ltd. Using the information provided, perform an analysis of the company's financial strength. Your report should include comments with respect to the financial strength of Coca-Cola Beverages, Ltd.

COCA-COLA BEVERAGES, LTD.
Consolidated Balance Sheets
As at December 31

	1993	1992
Assets		
Current assets:		
Cash	$ 13,480	$ 13,681
Accounts receivable	69,277	77,314
Inventories	51,624	68,369
Prepaid expenses	13,665	18,069
Income taxes recoverable	—	23,407
	$148,046	$200,840
Capital assets, net	307,579	393,162
Franchise assets	215,636	221,940
Deferred charges and other assets	36,288	8,765
	$707,549	$824,707
Liabilities and Shareholders' Equity		
Current liabilities:		
Accounts payable	$160,312	$116,909
Other current liabilities	24,643	12,185
Current portion of long-term debt	—	7,850
	$184,955	$136,944
Long-term debt	411,512	386,412
Deferred income taxes	—	37,005
Shareholders' equity	111,082	264,346
	$707,549	$824,707

R2.2 Balance sheet preparation. Presented below in alphabetical order are the balance sheet accounts of the Wong Company, Ltd., as of December 31, 1996:

Accounts payable	$ 27,000
Accounts receivable	17,000
Bonds payable (due 2006)	30,000
Buildings	39,000
Cash	?
Equipment	16,000
Land	29,000
Loan payable	14,000
Merchandise inventory	22,000
Mortgage payable	42,500
Patent	17,000
Retained earnings	37,000
Salaries payable	11,200
Share capital	20,000
Temporary investments	4,400

Required:

Prepare the December 31, 1996, balance sheet of the Wong Company, Ltd.

R2.3 Statement of changes in financial position. Terry Schmidt recently started a business that is to be operated as a corporation, Terra Interior Designs, Ltd. The following cash events transpired during the first few months after the business was established, but before operations commenced:

Terry invested cash of $19,000 for common shares.

Purchased equipment for $12,000.

Purchased land for $20,000.

Obtained a long-term loan of $20,000.

Land that originally cost $5,000 was sold for $5,000.

Made payments of $4,000 on the long-term loan.

Required:

a. Determine the cash balance at the end of the period.

b. Using the above information prepare a statement of changes in financial position for Terra Interior Designs, Ltd., for the year ended December 31.

2.12 REVIEW AND DISCUSSION QUESTIONS

Q2.1 Describe and provide an example of monetary and non-monetary, and current and non-current assets and liabilities.

Q2.2 Describe the different classifications for investments.

Q2.3 What are the appropriate titles for equity for a proprietorship, a partnership, a corporation, and a non-profit organization?

Q2.4 Distinguish between the concepts of liquidity and solvency.

Q2.5 Distinguish between contributed capital and retained earnings.

Q2.6 The balance sheet of Maple Leaf Gardens, Limited, discloses two different amounts and two different classifications for deferred compensation payable. In your own words explain what is meant by *deferred compensation payable* and explain the two different classifications.

Q2.7 Most companies present a classified balance sheet, that is, they divide both assets and liabilities into long-term and short-term items. Banks do not do that, but instead present an unclassified balance sheet that makes no distinction between current and long-term items. Why might an unclassified balance sheet be appropriate for a bank?

Q2.8 The current liability section of most balance sheets includes an item called *current payments on long-term debt.* If that item represents payments due on long-term debt, why is it included in current liabilities? Does the current asset section of those balance sheets include an item called *current amortization on long-term assets?* Why or why not?

Q2.9 The current assets and liabilities from The Meed Corporation's balance sheet are as follows (all dollar amounts in millions):

	1997	1996
Current assets:		
Cash	$ 21.1	$ 21.1
Accounts receivable	528.9	536.1
Inventories	394.6	381.0
Prepaid expenses	37.4	42.4
	$982.0	$980.6
Current liabilities:		
Accounts payable	$392.1	$412.5
Accrued wages payable	83.3	84.1
Other current liabilities	205.5	182.8
Current portion of long-term debt	12.7	12.6
	$693.6	$692.0

Included in accounts payable is an item entitled *outstanding cheques*. An outstanding cheque is a cheque that has been written, but it has not yet been processed by the bank. How does this item affect your perceptions of the company's liquidity? The company's current ratio? Its quick ratio? Its working capital?

Q2.10 Monsanto describes its credit standing with the following words (from the Management Discussion and Analysis segment reviewing the balance sheet).

Monsanto Maintains Strong Financial Position

Monsanto's financial position remained strong in 1994, as evidenced by Monsanto's current "A" or better debt rating. Financial resources were adequate to support existing businesses and to fund new business opportunities.

Working capital at year-end 1994 was at the same level as that of the prior year-end. Receivables increased primarily as a result of higher fourth quarter 1994 sales versus the prior year's fourth quarter sales. The increase in current liabilities principally related to the Agricultural Products restructuring and increased short-term debt . . .

Total short- and long-term debt at year-end 1994 was $258 million higher than that of the prior year-end. The additional long-term debt was used principally for capacity expansions. To maintain adequate financial flexibility and access to debt markets worldwide, Monsanto management intends to maintain an "A" debt rating. Important factors in establishing that rating are the ratio of total debt to total capitalization, which was 35 percent in 1994. . . .

Monsanto uses financial markets around the world for its financing needs and has available various short- and medium-term bank credit facilities, which are discussed in the notes to financial statements. These credit facilities provide the financing flexibility to take advantage of investment opportunities that may arise and to satisfy future funding requirements.

In your own words, describe Monsanto's interest in maintaining its "A" rating. Why might they be interested in that rating? What would you expect the company to do to preserve that rating?

Q2.11 The balance sheet presents a picture of a company's assets, liabilities, and equities as of a point in time. In general, the balance sheet reports items at their historical cost. Consider the typical line items reported in a balance sheet. As the manager of the company publishing the balance sheet, which items would you prefer to report at current market values? As a potential investor in the company, which items would you like to have market value information on? Discuss how the demand for market value information may or may not be consistent with the reporting notions of relevance and reliability.

Q2.12 The value of ratio analysis depends to a great extent on one's ability to interpret the ratios in the context of a company's particular environment. In this regard, discuss how the quick and current ratios for the following types of companies may or may not differ.

Defence contractor
Distillery
Hotel chain
Sports franchise

Q2.13 Consider the Maple Leaf Gardens balance sheet presented at the end of Chapter 1. Identify all the line items in that balance sheet that are based on certain subjective judgments and/or estimates of Maple Leaf Gardens management. What is the nature of each of those subjective decisions? Identify several such areas of judgment and discuss whether the judgmental discretion now allowed should be reduced via additional standard setting.

Q2.14 Consider the following terms which express important balance sheet ideas:

a. Net realizable value — present value.

b. Capital assets — intangible assets.

c. Liabilities — owners' equity.

Prepare a commentary on each of the above pairings, explaining how they are alike and how they are different in the context of a company's balance sheet.

Q2.15 Consider the following asset account titles taken from different companies' published financial statements. In addition to describing the account, these account titles also express important balance sheet ideas.

a. Contracts in Process.

b. Construction in Process.

c. Debt Issuance Costs.

Prepare a commentary on each of the above account titles, covering the following points: (1) why the item in question is considered an asset; (2) what kinds of costs might have been added to the account to achieve the current balance; and (3) when and how the cost of the asset will be allocated to future operations.

Q2.16 Consider the following typical business items:

a. A 10-ton, bulk-material, over-the-road truck.

b. A $1 million 90-day note payable.

c. 1,000 common shares.

d. Computer software designed to control inventory quantities.

How might these items be classified in different companies' balance sheets? Each item can be classified at least two different ways, and several could be classified more than two ways, depending on the company involved and the surrounding circumstances.

Q2.17 Review the list of key concepts and terms at the end of the chapter. If you have difficulty with a specific concept, refer to the discussion on the page number provided to gain a better understanding of the concept. Make a list of terms you do not thoroughly understand. When you have finished Chapter 3, refer back to this list to see if your understanding has improved.

Q2.18 We say that the accounting equation forces the right side of the balance sheet always to be in balance with the left side, or, in other words, every resource has a source. A company's earnings for the year, retained for use in the business, represent a source. Where might that source have been invested? Where would we find the equivalent of that source on the left-hand side of the balance sheet?

Q2.19 A number of sources of funds are available to a company, and those different sources are compensated in different ways. A supplier might sell steel to the company on a credit basis, asking for payment in full by 90 days. A bank would be willing to lend money to the company for periods of 90 days for any number of years. A shareholder, thinking that the shares can always be sold to someone else if need be, is willing to invest funds in the company. Where do these sources appear in the balance sheet? Where does the compensation required by the sources for the use of their funds appear in the income statement?

2.13 PROBLEMS

P2.1 Balance sheet equation: financing and investing activities. The following transactions were incurred by Dollard Company during the month of November:

1. A corporation was formed and share capital was issued for $20,000 cash.

2. Obtained a long-term bank loan of $35,000.

3. Purchased machinery for $27,000 cash.

4. Purchased an automobile for $22,000 cash.

5. Obtained a long-term mortgage for $40,000.

6. Purchased land for $45,000 cash.

Required:

a. Record the transactions for Dollard Company using the accounting equation.

b. Prepare a balance sheet for Dollard Company.

c. Prepare a statement of changes in financial position for Dollard Company.

P2.2 Balance sheet equation: financing and investing activities. The following transactions occurred during one month:

1. Jane formed a proprietorship and deposited $35,000 cash in the business bank account.

2. Obtained a long-term bank loan of $40,000.

3. Purchased land for $30,000 cash.

4. Purchased machinery for $27,000 cash.

5. Sold land for $10,000 cash that had originally cost $10,000.

6. During the period, Jane withdrew $7,000 cash from the proprietorship.

7. Paid $3,000 on principal of the bank loan.

Required:

a. Record the transactions using the accounting equation.

b. Prepare a balance sheet for Jane.

c. Prepare a statement of changes in financial position for Jane.

P2.3 Balance sheet equation: financing and investing activities. Presented below in alphabetical order are the accounts of the Hale Company as of December 31, 1996:

Bonds payable	$20,000
Buildings	25,000
Cash	8,000
Equipment	22,000
Land	17,000
Loan payable	42,000
Machinery	15,000
Share capital	25,000

Required:

Set up three columns corresponding to the accounting equation:

$$\text{Assets} = \text{Liabilities} + \text{Equity}$$

Place each of the above balances in the appropriate column. Total each column to ensure the equation is in balance.

P2.4 Journal entries: financing and investing activities. The following transactions were incurred by Camborne, Limited, during the month of September:

a. A corporation was formed and share capital was issued for $40,000 cash.

b. Obtained a long-term bank loan of $25,000.

c. Purchased land for $30,000 cash.

d. Obtained a long-term mortgage for $30,000.

e. Purchased machinery for $33,000 cash.

f. Paid $3,000 on principal of the bank loan.

g. Sold land for $7,000 cash that had originally cost $7,000.

h. Purchased a computer for $4,000 cash.

Required:

Prepare general journal entries for the above transactions.

P2.5 Journal entries: financing and investing activities. The following transactions occured during one month:

a. Terry formed a proprietorship and deposited $25,000 cash in the business bank account.

b. Purchased an automobile for $14,000 cash.

c. Obtained a long-term bank loan of $15,000.

d. Purchased machinery for $7,000 cash.

e. Purchased office equipment for $5,000 cash.

f. During the period, Terry withdrew $9,000 cash from the proprietorship.

g. Paid $2,000 on principal of the bank loan.

Required:

Prepare general journal entries for the above transactions.

P2.6 Partnership: financing and investing activities. The following transactions occurred during one month.

a. Tom and Jerry formed a partnership and each deposited $20,000 cash into a bank account.

b. Purchased a computer for $6,000 cash.

c. Purchased equipment for $8,000 cash.

d. During the period, Jerry withdrew $9,000 cash from the partnership and Tom withdrew $4,000 cash.

e. Obtained a long-term mortgage for $30,000.

f. Purchased land for $35,000 cash.

g. Paid $3,000 principal on the mortgage.

Required:

Prepare general journal entries for the above transactions.

P2.7 Account identification. Classify each of the following accounts:

a. Accounts Payable.

b. Prepaid Insurance.

c. Cash.

d. Share Capital

e. Supplies Inventory.

f. Rent Payable.

g. Land and Building.

h. Advance Deposit by Customer.

i. Loan Payable.

j. Accounts Receivable.

k. Retained Earnings.

l. Warranty Liability.

m. Temporary Investments.

n. Receivables from Employees.

P2.8 Comparisons of asset mix. Different companies have different assets for their use, largely because of the characteristics of their industry but also because of the maturity of the individual company and other company-specific factors. Individual companies fund those assets with different sources as well, depending on the cost and availability of capital to the industry and to the specific company.

Required:

a. Select five different companies — three in the same industry and two in completely different industries. For each company determine the percentage of assets represented by cash and cash equivalents, receivables, inventory, plant and equipment, and long-term investments and other assets. Comment on the similarities and the differences you noticed.

b. Calculate the current ratio for each of the five companies you selected. Compare the ratios for each of the companies, and explain what the ratio tells you about that company and about the group of companies in your sample.

P2.9 Current and non-current assets and liabilities. Consider the following account titles from 1996 balance sheets:

a. Accrued Wages.

b. Inventories.

c. Machinery and Equipment.

d. Long-Term Investments.

e. Deferred Income Taxes.

f. Other Liabilities.

g. Accumulated Amortization.

h. Prepaid Expenses.

i. Obligation under Capital Lease.

j. Goodwill.

Required:

Identify each account as either a current asset or a current liability, or a non-current asset or a non-current liability. Where you have a question about any item, make an assumption, and explain your assumption and your classification.

P2.10 Financial analysis. Collins Cutlery has a current ratio, based on its June 30, 1996, balance sheet, of 2:1. During the following six months, the following independent events took place.

a. Sold warehouse for cash.

b. Declared a cash dividend on common shares.

c. Sold merchandise on account (at a profit).

d. Retired mortgage notes that would have matured in 1999.

e. Paid cash for a patent.

f. Temporarily invested cash in government bonds.

g. Purchased inventory for cash.

h. Paid the cash dividend on common shares.

i. Purchased a computer and gave a two-year promissory note.

j. Collected accounts receivable.

k. Borrowed from bank on a 120-day promissory note.

Required:

For each of the above events, indicate the effect of that event on Collins' working capital and current ratio, and its ratio of total debt to equity. Make whatever assumptions are necessary to complete this exercise.

P2.11 Balance sheet preparation. Presented below in alphabetical order are the balance sheet accounts of the Grow Company as of December 31, 1996:

Accounts payable	$ 2,480
Accounts receivable	2,150
Bonds payable (due 1999)	8,000
Buildings	9,700
Cash	3,200
Share capital	25,000
Equipment	16,490
Income taxes payable	2,500
Inventory — raw material	1,800
Inventory — finished goods	4,200
Land	13,000
Temporary investments	1,500
Patent	12,000
Retained earnings	?
Trademark	8,000
Wages payable	750

Required:

Prepare the December 31, 1996, balance sheet of the Grow Company.

P2.12 Balance sheet accounts: assets. The Jones Company presents the following items in the asset side of its balance sheet. Explain why these items are considered assets for Jones Company. Comment on the source of the numbers attributed to those assets.

Newsprint inventory	$18,439
Investments in associated companies	71,896
Construction in progress	41,498

P2.13 Balance sheet accounts: liabilities. Contel Corporation lists the following items in the current liabilities section of the balance sheet. Explain what these items are and why they have been recorded by Contel as liabilities. Why are they current liabilities? Comment on the source of the numbers attributed to those liabilities.

Current maturities of long-term debt	$194,419
Interim borrowings	173,073
Accounts payable	478,579
Accrued taxes payable	67,088
Accrued interest payable	33,345
Accrued wage benefits	53,178
Other current liabilities	169,429

P2.14 Short-term and long-term debt. Snap-On Tools Corporation includes a footnote in its 1994 Annual Report describing its debt situation as follows:

At December 29, 1994, the Company had bank lines of credit totalling $101.3 million available for short-term borrowing, including support of commercial paper issuance. Of this amount, $100 million required compensating balances of 2 percent. Notes payable to banks totalled $11.5 million as of December 29, 1994, and $6.0 million as of December 30, 1993. Commercial notes payable totalled $65.0 million as of

December 29, 1994, and $31.0 million as of December 30, 1993. There were no short-term borrowings during 1988. Maximum short-term borrowings outstanding at the end of any month in 1994 and 1993 were $77.0 million and $37.0 million, respectively. The average outstanding borrowings were $56.7 million in 1994 and $16.6 million in 1993. The weighted average daily interest rates for 1994 and 1993 were 8.1 percent and 9.3 percent, respectively. The weighted average interest rates on outstanding borrowings at December 29, 1994, and December 30, 1993, were 8.1 percent and 8.7 percent, respectively.

Interest payments approximated $7.3 million and $3.8 million for 1994 and 1993, respectively.

The Company's annual maturities on its long-term debt due in the next five years are $.4 million for years 1991 through 1994 and $.2 million for 1995.

The Company's long-term debt consisted of the following for fiscal years ended (amounts in thousands):

	1994	1993
6.6% revenue bonds payable	$6,400	$6,500
Other	1,300	1,625
Less: current maturities	(425)	(425)
Total long-term debt	$7,275	$7,700

Required:

a. What amounts will Snap-On Tools report on its December 29, 1994, balance sheet as its short-term and long-term debt balances?

b. In your own words, what other interesting information did you gather from the footnote? Why might management have decided to make that information available to us?

P2.15 Quick ratio. The financial statements of Gold Medal Gym, Inc., include quick assets of $167,000 and current liabilities of $118,000.

a. Explain the impact each of the following transactions would have on the company's quick ratio:

(1) Merchandise costing $12,000 is purchased on account.

(2) Purchased exercise equipment for $14,000 cash.

(3) Invested $10,000 cash in a 60-day term deposit.

b. As a result of the above transactions, is the organization's financial position better or worse?

P2.16 Current ratio. The financial statement of Rideau Canal Canada, Ltd., include current assets of $174,000 and current liabilities of $97,000.

a. Explain the impact each of the following transactions would have on the company's current ratio:

(1) Made payments on account of $27,000.

(2) Collected payments on account of $33,000.

b. As a result of the above transactions, is the organization's financial position better or worse?

P2.17 Current ratio. The financial statements of Tunnel Mountain Resorts, Ltd., include current assets of $373,000 and current liabilities of $297,000.

a. Explain the impact each of the following transactions would have on the company's current ratio:

(**1**) Merchandise costing $15,000 is purchased on account.

(**2**) Made a payment of $20,000 on a long-term debt.

b. As a result of the above transactions, is the organization's financial position better or worse?

P2.18 Total debt-to-equity ratio. The financial statements of Halifax Marine Services include total debt of $199,000 and equity of $125,000.

a. Explain the impact each of the following transactions would have on the company's total debt-to-equity ratio:

(**1**) Made a payment of $10,000 on a long-term debt.

(**2**) Issued share capital for $15,000 cash.

(**3**) Collected accounts receivable of $8,000.

b. As a result of the above transactions, is the organization's financial position better or worse?

P2.19 Long-term debt-to-invested capital ratio. The financial statements of Burnaby Forest Products include long-term debt of $377,000 and shareholders' equity of $245,000.

a. Explain the impact each of the following transactions would have on the company's long-term debt-to-equity ratio:

(**1**) Made a payment of $5,000 on a long-term debt.

(**2**) Made a payment of $10,000 on accounts payable.

(**3**) Issued long-term bonds payable for $25,000.

b. As a result of the above transactions, is the organization's financial position better or worse?

P2.20 Statement of changes in financial position. Sarah Medlson recently started a business that she operated as a sole proprietorship. The following cash events transpired during the first few months after the business was established, but before operations commenced:

Sarah invested cash of $7,000.
Purchased equipment for $5,000.
Sarah withdrew $1,500 cash from the proprietorship.
Purchased land for $10,000.
Obtained a long-term loan of $20,000.
Land that originally cost $4,000 was sold for $4,000.
Made payments of $3,000 on the long-term loan.

Required:

a. Determine the cash balance at the end of the period.

b. Using the above information prepare a statement of changes in financial position for Sarah's business for the year ended December 31.

P2.21 Statement of changes in financial position. Jonathan Dempsey recently formed a corporation to operate a consulting business. The following cash events transpired during the first few months after the business was established, but before operations commenced:

Jonathan invested cash of $10,000 in share capital.
Purchased computer equipment for $6,000.
Obtained a long-term loan of $5,000.
Purchased office furniture for $3,000.
Made payments of $1,300 on the long-term loan.
The corporation paid dividends of $2,000.

Required:

a. Determine the cash balance at the end of the period.

b. Using the above information prepare a statement of changes in financial position for the year ended December 31.

P2.22 Balance sheet. Determine the missing amounts affecting the balance sheet in each of the independent cases below:

	A	B	C	D
Current assets	$38,000	?	$47,000	$24,000
Non-current assets	11,000	$25,000	?	69,000
Current liabilities	25,000	22,000	45,000	40,000
Non-current liabilities	?	17,000	6,000	18,000
Equity	11,000	29,000	43,000	?

P2.23 Balance sheet. Determine the missing amounts affecting the balance sheet in each of the independent cases below:

	A	B	C	D
Current assets	$47,000	?	$16,000	$25,000
Non-current assets	21,000	$35,000	?	74,000
Current liabilities	?	12,000	27,000	41,000
Non-current liabilities	30,000	23,000	10,000	60,000
Equity	11,000	41,000	32,000	?

P2.24 Balance sheet. Determine the missing percentage affecting the balance sheet in each of the independent cases below:

	A	B	C	D
Current assets	22%	?	31%	?
Non-current assets	?	53%	?	63%
Current liabilities	?	22	19	?
Non-current liabilities	37	?	44	33
Equity	51	33	?	28

P2.25 Statement of changes in financial position. Determine the missing amounts affecting the statement of changes in financial position in each of the independent cases below:

	A	B	C	D
Investing activities	$(27,000)	?	$(36,000)	$14,000
Financing activities	41,000	$33,000	?	15,000
Increase/(decrease) in cash	?	22,000	27,000	?
Beginning cash	23,000	?	20,000	16,000
Ending cash	?	11,000	?	?

P2.26 Classified financial statements. Describe how the following items would be disclosed on a properly classified financial statement:

a. Deferred income.

b. Land.

c. Current income taxes payable.

d. Deferred income tax charge.

P2.27 Classified financial statements. Describe how the following items would be disclosed on a properly classified financial statement:

a. Merchandise inventory

b. Retained earnings

c. Customer deposits

d. Footnotes

P2.28 Analysis of financial strength. Using the financial statements for Ted's Trucking presented in this chapter, analyze the financial strength of Ted's business. Comment on the significance of any ratios or other analysis you perform.

P2.29 Balance sheet. Using the information presented below, prepare a balance sheet.

Land	$ 80,000	Retained earnings	$113,000
Cash	46,000	Building	120,000
Inventory	62,000	Accounts payable	35,000
Accounts receivable	71,000	Share capital	70,000
Bank loan payable	30,000	Equipment	44,000
Mortgage payable	175,000		

P2.30 Financial strength analysis. Using the financial information presented for Petro-Canada and Gulf Canada Resources, Limited, perform a comparative analysis of the financial strength of the two companies. Your report should include comments on your findings.

PETRO-CANADA
Consolidated Balance Sheets
As at December 31

	1993	1992
Assets		
Current assets		
Cash and short-term	$ 129	$ 82
Accounts receivable	540	580
Inventories	443	460
Prepaid expenses	29	26
Income taxes	—	8
	$1,141	$1,156
Investments	88	80
Property and plant	4,027	3,865
Deferred charges	276	249
	$5,532	$5,350
Liabilities and Shareholders' Equity		
Current liabilities:		
Accounts payable	$ 919	$ 933
Income tax payable	53	—
Current portion of long-term debt	—	89
Short-term notes payable	—	86
	$ 972	$1,108
Notes payable	150	—
Long-term debt	902	868
Other liabilities	224	264
Deferred income taxes	510	467
Shareholders' equity	2,774	2,643
	$5,532	$5,350

GULF CANADA
Consolidated Balance Sheets
As at December 31

	1993	1992
Assets		
Current assets:		
Cash and short-term deposits	$ 685	$ 396
Accounts receivable	175	183
Other	66	77
	$ 926	$ 656
Investments, deferred	233	368
Capital assets, net	2,086	2,360
	$3,245	$3,384
Liabilities and Shareholders' Equity		
Current liabilities:		
Short-term loans	—	$ 94
Accounts payable	$ 127	143
Current portion of long-term debt	55	53
Current portion of other liabilities	27	29
Other	65	63
	$ 274	$ 382
Long-term debt	1,577	1,570
Other long-term liabilities	112	84
Deferred income taxes	105	138
Shareholders' equity	1,177	1,210
	$3,245	$3,384

P2.31 Financial strength analysis. Using the financial information presented for Ontario Hydro and Hydro Quebec perform a comparative analysis of the financial strength of the two companies. Your report should include comments on your findings.

ONTARIO HYDRO
Consolidated Balance Sheets
As at December 31

	1993	1992
Assets		
Fixed assets:		
Fixed assets in service	$46,978	$39,997
Less accumulated amortization	9,838	9,615
	$37,140	$30,382
Construction in progress	3,600	10,308
	$40,740	$40,690
Current assets:		
Accounts receivable	$ 1,207	$ 1,032
Fuel for electrical generation	662	1,345
Materials and supplies, at cost	283	351
Total current assets	$ 2,152	$ 2,728
Other assets:		
Deferred costs	1,396	2,394
Other assets	418	859
	$44,706	$46,671
Liabilities and Shareholders' Equity		
Long-term debt	$31,848	$31,238
Current liabilities:		
Bank indebtedness	$ 615	$ 635
Accounts payable	1,736	1,202
Current portion of long-term debt	1,837	2,796
Accrued interest	979	951
Short-term notes payable	1,109	898
	$ 6,276	$ 6,482
Other liabilities:		
Unamortized option premiums	853	—
Long-term accounts payable	631	503
Used nuclear fuel disposal costs	1,773	1,517
	$ 3,257	$ 2,020
Shareholders equity:		
Retained earnings	$ 3,325	$ 6,931
	$44,706	$46,671

HYDRO-QUEBEC
Consolidated Balance Sheets
As at December 31

	1993	1992
Assets		
Fixed assets:		
In service	$43,958	$39,926
Less accumulated amortization	7,295	6,736
	$36,663	33,190
Construction in progress	5,906	6,398
	$42,569	39,588
Current assets:		
Cash and temporary investments	639	1,329
Accounts receivable	1,335	1,329
Materials, fuel, and supplies	269	291
Total current assets	$ 2,243	2,949
Other Assets:		
Investments	180	181
Deferred costs	2,887	2,146
	$42,879	$44,864
Liabilities and Shareholders' Equity		
Long-term debt	$33,204	$31,174
Current liabilities:		
Accounts payable	$ 1,253	$ 1,101
Current portion of long-term debt	755	822
Accrued interest	1,086	1,053
Notes payable	119	19
	$ 3,213	$ 2,995
Other liabilities:		
Decommissioning of nuclear station	$ 28	$ 22
Perpetual debt	552	552
Total Liabilities	$36,997	$34,743
Equity:		
Share capital	$ 4,374	4,374
Retained earnings	6,508	5,747
	$47,879	$44,864

P2.32 Balance sheet. Alexa Hamilton began her repair business early this month. The balance sheet, prepared by an inexperienced bookkeeper, is shown below:

HAMILTON REPAIR BUSINESS
Balance Sheet
January 31, 1996

Assets		Liabilities and Equity	
Cash	$ 6,000	Parts inventory	$ 8,000
Accounts payable	17,000	Accounts receivable	13,000
Building	20,000	Land	12,000
Share capital	31,000	Equipment	15,000
		Mortgage payable	26,000
	$74,000		$74,000

Required:

Prepare a corrected balance sheet.

P2.33 Balance sheet. Zaba Industries, Ltd., had the following account balances as at December 31, 1996. Construct a balance sheet from the following information:

Patents	$80,000	Loan payable	$35,000
Accounts payable	25,000	Inventory	62,000
Retained earnings	?	Building and equipment	93,000
Mortgage payable	41,000	Cash	26,000
Bank loan	10,000	Common shares	70,000
Accounts receivable	37,000	Temporary investments	44,000

P2.34 Balance Sheet Equation. Terry Ziegler began a landscaping business on June 1st by investing $9,000 of her personal savings in the business. To start the business Terry purchased equipment for $2,500. Terry also obtained a bank loan for $5,000 and acquired a used truck for $7,000. During the month Terry withdrew $500 cash from the business to pay for personal expenses.

Required:

Use the balance sheet equation to summarize the transactions for Terry's business. Determine the ending cash balance for the business by preparing a statement of changes in financial position. As well, prepare a balance sheet.

P2.35 Classified balance sheet (Society of Management Accountants of British Columbia). The Milestone Moving and Storage firm provided the following accounts and balances. Unfortunately, some of the accounts in the ledger have been omitted by the computer programme. The list of accounts that follows shows the data available at February 28, 1993.

Cash	$ 1,815
Accounts Receivable	omitted
Prepaid Insurance	200
Office Supplies	450
Trucks	19,050
Building	5,000
Land	1,500
Notes Payable (due on August, 30, 1993)	2,500
Accounts Payable	omitted
D. Kelly — Capital	omitted
D. Kelly — Withdrawals	60
Interest Payable	100
Unearned Storage Fees	900
Accumulated Amortization — Building	1,000
Accumulated Amortization — Trucks	1,200

The following information is also available.

Total assets, $26,540.

Total liabilities, $4,100.

Net income, $1,050.

Required:

Prepare a classified balance sheet for the month of February 1993, showing the change in owners' equity. (It is necessary to calculate the omitted amounts.)

P2.36 Investing and financing activities (Published with permission of CGA Canada). The following information is available for Duke, Ltd.:

Cash proceeds from equipment sale	$200,000
Common shares issued	180,000
Long-term note issued for equipment	50,000
Dividends	24,000
Other equipment acquired	130,000

Required:

a. Determine the net cash provided by investing activities.

b. Determine the net cash provided by financing activities.

P2.37 Financial strength analysis. Using the financial information presented for John Labatt, Ltd., and the Molson's Companies, Limited, perform a comparative analysis of the financial strength of the two companies. Your report should include comments on your findings.

MOLSON'S COMPANIES, LIMITED
Consolidated Balance Sheets
As at March 31, 1994, and 1993
(dollars in thousands)

	1994	1993
Assets		
Current assets:		
Cash and short-term investments	$ 224,344	$ 208,590
Accounts receivable	395,770	358,395
Proceeds receivable from the sale of a 10% interest in Molson		
Breweries (note 2)	—	180,000
Inventories (note 9)	334,746	335,790
Prepaid expenses	43,342	37,202
Deferred income taxes	41,654	10,479
	1,039,856	1,130,456
Investments and other assets (note 20)	360,467	342,415
Property, plant, and equipment (note 11)	837,799	782,601
Intangible assets (note 12)	493,170	446,729
Deferred income taxes	16,906	13,426
	$2,748,198	$2,715,627
Liabilities		
Current liabilities:		
Bank indebtedness and short-term notes	$ 44,688	$ 275,168
Accounts payable	496,350	417,130
Provision for rationalization costs	137,273	136,156
Taxes payable	61,596	61,685
Dividends payable	10,602	10,886
Current instalments on long-term debt (note 13)	6,392	198
	756,901	901,223
Long-term debt (note 13)	505,670	412,415
Deferred gain (note 14)	95,893	117,311
Deferred consideration (note 2)	—	22,360
Deferred liabilities	77,398	89,718
Non-controlling interest	3,828	4,265
	1,439,690	1,547,292
Shareholders' Equity		
Capital stock (note 15)	449,551	449,302
Retained earnings	775,851	704,747
Unrealized translation adjustments (note 18)	83,106	14,286
	1,308,508	1,168,335
	$2,748,198	$2,715,627

JOHN LABATT, LIMITED
Consolidated Statements of Financial Position
As at April 30, 1994, and 1993
(millions)

	1994	1993
Assets		
Current assets:		
Cash and short-term investments	$ 368	$ 276
Accounts receivable and advances	376	286
Inventories (note 8)	193	192
Taxes recoverable	—	8
Prepaid expenses	93	85
Discontinued operations	72	340
	1,102	1,187
Fixed assets (note 9)	813	784
Other assets (note 10)	539	597
Discontinued operations	82	452
	$2,536	$3,020
Liabilities		
Current liabilities:		
Bank advances and short-term notes	$ 100	$ 88
Accounts payable and accrued charges	401	463
Deferred revenue	99	69
Taxes payable	52	—
Long-term debt due within one year	4	14
Discontinued operations	65	298
	721	932
Non-convertible long-term debt (note 11)	610	630
Deferred income taxes		
Continuing operations	86	93
Discontinued operations	—	48
	1,417	1,703
Convertible Debentures and Shareholders' Equity		
Convertible debentures (note 12)	91	111
Shareholders' equity:		
Share capital (note 13)		
Preferred shares	300	300
Common shares	363	486
Retained earnings	364	430
Cumulative translation adjustment	1	(10)
	1,028	1,206
	1,119	1,317
	$2,536	$3,020

On behalf of the Board

Samuel Pollock, Director   George S. Taylor, Director

P2.38 Financial strength analysis. Using the financial information presented for Imperial Oil Company, Limited, and Shell Canada Company, Limited, perform a comparative analysis of the financial strength of the two companies. Your report should include comments on your findings.

IMPERIAL OIL COMPANY, LIMITED
Consolidated Balance Sheet
As at December 31, 1993, 1992, and 1991
(millions)

	1993	1992	1991
Assets			
Current assets:			
Cash	$ 605	$ 265	$ 286
Marketable securities at cost	874	757	7
Accounts receivable	889	1,008	1,052
Inventories of crude oil	402	468	604
Materials, supplies, and prepaid expenses	129	140	178
Total current assets	2,899	2,638	2,127
Investments and other long-term assets	152	159	204
Property, plant, and equipment	9,389	9,965	10,760
Goodwill	356	373	400
Total assets	12,796	13,135	13,491
Liabilities			
Current liabilities:			
Accounts payable and accrued liabilities	1,157	1,316	1,529
Income taxes payable	436	247	110
Total current liabilities	1,593	1,563	1,639
Long-term debt (6)	2,030	2,222	2,356
Other long-term obligations	1,149	1,137	1,007
Commitments and contingent liabilities			
Total liabilities	4,772	4,922	5,002
Deferred income taxes	1,458	1,577	1,699
Shareholders' Equity			
Common shares (11)	2,977	2,977	2,977
Net earnings retained and used in the business:			
At beginning of year	3,659	3,813	3,999
Net earnings for the year	279	195	162
Dividends	(349)	(349)	(348)
At end of year	3,589	3,659	3,813
Total Shareholders' Equity	6,566	6,636	6,790
Total liabilities, deferred income taxes, and shareholders' equity	12,796	13,135	13,491

SHELL CANADA LIMITED

	1993	1992	1991
Assets			
Current assets			
Cash and short-term investments	(34)	128	36
Accounts receivable	709	695	766
Inventories (Note 10)			
Crude oil, products and merchandise	548	552	554
Materials and supplies	44	44	40
Prepaid expenses	39	97	96
	1,306	1,516	1,492
Investments, long-term receivables and other	245	159	126
Properties, plant and equipment (Note 4)	4,428	4,349	4,292
	5,979	6,024	5,910
Liabilities			
Current liabilities			
Short-term borrowings	73	—	—
Accounts payable and accrued liabilities	658	618	574
Income and other taxes payable	25	84	66
Current portion of long-term debt	315	147	188
	1,071	849	828
Site restoration	97	53	71
Long-term debt (Note 5)	1,005	1,279	1,110
Deferred income taxes	891	846	884
	3,064	3,027	2,893
Shareholders' Investment			
Capital stock (Note 6)			
100 4% Preference Shares	1	1	1
112 109 125 Class "A" Common Shares			
(1992–112 091 875; 1991–112 077 776)	523	523	522
	524	524	523
Contributed surplus	291	291	291
Retained earnings	2,100	2,182	2,203
	2,915	2,997	3,017
Commitments and contingencies (Note 14)			
	5,979	6,024	5,910

The consolidated financial statements have been approved by the Board of Directors.

Charles W. Wilson, *Director*   Peter J. G. Bentley, *Director*

P2.39 Financial strength ratios. Financial strength ratios for two companies are presented below. Comment on the relative financial strength of each organization.

ATLANTIC COMPANY

	1996	1995
Total debt-to-equity ratio	.88:1	1.01:1
Long-term debt-to-invested capital ratio	.47:1	.62 :1
Quick ratio	.71:1	.86 :1
Current ratio	.84:1	.99 :1

PACIFIC COMPANY

	1996	1995
Total debt-to-equity ratio	1.11:1	1.03:1
Long-term debt-to-invested capital ratio	.64 :1	.58 :1
Quick ratio	1.03:1	.97 :1
Current ratio	1.31:1	1.27:1

2.14 CASES

C2.1 Balance sheets tell a story. Presented below are six balance sheets. The balance sheet amounts are expressed as *percentages* of total assets in order to reflect relative amounts for each account. Each balance sheet represents a different company from a different industry. The industries and companies represented are:

Commercial bank

Supermarket chain

Advertising agency

Discount store chain

Electric utility

Chemical company

Match the industry with the appropriate column based on your understanding of some of the financial implications of operating in that industry. The identifications often require two or more distinguishing features.

	Industry					
	1	2	3	4	5	6
Assets						
Cash	11.3	5.1	.3	.5	.2	5.1
Accounts receivable	65.5	2.7	6.9	12.4	2.0	66.0
Inventory	—	27.2	3.1	12.8	52.7	—
Other current assets	—	2.2	3.9	7.4	2.2	7.7
Total current assets	76.8	37.2	14.2	33.1	57.1	78.8
Plant and equipment	2.2	60.3	74.8	34.5	41.9	7.6
Other assets	21.0	2.5	11.0	32.4	1.0	13.6
Total assets	100.0	100.0	100.0	100.0	100.0	100.0
Liabilities						
Notes payable	15.9	.7	2.9	10.3	.6	3.1
Accounts payable	73.5	23.6	3.8	10.3	21.9	56.3
Accrued taxes	—	1.5	.1	1.2	1.9	2.4
Other current liabilities	.6	4.9	4.3	7.5	8.1	7.7
Total current liabilities	90.0	30.7	11.1	29.3	32.5	69.5
Long-term debt	1.9	11.1	36.6	17.4	18.8	2.1
Other liabilities	1.7	7.9	12.0	7.9	1.4	6.5
Total liabilities	93.6	49.7	59.7	54.6	52.7	78.1
Equity	6.4	50.3	40.3	45.4	47.3	21.9
Total liabilities and equity	100.0	100.0	100.0	100.0	100.0	100.0

C2.2 An accounting game: the sheepherders (part one).* In the high mountains of Chatele, two sheepherders, Deyonne and Batonne, sit arguing their relative positions in life — an argument that has been going on for years. Deyonne says that he has 400 sheep, while Batonne has only 360 sheep. Therefore, Deyonne is much better off. Batonne, on the other hand, argues that he has 30 acres of land while Deyonne has only 20 acres; then too, Deyonne's land was inherited while Batonne had given 35 sheep for 20 acres of land 10 years ago. This year he gave 40 sheep for 10 additional acres of land. Batonne also makes the observation that 35 of Deyonne's sheep belong to another man, and Deyonne merely keeps them. Deyonne counters that he has a large one-room cabin that he built himself. He claims he has been offered three acres of land for the cabin. Besides these things, he has a plow (which was a gift from a friend and is worth a couple of goats), two carts (which were given him in trade for a poor acre of land), and an ox (which he acquired for five sheet). Batonne goes on to say that his wife has orders for five coats to be made of homespun wool, and that she will receive 25 goats for them. His wife has 10 goats already, three of which have been received in exchange for one sheep just last year. She has an ox, which she acquired in a trade for three sheep. She also has one cart, which cost her two sheep. Batonne's two-room cabin, even though smaller in dimension than Deyonne's, should bring him two choice acres of land in a trade. Deyonne is reminded by Batonne that he owes Tyrone three sheep for bringing up his lunch each day last year.

Required:

In your opinion, who is wealthier — Deyonne or Batonne?

---

*M. Carlson and J. W. Higgins, "A Games Approach to Introducing Accounting," *Accounting Education: Problems and Prospects* (Sarasota, FL: American Accounting Association, 1974).

Operating Activities: The Income Statement and the Statement of Changes in Financial Position

Objectives

After completing this chapter, you will be able to:
1. Discuss operating activities.
2. Record accounting transactions for operating activities using the preparer concepts: balance sheet equation, debits and credits, and general journal entries.
3. Define *revenues* and *expenses*.
4. Prepare an income statement, balance sheet, and statement of changes in financial position resulting from operating, investing, and financing activities.
5. Discuss the cash and accrual basis of accounting.
6. Analyze the management performance of an organization.

3.1 OPERATING ACTIVITIES

Operating activities are the day-to-day activities whereby the organization exchanges goods and services with other parties. Every organization has its own set of objectives and strategies, its own reason for being. Operating activities are the means of obtaining these objectives. Operating activities involve the providing of goods or services to customers, clients, or members. Part of the overall process of providing these goods and services requires the *use* of goods and services from sources outside the organization. This exchange of goods and services, in accounting terms, involves the recognition of revenues and expenses. The understanding of revenues and expenses and the income statement is the focus of this chapter.

In Chapter 2 we discussed the investing and financing activities of the organization. The investing and financing activities are disclosed in the balance sheet and the statement of changes in financial position. Operating activities are disclosed in the income statement and also have a strong influence on the statement of changes in financial position (also called the *cash flow statement*). Exhibit 3.1 illustrates the relationships among economic activities and the financial statements.

3.2 PREPARER CONCEPTS AND TECHNIQUES

Balance Sheet Equation

In Chapter 2 the concept of the balance sheet or accounting equation was introduced. Investing activities illustrated the acquisition and disposal of non-current assets, resulting in the use and receipt of cash. Financing activities, as well, illustrated the acquisition and redemption of non-current liabilities and equity. A sole proprietorship, Ted's Trucking, was used to demonstrate the impact investing and financing activities have on an organization. The accounting equation was used to summarize sample

E X H I B I T   3 . 1

Economic Activities and Financial Statements

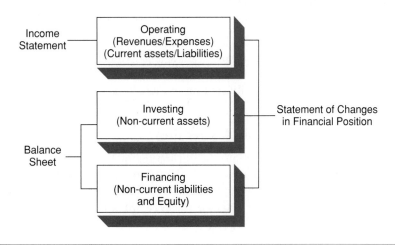

transactions, which were then used to develop a balance sheet and statement of changes in financial position for Ted's Trucking.

Ted had invested in land, building, and a truck. These resources had been financed by a loan, a mortgage, and Ted's personal capital of $19,000. If you were Ted and had $19,000, would you start a trucking business? If you did have $19,000, you would want to invest it carefully, to ensure you would receive an adequate return of your investment. If you were risk adverse, you might select a low-risk investment like Canada Savings Bonds. Many other possible investments exist. You would hope to invest wisely and have your $19,000 grow larger. You may or may not wish to invest in the trucking business. However, that is how Ted decided to invest his funds and he expects a return on his investment. He hopes his $19,000 will grow larger. To earn a return on his investment, Ted will provide delivery services to his customers. As well as providing delivery services to his customers, Ted will be required to receive goods and services. The exchange of goods and services impacts on the balance sheet equation as follows:

Goods and services *provided* (revenues) *increase* equity (credit).

Goods and services *received and used* (expenses) *decrease* equity (debit).

Debits and Credits

Now that Ted has established his trucking business with the initial investing and financing activities, he is ready to start operations. The accounting equation will now be used to illustrate operating activities for Ted's first month of operations. The operating activities will be combined with the investing and financing activities previously described in Chapter 2 (transactions 1–7). As previously mentioned in Chapter 2, the balance sheet equation is the basis of double-entry accounting. Double-entry accounting means that for *any* economic event, at least two activities occur, and, therefore, for each economic event debits must equal credits. Such activities are called *transactions*, and commonly involve an exchange of goods and services. Transactions 8–13, the operating transactions for Ted's Trucking for the month of January, are presented in the next section. They are summarized and combined with the financing and investing transactions previously recorded using the accounting equation and debits and credits.

3.3 ACCRUAL BASIS OF ACCOUNTING

The accrual basis of accounting is an important principle to adhere to when preparing meaningful financial statements. To facilitate the understanding of this important concept of accrual basis accounting, we will first examine cash basis accounting and then expand our illustration to include the accrual basis of accounting.

cash basis accounting
An accounting measurement system that records business transactions only when the underlying event has a cash effect.

Cash Basis Accounting

We will continue the illustration for Ted's Trucking developed in Chapter 2 to examine **cash basis accounting**. Under the cash basis of accounting revenues and expenses are recognized *only* when cash is exchanged. That is, revenues are recognized only when cash is received, regardless of when the goods or services were provided. Similarly, expenses are recognized *only* when cash is paid, regardless of when the goods or services were received. Any operating transactions made on account are not recognized under the cash basis of accounting. Transactions on account are economic events in which the goods and services are exchanged in the current period, with the cash settlement to be made in a subsequent period. In today's society, a large portion of the economic events that occur are on account. That is, the goods and services are exchanged today, with the cash settlement made several days later. In the business world, almost all transactions are conducted this way. Therefore, the use of the cash basis of accounting is *not* recommended under GAAP, except in very special circumstances. Traditionally, many smaller non-profit organizations have used the cash basis of accounting. However, the CICA Handbook recommends the accrual basis of accounting for all organizations, including non-profits. As a prelude to the discussion of the accrual basis of accounting, the operating transactions for Ted's Trucking are recorded using the cash basis of accounting. Ted's operating transactions are summarized below, using the accounting equation and debits and credits:

Cash Basis Accounting: Ted's Trucking

Transactions	Assets				=	Liabilities	+	Equity
	Cash	Land	Building	Truck		Loan	Mortgage	Capital
1–7 Investing and financing activities from Chapter 2.	Dr. 13,000	Dr. 4,000	Dr. 40,000	Dr. 10,000		Cr. 10,000	Cr. 38,000	Cr. 19,000
8 Goods/services provided; received $1,900 cash.	Dr. 1,900							Cr. 1,900
9 Goods/services received; paid $1,100 cash.	Cr. (1,100)							Dr. (1,100)
10 Goods/services provided; received a *promise* for payment of $1,800.	*No entry — cash basis of accounting*							
11 Goods/services received; *promised* to pay $1,300 later.	*No entry — cash basis of accounting*							
12 Cash payment of $200 received re: transaction 10. (Cash basis recognizes as revenue.)	Dr. 200							Cr. 200
13 Paid cash of $300 re: transaction 11. (Cash basis recognizes as expense).	Cr. (300)							Dr. (300)
Account totals	Dr. 13,700	Dr. 4,000	Dr. 40,000	Dr. 10,000		Cr. 10,000	Cr. 38,000	Cr. 19,700
	Total debits = 67,700					Total credits = 67,700		

For each of the above individual transactions debits equal credits. Therefore, when the transactions are summarized, total debits must equal total credits ($67,700).

As previously mentioned, the users of financial statements are not interested in individual transactions, but only the overall effect of these events. Therefore, the transactions for Ted's Trucking have been summarized and disclosed in financial statements (cash basis), which are explained in the next section.

Financial Statements: Cash Basis

The financial statements for Ted's Trucking have been prepared on the cash basis. The cash basis of accounting recognizes revenues and expenses *only* when there has been an exchange of cash. The cash basis balance sheet at January 31 is shown below:

TED'S TRUCKING
Balance Sheet (cash basis)
At January 31

Assets				
Cash	$13,700	Loan payable		$10,000
Land	4,000	Mortgage payable		38,000
Building	40,000			$48,000
Truck	10,000	**Equity**		
		Capital, Ted	$20,000	
		Withdrawals	(1,000)	
		Net income	700	19,700
	$67,700			$67,700

If you analyze Ted's capital account in the accounting equation, you will notice it has decreased from the original balance of $20,000 to an ending balance of $19,700. The balance sheet discloses this new equity balance. Equity has decreased by $300, and Ted is probably quite satisfied with his first month's operations. To provide additional information to the users of financial statements, and to more thoroughly explain the change in equity during the period, an operating statement or income statement is prepared.

The income statement summarizes the goods and services exchanged during the period. Goods and services provided are called *revenues*. Goods and services received and used are called *expenses*. If revenues exceed expenses, a net income has been earned during the period. If revenues are less than expenses, a net loss has been incurred. The balance sheet was earlier described as a photograph of an organization at a particular point in time. The income statement should be thought of as a video describing the organization's operating activities *over* a given time period. By summarizing the changes in equity during the period, an income statement may be prepared. The income statement for Ted's Trucking for the month ending January 31 is shown below:

TED'S TRUCKING
Income Statement (cash basis)
For the Month Ending January 31

Revenues:		
Trucking fees	$2,100	
Expenses:		
Operating expenses	1,400	
Net income	$ 700	

Thus, the income statement discloses the revenues earned and expenses incurred during the period. The income statement indicates Ted provided goods or services, that is, earned total revenues, of $2,100 during the month of January. Expenses were incurred or goods and services received and used for $1,400 during January. As revenues exceeded expenses by $700 during January, a net income has been earned. The net income of $700 or change in equity of $700 during the period is disclosed on the income statement. The other change in equity during the period was the cash withdrawal of $1,000 by Ted. Withdrawals or distributions to owners are not operating transactions and are *not* disclosed on the income statement. Withdrawals are a form of financing activity, where some of the owners' original capital has been returned to them. Withdrawals are disclosed on the statement of changes in financial position as a use of cash under financing activities. Distributions to owners also appear on the equity statement, which is discussed later in this chapter in Section 3.6.

As illustrated in Chapter 2, the change in cash during a period may be disclosed in a statement of changes in financial position. The statement of changes in financial position is also like a video disclosing events *during* a given period. Ted's operating activities are combined with the financing and investing transactions illustrated in Chapter 2 to prepare a statement of changes in financial position:

TED'S TRUCKING
Statement of Changes in Financial Position (cash basis)
For the Month Ending January 31

Operating activities:			
Net income			$ 700
Cash provided from operations			$ 700
Investing activities:			
Land purchase		$ (5,000)	
Land sale		1,000	
Building purchase		(40,000)	
Truck purchase		(10,000)	
Cash (used) for investing			$(54,000)
Financing activities:			
Loan payable		$ 10,000	
Mortgage payable		40,000	
Payment on mortgage		(2,000)	
Ted's withdrawals		(1,000)	
Ted's contributed capital		20,000	
Cash provided from financing			67,000
Increase in cash			$ 13,700
Cash — January 1			–0–
Cash — January 31			$ 13,700

During January, operating activities provided $700 cash, investing activities used $54,000, and financing activities provided $67,000. Overall during the month of January, cash increased by $13,700. We have used Ted's Trucking and the accounting equation to develop the three financial statements organizations most commonly prepare: the balance sheet, the income statement, and the statement of changes in financial position. These three statements are the vehicles used to communicate the language of accounting and the understanding of these statements is the focus of this text.

Accrual Basis of Accounting

accrual basis of accounting
An accounting measurement system that records the financial effects of transactions when a business transaction occurs without regard to the timing of the cash effects of the transaction.

The cash basis of accounting may present misleading information to the users of financial statements because the flow of cash may not coincide with the flow of economic events of the organization. The **accrual basis of accounting** requires economic events to be recognized in the accounting period in which they *occur*. Revenues are to be recognized in the period in which they are earned, that is, when the goods or services are *provided*, regardless of when the cash settlement is received. Similarly, expenses should be recognized when goods or services are *received and used*, regardless of when the cash payment is made. Expenses are generally thought to be the result of revenues being generated. That is, expenses are incurred for the sole purpose of

matching principle
When revenues are reported, the expenses incurred to generate those revenues should be reported in the same accounting period.

accounts receivable
Amounts due to a company from customers who purchased goods or services on credit.

accounts payable
Amounts owed to suppliers for merchandise purchased on credit but not yet paid for.

generating revenues. Thus, the **matching principle** requires revenues that have been earned to be matched with the expenses incurred to earn these same revenues.

The accrual basis of accounting actually involves the accruing of *promises to pay*. To adhere to the matching principle and to recognize revenues and expense transactions in the accounting periods in which they occur requires the recognition of receivables and payables, or promises for cash payments at a later date. Thus, when revenue is deemed to be earned, but cash has *not* been received, an asset **accounts receivable** is created to recognize the unpaid balance owing for the goods or services that have been rendered. Similarly, when an expense has been incurred, but not paid for, a liability **accounts payable** is created to recognize goods or services have been received. Under the going concern concept, it is assumed the accounting entity will be in operation long enough to collect or fulfil the promises for payment. The accrual basis of accounting is one of the most important fundamental concepts for the understanding and preparation of meaningful financial statements. We will continue to discuss these concepts in depth in the next two chapters.

The transactions for Ted's Trucking are summarized on the following page using the accrual basis of accounting. For each of the individual transactions in this example, debits equal credits. Therefore, when the transactions are summarized, total debits must equal total credits ($69,300).

Accruing Revenues and Expenses

To illustrate the accrual basis of accounting we will continue with the example of Ted's Trucking. General journal entries will be used to illustrate the *accrual basis* transactions 8 to 13. The first seven transactions described the financing and investing activities for Ted, and the related impact on assets, liabilities, and equity. Before recording the operating transactions, we need to expand the debit/credit rule and the accounting equation to include revenues and expenses.

Assets			Liabilities			Equity	
Debit Increase	Credit Decrease	=	Debit Decrease	Credit Increase	+	Debit Decrease	Credit Increase

Expenses		Revenues	
Debit Increase	Credit Decrease	Debit Decrease	Credit Increase

expenses
An outflow of assets, an increase in liabilities, or both, from transactions involving an enterprise's principal business activity.

revenues
The inflow of assets, the reduction in liabilities, or both, from transactions involving an enterprise's principal business activity.

Expense accounts are debited when they increase. The impact of an increase in an expense is to *decrease* equity. Expenses decrease equity. "**Expenses** are decreases in economic resources, either by way of outflows or reductions of assets or incurrences of liabilities, resulting from the revenue generating or service providing activities" (CICA Handbook 1000.38). Therefore, the debit to an expense account must be offset by a credit entry to reduce an asset account or a credit entry to increase a liability account.

An increase in revenues is recorded as a credit entry. Revenues increase equity. "**Revenues** are increases in economic resources, either by way of inflows or enhancements of assets or reductions of liabilities, resulting from the ordinary activities of an entity. Revenues of entities normally arise from the sale of goods, the rendering of services or the use by others of entity resources yielding rent, interest, royalties or

Accrual Basis of Accounting: Ted's Trucking

Transactions	Assets					=	Liabilities			+	Equity
	Cash	Accounts Receivable	Land	Building	Truck		Accounts Payable	Loan	Mortgage		Capital
1–7 Investing and financing activities from Chapter 2.	Dr. 13,000		Dr. 4,000	Dr. 40,000	Dr. 10,000			Cr. 10,000	Cr. 38,000		Cr. 19,000
8 Goods/services provided; received $1,900 cash.	Dr. 1,900										Cr. 1,900
9 Goods/services received; paid $1,100 cash.	Cr. (1,100)										Dr. (1,100)
10 Goods/services provided; received a *promise* for payment of $1,800.		Dr. 1,800									Cr. 1,800
11 Goods/services received; *promised* to pay $1,300 later.							Cr. 1,300				Dr. (1,300)
12 Cash payment of $200 received re: transaction 10.	Dr. 200	Cr. (200)									
13 Paid cash of $300 re: transaction 11.	Cr. (300)						Dr. (300)				
Account totals	Dr. 13,700	Dr. 1,600	Dr. 4,000	Dr. 40,000	Dr. 10,000		Cr. 1,000	Cr. 10,000	Cr. 38,000		Cr. 20,300

Total debits = 69,300   Total credits = 69,300

dividends" (CICA Handbook 1000.37). The credit to a revenue account must be offset by a debit increasing an asset account or a debit to decrease a liability account. If revenues exceed expenses, a net increase in equity occurs or a net income has been earned. If revenues are less than expenses, a net decrease in equity occurs and a net loss has been incurred for the period. The next set of transactions record the revenues and expenses for Ted's Trucking.

Transaction 8. During January Ted obtains his first delivery contract. Ted spends the next several days delivering freight as specified in the agreement, and receives $1,900 cash for services rendered. The asset Cash is increased by $1,900 and equity is increased by $1,900 for services rendered. The Cash account is debited to recognize the increase in assets. The credit entry is to a revenue account to recognize the increase in equity. Revenues *increase* equity.

```
8   Dr. Cash ........................................ 1,900
        Cr. Revenues ....................................      1,900
        Goods/services provided; $1,900 cash received.
```

Transaction 9. Ted receives goods and services related to operating expenses and pays $1,100. The asset Cash is decreased by $1,100 and equity is decreased by $1,100 for goods received. The Operating Expenses account is debited to recognize the increase in expenses. Expenses *decrease* equity. The credit entry is to the Cash account to recognize the decrease in assets.

```
9   Dr. Operating expenses ........................... 1,100
        Cr. Cash ........................................      1,100
        Goods/services received and used; paid $1,100 cash.
```

Transactions 8 and 9 for revenues and expenses were both cash transactions. As previously mentioned, it is probable business transactions would not immediately involve cash, but a *promise to pay* cash at a later date. Therefore, to illustrate the accrual method, we have added accounts receivable and accounts payable accounts to the illustration. Transactions 10 and 11 record accrued revenues and expenses. An **accrued expense** is an expense that has been incurred, but the cash payment has not been made for the goods or services received. An **accrued revenue** is revenue that has been earned, but cash has not been collected for the goods and services provided. A description of the accrual transactions follows.

accrued expense
An expense that has been incurred, but the cash payment has not been made for the goods or services received.

accrued revenue
Revenue that has been earned, but cash has not been collected for the goods and services provided.

Transaction 10. Ted delivers freight for a customer and receives an $1,800 promise to pay at a later date for the services rendered. The asset Accounts Receivable is increased by $1,800 and equity is increased by $1,800 for services rendered. Under the accrual basis of accounting the revenue is recognized in the period the services have been rendered, even though a cash payment has not been received. The asset Accounts Receivable is debited to recognize the increase in assets. The credit entry is to a revenue account to recognize the increase in equity. Revenues *increase* equity.

```
10  Accounts receivable.............................. 1,800
        Revenues ........................................      1,800
        Goods/services provided; received a promise for payment of $1,800.
```

Transaction 11. Ted receives a $1,300 invoice for goods/services used in January. The invoice has not been paid by the end of the month. Since the goods/services have been used, an expense has been incurred, even though the invoice has not been paid. Equity is decreased by $1,300 to recognize the expense. The liability Accounts

Payable is increased by $1,300 to recognize the unpaid liability. The Operating Expenses account is debited to recognize the increase in expenses. Expenses *decrease* equity. The credit entry is to Accounts Payable to recognize the increase in liabilities.

```
11  Operating expenses. . . . . . . . . . . . . . . . . . . . . . . . . . . . . . . . 1,300
        Accounts payable . . . . . . . . . . . . . . . . . . . . . . . . . . . . . . . .      1,300
        Goods/services received and used; promised to pay $1,300 later.
```

Thus the *accrual* operating transactions have been combined with the *cash* operating transactions. No distinction is made between the cash and non-cash revenue/expense transactions. Remember that revenues and expenses should be recognized when the event occurs, regardless of when the cash settlement is made. Before we formally summarize these additional transactions in financial statement format, an additional feature of accrual accounting should be discussed. When Accounts Receivable and Accounts Payable accounts are originally created, it is assumed payment will be made within a month or two. The next section examines payments on account.

Payments on Account

The accrual basis of accounting creates Accounts Receivables and Accounts Payable accounts on the assumption payments will ultimately be made for settlement of the balances owing. Transaction 12 illustrates a payment received on account. Transaction 13 is for a payment made on account. *Partial* payments have been illustrated to maintain ending balances in Accounts Receivable and Accounts Payable. Payments on account do *not* affect equity.

Transaction 12. Ted receives $200 cash on account for the services rendered in transaction 10. The asset Cash is increased by $200, offset by a $200 decrease in the asset Accounts Receivable. Cash is debited to recognize the increase in assets. The credit entry is to Accounts Receivable to recognize the decrease in assets.

```
12  Cash . . . . . . . . . . . . . . . . . . . . . . . . . . . . . . . . . . . . . . . . . 200
        Accounts receivable  . . . . . . . . . . . . . . . . . . . . . . . . . . . . .      200
        Payment received on account re: transaction 10.
```

Payments received on account do not affect equity, but merely represent an exchange of assets.

Transaction 13. Ted pays $300 on account for the services received in transaction 11. The asset Cash is decreased by $300 and the liability Accounts Payable is decreased by $300. Accounts Payable is debited to recognize the decrease in liabilities. The credit entry is to Cash to recognize the decrease in assets.

```
13  Accounts payable . . . . . . . . . . . . . . . . . . . . . . . . . . . . . . . . 300
        Cash . . . . . . . . . . . . . . . . . . . . . . . . . . . . . . . . . . . . . . . . .      300
        Made payment on account re: transaction 11.
```

Payments made on account do not affect equity, but merely represent an offsetting of liabilities and assets.

We have journalized the operating transactions for Ted's Trucking. Some operating transactions were completed on a cash basis and some were accrued. The operating transactions are combined with the investing and financing activities from Chapter 2 and presented in financial statements.

Financial Statements: Accrual Basis

The financial statements for Ted's Trucking have been prepared on the accrual basis. The accrual basis of accounting recognizes revenues and expenses in the period in which they *occur*, without regard to when the cash settlement has been made. The revised balance sheet at January 31 is shown below:

TED'S TRUCKING
Balance Sheet (accrual basis)
At January 31

Assets		Liabilities		
Cash	$13,700	Accounts payable		$ 1,000
Accounts receivable	1,600	Loan payable		10,000
Land	4,000	Mortgage payable		38,000
Building	40,000	**Equity**		
Truck	10,000			
		Capital, Ted	$20,000	
		Withdrawals	(1,000)	
		Net income	1,300	20,300
	$69,300			$69,300

As mentioned previously, the accrual basis of accounting necessitates the creation of Accounts Receivable and Accounts Payable accounts. These two new accounts are reflected on the revised balance sheet. Finally the other significant impact of accrual basis is on equity. The change in equity is reflected on the income statement for Ted's Trucking for the month ending January 31 shown below:

TED'S TRUCKING
Income Statement (accrual basis)
For the Month Ending January 31

Revenues:	
Trucking fees	$3,700
Expenses:	
Operating expenses	2,400
Net income	$1,300

The accrued revenues have been combined with the previously recorded cash revenues. The account Trucking Fees has been used to record revenues of $3,700 for the services provided to customers during the month of January. As well, the accrued expenses have been included with the previously recorded cash expenses. The accrual basis of accounting produces a net income of $1,300 for the month. The omission of accrued revenues and accrued expenses under the cash basis of accounting, caused net income to be understated by $600 (cash basis $700 versus $1,300 accrual basis).

Looking at the relationship between the balance sheet and income statement in a different way, we might diagram it as shown in Exhibit 3.2 on page 110.

The statement of changes in financial position for Ted's Trucking for the month ending January 31 is shown on the following page:

TED'S TRUCKING
Statement of Changes in Financial Position (accrual basis)
For the Month Ending January 31

Operating activities:		
Net income	$ 1,300	
Change in working capital items:		
Increase in accounts payable	1,000	
Increase in accounts receivable	(1,600)	
Cash provided from operations		$ 700
Investing activities:		
Land purchase	$ (5,000)	
Land sale	1,000	
Building purchase	(40,000)	
Truck purchase	(10,000)	
Cash (used) for investing		$(54,000)
Financing activities:		
Loan payable	$10,000	
Mortgage payable	40,000	
Payment on mortgage	(2,000)	
Ted's withdrawals	(1,000)	
Ted's contributed capital	20,000	
Cash provided from financing		67,000
Increase in cash		$ 13,700
Cash — January 1		–0–
Cash — January 31		$ 13,700

Exhibit 3.3 displays the relationship between the balance sheets, the income statement, and the statement of changes in financial position. Exhibits 3.2 and 3.3 show how the net income for a period flows into the end-of-period retained earnings balance. Please note that the addition to Retained Earnings for the period also results in some combination of increases in assets and/or decreases in liabilities. That has to be so because the basic accounting equation (i.e., Assets = Liabilities + Equity) requires the balance sheet to be in balance. The net addition to Retained Earnings for the year is, in fact, an aggregation of a variety of transactions during the period, which have affected a variety of balance sheet accounts. In addition, the balance sheet has been further affected by a variety of other, non-income transactions. Only in the simplest companies would the increase in Retained Earnings be directly traced to an increase in a specific asset account. Thus, in summary, investors can see whether their investment has increased (or decreased) over the year (or period) by comparing the equity section of the balance sheet from one point in time to the next. The income statement shows in detail how the operations of the company contributed to that increase (or decrease). It is worth saying again: The change in cash for the year is *not* the same as the change in Retained Earnings because those two numbers are the net aggregations of a great variety of transactions that affect many other balance sheet accounts, in addition to their impact on Cash or Retained Earnings.

The statement of changes in financial position for Ted's Trucking discloses *identical* amounts for investing and financing activities as previously indicated in Chapter 2. The cash provided from operations is $700. The operating activities section is typically the most complex section of the statement. In essence, to determine this amount one must work backwards from the accrual basis on which the income statement was prepared to determine a cash basis amount for net income. There are two methods that may be used to determine the cash provided or used in operations: the direct method and the indirect method.

E X H I B I T   3 . 2

Diagrammatic Relationship of the Balance Sheet, the Income Statement, and the Statement of Shareholders' Equity

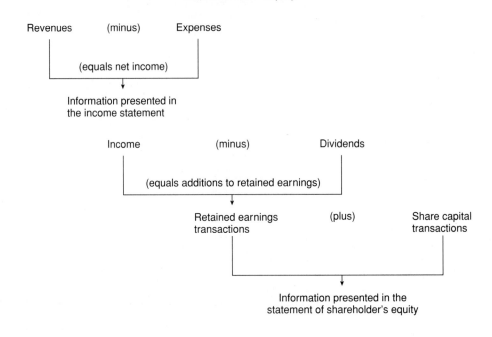

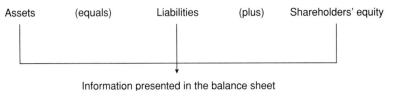

indirect method
A method of preparing the statement of changes in financial position whereby net income determined on the accrual basis of accounting is converted to the cash basis, to determine the cash provided/used in operating activities.

direct method
A method of preparing the statement of changes in financial position whereby the changes in the cash account resulting from the operating transactions, from the beginning to the end of the period, are analyzed.

The **indirect method** is the format used on Ted's statement. The accrual basis income of $1,300 was adjusted for the changes in current assets and current liabilities (working capital). Accounts Payable increased by $1,000, from zero at the beginning of the month to $1,000 at the end of the month. The $1,000 represents expenses included in the accrual basis income for which no cash has been disbursed. Similarly, Accounts Receivable increased by $1,600, from zero at the beginning of the month to $1,600 at the end of January. This $1,600 represents revenues accrued on the income statement for which no cash has been received. The net overall change in working capital items during the period was a decrease of $600 ($1,600 − $1,000). The indirect method is shown in Exhibit 3.4 on the following page.

The **direct method** analyzes the changes in the Cash account resulting from the operating transactions, from the beginning to the end of the period. As provided from the accounting equation, the operating transactions affecting Ted's Cash account for January are shown in Exhibit 3.5 on page 112. The statement of changes in financial position will be examined in more depth in Chapter 12.

EXHIBIT 3.3

Diagrammatic Relationship of the
Basic Financial Statements

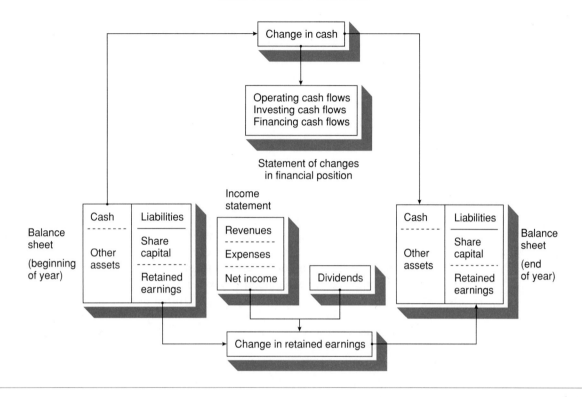

EXHIBIT 3.4

Cash Provided from Operations: Indirect Method

Operating Activities		Ted's Trucking
Net income (loss)		$1,300
Change in working capital items		
Increase in Accounts Payable	$1,000	
Increase in Accounts Receivable	(1,600)	(600)
Cash provided (used) in operations		$ 700

We used Ted's Trucking and the accounting equation to develop the three financial statements: the balance sheet, the income statement, and the statement of changes in financial position. As mentioned previously, although these statements may appear to be providing *all* the information, such is *not* the case. In the last set of statements no accrual was made for the interest owing on the mortgage or loan, and no amortization was recorded on the building. We will continue to develop additional areas of analysis in subsequent sections.

EXHIBIT 3.5

Cash Provided from Operations: Direct Method

Transaction	Amount
8	$1,900
9	(1,100)
12	200
13	(300)
Increase (decrease)	$ 700

3.4 ELEMENTS OF THE INCOME STATEMENT

The income statement, or statement of earnings, summarizes transactions that produce revenue for a company as a result of selling a product or service and transactions that result in expenses for the company. By summarizing revenues and expenses, the income statement presents a picture of the overall profitability of a company's operations.

Some argue that the income statement is the most important of the standard accounting statements because net income (or, colloquially, "the bottom line") is the basis for so many financial decisions. Management is rewarded or punished in a large part depending on whether actual income is or is not equal to planned income. Share prices rise or fall partly because the company reports net income higher or lower than the market's expectations. And, because of the frequently immediate reaction to its announcement, net income for the year is often taken to be the essence of that year's business activity.

The measurement of income under generally accepted accounting principles (GAAP) has been rigorously defined. This is probably because the evaluation of both companies and managements depends largely on the basis of reported net income. Recorded net income does not attempt to measure changes in values of the assets owned by a company, nor does it measure the company's qualitative accomplishments during the year. An accounting system could be designed to capture and report some or all of that type of information. However, faced with a trade-off between the reliability and relevance of presented information, the financial community has determined that a more reliable measure of income is more important than a broader, perhaps more relevant measure of income.

Most managers have supported a narrow definition of *income* because they prefer to be measured by a more concrete, more predictable measure of performance. For example, asset appreciation is *excluded* from the income statement in part because it is so hard to measure, in part because it fluctuates and suggests that a company's results are unstable, and in part because it is so completely out of management's control.

Fundamentally, management and analysts know that a living, functioning company is too complex to be represented simply by a single measure of performance. Maple Leaf Gardens, Limited, for example accomplished much more in 1994 than simply earning $1.69 per share. Thorough financial analysis requires considering all of the numbers in the income statement and asking about their relationships. What is the trend of net income? Does it appear that sales prices are keeping pace with cost increases or are they falling behind? To what degree was income depressed this year as a result of resolving a long-standing problem, and therefore clearing the way for increased income in the future?

The users of financial statements should also look beyond the income statement and ask about the company's cash flows and the strength of its balance sheet. Finally, to develop a complete picture of a company's results, financial statement users should go beyond the statements and investigate non-financial factors, including such things as a company's market share, customer loyalty, and new product development. A wise management provides footnotes and other textual commentaries describing the events of the year and encourages financial statement users to use the income statement only as a starting point for analysis.

Having said all of that, the financial community is occasionally too impatient to study a company in depth and, when pressured for immediate decisions, looks for shortcuts. Net income and earnings per share are the most commonly used shorthand measures of performance, and the income statement maintains its foremost position as the vehicle to report a company's financial results. The objective of this chapter is to help you understand the components of the income statement, how it is prepared, and how it can be used.

Terminology and Concepts

When first introduced to the income statement, people often think it strange that such an important topic should be encumbered by so many apparently overlapping and confusing terms. Perhaps the terminology problem can be traced to the attention given to the measurement of income — many people have looked at the subject from diverse viewpoints, and their different perspectives seem to have spawned many different words to express slightly different ideas. But perhaps it is simpler than that — perhaps the terminology problem is just a reflection of the inherent complexity of the subject. In any event, the words used are sometimes difficult. Because the topic is so important, it is useful to focus initially on the terminology used in connection with the income statement and to establish a common frame of reference for our subsequent discussions.

The term *revenues* refers to a company's actual (or promised) cash inflows resulting from a completed sale of the company's products or the satisfactory delivery of its services. *Revenues* are sometimes confused with *cash receipts*. Cash receipts may or may not pertain to revenues. To help you distinguish between a company's revenues and its cash receipts, consider the following. Cash inflows from the sale of shares or from borrowed money are not revenues but are financing transactions because the entity has continuing responsibilities to the providers of those funds. Cash deposits from a customer in advance of the delivery of a product or service are not revenues, nor will they be recognized as such until the "seller" completes its part of the bargain. In sum, revenues are those cash inflows (or expected cash inflows) that the company has earned and to which it is entitled to retain without qualification. Revenues are part of a company's income stream under accrual accounting. Some revenues also involve the receipt of cash, but others do not. Cash receipts, on the other hand, enter into the determination of a company's cash flows, which is the subject of the statement of changes in financial position.

sales
Sales suggests that the title to property has passed from a seller to a buyer. Most sales transactions qualify as revenue.

Sales, a legal term, suggests that the title to property has passed from a seller to a buyer. Most legal sales transactions qualify as revenue, but the accounting world is more interested in the substance of a transaction than in its legal form. Not all legal sales qualify as revenues for accounting purposes, however, as we shall see. When analyzing transactions, the accountant must look at the content of the economic event and not only its format.

gains
An increase in asset values, usually involving a sale unrelated to the principal revenue-producing activity of a business.

losses
Decreases in equity/net assets from peripheral or incidental transactions.

income
A generic term that may be used to indicate revenue from miscellaneous sources.

cost
The total acquisition value of an asset; the value of resources given up to acquire an asset.

net income
The difference between the aggregate revenues and aggregate expenses of an enterprise for a given accounting period; when aggregate expenses exceed aggregate revenues, the term *net loss* is used.

A *gain* is the net revenue a company earned as a result of a business transaction that is not a normal sale of products or delivery of services. "**Gains** are increases in equity/net assets from peripheral or incidental transactions and events affecting an entity" (CICA Handbook 1000.39). For example, a company that sells an excess piece of land that it had purchased earlier for possible expansion will recognize a gain in its income statement to the extent that the sales price of the land is more than the original cost. Conversely, if the sales price is less than the land's cost, the company will recognize a loss. "**Losses** are decreases in equity/net assets from peripheral or incidental transactions and events affecting an entity" (CICA Handbook 1000.40).

Income, a generic term, usually means revenue from sources other than product sales or from gain-producing transactions, such as interest income or rent income.

The term *expense* encompasses all actual or promised cash outflows, or allocations from prior years' cash outflows, which cannot be justified as an addition to an asset account or a reduction in a liability. To help you distinguish between expenses and cash payments, consider the following. As we said in Chapter 2, an accounting entry to record an expenditure must have two sides — one side is a reduction in cash, but whether the other side is an increase in an expense or an increase in an asset, or a reduction in a liability, depends on a careful analysis of the reason for the expenditure. Principal payments on debt are not expenses because they are simply the repayment of funds provided earlier by a lender. Dividends or withdrawals paid to the owners, are not expenses because they are financing transactions with the owners. Dividends are *not* an expense. An expenditure that creates a future value for the company may be considered an asset. If no measurable value results from an expenditure, it will be treated as an expense. Most often, an asset created in one year will become an expense in a future year.

An awkward word, **cost** is best understood when used in conjunction with an explanatory adjective such as *material cost, product cost*, or *transportation cost. Cost* is often a synonym for an actual or an expected expenditure, either an expense or an expenditure. You will hear management refer to the cost of a new machine, meaning the expenditure required for the asset. Or they will talk about the cost of a transaction, meaning the commission and delivery expenses incurred in connection with making a sale. The ambiguity of the term actually carries over to the traditional terminology used in preparing the income statement. The biggest deduction from revenue in the measurement of net income is referred to as the *cost of goods sold*, which is the total cost of the products removed from inventory and delivered to customers as a result of sales. For example, when a retail business sells a product for $75.00, it must also determine the cost of the product sold. If the product sold costs $50.00, the cost of the goods sold, $50.00 is matched with the sales revenue of $75.00. The other deductions from revenue on the income statement are selling expenses and general and administrative expenses, which are expenditures that were necessary for the operations of the business during the year.

The final financial result of all of an entity's operations for the year, **net income**, is the difference between total revenues (including product and service revenues, net gains from other transactions, and interest and other income) and the total of the cost of goods sold and operating expenses. The phrases *net income* and *net earnings* are often used interchangeably, and the income statement itself is often referred to as the *earnings statement*. There are a number of intermediate designations on the income statement, such as income from operations, income before extraordinary items, and income before taxes. Net income is the difference between revenues and expenses for the year, but it can also be seen as that part of the change in owners' equity from one year to the next that can be attributed to transactions with third parties — parties other than the owners.

profit
The excess of revenues over expenses for a single transaction.

Profit is a term that is occasionally a synonym for *income*. Most often profit (or loss) is used to describe the income (or loss) effect of an individual transaction. Unfortunately, some of these words are used casually in practice and are often used *interchangeably*. To understand what meaning is intended, it is important to consider the context in which a word is used and to focus on its meaning in that context.

3.5 INCOME STATEMENT

The income statement typically receives more attention from the users of financial information than the other financial statements. Users are particularly interested in the profitability of a company. The users may be even more interested or concerned if the company is incurring losses and not earning profits. When we review the financial statements of Ted's Trucking, one of our difficulties is that we lack a basis of comparison. Ted has started a new business and has no historical data for comparative purposes. Maple Leaf Gardens, Limited, statements have been prepared on a comparative basis, with the current year figures and the previous year's data. This presentation format allows for a relatively quick trend analysis to be completed, and a better understanding of the company's financial situation to be gained. The income statement for Maple Leaf Gardens, Limited, is presented below:

MAPLE LEAF GARDENS, LIMITED
Statements of Income
For the Year Ending June 30

	1994	1993
Revenues from operations	$62,693,174	$55,444,270
Investment and other income	850,022	754,089
	$63,543,196	$56,198,359
Expenses:		
Operating expenses	$53,175,423	$44,320,930
Depreciation	1,097,556	957,841
Amortization	1,545,663	1,969,962
	$55,818,642	$47,248,733
Operating income:	$ 7,724,554	$ 8,949,626
N.H.L. expansion fees (note 7)	3,112,931	525,333
Income before income taxes	$10,837,485	$ 9,474,959
Income taxes — current	$ 5,573,000	$ 5,212,000
Income taxes — deferred	(946,780)	(990,140)
	$ 4,626,220	$ 4,221,860
Net income	$ 6,211,265	$ 5,253,099
Earnings per share	$1.69	$1.43

Comparative analysis of the absolute amounts of the Maple Leaf Gardens, Limited, income statement indicates revenues from operations increased by approximately $7 million as compared to last year. Total operating expenses increased by over $8 million, resulting in a decrease in operating income of slightly over $1 million. A key figure on the statement is the income from N.H.L. expansion fees. The income from N.H.L. expansion fees was over $3 million in 1994, up significantly from 1993. The question that we should ask is: What is the anticipated income from N.H.L. expansion fees in the future? Will this source of income continue? The income statement of Maple Leaf Gardens makes reference to note 7, to enable users to answer this question and better interpret the financial situation of the company. A review of note 7 provides additional information on this source of revenue. Note 7 explains the particulars of the N.H.L. expansion fee and it appears the company's share of the expansion fee has been recognized in total in 1994 and 1993. Notes to financial statements, which are useful for the purposes of clarification or further explanation of the items in the financial statements, are considered an integral part of the financial statements and should be reviewed carefully.

The income statement and the accounting principles and concepts that influence its development are covered in depth in the next two chapters and throughout the remainder of the text.

3.6 EQUITY STATEMENTS

Proprietorships/Partnerships

"The financial statements of unincorporated businesses should include a statement setting out the details of the changes in owners' equity during the period and this statement should set out separately contributions of capital, income or losses, and withdrawals" (CICA Handbook 1800.07). Equity is comprised of two distinct elements: contributed capital and earned capital. Contributed capital represents the resources contributed by the owners of the organization. Earned capital is the cumulative net income/loss of the organization net of any distribution of resources to the owners. The total owner's equity is also displayed on the end-of-period balance sheet. But, to provide the users of financial reports more meaningful information, an equity statement may also be presented. A statement of owner's equity for the proprietorship Ted's Trucking is shown below:

TED'S TRUCKING
Statement of Owner's Equity
For the Month Ended January 31

Capital, Ted — January 1	$20,000
Net income	1,300
Withdrawals	(1,000)
Capital, Ted — January 31	$20,300

Ted's Trucking is a proprietorship and therefore uses a single equity account, a Capital account for the owner Ted. We have disclosed Ted's original investment of $20,000 as the beginning capital balance on January 1. To the beginning Capital balance is added the net income for the month of $1,300, and Ted's withdrawals of $1,000 are deducted to determine the ending balance of $20,300. Both capital contributed by Ted and that earned by the business is accumulated in the same account. With proprietorships and partnerships the distinction between contributed and earned capital becomes lost in the owner's capital account(s). A similar procedure is used for the equity statement of a partnership, except it is necessary to use a separate account for each partner. Therefore, if the partnership had four partners, the accounting system would require four capital accounts.

CHAPTER 3 Operating Activities

Corporations

If Ted's Trucking had been established as a corporation, the disclosure of the owner's equity would be slightly different. The name of the business would be suffixed by Limited or Ltd. For a corporation the equity is referred to as *shareholders' equity*. Ted's original contributed capital would be classified as *share capital*. The net income for the year would be accumulated in a retained earnings account. The distribution of resources to shareholders, called *withdrawals* for proprietorships and partnerships, are called **dividends** for corporations. Dividends are deducted from retained earnings when they are declared.

dividends
The distribution of the earned income of an enterprise to its owners.

TED'S TRUCKING, LIMITED
Statement of Shareholders' Equity
For the Month Ended January 31

Share capital		$20,000
Retained earnings — January 1	$ –0–	
Net income	1,300	
Dividends	(1,000)	
Retained earnings — January 31		300
Total shareholders' equity		$20,300

The total shareholders' equity balance is also disclosed on the equity section of the balance sheet. The most common practice for large corporations is to prepare two separate schedules: one schedule or statement for contributed capital or share capital, and a second schedule for earned capital or retained earnings for the period. Maple Leaf Gardens, Limited, discloses most of the particulars about its capital stock on the balance sheet, supplemented with footnote 6. Note 6 provides additional information on the capital stock of Maple Leaf Gardens, Limited: "During the fiscal 1994, the Corporation redeemed 500 common shares for total proceeds of $16,900 and reduced the authorized capital stock by 500 common shares." A statement of retained earnings is also provided to disclose the information on earned capital. The retained earnings statement of Maple Leaf Gardens, Limited, is shown below:

MAPLE LEAF GARDENS, LIMITED
Statement of Retained Earnings
For the Year Ended June 30

	1994	1993
Retained earnings — July 1	$14,808,800	$12,498,021
Net income	6,211,265	5,253,099
Dividends	(2,942,330)	(2,942,330)
Redemption of common shares	(16,895)	—
Retained earnings — June 30	$18,060,850	$14,808,800

Non-Profits

The equity statements of non-profit organizations typically use a single equity account referred to as Surplus, Unrestricted Surplus, Unappropriated Surplus, or Fund Balance. As well, non-profits do not recognize a net income, but the excess of revenues over expenses. The equity statement of the United Way of Canada is shown below:

UNITED WAY OF CANADA
Statement of Fund Balance
For the Year Ended December 31

Fund balance — January 1	$286,700
Excess of revenues over expenses	60,740
Fund balance — December 31	$347,440

3.7 ANALYZING THE INCOME STATEMENT

A variety of analysis techniques and approaches are available to the financial statement user. We discussed some of the different approaches in Chapter 2 to provide you with a basic understanding of financial statement analysis. It is important to again emphasize the significance of comparable data when performing financial analysis. Whether the user is analyzing absolute amounts, ratios, or trends, it is important to compare the data to similar financial data within or outside the organization. As previously mentioned, fundamental financial statement analysis would include the techniques listed in Exhibit 3.6. In Chapter 2, these analysis techniques were applied to the balance sheet. These same techniques will now be used to illustrate income statement analysis.

E X H I B I T 3 . 6

Financial Statement Analysis Techniques

Analyzing absolute Amounts   Trend analysis   Common-size statements   Ratio analysis

Trend Analysis

trend analysis
The analysis of ratios or absolute account balances over one or more accounting periods to identify the direction or trend of a company's financial health.

Trend analysis involves the comparison of financial data over time. For example, key figures like total revenues, total assets, and net income for the past 5 or 10 years may be presented in a series and analyzed to determine if any trends may be discovered in the organization's financial condition or operations. Many publicly held companies include 5- or 10-year summaries in their annual reports for this purpose. Frequently such financial information is presented in graphical format to facilitate its analysis and interpretation. A portion of Cineplex Odeon Corporation's five-year financial summary (in thousands of U.S. dollars) is presented below:

	Revenues				
	1989	**1990**	**1991**	**1992**	**1993**
Concession	$128,288	$134,318	$124,023	$125,374	$138,387
Box office	403,040	438,982	386,218	373,258	388,944

To facilitate trend analysis for the user, organizations may present their financial data in graphic format. A graphic illustration of Cineplex Odeon Corporation's five-year revenue data is presented on the next page.

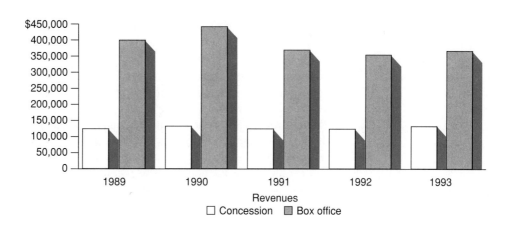

Cineplex Odeon Corporation
Five Year Financial Summary

Common-Size Statements

To illustrate common-size financial statements, Exhibit 3.7 presents Maple Leaf Gardens' common-size income statements for 1994 and 1993. An interpretation of vertical statements often parallels the interpretation of horizontal statements. Note that the common-size statements permit both a within-period analysis (e.g., in 1994, total

E X H I B I T   3 . 7

MAPLE LEAF GARDENS, LIMITED
Statements of Income
For the Year Ending June 30

	1994	Common-Size Percentage	1993	Common-Size Percentage
Revenues from operations	$62,693,174	98.7	$55,444,270	98.7
Investment and other income	850,022	1.3	754,089	1.3
Total revenues	$63,543,196	100.0	$56,198,359	100.0
Expenses:				
Operating expenses	$53,175,423	83.7	$44,320,930	78.9
Depreciation	1,097,556	1.7	957,841	1.7
Amortization	1,545,663	2.4	1,969,962	3.5
Total expenses	$55,818,642	87.8	$47,248,733	84.1
Operating income:	$ 7,724,554	12.2	$ 8,949,626	15.9
N.H.L. expansion fees	3,112,931	4.9	525,333	.9
Income before taxes	$10,837,485	17.1	$ 9,474,959	16.8
Income taxes — current	$ 5,573,000	8.8	$ 5,212,000	9.3
Income taxes — deferred	(946,780)	(1.5)	(990,140)	(1.8)
	$ 4,626,220	7.3	$ 4,221,860	7.5
Net income	$ 6,211,265	9.8	$ 5,253,099	9.3
Earnings per share	$1.69		$1.43	

EXHIBIT 3.8

Framework of Financial Statement Analysis

Financial Strength		Management Performance	
Liquidity	Solvency	Profitability	Asset Management

expenses were 87.8 percentage of total revenues) and across-period trend analysis (e.g., total expenses as a percentage of total revenues increased from 84.1 percent in 1993 to 87.8 percent in 1994).

To provide structure to financial statement analysis reference was previously made to the CICA research study "Using Ratios and Graphics in Financial Reporting." This CICA study provides an excellent framework for analysis. We have modified the framework for financial statement analysis recommended by the CICA research study so it is appropriate for an introductory level discussion of the topic. A basic framework of financial statement analysis is shown in Exhibit 3.8.

The financial strength of the organization was analyzed in Chapter 2, when the liquidity and solvency of organizations were investigated. Financial strength analysis focuses on the balance sheet elements.

Our analysis will now focus on the management performance of the organization. Analysis of management performance involves the analysis of profitability and asset management. **Profitability** refers to a company's overall income-generating ability, and **asset management** refers to the ability of a company's managers to utilize its assets effectively to produce a return for the company's creditors and owners. When analyzing management performance, much attention is focussed on the organization's operating activities and the analysis of the income statement.

An analysis of profitability may be undertaken using a number of different techniques. The absolute level of revenues, or net income, can be investigated over time (i.e., a trend analysis). As well, a series of profitability ratios can be calculated. A large number of different ratios are available to the financial statement user when it comes to the analysis of a company's profitability. We will illustrate only two profitability ratios in this chapter. Additional profitability analysis techniques will be examined in later chapters. Two of the more popular and useful ratios — earnings per share and return on equity — are discussed in the next section.

The income statement may also be used to reveal how effectively management is managing the organization's assets. Management is employed by the owners to control and manage the assets of the organization. We examine the total asset turnover ratio and the receivable turnover ratio to illustrate the concept of asset management. The management performance ratios are summarized in Exhibit 3.9.

profitability
The relative success of a company's operations.

asset management
A measure of management's ability to effectively utilize a company's assets to produce income.

earnings per share
A standardized measure of performance calculated as net income divided by the weighted-average number of common shares outstanding during an accounting period.

Profitability

Because the absolute level of net income is often difficult to compare between periods and among different companies (largely because the level of revenue-producing assets differs over time and between companies), it is an accepted practice for companies to report a standardized measure of their performance. Under GAAP, net income is divided by the number of shares of a company's share capital, and the resulting standardized measure of performance is called **earnings per share** (EPS). "Earnings per share represents the portion of the income for a period attributable to a share of issued capital of an enterprise. This information assists shareholders in evaluating the past

EXHIBIT 3.9

Ratio Analysis

Management Performance

Profitability	Asset Management
Earnings per share	Total asset turnover ratio
Return on equity ratio	Receivable turnover ratio

operating performance of a business, in forming an opinion as to its potential and in making investment decisions" (CICA Handbook 3500.01).

The rules followed in calculating earnings per share (EPS) are quite complex. For the purposes of this text, it is sufficient to understand that earnings per share results from dividing the number[1] of common shares outstanding during the year into the net income for the year that is available to the common shareholders.

$$\text{Earnings per share} = \frac{\text{Net income}}{\text{Number of common shares outstanding}^2}$$

At the end of each quarter and the end of each year, publicly held companies release earnings information for the period, in total and on a per share basis. The quarterly and annual reports are summarized in the financial press and then are used on an ongoing basis in calculating various stock market performance indicators. The determination of the earnings per share data provides meaningful information to the users of financial reports. The earnings per share figures may be disclosed in a footnote to the financial statements. Frequently, the earnings per share figure is disclosed as part of the income statement, as is the case with Maple Leaf Gardens, Limited. Maple Leaf Gardens disclosed earnings per share of $1.69 for 1994, and $1.43 for 1993. The absolute level of net income has increased to $6,211,265 in 1994, from $5,253,099 in 1993.

return on equity (ROE) A measure of profitability; a measure of the relative effectiveness of a company in using the assets provided by the owners to generate net income.

The second profitability ratio we will consider is the return on equity ratio. **Return on equity** (ROE), one of the most commonly used profitability measures, measures a company's profitability relative to the resources provided by its owners. It measures the adequacy of the return on capital invested by the owners. ROE is calculated as follows:

$$\text{Return on equity} = \frac{\text{Net income}}{\text{Equity}}$$

In general, the higher the ROE, the more profitable a company is thought to be. The return on equity for Maple Leaf Gardens, Limited, was 34.3 percent in 1994, compared to 35.3 percent in 1993. Although the return on equity has declined slightly from last year for Maple Leaf Gardens, the earnings per share and dollar value of net income has increased. To gain a better understanding of the profitability of Maple Leaf Gardens, Limited, additional analysis will be performed in later chapters.

---

[1] For ratios that use both balance sheet and income statement values, it is generally thought that the use of average balance sheet values provides the most useful information. The use of averages for balance sheet amounts avoids any distortions in analysis due to fluctuations in end-of-period balances. In many cases, sufficient information is not available to allow average amounts to be determined. Therefore, absolute amounts must be used. See the latter part of this section for a further discussion and illustration of ratios using average amounts.

[2] Earnings per share should be calculated using the weighted-average number of common shares outstanding. However, this information is not always readily available to the user. Therefore, as described in footnote 1 above, the end-of-period number of shares outstanding may have to be used. In practice, this is generally not a problem, because according to GAAP, the earnings per share figure should be disclosed as part of the organization's financial report.

Asset Management

total asset turnover ratio
A measure of an organization's utilization of available resources to generate revenues.

The **total asset turnover ratio** is a measure of an organization's utilization of available resources to generate revenues. This ratio examines a company's utilization of its revenue-producing assets. In general, the higher the ratio the better. A high turnover ratio indicates that management is effective in generating revenues from the assets it has at its disposal. A high turnover rate can also be problematic, however, if the reason for the high turnover is the liquidation of the company's assets. Similarly, a decreasing ratio may not necessarily indicate poor asset utilization. The total asset turnover is influenced by the turnover rate of the individual assets like receivables and inventory. Some assets like perishable inventory turn over quickly, while non-current assets turn over slowly. When using this ratio, it is important to compare it to the ratios of similar firms in the same industry or to the firm's previous ratios on a trend basis. The total asset turnover ratio is calculated as follows:

$$\text{Total asset turnover ratio} = \frac{\text{Sales (revenues)}}{\text{Total assets}}$$

accounts receivable turnover ratio
A measure of the effectiveness of receivable management.

A second indicator of the quality or effectiveness of a company's asset management is given by the **turnover ratio.** The quality of receivable management is usually evaluated in the context of the accounts (notes) receivable turnover ratio. The receivable turnover ratio is a measure of the rate at which a company's accounts and notes receivable are converted to cash. In general, a high ratio indicates excellent receivables management. The higher the ratio, the faster the organization is collecting its outstanding receivables. A low ratio, which means a slow collection process, may indicate serious problems in the sales-receivables-collection cycle. The ratio is calculated as follows:

$$\text{Accounts receivable turnover ratio} = \frac{\text{Sales (revenues)}}{\text{Accounts receivable}}$$

To illustrate the asset management ratios, consider again Maple Leaf Gardens' 1994 financial statements. Maple Leaf Gardens' asset management position in 1993 and 1994 compares very favourably. The receivable turnover ratio has improved significantly from 17.7 in 1993 to 36.1 in 1994. The total asset turnover ratio has improved marginally from 1.76 in 1993 to 2.07 in 1994. Both of these turnover ratios indicate Maple Leaf Gardens has sound asset management.

It is important to again emphasize the significance of comparable data when performing financial analysis. Whether the user is analyzing absolute amounts, ratios, or trends, it is crucial to compare the data to similar data within or outside the organization. Exhibit 3.10 provides a small sample of the comparative key business ratios available from Dun & Bradstreet Canada.

Consistency/Comparability in Ratio Analysis

The principle of consistency is used to assure comparative data is available for financial analysis. Consistency is also important with ratio analysis. Care must be taken to ensure the components of each ratio are similar to provide a consistent basis of comparison. The CICA research report "Using Ratios and Graphics in Financial Reporting" expressed a concern about the lack of consistency in calculating and using ratios. It is recommended that average values be used to calculate ratios that use both income statement and a balance sheet item (e.g., earnings per share, return on equity, and receivable and inventory turnovers). The use of average amounts is recommended to eliminate any fluctuations in year-end values that could distort the ratio analysis.

EXHIBIT 3.10

Ratio Guides

Industry	Return on Equity	Receivable Turnover
Florist	25.4	24.3
Shoe store	14.7	40.6
Air transportation	1.5	10.1
Theatres	7.8	—
Radio and television	4.6	8.1

Source: Dun & Bradstreet Canada.

However, in many instances, sufficient information is not available to allow for the determination of average balances for the two or more periods being analyzed and compared. Often, only two years' financial data are available to the user, the current and the immediately preceding period. An average could be determined for only the current year, but *not* the preceding year. If a ratio is calculated using an average amount for one period and an absolute amount for the other, this inconsistency could lead to a flaw in the analysis. Therefore, although it is highly desirable to use the average amount when calculating many ratios, if the information is not available for *all the periods* being analyzed, *averages should not be used* for any of the periods. Users should not calculate an average for one period and then try to compare it to another period in which an average could not be determined due to lack of information. It is important to determine ratios on a consistent basis to enhance the comparability of data. Therefore, in many instances, including examples and problems in this text, even though it is desirable to use average amounts, absolute amounts *should* be used because of the shortage of information.

The following data illustrate the use of average and non-average balances when calculating ratios:

	1997	1996
Company A		
Net income	$125,000	$ 75,000
Shareholders' equity	470,000	345,000
Company B		
Net income	40,000	30,000
Shareholders' equity	970,000	930,000

In this example financial data are available for only two years. It is not possible to determine the average shareholders' equity for 1996 (1995 data would be required). Therefore, when comparing the return on equity for each year, the year-end balance of shareholders' equity must be used. For Company A, the return on equity increased from 21.74 percent to 26.60 percent. If the average shareholders' equity is determined for 1997 and used for ratio purposes, a return of 30.67 percent is determined. It would be misleading to compare this to the 21.74 percent return for 1996 determined using *year-end* shareholders' equity. It is important that ratios be determined on a consistent basis to improve comparability. For Company B, due to the small change in shareholders' equity from 1996 to 1997, the difference is less significant (return on equity of 4.12% compared to 4.21%).

	1997	1996
Company A		
Percent return on equity	26.60 (125,000/470,000)	21.74 (75,000/345,000)
Percent return on *average* equity	30.67 [125,000/(470,000 + 345,000)/2]	n.a.*
Company B		
Percent return on equity	4.12 (40,000/970,000)	3.26 (30,000/930,000)
Percent return on *average* equity	4.21 [40,000/(970,000 + 930,000)/2]	n.a.

*n.a. = Not available.

In summary, in the preceding illustration, it would only be appropriate to use average values for 1997 if the data are *also* available to determine average amounts for 1996. We have emphasized the importance of comparative financial analysis. Exhibit 3.11 summarizes the different basis of comparison recommended for comparative financial analysis.

E X H I B I T   3 . 1 1

Comparative Analysis

Company A this year, compared to Company A last year.
Company A compared to Company B.
Company A compared to industry averages.

3.8 SUMMARY

The income statement and statement of changes in financial position have been presented to illustrate the operating activities of an organization. Ted's Trucking and the balance sheet equation were used to illustrate operating transactions and introduce the concepts of revenues and expenses. The income statement summarizes transactions that produce revenue for a company as a result of selling a product or service and transactions that result in expenses. It measures the overall profitability of the organization. The measurement of profitability is guided by a number of revenue and expense recognition conventions, principally the accrual concept and the matching principle.

The cash and accrual basis of accounting were used to prepare two sets of financial statements. The importance of understanding the accrual basis of accounting was emphasized. This chapter focussed on the income statement, and again illustrated the statement of changes in financial position. The impact of the accrual basis of accounting was disclosed on the four financial statements prepared by most organizations: the balance sheet, the income statement, the equity statement, and the statement of changes in financial position. The equity statement was illustrated for proprietorships and corporations.

Analysis of management performance was discussed, focussing on the income statement. The profitability and asset management of the organization were examined. Evaluating the profitability of operations may be accomplished through a trend analysis of net income or through the calculation of various profitability ratios such as earnings per share or return on equity. The importance of consistency and comparative financial analysis was emphasized.

This chapter should reinforce the concepts discussed in the first two chapters. A comprehensive set of review questions are provided to give feedback on your understanding of the language of accounting and your understanding of the material covered in the first three chapters. The next chapter looks at the accounting process and financial statement analysis.

3.9 KEY CONCEPTS AND TERMS

Accounts payable (p. 104)

Accounts receivable (p. 104)

Accounts receivable turnover
  ratio (p. 122)

Accrual basis of accounting (p. 103)

Accrued expense (p. 106)

Accrued revenue (p. 106)

Asset management (p. 120)

Cash basis of accounting (p. 100)

Cost (p. 114)

Direct method (p. 110)

Dividends (p. 117)

Earnings per share (p. 120)

Expenses (p. 104)

Gains (p. 114)

Income (p. 114)

Indirect method (p. 110)

Losses (p. 114)

Matching principle (p. 104)

Net income (p. 114)

Profit (p. 115)

Profitability (p. 120)

Return on equity ratio (p. 121)

Revenues (p. 104)

Sales (p. 113)

Total asset turnover ratio (p. 122)

Trend analysis (p. 118)

3.10 COMPREHENSIVE REVIEW QUESTIONS

R3.1 Analysis of financial strength and management performance. Shown below is financial information of Cineplex Odeon Corporation. Perform an analysis of financial strength and management performance of the company. Your report should include comments as to the company's financial position.

CINEPLEX ODEON CORPORATION
Consolidated Balance Sheet
At December 31, 1993, and 1992

	1993	1992
Assets		
Cash	$ 1,268	$ 1,350
Accounts receivable	19,640	21,578
Inventory	6,412	5,156
Other current assets	1,856	2,569
Total current assets	$ 29,176	$ 30,653
Capital assets	619,309	658,598
Long-term investments	42,524	45,580
Other assets	6,096	6,821
Total assets	$697,105	$741,652
Liabilities		
Accounts payable	$ 73,779	77,175
Deferred income	13,889	10,908
Income taxes payable	912	1,032
Other current liabilities	51,089	30,991
Total current liabilities	$139,669	$120,106
Long-term debt	324,852	413,500
Other long-term liabilities	32,197	9,080
Total liabilities	$496,718	$542,686
Total equity*	200,387	198,966
Total liabilities and equity	$697,105	$741,652

*Weighted-average shares outstanding: 1993, 106,730; 1992, 85,823.

CINEPLEX ODEON CORPORATION
Consolidated Income Statement
Year Ended December 31, 1993, and 1992

	1993	1992
Revenues:		
Admissions	$388,944	$373,258
Concessions	138,387	125,374
Other	18,899	20,091
	$546,230	$518,723
Expenses:		
Theatre operations	$440,214	$445,923
Cost of concessions	19,545	17,612
General and administrative	15,494	17,516
Depreciation and amortization	41,577	42,258
	$516,830	$523,309
Income (loss)	$ 29,400	$ (4,586)
Other income	1,267	558
Income before interest expense	$ 30,667	$ (4,028)
Interest expense	28,033	34,387
Income before income taxes	$ 2,634	$ (38,415)
Income taxes	1,665	1,298
Income (loss) from continuing operations	$ 969	$ (39,713)
Discontinued operations	(8,341)	(1,636)
Net loss	$ (7,372)	$ (41,349)

R3.2 Accrual versus cash basis accounting. McGregor and Epp is a professional accounting firm that was organized for business on May 1, 1996. John McGregor and Lowell Epp each contributed $15,000 cash for equal shares in the accounting partnership. The firm also borrowed $20,000 from the Bank of Montreal on July 1, 1996; the loan was to be paid in full on July 1, 1999, with interest at the rate of 11 percent annually.

The firm rented office space on May 1, paying two months' rent in advance. The regular monthly rental fee of $550 per month was to be paid on the first day of each month beginning on June 1. The company purchased a computer system and a fax machine in early July at a total cost of $4,500 cash. It is estimated the capital assets will be used for 4 years.

For the eight months ended December 31, 1996, the company had rendered $82,000 in accounting services. Of this amount, all but $11,000 had been collected by year-end. Another $7,600 in accrued revenues had not been recorded at December 31. Costs incurred and paid in cash by year-end included:

Utilities	$1,450
Salary — accounting clerk	6,800
Office supplies	1,760

Unpaid bills at year-end included a telephone bill for $180 and wages for the accounting clerk of $700. The partners have agreed to share profits and losses equally.

Required:

You have been retained by the firm to prepare a set of accounting statements as of December 31, 1996. Using the above information, prepare a balance sheet, an income statement, and a statement of changes in financial position using the accrual basis of accounting. As well, prepare an income statement using the cash basis of accounting. On the basis of your findings, comment on the performance of the partnership during its first eight months of operations.

3.11 REVIEW AND DISCUSSION QUESTIONS

Q3.1 Which subgroup(s) of financial statement readers is (are) likely to be most interested in the statement of changes in financial position and why?

Q3.2 Distinguish between accrued expenses and accrued revenues.

Q3.3 Why do you think the statement of changes in financial position is segregated into operating, financing, and investing activity sections? Identify other categorizations that accountants might have considered or that you believe would have merit.

Q3.4 Distinguish between dividends and withdrawals.

Q3.5 Assuming an organization has a September 30 year-end, the dates used for the statement of changes in financial position and the income statement are always "for the period ending September 30." The balance sheet date is "at September 30." Explain the reasoning behind the different date explanations.

Q3.6 Maple Leaf Gardens, Limited, previously had a fiscal year-end of May 31. In 1994 Maple Leaf Gardens changed its year-end to June 30. Why might an organization want to change the date of its fiscal year?

Q3.7 Distinguish between gains and sales.

Q3.8 Two accountants, arguing an income statement presentation issue, summarize the debate with these points:

Point: The income statement should report only the results of transactions directly related to the current period's operations of a company.

Counter-point: The income statement should report all transactions affecting the owners' interest in a company, except those involving dividends and capital stock.

Evaluate these two perspectives. Which one do you agree with, and why? Which of the following transactions do you feel should (or should not) be reported in a company's current income statement?

a. A gain on the sale of a subsidiary.

b. An unexpected loss due to a fire in the company warehouse.

c. The damages award received as settlement of a lawsuit.

d. A correction to the company's income statement from two years before.

e. Winning the grand prize of $40 million in the lottery — the CEO purchased the ticket using company funds.

Q3.9 It has frequently been noted that financial reporting can either adopt a balance sheet focus or an income statement focus, but that it is impossible to do both. The gist of such a statement is that if accounting focusses on the measurement of assets and liabilities, revenues and expenses become a function of how assets and liabilities are reported. Said another way, the basic equation must balance (Assets = Liabilities + Equity) and if two of the three factors (assets and liabilities) are prescribed, the third (equity) is whatever it takes to balance the equation. On the other hand, if the measurement of revenues and expenses is accounting's foremost concern (that is, equity), then the assets and liabilities reported on the balance sheet are determined by those revenue and expense measurements. Comment on these two views.

Q3.10 The Boston Celtics Limited Partnership presents the following footnote in their annual report:

> Revenues and expenses are recognized when revenues and the related costs are earned or incurred. Ticket sales and television and radio broadcasting fees generally are recorded as revenues at the time the game to which such proceeds relate is played. Team expenses, principally player and coaches' salaries, related fringe benefits and insurance, and game and playoff expenses, principally National Basketball Association attendance assessments, arena rentals and travel, are recorded as expense on the same basis. Accordingly, advance ticket sales and advance payments on television and radio broadcasting contracts and payments for team and game expenses not earned or incurred are recorded as deferred game revenues and deferred game expenses, respectively, and amortized ratably as regular season games are played. General and administrative and selling and promotional expenses are charged to operations as incurred.

Comment on the reasoning underlying such policies.

Q3.11 Consider yourself a prospective investor. Explain briefly how you might use the three basic financial statements (the balance sheet, the income statement, and the statement of changes in financial position) in your investment decision. What different insights would you expect those three different statements to provide for your investment decision?

Q3.12 In 1993, George Weston, Limited, reported net income for the year of $57 million (as reported in the statement of net income) and a net decrease in cash and cash equivalents of $24 million (as reported in the statement of changes in financial position). What do those two numbers mean to you as a potential investor in George Weston, Limited?

Q3.13 Review the list of new concepts or terms at the end of the chapter. If you have difficulty with a specific concept, refer to the discussion on the page number provided to gain a better understanding of the concept. Make a list of terms you do not thoroughly understand. When you have finished Chapter 4, refer back to this list to see if your understanding has improved.

Q3.14 A company acquired a building, paying a portion of the purchase price in cash and issuing a mortgage note payable to the seller for the balance.

a. In a statement of changes in financial position, what amount is included in investing activities for the above transaction?

b. In a statement of changes in financial position, what amount is included in financing activities for the above transaction?

Q3.15* A business executive was overheard saying: "I'm confused. Our business had a record net income this year. Both retained earnings and total assets are at an all-time high. How is it possible that we have less cash on hand at the end of this year than at the end of last year?" Does this statement reflect a flaw in accounting or a misunderstanding of accounting data? Briefly explain.

Q3.16 The statement of changes in financial position is a required basic financial statement.

a. What are the objectives of the statement of changes in financial position?

---

*Published with permission of CGA Canada

b. Identify two types of transactions that would be disclosed in a separate schedule with the statement of changes in financial position because they do not affect cash during the reporting period.

3.12 PROBLEMS

P3.1 Balance sheet equation: operating, financing, and investing activities. The following transactions were incurred by Stephan Company during the month of February:

1. A corporation was formed and share capital was issued for $25,000 cash.

2. Obtained a long-term mortgage for $50,000.

3. Purchased land for $30,000 cash.

4. Obtained a long-term bank loan of $25,000.

5. Purchased machinery for $20,000 cash.

6. Purchased an automobile for $26,000 cash.

7. Goods/services provided; received $3,200 cash.

8. Goods/services provided; received a promise for payment of $4,700.

9. Goods/services received; promised to pay $3,700 later.

10. Cash payment of $900 received on account re: transaction 8.

11. Paid cash of $1,200 on account re: transaction 9.

12. Goods/services received; paid $1,700 cash.

Required:

Using the accrual basis of accounting:

a. Record the transactions for Stephan Company using the accounting equation.

b. Prepare an income statement for Stephan Company.

c. Prepare a balance sheet for Stephan Company.

d. Prepare a statement of changes in financial position for Stephan Company.

P3.2 Balance sheet equation: operating, financing, and investing activities. The following transactions were incurred during the month of April:

1. James formed a proprietorship and deposited $40,000 cash in the business bank account.

2. Obtained a long-term bank loan of $25,000.

3. Purchased a building for $40,000 cash.

4. Purchased machinery for $12,000 cash.

5. Goods/services provided; received $7,200 cash.

6. Goods/services provided; received a promise for payment of $9,200.

7. Goods/services received; paid $8,400 cash.

8. Goods/services received; promised to pay $4,900 later.

9. Cash payment of $900 received on account re: transaction 6.

10. During the period, James withdrew $5,000 cash from the proprietorship.

11. Paid $1,000 on principal of the bank loan.

12. Paid cash of $1,800 on account re: transaction 8.

Required:

Using the accrual basis of accounting:

a. Record the transactions using the accounting equation.

b. Prepare an income statement for James.

c. Prepare a balance sheet for James.

d. Prepare a statement of changes in financial position for James.

P3.3 Journal entries: operating, financing, and investing activities. The following transactions were incurred by Dalton Company during the month of March:

1. A corporation was formed and share capital was issued for $50,000 cash.

2. Obtained a long-term bank loan of $65,000.

3. Purchased land for $40,000 cash.

4. Obtained a long-term mortgage for $25,000.

5. Sold land for $9,000 cash, that had originally cost $9,000.

6. Goods/services received; paid $5,900 cash.

7. Goods/services provided; received a promise for payment of $7,300.

8. Goods/services provided; received $8,800 cash.

9. Purchased a computer for $5,000 cash.

10. Goods/services received; promised to pay $5,300 later.

11. Cash payment of $3,100 received on account re: transaction 7.

Required:

Using the accrual basis of accounting, prepare general journal entries for the above transactions.

P3.4 Journal entries: operating, financing, and investing activities. The following transactions were incurred during the month of October.

1. Jonathan formed a proprietorship and contributed $10,000 cash; a used car that cost him $7,000 several years ago, which he recently had appraised at $4,000; and land that he originally bought for $6,000 and is presently valued at $11,500.

2. Purchased an automobile for $12,000 cash.

3. Obtained a long-term bank loan of $25,000.

4. Purchased machinery for $11,000 cash.

5. Purchased office equipment for $5,000 cash.

6. Jonathan withdrew $9,000 cash from the proprietorship.

7. Goods/services received; promised to pay $5,300 later.

8. Goods/services received; paid $5,900 cash.

9. Goods/services provided; received a promise for payment $7,300.

10. Paid $2,000 on principal of the bank loan.

11. Goods/services provided; received $8,800 cash.

12. Cash payment of $900 received on account re: transaction 9.

13. Paid cash of $1,200 on account re: transaction 7.

Required:

Using the accrual basis of accounting, prepare general journal entries for the above transactions.

P3.5 Partnership: operating, financing, and investing activities. The following transactions were incurred during the month of January:

1. Thelma and Louise formed a partnership and each deposited $25,000 cash into a bank account.

2. Purchased a vehicle for $16,000.

3. Purchased equipment for $8,000 cash.

4. Louise withdrew $4,000 cash from the partnership. Thelma withdrew $6,000 cash.

5. Obtained a long-term loan for $30,000.

6. Goods/services provided; received $5,500 cash.

7. Purchased land for $31,000 cash.

8. Goods/services received; paid $5,900 cash.

9. Goods/services provided; received a promise for payment of $9,900.

10. Paid $3,000 on principal on the long-term loan.

11. Goods/services provided; received $2,800 cash.

12. Cash payment of $3,700 received on account re: transaction 9.

Required:

Using the accrual basis of accounting, prepare general journal entries for the above transactions.

P3.6 Events and the affected accounts. Consider the following events, which were part of the activities of the Springtime Sales Company during the year:

1. Sales of merchandise on account.

2. Purchase of merchandise on account.

3. Purchase of a delivery truck, with a 10 percent down payment.

4. Sale of common stock for cash.

5. Purchase of a temporary investment.

6. Purchase of a three-year insurance policy for cash.

7. Amortization of one year's coverage of the insurance policy.

8. Payment of wages to hourly employees.

9. Payment of a dividend to shareholders.

Required:

For each of the above events, describe the nature of the accounts that would be affected (asset, liability, equity, etc.) and, in the context of the basic accounting equation, explain the rationale for your answer.

P3.7 Event analysis. The accounting records of the Floyd Corporation include the following entries:

a	Dr. Accounts Receivable	70,400	
	Cr. Revenue		70,400
b	Dr. Cash	78,960	
	Cr. Accounts Receivable		78,960
c	Dr. Operating Expenses	720	
	Cr. Supplies on Hand		720
d	Dr. Equipment	2,720	
	Cr. Cash		2,720
e	Dr. Accounts Payable	2,560	
	Cr. Cash		2,560
f	Dr. Notes Payable	20,000	
	Dr. Interest Expense	160	
	Cr. Cash		20,160
g	Dr. Dividends	12,800	
	Cr. Cash		12,800

Required:

For each entry, prepare a one-sentence description of the underlying event.

P3.8 Income statement preparation. On July 1, Tom and Sam Parks formed a window-washing business in downtown Toronto. The following information pertains to their first month's operations.

Total cash received	$2,400
Cash paid out:	
Purchased supplies	90
Truck rental	300
Paid employees	550
Paid July rent for office space	150

Although the Parks brothers expected most of their work to come from single engagements, they did enter into two contracts early in July. The first contract, with Budget Shoe Store, specified that Tom and Sam were to wash Budget's windows at a rate of $40 per month for a period of one year. In partial return for that favourable price, Budget Shoe Store paid the Parks brothers six months' cash in advance at the time of the contract. The second contract was with Economy Drugs. This contract was also for a one-year period and called for Tom and Sam to wash the drugstore's windows at a rate of $50 per month to be paid on the 10th of the month after the services are performed. The $50 payment for July services was subsequently received on August 10. There were no supplies on hand as of July 1 and supplies on hand at July 31 had cost $40.

Required:

Prepare an income statement for the Parks brothers for the month of July.

P3.9 Transaction analysis: cash versus accrual basis. The Midlands Corporation began the year with $10,000 cash, some other assets, some vendor payables, and $8,000 in owners' equity. During this current year, Midlands entered into a number of transactions, including the following:

1. Paid salaries of $700.

2. Purchased a $23,000 machine, giving a $23,000 note with an interest rate of 12 percent.

3. Paid dividends of $2,500.

4. Paid rent of $600.

5. Sold additional share capital for $8,000 cash.

6. Used $300 worth of supplies previously purchased.

7. Recorded amortization expense of $200.

8. Collected a $75 account receivable.

Required:

Determine the effect of each of the preceding transactions on a company's income statement and its cash balance. Under a column headed income statement, indicate whether the transaction results in a revenue or an expense and the dollar amount involved. Under the cash balance column, indicate whether the cash balance would increase or decrease and indicate the dollar amount involved. If a transaction has no effect on the income statement or the cash balance, indicate this in the appropriate column.

P3.10 Equity for proprietorships and corporations. Gerry Slowski started a business on January 21 by placing $26,000 cash in a bank account for the new business. During the first year, the business was successful, earning a net income of $17,000. During the year, $6,000 cash was distributed to Gerry.

Required:

a. Assuming the business was established as a corporation, prepare a statement of shareholder's equity for the year ended December 31.

b. Assuming the business was established as a proprietorship, prepare a statement of owner's equity for the year ended December 31.

P3.11 Income statement concepts. Each of the following concepts represent some important income statement ideas:

1. Gain versus income.

2. Loss versus expense.

3. Realized versus recognized.

4. Deferred versus prepaid.

Required:

Prepare a commentary explaining how the contrasted items are alike and how they are different, and how each of them might be considered in the presentation of the income statement.

P3.12 Asset or expense. The King Corporation reported net income of $5,000,000 in 1995, and it appears that 1996 will be much the same. During 1996, the company made the following expenditures:

1. $125,000 was spent to resurface the employee parking lot. That resurfacing has to be done every five years or so.

2. $250,000 was spent to upgrade the air cleaning system in the paint department. The system as it was had worked satisfactorily, but the provincial Department of Labour had recently promulgated new rules (effective three years from today) that would have required the changes the company made voluntarily.

3. $450,000 was paid to an architect for the design of a new research centre. The centre was the dream of the prior CEO, but has now been shelved because the new officers are more cautious about the future.

4. $300,000 was spent this year on the development of a new computer-based order entry system. The idea behind the new system is that salespeople in the field will be able to enter orders into the system directly, electronically, so that they can be shipped the very next day. Everyone hopes that the new system will enhance customer service and help stop a sales slide. The system appears to be on track, but another $200,000 will have to be spent before it will work as planned.

5. The company's plant was shut down for about three months this year because of the slow economy. The company struggled to find a way to keep their employees busy, so they could keep as many of them as possible. The employees agreed to accept half pay, and the company found maintenance work and training for them. At the end of the period, about 85 percent of the work force was still employed, and when the company went back to work, production resumed without a hitch. The maintenance work done by the employees in this time cost about $500,000; the training time cost the company another $400,000.

Required:

Prepare a memo discussing each of the above expenditures, discussing whether the other side of the entry should be an addition to an asset or an expense charge. Explain your position.

P3.13 Accrual basis of accounting. Tasha Cook prepared the financial report for the Childrens' Festival Foundation. The foundation is registered as a non-profit organization. Tasha simply used the cash basis of accounting to prepare a statement of revenues and expenditures. All cash receipts were recorded as revenue and all cash payments were recorded as expenditures. The statement indicated expenditures had exceeded revenues by $2,312. Expenditures for the period included the purchase of equipment for $5,500. It is estimated the equipment may be used for five years, with no residual value. Each year the Childrens' festival receives a $500 grant from the local Kinsmen/Kinette club. The club has approved payment of the grant but it had not been received when Tasha prepared the financial report. The week after the statement had been prepared, a number of unpaid invoices were received in the mail. These unrecorded expenditures totalled $2,456. Using the accrual basis of accounting, determine the net income for the period.

P3.14 Accrual basis of accounting. Jeanette Lough operates a small arts and crafts business as a sole proprietorship. Jeanette recently prepared the annual financial report for her business. Jeanette simply used the cash basis of accounting to prepare a statement of revenues and expenditures. All cash receipts were recorded as revenue and all cash payments were recorded as expenditures. The statement indicated a net income for the year of $6,013. A number of unpaid invoices were not recorded in the annual statement. These unrecorded invoices totalled $8,467. Cash payments included personal withdrawals Jeanette had made during the year totalling $4,320. Included in cash receipts were deposits from customers for work to be delivered next month. Such deposits from customers totalled $950. At the end of the accounting period, customers owed the business $1,750 for goods and services received during the year. Using the accrual basis of accounting, determine the revised net income for the period.

P3.15 Equity statement: corporation or proprietorship. During the current year, Susan Liske started a marketing consulting business. Susan invested $27,000 of her personal savings in the business. Her income statement for the year indicates a net income of $37,000. As well, at the end of the year Susan paid herself $8,000 as a return on her investment. Susan received no salary during the year.

Required:

Prepare a statement of owner's equity assuming Susan's business was established as:

a. A corporation

b. A proprietorship

P3.16 Partners' equity. For the fiscal year ending March 31, 1997, the partnership of Austman, Bailey & Carstens earned a net income of $153,000. The partners have agreed to share profits/losses equally. During the year, the partners had the following withdrawals: Austman $27,000, Bailey $33,000, and Carstens $19,000. The balance in each partner's capital account at the beginning of the year, April 1, 1996, was: Austman $67,000, Bailey $44,000, and Carstens $61,000.

Required:

Determine the total partnership equity, including each partner's ending capital balance.

P3.17 Partners' equity. For the year ending December 31, 1996, the partnership of Able, Best & Cane earned a net income of $81,000. The partners have agreed to share profits/losses equally. During the year, the partners had the following withdrawals: Able $7,000, Best $13,000, and Cane $9,000. The balance in each partner's capital account at the beginning of the year was: Able $23,000, Best $33,000, and Cane $22,000.

Required:

Determine the total partnership equity, including each partner's ending capital balance.

P3.18 Retained earnings. Determine the missing amounts affecting the shareholders' equity of a corporation in each of the independent cases below:

	A	B	C	D
Retained earnings — December 31, 1995	$50,000	?	$44,000	$73,000
Net income	15,000	$12,000	?	27,000
Dividends	?	5,000	7,000	10,000
Retained earnings — December 31, 1996	60,000	27,000	56,000	?

P3.19 Owner's equity. Determine the missing amounts affecting the owner's equity of a proprietorship in each of the independent cases below:

	A	B	C	D
Capital — December 31, 1995	$44,000	?	$88,000	$66,000
Net income	22,000	$32,000	?	25,000
Withdrawals	18,000	15,000	33,000	?
Capital — December 31, 1996	?	11,000	46,000	77,000

P3.20 Members' equity. Determine the missing amounts affecting the members' equity of a non-profit organization in each of the independent cases below:

	A	B	C	D
Unrestricted surplus — December 31, 1995	$32,000	?	$72,000	$99,000
Excess of revenues over expenses	?	$27,000	?	56,000
Transfer to restricted surplus	(15,000)	(3,000)	(20,000)	(25,000)
Unrestricted surplus — December 31, 1996	$57,000	33,000	97,000	?

P3.21 Statement of changes in financial position. Determine the missing amounts affecting the statement of changes in financial position in each of the independent cases below:

Activities	A	B	C	D
Operating	$45,000	?	$78,000	$55,000
Investing	(22,000)	$34,000	?	(36,000)
Financing	(28,000)	15,000	(33,000)	?
Increase/(decrease) in cash	?	7,000	41,000	(11,000)

P3.22 Statement of changes in financial position. Determine the missing amounts affecting the statement of changes in financial position in each of the independent cases below:

Activities	A	B	C	D
Operating	$38,000	?	$47,000	$(24,000)
Investing	(11,000)	$(25,000)	?	(15,000)
Financing	35,000	22,000	(45,000)	?
Increase/(decrease) in cash	?	17,000	6,000	(8,000)

P3.23 Income statement. Determine the missing amounts affecting the income statement in each of the independent cases below:

	A	B	C	D
Revenues	$56,000	?	$24,000	$88,000
Expenses	32,000	$34,000	27,000	?
Net income (loss)	?	11,000	?	19,000

P3.24 Income statement. Presented below is a common-size income statement. Determine the missing percentages affecting the income statement in each of the independent cases below:

	A	B	C	D
Sales	100%	100%	100%	?
Cost of sales	70	?	?	?
Gross profit	?	?	25	25%
Operating expenses	25	15	?	?
Net income (loss)	?	7	11	(5)

P3.25 Statement of changes in financial position. Determine the missing amounts affecting the statement of changes in financial position in each of the independent cases below:

	A	B	C	D
Operating activities	$25,000	$12,000	$(29,000)	$14,000
Investing activities	(10,000)	?	(84,000)	(19,000)
Financing activities	41,000	44,000	?	(31,000)
Increase/(decrease) in cash	?	24,000	27,000	?
Beginning cash	27,000	?	20,000	21,000
Ending cash	?	16,000	?	?

P3.26 Using the accounting equation. Applying the basic accounting equation to the Northfield Corporation at two successive year-ends yields the following results:

$$\text{Year-end assets} = \text{Liabilities} + \text{Equity}$$
$$1995: \$40,000 = \$30,000 + \$10,000$$
$$1996: \$35,000 = \$20,000 + \$15,000$$

Required:

Assuming that no dividends were declared and that no additional capital was invested by the owners, what amount would Northfield have reported as its net income or loss for the 1996 year? Please explain your answer in the context of the facts here.

P3.27 Maple Leaf Gardens, Limited, and the accounting equation. Think about the Maple Leaf Gardens' financial statements we have studied.

Required:

With reference to the accounting equation, describe in your own words how the following five transactions might affect Maple Leaf Gardens' financial statements:

a. The sale of share capital to a group of investors for $1 million.

b. The sale of a new issue of bonds to investors in the amount of $5 million.

c. Use of the proceeds of the share sale and the bond sale to retire a $6 million bank debt.

d. The purchase of $250,000 merchandise to be paid for within 30 days.

e. Results for the month of January indicating aggregate net income from all units of $2.5 million.

P3.28 Financial analysis. Ratios for two companies are presented below. Comment on the relative financial position of each organization.

WESTERN SERVICES, LIMITED

	1996	1995
Earnings per share	$1.96	$1.73
Return on equity	11.1%	9.9%
Total debt-to-equity ratio	3.13:1	2.97:1
Long-term debt-to-invested capital ratio	1.47:1	1.62:1
Total asset turnover	1.57:1	1.32:1
Receivable turnover	7.13:1	7.77:1
Quick ratio	1.11:1	.99:1
Current ratio	2.14:1	1.94:1

EASTERN SERVICES LIMITED

	1996	1995
Earnings per share	$3.23	$3.76
Return on equity	6.7%	8.1%
Total debt-to-equity ratio	2.67:1	2.88:1
Long-term debt-to-invested capital ratio	1.77:1	1.64:1
Total asset turnover	1.34:1	1.62:1
Receivable turnover	8.88:1	8.03:1
Quick ratio	1.03:1	1.07:1
Current ratio	2.44:1	2.17:1

P3.29 Statement of changes in financial position. Banister Corporation had the following transactions during the year ending December 31, 1996:

1. Issued share capital for $20,000.

2. Merchandise inventories decreased by $6,000.

3. Cash increased by $38,000.

4. Purchased machinery for $31,000.

5. Declared and paid cash dividends of $7,000.

6. Cash balance at January 1, 1996, was $24,000.

7. Accounts payable decreased by $12,000.

8. Equipment was sold for $16,000.

9. Net income was $56,000.

10. Accounts receivable increased by $10,000.

Required:

Using the above information, prepare a statement of changes in financial position for the year ended December 31, 1996.

P3.30 Statement of changes in financial position. Penhall Limited had the following transactions during the year ending December 31, 1996:

1. Temporary investments decreased by $17,000.

2. Cash increased by $8,000.

3. Prepaid insurance costs increased by $1,000.

4. Redeemed bonds for $20,000.

5. Purchased machinery for $20,000.

6. Issued share capital for $10,000 cash.

7. Merchandise inventories increased by $4,000.

8. Obtained a long-term loan for $13,000 and used the proceeds to purchase land.

9. Declared and paid cash dividends of $3,000.

10. Cash balance at January 1, 1996, was $21,000.

11. Accounts payable decreased by $8,000.

12. Equipment was sold for $27,000.

13. Net income was $24,000.

14. Accounts receivable decreased by $7,000.

15. Redeemed share capital for $4,000.

Required:

Using the above information, prepare a statement of changes in financial position for the year ended December 31, 1996.

P3.31 Statement of changes in financial position: partnership equity. Jack & Jill Home Cleaning is a partnership operated by Jack Simpson and Jill Yee. Jack & Jill Home Cleaning had the following transactions during the year ending December 31, 1996:

1. Jill contributed additional capital of $5,000.

2. Cleaning supplies inventory increased by $3,000.

3. Cash decreased by $9,000.

4. Purchased cleaning equipment for $11,000.

5. Jack withdrew $3,000 cash from the partnership.

6. Cash balance at December 31, 1996, was $8,000.

7. Accounts payable decreased by $3,000.

8. Equipment was sold for $12,000.

9. Net loss for the partnership was $7,000.

10. Accounts receivable decreased by $5,000.

Required:

a. Using the above information, prepare a statement of changes in financial position for the year ended December 31, 1996.

b. Prepare a schedule showing the changes in partners' capital accounts during the year. Jack and Jill have agreed to share profits and losses equally. On January 1, 1996, the balance in each partner's capital account was: Jill $4,000 and Jack $7,000.

P3.32 Statement of changes in financial position: proprietorship equity. Stan's Delivery Service is a sole proprietorship operated by Stan Yaworski. Stan's Delivery Service had the following transactions during the year ending December 31, 1996:

1. Net income was $3,000.

2. Accounts receivable increased $1,000.

3. Stan invested additional capital of $3,000.

4. Stationary supplies inventory decreased by $1,000.

5. Stan withdrew $1,000 cash.

6. Cash balance at January 1, 1996, was $2,000.

7. Purchased equipment for $7,000.

8. Accounts payable decreased $2,000.

9. Equipment was sold for $9,000.

Required:

a. Using the above information, prepare a statement of changes in financial position for the year ended December 31, 1996.

b. Prepare a schedule showing the changes in owners' equity during the year. On January 1, 1996, the balance in Stan's capital account was $2,000.

P3.33 Earnings per share. The financial statements of Winnipeg Copyrite, Ltd., include net income of $160,000 for the current year and the weighted average of common shares outstanding of 55,000. Earnings per share for the year were $2.91.

a. Explain the impact each of the following transactions would have on the company's profitability:

   (1) Incurred additional expenses of $17,000.

   (2) Issued 5,000 common shares.

   (3) Invested $20,000 in temporary investments.

b. As a result of the above transactions, is the organization in a better or worse financial position?

P3.34 Return on equity. The financial statements of Victoria Flowers, Ltd., show net income of $177,000 for the current year and total shareholders' equity comprised of share capital of $300,000 and retained earnings of $455,000. The net income of $177,000 has been included in the year-end retained earnings balance of $455,000. The return on equity for the year is 23.44 percent.

a. Explain the impact each of the following transactions would have on the company's profitability:

   (1) Incurred additional expenses of $22,000.

   (2) Issued 10,000 common shares for $5.00 each.

   (3) Invested $20,000 in inventory.

   (4) Paid dividends of $20,000.

b. As a result of the above transactions, is the organization in a better or worse financial position?

P3.35 Total asset turnover. The financial statements of Halifax, Limited, include total revenues of $2,112,000 for the current year and total assets of $733,000. The total asset turnover for the year is 2.88.

a. Explain the impact each of the following transactions would have on the company's asset management:

   (1) Earned additional revenues of $44,000.

   (2) Issued 10,000 common shares for $25,000 cash.

   (3) Invested $20,000 cash in machinery.

   (4) Paid cash dividends of $10,000.

b. As a result of the above transactions, is the organization in a better or worse financial position?

P3.36 Receivable turnover. The financial statements of Comox-Courtney, Limited, include total revenues of $3,765,000 for the current year and accounts receivable of $777,000. The receivable turnover for the year is 4.85.

a. Explain the impact each of the following transactions would have on the company's asset management:

    (1) Earned additional revenues of $277,000.

    (2) Issued 10,000 common shares for $30,000 cash.

    (3) Invested $50,000 in land.

    (4) Collected additional $55,000 on accounts receivable.

b. As a result of the above transactions, is the organization in a better or worse financial position?

P3.37 Financial analysis. Using the financial information presented for Pennington Stores, Limited, and Dalmys (Canada); Limited, perform a comparative analysis of the two companies. Your report should include comments with respect to your findings.

PENNINGTON STORES, LIMITED
Balance Sheets
(in thousands of dollars)

	January 29, 1994	January 30, 1993
Assets		
Current assets:		
Cash	$ 4,351	$ 4,564
Inventories	9,381	12,594
Prepaid expenses and sundry assets	529	563
Income taxes recoverable	198	221
	14,459	17,942
Capital assets, less accumulated amortization	24,511	26,170
Intangible asset	—	947
	$38,970	$45,059
Liabilities		
Current liabilities:		
Accounts payable	$ 8,330	$ 8,958
Current portion of retirement benefits	686	—
Current portion of mortgage payable	47	42
	9,063	9,000
Retirement benefits payable	1,698	320
Mortgage payable	6,619	6,666
	17,380	15,986
Shareholders' Equity		
Capital stock	337	337
Retained earnings	21,253	28,736
	21,590	29,073
	$38,970	$45,059

PENNINGTON STORES, LIMITED
Statements of Operations
(in thousands of dollars)

	52 Weeks Ended January 29, 1994	52 Weeks Ended January 30, 1993
Sales	$72,786	$73,307
Cost of sales, selling, and administrative expenses	73,000	71,682
Amortization	2,583	2,593
Interest expense	641	658
	76,224	74,933
Loss before income taxes and unusual items	3,438	1,626
Unusual items	3,975	—
Loss before income taxes	7,413	1,626
Income tax expense (recovery)	50	(567)
Loss for the period	$ 7,463	$ 1,059

DALMYS (CANADA) LIMITED
Balance Sheet
As at February 26, 1994
(in thousands of dollars)

	1994	1993
Assets		
Current assets:		
Cash and short-term investments	$ 7,385	$ 5,111
Accounts and sundry receivables	707	726
Inventory	9,774	10,666
Prepaid expenses	511	444
	18,377	16,947
Fixed	12,494	14,033
Deferred pension	443	298
	31,314	31,278
Liabilities		
Current liabilities:		
Accounts payable	13,288	15,483
Wages payable	1,786	1,887
Current maturity of obligations under capital leases	232	204
	15,306	17,574
Obligations under capital leases, less current maturity	863	1,095
Deferred lease inducements	73	—
Commitments **Shareholders' Equity**		
Capital stock	10,918	7,068
Retained earnings	4,154	5,541
	15,072	12,609
	31,314	31,278

DALMYS (CANADA) LIMITED
Statement of Operations
For the Year Ended February 26, 1994
(In thousands of dollars, except per share data)

	1994 $	1993 $
Sales	**111,569**	116,209
Cost and expenses:		
Cost of sales and selling, general and administrative expenses	**109,213**	111,005
Depreciation and amortization	**3,321**	3,429
Interest (net)	**(258)**	320
Interest on obligations under capital leases	**155**	184
	112,431	114,938
Net earnings (loss)	**(862)**	1,271
Net earnings (loss) per share	**(0.17)**	0.30

DALMYS (CANADA) LIMITED
Statement of Retained Earnings
For the Year Ended February 26, 1994
(In thousands of dollars)

	1994 $	1993 $
Balance — beginning of year	**5,541**	4,270
Net earnings (loss)	**(862)**	1,271
	4,679	5,541
Costs of issue (note 7)	**525**	—
Balance — end of year	**4,154**	5,541

P3.38 Financial analysis. Using the financial information presented for Shell Canada, Limited, and Imperial Oil, Limited, perform a comparative analysis of the two companies. Your report should include comments with respect to your findings.

SHELL CANADA, LIMITED
Consolidated Statement of Earnings and Retained Earnings
Year Ended December 31
($ millions)

	1993	1992	1991
Revenues:			
Sales and other operating revenues	**4,701**	4,492	4,732
Dividends, interest, and other income	**7**	55	55
	4,708	4,547	4,787
Expenses:			
Purchased crude oil, petroleum products, and other merchandise	**2,520**	2,556	2,784
Operating	**660**	586	636
Selling and general	**857**	814	900
Exploration and predevelopment	**66**	69	96
Depreciation, depletion, amortization, and retirements	**407**	352	321
Interest on long-term debt	**110**	119	118
	4,620	4,496	4,855
Unusual items (Loss) gain	**(52)**	14	57
Earnings:			
Earnings (loss) before income taxes	**36**	65	(11)
Income taxes	**18**	(15)	(23)
Earnings from continuing operations	**18**	80	12
Loss from discontinued operations	**—**	—	(138)
Earnings (loss)	**18**	80	(126)
Per class "A" common share (dollars):			
Earnings from continuing operations	**0.16**	0.72	0.11
Earnings (loss)	**0.16**	0.72	(1.12)
Retained Earnings:			
Balance at beginning of year	**2,182**	2,203	2,430
Earnings (loss)	**18**	80	(126)
	2,200	2,283	2,304
Dividends	**100**	101	101
Balance at end of year	**2,100**	2,182	2,203

SHELL CANADA, LIMITED
Consolidated Statement of Financial Position
At December 31
($ millions)

	1993	1992	1991
Assets			
Current assets:			
Cash and short-term investments	**(34)**	128	36
Accounts receivable	**709**	695	766
Inventories			
Crude oil, products, and merchandise	**548**	552	554
Materials and supplies	**44**	44	40
Prepaid expenses	**39**	97	96
	1,306	1,516	1,492
Investments, long-term receivables, and other	**245**	159	126
Properties, plant, and equipment	**4,428**	4,349	4,292
	5,979	6,024	5,910
Liabilities			
Current liabilities:			
Short-term borrowings	**73**	—	—
Accounts payable and accrued liabilities	**658**	618	574
Income and other taxes payable	**25**	84	66
Current portion of long-term debt	**315**	147	188
	1,071	849	828
Site restoration	**97**	53	71
Long-term debt *(Note 5)*	**1,005**	1,279	1,110
Deferred income taxes	**891**	846	884
	3,064	3,027	2,893
Shareholders' Investment			
Capital stock:			
100 4% preference shares	**1**	1	1
112 109 125 class "A" common shares			
(1992 — 112 091 875; 1991 — 112 077 776)	**523**	523	522
	524	524	523
Contributed surplus	**291**	291	291
Retained earnings	**2,100**	2,182	2,203
	2,915	2,997	3,017
Commitments and contingencies			
	5,979	6,024	5,910

The consolidated financial statements have been approved by the Board of Directors.

Charles W. Wilson, *Director*   Peter J.G. Bentley, *Director*

IMPERIAL OIL, LIMITED
Consolidated Balance Sheet
At December 31
(millions of dollars)

	1993	1992	1991
Assets			
Current assets:			
Cash	605	265	286
Marketable securities at cost	874	757	7
Accounts receivable	889	1,008	1,052
Inventories of crude oil	402	468	604
Materials, supplies, and prepaid expenses	129	140	178
Total current assets	2,899	2,638	2,127
Investments and other long-term assets	152	159	204
Property, plant, and equipment	9,389	9,965	10,760
Goodwill	356	373	400
Total assets	12,796	13,135	13,491
Liabilities			
Current liabilities:			
Accounts payable and accrued liabilities	1,157	1,316	1,529
Income taxes payable	436	247	110
Total current liabilities	1,593	1,563	1,639
Long-term debt	2,030	2,222	2,356
Other long-term obligations	1,149	1,137	1,007
Commitments and contingent liabilities			
Total liabilities	4,772	4,922	5,002
Deferred Income Taxes	1,458	1,577	1,699
Shareholders' Equity			
Common shares	2,977	2,977	2,977
Net earnings retained and used in the business:			
At beginning of year	3,659	3,813	3,999
Net earnings for the year	279	195	162
Dividends	(349)	(349)	(348)
At end of year	3,589	3,659	3,813
Total shareholders' equity	6,566	6,636	6,790
Total liabilities, deferred income taxes, and shareholders' equity	12,796	13,135	13,491

IMPERIAL OIL, LIMITED
Consolidated Statement of Earnings
For the Years Ended December 31
(millions of dollars)

	1993	1992	1991
Revenues:			
Operating revenues	8,795	8,972	9,440
Investment income	108	175	62
Total revenues	8,903	9,147	9,502
Expenses:			
Exploration	52	70	89
Purchases of crude oil and products	3,325	3,465	3,597
Operating	2,839	3,015	3,497
Commodity taxes	986	983	966
Depreciation and depletion	834	894	833
Financing costs	177	166	216
Total expenses	8,213	8,593	9,198
Unusual items	(122)	(101)	(31)
Earnings before income taxes	568	453	273
Income taxes	289	258	111
Net earnings	279	195	162

3.13 CASES

C3.1 Income statement and balance sheet. Susan Zipple began a consulting business by depositing $15,000 in a bank account opened in the name of the business. From the investment, she made a $5,000 down payment on a used automobile priced at $21,200 and signed a non-interest-bearing note payable for the balance. She also spent $1,200 for office supplies and paid $575 for advertising through which she gained a number of customers for her business.

On June 30, 1996, after six months in business, her records showed she had collected $22,400 in cash for services rendered and that customers still owed an additional $3,700 for services provided. She had purchased more supplies for cash, $750; however, supplies that had cost $885 were on hand unused at the period end. She had paid $1,150 on her personal credit card for gas and oil used in her automobile for business purposes, and carbon copies of credit card tickets showed she owed an additional $125 for gas and oil used during June. Through cash payments she had reduced the balance owed on the note payable signed at the time the vehicle was purchased by $5,600, but through use the automobile had amortized an amount equal to one-fifth of its cost.

Required:

Under the assumption the business had a total of $3,775 of cash on hand and in the bank at period-end, determine the amount of cash Susan had withdrawn from or the additional amount invested in the business. Prepare an income statement for the business showing the net income earned during the six months and a balance sheet as of June 30, 1996.

C3.2 Cash flow analysis. Gerald Houston began a small cleaning service by investing $12,000 of his personal savings in the business. Gerald also obtained a bank loan for $10,000. To start the business, Gerald purchased equipment for $3,000. He also acquired a used truck for $8,000. During the first month of operations, the business earned a net income of $7,200. Net income was determined using the accrual basis of accounting. Included in the determination of net income were the following items: accrued revenues of $900, and accrued expenses of $200. At the end of the month, Gerald is pleased to see the business has $17,500 cash in the bank.

Required:

Explain to Gerald the reason for his cash balance by preparing a statement of changes in financial position. In your opinion, has the first month of operations been successful?

C3.3 An accounting game: the sheepherders (part two).* A year has elapsed since you solved part one of the sheepherders game. After studying your solution to part one, Deyonne and Batonne grudgingly accepted your opinion as to their relative wealth at the end of last year. The passage of time has not diminished their penchant for argument, however. Now they're arguing about who had the largest income for the year just ended.

Deyonne points out that the number of sheep that he personally owns at year-end exceeds his personal holdings at the beginning of the year by 80, whereas Batonne's increase was only 20. Batonne replies that his increase would have been 60 had he not traded 40 sheep during the year for 10 additional acres of land. Besides, Batonne points out that he exchanged 18 sheep during the year for food and clothing items, whereas Deyonne exchanged only 7 for such purposes. The food and clothing has been pretty much used up by the end of the year. Batonne is happy because his wife made five coats during the year (fulfilling the orders she had at the beginning of the year) and received 25 goats for them. She managed to obtain orders for another five coats (again for 25 goats) — orders on which she has not yet begun to work. Deyonne points out that he took to making his own lunches this year; therefore, he does not owe Tyrone anything now. Deyonne was very unhappy one day last year when he discovered that his ox had died of a mysterious illness. Both men are thankful, however, that none of the other animals died or was lost.

Except for the matters reported above, each man's holdings at the end of the current year are the same as his holdings at the end of last year.

Required:

How would you, as an outside observer to this argument, define *income*? Given your definition, whose income — Deyonne's or Batonne's — was greater for the past year?

C3.4 Accrual versus cash basis accounting. Apex Machine Tool found itself with an exciting opportunity. A valued customer ordered a special tool and said that it would pay $10,000 a year in rent, over a 10-year period, for the use of the tool. Apex ran some numbers and estimated that the tool could be built for $60,000 ($25,000 in material, $10,000 in design cost, and $25,000 in labour and other factory costs), although it was clear that fabrication of the tool would take the better part of a year to complete.

On November 1, 1994, Apex's board of directors approved the project. During the next two months, all of the engineering was completed; during January 1995, the steel was ordered and received; the fabrication was completed during the rest of 1995; the tool was delivered to the customer in December 1995. To finance the purchase of the steel and pay for the cost of the engineering and fabrication, Apex borrowed $60,000 using the rental agreement from the customer as collateral. The bank insisted that the principle on the loan ($60,000) be repaid in equal annual instalments of $10,000 beginning December 31, 1996. The bank also insisted on annual interest payments, due December 31 each year, at 10 percent of the average amount of the loan outstanding during the year.

The customer is very happy with the tool but has said that it does not expect to have any use for it after the 10-year rental period. Apex plans to take the tool back at the end of the rental period and is sure that it will be good for many more years of useful service. At this time, however, Apex has no other customers in mind for the tool.

*M. Carlson and J. W. Higgins, "A Games Approach to Introducing Accounting," *Accounting Education: Problems and Prospects* (Sarasota, FL: American Accounting Association, 1974).

Required:

a. Create a time line for the 12 years beginning 1994 (as illustrated below) and indicate in words where, in which period, the events described above will fall using both cash basis and accrual basis accounting.

Cash basis
Accrual basis
|———— 1994 ————|———— 1995 ————|———— 1996 ————|

b. What is the nature of each purchase, using the cash basis of accounting? Put a label on each of these events, on each side of the line. For example, using the cash basis of accounting, what is the nature of the steel purchase in the early part of 1995?

c. Describe in your own words how the management of Apex might have applied the matching concept and the allocation concept to the above situation, and how its judgments might have been affected by the notion of conservatism.

CHAPTER 4

The Accounting Process and Financial Statement Analysis

―――――――― **Outline** ――――――――

- 4.1 Accounting Systems
- 4.2 The Accounting Cycle
- 4.3 Adjusting Entries
- 4.4 Closing Entries
- 4.5 Accounting Cycle: An Illustration
- 4.6 Analyzing Financial Statements: An Illustration
- 4.7 Summary
- 4.8 Key Concepts and Terms
- 4.9 Comprehensive Review Question
- 4.10 Review and Discussion Questions
- 4.11 Problems
- 4.12 Cases

―――――――― **Objectives** ――――――――

After completing this chapter, you will be able to:
1. Describe the eight steps in the accounting cycle.
2. Record general journal entries for adjusting and closing entries.
3. Explain the impact of adjusting entries on financial statements.
4. Prepare an income statement and balance sheet from trial balance information.
5. Analyze the financial strength and management performance of an organization, using trend analysis, common-size statements, and ratios.

150

I n the previous chapters, we examined financial statements and discussed fundamental accounting concepts. This chapter discusses and illustrates the accounting process by which an organization records the financial results of its economic activities, and then reports those results in its financial statements.

4.1 ACCOUNTING SYSTEMS

As noted in Chapter 1, the purpose of accounting is to measure the financial impact of economic events and transactions as they affect an organization and to communicate those financial results to various accounting information users. Thus, the basic processes of accounting involve measuring, recording, reporting, and analyzing financial information.

In this chapter, we examine the process of measuring, recording, and reporting. We will have more to say about measuring assets and liabilities in subsequent chapters as we discuss accounting for individual assets and liabilities. The principal focus of this chapter, however, is on the recording process. We have elected to devote considerable attention to the recording process because that process provides the foundation for much of the remaining, more sophisticated accounting discussion. The users of accounting information need *not* know all the details of the mechanics of accounting record-keeping; however, to interpret accounting information effectively, having a good understanding of the basic accounting process is helpful.

A diagram, previously presented in Chapter 1, that illustrates the process of preparing a company's financial statements is shown in Exhibit 4.1. The process of preparing the financial statements is subject to the control of management and the influence of the independent auditor.

Financial statements are nothing more than the summary of an organization's transactions and a variety of financial judgments made by management. Those transactions and judgments are subject to the organization's internal control system, which assures that all record-keeping is correct and complete. The financial reporting system sorts all transactions and judgments into similar or related groupings and then aggregates that input so that the summarized financial statements can be prepared. The summarization of that data and their presentation in the financial statements must follow the requirements of GAAP.

Internal Control Systems

An internal control system is a set of procedures and policies designed to assure that all transactions and all necessary judgments have been recognized and that they are classified and correctly described in the accounting records. The internal control system involves the designing and maintaining of accounting records and selecting and applying accounting policies that will safeguard the organization's assets and assist with the prevention and detection of error and fraud. Management is responsible for maintaining a system of internal control that ensures that all transactions are recognized, that all judgments are made, and that the raw data are summarized and presented fairly. Management establishes the system and uses internal auditors and other systems checks to monitor its performance. As a member of the management team, the accountant plays an important role in the design and implementation of the internal control and financial reporting systems. Most large organizations have sophisticated systems of internal control, but some organizations may have very few controls in place.

E X H I B I T   1 . 4

The Financial Reporting Process

Management's Responsibilities

Design, implement, and maintain	Determine how GAAP are to be applied	Review and sign off
Internal Control System	**Financial Reporting System**	**Financial Statements**
Test effectiveness (GAAS)	Evaluate application of GAAP	Express a professional opinion

Independent Auditor's Activities

Financial Reporting Systems

The financial reporting system sorts all of the transactions and judgments into similar or related groupings and then aggregates that input so that the summarized financial statements can be prepared. The summarization of that data and their presentation in the financial statements must follow the requirements of GAAP. The reliability of the financial statements is directly dependent on the systems that generate the statements. An organization with weak controls and a poor reporting system will generally produce unreliable, less meaningful financial statements. At the culmination of the process, management evaluates the resulting financial statements to be sure the results make good economic sense before the statements are released to third parties.

Measuring

A wide variety of information about an organization might be useful to investors and other third parties. However, accounting systems measure, record, and report only those events and transactions that can be objectively measured. For example, it may be quite significant that the president of a company resigned or that a new president has been hired, and a press release describing those events may be given wide distribution. However, because the economic consequences of this type of qualitative event are very difficult to measure objectively, it will neither be recorded in the accounting records of the company nor reported in the company's financial statements. The cost of any severance pay due the resigned president can be measured objectively and thus will be recorded as an obligation in the company's accounts and reflected in its financial statements.

Measurement questions are frequently difficult. Although most economic events and transactions (e.g., sales of merchandise for cash, purchases of equipment, payment of salaries) can be measured relatively easily, the more complex events and transactions (e.g., sales on credit terms, expenditures for research and development, the purchase of another business) present more serious measurement problems, as we will see in later chapters.

Imagine the spectrum of possible transactions on a continuum that looks like this:

Impact is apparent and measurable.	Impact is likely and estimable.	Impact is uncertain and unmeasurable.

EXHIBIT 4.2

Typical Chart of Accounts

Financial Statement Element	Account Numbers
Assets	100–199
Liabilities	200–299
Equity	300–399
Revenues	400–499
Expenses	500–599
Miscellaneous	600–699

Accounting attempts to deal with all of those events and transactions that are, at best, objectively measurable and at least reasonably estimable. For example, at the left side of the spectrum, the purchase of merchandise is recorded quite routinely at the amount to be paid to a vendor. In the middle of the spectrum, a probable product recall is recognized in the financial statements, assuming that the cost of the recall can be estimated with a reasonable degree of certainty. Other events and transactions, the financial effects of which cannot be reasonably foreseen or quantified, must be communicated to third parties who have an interest in the company through other communication channels. As an example of an event at the right side of the spectrum, think about a company that is ready to bring a potentially dramatic new product to market; the event will almost certainly be described in press reports and in the president's letter in the annual report to shareholders. But because the financial success of the new product is not known and because its impact cannot be measured until the market reacts, the event of the new product launch is not recognized in the financial statements. As you can imagine, management depends on its accounting systems to deal with the events and transactions on the left-hand side of the continuum and spends more of its time attempting to estimate fairly the effects of those transactions in the middle and to communicate thoroughly the effects of those transactions on the right.

Chart of Accounts

chart of accounts
A list of the general ledger accounts used by an enterprise in its accounting system.

A basic component of the accounting system is the selection and description of the accounts to be used in the reporting system. Although the needs of all organizations may differ, a generalization with respect to account numbers may be made. Most organizations follow a numbering system similar to the basic **chart of accounts** presented in Exhibit 4.2.

Most organizations provide additional subcodes for different departments or geographic areas. The design of the chart of accounts takes into consideration the needs of users within and outside the organization. Generally, it is thought that the more information provided for the user, the better. However, the constraints of materiality and costs versus benefits influence the design of the chart of accounts. The materiality principle states that an item of information is considered to be material or significant if it is probable that its omission or misstatement would influence or change a decision of a user. It may be helpful to some users to see five different bank accounts on the balance sheet, but it probably will not really provide them with a significant amount of information, or change any decisions they make related to the organization. The other

EXHIBIT 4.3

Steps in the Accounting Cycle

1. Identifying source documents
2. Journalizing
3. Posting
4. Preparing a trial balance
5. Recording adjusting entries
6. Preparing financial statements
7. Recording closing entries
8. Preparing a post-closing trial balance

consideration is the cost of providing very detailed information to the users. The concept of costs versus benefits states that the benefits expected to arise from providing information in the financial statements should exceed the cost of doing so. The design of the chart of accounts is part of management's responsibility for system design and a matter of professional judgment.

4.2 THE ACCOUNTING CYCLE

accounting cycle
The process or steps necessary to prepare financial statements.

The financial reporting system designed by management is comprised of a number of different elements and procedures. A vital part of the financial reporting system is the various components of the accounting cycle. The **accounting cycle** is the process or steps to be completed to prepare financial statements. It is referred to as a *cycle,* because the steps must be completed each time financial statements are prepared. The accounting cycle involves the recording, summarizing, and classifying of financial information on a periodic basis. While no two organizations are the same, all organizations follow primarily the same process. The typical steps in the accounting cycle are listed in Exhibit 4.3.

1. Identifying Source Documents

source document
Any document used to record financial information related to the economic activities of the organization.

The first step in the accounting cycle is designing and identifying all necessary source documents. A **source document** is any document used to record financial information related to the economic activities of the organization. Examples of source documents are invoices, cheques, receipts, and other documents peculiar to specialized industries. When management designs the system of internal control, one important consideration is the number of copies that are required of each document. For example, several copies of a sales invoice may be needed: one for the customer, one for the shipping department, and one for the accounting department. The size of the organization, the volume of transactions, and the level of control desired influence the design and flow of documents through the organization. The subject of internal control is very broad and beyond the scope of an introductory text on accounting. However, students should be aware of the importance of internal controls and the role they play in the financial reporting system. Once the various source documents have been identified, they provide the basis for recording financial information about the organization.

2. Journalizing

journalizing
The recording of the financial information from the source documents to a journal.

posting
An accounting process involving the transfer of financial data from the general journal to the general ledger.

general ledger
An accounting data file containing aggregate account information for all accounts listed in an enterprise's chart of accounts.

t-accounts
An accounting information file usually associated with the general ledger. The T divides the account into a left and right side, to facilitate the recording of debit and credit entries.

trial balance
A listing of the account balances from the general ledger designed to verify that the sum of the accounts with debit balances equals the sum of the accounts with credit balances.

adjusting entries
Journal entries recorded to update or correct the accounts in the general ledger.

The second step in the accounting cycle, **journalizing,** is the recording of the financial information from the source documents to a journal. Depending on the size and type of operating activities of the organization, a number of different journals may be used as part of the financial reporting system. Small organizations may use only two journals, a cash receipts journal and a cash payments journal. An automobile dealership commonly uses several journals: new vehicle sales, used vehicle sales, service and mechanical, parts, warranty, and body shop journals. All organizations also use a general journal for adjusting and correcting entries. The general journal format was illustrated previously in Chapters 2 and 3.

3. Posting

After a series of transactions have been journalized in the financial reporting system, those entries are then aggregated by account. This aggregation process is called **posting** because the individual entries are posted from the journal to the affected accounts contained in the **general ledger.** The general ledger is comprised of a number of **T-accounts.** A manual or computerized accounting system will use a different format for its general ledger than the one found in most accounting textbooks. This book uses T-accounts as illustrated previously. The "T" simply divides the account into left and right sides to facilitate the recording of debit and credit entries.

4. Preparing a Trial Balance

The next step is the preparation of a trial balance. The **trial balance** is a list of the account balances from the general ledger. The trial balance has two uses: (1) it provides an opportunity to examine the aggregated results of the individual entries to see whether the resulting balances make sense as compared to what management expected them to be; and (2) it provides an opportunity to see whether the sum of the accounts' ending debit balances equals the sum of the accounts' ending credit balances. If that review of the trial balance identifies any errors or omissions, they are corrected with adjusting entries. Depending on the extent of the adjustments, an *adjusted* trial balance may be prepared to prove that the system is now ready to produce the financial statements. Although the trial balance does not provide any guarantee that the information in each account is accurate, it does verify that the overall recording and posting processes have been completed in a numerically consistent fashion (Dr. = Cr.).

5. Recording Adjusting Entries

In addition to the entries that have been made on an ongoing day-to-day basis, some **adjusting entries** are normally required as of the end of the period. At the end of each accounting period, whether it's month-end or year-end, the accountant and other members of the management team are responsible for providing meaningful financial statements to the users. Management must ask questions about the measurement of assets and liabilities, and the recognition of revenues and expenses. Is inventory reflected in the accounts at a realistic value? Is there any obsolete inventory? Are all the receivables fully collectible? Have *all* liabilities been recorded? Depending on the answers to such introspective questions, additional entries may be required to adjust the balances in the accounts before the financial statements can be prepared. In Chapters 2 and 3 the statements prepared for Ted's Trucking purposely *omitted* adjusting entries. In just about *all* cases, a number of adjusting entries are required before meaningful statements can be produced. Another trial balance may be prepared, once the adjusting entries have been recorded. A number of different adjusting entries are illustrated in Section 4.3.

6. Preparing Financial Statements

After the adjusting entries have been recorded, the balance sheet, the income statement, and the statement of changes in financial position can be prepared. To prepare the statements management uses the data from the *adjusted* trial balance, which includes all adjusting entries, and presents that data in the way that most meaningfully communicates the company's results. During the preparation of the financial statements, some accounts can be aggregated, but other balances may have to be disaggregated and very significant transactions may have to be reported separately. In addition, the reporting process goes beyond the presentation of the account balances — management generally decides that for a full and fair presentation of the company's results, supplemental footnotes are required. In the end, management must satisfy itself that the resulting financial presentation is fair and in accordance with GAAP.

7. Recording Closing Entries

closing entries
Accounting data entries prepared at the end of an accounting period; designed to close or set equal to zero the temporary accounts.

temporary accounts
Those accounts that are closed at the end of each accounting period, for example, the income statement accounts, dividends, and the income summary.

post-closing trial balance
A listing of the account balances from the general ledger, after the accounts have been closed.

Finally, after all necessary and appropriate adjustments to the accounts have been made, and the financial statements have been issued, a series of entries are made to transfer information pertaining to the period's operations (as contained in the revenue and expense accounts) to the cumulative Retained Earnings account. These entries are called **closing entries** because they close, or set equal to zero, all of the income statement accounts. In addition to closing out the income statement accounts, closing entries are also used to close the corporation's Dividends Declared account by transferring its balance to Retained Earnings. For a proprietorship, the Withdrawals account is closed to the owner's capital account. The accounts that are closed at the end of an accounting period are referred to as **temporary accounts**.

The closing entry process is an important phase in the functioning of an accounting system. Not only does it provide the necessary link between the income statement, the balance sheet, and the statement of owners' equity, but also it serves an important information maintenance role. That is, the income statement measures the performance of the organization for a given period of time. As such, the income statement accounts should contain only information pertaining to the current accounting period. By setting the income statement account balances equal to zero at the end of each period, the closing entry process ensures that no operations-related data from a previous accounting period are carried forward into a succeeding operating period. Closing entries are only prepared *once* a year, at the end of the fiscal year.

8. Preparing a Post-Closing Trial Balance

After the closing entries have been journalized and posted to the general ledger, the final step in the accounting cycle is the preparation of another trial balance: the post-closing trial balance. The purpose of the **post-closing trial balance** is to prove the mathematical accuracy of the recording process, and to ensure the general ledger is in

Adjusting Entries

Accruals		Allocations	
Expenses: Interest Salaries Taxes	Revenues: Sales Interest	Expenses: Amortization Supplies Prepaid costs Bad debts Investment losses Inventory losses	Revenues: Deposits Unearned revenue

permanent account
Those accounts, principally the balance sheet accounts, that are not closed at the end of an accounting period.

balance for the beginning of the next fiscal year. The post-closing trial balance *must* contain only balance sheet or permanent accounts. A **permanent account** is a general ledger account that is not closed at year-end.

4.3 ADJUSTING ENTRIES

Depending on the organization, very few or a large number of adjusting entries are required before the financial statements can be prepared. As well, the types of entries required vary with different organizations. To add structure and facilitate the understanding of adjusting entries, we have summarized them into two groups: accruals and allocations.

accruals
Accruals relate to adherence of the accrual basis of accounting. An accrued expense is an expense that has been incurred, but it has not been paid for, and it has not been recorded.

Accrual entries adhere to the accrual basis of accounting. An accrued expense is an expense that has been incurred, but it has not been paid for and it has not been recorded. An accrued revenue is revenue that has been earned, but no payment has been received and no entry has been recorded to recognize the revenue. Accruals also impact assets and liabilities.

allocation
Allocations pertain to the apportionment of revenues and expenses to different accounting periods.

Allocation entries pertain to the apportionment of revenues and expenses to different accounting periods. Frequently, economic activities overlap more than one accounting period. Allocations are necessary to distribute the appropriate amount of revenue or expense to the correct accounting period. Allocations also impact asset and liability values at the end of the accounting period in question. Exhibit 4.4 summarizes a number of possible adjusting entries. This list should not be considered all inclusive, but only a representation of a number of different adjusting entries.

Accrued Expenses

An adequate internal control system ensures that all source documents are accounted for and the related accounting entries recorded in the financial reporting system. When an accrued expense has been incurred but not recorded and not been paid, an adjusting entry must be recorded to recognize the expense and also include the creation of a related payable or liability account. Three examples of accrued expenses are illustrated: accrued expenses for interest, salaries, and taxes.

Financing with short- and long-term liabilities will include an obligation to make periodic payments of interest and principal. The reductions to the principal or the liability are recorded only when paid. However, as interest is incurred over time, it should be accrued at the end of the accounting period. Assuming the organization has a

$1,000 loan with interest at 10 percent, $100 interest expense (.10 × $1,000) is accrued at the end of the period. The adjusting entry if the interest has not been paid is:

```
Interest Expense . . . . . . . . . . . . . . . . . . . . . . . . . . . . . . . . . . . . . . . . 100
      Interest Payable  . . . . . . . . . . . . . . . . . . . . . . . . . . . . . . . . . . . . .        100
      Adjusting entry for accrued interest.
```

Similarly, when the accounting period ends on a date other than a payday, salaries are owed to employees at the end of the period. Assuming salaries of $200 remain unpaid at the end of the period, the following adjusting entry for accrued salaries is required:

```
Salaries Expense. . . . . . . . . . . . . . . . . . . . . . . . . . . . . . . . . . . . . . . . 200
      Salaries Payable . . . . . . . . . . . . . . . . . . . . . . . . . . . . . . . . . . . . . .        200
      Adjusting entry for accrued salaries.
```

The final example of an accrued expense is for taxes that have been incurred but have not been paid at the end of the accounting period. Most organizations record adjusting entries for accrued expenses to recognize the goods and services received but not paid for or recorded in the accounting system. The entry for accrued taxes of $300 is:

```
Taxes Expense . . . . . . . . . . . . . . . . . . . . . . . . . . . . . . . . . . . . . . . . 300
      Taxes Payable  . . . . . . . . . . . . . . . . . . . . . . . . . . . . . . . . . . . . . . .        300
      Adjusting entry for accrued taxes.
```

Accrued Revenues

When accrued revenue has been earned but no payment has been received, the adjusting entry must recognize the revenue that has been earned and also include the creation of a related receivable account. Accrued revenues may include sales and interest income. At the end of each accounting period, a quantity of goods and services will have been supplied to customers, for which no payment has been received. An adjusting entry to accrue these revenues and create the accounts receivable will be necessary. Assuming accrued revenues of $400 at the end of the period, the adjusting entry is:

```
Accounts Receivable  . . . . . . . . . . . . . . . . . . . . . . . . . . . . . . . . . . . . 400
      Sales. . . . . . . . . . . . . . . . . . . . . . . . . . . . . . . . . . . . . . . . . . . . . . .        400
      Adjusting entry for accrued revenues.
```

At the end of the period, interest on investments will be earned but may not have been received in cash. An adjusting entry to accrue interest income of $500 follows:

```
Interest Receivable  . . . . . . . . . . . . . . . . . . . . . . . . . . . . . . . . . . . . . 500
      Interest Income . . . . . . . . . . . . . . . . . . . . . . . . . . . . . . . . . . . . . . .        500
      Adjusting entry for accrued interest revenue.
```

Cost Allocations

Cost allocation relates to a cash expenditure that has been *previously* recorded and that covers more than one accounting period. The adjusting entry recognizes the expense and the associated reduction of a related asset. Expense allocations may include such items as amortization, supplies, prepaid costs, bad debts, and the decline in the value of investments and inventory.

During the accounting period, supplies are purchased and used as needed. At the end of the period, in most cases, a quantity of unused supplies is still on hand. Assume

$2,200 of supplies were purchased during the year, and $500 remained on hand at the end of the period. How the original purchase entry was recorded will influence how the adjusting entry is to be made. If the original purchase entry was made to the asset account Supplies, an adjusting entry to reduce the asset to $500 is required. The entry also recognizes the quantity used during the period ($2,200 − $500 = $1,700) as Supplies Expense.

```
Supplies Expense .....................................  1,700
    Supplies .........................................              1,700
    Adjusting entry allocating supplies.
```

If the bookkeeper determined that because supplies are used frequently the purchase entry for $2,200 was made to Supplies Expense, then the required adjusting entry creates the Supplies asset account for $500 and reduces the Supplies Expense to $1,700 ($2,200 − $500 = $1,700).

```
Supplies ............................................  500
    Supplies Expense .................................              500
    Adjusting entry allocating supplies.
```

The adjusting entry for insurance also depends on how the original entry was recorded. Assume the acquisition of a three-year insurance policy for $2,400 at the beginning of the year. The adjusting entry must allocate one-third or $800 to Insurance Expense and two-thirds or $1,600 to the current asset, Prepaid Insurance. Assuming the original entry for $2,400 was made to the Prepaid Insurance account, the adjusting entry would be:

```
Insurance Expense ...................................  800
    Prepaid Insurance ................................              800
    Adjusting entry allocating insurance.
```

At the end of each accounting period, management must estimate the collectibility of its accounts receivable. The different methods of estimating uncollectible accounts are discussed in Chapter 6. At this point, it should be recognized that an adjusting entry allocating a portion of the asset to an expense account is required for accounts receivable, similar to the entries for insurance and supplies. Management's original intent is not to incur any losses from uncollectible accounts. However, even with the best control procedures most organizations incur losses from uncollectible accounts. Assume that at the end of the period, accounts receivable of $17,200 remain uncollected. If management estimates only $16,300 of these accounts will be collected, the adjusting entry is:

```
Bad Debt Expense....................................  900
    Allowance for Doubtful Accounts ..................              900
    Adjusting entry for estimating uncollectible accounts.
```

The Bad Debt Expense account reflects the estimated uncollectible accounts receivable. As the uncollectible accounts are only *estimated*, the amount is *not deducted* directly from the asset Accounts Receivable. Instead, a contra account called Allowance for Doubtful Accounts is used. On the balance sheet this account's balance of $900 is deducted from the asset Accounts Receivable balance of $17,200. The difference of $16,300 is called the *net realizable value*.

The principle of conservatism requires investments to be written down when their market value falls *below* their original cost. No adjustment is made when the market value exceeds the cost of the investments. Assume that at the end of the period investments with a cost of $7,700 have a market value of only $6,600. The required adjusting entry would be:

```
Loss on Investments  . . . . . . . . . . . . . . . . . . . . . . . . . . . . . . . .   1,100
     Investments  . . . . . . . . . . . . . . . . . . . . . . . . . . . . . . . . . . . . . . . .       1,100
     Adjusting entry to recognize the decrease in the value of investments.
```

A similar adjusting entry is required when the value of merchandise inventory declines. Although organizations try to avoid owning obsolete or damaged inventory, firms handling large volumes of merchandise will unavoidably incur such losses. Assuming the value of a firm's inventory has decreased by $1,500, the following adjustment is needed:

```
Loss on Inventory  . . . . . . . . . . . . . . . . . . . . . . . . . . . . . . . . .   1,500
     Inventory  . . . . . . . . . . . . . . . . . . . . . . . . . . . . . . . . . . . . . . . . . . .       1,500
     Adjusting entry to recognize the decrease in value of inventory.
```

As well, losses on investments and inventory are often recorded in a contra account, similar to the Allowance for Doubtful Accounts. These issues will be examined in detail in later chapters.

Revenue Allocations

Revenue allocations relate to situations where the organization has been paid in advance for goods or services to be performed at a later date. When the payment is first received, a liability account is created. The adjusting entry is made when the goods and services have been provided to the customer. At that point in time, the revenue is earned and the obligation under the liability has been fulfilled. Two examples are provided: one when a deposit (liability) account was used and one when an unearned revenue (liability) account was used.

Organizations selling expensive durable goods like automobiles frequently require customers to make a deposit when the order is placed. When the cash deposit is received, a liability (Customer Deposits) is credited. When the vehicle is delivered to the customer, the total selling price is collected and the revenue is recognized as earned. In addition, once delivery of the vehicle has occurred, the firm no longer has a liability to the customer. An adjusting entry is needed to eliminate the liability and reclassify the deposit as sales revenue:

```
Customer Deposits  . . . . . . . . . . . . . . . . . . . . . . . . . . . . . . . . .   500
     Sales . . . . . . . . . . . . . . . . . . . . . . . . . . . . . . . . . . . . . . . . . . . . . .       500
     Adjusting entry to allocate revenues/liabilities.
```

A similar entry is required for unearned revenue. Unearned revenue is similar to customer deposits in that a customer had paid in advance for a good or service to be provided at a later date. When the advance payment is received, the *liability* account, Unearned Revenue, is credited. Once the goods and services have been provided, the liability no longer exists and revenue has been earned. The adjusting entry would be:

```
Unearned Revenue  . . . . . . . . . . . . . . . . . . . . . . . . . . . . . . . . .   1,300
     Revenue Earned  . . . . . . . . . . . . . . . . . . . . . . . . . . . . . . . . . . . . .       1,300
     Adjusting entry to allocate revenues/liabilities.
```

Amortization

amortization
A systematic allocation process that allocates the acquisition cost of a long-lived asset over the estimated useful life of the asset.

Amortization is an important concept for users of financial statements to understand. The concept of amortization is often misunderstood. We could discuss the many misunderstandings about amortization, but that may simply reinforce those ideas. Users of financial statements should realize that **amortization** is the allocation of the cost of a long-lived asset over its estimated useful life. Therefore, from an income statement perspective, amortization is simply an expense, similar to other expenses necessary to earn revenue, to be matched against revenue in a given time period. From a balance sheet perspective, amortization is a reduction in the net book value of a long-lived asset as a result of the asset being used in the current accounting period. The concept of amortization will be covered in depth in later chapters. To illustrate the impact of amortization on the financial statements, we return to the illustration for Ted's Trucking.

One of Ted's original investing transactions was the purchase of a used truck for $10,000. When organizations acquire any long-lived assets, there is always some uncertainty with respect to how long the asset will be used by the organization, and what will be the value of the asset at the end of its useful life. To properly account for long-lived assets, it is necessary to *estimate* the asset's **useful life** and the asset's **residual value** at the end of its useful life. An asset's useful life is simply the time period that the organization estimates it will *use* the asset. The asset's useful life may often be shorter than its total life. For example, automobiles may typically have total lives of 10 years or longer. However, most organizations, for reliability reasons, prefer to use the vehicles for only three or four years. They then sell the vehicle and acquire a new vehicle and start the process over again. We will assume Ted has decided to use his truck for three years. Ted has also estimated the truck will have a residual value at the end of the truck's useful life (3 years) of $2,800. Amortization on a straight-line basis is determined as follows:

useful life
The time period that is estimated for the asset to be used by the organization.

residual value
The amount that is expected to be recovered when an asset is retired, removed from active use, and sold.

accumulated amortization
A contra asset account deducted from the acquisition cost of a capital asset that represents the portion of the original cost of an asset that has been allocated to prior accounting periods.

contra account
(contra asset, contra liability) An account that is subtracted from a related account; for example, accumulated amortization is subtracted from the Building or Equipment account.

$$\text{Amortization} = \frac{\text{Cost of asset} - \text{Residual value}}{\text{Estimated useful life}}$$

Amortization on Ted's truck is:

$$(\$10,000 - \$2,800)/3 \text{ years} = \$2,400 \text{ per year}$$

The amortization on Ted's truck has been estimated at $2,400 a year. If we wish to prepare financial statements for Ted's Trucking's first month of operations, the annual amortization must be converted to a monthly basis:

$$\$2,400/12 \text{ months} = \$200 \text{ per month}$$

Dr. Amortization Expense 200
    Cr. Accumulated Amortization 200
    Adjusting entry to record amortization.

Amortization is similar to other expenses and therefore decreases equity. Amortization expense is disclosed on the income statement with the other expenses. The offsetting credit entry is a decrease in the asset. However, the entry is *not* made directly to the asset account, but to a contra account called **Accumulated Amortization.** A **contra account** has the opposite balance of the asset account and is used to offset the asset balance. The contra account is disclosed on the financial statements together with its related asset account to determine the net book value of the asset. Over the life of a capital asset, the Accumulated Amortization account is used to accumulate and sum-

---

EXHIBIT 4.5

Annual Closing Entries

1. Close all revenue accounts to the Income Summary account.
2. Close all expense accounts to the Income Summary account.
3. Close the Income Summary account to Retained Earnings (Capital).
4. Close Dividends (Drawings) to Retained Earnings (Capital).

---

marize each period's amortization. At the end of the asset's useful life, the asset account less the Accumulated Amortization account should equal the asset's residual value.

The balance sheet presentation of the contra account Accumulated Amortization is shown below:

Capital assets:	
Truck	$10,000
Less: accumulated amortization	200
	$ 9,800

The capital asset has a net book value of $9,800. As can be seen from the journal entry for amortization, amortization does *not* involve the use of cash. Therefore, when the statement of changes in financial position (cash flow statement) is prepared, an adjustment must be made to adjust for the non-cash item amortization. This adjustment is similar to the adjusting entries for current working capital items related to accrued expenses and revenues. Amortization expense is deducted when determining net income. However, it should *not* be considered when determining net income on a cash basis or what we call *cash provided from operating activities*. Therefore, since amortization expense is deducted when determining net income, it must be added back on the statement of changes in financial position when determining cash provided from operations:

Operating activities:	
Net income	$1,100
Add back: Non-cash items:	
Amortization *expense*	200
	$1,300

Once non-cash items like amortization have been added back, the other elements of the operating activities may be included to complete the statement of changes in financial position.

4.4 CLOSING ENTRIES

The concepts associated with closing entries were previously discussed in this chapter. To review, closing entries are made *only* at the end of the accounting period. Closing entries clear the temporary revenue and expense accounts to zero balances at the end of the period. As well, closing entries transfer the net income/loss and any distributions to owners to the Retained Earnings account (Capital account for proprietorships). Exhibit 4.5 lists the four closing entries to be made each year.

The Income Summary account is a temporary account used to facilitate the closing process. Use of the Income Summary account avoids polluting the equity account with a number of closing entries. Thus, the only closing entries made directly to Retained Earnings are entries to transfer the net income or loss for the year, and to close the Dividends account.

Proprietorships/Partnerships

The four closing entries are illustrated for the proprietorship Ted's Trucking. The first two closing entries, closing the revenue and expense accounts to Income Summary, would conceptually be the same for *all* organizations. Entries 3 and 4 for a partnership would include Capital and Drawings accounts for *each* of the partners.

1	Income Summary	2,600	
	Amortization Expense		200
	Supplies Expense		400
	Legal Expense		900
	Fuel Expense		500
	Utility Expense		600
	Entry to close all the expense accounts.		
2	Trucking Fees	3,700	
	Income Summary		3,700
	Entry to close all the revenue accounts.		
3	Income Summary	1,100	
	Capital, Ted		1,100
	Entry to close the Income Summary account and transfer net income to equity.		
4	Capital Ted	1,000	
	Drawings, Ted		1,000
	Entry to close the Drawings account to equity.		

Corporations

Closing entries for a corporation would be similar to those illustrated for Ted's Trucking, except a corporation would use a Retained Earnings account in lieu of a Capital account, and a Dividends account in lieu of a Drawings account.

Non-Profits

Closing entries for a non-profits would be very similar to entries 1 and 2 illustrated for Ted's Trucking. Non-profits would *not* use a Retained Earnings account or a Capital account, but some type of Surplus account. The Surplus account for non-profit organizations may be called a number of different titles: Fund Balance, Unappropriated Surplus, or Unrestricted Surplus. Since non-profits do not have owners, closing entry 4 is not required.

4.5 ACCOUNTING CYCLE: AN ILLUSTRATION

To illustrate the accounting cycle and the preparation of financial statements, we trace the business activities of Blue Ridge Hardware Company, Ltd., from its first transaction through the end of its first year of operations. This illustration assumes a manual accounting system, since it is easier to see the development of the entries and the flow of those entries through the accounts into the final financial statements using the paper trail of a manual system.

First Year of Operations

In the following pages, the basic business transactions that a small retailer might encounter during the first year of operations are presented in general journal format. This illustration outlines the entries required as a result of those transactions. Finally, the accounting process is completed with the preparation of a trial balance and the formal financial statements. For simplicity in this illustration, all similar transactions that occurred throughout the year have been grouped and only the yearly totals are recorded. For example, transaction 5 in the following illustration reflects the total merchandise purchased by the business on account throughout the entire year. On the company's books, however, each purchase of merchandise inventory made throughout the year would have been recorded separately and chronologically. The first two steps in the accounting cycle, analyzing the source documents and journalizing, are combined in the illustration.

Transaction 1. On April 1, 1995, two friends formed the Blue Ridge Hardware Company and filed for a corporate charter. Each invested $5,000 cash in the new company and received 5,000 shares for the investment. For the company's records, the following entry is required:

```
1   Dr. Cash . . . . . . . . . . . . . . . . . . . . . . . . . . . . . . . . . . . . . . . . . 10,000
        Cr. Share Capital . . . . . . . . . . . . . . . . . . . . . . . . . . . . . . . . .      10,000
    Issued 10,000 shares of share capital.
```

GAAP say that a company may not generate income as a result of transactions with its owners. This receipt of cash increases equity but not retained earnings. It impacts the balance sheet but not the income statement.

Transaction 2. Also on April 1, 1995, a three-year lease was signed for the building in which the hardware store is located. The lease called for a monthly rental of $300 and was cancellable by either the lessor or the lessee (Blue Ridge Hardware) with at least 60 days' advance notice.

```
2   No entry is needed.
```

This business transaction does *not* affect the financial resources or obligations of Blue Ridge Hardware at this time. Even though the business signed the lease, the contract is an executory agreement that will be consummated over time. An *executory contract* is a binding agreement that requires fulfilment of obligations in the *future*. Because the business uses the building, the monthly lease payments are recorded (see transaction 11). However, on the day that this particular lease is signed, no assets or liabilities of the hardware store are affected, and, hence, no amounts need to be entered into the accounts.

Transaction 3. A total of $7,500 was borrowed from a local bank on April 1, 1995. Repayment is to be made over a five-year period, and interest at 12 percent per year is due annually on March 31 on the unpaid balance:

```
3   Dr. Cash . . . . . . . . . . . . . . . . . . . . . . . . . . . . . . . . . . . . . . . . 7,500
        Cr. Bank Loan Payable . . . . . . . . . . . . . . . . . . . . . . . . . . . . . . .      7,500
    Received loan from bank.
```

This receipt of cash is not a revenue item because it must be paid back sometime in the future. Note that the loan carries with it an obligation to pay interest on the borrowed funds. That commitment is not recorded when the loan proceeds are received because (like the lease payments in transaction 2) interest accrues over time and is recorded only as times elapses — usually at the end of each accounting period during the adjusting entry process.

Transaction 4. During the month of April, store equipment was purchased for $10,000 cash:

```
4  Dr. Store Equipment . . . . . . . . . . . . . . . . . . . . . . . . . . . . . . 10,000
       Cr. Cash . . . . . . . . . . . . . . . . . . . . . . . . . . . . . . . . . . . .      10,000
       Purchased store equipment.
```

Transaction 5. During the year, merchandise inventory in the amount of $57,400 was purchased on credit. Payment was usually due within 30 days of the purchase date:

```
5  Dr. Merchandise Inventory . . . . . . . . . . . . . . . . . . . . . . . . . 57,400
       Cr. Accounts Payable . . . . . . . . . . . . . . . . . . . . . . . . . . . .      57,400
       Purchased merchandise inventory on account.
```

The purchase of equipment in transaction 4 is simply an exchange of one asset for another. Similarly, the purchase of inventory in transaction 5 is also treated as the acquisition of an asset even though the various suppliers have not yet been paid. The inventory purchase transaction recognizes the payment promise that Blue Ridge Hardware made when it ordered and received the merchandise. The fulfilment of that promise to pay is recognized as a separate, subsequent transaction (e.g., see transaction 10). The equipment and the inventory are both considered to be assets because they both have continuing value and because both will help the store generate future cash flows from future operations. Because the expense associated with these cash payments will benefit future operations and because we want to match that expense with the related benefit, we treat the expenditures as assets today and charge them to expenses in future transactions (e.g., see transactions 8 and 17).

Transaction 6. During the year, cash sales amounted to $29,800.

Transaction 7. During the year, sales on account or credit sales amounted to $44,700:

```
6  Dr. Cash . . . . . . . . . . . . . . . . . . . . . . . . . . . . . . . . . . . . . 29.800
       Cr. Sales . . . . . . . . . . . . . . . . . . . . . . . . . . . . . . . . . . . .      29,800
       Cash sales for the period.
7  Dr. Accounts Receivable . . . . . . . . . . . . . . . . . . . . . . . . . . 44,700
       Cr. Sales . . . . . . . . . . . . . . . . . . . . . . . . . . . . . . . . . . . .      44,700
       Sales on account for the period.
```

These two types of sales (i.e., transactions 6 and 7) can be considered revenues for the company because they result from consummated transactions with third-party customers and because they represent completion of the seller's earnings process. The company has no obligation to return any amount of these sums and has no obligation to do any further work for the third-party customers. Note that the credit sales are treated as revenues just as though they had been collected in cash. The collection of those receivables is treated as a separate transaction affecting only the balance sheet (e.g., see transaction 9).

Transaction 8. The cost of merchandise sold during the year totalled $45,000:

```
8  Dr. Cost of Goods Sold . . . . . . . . . . . . . . . . . . . . . . . . . . . 45,000
       Cr. Merchandise Inventory . . . . . . . . . . . . . . . . . . . . . . . .      45,000
       Cost of merchandise sold during the period.
```

This entry *matches* the cost of the merchandise sold with the revenue generated by its sale (transactions 6 and 7). The amount of the original purchase price of the merchandise that is to be allocated to the sale transaction is typically the subject of considerable study and analysis by financial managers and will be covered in detail in later chapters of this book.

Transaction 9. Collections of cash from accounts receivable totalled $40,500:

```
 9   Dr. Cash ...................................... 40,500
         Cr. Accounts Receivable .............................    40,500
     Payments received on account.
```

Transaction 10. Payments for merchandise inventory previously purchased on credit amounted to $53,600:

```
10   Dr. Accounts Payable ............................ 53,600
         Cr. Cash ......................................    53,600
     Payments made on account.
```

Transactions 9 and 10 are examples of transactions that affect only the balance sheet — they represent an exchange of one asset for another or a settlement of a liability using an asset. The revenue or expense aspect of these transactions was recognized earlier because of the recognize-all-promises nature of the accrual basis of accounting.

Transaction 11. Cash paid for building rent for the year totalled $3,600:

```
11   Dr. Rent Expense ............................... 3,600
         Cr. Cash ......................................    3,600
     Paid rent for the year.
```

Transaction 12. Cash wages paid to employees totalled $14,600.

Transaction 13. Cash paid for utilities amounted to $450.

Transaction 14. On March 31, 1996, interest on the bank loan for the first year of $900 was paid.

Transaction 15. Federal and provincial income taxes paid during the year amounted to $600.

```
12   Dr. Wage Expense ............................. 14,600
         Cr. Cash ......................................    14,600
     Paid wages during the year.
13   Dr. Utility Expense................................ 450
         Cr. Cash ......................................    450
     Paid utilities for the year.
14   Dr. Interest Expense ............................. 900
         Cr. Cash ......................................    900
     Paid interest for the year.
15   Dr. Income Tax Expense ........................... 600
         Cr. Cash ......................................    600
     Paid income taxes for the year.
```

Transactions 11, 12, 13, 14, and 15 recognize the various operating expenses for the store for the current period. These transactions are charged to expenses — that is, they are not added to an asset — because they create no measurable *future* value for the company and, therefore, require no allocation to a future period and because they assisted in generating the company's revenues for the current period and should, therefore, be matched with those revenues.

Transaction 16. Cash dividends of $2,000 were declared and paid:

```
16  Dr. Dividends .................................. 2,000
        Cr. Cash ....................................... 2,000
    Dividends were declared and paid.
```

Repeating an earlier observation, dividends are *not* an expense of the business but are understood to be distributions of profits to owners. As such, a dividend declaration affects only the balance sheet — it is a distribution of the income that is included in Retained Earnings for the year. The Dividends account is a contra shareholders' equity account and when the accounts for the year are closed, it is netted to the Retained Earnings account as a partial offset to the earnings for the year.

The 16 entries presented here represent the investing, financing, and operating activities of Blue Ridge Hardware Company, Ltd., for its first year of operations. The next step in the accounting cycle is the *posting* of the transactions from the general journal to the general ledger. Once the transactions have been posted to their individual accounts in the general ledger, a trial balance should be prepared to ensure the mathematical accuracy of the journalizing and posting procedure. We will assume the ledger is in balance (Dr. = Cr.) and omit the trial balance until after the adjusting entries have been recorded.

Transaction 17 (adjusting entry). At year-end, the owners estimated that the store equipment had a 10-year useful life and that 1 year had passed. Hence, an adjusting entry was made to allocate $1,000 of the original cost of the equipment (see transaction 4) to expense in this first period:

```
17  Amortization Expense ........................... 1,000
        Accumulated Amortization ........................... 1,000
    Adjusting entry for amortization.
```

Some portion of the original cost of the store equipment was used to produce the revenues earned in this period. Under GAAP, the cost of long-lived assets must be allocated to specific accounting periods. The usual way to accomplish this allocation is to estimate the useful life of the asset and to charge a pro rata portion of the cost of that asset to expense each elapsed year. This process of allocation is called *amortization*. At times it will be useful to know the original cost of a company's capital assets. Therefore, rather than reduce the asset account directly, the annual amortization allocation is credited to a contra asset account called Accumulated Amortization. This contra account is reported on the balance sheet as a deduction from the Store Equipment account, thereby not only preserving the original cost of the equipment but also reporting its net unamortized cost. The unamoritzed cost is often referred to as its *net book value*.

Transaction 18 (adjusting entry). A number of accrued expenses remained unpaid and unrecorded at the end of the period. Blue Ridge Hardware estimated that when the March bills were all processed, the company would owe an additional $200 for utilities and an additional $2,300 in taxes. As well, wages earned by employees but not yet paid were $700 as of March 31, 1996.

```
18  Dr. Utility Expense................................. 200
        Cr. Accounts Payable ............................. 200
    Adjusting entry for accrued utility expense.
```

Transaction 19 (adjusting entry). Blue Ridge estimated that the company owes an additional $2,300 in income taxes.

```
19  Dr. Income Tax Expense ........................... 2,300
        Cr. Income Taxes Payable ........................... 2,300
    Adjusting entry for accrued income tax expense.
```

Transaction 20 (adjusting entry). Wages earned by employees but not yet paid were $700 as of March 31, 1996.

```
20  Dr. Wage Expense  . . . . . . . . . . . . . . . . . . . . . . . . . . . . . . . . . 700
        Cr. Wages Payable  . . . . . . . . . . . . . . . . . . . . . . . . . . . . . .        700
        Adjusting entry for accrued wage expense.
```

Once all the adjusting entries have been completed, we are just about ready to prepare the financial statements. As with the day-to-day transactions, the adjusting entries are entered in the journal and then posted to the general ledger.

We can now derive the individual account balances for Blue Ridge Hardware as of March 31, 1996. First, we establish a separate account for each specific asset, liability, owners' equity, revenue, and expense account. Together these accounts form the chart of accounts for Blue Ridge hardware. Since April 1, 1995, was the first day of operations, the beginning balance in each account is $0. Second, we record (i.e., post) each entry in the appropriate ledger account and then determine the fiscal year-end *balance* of each account. The results of the posting step in the accounting cycle, the year-end balances in the ledger, are shown in Exhibit 4.6.

To verify that the company's account are in balance, we prepare a trial balance using the general ledger account balances. Since the adjusting entries have been journalized and posted to the ledger, it is called an **adjusted trial balance.** The adjusted trial balance for Blue Ridge Hardware is in balance, suggesting that an equivalent amount of debits and credits were posted to the accounts. However, a balanced trial balance does not ensure the accuracy of the data in the particular accounts. Each account has its **normal balance.** An account's normal balance is its positive or increase side of the debit/credit, accounting equation rule. Therefore, assets have normal balances of debits, and liabilities have normal balances of credits. Equity and revenue accounts would normally have a credit balance and expenses a debit balance.

adjusted trial balance
A listing of the account balances from the general ledger, after the adjusting entries have been recorded.

normal balance
An account's normal balance is its positive or increase side of the debit/credit, accounting equation rule.

BLUE RIDGE HARDWARE COMPANY, LTD.
Adjusted Trial Balance
March 31, 1996

Account	Debit	Credit
Cash	$ 2,050	
Accounts receivable	4,200	
Inventory	12,400	
Store equipment	10,000	
Accumulated amortization		$ 1,000
Accounts payable		4,000
Wages payable		700
Income taxes payable		2,300
Bank loan payable		7,500
Share capital		10,000
Retained earnings		–0–
Dividends	2,000	
Sales		74,500
Cost of sales	45,000	
Rent expense	3,600	
Wage expense	15,300	
Utility expense	650	
Income tax expense	2,900	
Interest expense	900	
Amortization expense	1,000	
Total	$100,000	$100,000

EXHIBIT 4.6

BLUE RIDGE HARDWARE CO.
General Ledger

Cash

	Debit		Credit
(1)	10,000	(4)	10,000
(3)	7,500	(10)	53,600
(6)	29,800	(11)	3,600
(9)	40,500	(12)	14,600
		(13)	450
		(14)	900
		(15)	600
		(16)	2,000
2,050			

Accounts Receivable

	Debit		Credit
(7)	44,700	(9)	40,500
	4,200		

Inventory

	Debit		Credit
(5)	57,400	(8)	45,000
	12,400		

Share Capital

	Debit		Credit
		(1)	10,000
			10,000

Dividends

	Debit		Credit
(16)	2,000		
	2,000		

Rent Expense

	Debit		Credit
(11)	3,600		
	3,600		

Accumulated Amortization

	Debit		Credit
		(17)	1,000
			1,000

Sales

	Debit		Credit
		(6)	29,800
		(7)	44,700
			74,500

Cost of Sales

	Debit		Credit
(8)	45,000		
	45,000		

Utility Expense

	Debit		Credit
(13)	450		
(18)	200		
	650		

Interest Expense

	Debit		Credit
(14)	900		
	900		

Store Equipment

	Debit		Credit
(4)	10,000		
	10,000		

Accounts Payable

	Debit		Credit
(10)	53,600	(5)	57,400
		(18)	200
			4,000

Wage Expense

	Debit		Credit
(12)	14,600		
(20)	700		
	15,300		

Income Tax Expense

	Debit		Credit
(15)	600		
(19)	2,300		
	2,900		

Amortization Expense

	Debit		Credit
(17)	1,000		
	1,000		

Bank Loan Payable

	Debit		Credit
		(3)	7,500
			7,500

Income Taxes Payable

	Debit		Credit
		(19)	2,300
			2,300

Wages Payable

	Debit		Credit
		(20)	700
			700

The next step in the accounting process is preparing the income statement, a balance sheet, and a statement of changes in financial position. Visualize the management of Blue Ridge Hardware as they study the account balances in the trial balance, as they think about the kinds of transactions summarized in each account, and as they decide how the accounts should be displayed in the financial statements. On one level, the process is relatively easy: The temporary accounts — which include the revenue and expense accounts — appear on the income statements and the permanent accounts — which include the assets, liabilities, and owners' equity accounts — appear on the balance sheet. The temporary accounts are called *temporary* because they are used during *only one* accounting period and closed out. At the beginning of the following year they are opened again to measure the results of operations for that new year. Permanent accounts are called *permanent* because the balances carry forward from one year to the next. On a different level, the process of preparing financial statements from a trial balance is more difficult. Management must decide which accounts can be combined, which should be presented as separate line items on the statements, and which accounts must be analyzed (i.e., broken down into more detail). The objective of this process is to be sure that the financial statements include enough information to present a fair picture of the company without obscuring reality with too much detail. To put yourself in the situation of the Blue Ridge Hardware owners, study the trial balance and the ledger accounts and see how those data were organized into the resulting financial statements.

BLUE RIDGE HARDWARE COMPANY, LTD.
Income Statement
For the Year Ending March 31, 1996

Sales		$ 74,500
Cost of sales		45,000
Gross profit		$ 29,500
Rent expense	$ 3,600	
Wage expense	15,300	
Utility expense	650	
Interest expense	900	
Amortization expense	1,000	21,450
Income before taxes		$ 8,050
Income tax expense		2,900
Net income		$ 5,150

BLUE RIDGE HARDWARE COMPANY, LTD.
Balance Sheet
As at March 31, 1996

Assets		Liabilities	
Current assets:		Current liabilities:	
Cash	$ 2,050	Accounts payable	$ 4,000
Accounts receivable	4,200	Wages payable	700
Inventory	12,400	Income taxes payable	2,300
Total current assets	$18,650	Total current liabilities	$ 7,000
		Long-term liabilities:	
Capital assets:		Bank loan payable	7,500
Store equipment	$10,000	Total liabilities	$14,500
Accumulated amortization	(1,000)	**Shareholders Equity**	
	$ 9,000	Share capital	$10,000
Total assets	$27,650	Retained Earnings*	3,150
		Total equity	$13,150
		Total liabilities and equity	$27,650

*Net income of $5,150 less dividends of $2,000.

BLUE RIDGE HARDWARE COMPANY, LTD.
Statement of Changes in Financial Position
For the Year Ending March 31, 1996

Operating activities:		
Net income	$ 5,150	
Items not involving cash:		
Amortization	1,000	
Change in working capital items:		
Accounts payable	4,000	
Accounts receivable	(4,200)	
Inventory	(12,400)	
Wages payable	700	
Income taxes payable	2,300	$ (3,450)
Investing activities:		
Store equipment		(10,000)
Financing activities:		
Bank loan	$ 7,500	
Share capital issued	10,000	
Dividends paid	(2,000)	15,500
Increase in cash		$ 2,050
Cash — April 1, 1995		–0–
Cash — March 31, 1996		$ 2,050

The next to last step in the accounting cycle requires closing entries to be made at the end of the year. To ensure that you understand the closing entry process and the linkage between net income and retained earnings, we suggest that you trace the closing entries from the general journal to the ledger accounts. After this posting, all temporary accounts *must* have a zero ending balance, and the net income of Blue Ridge Hardware will have been transferred to Retained Earnings.

1 Income Summary 69,350
      Cost of Sales   45,000
      Rent Expense   3,600
      Wage Expense....................................   15,300
      Utility Expense   650
      Income Tax Expense   2,900
      Interest Expense..................................   900
      Amortization Expense   1,000
   Entry to close all expense accounts.

2 Sales 74,500
      Income Summary 74.500
   Entry to close the revenue account.

3 Income Summary 5,150
      Retained Earnings   5,150
   Entry to close the Income Summary account and transfer net income to equity.

4 Retained Earnings 2,000
      Dividends   2,000
   Entry to close the Dividend account to equity.

The final step in the accounting cycle is to prepare the post-closing trial balance. The post-closing trial balance *must* contain only the permanent accounts (i.e., balance sheet accounts), as all the temporary accounts (i.e., income statement accounts) have been cleared to zero balances.

BLUE RIDGE HARDWARE COMPANY, LTD.
Post-Closing Trial Balance
March 31, 1996

Account	Debit	Credit
Cash	$ 2,050	
Accounts receivable	4,200	
Inventory	12,400	
Store equipment	10,000	
Accumulated amortization		$ 1,000
Accounts payable		4,000
Wages payable		700
Income taxes payable		2,300
Bank loan payable		7,500
Share capital		10,000
Retained earnings		3,150
Total	$28,650	$28,650

4.6 ANALYZING FINANCIAL STATEMENTS: AN ILLUSTRATION

Now that the accounting process is complete and the financial reports of Blue Ridge Hardware have been prepared, let us briefly consider what these reports reveal about the organization. The first stage of any analysis is to examine the absolute amounts presented in the statements. This can be followed by a trend analysis examining financial data for a series of three to five years. Common-size financial statements assist trend analysis and provide a more in-depth analysis of individual years' information and facilitate a comparison between one or more periods. Finally, ratio analysis can be used to facilitate the analysis between statements and different accounting periods. To provide an opportunity for comparative analysis, we have assumed it is one year later, and Blue Ridge Hardware has completed its second year of operations.

Analysis of Financial Statement Amounts

A comparative income statement, retained earnings statement, balance sheet, and statement of changes in financial position for Blue Ridge Hardware Company are presented below.

BLUE RIDGE HARDWARE COMPANY, LTD.
Income Statement
For the Year Ending March 31

	1997	1996
Sales	$106,300	$74,500
Cost of sales	66,900	45,000
Gross profit	$ 39,400	$29,500
Rent expense	$ 4,080	$ 3,600
Wage expense	21,400	15,300
Utility expense	790	650
Interest expense	830	900
Amortization expense	1,300	1,000
Income tax expense	$ 3,600	$ 2,900
Total expenses	$ 32,000	$24,350
Net income	$ 7,400	$ 5,150

The income statement indicates that for the year ended March 31, 1996, Blue Ridge Hardware earned net income of $5,150 on net revenues of $74,500. Since most companies have more expenses than sales during their initial building years, they often lose money during their first year (or years) of operations; hence, it is encouraging that Blue Ridge Hardware achieved a positive net income — its sales volume exceeded its cost of operations. On the basis of these earnings, the organization declared and paid a dividend in the amount of $2,000. And, since the full amount of net income for the period was not distributed as a dividend, the owners' investment in the organization grew by $3,150. Several important points here merit restatement. First, dividends are *not* reported as an expense of the business on the income statement but instead are a distribution of the company's income to its shareholders. Second, to the extent that the income for the period is not distributed as dividends, it has the same effect as if the owners had invested that amount of new funds in the organization. For the year ended March 31, 1997, net income has improved to $7,400 on increased sales of $106,300. Expenses have increased by nearly $8,000 ($32,000 − $24,350), but have been more than offset by an increase in gross profit during the year of about $10,000 ($39,400 − $29,500).

BLUE RIDGE HARDWARE COMPANY, LTD.
Retained Earnings Statement
For the Year Ending March 31

	1997	1996
Beginning retained earnings — April 1	$ 3,150	$ –0–
Net income	7,400	5,150
Less: *dividends*	–0–	(2,000)
Ending retained earnings — March 31	$10,550	$ 3,150

During the year ending March 31, 1997, no dividends were distributed to shareholders. Apparently, the company has decided to retain its earnings within the organization to finance future operations. Not declaring and paying dividends also improves the company's cash flow position, which is indicated on the statement of changes in financial position. The ending retained earnings balances are carried forward to the shareholders' equity section of the balance sheet, illustrating the interrelationship of the income statement and the balance sheet.

BLUE RIDGE HARDWARE COMPANY, LTD.
Balance Sheet
As at March 31

	1997	1996		1997	1996
Assets			**Liabilities**		
Current Assets:			Current Liabilities:		
Cash	$ 1,420	$ 2,050	Accounts payable	$ 7,200	$ 4,000
Accounts receivable	8,700	4,200	Wages payable	1,100	700
Inventory	15,130	12,400	Income taxes payable	1,800	2,300
Total current assets	$25,250	$18,650	Total current liabilities	$10,100	$ 7,000
Capital assets:			Long-term liabilities:		
Store equipment	$13,000	$10,000	Bank loan payable	5,300	7,500
Accumulated amortization	(2,300)	(1,000)	Total liabilities	$15,400	$14,500
	$10,700	$ 9,000	**Shareholders' Equity**		
Total assets	$35,950	$27,650	Share capital:		
			10,000 shares issued	$10,000	$10,000
			Retained earnings	10,550	3,150
			Total equity	$20,550	$13,150
			Total liabilities and equity	$35,950	$27,650

With respect to the financial condition of the organization, the balance sheet at March 31, 1997, reveals that at year-end, Blue Ridge Hardware has the following:

Total assets (and total equities) of $35,950 (1996 — $27,650).

Total liabilities of $15,400 (1996 — $14,500).

Shareholders' equity of $20,550 (1996 — $13,150).

All of the above figures indicate significant growth for the company during the year. The shareholders' equity, or the company's net worth, is the value that would remain if all assets could be converted to cash at their balance sheet values and then used to satisfy all existing liabilities. The liquidation of a company, however, is a rare event, and it is also unlikely that the cash liquidation value of the assets would exactly equal their book values. Consequently, an alternative description of owners' equity or net worth is to say that it is the net book value of all assets minus the book value of all liabilities.

The balance sheet also reveals that Blue Ridge Hardware has current assets totalling $25,250 (1996 — $18,650), which exceeds not only its total current liabilities of $10,100 (1996 — $7,000) but also total current and long-term liabilities of $15,400 (1996 — $14,500). This indicates that the organization is relatively secure in terms of its ability to pay off its outstanding obligations. However, it appears accounts receivable and inventory have increased significantly during the year. These two items merit further investigation and will be analyzed in a subsequent section on ratio analysis.

BLUE RIDGE HARDWARE COMPANY, LTD.
Statement of Changes in Financial Position
For the Year Ending March 31

	1997	1996
Operating activities:		
Net income	$ 7,400	$ 5,150
Items not involving cash:		
Amortization	1,300	1,000
Change in working capital items:		
Accounts payable	3,200	4,000
Accounts receivable	(4,500)	(4,200)
Inventory	(2,730)	(12,400)
Wages payable	400	700
Income taxes payable	(500)	2,300
Cash provided (used) from operations	$ 4,570	$ (3,450)
Investing activities:		
Store equipment	$(3,000)	$(10,000)
Cash provided (used) from investing	$(3,000)	$(10,000)
Financing activities:		
Bank loan	$(2,200)	$ 7,500
Share capital issued	–0–	10,000
Dividends paid	–0–	(2,000)
Cash provided (used) from financing	$(2,200)	$ 15,500
Increase (decrease) in cash	$ (630)	$ 2,050
Cash — Beginning balance, April 1	2,050	–0–
Cash — Ending balance, March 31	$ 1,420	$ 2,050

The statement of changes in financial position for the year ended March 31, 1996, reveals that the organization generated a net cash inflow from financing activities in the amount of $15,500 and spent $10,000 in cash on investing activities. An additional $3,450 was spent in support of the company's operations, leaving a net cash balance of $2,050 at year-end. To ensure the continued success of the organization, it is important for Blue Ridge Hardware to become a net positive generator of cash flows from operations. Clearly, the company will become viable only if the cash flows from operating activities become positive. As can be seen for the period ending March 31, 1996, a positive cash flow from operations of $4,570 was achieved. During 1997, investing activities decreased to $3,000 and financing activities included a significant reduction on the bank loan of $2,200. Overall, cash decreased $630 during the year. This decrease could have been avoided by making a smaller payment on the bank loan.

Trend Analysis

It is difficult to perform trend analysis for Blue Ridge Hardware, as it has only been in operation for two years. The foregoing analysis has indicated a positive trend in most financial statement items. To facilitate trend analysis common-size statements are presented.

BLUE RIDGE HARDWARE COMPANY, LTD.
Common-Size Income Statement
For the Year Ending March 31

	1997		1996	
Sales	$106,300	100.0%	$74,500	100.0%
Cost of sales	66,900	62.9	45,000	60.4
Gross profit	$ 39,400	37.1	$29,500	39.6
Rent expense	$ 4,080	3.9	$ 3,600	4.8
Wage expense	21,400	20.1	15,300	20.6
Utility expense	790	.7	650	.9
Interest expense	830	.8	900	1.2
Amortization expense	1,300	1.2	1,000	1.3
Income tax expense	$ 3,600	3.4	$ 2,900	3.9
Total expenses	$ 32,000	30.1	$24,350	32.7
Net income	$ 7,400	7.0%	$ 5,150	6.9%

Common-size statements permit both a within-period analysis (e.g., in 1997, total expenses were 30.1 percentage of total revenues) and across-period trend analysis (e.g., total expenses as a percentage of total revenues decreased from 32.7 percent in 1996 to 30.1 percent in 1997). Net income as a percentage of sales was about the same each year, 7.0 percent in 1997 compared to 6.9 percent in 1996. However, cost of sales did increase by 2.5 percent from the previous year (62.9 – 60.4). Individual expenses decreased on a percentage basis over the two-year period. However, wage expense continues to represent a very large portion of expenses in total dollars, as well as on a percentage basis.

The common-size balance sheets reveal significant changes in the following items: accounts receivable increased 9.0 percent (24.2 – 15.2), accounts payable increased 5.5 percent (20.0 – 14.5), the bank loan decreased 12.4 percent (14.7 – 27.1), and total equity increased nearly 10 percent (57.2 – 47.6).

BLUE RIDGE HARDWARE COMPANY LTD.
Common-Size Balance Sheet As at March 31

Assets	1997		1996	
Current assets:				
Cash	$ 1,420	3.9%	$ 2,050	7.4%
Accounts receivable	8,700	24.2	4,200	15.2
Inventory	15,130	42.1	12,400	44.9
Total current assets	$25,250	70.2	$18,650	67.4
Capital assets:				
Store equipment	$13,000	36.2	$10,000	36.2
Accumulated amortization	(2,300)	(6.4)	(1,000)	(3.6)
Total capital assets	$10,700	29.8	$ 9,000	32.6
Total assets	$35,950	100.0	$27,650	100.0%

Liabilities	1997		1996	
Current liabilities:				
Accounts payable	$ 7,200	20.0%	$ 4,000	14.5%
Wages payable	1,100	3.1	700	2.5
Income taxes payable	1,800	5.0	2,300	8.3
Total current liabilities	$10,100	28.1	$ 7,000	25.3
Long-term liabilities:				
Bank loan payable	$ 5,300	14.7	7,500	27.1
Total liabilities	$15,400	42.8	$14,500	52.4
Shareholders' Equity				
Share capital — 10,000 shares issued	$10,000	27.8	$10,000	36.2
Retained earnings	10,550	29.4	3,150	11.4
Total equity	$20,550	57.2	$13,150	47.6
Total liabilities and shareholders' equity	$35,950	100.0	$27,650	100.0%

Most annual reports include financial data in graphical format to facilitate the user's understanding of the financial information. As no generally accepted standards exist for the presentation of financial information in a graphical format, a number of different graphs may be seen in annual reports. We present a sample of financial graphs using information from the financial statements of Blue Ridge Hardware.

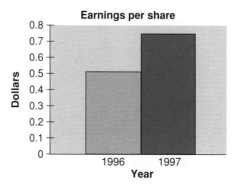

A bar graph illustrates the growth in earnings per share of Blue Ridge Hardware during its first two years of operation. Earnings per share have increased from $.515 in 1995 to $.740 in 1996. The graph helps to illustrate the significance of the increase in earnings during the period.

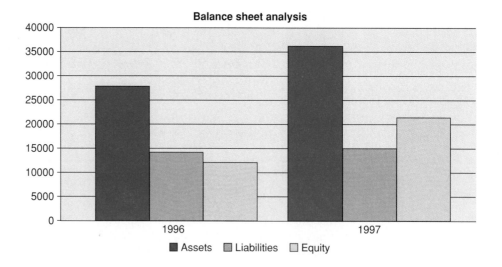

A bar graph has also been used to indicate the growth of Blue Ridge Hardware during the period. The graph shows a significant increase in assets and equity, and a stable liability position during the period. Assets have increased from $27,650 in 1996 to $35,950 in 1997. As well, equity has increased from $13,150 in 1995 to $20,550 in 1996. During the same period, liabilities have increased by only a small amount from $14,500 in 1996 to $15,400 in 1997.

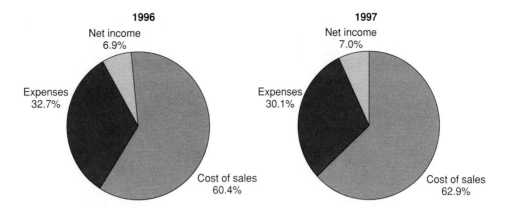

Pie graphs illustrate the breakdown of sales dollars for Blue Ridge Hardware for 1996 and 1997. In 1996 cost of sales comprised 60.4 percent of sales, total expenses 32.7 percent, and net income 6.9 percent. The graph does not really illustrate any significant changes for 1997. In 1997, cost of sales represented 62.9 percent, total expenses 30.1 percent, and net income 7.0 percent. In this case, graphical presentation may be misleading, indicating what appears to a very small change in operations. Earlier analysis using common-size statements indicated more concern over the 2.5 percent increased in cost of sales and the relatively large percentage of total expenses represented by wage expense. One of the purposes of this illustration is to remind the user of financial information to carefully analyze all information, and particularly analyze any graphical information with care.

Ratio Analysis

One of the most common and useful means of financial analysis is the use of ratios. The financial strength ratios from Chapter 2 and the management performance ratios from Chapter 3 are used to further analyze the financial statements of Blue Ridge Hardware Company, Ltd.

Liquidity Analysis

	1997	1996
Quick Ratio	1.00:1 [(1,420 + 8,700)/10,100]	.89:1 [(2,050 + 4,200)/7,000]
Current ratio	2.50:1 (25,250/10,100)	2.66:1 (18,650/7,000)

The firm's 1996 liquidity position has not changed significantly compared to 1995. The quick ratio has improved slightly to 1.00:1 in 1996 from .89:1 in 1995. The current ratio weakening during the year, from 2.66:1 in 1995 to 2.50:1 in 1996.

Solvency Analysis

	1997	1996
Total debt-to-equity ratio	.75:1 (15,400/20,550)	1.10:1 (14,500/13,150)
Long-term debt-to-invested capital ratio	.21:1 [5,300/(5,300 +20,550)]	.36:1 [7,500/(7,500 + 13,150)]

Solvency ratios have improved significantly during the year. The total debt-to-equity ratio decreased to .75:1 from 1.10:1 in 1995. As well, the long-term debt-to-invested capital ratio improved during the period, from .36:1 in 1996 to only .21:1 in 1997. This improvement was the result of a reduction in long-term debt, combined with an increase in equity during the period.

Profitability Analysis

	1997	1996
Earnings per share	$.740 ($7,400/10,000)	$.515 ($5,150/10,000)
Return on equity	36.00% (7,400/20,550)	39.16% (5,150/13,150)

Profitability has improved during the year. The earnings per share increased from $.515 in 1996 to $.740 in 1997. While the return on equity actually decreased during the same period, from 39.16 percent in 1996 to 36.00 percent in 1997, it should still be noted that a return on equity of 36.00 percent is very respectable, especially when compared to most standard investment opportunities.

Asset Management Analysis

	1997	1996
Total asset turnover	2.96 (106,300/35,950)	2.69 (74,500/27,650)
Receivable turnover	12.21 (106,300/8,700)	17.73 (74,500/4,200)

The total asset turnover ratio indicates management has been more efficient with its overall asset management, increasing to 2.96 in 1997 from 2.69 in 1996. However, the receivable turnover ratio indicates a significant drop, from 17.73 in 1996 to only 12.21 in 1997. This may indicate a possible problem with the collection of accounts receivables, which should be watched closely in subsequent periods.

We have used the comparative financial statements of Blue Ridge Hardware, Ltd., to illustrate financial statement analysis. We compared the figures for a two-year period, looking at absolute amounts, trends, common-size statements, and ratios. What did this analysis tell us about Blue Ridge Hardware? Overall, we found that Blue Ridge Hardware is in a relatively good financial position. The liquidity position is good and the solvency position is very good. Accounts receivable and inventory levels should be watched carefully to ensure they do not rise to unacceptable levels in future periods. Blue Ridge has been profitable during its first two years of operation, which is encouraging for a new organization. Additional comparative analysis can be performed if financial data for the hardware industry are available. Industry data would invariably help to confirm or dispute our previous findings.

4.7 SUMMARY

The purpose of this chapter has been to discuss and illustrate the accounting process used in preparing accounting reports. This process involves several distinct activities: designing the financial reporting system, analyzing business transactions to assess their financial effect on the assets, liabilities, and equities of an organization, recording this analysis in various data files, verifying the accuracy of the recording process, and, finally, preparing and analyzing the financial statements.

Blue Ridge Hardware Company, Ltd., was used to illustrate the steps in the accounting cycle: identifying source documents, journalizing, posting, preparing a trial balance, recording adjusting entries, preparing financial statements, recording closing entries, and preparing a post-closing trial balance. The financial statements of Blue Ridge Hardware were used to illustrate financial statement analysis techniques.

Although it is important for you to understand how accounting reports are prepared and how the accounting system operates, our principal goal is to ensure that you understand fully how accounting reports communicate and what they reveal about the operations and financial condition of the organization. Thus, in the chapters that follow, we focus our attention not on the process of financial statement preparation but on analyzing important business transactions for the purpose of accounting and of understanding what information the accounting statements convey.

4.8 KEY CONCEPTS AND TERMS

Accounting cycle (p. 154)	**Journalizing** (p. 155)
Accruals (p. 157)	**Normal balance** (p. 168)
Accumulated amortization (p. 161)	**Permanent account** (p. 157)
Adjusted trial balance (p. 168)	**Post-closing trial balance** (p. 156)
Adjusting entries (p. 155)	**Posting** (p. 155)
Allocation (p. 157)	**Residual value** (p. 161)
Amortization (p. 161)	**Source document** (p. 154)
Chart of accounts (p. 153)	**T-accounts** (p. 155)
Closing entries (p. 156)	**Temporary accounts** (p. 156)
Contra account (p. 161)	**Trial balance** (p. 155)
General ledger (p. 155)	**Useful life** (p. 161)

4.9 COMPREHENSIVE REVIEW QUESTION

R4.1 Accounting cycle. Sally Smith started her own business as a proprietorship on January 1, and completed the following transactions for the year ending December 31.

1. Sally invested $2,000 of her personal savings in the business.

2. Paid $50 cash for office supplies.

3. Purchased equipment for $300 on account.

4. Earned revenue of $100, paid in full.

5. Paid $200 on account (re: purchase of equipment).

6. Earned revenue of $300, to be paid later.

7. Paid utility bill for $25.

8. Collected $150 on account.

Required:

a. Record the transactions in the general journal.

b. Post the transactions to the general ledger (T-accounts).

c. Prepare adjusting entries (journalize and post to T-accounts) based on the following information:

Equipment has a 10-year life and no residual value.
At the end of the accounting period $10 of office supplies were on hand.
Included in revenues is $20 received in advance (unearned revenue).

d. Prepare a trial balance.

e. Prepare financial statements for the year ending December 31.

f. Prepare closing entries (journalize and post to T-accounts).

g. Prepare a post-closing trial balance.

4.10 REVIEW AND DISCUSSION QUESTIONS

Q4.1 Distinguish between the general ledger and the general journal.

Q4.2 What is the purpose of adjusting entries? How frequently should adjusting entries be prepared?

Q4.3 Describe the purpose of closing entries. How frequently are closing entries prepared?

Q4.4 What purposes are served by the preparation of a trial balance, balance sheet, and income statement? How frequently should they be prepared?

Q4.5 Describe at least five events that a company is likely to experience that would not be measured, recorded, and reported in the company's financial statements.

Q4.6 Visualize the millions of transactions that a large company would engage in throughout a year with a variety of other parties, for differing dollar amounts, and for different purposes. Identify some of the ways in which errors might enter the accounting cycle and suggest internal controls that might minimize the likelihood of those errors occurring and/or going undetected.

Q4.7 The accounting cycle described in this chapter is a standard approach employed by most companies, who will then often modify it to better suit their needs. Discuss some of the unique circumstances of particular companies that would possibly lead to slight modifications and/or customizations of the accounting cycle.

Q4.8 The income statements prepared by Atlantic Coast Manufacturing Company detail the company's results of operations for the year ended December 31. Some of the line items from that income statement appear below. For each of these items, describe in your own words what the source of the numbers might have been.

a. Sales — $500,000.

b. Payroll expense — $250,000.

c. Bad debt expense — $25,000.

d. Computer amortization — $30,000.

e. Selling expense — $75,000.

Q4.9 Great Lakes Services, Ltd., maintains cash in a box at the reception desk and in the plant for buying stamps and paying for other small expenses; each box usually contains $250. The company maintains three different bank accounts with a local bank. One is its general corporate account with an average balance of $1 million; another is the factory payroll account with an average balance of $250,000; and the third is the executive payroll account with an average balance of $50,000. The company usually has between $100,000 and $200,000 of excess cash invested in short-term investments. Great Lakes Services has total assets of $10 million and a net worth (Net worth = Assets − Liabilities) of $4 million. How many general ledger accounts should the company maintain to collect the transactions affecting its cash and its cash-equivalent items? How many line items should the company present on its balance sheet to describe its cash and cash-equivalent items? Please explain the reasoning behind your answers.

Q4.10 Describe each of the following in your own words. Explain how each enters into recording and processing financial data and in preparing and presenting financial statements.

a. Permanent and temporary accounts.

b. Adjusting entries and closing entries.

c. The trial balance.

Q4.11 As you worked through the accounting process illustrated by the Blue Ridge Hardware example, you learned something about the accounting process and you enhanced further your understanding of accounting concepts. That understanding will be developed further in subsequent chapters, but it will be useful to articulate your developing understanding as it grows. In that context, describe the following in your own words:

a. The difference between an asset and an expense.

b. The impact of accrual accounting on the measurement of operating results.

c. The concept of amortization.

Q4.12 Using the financial statements for Maple Leaf Gardens, Limited, provided in Chapter 1, briefly describe the possible adjusting entries that were required in the preparation of their annual statements.

Q4.13 Review the list of key concepts and terms at the end of the chapter. If you have difficulty with a specific concept, refer to the discussion on the page number provided as a reference to gain a better understanding of the concept. Make a list of terms you do not thoroughly understand. When you have finished Chapter 5, refer back to this list to see if your understanding has improved.

Q4.14 If you were given a company's year-end balance sheets and annual income statements together with a record of dividends declared for a series of years and were asked to prepare a statement of changes in financial position for the company, what additional information concerning retained earnings, income taxes, long-term investments, and property, plant, and equipment (net) would you like to have? What would you do if you could not get such additional information?

Q4.15 When preparing an organization's year-end financial statements, as part of the accounting process the organization may prepare three different trial balances. Name these trial balances and briefly describe their purposes.

Q4.16 Identify whether each of the following is properly classified as an operating, investing, or financing activity in a statement of changes in financial position. Explain your rationale.

a. Receipts from sales of property, plant, and equipment.

b. Interest payments to lenders and other creditors.

c. Proceeds from issuing equity instruments.

d. Payments to acquire long-term debt instruments.

Q4.17 When Zenith Enterprises prepared its annual report, the accountant failed to record adjusting entries for amortization of $2,300 and an accrued revenue of $1,000. Explain the impact this error will have on the financial statements.

4.11 PROBLEMS

P4.1 Conservatism, net income determination. Holiday Travel, Limited, has completed its first year of operations. The company's accountant has prepared a draft copy of an income statement showing a net income before adjustments of $13,300. A discussion with the accountant reveals the following information, which was not taken into consideration when drafting the income statement:

Bad debts are estimated at 3 percent to 7 percent of sales. Sales for the current year were $147,500.

Computer equipment and a computerized reservation system costing $14,000 is estimated to have a useful economic life of four to six years.

Temporary investments that cost $7,200 have a market value of $7,650.

Holiday Travel, Limited, has no previous basis on which to base its adjustments because this is its first year of operations. You have been asked to determine a revised net income figure based on the most conservative, but reasonable estimates using the information given. As well, your report should include a brief description of the accounting principle of conservatism with particular reference to the financial report of Holiday Travel, Limited.

P4.2 Maximizing net income. Cougar Athletics, Ltd., has completed its first year of operations. The company's accountant has prepared a draft copy of an income statement showing a net income before adjustments of $11,100. A discussion with the accountant reveals the following information, which has not been taken into consideration when drafting the income statement:

Accrued interest revenue of $1,200 has not been included in net income.

Bad debts are estimated at 3 to 6 percent of sales. Sales for the current year were $155,000.

Exercise equipment costing $15,000 is estimated to have a useful economic life of four to six years.

There is no previous experience on which to base adjustments because this is the first year of operations for the company. The objective of financial reporting for the company is to maximize its profits each year. You have been asked to determine a revised net income figure.

P4.3 Closing entries. Using the information provided in the financial statements of Maple Leaf Gardens, Limited, provided in Chapter 1, prepare the closing entries.

P4.4 Income statement. Determine the missing amounts affecting the income statement in each of the independent cases below:

	A	B	C	D
Sales	$47,000	?	$66,000	$88,000
Cost of sales	21,000	$32,000	?	45,000
Gross profit	?	22,000	27,000	?
Operating expenses	30,000	?	10,000	26,000
Net income (loss)	?	11,000	?	?

P4.5 Statement preparation. The following information was taken from the trial balance for Kingston Corporation for the year ended December 31, 1996. Kingston has 10,000 shares of share capital issued and outstanding.

Accounts payable	$22,200
Advertising expense	3,500
Cash	1,100
Dividends paid	7,500
Income tax expense	10,000
Interest expense	1,200
Building (net)	25,000
Amortization expense	800
Notes payable	4,000
Office salaries	25,000
Office supplies used	1,500
Salaries payable	800
Accounts receivable	25,300
Share capital	50,000
Cost of goods sold	228,000
Sales	285,000
Income tax payable	4,000
Land	32,600
Merchandise inventory	32,000
Long-term debt	15,000
Notes receivable	4,800
Office supplies inventory	700
Retained earnings, 1/1/96	18,000

Required:

a. Prepare an income statement, a balance sheet, and a statement of shareholders' equity for the Kingston Corporation as of December 31.

b. Complete a ratio analysis of Kingston Corporation. Include comments on your analysis.

c. Prepare a common-size income statement and balance sheet for Kingston Corporation.

P4.6 Transaction analysis. Prepare general journal entries for the following transactions:

a. Selling share capital.

b. Signing a three-year lease on a building.

c. Paying three months' rent in advance.

d. Purchasing supplies for cash.

e. Purchasing equipment on account.

f. Purchasing merchandise on account.

g. Obtaining a six-month bank loan.

h. Selling merchandise for cash.

i. Selling merchandise on account.

j. Paying an account payable.

k. Paying property taxes.

P4.7 Transaction analysis. Prepare general journal entries for the following transactions:

a. Sold additional shares of share capital.

b. Borrowed money from a local bank and signed a note.

c. Purchased supplies for cash.

d. Rendered services and collected cash for those services.

e. Rendered services to customers who agreed to pay for those services within 30 days.

f. Purchased supplies on account.

g. Paid salary expense.

h. Paid office rent.

i. Collected cash from customers for whom services were previously performed.

j. Paid interest on the loan.

k. Used supplies in connection with performing services.

l. Repaid part of the bank loan principal.

m. Paid cash dividends to shareholders.

P4.8 Journalizing, posting, and preparing a trial balance. The following transactions were incurred by Leipert Enterprises during the month of May:

1. A corporation was formed and share capital was issued for $40,000 cash.

2. Obtained a long-term bank loan of $45,000.

3. Purchased land for $27,000 cash.

4. Goods/services received and used; paid $7,000 cash.

5. Obtained a long-term mortgage for $20,000.

6. Goods/services provided; received a promise for payment of $6,500.

7. Goods/services provided; received $6,600 cash.

8. Purchased office equipment for $6,100 cash.

9. Goods/services received and used; promised to pay $4,800 later.

10. Cash payment of $2,500 received on account re: transaction 6.

11. Sold land for $4,000 cash that had originally cost $4,000.

Required:

Using the accrual basis of accounting:

a. Prepare general journal entries for the above transactions.

b. Post the journal entries to the general ledger (T-accounts).

c. Prepare a trial balance.

P4.9 Account analysis. Up-n-Down Corporation has published annual financial statements since it first sold shares to a group of nonfamily-member investors. The company's balance sheets at December 31, 1995, and 1996, were as follows:

	1995	1996
Cash	$ 222	$ 17
Accounts receivable	7,523	8,003
Allowance for doubtful accounts	(116)	(170)*
Inventories	6,745	5,848
Prepaid insurance	805	632*
Deferred catalogue costs	1,519	2,483*
Land and buildings	4,344	4,344*
Equipment	2,858	3,268*
Accumulated amortization	(1,682)	(2,457)*
Total assets	$22,218	$21,968
Accounts payable	$ 8,022	$ 6,801
Bank borrowings	7,445	6,925*
Salaries payable	453	585
Taxes payable	1,111	1,298
Share capital	3,110	3,110*
Retained earnings	2,077	3,249*
Total liabilities and equity	$22,218	$21,968

Required:

For each of the accounts starred above, describe the transactions that might have accounted for the changes in the balances between the two years. Your descriptions should indicate whether the entry used to record the transaction(s) increased or decreased the account and what other accounts might have been affected by the other side of the entry.

P4.10 Account analysis. The T-account below depicts a number of transactions that increased and decreased the Cash account of Holcum, Ltd.

Cash

Balance — January 1	–0–		(e)	Paid for store equipment	10,000
(a) From share capital	10,000		(f)	Cash sales returned	500
(b) Bank loan payable	9,000		(g)	Paid merchandise	
(c) Cash sales	30,300			suppliers	53,600
(d) Collections on account	40,500		(h)	Paid rent	3,600
			(i)	Paid employees	14,600
			(j)	Paid for utilities	450
			(k)	Paid income tax	600
			(l)	Paid other expenses	500
			(m)	Loan payment, 1,500 on	
				principal, 450 interest	1,950
			(n)	Paid dividends	1,500
Balance — December 31	2,500				

Required:

For each of the identified entries (a through n), prepare a general journal entry.

P4.11 Resources and sources. Resourceful Products, Incorporated, includes the following asset accounts in its balance sheet.

a. Cash

b. Land

c. Merchandise inventory

d. Accounts receivable

e. Delivery truck

f. Factory building

g. Investments

Required:

Thinking about the basic accounting equation, where every resource has a source, list the most likely source or sources for each of the resources identified above.

P4.12 Event analysis. The accounting records of Cecil, Inc., include the following entries:

a.	Dr. Rent Expense	4,500	
	Cr. Prepaid Rent		4,500
b.	Dr. Unearned Revenue	27,000	
	Cr. Passenger Revenue		27,000
c.	Dr. Salaries Expense	4,950	
	Cr. Salaries Payable		4,950
d.	Dr. Repairs Expense	7,800	
	Cr. Accounts Payable		7,800
e.	Dr. Maintenance Expense	5,550	
	Cr. Spare Parts on Hand		5,550
f.	Dr. Accounts Receivable	3,800	
	Cr. Office Equipment		3,800
g.	Dr. Land	24,500	
	Cr. Cash		2,450
	Cr. Notes Payable		22,050
h.	Dr. Cash	6,900	
	Cr. Accounts Receivable		6,900
i.	Dr. Cash	12,000	
	Cr. Share Capital		12,000

Required:

For each entry, prepare a one-sentence description of the underlying event.

P4.13 Account balances. The Detail Corporation located in Taber, Alberta, maintains a complex accounting system because management likes to have a fully detailed financial statement every month, covering all phases of the company's operations, for their evaluation and planning meetings. Some of the accounts the company maintains are:

1. Cash in Bank.

2. Allowance for Doubtful Accounts.

3. Inventory.

4. Forklift Trucks.

5. Accumulated Amortization.

6. Flour Sales.

7. Interest Expense.

Required:

a. For each of the above accounts, indicate whether the account balance would normally be a debit balance or a credit balance. Provide a single sentence explaining why, in concept, the balance might normally be on that side.

b. For each of the above accounts, describe the nature of the entries that might affect the accounts; as part of that description, provide one illustrative entry affecting the debit side of the account and one affecting the credit side of the account.

P4.14 More complex events and the affected accounts. Consider the following series of events that were part of the activities of the Onetime Manufacturing Company during the year:

a. On June 30, the Treasurer called the company's banker and asked her to buy a short-term investment. The investment cost $100,000 and carried an interest rate of 10 percent, interest to be paid at maturity. At December 31, the company still had the investment.

b. On March 31, the company bought a lift truck to help move material around in the factory. The truck cost $25,000, but the dealer agreed to finance $20,000 of the purchase price. The company signed a five-year note for $20,000, at 10 percent interest.

c. To prepare for a substantial expansion, the company sold $10,000,000 of 10-year, 8 percent bonds on October 1. An investment banker helped put together the offering document, and a lawyer researched the legal aspects of the offering. The total of the professional fees paid to these two firms was $75,000. The bonds require semiannual interest payments and require that the principle be paid in full at maturity.

d. The company owned a piece of land next to its main plant, which they intended to use for the expansion discussed in c above. During December, the company paid an engineering company $50,000 to make soil tests on the land, and paid an architect $50,000 for a preliminary drawing of the anticipated new plant expansion. By the time December 31 had come, however, the economy had softened substantially, and there was now considerable question as to whether the market was really ready to buy more of the company's products. It was decided to put the expansion plans on the back burner for at least a year.

Required:

For each of the above events, describe the nature of the accounts that would be affected (asset, liability, equity, etc.) at the date of the event and as of December 31, and, in the context of the basic accounting equation, explain the rationale for your answer.

P4.15 Transaction analysis. The Bash Company, a retailer, was formed on July 1, 1996. During the month of July, the corporation experienced 11 different business transactions. At the end of the month, Bash prepared the following trial balance:

BASH COMPANY
Trial Balance
July 31, 1996

Account	Debit	Credit
Cash	$103,000	
Accounts receivable	6,500	
Inventory	10,000	
Equipment	120,000	
Accumulated amortization		$ 500
Accounts payable		50,000
Loan payable		120,000
Interest payable		1,000
Salaries payable		8,000
Share capital		50,000
Retained earnings		?
Total	$239,500	$239,500

Note the following:

1. All sales were on account.

2. All asset purchases were on credit, and no payments were made against these liabilities during the month.

3. No cash was paid for any of the expenses incurred during the month.

Required:

Based on the data contained in the trial balance, prepare the accounting entries for the transactions that occurred during July. The transactions may be recorded in any order.

P4.16 Transaction analysis. Below is a partial list of business events entered into by Duncan Wholesale Sporting Goods during the first fiscal quarter of 1996. Determine how each event, as of the date it occurred, would be recognized, if at all, in the 1996 financial statements. If the event should not be recognized, write not recognized. If the event should be recognized now for financial reporting purposes, indicate how (+ or −) and by what dollar amount each of the following financial statement components would be affected (if there is no change in a particular column, leave that space blank): cash flow, net current assets (current assets minus current liabilities), total assets, net assets (total assets minus total liabilities), and net income. (M = Million.) Hint: Set up a table with the financial statement components as column heads as shown below. Enter + or − and dollar amount or not recognized.

Cash Flow	Net Current Assets	Total Assets	Net Assets	Net Income

a. Purchased $8M of merchandise on account.

b. Sold merchandise for $5M cash (entry for sales only).

c. Recognized $4M cost of merchandise just sold (entry for cost only).

d. Borrowed $4M cash, issuing a 90-day, 10 percent note.

e. Paid $4M loan (*d* above) plus $.1M interest (for 90 days).

f. Received an order for $3M of merchandise to be shipped next quarter.

g. Collected a $.5M account receivable.

h. Bought equipment for $1M cash.

i. Signed a year's rental agreement for office space for $.1M a month.

j. Sold for $.4M cash a long-term investment that had cost $.5M (in prior years, the investment's market value fluctuated between $.6M and $.7M).

k. Paid cash dividends of $.2M.

l. The company has been told that its warehouse and material-handling equipment shown at $10M net would cost $15M if replaced today

m. Paid a $.3M account payable.

n. Recognized $.4M annual amortization on equipment.

o. Bought a $6M machine, paying $2M in cash and signing a 10-year note for the balance.

p. The board of directors authorized $10M for capital expenditures to be made next year.

q. Received notice of a lawsuit against the company for $1M.

r. Sold a machine that had a book value of $1.5M for $2.0M cash.

s. Discovered that, because of obsolescence, inventory that cost $.8M was estimated to have a net realizable value of only $.5M.

t. An account receivable of $.2M from a sale made during 1994 was determined to be uncollectible.

P4.17 Transaction analysis: Computer Corner, Inc. In the fall of 1995, Gary Reed inherited $100,000. He promptly quit his job, and he and his wife Connie decided to take $75,000 of the inheritance and start their own business. In January 1996, the Reeds opened Computer Corner, Inc., a small retail computer store. At the end of 1996, the trial balance of Computer Corner, Inc., appeared as follows:

COMPUTER CORNER, INC
Trial Balance
December 31, 1996

Account	Debit	Credit
Cash	$ 23,700	
Accounts receivable	39,300	
Accumulated amortization		$ 2,500
Allowance for doubtful accounts		4,000
Inventory	65,000	
Prepaid rent	4,000	
Property and equipment	25,000	
Accounts payable		25,000
Loan payable		30,000
Interest payable		3,000
Salaries payable		3,500
Common stock		75,000
Retained earnings		14,000
Total	$157,000	$157,000

The following information pertains to the business during its first year of operation:

1. Signed a five-year lease in January that stipulated a monthly rent of $4,000.

2. Borrowed $30,000 in January from a local bank. The term of the loan was five years and the interest rate was 10 percent.

3. Cash sales for the year totalled $200,000. Credit sales for the year totalled $180,000.

4. Inventory purchased during the year totalled $280,000. All inventory purchases were on an accounts payable basis.

5. Purchases of property and equipment for the year totalled $25,000 and were paid in cash.

6. Operating expenses for the year included the following:

Supplies	$ 3,500
Utilities	3,000
Insurance	2,000
Salaries	70,000
Advertising	6,500
	$85,000

Included in the salaries figure was $50,000 attributable to Gary and Connie Reed.

7. The Reeds withdrew $8,000 during the year that was not salary related.

Required:

Based on the information presented above in items 1–7 and in the December 31, 1996, trial balance, prepare the journal entries to record the activities of Computer Corner, Inc., for 1996, including the initial investment by the owners. Your entries do not need to be recorded in any particular sequence.

P4.18 Adjusting and closing entries, and preparation of income statement and balance sheet. Two trial balances as of December 31, 1996, for Terry's Repair Service are shown below. All accounts have normal balances. One trial balance includes the account balances before any adjusting entries having been made. The second trial balance reflects the account balances including all appropriate adjustments. Terry's Repair Service has a December 31 year-end.

	Trial Balance before Adjustments	Trial Balance after Adjustments
Accounts payable	$ 6,000	$ 7,000
Accounts receivable	9,000	12,000
Accumulated amortization	1,000	2,000
Advances from customers	1,000	2,000
Advertising expense	4,000	5,000
Building	20,000	20,000
Capital, Terry	19,000	19,000
Cash	5,000	5,000
Amortization expense	–0–	1,000
Insurance expense	–0–	1,000
Land	10,000	10,000
Mortgage payable, due 1999	25,000	25,000
Prepaid insurance	4,000	3,000
Revenues	27,000	29,000
Salaries expense	15,000	15,000
Supplies on hand	6,000	4,000
Supplies expense	–0–	2,000
Withdrawals, Terry	6,000	6,000

Required:

a. Prepare general journal entries to record the adjusting entries.

b. Prepare an income statement for Terry's Repair Service.

c. Prepare a balance sheet for Terry's Repair Service.

d. Prepare general journal entries to record the closing entries.

P4.19 Balance sheet classifications. Zipper, Limited, prepares a classified balance sheet each year with the following classifications: current assets, capital assets, current liabilities, long-term liabilities, and shareholders' equity. Zipper, Limited, has a December 31 year-end. Shown on the next page is a **partial** trial balance for Zipper, Limited: All accounts have a normal balance.

Adjusted Trial Balance
December 31

Accounts payable	$24,000
Accounts receivable	35,000
Accumulated amortization	19,000
Advances from customers	4,000
Allowance for doubtful accounts	3,000
Bad debt expense	1,000
Bonds payable	20,000
Cash	11,000
Common shares (no par value)	15,000
Amortization expense	5,000
Dividends declared	5,000
Equipment	59,000
Interest expense	3,000
Interest payable	5,000
Land	21,000
Mortgage payable	27,000
Patent	18,000
Patent expense	3,000
Prepaid rent	4,000
Preferred shares (no par value)	7,000
Rent expense	5,000
Retained earnings	12,000
Revenues	49,000
Temporary investments	15,000

Required:

a. Determine the following:

(1) Total current liabilities of Zipper, Limited, on December 31.

(2) Total capital assets of Zipper, Limited, on December 31.

(3) Total current assets of Zipper, Limited, on December 31.

b. Prepare an income statement for the year ended December 31.

c. Prepare closing entries.

P4.20 Adjusting entries. For each of the unrelated accounts given below, the unadjusted balances and the balances they should have after adjusting entries have been made are indicated. You may assume all accounts have their normal balances.

		Unadjusted Balance	Adjusted Balance
1	Supplies on hand	$ 940	$ 410
2	Prepaid insurance	560	340
3	Customer deposits	880	370
4	Accumulated amortization	4,000	4,800
5	Interest receivable	–0–	300
6	Salaries payable	–0–	990

Required:

For each item listed above prepare the most probable general journal entry for each adjustment.

P4.21 Adjusting and Closing entries (*Published with permission of CGA Canada*). The December 31 unadjusted and adjusted trial balances of Jane's Shoppe appear below:

	Unadjusted Balance		Adjusted Balance	
	Dr.	Cr.	Dr.	Cr.
Cash	$ 2,875		$ 2,875	
Accounts receivable	2,000		2,000	
Shop supplies	1,762		725	
Shop equipment	5,125		5,125	
Accumulated amortization		$ 725		$ 1,200
Accounts payable		575		575
Jane Tone, capital		5,500		5,500
Jane Tone, withdrawals	30,000		30,000	
Revenue from repairs		55,785		55,585
Rent expense	2,500		2,400	
Wages expense	18,250		18,638	
Miscellaneous expense	73		73	
	$62,585	$62,585		
Shop supplies expense			1,037	
Amortization expense			475	
Wages payable				388
Advances from customers				200
Prepaid rent			100	
			$63,488	$63,488

Required:

a. Prepare the indicated adjusting entries.

b. Prepare the resulting closing entries.

P4.22 Chart of accounts. Using the adjusted trial balance provided on page 168, prepare a chart of accounts for the Blue Ridge Hardware Company, Ltd.

P4.23 Ratio analysis. For the year ended March 31, Flutie, Ltd., had total assets of $123,000 and total liabilities of $64,000. Included in the total liabilities were current liabilities of $44,000. Net income for the year was $22,000. In determining the preceding balances, the accountant failed to make the following adjusting entries: accrued revenues of $21,000, amortization expense of $13,000, and accrued expenses of $3,000. Determine the revised net income, the return on equity ratios, and the long-term debt-to-invested capital ratios before and after the adjustments are considered. Do you think the omission of the adjusting entries will have a material impact on the financial statements of Flutie, Ltd.?

P4.24 Impact of adjusting entries. Beare Enterprises, Ltd., has completed its first year of operations. The company's accountant has prepared a draft copy of an income statement showing a net income before adjustments of $62,500. A discussion with the accountant reveals the following information, which has not been taken into consideration when drafting the income statement:

Accrued interest revenue of $800 has not been included in net income.

Bad debts are estimated at 3 to 5 percent of sales. Sales for the current year were $225,000.

Machinery costing $24,000 is estimated to have a useful economic life of 8 to 10 years, with no residual value.

Accrued expenses of $3,300 have not been included in net income.

There is no previous data on which to base adjustments because this is the first year of operations for the company. The objective of financial reporting for the company is to maximize its profits each year. You have been asked to determine a revised net income figure.

P4.25 Adjusting entries. For each of the *unrelated* accounts given below, the unadjusted balances and the balances they should have after adjusting entries have been made are indicated. All accounts have their normal balances.

		Unadjusted Balance	Adjusted Balance
1	Supplies expense	$ 870	$ 1,150
2	Prepaid rent	2,500	2,650
3	Sales	56,700	59,200
4	Accumulated amortization	20,200	22,800
5	Interest expense	3,100	4,000
6	Salaries payable	1,000	1,400

Required:

For the accounts listed above, prepare the most probable general journal entry for each adjustment.

P4.26 Financial statement preparation. Using the following information taken from the trial balance of Shaw Enterprises, Ltd., prepare an income statement and a classified balance sheet for the year ending December 31:

Accounts receivable	$ 35,100
Accounts payable	32,000
Accumulated amortization	5,000
Advertizing expense	7,500
Building	30,000
Cash	6,100
Cost of goods sold	216,000
Amortization expense	1,300
Dividends paid	7,000
Income tax expense	10,000
Income tax payable	7,000
Interest expense	3,200
Land	20,600
Long-term debt	16,000
Merchandise inventory	23,000
Notes receivable (due in two years)	7,800
Salaries expense	18,000
Salaries payable	800
Sales	275,000
Share capital	33,000
Supplies expense	2,500
Supplies inventory	1,700
Retained earnings, January 1	21,000

P4.27 Statement of changes in financial position. Tom's Cleaning Service is a sole proprietorship operated by Tom Slater. Tom's Cleaning Service had the following transactions during the year ending December 31, 1996:

Net income for the proprietorship for 1996 was $17,000.

Accounts receivable increased $6,000 during the year.

Tom invested additional capital of $4,000.

Supplies inventory increased by $2,000.

Tom withdrew $2,000 cash from the proprietorship.

Cash balance at January 1, 1996, was $7,000.

Amortization expense for the year was $6,000.

Purchased equipment for $11,000.

Obtained a long-term loan of $10,000.

Accounts payable increased $3,000 during the year.

Equipment with accumulated amortization of $6,000 that originally cost $11,000 was sold for $5,000.

Required:

a. Using the above information, prepare a statement of changes in financial position for the year ended December 31, 1996.

b. Prepare a schedule showing the changes in owner's equity during the year. On January 1, 1996, the balance in Tom's capital account was $7,000.

P4.28 The accounting process. Gerry Gowan started her own business as a proprietorship and completed the following transactions for the year ending December 31.

1. Gerry invested $3,000 of her personal savings in the business.

2. Paid $50 cash for office supplies.

3. Purchased equipment for $450 on account.

4. Earned revenue of $100; paid in full.

5. Paid $200 on account re: purchase of equipment.

6. Earned revenue of $300; to be paid later.

7. Paid utility bill for $25.

8. Collected $100 on account.

Required:

a. Record the transactions in the general journal.

b. Post the transactions to the general ledger (T-accounts).

c. Prepare adjusting entries (journalize and post to T-Accounts) based on the following information:

Equipment has a five-year life and no residual value.
At the end of the accounting period, $25 of office supplies were on hand.
Included in revenues is $10 received in advance (unearned revenue).

d. Prepare a trial balance.

e. Prepare financial statements for the year ending December 31.

f. Prepare closing entries (journalize and post to T-accounts).

g. Prepare a post-closing trial balance.

P4.29 Financial analysis. Using the financial information presented below for Andres Wines, Ltd., perform a comparative analysis of the company. Your answer should include comments on your findings.

ANDRES WINES, LTD.
Consolidated Balance Sheets
As at March 31, 1994, and March 31, 1993

	1994	1993
Assets		
Current assets:		
Cash and short-term investments	$11,994,807	$20,261,558
Accounts receivable	5,119,971	4,539,764
Inventories of wine and supplies	20,613,067	20,940,719
Prepaid expenses	415,539	528,353
	38,143,384	46,270,394
Fixed assets	11,786,537	10,937,533
	$49,929,921	$57,207,927
Liabilities		
Current liabilities		
Accounts payable and accrued liabilities	$ 4,340,519	$ 3,162,957
Dividends payable	666,660	661,451
Income and other taxes payable	1,098,450	1,122,898
Current portion of long-term debt	175,000	175,000
	6,280,629	5,122,306
Long-term debt	1,091,000	1,301,000
Deferred income taxes	1,266,000	1,514,000
Minority interest in net assets of subsidiary companies	302,653	289,842
	8,940,282	8,227,148
Shareholders' Equity		
Capital stock*	3,220,492	2,332,367
Retained earnings	37,769,147	46,648,412
	40,989,639	48,980,779
	$49,929,921	$57,207,927
*Number of shares outstanding	4,593,404	4,491,404

Signed on behalf of the Board

Director

Director

ANDRES WINES, LTD.
Consolidated Statements of Earnings
For the Years Ended March 31, 1994, and March 31, 1993

	1994	1993
Sales	$55,835,190	$56,359,652
Costs and expenses:		
Manufacturing, selling, and administration	47,816,935	47,471,626
Depreciation	1,221,164	1,235,989
Interest on long-term debt	144,332	162,269
	49,182,431	48,869,884
	6,652,759	7,489,768
Provision for income taxes:		
Current	2,839,000	3,118,000
Deferred	(248,000)	(73,000)
	2,591,000	3,045,000
	4,061,759	4,444,768
Minority interest in net earnings of subsidiary companies	13,483	18,290
Net earnings for the year	$ 4,048,276	$ 4,426,478
Earnings per share:		
Basic	$ .88	$ .99
Fully diluted	$ .87	$ .96

ANDRES WINES, LTD.
Consolidated Statements of Retained Earnings
For the Years Ended March 31, 1994, and March 31, 1993

	1994	1993
Balance — beginning of year	$46,648,412	$44,841,538
Net earnings for the year	4,048,276	4,426,478
	50,696,688	49,268,016
Dividends:		
Class A and Class B	12,907,552	2,599,615
Preference	19,989	19,989
	12,927,541	2,619,604
Balance — end of year	$37,769,147	$46,648,412

P4.30 Financial analysis. Using the financial information presented below for Coca-Cola Beverages, Ltd., perform a comparative analysis of the company. Your answer should include comments on your findings.

COCA-COLA BEVERAGES, LTD.
Consolidated Balance Sheets
As at December 31
(in thousands)

	1993	1992
Assets		
Current assets:		
Cash	$ 13,480	$ 13,681
Trade accounts receivable	69,277	77,314
Income taxes recoverable	—	23,407
Inventories	51,624	68,369
Prepaid expenses and other assets	13,665	18,069
	148,046	200,840
Land, buildings, and equipment	283,072	393,162
Assets to be sold	24,507	—
Deferred income taxes	25,505	—
Deferred pension surplus	10,783	8,765
Franchise assets	215,636	221,940
	$707,549	$824,707
Liabilities and Shareholders' Equity		
Current liabilities:		
Accounts payable and accrued expenses	$160,312	$116,909
Due to related companies	24,643	12,185
Current portion of long-term debt	—	7,850
	184,955	136,944
Long-term debt	411,512	386,412
Deferred income taxes	—	37,005
	596,467	560,361
Shareholders' equity:		
Share capital*	271,879	280,688
Deficit	(160,797)	(16,342)
	111,082	264,346
	$707,549	$824,707
*Number of shares outstanding	40,102	40,102

Approved by the Board,

Director

Director

COCA-COLA BEVERAGES, LTD.
Consolidated Statements of Earnings (Loss) and Retained Earnings (Deficit)
Year Ended December 31,
(in thousands except per share amounts)

	1993	1992
Net operating revenues	$ 882,257	$894,967
Cost of sales	556,604	604,132
Gross profit	325,653	290,835
Selling, administrative, and general expenses	299,271	305,968
Amortization of franchise assets	6,304	6,234
Operating income (loss)	20,078	(21,367)
Interest expense	45,086	45,624
Other deductions	1,705	4,671
Restructuring provision	165,500	—
Loss before income taxes	(192,213)	(71,662)
Income tax recovery	53,180	26,613
Net loss for the year	(139,033)	(45,049)
Preferred share dividends	(3,918)	(4,938)
Net loss available to common shareholders	$(142,951)	$ (49,987)
Net loss per common share	$ (3.56)	$ (1.25)
Retained Earnings (Deficit)		
Balance at beginning of year	$ (16,342)	$ 35,649
Net loss for the year	(139,033)	(45,049)
Dividends		
Common shares	(1,504)	(2,004)
Preferred shares	(3,918)	(4,938)
Balance at end of year	$(160,797)	$ (16,342)

P4.31 Financial analysis. Using the financial information presented below for Maple Leaf Foods, Inc., perform a comparative analysis of the company. Your answer should include comments on your findings.

MAPLE LEAF FOODS, INC.
Consolidated Balance Sheets
As at December 31
(in thousands of Canadian dollars)

	1993	1992
Assets		
Current assets:		
Cash and cash equivalents	$ 204,993	$ 253,118
Accounts receivable	230,685	224,301
Inventories	208,407	191,909
Prepaid expenses	10,276	9,239
	654,361	678,567
Investments in associated companies	49,268	58,528
Property and equipment	562,433	521,832
Other assets	49,107	35,040
Goodwill	185,534	125,051
	$1,500,703	$1,419,018
Liabilities and Shareholders' Equity		
Current liabilities:		
Accounts payable and accrued charges	$ 347,709	$ 290,695
Income and other taxes payable	21,515	50,072
Current portion of long-term debt	4,627	2,299
	373,851	343,066
Long-term debt	47,553	46,089
Deferred income taxes	42,767	39,825
Minority interest	50,593	45,410
Shareholders' equity:		
Share capital* and contributed surplus	840,632	840,392
Retained earnings	140,665	101,274
Unrealized foreign currency adjustment	4,642	2,962
	985,939	944,628
	$1,500,703	$1,419,018
*Number of shares outstanding	80,856	80,872

On behalf of the Board:

G.B. Ballantyne   L.N. Rose
Director   Director

MAPLE LEAF FOODS, INC.
Consolidated Statement of Earnings
Years Ended December 31
(in thousands of Canadian dollars except per share amounts)

	1993	1992
Sales	$3,034,917	$2,750,512
Cost of products sold	2,633,547	2,357,896
Selling, research, and administrative expenses	240,784	239,039
Depreciation	49,676	44,417
Amortization of goodwill	4,483	3,543
	2,928,490	2,644,895
Earnings from operations	106,427	105,617
Interest income	7,264	8,088
Other income	9,223	7,854
	16,487	15,942
Earnings before income taxes	122,914	121,559
Income taxes	45,603	46,270
Earnings before minority interest	77,311	75,289
Minority interest	7,190	6,107
Net earnings from continuing operations	70,121	69,182
Discontinued operations	—	3,311
Net earnings	$ 70,121	$ 72,493
Earnings per share		
Net earnings from continuing operations	$ 0.87	$ 0.86
Net earnings	0.87	0.90

MAPLE LEAF FOODS, INC.
Consolidated Statements of Retained Earnings
Years Ended December 31
(in thousands of Canadian dollars)

	1993	1992
Retained earnings, beginning of year	$ 101,274	$ 59,494
Net earnings	70,121	72,493
Dividends declared	(30,730)	(30,713)
Retained earnings, end of year	$ 140,665	$ 101,274

P4.32 Adjusting and closing entries, income statement (*Published with permission of CGA Canada*). The unadjusted trial balance was compiled from the records of Will Power's proprietorship at December 31:

Trial Balance

	Dr.	Cr.
Cash	$ 6,500	
Accounts receivable	100,000	
Inventory	45,000	
Supplies	2,270	
Prepaid insurance	2,840	
Equipment	75,000	
Accumulated amortization		$ 11,100
Accounts payable		5,000
Will Power, capital		182,000
Will Power, withdrawals	29,500	
Sales		416,307
Cost of goods sold	263,177	
Advertizing expense	1,250	
Rent expense	21,000	
Salaries expense	61,870	
Office expense	6,000	
	$614,407	$614,407

Additional data:

1. Expired insurance, $2,655.

2. Amortization on equipment, $7,900.

3. Supplies on hand, $550.

4. Uncollectible accounts, $2,000.

5. Estimated warranty expense, $4,450.

Required:

a. Prepare the adjusting entries.

b. Prepare the closing entries.

c. Prepare an income statement.

P4.33 Adjusting entry analysis (*Published with permission of CGA Canada*). Robin Company has completed 25 percent of its contract with Kinsman, Ltd., and has made the following adjusting entry on December 31.

```
Dr. Unearned Revenue  . . . . . . . . . . . . . . . . . . . . . . . . . . . . . .  4,325
   Cr. Fees Earned  . . . . . . . . . . . . . . . . . . . . . . . . . . . . . . . .        4,325
```

Required:

a. What must have been the original journal entry related to this contract with Kinsman, Ltd.?

b. State whether each of the following financial statement items are affected by the adjusting entry and if so by how much?

(1) Assets

(2) Liabilities

(3) Shareholders' equity

(4) Revenues

(5) Expenses

P4.34 Cash flow analysis (*Published with permission of CGA Canada*). The president of Take-It-For-Granite Rock Company has asked its accountant, Adam Upp, CGA, to determine how much cash was paid to merchandise creditors during the year. Adam extracted the following data:

Accounts payable, January 1, $12,000
Accounts payable, December 31, $8,000
Inventory, January 1, $40,000
Inventory, December 31, $48,000
Cost of goods sold, $290,000

Required:

Prepare a brief report for the president.

P4.35 Financial statement preparation, closing entries (*Society of Management Accountants of British Columbia*). Your friend Paul Price has operated Paul's Pool Repair Service for three months. He has never kept any bookkeeping records. He would like you to give him a picture of his financial situation. Paul provides you with the following information:

1. On May 1, Paul started the business with $10,000 cash from his savings.

2. Paul purchased some tools for $3,800 on May 1. These tools are foreign made and because of a change in the exchange rate, today they are worth only $3,200 new. Paul figures these tools will have to be replaced at the end of three years, at which time they will have no salvage value.

3. On May 1, Paul also purchased some used equipment from Harry's Pool Repair Service. The equipment had cost Harry $4,000 three years ago and had an estimated total life of seven years. Harry sold the equipment to Paul for $1,600. The total estimated life of the equipment has not changed.

4. Supplies of $500 were purchased during the period. Paul estimates $200 are still in inventory at July 31.

5. Paul paid $250 in wages for occasional help, and $100 is still owed July 31.

6. Paul has a rental truck. Rent of $900 was paid May 1 in advance for a three-month period. Mileage charges totalled $175. $50 remains unpaid. The truck rental has been renewed, but not paid.

7. Paul has sent invoices to his customers for all work performed so far. Total billings are $6,400. Of this, $3,300 has been remitted.

8. Paul took drawings of $2,000. He also took $50 worth of supplies home for personal use.

Required:

a. Prepare a balance sheet for July 31, and an income statement for the three-months period of operations.

b. Prepare closing journal entries for July 31.

P4.36 Adjusting entries (*Society of Management Accountants of British Columbia*). Azure Manufacturing prepares monthly financial statements. Its fiscal year is February 1 to January 31. The following information is available at Wednesday, February 28, 1997:   Wednesday

1. Salaries and wages are paid to employees each Friday. The weekly salary payroll is $15,000. Wage earned, but not paid, total $26,000.

2. Office premises are leased on an annual basis. On February 1, 1997, Azure made its quarterly payment of $3,000, in advance, and recorded the full amount as rent expense.

3. Manufacturing premises are owned. The land was purchased five years ago for $92,000. An appraisal prepared during the month indicated the land has a current market value of $155,000.

4. Azure owns manufacturing equipment that cost $72,000, with an estimated residual value of $6,000. It is expected the equipment will have a useful life of 60,000 machine hours. Equipment usage records show 33,600 hours of use to January 31, 1997, and 34,400 hours used to February 28, 1997.   15 months

5. Azure entered into two agreements with customers to manufacture skyhooks. The first contract was signed February 3, 1990, and was for production of 6,000 units at a total price of $18,900. Azure had expected to fill this order during February and, thus, recorded the sale on February 3. Due to a dispute over specifications, no units have been produced.

   The second contract, for 9,000 units at a total price of $27,900, was signed February 28, 1997. Production will be completed by March 31. No cash has been received for either of these contracts.

6. Interest accrued on Azure's debts consists of:

   Mortgage payable $2,000
   Equipment loan $500

Required:

Prepare all necessary adjusting journal entries for February 28, 1997. If an adjustment is not required, indicate the reason.

P4.37 Adjusting entries, balance sheet, income statement (*Society of Management Accountants of British Columbia*). Shown below is the unadjusted trial balance and other information relating to Randy Savage, a chartered surveyor.

RANDY SAVAGE, CHARTERED SURVEYOR
Trial Balance
December 31, 1996

Cash	$ 53,558	
Accounts receivable	15,500	
Allowance for doubtful accounts		$ 1,150
Survey supplies	2,120	
Unexpired insurance	840	
Capital assets	28,880	
Accumulated amortization		3,480
Note payable		6,000
Randy Savage, capital		64,640
Randy Savage, drawings	40,000	
Revenue from fees		110,000
Rent expense	10,010	
Salaries expense	32,180	
Utilities expense	1,412	
Miscellaneous office expense	770	
	$185,270	$185,270

1. Service performed for clients but not recorded by December 31, 1996, were $4,500.

2. An aging of adjusted accounts receivable has determined that 8 percent of the balance will probably not be collected.

3. Insurance expired during the year was $270.

4. Capital assets are being amortized at a rate of 10 percent of cost per year.

5. Rent on the building is $770 per month. The rent for 1996 has been paid, as has that for January 1991.

6. Salaries earned but unpaid at December 31, 1996 were $2,180.

7. The terms and conditions of the note payable are as follows:

Date borrowed:	December 1, 1996
Term:	90 days
Interest rate:	12% per annum

Required:

a. Prepare adjusting entries for December 31, 1996, from the information given above. No narratives are necessary.

b. Prepare in good form an income statement and a balance sheet for the year ending December 31, 1996. Ignore income taxes.

P4.38 Adjusting entries (*Society of Management Accountants of British Columbia*). Poison Printers had their first year-end December 31, 1996. Below are some of the 1996 transactions:

Jan. 2   Bought office supplies for $5,000 cash. At year-end $2,400 of supplies were still on hand.

July 1   Bought an offset printing machine for $20,000 cash and started using it. The machine has an estimated salvage value of $4,000 at the end of its estimated four-year life, and is to be amortized by the straight-line method.

Sept. 1   Bought a $9,600, two-year insurance policy for cash. The policy came into effect on this date.

Dec. 1   Received a $30,000, 90-day 9 percent note from a customer, replacing an account receivable in the same amount.

15   Rented out excess office space for a six-month period starting on this date, and received a $640 cheque for the first month's rent.

Required:

Use dates, but explanations are not required.

a. Prepare transaction journal entries for the above transactions.

b. Prepare any required December 31 adjusting journal entries.

P4.39 Adjusting and closing entries (*Published with permission of CGA Canada*). The December 31, 1996, trial balance for Glover Company, which provides sales and service to clients, was as presented below:

GLOVER COMPANY
Trial Balance
As at December 31, 1996

	Dr.	Cr.
Cash	$ 21,850	
Accounts receivable	23,600	
Allowance for doubtful accounts		$ 1,500
Merchandise inventory	18,750	
Unexpired insurance	5,600	
Machinery	710,500	
Accumulated amortization — machinery		186,200
Land	100,000	
Notes payable, 6%		360,000
Unearned service revenue		140,200
Common shares		145,400
Retained earnings		16,400
Dividends	6,200	
Sales		214,600
Sales discounts	500	
Sales returns	700	
Purchases	61,000	
Purchase returns		1,000
Administration expense	1,200	
Advertizing expense	8,100	
Interest expense	3,200	
Salaries expense	96,700	
Maintenance expense	5,400	
	$1,065,300	$1,065,300

The following additional information is provided for your consideration on December 31.

1. An aging analysis revealed that total receivables likely to be collectible amounted to $21,600.

2. An analysis of the prepaid insurance account reveals that $1,700 of the insurance premiums paid before December 31, was for insurance coverage in the next year.

3. The note payable was issued on December 1 and is due on February 28, next year.

4. The machinery has an estimated residual value of $20,000 and is amortized using the straight-line method over a 10-year period.

5. Unrecorded wages since the last payroll amounted to $300 as of December 31.

6. Upon examination of amounts collected from clients in advance for services, it is estimated that 70 percent of contracts with these clients have been completed.

Required:

a. Prepare a journal entry for each of the above items which requires an adjusting entry. If no journal entry is required then you must provide a comment which supports your answer. Round all amounts to the nearest dollar.

P4.40 Ratio analysis. For the year ended December 31, Demiee, Limited, had current assets of $92,000. Included in the current assets were quick assets of $39,000. On December 31 Demiee had current liabilities of $69,000. In determining the preceding balances, the accountant failed to make the following adjusting entries: amortization expense for $17,000, supplies used for $9,200, and accrued expenses for $14,000. Determine the quick and current ratios, before and after the adjustments are considered. Do you think the omission of the adjusting entries will have a material impact on the ratio analysis?

4.12 CASES

C4.1 Transaction analysis: Garland Creations, Inc.* Sandy Lawson had been determined to own her own company after completing her MBA. As an accomplished seamstress, she had always had a little business on the side making clothes for friends and specialty stores. The success of the Cabbage Patch dolls convinced her that there was money in stuffed toys. She decided that there was an unexploited niche for a family of animals, each having its own personality.

She took the savings of $7,044 that she had accumulated over the years and, with $263 worth of materials, set out to realize her dreams. Her family was very supportive and lent her $6,000 on a short-term note. She used $3,000 of this to purchase the specialized sewing equipment that she needed to make the animals.

From her years in the clothing business, she managed to find a supplier willing to let her have 90 day credit and invested in an additional $7,364 of materials on 90-day credit terms. Her own car was on its last legs, so she purchased a good secondhand pickup truck for $6,600 that she financed through a bank with a $1,600 deposit. One of her family members had an unused garage where she could set up her equipment. Installation of the equipment cost her $1,053. A year's insurance to cover the equipment cost an additional $1,000. A variety of different supplies necessary to get her operations off the ground absorbed another $963.

By the end of the first six months, she had made a substantial payment to her supplier, leaving a balance owed of $3,726 in the account. Sales had gone well and brought in a very welcome and reassuring inflow of cash totalling $12,325. She attributed these sales partly to the advertizement that she had run in a trade magazine that had cost her $2,442.

---

*This case was prepared by Michael F. van Breda. Copyright 1988 by Michael F. van Breda.

Although she had not been able to repay her family or the bank any of the capital that they had lent her, she had paid the family $360 in interest. Wages had totalled $10,697.

While everyone else headed off for New Year's Eve parties, Sandy Lawson sat down at her desk to determine how well her business had done in the first six months of its life. She had worked extremely hard making stuffed toy animals and was proud of the different personalities that she had been able to create. They surrounded her on all sides as she pored over the numbers.

The results, as she figured them, were very pleasing to her. They appear below.

GARLAND CREATIONS
Income Statement
For Six Months Ended December 31, 1989

Revenue		$12,325
Opening inventory	$ 263	
Purchases	7,364	
Wages	10,697	
Prepaid expenses	2,053	
Supplies	963	
Total	$21,340	
Less: closing inventory	16,005	
Cost of goods sold		5,335
Gross margin		$ 6,990
Advertizing expenses		2,442
Interest expense		360
Net income		$ 4,188

GARLAND CREATIONS
Balance Sheet
As of December 31, 1989

Cash	$ 616
Inventory	16,005
Current assets	$16,621
Equipment	3,000
Truck	6,600
Total assets	$26,221
Accounts payable	$ 3,726
Notes payable	6,000
Current liabilities	$ 9,726
Bank loan	5,000
Capital	7,307
Retained earnings	4,188
Total equities	$26,221

Required:

a. Using the description of events in the case and the financial statements provided, replicate the journal entries and the T-accounts Sandy prepared to record the first six months of her business.

b. Where you believe it appropriate, adjust her accounting to better reflect the events. Revise her statements accordingly.

c. Comment on how well the business has done.

C4.2 Overview of the accounting cycle: Photovoltaics, Inc.*

Photovoltaics, Inc., is a manufacturer and distributor of photovoltaic solar energy units. The company was founded in 1990 by Arthur Manelas and Harry Linn. Manelas, formerly a research scientist, had been operating a small photovoltaic manufacturing company when Linn, a marketing consultant to industry and himself an owner of a solar energy company, proposed the joint venture.

The founders planned to take advantage of a major shift in consumer attitudes from fossil fuel energy production to cleaner, cheaper energy generation using wind, water, or sun. The joint venture would merge Linn's marketing experience and access to capital with Manelas' prior manufacturing knowledge and government patent on the photovoltaic unit.

The development of photovoltaic technology had begun in 1954 when scientists at the Bell Laboratories found that crystals of silicon could turn sunlight into electricity. The scientists observed that an electric current was produced when photons, or light energy, would strike silicon atoms, thereby causing electrons to be released. The first application of this technology involved the space program: using photovoltaic solar cells to power the Vanguard I satellite in 1958.

Today, photovoltaic cells are used to power buoys in shipping channels, transmitters on mountain tops, and communication equipment on offshore drilling platforms. In remote locations in Indonesia, Africa, and Australia, where electrical service neither exists nor is cost justified, photovoltaic arrays are used to generate electricity to power such life-sustaining equipment as water pumps and medical refrigerators storing vaccines.

Compared with power generated from such traditional sources as hydroelectric-, coal-, or oil-fueled plants, early photovoltaic arrays were prohibitively expensive (e.g., $2,000 per peak watt). Recent technological advances, however, made the cells so efficient and economical (i.e., $1.85 per peak watt) that they were now competitive with existing alternative energy sources. Elmer B. Kaelin, president of the Potomac Edison Company, warned utility executives that the day was quickly approaching when "homeowners will have every incentive to install solar collectors and pull the plug on the electric company."

Convinced that excellent market opportunities for the solar arrays existed, Linn began preparing a prospectus that could be used to help raise capital to significantly expand Manelas' current operations. The two founders had located a manufacturing facility in Lethbridge, Alberta, that would cost approximately $8 million to acquire and equip with updated production equipment. Based on his prior experience, Linn knew that prospective investors would expect to see the following:

A statement of financial position classifying the company's assets and equities as they would appear at the preproduction stage.
A pro forma earnings statement for the first year of operations.
A pro forma balance sheet as it would appear at the end of the first year of operations.
A pro forma cash flow statement for the first year of operations.

In anticipation of preparing these reports, Linn collected the following information and arrived at the following projections:

---

*This case was prepared by Kenneth R. Ferris. Copyright 1990 by Kenneth R. Ferris.

Data related to preproduction transactions:

1. Ten million shares of common stock (par value $1) were authorized for sale by the charter of incorporation. Manelas received 500,000 shares in exchange for rights to the photovoltaic patent, and Linn received an equal number of shares after capitalizing the firm with $500,000 in personal funds.

2. Incorporation and attorney's fees amounted to $27,000.

3. The $8 million purchase price of the manufacturing facility and equipment was to be allocated as follows: building — $4.5 million, land — $750,000, and equipment — $2.75 million. In addition, raw materials and partially completed solar units had been purchased on credit from Manelas' original manufacturing company at a cost of $1.3 million. A note, secured by the inventory itself and accruing interest at a rate of 10 percent per annum on the unpaid balance, was issued to Manelas.

Projected data:

4. Sales of common stock to independent investors and venture capitalists would total 2.5 million shares. A selling price of $3.25 per share was set and transaction costs of 1.5 percent of the stock proceeds were projected.

5. Revenues from the sale of solar arrays for the first year were projected to be $480,000, with one-fifth of this amount estimated to be uncollected by year-end. The company had decided to follow a particularly rigid credit policy until operations were well established; hence, no provision for bad debts would be established because no uncollectible accounts were anticipated.

6. Cash purchases of raw materials were estimated at $70,000; the cost of units sold was projected at $215,000.

7. Insurance on the building, equipment, and inventory was expected to cost $2,700 per year.

8. Labour costs were estimated at $72,000; selling and administrative costs were projected at 2 percent of gross sales.

9. The useful life of the acquired assets were estimated as follows: building — 20 years and equipment — 10 years. Linn decided to write the patent off over its legal life of 17 years and the organizational costs (i.e., incorporation and attorney fees) over 5 years.

10. Salaries to Linn and Manelas were set at $20,000 each for the first year.

11. No principal repayments would be made on the 10 percent notes issued to Manelas during the first year of operations.

12. Income taxes would be calculated as follows:

Income Level	Tax Rate
$0–50,000	15%
$50,000–75,000	25
75,001–100,000	34
100,001–335,000	39
335,001–above	34

The company would be required to pay 80 percent of its taxes by year-end.

13. Fifty percent of net income after taxes would be distributed to investors as dividends.

Required:

a. Consider the informational needs of a developing company. Design an efficient accounting system for Photovoltaics, Inc. What accounts would be needed?

b. Prepare the three accounting statements needed for the prospectus.

c. As a prospective investor in the company, what factors would you look for in the accounting statements to help you decide whether or not to invest in the venture?

Accrual Basis of Accounting: Revenue Recognition

---- **Objectives** ----

After completing this chapter, you will be able to:
1. Discuss and apply revenue recognition concepts.
2. Discuss and apply expense recognition concepts and the matching principle.
3. Explain the importance of adjusting entries in preparing meaningful financial statements.
4. Describe different income statement classifications.
5. Analyze the financial statements using gross profit analysis and inventory turnover analysis.

Chapter 5 is the capstone chapter to Part I of the text. Part I may well be the most important section of the text, since it is here that we have explained the principles of the language of accounting and examined the basic financial reports. We have discussed generally accepted principles and illustrated the steps in the accounting cycle. We have introduced financial analysis as a means of understanding financial reports and the organizations behind the statements. In later chapters we will examine different methods of accounting for amortization and inventory costing models. We will look at the liabilities created when accounting for leases and pensions. Before we go on and examine the individual financial statement elements in more detail, this chapter reinforces the basic concepts and accounting procedures introduced in the first four chapters.

Chapter 2 discussed the investing and financial activities of the organization. The acquisition of non-current assets and the financing of such assets by issuing long-term debt or common shares is primarily a start-up activity of a firm. Financing and investing activities, while important to the firm, are not frequent or high in volume. The greatest portion of all organizations' activities involves operating transactions. Chapter 3 focussed on operating activities and the income statement. The key concepts related to the income statement are the matching principle, the accrual basis of accounting, and the recognition of revenues and expenses. These important concepts are the focus of this chapter. The income statement or operating transactions, of course, impact on the balance sheet and the statement of changes in financial position. The interrelationships of the basic financial statements are depicted in Exhibit 5.1.

E X H I B I T   5 . 1

Interrelationships of the Basic Financial Statements

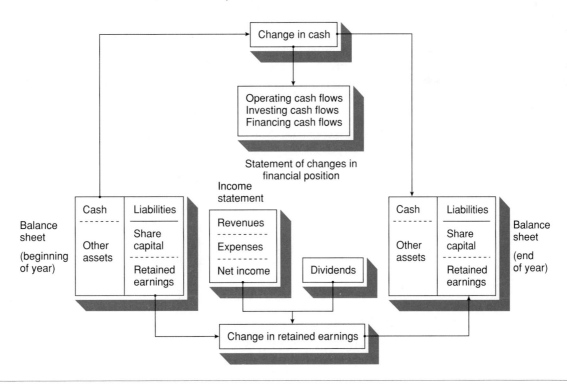

5.1 REVENUE RECOGNITION

Decisions about revenue recognition are among the most important accounting decisions a manager must make. For a simple transaction, for example, a retail sale of merchandise for cash, it is easy to determine which period's income statement should benefit — the revenue is recognized in the period when the merchandise and the cash are exchanged. For more complex transactions, such as the sale of a partially completed building in exchange for cash and a long-term note receivable, it is much more difficult to know whether a sale has really occurred and to decide *when* the revenue should be recognized. Should the sale be included in the income statement in (1) the period in which the parties agreed to the transaction, (2) the period the building is completed, or (3) the period the note is finally paid off in cash? Take a moment and think about when revenue should be recognized in the sale of a life insurance policy, the construction of a submarine for the Navy, or the provision of legal services. The recognition of revenue and the matching of related expenses is really a question of *timing*. Revenue and expense recognition involves the allocation of revenues and expenses to different accounting periods — that is adherence to the periodic concept. This process involves different estimates and the use of professional judgment to produce meaningful financial statements. If the users wished only reliable, objective information, they could wait until the end of the life of the organization to determine the extent of all revenues earned and expenses incurred. This would not, however, provide users with timely, relevant information. Therefore, revenues and expenses are recognized and allocated over the life of the organization.

Revenue should be recognized when certain performance requirements have been met.

> In a transaction involving the sale of goods, performance should be regarded as having been achieved when the following conditions have been fulfilled:
> (a) the seller of the goods has transferred to the buyer the significant risks and rewards of ownership, in that all significant acts have been completed and the seller retains no continuing managerial involvement in, or effective control of, the goods transferred to a degree usually associated with ownership; and
> (b) reasonable assurance exists regarding the measurement of the consideration that will be derived from the sale of goods, and the extent to which goods may be returned. (CICA Handbook 3400.07)

To make revenue recognition decisions — that is, to decide whether a company is entitled to recognize revenue from a transaction of the *current* period — management must answer three important questions:

1. Has the seller *transferred to the buyer substantially all of the risk/rewards* associated with the product sold or service provided?
2. Has the seller earned the *right to the proceeds* from this sale because the seller has completed his or her share of the transaction?
3. Is the *collectibility of proceeds* from this sale assured with a reasonable degree of certainty?

Transfer of Risk and Rewards

Has the seller transferred to the buyer substantially all of the risk and any rewards associated with the product sold or service provided? A seller almost always retains some risk related to an item sold as the result of its customer service policies, which provide for product return or repair under warranty. To qualify for revenue recognition at the time of an exchange, however, the transaction must burden the seller with only ordinary business risks that can be estimated with a reasonable degree of certainty, and provide an opportunity to benefit from any potential rewards. Almost every consumer product company recognizes revenue when its products are delivered to the customer, and such companies simultaneously recognize an expense and liability for the estimated warranty services that may be required. That is, the warranty expense is matched in the same period the sales revenue was recognized. If those future expenses cannot be estimated with reasonable accuracy — because, for example, it is a very new product and there is not sufficient experience to estimate what the rate of warranty repair will be — the sale itself should not be recorded but should be treated as a liability called *deferred revenue*. In such a case, the revenue would be deferred until the ultimate results from the transaction can be estimated more precisely.

Right to the Proceeds

Has the seller earned the right to the proceeds from this sale by having *completed* a substantial portion of his or her share of the transaction? The seller of a software package can answer that question affirmatively when the disks and the manuals are delivered to the customer — in that case, the delivery completes the earnings process because the company need do nothing more to the product to satisfy the customer. On the other hand, the producer of a custom-designed software cannot answer that question affirmatively until the software has been programmed, debugged, and tested successfully on the customer's hardware. Only when all of that has been done can the seller say that the earnings process is complete, and only then can the sale be recognized in the seller's income statement. In some very predictable long-term contract situations, the seller may be able to say that the earnings process is complete in phases and, as each phase is completed, recognize a pro rata share of the total expected revenue on the contract and the total expected cost of fulfilling that contract. This accounting convention is referred to as *percentage-of-completion* accounting and is illustrated in Section 5.2. Aside from that unique exception, however, sale transactions can be recorded as revenue only when management can objectively affirm that the company's earnings process has been completed.

Collectibility of the Proceeds

Can we objectively measure the collectibility of the proceeds from this sale with a reasonable degree of certainty? Under accrual accounting, a seller makes no distinction between cash sales and credit sales on the assumption that collectibility of any resulting receivable is reasonably assured and that any credit loss can be estimated and recorded coincident with recognizing the revenue. However, when the terms of a transaction or the financial status of a buyer raise serious questions about the collectibility of the receivable resulting from the sale, recognition of the revenue should be deferred until that credit question is resolved. In some questionable collectibility situations, the seller may be entitled to recognize revenue on an instalment basis; that is, the seller will recognize a pro rata portion of the total expected revenue and a pro rata portion of the total expected cost of the sale, as the cash payments are received. The question of collectibility is similar to the first question regarding transfer of risk — management must be able to estimate reasonably the amount of loss the company will incur as the result of a possible bad debt. If that loss cannot be reasonably estimated based on experience, the recognition of revenue must be deferred until that uncertainty is resolved.

Most companies' sales transactions are straightforward, and the financial statement user can assume that the preceding three questions were asked and answered in a routine fashion. However, when a company's business is complex, the footnotes to the financial statements will describe the revenue recognition policies being followed. For example, in General Motors' annual report, the company explains that it records a sale when it ships a car to an independent dealer rather than when the car is sold to the ultimate buyer. GM evidently follows that practice because it is confident that the dealer has assumed all substantive risk at the time of shipment.

Revenue Cases

Occasionally, a management group feels pressured to produce increasing net income numbers — the pressure may be from higher-level management or shareholders who want the company to perform well — and someone in the group will provide an inadequate or incorrect answer to one of the revenue recognition questions. Unless one of the other members of the group protests, the company's income will be misstated. That misstatement may keep income high for a period and forestall a day of reckoning in the marketplace. However, an incorrect answer to a revenue recognition question almost always becomes public, and the human and corporate cost to correct such misstatements is usually very great. Three cases involving misstatement are illustrated. You will note that in these cases more than one revenue recognition question was asked, and more than one *wrong* answer was given.

Case 1

A manufacturer of designer jeans maintained a policy of selling only to customers whose accounts receivable were current (i.e., if there was an unpaid balance, it included only the most recent month's purchases). However, at the end of a quarter when sales were below budget, an order came in from a major customer whose account was 90 days past due. At the direction of the CEO, the company recorded the sale in the period when the order was received but held the delivery, setting the jeans aside in the warehouse. The customer was told that the merchandise would be shipped when the customer's account was paid up to a current status. That transaction did *not* qualify for revenue recognition in the period when the order was received because, by the manufacturer's own policies, there was a question as to the collectibility of the receivable. Because of its refusal to ship the merchandise, the manufacturer retained all risk on the goods "sold." (Who bore the risk, for example, of a fire in the warehouse or of a dramatic change in styles?) Revenue could have been recognized in the period when the customer's account status was acceptable and when the product was shipped to the customer.

Case 2

A manufacturer of computer equipment maintained a policy to recognize revenue when its products were shipped, pursuant to a valid customer order. So long as the products were on the leading edge of technology, the policy was appropriate because shipment by the manufacturer was the equivalent of customer acceptance. However, there came a time when the competition caught up with the company's products, and customers frequently accepted shipment subject to testing against a competing product in their own installations. (Had the customer accepted all risk for the equipment?) The company's products didn't always win out against competitors, and many of its shipments were returned. When the business circumstances changed, the company's revenue recognition policies *should* have changed to recognize revenue only in the period when it had formal customer acceptance in hand. Only then could the company be sure that the risk had been transferred on the "sales" and that collectibility could be estimated with any reasonable degree of certainty.

Case 3

An operator of a computer service bureau also ran a school in which students from disadvantaged neighbourhoods were trained on word processors and other computer equipment. The teaching was provided by computer-driven programmed instruction, and the students worked on their programs in labs under the direction of proctors. The tuition was paid periodically by government grants as the students completed phases of the program. The company recognized all of the revenue from the course (less a provision for dropouts) as soon as a student signed up for the course. (Had the company essentially completed its portion of the transaction?) Revenue should not, however, have been recognized up front when the students signed up because to complete the earnings process and to ensure their estimates of dropouts, the company had to coach the students through the training and encourage their completion of the course work. Revenue should have been recognized only in the periods when the students completed phases of their course work, and the company completed that phase of its earnings process.

5.2 REVENUE RECOGNITION METHODS

Different revenue recognition methods exist to cover unusual situations or the peculiarities of special industries. Many organizations simply recognize revenue at the point of sale. At the time of sale, generally all the revenue recognition criteria have been met. That is, the buyer has accepted substantially all of the risk associated with the product or service provided, the seller has earned the right to the proceeds from the sale, and the collectibility of the proceeds is reasonably assured. The *point-of-sale* method of revenue recognition is by far the most commonly used method. However, circumstances may exist when it is deemed more appropriate to recognize revenue *before* the time of sale. When an organization is relatively sure its product can be sold and the selling price is known, and collectibility assured, it may recognize revenue at the *completion of production*. For long-term construction projects that spread over two or more accounting periods, to defer any revenue recognition to the point of sale would be misleading. For long-term contracts the *percentage-of-completion* method or the *completed-contract* method may be used. Other industries and circumstances may require revenue to be recognized *after* the time of the sale. When the point-of-sale method is used, the collectibility of the proceeds from the sale are reasonably assured. At the same time, it is realized some accounts may prove to be uncollectible. Therefore, the point-of-sale method would normally also provide for the recognition of bad debt expense for estimated uncollectible accounts to be matched against the revenue recognized. In situations where the collectibility of cash is very uncertain, the *instalment sales* or the *cost recovery* methods are deemed appropriate. These revenue recognition methods are discussed below and summarized in Exhibit 5.2.

For long-term contracts the revenue recognition criteria are not as straightforward as with the point-of-sale method. Uncertainty exists as to the transfer of the risks and rewards associated with the asset. The rights to the proceeds are usually established by contract. The collectibility of the proceeds may be in doubt because of the length of the contract. For example, the construction of a large building or factory may take several years. The length of the project will increase its level of risk and uncertainty. The percentage-of-completion method or the completed-contract method may be used to account for long-term contracts. The annual report of CAE, Inc., provided information on the company's policy of revenue recognition for long-term contracts:

> Revenue from long-term commercial and military contracts is recognized using percentage of completion method, where sales, earnings and unbilled accounts receivable are recorded as related costs are incurred. Profit sales are adjusted

EXHIBIT 5.2

Revenue Recognition Methods

When Revenue Recognized

Before Sale (During/end of production)	Time of Sale	After Sale (Cash collection)
Percentage-of-completion method		Instalment sales method
Completed-contract method	Point-of-sale method	
Completion-of-production method		Cost recovery method

currently as a result of revisions to projected contract revenues and estimated cost at completion. Losses, if any, are recognized fully when first anticipated. All other revenue is recorded and related costs transferred to cost of sales at the time the product is shipped or the service is provided.

Percentage-of-Completion Method

percentage-of-completion method A revenue recognition method in which total contract revenues are allocated between several accounting periods on the basis of the actual work completed.

"Percentage of completion method is a method of accounting that recognizes revenue proportionately with the degree of completion of goods or services under a contract" (CICA Handbook 3400.05). The percentage-of-completion method is used when performance consists of the execution of more than one act and revenue is to be recognized upon the completion of each act. Revenue should be recognized on a proportionate basis, dependent on the costs incurred to date and the estimated percentage of completion.

Completed-Contract Method

completed-contract method A revenue recognition method in which contract revenues are unrecognized until the contract is substantially completed.

"Completed contract method is a method of accounting that recognizes revenue only when the sale of goods or the rendering of services under a contract is completed or substantially completed" (CICA Handbook 3400.04). The completed-contract method defers the recognition of any revenue until the long-term project is completed. The completed-contract method is deemed appropriate when performance consists of the execution of a single act or when the organization cannot reasonably estimate the extent of progress toward completion.

Completion-of-Production Method

completion-of-production method If upon completion of production the revenue recognition criteria have been met, it is appropriate to recognize revenue at that time.

If upon **completion of production** the revenue recognition criteria have been met, it is appropriate to recognize revenue at that time. This method is not used extensively, but may be appropriate for some organizations. The prime criteria would be reasonable assurance that the product can be sold, at a determinable price, and that an identifiable seller exists. If the organization has a very saleable product, and a creditworthy customer, revenue may be recognized prior to the point of sale, that is, on the completion of production.

Point-of-Sale Method

point of sale
At the point of sale, goods or services are rendered in exchange for cash or a promise to pay (receivable).

The point-of-sale method is the most commonly used revenue recognition method. At the **point of sale**, goods or services are rendered in exchange for cash or a promise to pay (receivable). The risk of ownership is transferred to the buyer and the proceeds from the sale are earned by the seller. Any uncertainty with respect to the collectibility of the proceeds is provided for by matching bad debt expense against the earned revenue. As a result, the criteria for revenue recognition have been met. All related expenses should be matched in the same period revenue is recognized. Most retail transactions occur in this manner.

Instalment Sales Method

instalment sales method
A method of recognizing revenue that parallels the receipt of cash.

In situations where uncertainty exists as to the collectibility of the proceeds of the transactions, revenue recognition is deferred until the proceeds are collected. Organizations that have a large portion of sales returns may also wish to delay revenue recognition. Under the **instalment sales method**, it is assumed such uncertainties do exist. Therefore it is deemed appropriate to recognize revenue *only* as cash is received. The instalment sales basis is not widely used. Many managers would not wish to be involved in transactions with high levels of risks and uncertainties. However, the instalment sales method is often used in the real estate and publishing industries.

Cost Recovery Method

cost recovery method
Under the cost recovery method, all costs incurred must be recovered before any profit is recognized.

The **cost recovery method** is only used for high-risk transactions, in which the realization of any profit is highly speculative. Under this method *all* costs incurred must be recovered *before* any profit is recognized. The cost recovery method is not commonly used. Most managers would be averse to entering into such highly speculative business transactions.

Revenue Recognition Methods: An Illustration

We now illustrate the accounting for the different revenue recognition methods. Most revenue transactions involve additional expenses to be matched against the revenue recognized. However, not all relevant expenses are illustrated herein. We illustrate only those methods that are appropriate due to the assumed circumstances of the example.

Banman Construction has a contract to construct an office building in downtown Moose Jaw. The contract price is $7,000,000, with estimated costs of $5,400,000. It is estimated the project will take three years to complete. At the end of the first year, costs of $2,200,000 had been incurred. In the second year additional costs of $1,900,000 were incurred. In Year 3 costs of $1,300,000 were incurred and the project was completed. Exhibit 5.3 summarizes the revenue and related costs to be recognized each under each method.

Percentage-of-completion method. The percentage-of-completion method is a complex method, dealing with holdbacks, construction in progress, and other complexities. An intermediate accounting text should be referred to for coverage of these additional issues. The basic concept of spreading the recognition of revenue over more than one accounting period is illustrated in the following entries. The percentages of completion were determined in Exhibit 5.3.

E X H I B I T   5 . 3

	Completed-Contract Method			Percentage-of-Completion Method		
Year	Revenue	Expense	Net	Revenue	Expense	Net
1	—	—	—	$2,850,000*	$2,200,000	$ 650,000
2	—	—	—	2,460,000†	1,900,000	560,000
3	$7,000,000	$5,400,000	$1,600,000	1,690,000‡	1,300,000	390,000
Totals	$7,000,000	$5,400,000	$1,600,000	$7,000,000	$5,400,000	$1,600,000

*($2,200,000/$5,400,000)=41%; .41($7,000,000)=$2,850,000.

†($1,900,000/$5,400,000)=35%; .35($7,000,000)=$2,460,000.

‡($1,300,000/$5,400,000)=24%; .24($7,000,000)=$1,690,000.

```
Year 1   Accounts Receivable ........................  2,850,000
             Revenue — Construction  ...........................2,850,000
         Revenue recognized (41% complete).
         Cost of Construction ........................  2,200,000
             Cash, Payables, etc. ..............................2,200,000
         Cost of construction (41%).
Year 2   Accounts Receivable ........................  2,460,000
             Revenue — Construction  ...........................2,460,000
         Revenue recognized (35% complete).
         Cost of Construction ....................... 1,900,000
             Cash, Payables, etc. ..............................1,900,000
         Cost of construction (35%).
Year 3   Accounts Receivable ........................  1,690,000
             Revenue — Construction  ...........................1,690,000
         Revenue recognized (remaining 24%).
         Cost of Construction ....................... 1,300,000
             Cash, Payables, etc. ..............................1,300,000
         Cost of construction (remaining 24%).
```

The percentage-of-completion method recognizes a portion of the total revenue each year based on the percentage of the project that has been completed at each year-end. All related expenses should be matched in the appropriate accounting period.

Completed-contract method. The entries to recognize the revenue using the completed-contract method are shown below. The percentages of completion were determined in Exhibit 5.3. No revenue is recognized until Year 3 when the project is fully completed.

```
Year 1   No revenue is recognized in Year 1.
         Cost of Construction Inventory ...............  2,200,000
             Cash, Payables, etc. ..............................2,200,000
         Cost of construction (41%).
Year 2   No revenue is recognized in Year 2.
         Cost of Construction Inventory ...............  1,900,000
             Cash, Payables, etc. ..............................1,900,000
         Cost of construction (35%).
Year 3   Accounts Receivable ........................  7,000,000
             Revenue — Construction  ...........................7,000,000
         100% of revenue is recognized in Year 3.
         Cost of Construction Inventory ...............  1,300,000
             Cash, payables, etc. ..............................1,300,000
         Cost of construction (remaining 24%).
         Cost of Construction .......................  5,400,000
             Cost of Construction Inventory .....................5,400,000
         To transfer the total cost from inventory.
```

The Year 3 entry records all of the revenue. It is unlikely any organization would delay trying to collect their accounts receivable until the project had been completed. To help finance the project, progress billings would have been made during the construction progress. These entries have not been illustrated.

Completion of production method. When the revenue recognition criteria have been met to enable the recognition of revenue upon completion of production, an inventory account must be established. The inventory account for the finished product is valued at the selling price of the product. The revenue is recognized and the costs matched against this same revenue. Later, at the point of sale, since revenue has already been recognized, an entry is made to eliminate the inventory account and create an accounts receivable account from the customer. It is assumed these transactions *all* take place in Year 1. The entries to recognize the revenue using the completion of production method are shown below:

```
Year 1   Finished Goods Inventory . . . . . . . . . . . . . . . . . . . .  7,000,000
              Sales . . . . . . . . . . . . . . . . . . . . . . . . . . . . . . . . . . . . . . .7,000,000
         Revenue recognized at the end of production.
         Cost of Goods Sold  . . . . . . . . . . . . . . . . . . . . . . .  5,400,000
              Cash, Payables, etc.  . . . . . . . . . . . . . . . . . . . . . . . . . . .5,400,000
         Cost of goods sold matched against revenue earned.
         Accounts Receivable . . . . . . . . . . . . . . . . . . . . . . .  7,000,000
              Finished Goods Inventory . . . . . . . . . . . . . . . . . . . . . . . . .7,000,000
         At the point of sale, the inventory account is reclassified as a receivable.
```

Point-of-Sale Method. The point-of-sale method of revenue recognition has been assumed for many previously illustrated transactions. Assuming the total sale is made in Year 1, the entries to recognize the revenue at the point of sale are shown below:

```
Year 1 Accounts Receivable . . . . . . . . . . . . . . . . . . . . . . .  7,000,000
              Sales . . . . . . . . . . . . . . . . . . . . . . . . . . . . . . . . . . . . . . .7,000,000
         Revenue recognized at the point of sale.
         Cost of Goods Sold  . . . . . . . . . . . . . . . . . . . . . . .  5,400,000
              Inventory . . . . . . . . . . . . . . . . . . . . . . . . . . . . . . . . . . . . . .5,400,000
         Cost of goods sold matched against revenue earned.
```

Instalment Sales Method. When the instalment sales method is used, uncertainty exists as to the collectibility of the proceeds. Therefore, no revenue is recognized until cash is received, and any costs associated with the product are treated as inventory until cash is collected. When the cash is collected, the revenue is recognized and the related costs matched against the revenue. The data from Exhibit 5.3 have been used. The costs of the project are classified as inventory and then allocated and matched against revenue as cash payment is received. The entries to recognize the revenue on an instalment sales basis are shown below:

```
Year 1   Inventory  . . . . . . . . . . . . . . . . . . . . . . . . . . . . . . .  5,400,000
              Cash, Payables, etc.  . . . . . . . . . . . . . . . . . . . . . . . . . . .5,400,000
         Costs of the finished project.
Later    Cash . . . . . . . . . . . . . . . . . . . . . . . . . . . . . . . . . . .  2,100,000
              Sales . . . . . . . . . . . . . . . . . . . . . . . . . . . . . . . . . . . . . . .2,100,000
         Only when the cash is received is revenue recognized (2,100,000/
         7,000,000=30%).
         Cost of Goods Sold  . . . . . . . . . . . . . . . . . . . . . . .  1,620,000
              Inventory . . . . . . . . . . . . . . . . . . . . . . . . . . . . . . . . . . . . . .1,620,000
         30% of the total cost (.30×5,400,000) is matched against 30% of the total
         revenue of 2,100,000.
```

Revenue would continue to be recognized only when cash was received until the receivable had been collected in full. If the total amount of the contract is not collected, the balance in the inventory account would be written off as a loss.

Cost Recovery Method. The cost recovery method is similar to the instalment sales method, for uncertainty exists as to the collectibility of the proceeds of the contract. The cost recovery method is only used when *extreme* uncertainty exists with respect to the collectibility of the cash payments. Before *any* revenue is recognized all costs must be recovered. This method is not allowable for income tax purposes. The entries to recognize the revenue on the cost recovery basis are shown below:

```
Year 1   Inventory . . . . . . . . . . . . . . . . . . . . . . . . . . . . . .  5,400,000
              Cash, Payables, etc. . . . . . . . . . . . . . . . . . . . . . . . .5,400,000
         Costs of the finished project.
Later    Cash . . . . . . . . . . . . . . . . . . . . . . . . . . . . . . . . .  2,100,000
              Inventory . . . . . . . . . . . . . . . . . . . . . . . . . . . . . .2,100,000
         When cash is received, no revenue is recognized until costs have been
         recovered.
         Cash  . . . . . . . . . . . . . . . . . . . . . . . . . . . . . . . . .  2,100,000
              Inventory . . . . . . . . . . . . . . . . . . . . . . . . . . . . . .2,100,000
         Second payment received; total costs have not been recovered, so no
         revenue has been recognized.
         Cash  . . . . . . . . . . . . . . . . . . . . . . . . . . . . . . . . .  2,800,000
              Inventory . . . . . . . . . . . . . . . . . . . . . . . . . . . . . .1,200,000
              Revenue  . . . . . . . . . . . . . . . . . . . . . . . . . . . . . .1,600,000
         Total costs have been recovered. Any excess can now be recognized as
         revenue.
```

5.3 EXPENSE RECOGNITION

In preparing the income statement, questions concerning the recognition of both revenue and expenses must be addressed. Although the challenges to revenue recognition may be the most dramatic questions posed to management in connection with the preparation of the income statement, measurement of net income is also affected by costs and expenses. And, in fact, management must address similar questions regarding the recognition of expenses.

1. Have we included (*matched*) in our income statement all of the costs and expenses associated with the benefits (revenues) we realized during the year?
2. As we prepared these financial statements, have our judgments and estimates been appropriately *conservative*?
3. Do all of our assets still have the *potential to earn* future cash flows equal to their current costs? Have we recorded as liabilities all of the future expenditures we are likely to have to make?

Matching Principle

Have we included in our income statement all of the costs and expenses associated with the benefits we realized during the period? In an accrual accounting system, management's first obligation is to match expenses with revenues in the accounting period in which the benefits are realized. Some benefits are transaction based — the obvious example being sales to customers. In the case of sales, the matching principle requires that all costs and expenses connected with the sale be recognized in the

E X H I B I T 5 . 4

Matching Principle

```
                        ┌─────────────────────┐
                        │  Revenues (sales)   │
          ┌────────────→│  generate and are   │←────────────┐
          │             │     matched by      │             │
          │             └─────────┬───────────┘             │
          │                       │                         │
┌─────────┴────────┐   ┌──────────┴─────────┐   ┌───────────┴────────┐
│ Prior Period Cost│   │ Current Period Costs│   │ Future Period Costs│
│                  │   │                    │   │                    │
│ Cost of goods    │   │ Commissions expense│   │ Warranty expense   │
│ sold (inventory) │   │ Advertizing expense│   │ Bad debts expense  │
│ Insurance expense│   │ Operating expenses │   │                    │
│ Amortization     │   │ Interest expense   │   │                    │
│ expense          │   │                    │   │                    │
└──────────────────┘   └────────────────────┘   └────────────────────┘
```

same accounting period as the related revenue. Those costs and expenses to be matched against sales include some prior period costs that have been deferred as inventory until the period in which the product is sold. Other costs include the actual current period costs to make the sale, such as commissions, as well as certain future costs, such as the estimated cost of warranty work and estimated losses due to bad debts. Some benefits also flow to the company with the passage of time. For example, interest expense is an expense of the current period because the company has had the use of the borrowed funds for the period. Or an insurance premium paid in advance to cover three years' of insurance is recorded orginally as an asset (Prepaid Insurance); that asset is then allocated to insurance expense, one-third in each of the covered years. The application of the matching principle requires some thought — management must look carefully at the benefits realized during the *current* period and then think carefully about all the prior, current, and future expenses that might be connected with those benefits. Exhibit 5.4 displays the interrelationship of expenses from prior, current, and future periods with *current* period revenues, and the matching of revenues and expenses.

The matching principle may be explained in terms of the cause and effect relationship that exists between revenues and expenses. Some revenues cause expenses to be incurred and some expenses directly generate revenues. For example, when a revenue is earned, it causes a commission expense to be incurred and paid to the sales staff. Similarly, when advertising expenses are incurred, it is anticipated they will cause revenues to be earned. Most revenues and expenses have this cause and effect relationship, either directly or indirectly. It is management's responsibility to ensure these cause and effect relationships are *matched* in the appropriate accounting period. This normally requires adjusting entries to be made to allocate revenues and expenses among prior, current, and future periods. Maple Leaf Gardens, Limited, through its ownership of the Toronto Maple Leaf Hockey Club, has a number of employment contracts calling for advance payments (signing bonuses). These payments are made in anticipation of future revenue generation. Therefore, the expenditure is set up as a non-current asset called *Deferred Charges*. The financial statement note on deferred charges states:

The corporation has entered into employment contracts with certain of its employees which provide for initial cash payments. These cash payments are reflected on the balance sheet as deferred charges and are being amortized on a straight-line basis over the life of the employment contracts. Any unamortized balance relating to a terminated contract is written off in the period of termination.

Conservative Judgments and Estimates

As we prepared these financial statements, have our judgments and estimates been appropriately conservative? The decision as to whether an expenditure is an expense of the current period or whether it is an asset and is to be allocated to expense in future periods is sometimes a difficult one. Some managers argue that an expenditure has a clear benefit and should, therefore, be allocated to future periods. Others argue that the benefit is tenuous and the expense should, therefore, be recognized immediately. For example, some argue logically that an advertizing campaign is sure to build product awareness and customer loyalty. Because those benefits will produce future sales, it might be argued that some portion of those advertizing expenditures should be treated as an asset and deferred into future periods so that they can be matched against future sales. However, because those future benefits are uncertain (and because they are very difficult to measure), the principle of conservatism forces companies to recognize those expenditures as expenses in the period they are incurred.

In practice, management is often tempted to be optimistic. After all, an entrepreneur who has devoted three years to developing a new product must believe strongly in that product to have devoted so much time to it. It naturally follows that the entrepreneur is confident of success and, therefore, wants to match the costs of that product development with the expected future sales. Determining whether they have been appropriately conservative requires an extraordinary amount of objectivity from a responsible management group. It is also possible, however, to be too conservative. An overly conservative approach to the asset/expense decision results in an unduly pessimistic income statement for the current period and an unrealistically profitable picture in subsequent years. As in all key management decisions, the answer is balance: management must balance its application of the matching principle, which requires the deferral of some expenses until future periods, with its application of the conservatism principle, which stipulates that the only surprises that should arise in future years should be pleasant surprises.

Asset Earning Potential

Do all of our assets still have the potential to earn future cash flows equal to their current costs? Have we recorded as liabilities all of the future expenditures we are likely to have to make? In addition to our challenge of the income statement, we ought to challenge the balance sheet as well. GAAP require that an impairment of an asset and the recognition of a liability be recorded — and a charge to expense be recorded as well — when it is probable that an asset impairment/liability incurrence has occurred and when the amount of the expense can be estimated reasonably. In this context, *probable* is understood to mean that a future event confirming the impairment/incurrence is likely to occur.

Some expenses are probable because they are a natural consequence of a company's activities. For example, it is probable that a company that sells a consumer product with a warranty will incur some warranty expense, and so an estimate of that expense is recorded in the period in which the sales are recorded. Ford Motor Company of Canada, Limited, disclosed the following footnote on its accounting for product warranty costs: "Anticipated costs related to product warranty are recorded at the time of the sale of the products." Other expenses are probable because of forces outside the company, and so are recorded in the period that the outside events become probable. For example, a fashion goods manufacturer knows that its inventory is subject to obsolescence and so analyzes the inventory periodically and records an adjustment to the carrying value of its unsold products when they become unfashionable and difficult to sell.

Some expenses become probable over time as the asset impairment becomes more serious or the threat of a liability becomes more tangible. For example, when a company is sued, its lawyers are not likely to be able to estimate the probability of losing the suit or the possible cost of such a loss. As time goes on, however, they form a clearer picture of the litigation and have a better estimate of winning or losing. At an intermediate stage in the litigation, they may develop an opinion as to the probability of losing the suit, but they still may be a long way from being able to estimate the cost of such a loss. Thus, the company may be required to include a *footnote* to its financial statements warning of the possibility of such a loss, but the expected future liability is not recognized in the balance sheet, nor is the expense recognized in the income statement. Eventually, a time will come when a settlement is under discussion or when a judgment has been reached and the dollar cost of that lawsuit loss can be reasonably estimated. At that time, the liability and the expense connected with that lawsuit are recorded in the financial statements. Du Pont Canada, Inc., included a footnote in its annual report disclosing its commitments and contingent liabilities: "The company is subject to various lawsuits and claims arising out of the normal course of business. In the opinion of company counsel, any liability resulting from lawsuits and claims would not materially affect the consolidated financial position of the company."

As you have thought about the three revenue recognition questions and the three expense recognition questions, perhaps you have realized that the critical issues have to do with *timing*. Because the income statement presents the results of operations for a given period of time, all of the critical questions having to do with the preparation of the income statement are timing issues — when, in which period, should an event be recognized? For example, an expenditure for a new roof can be added to the cost of a building and amortized over the building's remaining life or it can be charged to maintenance expense all at once at the time of the expenditure. Intellectually, we might debate the nature of the expenditure — whether the new roof is an addition to the building or whether it is simple maintenance — but the practical effect of that debate would be a focus on the timing of the impact of that expenditure on net income. Because an income statement measures results over one period of time, and because income statements for a period of years measure trends of income, the timing of revenue recognition and expense recognition are critical. Management must use professional judgment to make those decisions as objectively as possible, to produce the fairest measure of results of operation for the period.

Expense Cases

To help you review your understanding of expenses and expense recognition, consider the following three cases. Note the expense questions asked and how they were answered in each case.

Case 1

A manufacturer of high-tech products was faced with increasing competition and was forced to produce new models of its product before all of the engineering was complete. To meet production schedules, it was necessary to do significant handwork on each unit, which was very expensive. It was decided to send that handwork to a subcontractor because of its cheaper labour rate. Apparently arguing that a failure in tool design caused the production problem and required the handwork, management had the subcontractor bill the handwork as tooling. The manufacturer accounted for those tooling charges as long-term assets and amortized them against income over five years. (Did the handwork have the potential to earn future cash flows?) The subcontractor agreed to the mislabelled billings because the job was important to their own income. Clearly, the handwork added no new value to the manufacturer and should have been accounted for as part of the current period's cost of sales. The fraud was uncovered when an employee of the subcontractor finally "blew the whistle" on the mislabelled billings.

Case 2

A cable TV company was experiencing much greater growth than it had anticipated. Management was concerned that the growth could not be sustained and so decided to "park" some of its current income for future years. To do so, it set up reserves and charged current operations with expenses for possible inventory obsolescence. (Were all costs and expenses associated with the current year's revenues appropriately recognized?) In later years, the growth did begin to slow down and eventually slowed disastrously. Rather than recognizing the effect of that slowdown in the income statement, management drew down on some of those reserves, crediting current income with a reversal of the prior years' expenses. This only postponed the inevitable, however, and the company eventually entered bankruptcy. The shareholders sued management because they were misled on the up side and the down side of the company's business cycle. The shareholders argued that they wanted to know the naked facts about the company's earnings, period by period, and that they had been misled by management's "smoothed" results.

Case 3

A bank had substantial loans outstanding to oil and gas producers at a time when oil prices collapsed. Looking at the collateral behind its loans, the bank realized that, under current conditions, the collectibility of these loans was very questionable. Management delayed making any addition to the bank's loan-loss reserve (and taking a current period charge to bad debts expense) because it had some studies suggesting that oil prices would eventually recover. (Were the bank's judgments and estimates sufficiently conservative?) Oil prices did not recover sufficiently, however, and the bank's major borrowers eventually collapsed. When that occurred, the bank had to make a major addition to its loan-loss reserve. The shareholders sued, arguing that management knew about the probability of the loan-loss problem much earlier and had it accounted for the probable losses conservatively, the shareholders would have had a fairer picture of the bank's operations much sooner.

Expense Recognition: An Illustration

The implementation of the matching principle requires management to carefully examine its current period revenues and determine which costs and expenses should be matched against that revenue. Such costs may have been incurred in the current period, or in prior or future periods. The operating activities of Rom's Computer Sales, Inc., will be used to illustrate expense recognition and the matching principle.

During the current period, the month of November, Rom's Computer Sales recognized revenue at the point of sale, for a total of $208,000. All revenue transactions were for the sale of computer equipment. During the month of November, $7,200 was incurred for advertising expenses. Loan payments during November included interest expense of $2,800 and loan principle payments of $9,900. Commission expense paid to sales staff for November is based on 5 percent of total sales for the current period. Other operating expenses for November were $11,300. The current period transactions are summarized below:

```
1.  Cash . . . . . . . . . . . . . . . . . . . . . . . . . . . . . . . . . . . . . . . . . . . 208,000
        Sales . . . . . . . . . . . . . . . . . . . . . . . . . . . . . . . . . . . . . . . . . .      208,000
        Sales for the current period.
2.  Advertizing Expense . . . . . . . . . . . . . . . . . . . . . . . . . . . . . . .   7,200
        Accounts Payable  . . . . . . . . . . . . . . . . . . . . . . . . . . . . . . .        7,200
        Advertizing for the current period.
3.  Interest Expense  . . . . . . . . . . . . . . . . . . . . . . . . . . . . . . . .   2,800
    Loan Payable  . . . . . . . . . . . . . . . . . . . . . . . . . . . . . . . . . . .   9,900
        Cash . . . . . . . . . . . . . . . . . . . . . . . . . . . . . . . . . . . . . . . . .       12,700
        Loan payments during the period.
4.  Commission Expense . . . . . . . . . . . . . . . . . . . . . . . . . . . . . 10,400
        Cash . . . . . . . . . . . . . . . . . . . . . . . . . . . . . . . . . . . . . . . . .       10,400
        Commission of 5% of sales was paid during the period (.05×208,000).
5.  Operating Expenses . . . . . . . . . . . . . . . . . . . . . . . . . . . . . . 11,300
        Accounts Payable  . . . . . . . . . . . . . . . . . . . . . . . . . . . . . . .       11,300
        Operating expenses for the current period.
```

Expenses incurred during the current period are usually easily identified and matched against the current period's revenues. Care must be taken to ensure costs incurred in previous periods that relate to the current period are identified and matched with current period revenues. A major expenditure from prior periods is the acquisition of inventory for resale. Prior to the month of November, the company would have acquired computer equipment for resale to its customers. When the revenue is recognized in the current period, the cost of goods sold must be determined. The cost of goods sold for November was $156,000. The identification of other expenses may require the use of adjusting entries. For example, insurance costs previously incurred, to be allocated to the current period, totalled $1,100. Amortization of capital assets, previously acquired, for the current period was $2,300. The *adjusting* entries for prior period cost allocations are summarized below:

```
6.  Cost of Goods Sold . . . . . . . . . . . . . . . . . . . . . . . . . . . . . . 156,000
        Inventory  . . . . . . . . . . . . . . . . . . . . . . . . . . . . . . . . . . . . .      156,000
        Cost of goods sold for the period.
7.  Insurance Expense . . . . . . . . . . . . . . . . . . . . . . . . . . . . . . .   1,100
        Prepaid Insurance  . . . . . . . . . . . . . . . . . . . . . . . . . . . . . . .        1,100
        Insurance allocated to the period.
8.  Amortization Expense . . . . . . . . . . . . . . . . . . . . . . . . . . . . .   2,300
        Accumulated Amortization . . . . . . . . . . . . . . . . . . . . . . . . . .        2,300
        Amortization allocated to the period.
```

Management must take care to ensure any possible future period costs related to the current period are recognized in the current period and matched against current period revenues. Two such items are warranty costs and bad debt losses. Although such costs may not actually be incurred until future periods, the *cause* of such costs was the sale made in the *current* period. Therefore, since the revenue has been recognized in the current period, any and all related expenses should be matched in the same period. This will require an adjusting entry, and an *estimate* of the future costs to be incurred. Such estimates are typically based on the experiences of past accounting periods. For Rom's Computer Sales, past experience indicates warranty costs average 4 percent of sales and bad debt losses average 1 percent of sales. The *adjusting entries* for possible future period costs are summarized below:

```
9.  Warranty Expense . . . . . . . . . . . . . . . . . . . . . . . . . . . . . . . .   8,320
        Estimated Warranty Liability . . . . . . . . . . . . . . . . . . . . . . . . .        8,320
        Estimated warranty costs for the period (.04 × 208,000).
10. Bad Debt Expense . . . . . . . . . . . . . . . . . . . . . . . . . . . . . . . .   2,080
        Allowance for Doubtful Accounts  . . . . . . . . . . . . . . . . . . . . .        2,080
        Estimated uncollectible accounts for the period (.01 × 208,000).
```

The preceding example has been used to illustrate the care that must be taken to ensure the proper matching of expenses and revenues within any given time period. This example also reinforces the importance of adjusting entries in preparing meaningful financial statements.

5.4 INCOME STATEMENT CLASSIFICATION

Traditionally, income statements are prepared with revenues listed first, followed by various categories of expense deductions, to arrive at a bottom line or net income. Income statements may be condensed for brevity, or expanded for detail, providing many useful subtotals. For example, one important subtotal is the gross margin or gross profit, calculated as net sales minus the cost of sales or services. Another subtotal is income from continuing operations, which measures the profitability of a company's principal line of business activity. How an income statement is prepared depends on the type of organization and the needs of its users.

Service and Merchandise Organizations

In Chapter 3 an income statement for a service organization, Ted's Trucking, was illustrated. There are many other service organizations, for example, medical or legal practices. Service organizations have a simple revenue section on their income statements. In many instances they use only one revenue account, and have no direct cost of sales to be matched with revenues. The expenses are simply deducted from revenues to determine the net income (loss):

SERVICE ORGANIZATION
Income Statement
For the Period Ending December 31

Revenues	$20,000
Expenses	15,000
Net income	$ 5,000

For merchandise organizations the income statement is more complex because of the need to account for the cost of the merchandise sold. Before the operating expenses are deducted from revenues, an additional step is added to the income statement. That step is the determination of gross profit. **Gross profit** is sales revenue less the cost of the merchandise sold.

gross profit (gross margin) A measure of a company's profit on sales calculated as net sales minus the cost of goods or services sold.

MERCHANDISE ORGANIZATION
Income Statement
For the Period Ending December 31

Sales	$50,000
Cost of sales	30,000
Gross profit	$20,000
Expenses	15,000
Net income	$ 5,000

The accounting for the cost of sales or the cost of goods sold is a complex problem because of the large volume of transactions recorded by most organizations. Try to imagine the number of transactions a large retail store like The Hudson Bay Company would process during a busy Saturday. Next consider how many transactions would be recorded across Canada on a yearly basis. With the advent of computers, many organizations use sophisticated systems with scanning devices to facilitate the accounting for the cost of goods sold and the accounting for inventory. The two methods that may be used to account for the cost of goods sold are the perpetual and the periodic inventory methods. The accounting for inventory and cost of goods sold is examined in Chapter 7.

Income from Continuing Operations

income from continuing operations
Continuing results are those that can reasonably be expected to reoccur in future periods and are usually included in income from continuing operations

The results of a company's operations are frequently broken down into recurring and non-recurring categories. Recurring (or continuing) results are those that can reasonably be expected to reoccur in future periods and are usually included in **income from continuing operations**. In the minds of many financial analysts, the income from continuing operations is the most important indicator of a company's performance because of its value in predicting future earnings performance. Non-recurring income (or losses), on the other hand, refers to events or transactions that are not expected to recur in future periods. This category includes extraordinary items (such as loss due to fire or natural phenomena), as well as discontinued operations. GAAP define (and provide explicit accounting treatment for) extraordinary items and discontinued operations.

Discontinued Operations

discontinued operations
When a company decides to divest itself of a division, a subsidiary, or other business segment.

net income from discontinued operations
All of the final period's sales and expenses related to discontinued operations should be netted together and reported in a single line on the income statement.

"Discontinued operations are the operations of a business segment that has been sold, abandoned, shut down or otherwise disposed of, or that is subject to a formal plan of disposal" (CICA Handbook 3475.02). **Discontinued operations** are when a company decides to divest itself of a division, a subsidiary, or other business segment (so long as it is a separate, major line of business). All of the final period's sales and expenses related to that segment should be netted together and reported in a single line on the next income statement with the designation **net income from discontinued operations**. That line item, for the period when the divestiture decision is made, *also* includes an estimate of the loss to be incurred on the sale of the division or segment (it would not include an estimated gain, of course). All prior periods' income statements presented for comparative purposes should be restated to place the results of that to-be-sold-segment in the discontinued operations line. Rio Algom, Limited, disclosed discontinued oeprations as part of their annual report:

> On October 7, 1993, the Corporation sold its potash operations, carried on by the Potash Company of America Division (PCA), to the Potash Corporation of Saskatchewan (PCS) for proceeds of approximately $202.3 million. Accordingly, the potash operations have been accounted for as discontinued operations in these financial statements. These operations consist of the underground potash mine near Sussex, New Brunswick, the solution mine near Saskatoon, Saskatchewan, and the Division's sales operations based in Darien, Connecticut. The Corporation used approximately $95.8 million of the proceeds to repay the PCA debt.

Extraordinary Items

Because of the importance attached to the net income figure, only one figure in the income statement is so designated, and all items of revenue and expense are included in the determination of that amount. Certain events are so unusual and significant that they are called **extraordinary items** and, hence, warrant separate disclosure on the income statement. When extraordinary items are reported on the income statement, an intermediate subtotal is designated **net income before extraordinary items**. To guard against the liberal use of the extraordinary item presentation, GAAP define an extraordinary item as being both *unusual* (possessing a high degree of abnormality and clearly unrelated to the normal business of the entity) and *infrequent* (not reasonably expected to reoccur in the near future).

The CICA Handbook states:

> Extraordinary items are items which result from transactions or events that have all of the following characteristics:
> (a) they are not expected to occur frequently over several years;
> (b) they do not typify normal business activities of the entity; and
> (c) they do not depend primarily on decisions or determinations by management or owners. (CICA Handbook 3480.02)

Examples of extraordinary items include losses from natural disasters (fires, floods, tornadoes) and expropriations by governments. Extraordinary items are to be disclosed net of any applicable income taxes as a separate line item on the income statement. Earnings per share figures should be disclosed both before and after extraordinary items. As might be expected, extraordinary item presentation in published financial statements is generally quite rare. The Alberta Natural Gas Company, Ltd., disclosed the following note on an extraordinary item in its annual report:

> Extraordinary items were recorded for the nonrecurring consequences of the Sterlington fire and explosion. The 1993 gain represents the proceeds from the IMC fertilizer settlement and the 1992 gain represents an "involuntary conversion" book gain arising from insurance proceeds received to rebuild the damaged plant. The following is a summary of the extraordinary items:

Year Ended December 31	1993	1992
Gain	$31,822	$56,733
Expenses	(4,010)	(20,429)
Income and other taxes	(12,416)	(16,123)
Net	$15,396	$20,181

Silverado Mines, Ltd., also disclosed a footnote on an extraordinary item in its annual report:

> Effective November 29, 1993 the Company's long term debt of $3,242,325, including accrued interest for the year of $308,665, was extinguished by payment of $2,000,000 to Marubeni America Corporation. The resulting gain on forgiveness of debt of $1,242,325, together with forgiveness of accounts payable of $52,289 (for a total forgiveness of debt of $1,294,614) has been classified as an extraordinary item.

Changes in Accounting Policy

The consistency concept discussed in Chapter 1 requires consistent application of accounting methods from one year's financial statements to the next to facilitate yearly comparisons of financial results. Consistency is a goal, however, not a categorical requirement. As the economic conditions that a company faces change, sometimes changing the accounting methods and policies it has used to depict its operations is also beneficial. A change in accounting policy may be made "if it is considered that the change would result in a more appropriate presentation of events or transactions in the financial statements of the enterprise" (CICA Handbook 1506.02). When a company implements an accounting policy change, the current period's income statement is prepared using that new policy as if it had been adopted on the first day of the period. A **change in accounting policy** should be applied retroactively, with the statements for prior periods restated for purposes of comparability. A footnote is the appropriate disclosure to describe the change in accounting policy and the effect of the change on the financial statements. AFS Interculture Canada dislcosed with a footnote a change in accounting policy:

change in accounting policy
A change in accounting policy may be made "if it is considered that the change would result in a more appropriate presentation of events or transactions in the financial statements of the enterprise." (CICA Handbook 1506.02).

> To better reflect the nature of the organization's current operations, AFS has changed both its revenue recognition policy and its fiscal year end. Fees and contributions are now recognized in the year participants depart for their host counties. The fiscal year has been changed to a calendar year basis, and the organization had a short September-December fiscal year to phase in this change.

The Island Telephone Company, Limited, changed its revenue recognition method:

> In 1992, the Company changed its method of accounting for the telephone directory to recognize the related revenue and expenses at the time of the issue of the directory. Previous, these revenues and expenses were recognized over the 12 months following the issue. This accounting change was applied on a prospective basis and resulted in an increase in net income of $163,500 in 1992.

Additional discussions and illustrations of changes in accounting policies are presented in Chapter 8.

Subsequent Events

Subsequent events are economic activities that occur after the financial statement date that may influence the decisions of financial statement users. If the subsequent event relates to conditions that existed at the financial statement date, and if the economic impact of the event is significant, the statements should be adjusted to reflect the subsequent event. "Financial statements should be adjusted when events occurring between the date of the financial statements and the date of their completion provide additional evidence relating to conditions that existed at the date of the financial statements" (CICA Handbook 3820.06). Other subsequent events that do not relate to existing conditions, but are considered to have a significant effect on future operations, are typically disclosed in a footnote to the financial statements. "Financial statements should not be adjusted for, but disclosure should be made of, those events occurring between the date of the financial statements and the date of their completion that do not relate to conditions that existed at the date of the financial statements but: (a) cause significant changes to assets or liabilities in the subsequent period; or (b) will, or may, have a significant effect on the future operations of the enterprise" (CICA Handbook 3820.10). John Labatt, Limited, used a footnote to disclose the following subsequent event: "On July 6, 1994, the Board of Directors of the Company approved an agreement in principle to acquire 22% of a brewing business in Mexico, subject to certain conditions, for US$510 million." A similar footnote disclosure was used by Dofasco, Inc., to disclose its subsequent event: "On February 28, 1994 the Corporation announced the sale of its wholly-owned subsidiary National Steel Car Limited, a Hamilton based manufacturer of railway cars and specialized rolling stock."

Subsequent events emphasize the importance of the use of footnotes in financial statement disclosure. Users should carefully analyze all footnotes provided in the annual report and not solely focus on the financial data.

5.5 INDUSTRY EXAMPLES OF REVENUE/EXPENSE RECOGNITION

Footnote Disclosure

The earlier sections of this chapter discussed the concepts of revenue and expense recognition. In most cases it is a matter of timing, that is, determining whether the item should be recognized in the current period or deferred until a later accounting period. In Chapter 4, in the section discussing adjusting entries, it was mentioned that adjusting entries may be placed in one of two general categories. One was *accruals*, which simply assumed adherence to the accrual basis of accounting. Under GAAP it is assumed that unless otherwise stated the organization is following the accrual basis. The second type of adjusting entry was called *allocations*. Allocations relate to revenues or expenses for which payment has been previously made, but not *all* of the goods or services have been exchanged. Therefore, assets like prepaid expenses or depreciable assets, and liabilities like unearned revenues or customer deposits must be established. Numerous examples of revenue and expense deferral are available in the real world, some of which are illustrated here.

Many annual reports contain a footnote explaining the organization's revenue recognition policies. The annual report of the Canadian Red Cross Society contained the following note on revenue and expenditure recognition: "Revenues and expenditures of the Society are accounted for on the accrual basis of accounting whereby revenues are recognized in the year in which they are earned and expenditures are recognized in the year incurred as a result of the receipt of goods or services and the creation of a legal obligation to pay." The Canadian Red Cross Society footnote confirms the use of the accrual basis of accounting that is so important for the preparation of meaningful financial statements.

Many organizations are paid in advance for goods or services to be provided at a later date. The receipt of the advance payment gives rise to a liability account for deferred revenue. Deferred revenue is a non-monetary liability to provide goods or services at a later date. When that time in the future arrives, an adjusting entry is required to transfer the earned revenue from the liability account to the appropriate revenue account. Thompson Corporation recognizes deferred revenue for tours and subscriptions: "Inclusive tour revenue is included in deferred revenue until the date of tour departure. Subscription revenue received in advance of the delivery of services or publications is included in deferred revenue and as services are rendered or publications sent to subscribers the proportionate share is recognized as revenue." Maple Leaf Gardens, Limited, also recognizes deferred income for events and services to be provided in the future: "Deferred income represents payments received in advance for events and services which have not yet been performed. These amounts will be recorded in income as earned." Cineplex Odeon Corporation disclosed a footnote on deferred income very similar to that of Maple Leaf Gardens, Limited: "Advance payments received under strategic marketing relationship with a major supplier, advance sales of admissions, the sale of gift certificates and income from certain promotional programs are included as deferred income, and are recognized as income when services are rendered."

The annual report of the Canadian Red Cross Society contained an additional footnote on revenue recognition pertaining to the revenue for government grants and other revenues that are deferred until the subsequent year: "Deferred revenue includes amounts received from government grants, campaigns and the United Way, and in respect of programs which are applicable to future periods, mainly the following fiscal year."

The matching principle requires the recognition of expenses in the appropriate accounting period. Many expenditures are incurred that will benefit future accounting periods. In subsequent periods adjusting entries are necessary to allocate the expenses to the period in which the matching revenues have been earned. A number of footnotes from Canadian annual reports are shown to illustrate expense allocations. Hydro-Québec disclosed a footnote on the accounting for its marketing programs: "Hydro-Québec has implemented a number of marketing programs aimed at consumption management, energy conservation and market optimization. The deferred expenses related to these programs are amortized on a staight-line basis over a period not exceeding five years after the year in which they are incurred."

The marketing costs of Hydro-Québec and the deferred charges of Maple Leaf Gardens, Limited, are examples of expenditures made in advance of their anticipated benefit. Therefore, they are established as assets, with their costs to be allocated to future periods. As well, some organizations anticipate expenses that have yet to be incurred. An example of such costs is that of warranty costs. Camco, Inc., disclosed a footnote on its product warranty costs: "Anticipated future costs of product warranties are charged to operations in the year the product is sold." The warranty expense is recorded and matched against the sales revenue in the accounting period the sale is made. The warranty expense and warranty liability must be *estimated* based on past experience. Many organizations have similar adjustments for anticipated expenses and the related liabilities. Greyhound Lines of Canada, Ltd., uses a liability account called Reserve for Injuries and Damages. Its footnote explains: "The Company's potential cost of settling claims for injuries and damages is provided annually on the basis of management's and counsel's assessments of the specific liability for each claim."

Airlines must make adjusting entries in each accounting period to recognize the estimated cost of the frequent flyer programs. PWA Corporation's note on its frequent flyer program states: "The incremental costs of providing travel awards under the Corporation's 'Canadian Plus' and affiliated carrier's frequent flyer programs are accrued as the entitlements to such awards are earned." PWA Corporation also disclosed a footnote related to deferred charges: "Pre-operating costs related to the introduction of new types of aircraft and computer systems development costs are amortized over various periods up to 5 years."

Most organizations have a number of deferred income and deferred charges to be allocated each accounting period. Properly recorded adjusting entries accomplish this task. Under GAAP, the accrual basis of accounting helps provide the users of financial reports the most meaningful information.

EXHIBIT 5.5

Ratio Guides

Industry	Gross Profit Margin Ratio	Inventory Turnover Ratio
Women's clothing	43.0%	5.6
Gas/service stations	18.6	27.3
Food stores	22.3	15.4
Farm machinery	15.5	2.6
Gold mining	49.4	13.1
Building contractors	14.5	6.3

Source: Dun & Bradstreet, Canada.

5.6 ANALYZING FINANCIAL STATEMENTS

Ratio Analysis

Now that we have examined the cost of goods sold in greater depth, two additional management performance ratios may be illustrated. One of the most commonly used profitability ratios used to measure management performance is the gross profit margin ratio. The **gross profit margin ratio** indicates the percentage of each dollar of revenue that is realized as gross profit after deducting the cost of goods or services sold. It represents the profit available to cover a company's other operating expenses, such as selling and administrative expenses, interest, and taxes. It provides an indicator of a company's pricing policies. It is calculated as follows:

gross profit margin ratio
A measure of profitability that assesses the percentage of each sales dollar that is recognized as gross profit.

$$\text{Gross profit margin ratio} = \frac{\text{Gross profit}}{\text{Sales (net)}}$$

Generally a high gross profit margin is good. However, if the profit margin is too high, it may mean the loss of potential customers to competitor firms. The gross profit margin can vary greatly with different products. As indicated in Exhibit 5.5, 43.0 percent is the average gross profit percentage on women's clothing, compared to only 15.5 percent on farm machinery. As with other ratios, comparative data are the most useful.

The quality of a company's inventory management is often revealed by the inventory turnover ratio. The **inventory turnover ratio** measures the number of times that the average level of inventory on hand was sold, or turned, during an accounting period and is calculated as follows:

inventory turnover ratio
A measure of the effectiveness of inventory management calculated as the cost of goods sold for a period divided by the average inventory held during that period.

$$\text{Inventory turnover ratio} = \frac{\text{Cost of goods sold}}{\text{Inventory}}$$

As mentioned previously, it is desirable to average figures for items like inventory. However, only end-of-period inventory values may be available to the user. In general, the higher the inventory turnover ratio, the more profitable a company is and the more effective the inventory management is thought to be. A high turnover rate also helps to reduce the potential of loss due to product obsolescence or deterioration. If the turnover ratio is too high, however, it may indicate that the company is losing sales opportunities because inventory levels are inadequate. Unfortunately, there is no ideal turnover rate, and to judge the effectiveness of inventory management, it is important to compare this ratio to that of prior periods, to industry averages, or to competitor ratios (see Exhibit 5.5).

EXHIBIT 5.6

Financial Statement Analysis Ratios

Financial Strength		Management Performance	
Liquidity	**Solvency**	**Profitability**	**Asset Management**
Quick ratio	Total debt-to-equity ratio	Earnings per share	Total asset turnover ratio
Current ratio	Long-term debt-to-invested capital ratio	Return on equity	Receivable turnover ratio
		Gross profit margin ratio	Inventory turnover ratio

Exhibit 5.5 provides a sample of the comparative gross profit margin ratio and inventory turnover ratios available from Dun & Bradstreet Canada. Industries with perishable goods like food stores must have a higher inventory turnover ratio than a firm selling durable goods like farm machinery.

Exhibit 5.6 is provided as a summary of the ratios discussed in the first five chapters of text. The table of ratios should not be considered to be all inclusive, but a sample of ratios commonly used to measure financial strength and management performance. As we explore additional complexities of financial statements, additional ratios and analysis techniques will be discussed.

Assessing Risk

The analysis of profitability is not an end in itself but is often undertaken as part of a broader assessment of the relative riskiness of a company. In the case of a lending institution evaluating the desirability of lending funds to a company, the principal focus is on default risk. In the case of an investment or brokerage house evaluating the desirability of investing funds in a company, the principal focus is on operational risk. **Default risk** refers to the probability that a company will be unable to meet its short-term or long-term obligations. The liquidity and solvency ratios discussed in Chapter 2 provide a good assessment of the probability of default risk. **Operational risk**, on the other hand, refers to the probability that a company will experience unforeseen or unexpected events or factors that consequently will reduce or impair its revenue and earnings streams (and, implicitly, its cash flow stream). These factors or events may be economywide (e.g., general inflation, recession, or high interest rates), industrywide (e.g., increased competition, changes in technology, or raw material/labour constraints), or firm specific (e.g., labour disputes, equipment failure, or product safety considerations).

Assessing the operational riskiness of a company involves, in part, developing an understanding of a company's marketplace, its competition, its sensitivity to inflation and interest rate changes, and its ability to respond to new opportunities. By analyzing the resiliency of past operations to prior economic changes, it is possible to formulate assessments as to how well (or poorly) current and future operations might respond to future economic changes and opportunities.

Future-Oriented Financial Information

The ability to assess operational and default risk is tied in part to the ability to generate insightful future-oriented financial statements. **Future-oriented financial statements** are projected or forecasted financial statements. The annual reports and audited finan-

default risk
The probability that a company will be unable to meet its short-term or long-term obligations.

operational risk
The probability that unexpected events will occur and consequently reduce or impair the revenue, earnings, and cash flow streams of a company.

future-oriented financial information
Projected or forecasted financial statements.

EXHIBIT 5.7

BLUE RIDGE HARDWARE COMPANY., LTD.
Income Statement
For the Year Ending March 31, 1996

Sales		$74,500	100.0%
Cost of sales		45,000	60.4
Gross profit		$29,500	
Rent expense	$ 3,600		4.8
Wage expense	15,300		20.6
Utility expense	650		0.9
Interest expense	900		1.2
Amortization expense	1,000	21,450	1.3
Income before taxes		$ 8,050	
Income tax expense		2,900	3.9
Net income		$ 5,150	6.9

cial statements are based on historical data. Users of financial information are interested in future operations and organizations. Forecasts are crucial to lending and investment decisions, for example, because the repayment of debt and the payment of future dividends depend substantially on a company's future profitability. The ability to forecast future operations of any type are dependent on the reliability of the crystal ball used. Most users would not have access to the necessary information to prepare a complete set of future-oriented financial statements. However, most users would prepare some type of future-oriented analysis to help with their financial decisions. Users may try to forecast a best-case/worst-case scenario to establish the limits of their default risk or operational risk.

Some organizations may include future-oriented financial statements as part of their annual report. Section 4250 of the CICA Handbook provides standards for the presentation and disclosure of future-oriented financial information. The intent of the section is to ensure that users do not confuse the forecast or projected financial data with actual historical data. General requirements for the presentation of future-oriented financial information include:

■ Use of the same GAAP as used for the historical statements.

■ A *cautionary* note to the effect that actual results achieved for the forecast period *will* vary from the information presented and that the variations may be *material*.

■ Disclosure of significant assumptions underlying future-oriented financial information.

■ Use of assumptions based on the judgment of management.

Users should take into consideration that the organization and its management present future-oriented financial information from a biased position and users should make financial decisions accordingly.

To illustrate the development of a future-oriented income statement, we return to our example of Blue Ridge Hardware Co. In Chapter 4, we used the transactions of Blue Ridge Hardware Co. as a basis for preparation of financial statements for the first year of operations. As a starting point for preparing a future-oriented income statement, it is useful to understand the relationship between the various income statement accounts. One way to do this is to prepare a *common-size* income statement. Exhibit 5.7

EXHIBIT 5.8

BLUE RIDGE HARDWARE COMPANY, LTD.
Forecast Income Statement
For the Year Ending March 31, 1997

Sales*		$85,675
Cost of sales†		48,835
Gross profit		$36,840
Rent expense	$ 3,600	
Wage expense	15,300	
Utility expense	650	
Interest expense	900	
Advertizing expense‡	2,000	
Amortization expense	1,000	23,450
Income before taxes		$13,390
Income tax expense§		4,820
Net income		$ 8,570

Assumptions:

* Sales projected to increase by 15% (.15)($74,500).

† Cost of sales projected to decrease to 57% (.57)($85,675).

‡ Projected additional expense of $2,000 for advertizing.

§ Tax expense projected to remain at 36% (.36)($13,390).

presents such a statement for Blue Ridge Hardware for the first year of operations. If multiple periods of data are available, it is best to prepare common-size statements for several periods to determine whether the percentage relationships vary significantly between periods or at various levels of activity.

Since a common-size income statement relates all other account balances to the revenue figure, the most important projection is that of revenues. For illustrative purposes, let us assume that Blue Ridge Hardware is considering an advertising campaign as a means to generate additional future sales. On the basis of discussions with a local advertising agency, Blue Ridge anticipates an expenditure of $2,000 for print advertizing to produce a 15 percent growth in sales.

To service the expected increase in customer demand, an additional investment in inventories will be required. However, the cost of merchandise is not expected to increase linearly with sales because volume purchase discounts will be available and will lower the overall cost. Thus, the cost of sales is projected to decline to 57 percent of revenues from the 1996 level of 60.4 percent. All other outlays for operating expenses are expected to remain fixed in amount since no new employees or store operating hours will be required to handle the expected growth in sales. Further, income taxes are anticipated to remain at the 1996 level of 36 percent of pretax income (i.e., $2,900/$8,050).

Using these assumptions, it is possible to prepare a future-oriented income statement for 1997 to assess the relative impact of the advertising campaign on Blue Ridge Hardware's profitability. Exhibit 5.8 presents a future-oriented income statement for the year ended March 31, 1997, which reveals that net income after taxes is projected to grow to $8,570, or an increase of $3,420 ($8,570 − $5,150). Thus, if our assumptions are reasonable, it is clear that the profitability of the company is substantially enhanced by the advertising campaign. Since advertising may help develop long-term customers, the effects may also have a carryover effect beyond 1998.

Just as the preparation of a future-oriented income statement was used to evaluate the desirability of undertaking an advertizing campaign, future-oriented statements may also be used to evaluate the desirability of lending money to Blue Ridge Hardware or of investing in it. A future-oriented statement of changes in financial position and a future-oriented balance sheet could also be produced.

5.7 SUMMARY

This chapter has discussed revenue and expense recognition concepts and illustrated different recognition methods. Revenue recognition methods illustrated included the point-of-sale, percentage-of-completion, completed-contract, completion of production, instalment sales, and the cost recovery methods. Footnotes from the annual reports were presented to reinforce the recognition concepts and methods. The classification of the income statement was examined, including classification of discontinued operations, extraordinary items, and changes in accounting policy. Analyzing financial statements was revisited, including the assessment of risk and future-oriented financial information.

The first five chapters have presented an overview of the language of accounting and the basic financial reports used to convey the language. The remaining chapters examine closely each of the financial statement elements.

5.8 KEY CONCEPTS AND TERMS

Change in accounting policy (p. 233)
Completed-contract method (p. 220)
Completion-of-production
   method (p. 220)
Cost recovery method (p. 221)
Default risk (p. 237)
Discontinued operations (p. 231)
Extraordinary item (p. 232)
Future-oriented financial
   statements (p. 237)
Gross profit (p. 230)
Gross profit margin ratio (p. 236)

Income from continuing
   operations (p. 231)
Instalment sales method (p. 221)
Inventory turnover ratio (p. 236)
Net income before extraordinary
   items (p. 232)
Net income from discontinued
   operations (p. 231)
Operational risk (p. 237)
Percentage-of-completion
   method (p. 220)
Point-of-sale method (p. 221)

5.9 COMPREHENSIVE REVIEW QUESTION

R5.1 Financial analysis. Alberta Natural Gas, Ltd. (ANG), is a Calgary-based corporation that has been active in the natural gas industry for more than 30 years. Originally a transporter of natural gas, ANG expanded its operations to include natural gas liquids (NGL) and ethane extraction, and natural gas and NGL marketing. The corporation further diversified into the production and marketing of speciality chemicals. Presented below is Alberta Natural Gas Company's comparable financial statements for the year ended December 31. Perform an analysis of the financial strength and management performance of the company. Your report should include comments as to the financial position of the company.

ALBERTA NATURAL GAS COMPANY, LTD.
Consolidated Statement of Income
Year Ended December 31

	1993	1992
Revenues	$662,693	$572,819
Expenses:		
Operating and maintenance	$521,016	$409,079
Selling and administrative	49,598	50,079
Amortization and amortization	22,619	15,246
Property taxes/other expenses	4,793	5,139
	$598,026	$479,901
Operating income	$ 64,667	$ 47,918
Other income	13,705	4,684
Interest expense	(16,397)	(19,422)
Income before income taxes	$ 61,975	$ 33,180
Income taxes	(28,577)	(15,381)
Income from continuing operations	$ 33,398	$ 17,799
Discontinued operations	790	(20,075)
Extraordinary items	15,396	20,181
Net income	$ 49,584	$ 17,905

ALBERTA NATURAL GAS COMPANY, LTD.
Balance Sheet
As at December 31

	1993	1992
Assets		
Current assets:		
Cash	$ 13,668	$ 39,501
Accounts receivable	115,571	86,132
Income taxes receivable	—	10,876
Inventories	57,495	38,551
Other	4,512	3,950
Total current assets	$191,246	$179,010
Investments	38,532	18,489
Property, plant, and equipment — net	376,474	289,752
Goodwill and other	34,364	22,021
	$640,616	$509,272
Liabilities and Shareholders' Equity		
Current liabilities:		
Notes payable	$ 79,445	$ 22,009
Accounts payable	101,968	86,463
Deferred income taxes	16,426	16,361
Current portion of long-term debt	—	60,000
Total current liabilities	$197,839	$184,833
Long-term debt	176,748	111,813
Deferred income taxes	58,273	43,150
Total liabilities	$432,860	$339,796
Shareholders' equity:		
Share capital*	$113,701	$113,099
Retained earnings	94,055	56,377
Total shareholders' equity	$207,756	$169,476
	$640,616	$509,272

*Weighted-average shares oustanding: 1993 — 25,697; 1992 — 25,654

5.10 REVIEW AND DISCUSSION QUESTIONS

Q5.1 Distinguish between the instalment sales and the point-of-sale methods of revenue recognition.

Q5.2 Describe the purpose of the receivable turnover ratio compared to the inventory turnover ratio.

Q5.3 Distinguish between the percentage-of-completion and the completed-contract methods of accounting for long-term contracts.

Q5.4 Distinguish between sales and the cost of goods sold.

Q5.5 Distinguish between gross profit and net income.

Q5.6 Contrast the point-of-sale and the instalment sales methods of revenue recognition.

Q5.7 Contrast the income statements of a merchandise firm and a service organization.

Q5.8 Compare an income statement for an accounting practice and an income statement for a retail shoe store.

Q5.9 Contrast the accounting for discontinued operations with the accounting for extraordinary items.

Q5.10 Distinguish between default risk and operational risk. Discuss how you would assess the two different types of risk associated with a firm.

Q5.11 Contrast historical financial statements as compared to future-oriented financial information. Your discussion should consider the qualitative criteria of relevance and reliability.

Q5.12 (*Published with permission of CGA Canada*) "In the past we used strictly cash basis accounting for our merchandising business. At year end a tax accountant would adjust our statement to an accrual basis to satisfy Revenue Canada. Now that we have grown bigger we have switched to accrual accounting."

a. What changes are made immediately to the business's balance sheet to reflect the change-over to accrual accounting?

b. How will the income statement differ as a result of the changeover?

Q5.13 Flowers Industries bakes and distributes bread and other bakery products. In 1994 the company began a program of selling its distribution routes to its salespeople in an effort to give those people an increased stake in the business and provide them with an incentive to develop the territory more fully. Flowers includes the footnote below in its financial statements for 1996. Do you agree with Flowers' policy? Why or why not?

> **Long-Term Notes Receivable and Deferred Income**
> The company has sold a portion of its routes to independent distributors. The income from these sales is recognized as the cash payments are received.
>   The amounts due under the notes receivable from the distributors of $21,595,000 and $14,448,000 have also been included in deferred income at July 2, 1996 and June 27, 1995, respectively. At July 2, 1996 and June 27, 1995, $20,112,000 and $13,476,000, respectively, are included in other long-term assets.

Q5.14 General Motors' income statement for 1995 included a special charge of $3.3 billion, which it described as a special provision for scheduled plant closings and other restructurings. The charge is described in Note 7, as follows:

NOTE 7. Special Provision for Scheduled Plant Closings and Other Restructurings
In 1995, a special restructuring charge of $3,314.0 million was included in the results of operations to provide for the closing of four previously idled assembly plants, as well as provide for other North American manufacturing and warehouse operations which will be consolidated or cease operating over the next three years. As a result, consolidated net loss was increased by $2,087.8 million or $3.47 per share of $1-⅔ par value common stock. A similar provision was made in 1991 in the amount of $1,287.6 million for costs associated with scheduled plant closings and other restructurings of foreign operations that were reasonably estimable at the time.

   During 1995, 1994, and 1993, a net of $1,731.7 million, $148.1 million, and $218.6 million, respectively, was charged against these reserves.

Discuss the appropriateness of charging the 1995 income with this expense. Is it an appropriate charge against 1995, as opposed to 1996 or 1997? Why or why not? Why should it not be reallocated back to 1994 or prior years?

Q5.15 Greenman, Limited, produces jet fighters and has other defence department contracts for production and research projects. The company describes its revenue recognition policies in the following footnote:

Revenue recognition
Sales under fixed-price production contracts are recorded at the time of delivery. Sales, including fees earned, under cost-reimbursement and research, development, test, and evaluation contracts are recorded as costs are incurred.

   Certain contracts contain cost and/or performance incentives. Such incentives are included in sales at the time actual performance can be related to the target and the earned amount can be reasonably determined. Accordingly, earnings recorded in one period may include adjustments related to sales recorded in a prior period. Losses on contracts are recorded when they become known.

Comment on the reasoning underlying these policies.

Q5.16 The following information is provided concerning the operations of Moore Corporation, Limited. "At December 31, certain lawsuits and other claims arising in the ordinary course of business were pending against the Corporation. While the outcome of these matters is not determinable, management believes that the ultimate resolution of these matters will not have a material effect on the Corporation's financial position or results in operations." Explain how such information should be disclosed in the annual financial reports of the corporation.

Q5.17 Review the list of key concepts and terms at the end of the chapter. If you have difficulty with a specific concept, refer to the discussion on the page number provided as a reference to gain a better understanding of the concept. Make a list of terms you do not thoroughly understand. Refer back to the list periodically to see if your understanding has improved. Before starting Chapter 6, review the key concepts and terms at the end of Chapters 1 to 4.

Q5.18 Sears Canada, Inc., included the following footnote in its annual report. Which revenue/ expense recognition concepts pertain to this note? What adjusting entry would be required each year?

Prepaid advertizing
Catalogue production costs are deferred and amortized over the life of each catalogue on the basis of the estimated sales from the catalogue.

Q5.19 Rogers Communications, Inc., included the following footnote in its annual report. Which revenue/expense recognition concepts pertain to this note? What adjusting entry would be required each year?

Prepayments for services

Prepayments for services include subscriber deposits and amounts received from subscribers related to services to be provided in future periods.

Q5.20 The Heart and Stroke Foundation of Canada included the following footnote in its annual report. Which revenue/expense recognition concepts pertain to this note? What adjusting entry would be required each year?

Revenue recognition

Revenue from grants, pledges and donations is normally recognized on a cash basis. Certain committed grants, from governmental and similar agencies, and pledges from large corporations are accounted for on an accrual basis.

Q5.21 OXFAM-Canada included the following footnote in its annual report. Which revenue/ expense recognition concepts pertain to this note? What adjusting entry would be required each year, assuming OXFAM is able to fulfil its obligations under the terms of the grant? What adjusting entry would be required each year, assuming OXFAM is not able to fulfil its obligations?

Deferred revenue

Deferred revenue consists of grants and contributions designated for the purpose of funding various specified projects. Under the terms of the grants and contributions, OXFAM-Canada may be required to repay funds received should they not be able to fulfil their funding obligations or obtain approval to fund alternate projects.

Q5.22 A college friend has been quite successful with a computer software company she began shortly after graduation. The company now needs more money for expansion, and your friend is about to sell stock to a select group of investors. She has been preparing financial statements for her company for her own use but will now have to prepare financial reports for outsiders. Explain to your friend the advantages and disadvantages of adopting aggressive accounting policies or conservative accounting policies. Give as many examples as you can, together with your overall explanation.

Q5.23 You are the president of a small computer company that led the market in the introduction of a low-priced lap-top computer. With a manufacturing cost of $1,500 and a retail price of $3,000, the company did quite well. In the last several years, products of the major companies in the industry have surpassed your original product due to a few technical refinements. You are now ready to introduce Version 2 of your product, which will be a dramatic leap over the competition. However, you still have about 5,000 units of the earlier model. Your salespeople tell you that you have only two alternatives. The salespeople are confident that the units can be sold to college students at a discounted price of $500 each. Alternatively, it may be possible to sell those units at full retail price in some less-developed countries. How (and why) should this choice be reflected in your company's financial statements?

Q5.24 Since you won $100,000 in the lottery, you have been besieged with proposals to invest your gains. Most recently, Harry Schultz, president of Schultz Corporation, has suggested that you invest $50,000 in the common stock of his company's manufacturing subsidiary. He has shown you the financial statements of the subsidiary and they look promising. On the balance sheet, you see that the assets are mostly raw material inventory and production equipment. The liabilities are quite small and consist mostly of ordinary trade payables to creditors. The income statements show a steady growth in sales and a very satisfactory return. You understand that Schultz Corporation as a whole has not been doing well recently because of price-cutting competitors. The president assures you that the manufacturing side of the business is quite healthy and urges your investment. Would you buy an equity interest in the manufacturing subsidiary? Why or why not? If you are uncertain about making the investment at this time, outline the additional information you would like to have before making that investment, and explain why that information might be important to you.

5.11 PROBLEMS

P5.1 Cash provided from operations (*Published with permission of CGA Canada*). The following information is extracted from the records of Roberts Company:

ROBERTS COMPANY
Income Statement
For the Month Ended November 30

Sales		$150,000
Cost of goods sold		83,000
Gross profit		$ 67,000
Operating expenses:		
Wages	$30,000	
Rent	9,000	
Interest	1,000	
Amortization	11,000	51,000
Net income		$ 16,000

Additional data:

1. During November, the Accounts Receivable balance increased by $14,500.

2. Roberts' Accounts Payable increased by $17,600 during the month.

3. The Wages Payable balance increased by $1,900 during the month.

4. Rent Payable decreased by $1,500 during October and by $1,600 during November.

5. The Interest Payable account had the same balance on November 30 as it did on November 1.

Required:

Prepare a statement to show how much cash was provided by operations for Roberts Company for the month of November.

P5.2 Income statement concepts. Consider the following comparisons, each of which suggest some important income statement decisions:

a. Asset versus expense.

b. Earned versus unearned.

c. Current period charge versus future period charge.

d. Current period charge versus prior period charge.

e. Operating items versus extraordinary items.

Required:

Prepare a commentary on each of the above concepts, explaining how the contrasted items are alike and how they are different, and the factors that might require them to be treated differently on the income statement.

P5.3 Revenue recognition. Consider the following unique company situations:

1. The Canadian Health Club sells lifetime memberhsips, costing $1,200, that allow the member unlimited use of any of the club's 100 facilities around the country. The initiation fee may be paid in 24 monthly instalments, with a 1 percent interest charge on the unpaid balance.

2. Universal Motors has always offered a limited, 24-month warranty program on its cars. But to counter the incredible competition in the industry, the company has come to the conclusion that they must do something more. With that in mind, they have developed a new program: For a $500 payment at the time of purchase, the customer can buy a five-year warranty that will cover replacement of almost all parts and will include labour. The purchased warranty expires at the end of five years or when the customer sells the car, whichever occurs first.

3. Community Promotions Corporation sells coupon books that give the holder a 10 percent discount (up to $10) from any of 25 participating merchants. The buyer of the coupon book pays $50 for the book, but obviously can realize up to $250 in benefits. Community Promotions convinces the merchants to participate in the program at no cost, arguing that they will build traffic and have the opportunity for repeat business from the coupon book holders.

4. Household Furnishings Emporium sells appliances and furniture with instalment contracts. Those contracts usually carry interest rates of 16 percent or more. When the company has accumulated $200,000 of contracts with a year or more to go, they sell the contracts to a finance company on a non-recourse basis. The company continues to service the contracts and is paid a service fee that is based on the cash they collect and turn over to the finance company. If a contract goes bad, Household turns it over to a collection agency and has no further responsibility for it. In January the company sold contracts with a face value of $250,000 and received $275,000 in cash.

5. Neighbourhood News, Inc., prints and distributes a weekly newspaper throughout the county. Local merchants order a certain number of the papers each week, and pay for them on delivery. The company always takes back any unsold papers, however, and gives the merchant credit.

Required:

For each of the above situations, prepare a short paper describing the revenue recognition policy the company ought to follow, and explain the basis for your recommendation.

P5.4 Income statement classification. Net income for the Multi Corporation, for the year ended December 31, is $10,000,000. There is some debate, however, about the presentation of the income statement, and the classification of certain events that could be considered material to that net income. In thinking about these items, it will be important to know that Multi manufactures and distributes a line of automobile aftermarket accessories, which are sold through Sears and other major retail outlets. The events that follow all occurred, or were recognized, during the year.

1. A fire destroyed a company warehouse in Ontario. The loss was $2,500,000, half of which was covered by insurance.

2. The company completed a defence contract that produced a $1,250,000 profit. The contract used excess capacity in the plant, and the gross margin went directly to the bottom line. The company hopes to bid on similar contracts, but is not sure that there will be a repeat opportunity.

3. An order of seat covers for an East Coast auto parts chain was found to be defective and was returned and scrapped. The loss on the order was $250,000, and the company gave the customer an additional discount of $500,000 on future orders in the hopes of protecting the relationship.

4. The company spent $1,000,000 on the development of a direct mail catalogue. The catalogue probably has a useful life of 24 months. In the first three months of the mail order operations, sales exceeded expectations substantially.

5. To ensure its source of merchandise, the company has made investments in several Pacific Rim supplier companies. An opportunity came to sell one of those investments at a substantial gain. The company agreed to the sale, received $4,000,000 in cash, realized a $2,000,000 gain, and invested the entire proceeds in a new supplier just beginning business in Mexico.

6. A loan to a manufacturer of car radios was written off this year. In fact, it had been clear for some time that the $1,500,000 note was worthless, but the radio maker was part of a complex of companies, some of whom were important to Multi. Multi's CEO had elected to keep a low profile with regard to the radio maker and had refused to press for payments of principal or interest, for fear of alienating the other companies in the group. But now, other sources had been found so that the complex was less significant as a supplier, and Multi forced the hand of the radio maker, pushing it into bankruptcy.

Required:

Prepare a paragraph discussing each event and describing how the item should be treated in Multi's income statement. Should the item be classified as unusual, extraordinary, or ordinary? Should the item be carried forward into next year (as an asset)? Be sure to explain the rationale for your decision.

P5.5 Quarterly income statements. Li'l Tyke sells toys in its own stores throughout the West. It is a very seasonal business, with about 80 percent of sales coming in the period November 15 to December 31. Unfortunately, to have a presence in the market for those peak times, the store must remain open all year around. The company struggles to present a reasonable picture of its operations during the early part of the year, and it worries particularly about the requirement to present quarterly reports to its shareholders. The president has come up with several ideas to deal with this problem, and he asked you to consider these suggestions:

1. Everyone agrees that the company sells its toys at a higher markup during its peak season, but no one knows for sure how much the difference might be. The real margin for the year is not known until the year-end inventory is counted and the real cost of sales is determined. The president proposes to use last year's actual gross margin percentage to determine the gross margin for each of the first three quarters. He will determine an actual gross margin after the year-end inventory and will use that number to prepare the income statement for the year as a whole. That gross margin will also be used to develop the gross margins for the first three quarters of the next year.

2. Most of the company's advertising is spread evenly over the period September 1 through December 15. The president has negotiated with the advertizing agency to allow the company to pay for those advertizements during the month of December. He proposes to expense the advertizing expense 20 percent in the third quarter and 80 percent in the fourth quarter, which is approximately proportionate to the way sales are realized during the six-month period.

3. The president has also negotiated with the landlords of most of the store locations to allow the company to pay the rent in a lump-sum total in the month of December. He proposes to expense the rent over the year on a pro rata basis, following the expected sales pattern.

Required:

Prepare a brief paragraph discussing each of the president's proposals for the Li'l Tyke's quarterly income statements. Do you agree with his plans? Why or why not?

P5.6 Revenue recognition. At the beginning of 1996, John Cornell decided to quit his current job as construction supervisor for Walsh, Inc., a construction company headquartered in Regina, Saskatchewan, and formed his own company. When he resigned, he had a written contract to build a custom home in Estevan, Saskatchewan, at a price of $400,000. The full price was payable in cash when the house was completed and available for occupancy.

By year-end 1996, Cornell's new company, Distinctive Homes, Inc., had spent $50,000 for labour, $107,740 for materials, and $3,800 in miscellaneous expenses in connection with construction of the home. Cornell estimated that the project was 70 percent complete at year-end. In addition, construction materials on hand at year-end cost $2,600.

During the year, Distinctive Homes, Inc. had also purchased a small run-down house for $95,000, spent $32,000 fixing it up, and then sold it on November 1, 1995, for $175,000. The buyer paid $25,000 down and signed a note for the remainder of the balance due. The note called for interest payments only, at a rate of 12 percent per year, with a balloon payment for the outstanding balance at the end of 1997.

John's wife, Karen, was employed to keep the accounting records for Distinctive Homes, Inc., and on December 31, she prepared the following statement:

Assets		Debts and Capital	
Cash	$ 21,000	Accounts payable	$ 44,600
Material on hand	2,600	Owner's investment	242,540
House renovation contract	150,000	Sale of renovated house	175,000
Construction in progress	161,540		
Cost of renovated house	127,000		
	$462,140		$462,140

After reviewing the statement, John and Karen got into a discussion concerning the level of income the company earned during the year. John argued that the entire profit on the sale of the renovated home, along with 70 percent of the expected profit from the construction contract, had been earned. Karen, on the other hand, maintained that the profit on the renovation should be recognized only to the extent of the cash actually collected and that no profit should be recognized on the new home construction until it was completed and available for occupancy.

After discussing the problem at length, John and Karen agreed there were four possible alternative approaches to measuring the company's income:

1. Report the entire amount of renovation income and the proportionate amount of construction contract income.

2. Report the entire amount of renovation income but none of the construction contract income.

3. Report the renovation income in proportion to the amount of cash received and the construction contract income in proportion to the amount of work completed.

4. Report the renovation income in proportion to the amount of cash received but none of the construction contract income.

Required:

Prepare the balance sheets and income statements that would result under each of the above four approaches. Which set of statements do you believe best reflects the results of Distinctive Homes, Inc., for 1996?

P5.7 Revenue recognition. Supercolider, Inc., is an independent research and development laboratory that undertakes contractual research for a variety of corporate and governmental clients. Occasionally, scientists at the laboratory undertake independent research, which, if successful (i.e., results in new products, designs, or technology), is then marketed by the company. In January 1993, scientists at Supercolider began work on a number of minor research projects involving high-speed atom smashing. During 1993, costs incurred in these efforts amounted to $363,000. In May 1994, promising results emerged and were reported to the Department of Energy. Development costs incurred in 1994 through the end of May totalled $204,000.

At this point, Supercolider tried to secure a government contract to support the remainder of the research effort. The Department of Energy (DOE) was reluctant, however, to commit substantial sums until further tests had been completed. Nonetheless, to ensure that it retained the "first right of refusal," the DOE gave Supercolider a "seed grant" of $50,000 to help support the continuation of the studies; this grant carried a stipulation that the DOE would retain the right to acquire the results, patents, and copyrights from the research any time on or before December 31, 1995, for $2,400,000.

Further testing proved favourable, although additional development costs incurred amounted to $325,000 in 1994 and to $210,000 in 1995. On December 28, 1995, the DOE exercised its right and agreed to purchase the results, patents, and copyrights from the research. As previously agreed, the DOE paid Supercolider $300,000 immediately, with the remainder of the contract price payable in seven equal annual instalments beginning on December 31, 1996, through December 31, 2002. On March 1, 1996, Supercolider delivered all scientific and legal documents, test results, and samples to the DOE offices.

Required:

Evaluate the facts of this case and determine when Supercolider, Inc., should recognize the various revenue streams associated with its work on this project. Also determine when Supercolider should recognize the various developmental costs. Be prepared to substantiate your position.

P5.8 Statements classification. Describe how the following items would be disclosed on a properly classified financial statement.

a. Earnings per share.

b. Extraordinary items.

c. Dividends declared.

d. Deferred charge.

P5.9 Classified income statement. Determine the missing amounts affecting the income statement in each of the independent cases below:

	A	B	C	D
Sales	$53,000	?	$62,000	$81,000
Cost of sales	22,000	$32,000	?	39,000
Gross profit	?	22,000	33,000	?
Operating expenses	28,000	?	10,000	21,000
Extraordinary item	(11,000)	7,000	?	(2,000)
Net income (loss)	?	11,000	16,000	?

P5.10 Classified income statement. Determine the missing amounts affecting the income statement in each of the independent cases below:

	A	B	C	D
Sales	$77,000	?	$67,000	$72,000
Cost of sales	46,000	$42,000	?	37,000
Gross profit	?	31,000	38,000	?
Operating expenses	28,000	?	16,000	18,000
Extraordinary item	12,000	(8,000)	?	(3,000)
Discontinued operations	?	(17,000)	6,000	(4,000)
Net income (loss)	(11,000)	(7,000)	22,000	?

P5.11 Gross profit analysis. Reliable Auto Body Service is a small vehicle repair shop. Reliable specializes in auto body repair and paint jobs. Reliable performs two types of jobs: retail sales and insurance claims. During the past few weeks, the weather has been extremely poor, with heavy snowy blizzards followed by icy winter conditions with freezing rain. As a result of these poor weather conditions, the region has seen numerous "fender-benders" and serious automobile accidents. These conditions have been excellent for business. During the most recent month, Reliable had retail labour sales of $34,000, and retail parts sales of $29,000. The insurance repairs have been very good during this period with labour sales of $52,000 and related parts sales of $44,000. Gross profit percentages of sales were:

Retail labour	60%
Insurance labour	55
Retail parts	30
Insurance parts	25

Determine the total gross profit in dollars earned during the month.

P5.12 Gross profit analysis. Dependable Auto Service is a vehicle repair shop. Dependable performs two types of jobs: retail sales and warranty repairs for a large auto dealership. During the most recent month, Dependable had retail labour sales of $51,000, combined with retail parts sales of $38,000. The warranty repairs have been very good during this period with labour sales of $67,000 and related parts sales of $49,000. Cost of sales were:

Retail labour	$22,000
Warranty labour	34,000
Retail parts	27,000
Warranty parts	36,000

Determine the total gross profit in dollars earned during the month, and the gross profit margin ratio for each sales category.

P5.13 General journal entries. Rosa Maclean has decided to open an automobile dealership, Rose Valley Auto Sales, Ltd. During the first month the following transactions occurred:

1. Rosa opens a bank account for the dealership and deposits $200,000 of her personal savings.

2. Purchases service equipment for $50,000 and parts shelving for $20,000, paying $40,000 cash and obtaining a bank loan for the balance.

3. The parts manager purchases parts on credit for $80,000.

4. Payment of $10,000 for parts previously purchased on credit.

5. Payment on bank loan of $2,000.

6. New car sales manager purchases 40 new vehicles at an average cost of $16,500, financed through a bank loan.

7. During the month, the service department has sales on account of $50,000 (gross profit 60%).

8. During the month, the parts department has sales on account of $75,000 (gross profit 30%).

9. At month-end the following payments were made:

Service manager's salary	$3,500
Parts manager's salary	3,200
Utilities expense	1,500

10. The new vehicle department sold a new vehicle for $19,000 cash that had an original invoice cost of $17,300.

Required:

a. Prepare general journal entries for the above transactions.

P5.14 Statement classification. Describe how the following items would be disclosed on a properly classified financial statement:

a. Deferred income.

b. Contingent liabilities.

c. Earnings per share.

d. Discontinued operations.

e. Amortization methods used.

P5.15 Income measurement. At the beginning of 1996, M. Carlson, the owner and operator of a large agricultural concern, had no inventories on hand. During 1996, however, his company produced 80,000 bushels of corn, 100,000 bushels of soybeans, and 160,000 bushels of barley. Upon completion of the harvest, Carlson sold one-half of each of his crops at the following prices: corn, $4.50 per bushel; soybeans, $3.25 per bushel; and barley, $2 per bushel. At year-end, the remaining half of Carlson's crop was unsold.

To operate the company, Carlson incurred costs during 1996 of $370,000, including $100,000 in amortization on his buildings and equipment. Moreover, Carlson estimates that his selling and delivery costs on the crops average $0.42 per bushel; these costs are included in his total operating costs given above. Finally, the commodities price quotations reported in *The Globe and Mail* at year-end revealed that the current market price per bushel for each of the crops was as follows: corn, $5 per bushel; soybeans, $3.47 per bushel; and barley, $2.20 per bushel.

Presented is the balance sheet for M. Carlson, Inc., as of January 1, 1996:

M. CARLSON., INC.
Balance Sheet
As of January 1, 1996

Assets		Liabilities	
Cash	$ 75,000	Accounts payable	$ –0–
Land	300,000	**Equity**	
Building & equipment	750,000	Capital stock	550,000
Accumulated amortization	(350,000)	Retained earnings	225,000
	$775,000		$775,000

Required:

Prepare an income statement and balance sheet for the company as of December 31, 1996. Prepare a list of the accounting policy decisions that you made in arriving at these statements.

P5.16 Accrual versus cash basis accounting. Meredith, Miller and Associates, Inc., is a management consulting group that was organized for business on August 1, 1996. Greg Meredith and Kate Miller each contributed $20,000 cash for share capital in the new company. The firm also borrowed $15,000 from a local bank on September 1, 1996; the loan was to be paid in full on August 30, 1997, with interest at the rate of 12 percent annually.

The new company rented office space on September 1, paying two months' rent in advance. The regular monthly rental fees of $600 per month were to be made on the first day of each month beginning on November 1. The company purchased equipment in early August at a total cost of $3,600 cash. The owners estimated that the useful life of the office equipment was three years, with no residual value.

For the five months ended December 31, 1996, the company had rendered $31,000 in consulting services. Of this amount, $19,000 had been collected by year-end. Other costs incurred and paid in cash by year-end included:

Utilities	$ 550
Part-time typist/secretary	6,000
Miscellaneous office supplies	325

Unpaid bills at year-end included a telephone bill for $75 and wages for the typist-secretary of $600.

Required:

You have been retained by the firm of Meredith, Miller and Associates, Inc., to prepare a set of accounting statements as of December 31, 1996. Using the above information, prepare a balance sheet, an income statement using the accrual basis of accounting, an income statement using the cash basis of accounting, and a statement of changes in financial position. On the basis of your findings, be prepared to comment on the performance of the company during its first five months of operations.

P5.17 Accrued interest income (*Published with permission of CGA Canada*). A company accountant was overheard saying, "We regularly record the accrual of interest income. If it becomes certain, however, that the interest income will not be received, we discontinue its recognition. Not only do we stop accruing interest, but we actually reverse any interest which has been accrued on the books but not received."

Required:

a. Can this action be justified by GAAP?

b. What entry would probably be made to reverse the accrued interest?

P5.18 Construction in progress (*Published with permission of CGA Canada*). On January 2, Bush Construction Company entered into a contract to complete an office building for a fee of $10,000,000. On that date the estimated cost to complete the building was estimated at $8,500,000.

Required:

a. Assuming that Bush completed 40 percent of the construction at a cost of $3,600,000, calculate the amount of income that should be recognized.

b. In the next year the construction costs were $4,100,000 and the project was 90 percent complete. Calculate the amount of income to be recognized by Bush for the year.

P5.19 Analysis of an error for unrecorded sales. The partial income statement of Stoney Plain Enterprises, Ltd., for the year ended December 31 is shown below:

Sales	$182,000
Cost of goods sold	97,000
Gross profit	$ 85,000

A few days after the financial statements of Stoney Plain Enterprises, Ltd., had been prepared and distributed to the shareholders, an accounting error was discovered. It was determined that invoices for sales on account totalling $11,000 had not been included in the financial report. The correct amount for the sales figure should be $193,000. The ending Accounts Receivable balance was understated by $11,000.

Required:

a. Determine the impact of this error on gross profit, the gross profit margin ratio, and the accounts receivable turnover ratio. Assume the Accounts Receivable balance was $26,000 on January 1 and $21,000 on December 31.

b. Explain the impact of the error on the statement of changes in financial position.

c. Would you consider the error to have a material impact on the financial statements of Stoney Plain Enterprises, Ltd.?

P5.20 Gross profit analysis. The financial statements of Victorian Country Gardens, Ltd., include average Accounts Receivable and Inventory balances of $72,000 and $87,000 respectively. An analysis of the financial statements determines the accounts receivable turnover ratio for the period to be 5.72. The inventory turnover ratio for the same period is 3.46. Determine the dollar value of gross profit for the period and the gross profit ratio.

P5.21 Gross profit analysis. The financial statements of the Royal Dance Theatre include average Accounts Receivable and Inventory balances of $13,000 and $16,000 respectively. An analysis of the financial statements determines the accounts receivable turnover ratio for the period to be 6.64. The inventory turnover ratio for the same period is 4.55. Determine the dollar value of gross profit and the gross profit ratio for the period.

P5.22 Turnover analysis. The partial income statement of Summerside Enterprises, Ltd., for the year ended January 31 is shown below:

Sales	$118,000
Cost of sales	87,000
Gross profit	$ 31,000

The accounts receivable turnover ratio for the period is 5.22. The inventory turnover ratio for the same period is 4.40. Determine the average Accounts Receivable and Inventory balances for the period.

P5.23 Turnover analysis. The partial income statement of Dawson Creek Parts & Services, Limited, for the year ended October 31 is shown below:

Sales	$789,000
Cost of sales	613,000
Gross profit	$176,000

The accounts receivable turnover ratio for the period is 3.47. The inventory turnover ratio for the same period is 2.77. Determine the average Accounts Receivable and Inventory balances for the period.

P5.24 Industry specific accounts. The following account titles were selected from annual reports published by various major companies:

a. Amortization of Special Tools.

b. Dealer Desposits.

c. Accrued Marketing.

d. Timber and Timberlands, Net of Timber Amortization.

e. Leasehold Costs, Improvements, Store Fixtures, and Equipment.

f. Exploration Expense.

g. Charge for Discontinuing Automatic Blanket Operations.

h. Operating Revenues:
   Local Service
   Interprovincial Access
   Intraprovincial Access
   Toll Other

Required:

For each of the above account titles, indicate whether the account is a balance sheet account or an income statement account. For each account describe the kinds of event(s) that might be reflected in the account.

P5.25 Financial analysis. Big Rock Brewery, Ltd., is a regional producer and marketer of speciality draught and bottled beer located in Calgary, Alberta. Founded in 1985, the company's products are currently marketed in the prairie provinces and also through independent distributors in the United States. Presented below is Big Rock's comparable statement of income and retained earnings for the year ended March 31, and balance sheet at March 31.

BIG ROCK BREWERY, LTD.
Statement of Income and Retained Earnings
Year Ended March 31

	1994	1993
Sales	$16,140,745	$12,730,373
Government commissions/taxes	6,572,458	5,694,524
Cost of sales	4,363,698	3,258,163
Gross profit	$ 5,204,589	$ 3,777,686
Expenses:		
Amortization	$ 414,946	$ 212,664
Selling and administrative	2,756,846	2,078,767
Interest on long-term debt	12,891	12,775
Interest on other debt	—	40,379
Loss (gain) on disposal of capital assets	(79,815)	5,864
	$ 3,104,868	$ 2,350,449
Operating income	2,099,721	$ 1,427,237
Income taxes	792,000	502,500
Net income for the year	$ 1,307,721	$ 924,737
Retained earnings beginning	1,745,365	820,628
Retained earnings ending	$ 3,053,086	$ 1,745,365

BIG ROCK BREWERY, LTD.
Balance Sheet
As at March 31

	1994	1993
Assets		
Current assets:		
Cash	$ 311,960	$ 53,851
Accounts receivable	1,177,089	1,212,178
Inventories	943,033	711,312
Prepaid expenses	67,138	72,763
Total current assets	$ 2,499,220	$2,050,104
Property, plant, and equipment — net	7,959,570	6,986,401
Other assets	10,000	10,000
	$10,468,790	$9,046,505
Liabilities and shareholders' equity		
Current liabilities:		
Bank indebtedness	—	$ 761,474
Accounts payable	$ 609,357	391,595
Income tax payable	392,663	59,987
Current portion of long-term debt	80,400	80,400
Total current liabilities	$ 1,082,420	$1,293,456
Long-term debt	89,000	79,400
Deferred income taxes	881,500	565,500
Total liabilities	$ 2,052,920	$1,938,356
Shareholders' equity:		
Share capital*	5,362,784	5,362,784
Retained earnings	3,053,086	1,745,365
Total shareholders' equity	$ 8,415,870	$7,108,149
	$10,468,790	$9,046,505

*Common shares outstanding: 1994 — 4,406,200 and 1993 — 4,406,200.

Required:

Prepare a report to evaluate the financial position of Big Rock Brewery, Ltd. Perform the financial analysis you deem necessary to explain the operations of Big Rock.

5.26 Sales returns. In December, Barton Industires, Inc., disclosed that it would restate its results for the third quarter because a sale it had booked was returned during the fourth quarter. According to a news release by the maker of oil field equipment, the restatement would reduce its third-quarter revenues from $8.1 million to $7.1 million, and its net income from $1.0 million to $400,000.

Required:

Determine the accounting entries required for the third quarter restatement. Ignore any income taxes.

P5.27 Income statement, cash flow analysis (*Published with permission of CGA Canada*). Betty Hill realized a long-standing ambition of being her own boss when she opened Colour World paint store. The venture was made possible by a $100,000 inheritance from her late aunt. When Betty started the business on January 2, Delta Valley, a rapidly expanding community, had no such store, and it appeared to her that the business would succeed. On January 2, Betty deposited $105,000 in a bank account under the name of Colour World. She then paid $24,000 cash for store equipment, which she expected would last for 10 years with no residual value. She also paid $7,200 in advance for six months' store rent.

Betty decided to mark her merchandise for sale at 30 percent above cost — that is, an item that cost $10 was marked to sell for $13. This markup was 5 to 10 percent lower than in nearby Burnaby and Vancouver — this she believed would entice customers not only from Delta Valley but nearby communities as well.

On June 30, six months after opening her store, Betty has come to you for advice. She tells you she cannot understand why her cash balance is only $100, especially when business has been so good.

Your examination of Colour World records indicates the following:

- Purchases of merchandise were $300,000; all of the purchases were paid for except for $20,000, which is due on July 31.
- Expenses (other than rent) paid during the first six months amounted to $28,000; $1,400 of expenses remain outstanding and unpaid.
- Accounts receivable amounted to $58,200.
- Inventory on June 30 amounted to $75,000.

Required:

a. Prepare, in good form, an income statement for Colour World.

b. Prepare a schedule in good form that explains the $100 cash balance by showing the cash receipts and cash disbursements during the first six months ended June 30.

P5.28 Annual report information. The following list identifies a number of items that might tell you something about a company. Study this list from the standpoint of a potential investor.

1. Brief history of business.

2. Financial statements for last five years (audited if possible).

  a. Balance sheets.

  b. Income statements.

3. Evaluation of labour relations and terms of union contracts.

4. Description, age, and general evaluation of plants, manufacturing equipment, warehouses, branches, and delivery equipment, owned or leased.

5. Trend of sales of each of principal products for five years.

6. Description of corporate structure.

7. Number of employees.

8. Explanation of unusual items on financial statements.

9. List of officers and directors, and their affiliations and background.

10. Principal competitors — comparative share of market.

11. Share distribution, number of shareholders.

12. Description of marketing and distirbution methods and areas.

13. Details of debt.

14. Status of income tax audit and liability.

15. Percentage of ownership of share available for acquisition.

16. Description and cost of fringe benefits (insurance, medical, pensions).

17. Details of unrecorded and contingent liabilities.

18. Description of any option, incentive, or profit sharing plans.

19. Organization, functions of principal executives, and their ages.

20. Description of principal customers — share of business.

21. Projection of sales and earnings over next five years.

22. Willingness of management to continue in business.

23. Terms of principal contracts and leases.

24. Extent of export sales.

25. Major capital expenditures presently authorized.

26. Status of litigation and any other claims or suits against the company.

27. Extent of advertizing.

28. Estimate of major capital expenditures required over next five years.

29. Copies of annual reports to shareholders.

30. Copy of charter and bylaws.

31. Cost of capital.

32. Social responsibility activities.

33. Major subsidiaries and affiliates.

Required:

Prepare a brief paper identifying the top 10 items from the list that you would want to be able to study and review. Why did you select those items? Which would you expect to find in the company's annual report to shareholders?

P5.29 Financial statements.   Michelle Mason decided to operate a concession in a local recreation area for the months of May, June, July, and August. Although she kept no accounting records, Michelle was careful to process all funds related to operations through a bank account opened specifically for that purpose. An analysis of all deposits and cheques written for the four months is summarized below:

Deposits

Michelle's investment of personal funds	$ 1,750
Food sales	9,420
Other revenue	300
Short-term bank loan	2,000
Total deposits	$13,470

Cheques

Cleaning supplies purchased	$ 945
Utilities	330
Cost of food sales	4,600
Wages to assistant	1,200
Insurance premiums	165
Loan interest	105
Withdrawals — Michelle	810
Total cheques	$ 8,155
Cash balance — August 31	$ 5,315

A discussion with Michelle reveals the following additional information:

1. Other revenue includes all revenue earned except for $250 from a company that scheduled an event for the last weekend in August. This account has not been collected at August 31.

2. A deposit of $150 was paid in advance and included in food sales. The related event could not be scheduled during the summer and the deposit must be refunded.

3. Cleaning supplies on hand at the end of August totalled $170.

4. The insurance premiums represent coverage for the months of May, June, July, and August.

5. All payments due were paid except for an invoice for cleaning supplies of $120, which remains unpaid at August 31.

6. Michelle estimates the utility bill for August when received will be $110.

7. Interest on the loan accrued and unpaid at August 31 was $75.

8. Wages to an assistant for $175 were unpaid at August 31.

Required:

a. Prepare an income statement for the four months ending August 31.

b. Prepare a balance sheet at August 31.

P5.30 Comprehensive financial statements. Shown below are two trial balances for Batton Company. All accounts have normal balances. Batton has a December 31 year-end. The trial balance shown for December 31, 1996, was prepared after the books were closed at year-end. The trial balance for February 28, 1997, was prepared after including any necessary adjusting entries for the two-month period.

	Adjusted Trial Balance at February 28, 1997	Post-Closing Trial Balance at December 31, 1996
Accounts payable	$ 31,000	$38,000
Accounts receivable	22,000	17,000
Accumulated amortization	20,000	15,000
Advances from customers	4,000	3,000
Cash	6,000	5,000
Common shares	15,000	14,000
Cost of sales	70,000	
Amortization expense	5,000	
Dividends declared	4,000	
Equipment	45,000	40,000
Interest expense	7,000	
Interest payable	5,000	6,000
Land	21,000	19,000
Merchandise inventory	13,000	12,000
Mortgage payable	36,000	28,000
Patent	18,000	21,000
Patent expense	3,000	
Prepaid rent	4,000	2,000
Rent expense	5,000	
Retained earnings	12,000	12,000
Sales	115,000	
Wages expense	15,000	

Required:

a. Prepare an income statement for Batton Company for the two months ending February 28, 1997.

b. Prepare a retained earnings statement as at February 28, 1997.

c. Prepare a balance sheet as at February 28, 1997.

d. Prepare a statement of changes in financial position for the two months ending February 28, 1997.

P5.31 Financial analysis. Presented below is Blaze Limited's comparable financial statements for the year ended December 31. Perform an analysis of financial strength and management performance of the company. Your report should include comments as to the company's financial position.

BLAZE, LIMITED
Income Statement
For the Year Ended December 31

	1996	1995
Sales	$662,000	$572,000
Cost of goods sold	450,000	410,000
Gross profit	$212,000	$162,000
Expenses:		
Operating and maintenance	$ 71,000	$ 69,000
Selling and administrative	49,000	50,000
Amortization	22,000	15,000
	$142,000	$134,000
Income before income taxes	$ 70,000	$ 28,000
Income taxes	(32,000)	(11,000)
Net income	$ 38,000	$ 17,000

BLAZE, LIMITED
Balance Sheet
As at December 31

	1996	1995
Assets		
Current assets:		
Cash	$ 13,000	$ 49,000
Accounts receivable	99,000	76,000
Inventories	73,000	60,000
Supplies	34,000	16,000
Total current assets	$219,000	$201,000
Long-term investments	38,000	18,000
Property, plant, and equipment	376,000	254,000
Accumulated amortization	(34,000)	(22,000)
	$599,000	$451,000
Liabilties and Shareholders Equity		
Current liabilities:		
Notes payable	$ 79,000	$ 72,000
Accounts payable	96,000	86,000
Current portion — long-term debt	15,000	10,000
Total current liabilities	$190,000	$168,000
Long-term debt	176,000	140,000
Total liabilities	$366,000	$308,000
Shareholders' equity:		
Share capital*	$139,000	$ 87,000
Retained earnings	94,000	56,000
Total shareholders' equity	$233,000	$143,000
	$599,000	$451,000

*Weighted-average shares outstanding: 1996: 36,000 shares; 1995: 25,000 shares.

P5.32 Cash and accrual basis of accounting (*Society of Management Accountants of British Columbia*). You have been asked to examine the books of the True Machine Maintenance Company. The company sells maintenance contracts to service chain saws. The owner has tried to keep his books and did so on a cash basis. After some investigation, you discover the following incomplete facts:

Account Balances

Accounts*	June 30	July 31
Maintenance contracts Revenue	$ 600	$3,600
Cash	1,200	1,500
Rent expense	1,500	3,000

*Note: This is not a complete list of all accounts.

1. During the month of July maintenance contracts were sold for a value of $3,000 cash.

2. The terms of the maintenance contracts were for limited service spread evenly over a six-month period, starting July 1.

3. True Machine Maintenance rents its premises and pays quarterly in advance. The rent was last paid on July 1.

4. On July 3 True Machine Maintenance purchases equipment for $20,000. Of this amount, only an advance of $1,000 was paid on July 15. The balance is due on October 1 with no interest.

5. During July work performed under the maintenance contracts cost True Machine Maintenance $200 for labour and materials, paid in cash.

6. The company's policy is to amortize its capital assets straight line over 10 years.

Required:

a. Prepare an income statement for June 30–July 31 on an accrual basis.

b. Prepare an income statement for June 30–July 31 on a cash basis.

P5.33 Financial statements (*Society of Management Accountants of British Columbia*). Mr. Lonely, a sole proprietor, started business on January 31, 1996, with $10,000 of his own capital.

During 1996 the following occurred: Credit sales were $70,000, while cash sales totalled $12,120. Mr. Lonely made cash purchases of $45,200, of which $7,312 remained unsold at year-end. Premises were rented on February 1. Rent was $800 per month, paid quarterly in advance. On March 1, Mr. Lonely purchased furniture for $12,000, which is expected to last for 10 years. After 10 years, the furniture is expected to be worth 10 percent of the cost.

On May 1, a three-year insurance policy was purchased for $900. On June 1, equipment was purchased for $9,240. It is expected to last seven years with no residual value. (The straight-line method of amortization is used for all depreciable assets.)

Mr. Lonely received a 10 percent $10,000 bank loan on September 30. Interest is payable annually, while the principal is due in four years. During the year, Mr. Lonely took home $14,000 in cash and $1,100 worth of inventory from the firm. Supplies purchased during the year were $700. Unused supplies on hand at December 31 were $420. Cash on hand at December 31 was $3,480. Ten percent of credit sales remain uncollected, while 1 percent of credit sales are expected to be uncollectible.

Mr. Lonely has come to you, his friend, to sort out his finances.

Required:

Prepare in good form an income statement and balance sheet for the period ending December 31, 1995. Ignore income taxes.

P5.34 Revenue recognition (*Society of Management Accountants of British Columbia*). Akeems Fitness Centre opened for business on April 1 with the following membership fee schedule:

Ten trial sessions	$ 30
One-year membership	180
Two more year membership	312
Three-year membership	396

The owner expected prospective members would pay for the 10 trial sessions; then, if interested, pay for a membership. The first three months' receipts are shown below:

		Number Sold	Dollars Received
April	Trials	30	$ 900
	One-year memberships	10	1,800
May	Trials	20	600
	One-year memberships	10	1,800
	Two-year memberships	5	1,560
June	Trials	20	600
	One-year memberships	20	3,600
	Two-year memberships	10	3,120
	Three-year memberships	5	1,980
Total receipts			$15,960

Assumptions:

1. All membership and trial session receipts are received in cash at the beginning of the month.

2. All trial sessions must be used up in the month paid for.

Required:

a. Using accrual accounting, what amount of revenue should be recognized in the first quarter ended June 30?

b. If your answer to *a.* is different than $15,960, where would the balance of the receipts be shown in the financial statements?

P5.35 Financial statement preparation (*Society of Management Accountants of British Columbia*). Tahiti, Ltd., is a two-year-old publicly traded manufacturing company. Below is incomplete information relating to the financial year, which ended December 31.

January 1	Balances	December 31	Balances
Inventory	$43,200	Accounts payable	$32,900
Accounts payable	–0–	Dividends payable	10,000
Accounts receivable	50,000		
Retained earnings	62,400		

1. Sales were $787,500

2. Cash dividends paid were $10,000.

3. Payments to suppliers were $267,090.

4. Collections from customers were $619,410.

5. 12 percent, 10-year bonds payable are outstanding.

6. Gross profit margin is 60 percent.

7. Total expenses were $352,000.

8. Total liabilities are equal to 50 percent of current assets.

9. Bond interest expense is $12,000 per year.

10. All sales and purchases are on credit.

11. Amortization expense (machinery) using the straight-line method of amortization, based upon a five-year life, is $40,000 per annum.

Required:

From the information above, prepare a balance sheet and a statement of retained earnings for the period ending December 31.

P5.36 Income Statement (*Society of Management Accountants of British Columbia*). Kieron Logging Supplies, Inc., sells logging equipment. An alphabetical listing of account balances as at September 1, 1996, is as follows:

Acounts payable	$425,000
Accounts receivable	219,000
Allowance for doubtful accounts	12,500
Building	565,000
Cash	187,000
Common shares (750 shares issued and outstanding)	275,000
Dividends payable	35,000
Inventory	395,000
Land	410,000
Mortgage payable	585,000
Retained earnings	444,200

All accounts had normal debit or credit balances. Information relative to the fiscal year follows:

1. Of the total sales of $2,745,000, credit sales were $1,875,000.

2. Collections on accounts receivable were $1,675,000. Bad debt expense for the year was $10,500.

3. Kieron Logging Supplies, Inc., made purchases of $1,775,000, all on credit. Goods totalling $42,725 were determined to be unsatisfactory and were returned to the suppliers. Payments to suppliers totalled $1,485,000.

4. Deposits received from customers in advance on special orders totalled $72,000. As of the company's year-end, no work had been performed on these orders.

5. Ending inventory was $286,500.

6. The dividends were paid.

7. Since the building was acquired in late August 1996, no amortization had been recorded on it for that year. The building has an estimated residual value of $65,000 and is to be amortized over a 40-year period.

8. The company paid $15,000 for transportation-in, and $7,200 for transportation-out.

9. Kieron Logging Company had made total mortgage payments of $85,000, of which $74,800 represented interest on the mortgage.

10. Other operating expenses incurred and paid were:

Advertizing	$ 22,000
Salaries	85,000
Utilities	5,500
Telephone	1,750
Property taxes	4,200
Income taxes	184,000

Required:

Prepare a detailed income statement for year ending August 31, 1997. All calculations should be shown.

P5.37 Financial analysis. The financial statements of The Toronto Sun Publishing Corporation and Thompson Corporation are presented below. Prepare a financial analysis to evaluate the financial positions of the two companies. Perform any analysis you deem necessary given the information provided.

THE TORONTO SUN PUBLISHING CORPORATION
Consolidated Statements of Retained Earnings
(in thousands)

	Year Ended December 25, 1993	Year Ended December 26, 1992
Retained earnings — Beginning of year	$128,944	$131,300
Net (loss) earnings for the year	(51,163)	2,358
	$ 77,781	$133,658
Dividends	4,788	4,714
Retained earnings — End of year	$ 72,993	$128,944

THE TORONTO SUN PUBLISHING CORPORATION
Consolidated Statements of Earnings
(in thousands)

	1993	1992
Revenue:		
Newspaper operations	$289,251	$290,975
Commercial printing	39,459	39,399
	$328,710	$330,374
Operating expenses:		
Wages and employee benefits	$149,265	$147,815
Newsprint and ink	57,698	56,551
Departmental operating expenses	98,800	104,047
Depreciation and amortization	17,185	16,662
Amortization of goodwill and intangibles	3,180	3,075
	$326,128	$328,150
Operating profit:		
Provision for early retirement and voluntary buyout programs	(10,102)	—
Adjustment of carrying value of U.S. holdings	(46,647)	—
Interest expense on long-term debt	—	(399)
Other net interest expense	(544)	(609)
Foreign exchange gain	15	136
	$ (54,696)	$ 1,352
Income taxes provided	(239)	(3,689)
Minority interest	3,772	4,695
Net (loss) earnings for the year	$ (51,163)	$ 2,358

THE TORONTO SUN PUBLISHING CORPORATION
Consolidated Balance Sheets
(in thousands)

Assets

	December 25, 1993	December 26, 1992
Current assets:		
Cash and short-term investments	$ 5,859	$ 6,790
Accounts receivable	48,934	46,642
Inventory	5,916	4,968
Prepaid expenses	3,352	2,869
Employee share purchase loans	1,162	1,303
	$ 65,223	$ 62,572
Fixed assets	149,021	151,076
Goodwill	73,650	88,569
Investment	—	28,875
Newspaper circulation	17,000	17,500
Other assets	5,694	6,523
	$310,588	$355,115

Liabilities

	December 25, 1993	December 26, 1992
Current liabilities:		
Bank term loan	—	$ 5,850
Accounts payable	$ 43,128	30,963
Income taxes payable	291	556
Deferred subscription revenue	9,731	8,921
Due to related company	13,939	10,592
	$ 67,089	$ 56,882
Deferred income taxes	5,396	6,542
Minority interest	8,396	10,348
	$ 80,881	$ 73,772

Shareholder's Equity

	December 25, 1993	December 26, 1992
Capital stock		
Authorized — unlimited number of common shares		
Issued and fully paid — 24,215,437 shares (December 26, 1992 — 23,811,167)	$155,616	$150,890
Retained earnings	72,993	128,944
Cumulative translation adjustment	1,098	1,509
	$229,707	$281,343
	$310,588	$355,115

THOMPSON CORPORATION
Conslidated Balance Sheet
(millions of U.S. dollars)

	December 31	
	1993	**1992**
Assets		
Current assets:		
Cash	$ 496	$ 315
Accounts receivable	671	658
Inventories	272	255
Prepaid expenses	331	263
	$1,770	$1,491
Property and equipment	1,378	1,353
Aircraft and spares	681	587
Publishing rights and circulation	2,611	2,667
Goodwill	1,412	1,450
Other assets	361	359
	$8,213	$7,907
Liabilities and Shareholders' Equity		
Current liabilities:		
Short-term indebtedness	$ 178	$ 29
Accounts payable	914	841
Deferred revenue	552	470
Current portion of long-term debt	15	41
	$1,659	$1,381
Long-term debt	2,612	2,589
Finance leases	381	394
Other liabilities	300	261
Deferred income taxes	269	275
	$5,221	$4,900
Shareholders' equity:		
Share capital	$ 728	$ 725
Cumulative translation adjustment	(335)	(298)
Retained earnings	2,599	2,580
	$2,992	$3,007
	$8,213	$7,907

THOMPSON CORPORATION
Conslidated Statement of Earnings and Retained Earnings
(millions of U.S. dollars)

	December 31	
	1993	**1992**
Sales	$5,849	$5,980
Cost of sales, selling, marketing, general, and administrative expenses	(4,868)	(5,058)
Depreciation	(250)	(234)
Operating profit before amortization and unusual charges	$ 731	$ 688
Amortization	(113)	(117)
Unusual charges	(100)	(170)
Operating profit after amortization and unusual charges	$ 518	$ 401
Corporate	(16)	(17)
Net interest expense and other financing costs	(175)	(164)
Income taxes	(50)	(54)
Earnings	$ 277	$ 166
Retained earings at beginning of year	2,580	2,668
Dividends delcared on common shares	(258)	(254)
Retained earnings at end of year	$2,599	$2,580

5.12 CASES

C5.1 The cost of ill-gotten sales: RJR Nabisco. On September 21, 1989, RJR Nabisco announced that it would end the practice of trade loading in its domestic cigarette distribution business. According to a news release, the discontinuation of this merchandising practice would cause RJR, acquired by Kohlberg, Kravis Roberts in late 1988 in a $25 billion leveraged buyout, to forgo $340 million in operating income in the last six months of 1989. The news release reported that the practice was discontinued "to curb excess inventories."

Trade loading refers to a marketing practice in which manufacturers attempt to induce wholesale customers (known as *trade*) to purchase more inventory than they can currently sell. According to RJR officials, trade loading is a common practice in many industries, such as the food and beverage industry, and has been shown to be a highly effective marketing tool. For example, in spite of declining cigarette sales, RJR officials reported that trade loading had resulted in excess wholesaler purchases of more than 18.5 billion cigarettes as of January 1989, or approximately a six weeks' supply.

Trade loading typically involves push and/or pull price promotions. A push promotion, for example, involves a price discount from the manufacturer to the wholesaler, whereas a pull promotion involves a price discount (also financed by the manufacturer) from the wholesaler to the retailer. In the case of RJR, the timing of trade loading promotions was synchronized with industry pricing patterns. Beginning in 1983, tobacco manufacturers effectively institutionalized the practice of price increases (only) in June and December. Wholesalers typically responded to the anticipated price increases by purchasing large quantities of inventories just prior to the quarter ending June and December so that the inventory could be resold to retailers at the new, higher prices.

As a way to induce similar inventory purchases in the quarters ending in March and September, RJR and other tobacco producers instituted the push/pull price promotions. Thus, significant selling and shipping could be anticipated by tobacco producers at the end of each quarter.

In spite of the costs associated with maintaining and warehousing the excess inventory, whole-saler-distributors became heavily dependent on trade loading. According to *Fortune* magazine, "Many would be breakeven operations or money losers if they did not get a quarterly surge from the load." Wholesaler-distributors also benefit, however, from the tobacco industry's generous product return policy: Cigarettes that manufacturers regard as too stale to sell (i.e., those that are six months old) are eligible for a full return. In spite of this generous return policy, however, distributors frequently sold stale cigarettes because of their higher profit margin, a practice that concerned many manufacturers worried about product quality and customer satis-faction.

Required:

Evaluate the practice of trade loading. What are the costs and benefits of this practice? What are the implications of trade loading for the quality of reported earnings and assets? Why would RJR Nabisco stop this practice?

C5.2 Revenue recognition under long-term contracts: Buildmore Construction Company. In June 1996, Buildmore Construction Company (BCC) was employed by the city of Sudbury to assist in constructing its new Trade Centre complex. BCC was to construct the superstructure of a multistorey office building as part of the city's downtown redevelopment. The construction agreement called for work to begin no later than August 1996 and required the company to construct the concrete frame for the complex.

Under the terms of the three-year contract, BCC was to receive a total of $10 million in cash payments from the city of Sudbury, to be paid as follows: 25 percent when the project is 30 percent complete, 25 percent when the project is 60 percent complete, and the remaining 50 percent when the project has been fully completed (including all necessary building approvals). The contract, which was of a fixed price variety and hence did not provide for cost overrun recoupment, required that completion estimates be certified by an independent engineering consultant before any cash progress payments would be made.

In preparing its bid, BCC had estimated that the total cost to complete the project would be $8.3 million, assuming no cost overruns. Hence, under optimal conditions, the company anticipated a profit of approximately $1.7 million.

During the first year of the contract, BCC incurred actual costs of $2.49 million, and on June 30, 1997, the engineering consulting firm of C. Likert & Associates determined that the project had attained a 30 percent completion level. In the following year, BCC incurred actual costs of $3.1 million. As of June 30, 1998, the firm of C. Likert & Associates determined that the project had attained at least a 60 percent completion level. In their report to the City Authority, however, the consulting engineers noted that BCC might be facing a potential cost overrun situation. In response to this observation, the directors of BCC noted that they had anticipated that a number of economies of scale would arise during the final phases of construction and thereby offset any prior cost overruns.

By May 1999, BCC had completed the remainder of the project. Actual costs incurred during the year to June 30, 1996, amounted to $3.11 million. The firm received a certification for the fully completed work.

Prior to issuing the 1997 annual report, the controller's office of BCC determined that the proceeds from the Trade Centre contract would be accounted for using the completed-contract method. Under this approach, the recognition of income is postponed until essentially all work on the contract has been completed. This method previously had been utilized by the company to account for construction contract income, and it appeared to be a prudent alternative, given the possibility of some cost overrun during the life of the current contract.

Under the completed-contract approach, revenues (and thus expenses) are recognized on completion or substantial completion of a contract. In general, a contract is regarded as substantially complete if the remaining costs to complete the project are insignificant in amount. Funds expended under the contract are accounted for in an asset account, Construction in Progress, while progress payments received during the construction phase are accounted for in a Deferred or Unearned Revenue account. Although income is not recognized until completion of the contract, any expected losses should be recognized immediately when identified.

Required:

a. Assuming that BCC had no other sources of revenues or expenses, determine the level of profits to be reported for the years ended June 30, 1997, 1998, and 1999, utilizing the following revenue recognition methods:

(1) Percentage of completion.

(2) Completed contract.

(3) Cash basis. (Note: Assume that the City Authority remits cash payments on the same day as work completion certification.)

b. Which set of results (from part *a*) best reflects the economic performance of the company over the period 1997–1999? What criteria did you apply in the foregoing assessment?

c. What are the advantages and disadvantages of each of the methods in part *a*?

C5.3 Revenue and expense recognition. Entertainment Arts, Inc., (EAI), develops videotapes using animation (much like standard cartoons) and moving clay models (like the dancing raisins). The videos were prominent parts of cable TV fare during after-school hours. They had proven to be very popular with the 8-to-12-year-old market, and many of the featured characters were well known to the members of that age group. Each video cost about $150,000 to make, but because the target audience group was constantly being replenished, it could be shown an infinite number of times. As each video was made, its cost was added to an asset account. The cost was amortized over 10 years to reflect the possibility that changed styles would ultimately make the video obsolete. At the time of this case, EAI had 92 films in its asset pool, with an average age of 3.5 years and an aggregate unamortized cost of $11,000,000.

The company received a proposal for a license on EAI characters from an agent who represented a number of manufacturers of children's products. Three companies asked for an exclusive right to use EAI characters in their markets for a three-year period, and each proposed to pay EAI a 1 percent royalty on any of its products' sales where the product used an EAI character in its design. The agent asked EAI for a commission of $75,000 as compensation for bringing all of the parties together. EAI asked for details, and the agent explained the three companies' plans as follows:

	Planned Annual Sales of EAI-Related Products
Lunch box manufacturer	$1,500,000
Clothing manufacturer	3,500,000
Toy manufacturer	5,000,000

EAI argued that it would be giving something up by signing this agreement, and that it wanted more for its sacrifice than the 1 percent royalty proposed. So EAI countered with this proposal:

	Minimum Annual Royalty Payable	1 Percent Royalty on Annual Sales over
Lunch box manufacturer	$10,000	$1,000,000
Clothing manufacturer	25,000	2,500,000
Toy manufacturer	40,000	4,000,000

After some further negotiating, a three-year contract was signed: The manufacturers agreed on the guaranteed minimum royalty but insisted that the annual minimum payments would be paid at the end of each year, at the same time the obligation for any additional royalty was due. And, as a concession to complete the deal, the agent agreed to reduce her commission to $60,000.

1. What should EAI's revenue recognition policies be for this licence agreement? Please explain all the considerations that entered into your policy proposal.

2. What should EAI's accounting policy be with regard to the aggregate unamortized cost of the videos ($11,000,000) as a result of this transaction? Please explain.

3. What should EAI's accounting policy be with regard to the $60,000 commission paid?

Please explain.

C5.4 Financial statement disclosure. You are the president of a small paint manufacturer located in southern Ontario. Your paint products are sold throughout Canada. Because the economy has been flat, your business has been hurt. Nonetheless, sales for 1996 were about $25 million and net income was about $3 million. It is now February 1997, and as you begin to draw together the data you need for your company's 1996 report to shareholders, the production people bring you distressing news. It appears that one lot of paint that was shipped last year is defective. If it is applied when the weather is at all humid, the paint blisters and peels very badly. They have already notified the distributors and begun a recall, but it appears that some of that batch has gotten into the retail distribution network and in fact has been sold to contractors and homeowners. Production people estimate the cost of recalling the entire lot at $300,000. However, if anyone has actually used the paint on a job site, the paint will have to be scraped off carefully and thoroughly. There obviously is no way to know how much of the paint might have been sold to end users and how much of it might have been applied on specific jobs.

How should this event be reflected in the company's financial statements?

PART II

Measuring and Reporting Assets

Cash, Temporary Investments, and Receivables

--------- **Objectives** ---------

After completing this chapter, you will be able to:
1. Describe the measurement and valuation of cash, receivables, and temporary investments.
2. Apply the accounting procedures for quick assets: bank reconciliations, lower of cost or market rule for temporary investments, and the allowance method for receivables.
3. Record transactions for the different quick assets, acquisitions, disposals, and adjustments.
4. Explain and apply financial statement disclosure for cash, receivables, and temporary investments.
5. Perform financial analysis to evaluate cash, receivables, and temporary investments.

In the previous chapters, we introduced some of the fundamental concepts involved in preparing financial statements. In a sense, the preceding chapters attempted to demystify the language of accounting, and financial statements. It is important not to lose sight of the fact that many challenges are inherent in management's desire to report on the financial condition and results of operations for the organization. Organizations are engaged in diverse and different activities, and run by managers with different ideas of how best to achieve certain results, all to the satisfaction of absentee owners who have their own agendas. In light of such circumstances, if the formulation of generally accepted accounting principles seems an imposing task, it is. We must remember that the overall objective of financial reporting is to provide useful information to decision makers. Such an objective necessitates a closer look at the various components making up the financial statements, so the user will be able to better comprehend the financial story those statements tell.

Consider the fact that the assets reported on a company's balance sheet may be used in a variety of capacities to benefit the company. For example, one asset, cash, may be used to buy inventories or pay employee salaries. Inventories, another asset, may be sold to produce revenues and, hence, new cash inflows. Machinery and equipment may be used to produce new inventory units to sell to customers. Thus, each asset category on the balance sheet effectively serves one or more specialized functions within a company.

In this chapter, we focus on the accounting for cash, temporary investments, and receivables. Although these current assets differ as to their origin, they have similar attributes. All, for example, are liquid assets; temporary investments and receivables can be readily converted into cash. They are subject to valuation adjustments for financial reporting purposes — accounts receivable are reported at their net realizable value (i.e., the amount of cash flows expected to be realized when they are liquidated), and temporary investments are reported at the lower of cost or market value.

Our objective in this chapter is to learn how these current assets arise, how they are accounted for, how they can be managed, controlled, and utilized effectively, and how they may be analyzed. We begin with a consideration of the accounting for cash.

6.1 CASH

Cash Management

cash management
The management of cash involves the efficient management of any excess cash and proper cash planning to avoid cash shortages.

The management of cash involves two aspects. Firstly, management is responsible for ensuring the organization has sufficient cash available to meet its day-to-day activities. To accomplish this objective typically involves some form of cash planning or budgeting. When cash deficiencies are anticipated, management may factor or sell its receivables to obtain cash in the short term. In addition, management may find it necessary to pledge receivables or other assets as security for loans to supply needed cash during peak activities during the year. Most businesses are seasonal to a certain degree, and, as a result, have peaks and valleys with respect to their needs for cash. Proper cash budgeting can help avoid any unpleasant surprises during the year. The second element of **cash management** is the efficient management of any excess cash. This simply requires the short-term investment of excess funds to earn a return on the excess cash resources. An additional element of cash management is the proper control of cash.

internal control
The policies and procedures implemented by management to safeguard a company's assets and its accounting system against misapplication or misuse.

Internal Control

As previously described in Chapter 1, management is responsible for the design and maintenance of an adequate system of **internal control.** An internal control system is an important component of the financial reporting system required to produce meaningful financial statements. An internal control system helps ensure the safeguarding of the resources of the organization and minimizes the potential losses due to fraud. The basic principles of internal control for the most part seem to be common sense. However, many organizations fail to properly implement good internal control systems. Most internal control systems involve a number of interrelated steps or processes. Frequently, employees take shortcuts that make their daily routines a little easier; however, their shortcuts may be eliminating some or all of the controls that were built into the accounting system. Individual employees are often not aware of the impact their individual tasks have on the overall accounting system and the controls established within the system. It is important that the significance of the individual processes be communicated to the individuals performing the tasks.

The subject of internal control is very broad, and will not be covered in-depth in this text. However, a basic understanding of systems and controls is helpful to the understanding of financial reports. We now describe some fundamental concepts of internal control.

The assigning of **responsibility** is a basic element of a sound internal control system. It is important that all employees clearly understand what tasks they are and are not responsible for. It is also important that all company policies and procedures be properly documented to facilitate the communication of responsibilities.

Separation of duties is another basic concept of internal control. The basic premise is that the individual who has *custody* of an asset must be different from the person who is responsible for *accounting* for the asset. The purpose of this separation is to avoid assigning complete responsibility for an activity to one person. If an activity can be subdivided, it is generally thought control is enhanced, as the different individuals involved in the process serve as checks on each other. For fraud or theft to be committed, collusion among all parties involved in the process is required.

Insurance and **bonding** are a fundamental means of safeguarding the assets of the organization. If an organization does not have fire insurance, and the organization has the misfortune of having a fire that destroys some of its assets, a substantial loss would be incurred. With insurance coverage the loss would be minimized or possibly totally recovered depending on the specifications of the insurance policy. Bonding is really the same as insurance, except it pertains to safeguarding the organization against losses due to theft or fraud committed by its employees. Should an employee steal from their employer, the organization would be reimbursed for any losses caused by the *bonded* employee.

Cash Control

As cash is the most liquid of all assets, a proper control system for cash is especially important. The previously mentioned concepts of internal control can be applied to the control of cash. The concept of responsibility is particularly relevant to the handling of cash. Only a restricted number of efficient employees should process cash. As well, proper internal control procedures require the separation of the duties of handling cash and the related accounting for cash. The task of processing cash receipts should also be separated from the processing of cash payments. As well, organizations should have a policy of bonding employees who handle cash.

Internal control procedures specific to cash include: making frequent deposits, making all payments by cheque, requiring two signatures on all cheques, using a petty cash fund, and making monthly bank reconciliations. To ensure the safeguarding of cash it is wise to make bank deposits daily or even more frequently if large sums of cash are

responsibility
The assigning of responsibility is a basic element of a sound internal control system.

separation of duties
A basic concept of internal control. The basic premise is that the individual who has custody of an asset must be different from the person who is responsible for accounting for the asset.

insurance
A fundamental means of safe guarding the assets of the organization and a basic principle of internal control.

bonding
The same as insurance, except it pertains to safeguarding the organization against losses due to theft or fraud committed by employees.

processed by the organization. By making frequent deposits the responsibility for the safeguarding of cash is passed on to the bank. All cash payments should be made by cheque. This minimizes the handling of cash and also the cheque itself provides documentation for the transaction, which is easily lost with cash transactions. Most organizations have two signatures required on all cheques. This procedure provides a sharing of responsibilities and also a double check to ensure cash payments are only for properly authorized expenditures. A **petty cash fund** should be used *only* for small cash expenditures. The petty cash fund may contain only $100.00. It is used for infrequent small expenditures to avoid the process of issuing a cheque for immaterial items.

A bank reconciliation should be prepared on a monthly basis to assist in the control of cash. A **bank reconciliation** compares the accounting for cash recorded by the bank to the accounting for cash recorded by the company. The purpose of the bank reconciliation is to help ensure no errors have been recorded by the company or the bank in the accounting for cash. In addition, the bank reconciliation is necessary to determine the correct cash balance for financial reporting purposes at the end of the accounting period. Without a bank reconciliation, not only is the Cash account not accurately presented, but other balance sheet and income statement accounts may be under- or overstated as well. It may be argued that many of these misstatements are immaterial in nature. However, the degree of significance or materiality of the unrecorded items cannot be determined without completing a bank reconciliation. A bank reconciliation is a schedule prepared to account for *timing differences* as to when cash transactions are recorded by the company and recorded by the bank. In the long term, the same transactions will be recorded by both parties. However, in the short term, a number of transactions may be outstanding and remain unrecorded by either party. Let's consider an example. Suppose you receive a cheque for the small amount of $3.27. The issuing party records the cash payment in its accounting records today. You put the cheque in the "junk" drawer of your desk, and it stays there for three months before you actually cash the cheque. During the three-month period, the cheque has been recorded by the issuing company, but not received and processed by their bank. Such an item is referred to as an *outstanding cheque*. Such timing differences are commonplace. The basic steps of a bank reconciliation are illustrated in Exhibit 6.1.

Items commonly to be added or subtracted in the accounting records include items recorded by the bank but not yet entered in the accounting records such as service charges, loan payments, collections on account made by the bank on our behalf, or non-sufficient funds (NSF) cheques. Items commonly to be added or subtracted to the bank record side of the reconciliation include items added or subtracted in the accounting records but not yet entered in the bank records such as outstanding deposits or outstanding cheques. An **outstanding deposit** is a deposit The managethat has been recorded in the accounting records but not yet received or recorded by the bank. Similarly, an **outstanding cheque** is a cheque that has been recorded in the accounting records but not yet received or recorded by the bank.

The following example illustrates a bank reconciliation. On October 31 the accounting records indicated a cash balance of $4,352. The October 31 bank statement showed a balance of $3,971. Which of these balances should appear on the October 31 balance sheet? In almost all cases neither of these figures would be the appropriate figure to disclose on the financial statements, because of timing differences between when transactions had been recorded in the accounting records and by the bank. Additional information for October includes an outstanding deposit of $1,412 and outstanding cheques as follows: #712 $300, #717 $127, and #721 $432. During Octo-

---

petty cash fund
Used for small cash expenditures.

bank reconciliation
A bank reconciliation compares the accounting for cash recorded by the bank to the accounting for cash recorded by the company.

outstanding deposit
A deposit that has been recorded in the accounting records, but not yet received or recorded by the bank.

outstanding cheque
A cheque that has been recorded in the accounting records, but not yet received or recorded by the bank.

EXHIBIT 6.1

Bank Reconciliation Steps

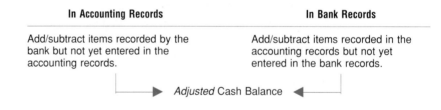

In Accounting Records	In Bank Records
Add/subtract items recorded by the bank but not yet entered in the accounting records.	Add/subtract items recorded in the accounting records but not yet entered in the bank records.

Adjusted Cash Balance

ber the bank had incorrectly deducted $57 from the account. This error will be corrected by the bank on the November bank statement. Service charges deducted by the bank for October totalled $27. The bank had returned an NSF cheque for $175. Cheque #702, a payment on account was, incorrectly entered in the accounting records for $317. The actual amount of cheque #702 was $371. During October the bank collected a note receivable of $500, charging a collection fee of $15. The bank reconciliation for October is shown below:

Bank Reconciliation — October 31

Accounting Records		Bank Records	
Balance	$4,352	Balance	$3,971
		Outstanding deposit	1,412
NSF cheque	(175)	Outstanding cheques:	
Note receivable	500	#712	(300)
Collection fee	(15)	#717	(127)
Error ($371 – $317)	(54)	#721	(432)
Service charge	(27)	Bank error	57
Adjusted cash balance	$4,581	Adjusted cash balance	$4,581

The October 31 balance sheet would show an adjusted cash balance of $4,581. When the *adjusted* cash balance has been determined, adjusting entries are required to adjust the *accounting* records for the previously unrecorded transactions. The adjusting entries are necessary to properly disclose the related income statement and balance sheet accounts (e.g. expenses, receivables, and payables). No adjustments are made to the bank's records. The bank will process the outstanding items, and they should appear on the next month's bank statement. In some instances, items will take more than one month to clear the system and be processed. Bank reconciliations are a good control procedure that may be used by individuals, as well as by business or government organizations. The adjusting entries for the October 31 bank reconciliation follow:

```
Dr.  Service Charge Expense . . . . . . . . . . . . . . . . . . . . . . . . . . . . . . . 27
     Cr.  Cash . . . . . . . . . . . . . . . . . . . . . . . . . . . . . . . . . . . . . . . . . .        27
     Unrecorded service charges.
Dr.  Cash . . . . . . . . . . . . . . . . . . . . . . . . . . . . . . . . . . . . . . . . . . . 485
Dr.  Service Charge Expense . . . . . . . . . . . . . . . . . . . . . . . . . . . . . . 15
     Cr.  Note Receivable . . . . . . . . . . . . . . . . . . . . . . . . . . . . . . . . . .       500
     Collection of note receivable.
```

```
Dr.  Accounts Receivable . . . . . . . . . . . . . . . . . . . . . . . . . . . . . . . 175
       Cr.  Cash  . . . . . . . . . . . . . . . . . . . . . . . . . . . . . . . . . . . . . . . .      175
     NSF cheque returned by bank.
Accounts Payable  . . . . . . . . . . . . . . . . . . . . . . . . . . . . . . . . . . . 54
       Cash . . . . . . . . . . . . . . . . . . . . . . . . . . . . . . . . . . . . . . . . . .       54
     Error cheque #702.
```

Financial Statement Disclosure: Cash

Some organizations have several different cash accounts, for example, an account for cash on hand, petty cash, and an account for each different bank account. However, for financial reporting purposes, most organizations would disclose only a single figure for cash, classified as a *current asset*. If cash is negative, which *is* possible if the organization writes more cheques than there is cash available to cover the cheques, the negative cash balance should be classified as a *current liability*. A negative cash balance, or bank overdraft, is in effect a short-term loan from the bank to cover the outstanding cheques. Frequently cash is disclosed as cash and equivalents, as it also includes short-term investments maturing in less than three months.

Following are some examples of how organizations disclose cash. Northern Telecom, Limited, disclosed its cash equivalents as follows: "All highly liquid investments with original maturities of three months or less are classified as cash and short-term investments." Coca-Cola Beverages, Ltd., had a similar disclosure for its cash: "Cash is defined as cash on account plus demand deposits and short-term investments with maturities of three months or less. Outstanding cheques are classified as accounts payable." Coca-Cola Beverages, Ltd., classified its outstanding cheques as accounts payable, since an outstanding cheque has not been cashed by the recipient by the end of the accounting period, and is in effect the same as a unpaid account. Maple Leaf Foods, Inc., disclosed its cash and cash equivalents as follows: "Cash and cash equivalents are comprised of cash and short-term securities. The carrying value of these items, which are carried at cost or amortized cost as appropriate, approximates fair market value."

Short-term investments with maturities of three months or less are frequently classified with cash and equivalents. Investments with maturities of more than 3 months, but less than 12 months are classified as temporary investments. "The following should be excluded from current assets: (a) cash subject to restrictions that prevent its use for current purposes; (b) cash appropriated for other than current purposes" (CICA Handbook 3000.01).

Analyzing Cash

The analysis of cash is closely related to the financial strength analysis discussed in Chapter 2. When analyzing cash, it should be considered in conjunction with the analysis of the other quick assets, temporary investments, and receivables. The liquidity ratios previously discussed are influenced by the level of cash available at the end of each period. The absolute amount of cash and equivalents should be compared from period to period. For Maple Leaf Gardens, Limited, cash decreased from approximately $12 million in 1993 to $10 million in 1994. This at first appears to be a significant decrease in liquid assets. However, further analysis (previously discussed in Chapter 2) reveals that working capital and the current and quick ratios have all increased during the same period. A review of the statement of changes in financial position also provides information on the changes in cash during the period. As with all analysis, comparative financial data, either within or outside the organization, greatly enhances the analysis.

6.2 TEMPORARY INVESTMENTS

temporary investments
Short-term investments in the shares or bonds of other corporations.

If an investment is to be held less than a year, and longer than three months, it is classified as a **temporary investment** and thus a current asset. "Investments should be classified as current assets only if capable of reasonably prompt liquidation. Such investments would include not only temporary holdings of marketable securities but also other investments, such as treasury bills, investment certificates and call loans" (CICA Handbook 3010.02). If management's intent is to hold a particular investment for a period exceeding one year, the financial reporting requirements resulting from that long-term intention differ from the requirements for reporting temporary investments. These requirements are discussed in the appendix to Chapter 8. The accounting for temporary investments will now be discussed.

Acquisition Cost

The management of temporary investments principally involves the managerial concern of how best to invest a company's surplus cash until such funds are needed to support its regular operations. The term *temporary investments* refers to the investment of surplus cash resources in the securities (e.g., shares and bonds) of other corporate entities. A readily accessible market for these securities makes them highly liquid investments. The acquisition cost of the temporary investment would include the purchase price of the security *plus* any commissions or relevant taxes. Typically the temporary investment of excess cash would be held for a few months and then sold and converted back to cash. The proceeds on the sale of the temporary investment would include the selling price of the security *less* any commissions or relevant taxes. If the proceeds exceed the acquisition cost, a gain on sale of temporary investments would be recognized on the income statement. If the proceeds are less than the acquisition cost, a loss on sale of temporary investments would be recognized on the income statement. When the sale of investments involves the multiple purchases of the same security at *different* acquisition prices, the weighted-average cost of the temporary investments should be used to determine the disposal value and the resulting gain or loss.

Market Value

With few exceptions the historical cost principle is used to value assets. In special situations assets may be valued at market value. Chapter 5 presented revenue recognition methods. When revenue is recognized at the completion of production, before the point of sale, the produced inventory is valued at its anticipated selling price. Another exception to the use of historical costs is the use of market values for temporary investments, when the lower-of-cost-or-market rule is applied. Sophisticated financial markets exist for most investments, making the determination of market values very easy.

Lower of Cost or Market

When temporary investments are held at the end of the accounting period, management must determine the value of the investment to be disclosed in the financial statements. As with the net realizable value considerations associated with accounts

EXHIBIT 6.2

Financial Reporting of Temporary Investments

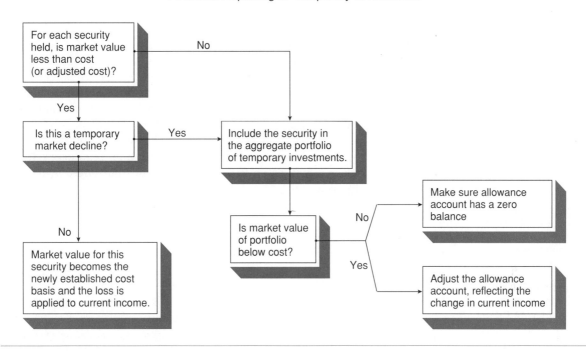

receivables and other assets, the accounting for these highly liquid temporary investments involves the application of the *conservatism principle* through the use of the **lower-of-cost-or-market** method. The Interprovincial Pipe Line System, Inc., annual report had a footnote describing adherence to the lower-of-cost-or-market rule: "Cash includes short term deposits, which are highly marketable securities with a maturity of three months or less when purchased. Short term investments, which are marketable securities with a maturity of more than three months when purchased, are valued at the lower of cost and market."

As we consider the specific issues involved, the principal focus will be on equity (share) investments, which management intends to hold for less than a year, thus rendering them in the current asset category for balance sheet presentation purposes. Exhibit 6.2 summarizes the financial reporting issues of the lower-of-cost-or-market method of accounting for temporary investments.

lower of cost or market
A method to value temporary investments; the lower of an asset's cost basis or current market value is used to value the asset account for balance sheet purposes.

Temporary Declines in Value

The initial step in accounting for temporary investments, as the diagram in Exhibit 6.2 indicates, is to compare the current market value of each separate equity security with its recorded cost. If the market value is less than its cost, management must determine whether that decline is permanent or temporary, an important determination that affects the way in which the decline is handled.

Temporary declines in value are viewed as short-term fluctuations that are anticipated to *reverse* themselves in the short-term. For example, if 500 shares of Canuck, Ltd., were purchased in September at a price of $100 per share and if at year-end the shares were trading at $86 per share, assuming no permanent impairment of the stock's value, the decline in share price would be considered temporary. If, on the other hand, Canuck, Ltd., had one of its leading revenue-producing products found to be environmentally hazardous, the decline in share price might reasonably be judged to be permanent.

If management decides that a market decline in the value of an individual security that it holds as a short-term investment is indeed temporary, that security need not be accounted for further on an individual basis and is aggregated with (1) other temporary investments also exhibiting temporary declines *and* with (2) those temporary investments whose market values are in excess of their cost. Then, if the market value of this portfolio of aggregated securities is lower than its *aggregated* cost, an accounting entry must be made to reflect this overall decline in portfolio value. This portfoliowide application of the lower-of-cost-or-market valuation method is accomplished by creating a contra asset account, **Allowance for Market Decline in Temporary Investments**. The adjusting entry is recorded to the **valuation allowance**, and current income is reduced by recording an **unrealized loss**. The Clearly Canadian Beverage Corporation in its note on short-term investments included comments on its valuation allowance:

allowance for market decline in temporary investments
A contra asset account deducted from the cost basis of temporary investments.

valuation allowance
A contra account used to record the market decline in temporary investments.

unrealized loss (gain)
A loss (gain) that is recognized in the financial statements but is not associated with an asset sale.

	1994	1993
Government of Canada Bonds, at market	$ —	$21,793,000
Other, at market	12,633,000	—
	$12,633,000	$21,793,000

The carrying value of short-term investments is net of a valuation allowance of $232,000 (1993 — $653,000) recorded to reflect the decline in the market value of these investments.

Recall from an earlier chapter that a loss represents a reduction in the value of an asset held by a company, whereas a gain represents an increase in an asset value. Neither losses nor gains relate to the principal business activity of a company, although both must be reported on the income statement. Hence, losses should not be confused with expenses, nor gains with revenues. It is also important to note that this portfolio loss is *unrealized*. That is to say, the loss *does exist* today; but it has not been consummated through a sale of the investment. When the investment is sold, the loss would become *realized*. The fact that the loss is unrealized, however, does not preempt the need to recognize it in the accounts and the income statement.

Consider, for example, the portfolio of temporary investments in Exhibit 6.3. In this example, the aggregate market value of the portfolio at the end of Month 1 is $71,000 as compared with an aggregate recorded cost of $75,000. Assuming that management judges the decline in the value of Investments 2 and 3 to be *temporary*, the following adjusting entry would be recorded at the end of Month 1:

```
Dr.  Unrealized Loss . . . . . . . . . . . . . . . . . . . . . . . . . . . . . . . .  4,000
      Cr.  Allowance for Market Decline . . . . . . . . . . . . . . . . . . . . . . . .     4,000
      To record the decline in the market value of the portfolio of temporary investments.
```

The rationale for decreasing this period's net income, and, hence, owners' equity in this way (i.e., recording an unrealized loss on the income statement) is that management expects to hold a temporary investment for less than one year. Therefore, it is assumed that a portfolio market decline below cost, even if temporary, will not reverse

EXHIBIT 6.3

Portfolio of Temporary Investments

	At the End of Month 1			At the End of Month 2		
	Recorded Cost	Market Value	Gain (Loss)	Recorded Cost	Market Value	Gain (Loss)
Investment 1	$20,000	$22,000	$ 2,000	$20,000	$23,000	$ 3,000
Investment 2	30,000	25,000	(5,000)	30,000	27,000	(3,000)
Investment 3	25,000	24,000	(1,000)	25,000	24,000	(1,000)
	$75,000	$71,000	$ (4,000)	$75,000	$74,000	$ (1,000)

itself before the securities in the portfolio are sold. The accounting convention of conservatism therefore leads to the practice of recognizing the loss immediately, even though it has not yet been realized via an actual sale of securities.

Applying the same process to the portfolio at the end of Month 2, we find that the aggregate value of the portfolio is only $1,000 ($75,000 − $74,000) below its original cost. The valuation allowance, however, has a $4,000 credit balance carried over from Month 1, so the valuation allowance account must be adjusted to reflect the $3,000 recovery. The adjusting entry to reduce the allowance account to $1,000 at the end of Month 2 would be:

```
Dr.  Allowance for Market Decline . . . . . . . . . . . . . . . . . . . . . . .  3,000
     Cr.  Unrealized Gain . . . . . . . . . . . . . . . . . . . . . . . . . . . . . . . .      3,000
     To record the increase in the market value of the portfolio of temporary investments.
```

This adjustment leaves a $1,000 balance in the contra asset account, which represents the difference between the portfolio's current aggregate market value ($74,000) and its aggregate cost (still $75,000).

But what if the aggregate market value of the portfolio is higher than its aggregate cost? Imagine, for instance, that the market value of the temporary investments portfolio in Exhibit 6.3 at the end of Month 2 is $77,000 (i.e., $2,000 in excess of its cost). It is important to remember that the lower-of-cost-or-market method of valuing investments precludes those investments from being reported on the balance sheet at an amount *higher* than their original cost (in this example, $75,000). In such a case, any existing balance in the Allowance for Market Decline account must be brought to *zero*; to do this, the entry above would be for $4,000 instead of $3,000.

A subtle but important point to note at this juncture is that even though the application of the lower-of-cost-or-market guidelines precludes reporting temporary investments at a value above recorded cost, it does not preclude the implicit reporting of an *individual* security at a value above its recorded cost. Indeed, the application of lower of cost or market on a portfoliowide basis provides for *netting* individual security market gains and losses in determining the target balance to be reported in the contra asset allowance account. Such a netting of gains and losses is quite consistent with the portfolio theory of managing investments in equity securities. That is, one way investors can diversify their investment risk is to hold a portfolio of investments in a variety of companies — the classic notion of "don't put all your eggs in one basket." If *only* market declines were considered in reporting for temporary investments, the Month 1 targeted allowance account balance of $4,000 in Exhibit 6.3 would have been $2,000 more, or $6,000. In effect, under the portfolio approach to lower of cost or market, the

$2,000 unrealized gain on Investment 1 is implicitly being recognized. Given the readily available and objective sources for determining the market value of these securities (e.g., stock exchange quotes), this slight modification is not viewed as a significant violation of the conservatism principle. In fact, given the overriding concern of providing useful information to financial statement users, the modification of the lower-of-cost-or-market method for temporary investments is both necessary and desirable.

Conservatism: Lower of Cost or Market

The principle of conservatism states when uncertainty exists, estimates of a conservative nature should attempt to ensure that assets are not overstated and losses are not understated. It is generally believed that users of financial reports are better served with information that understates income and assets, rather than reports that overstate income and assets. The conservatism principle also states when two acceptable accounting policies are available, the policy providing the lowest asset value, or the highest expense value should be used. Conservatism may be applied to the lower-of-cost-or-market rule for temporary investments by analyzing investments on an *individual* basis. The previous illustration applied the lower-of-cost-or-market rule on an aggregate or portfolio basis. The portfolio approach actually nets losses and gains on individual investments when determining the aggregate adjustment between cost and market values. The more conservative approach is now illustrated.

Let's reconsider the portfolio of temporary investments in Exhibit 6.3. The total market value of the current portfolio at the end of Month 1 is $71,000 as compared with an aggregate recorded cost of $75,000. Under the aggregate approach an unrealized loss of $4,000 has been recorded. If instead the lower-of-cost-or-market rule is applied to the investments on an *individual* basis, both Investments 2 and 3 would be written down, for a total of $6,000. The market value of Investment 1 is above its cost and is not adjusted. The following adjusting entry would be recorded at the end of Month 1:

```
Dr.  Unrealized Loss . . . . . . . . . . . . . . . . . . . . . . . . . . . . . . . . . .  6,000
     Cr.  Allowance for Market Decline . . . . . . . . . . . . . . . . . . . . . . . . .      6,000
     To record the decline in the market value of the individual temporary investments.
```

As with the aggregate approach to the lower of cost or market an unrealized loss is recognized on the income statement and the allowance account is used to record the decline in market value.

Applying the same process to the individual investments at the end of Month 2, we find that the market value of the individual Investments 2 and 3 is only $4,000 below its original cost. The valuation allowance, however, has a $6,000 credit balance carried over from Month 1, so the valuation allowance account must be adjusted to reflect the $2,000 recovery. The adjusting entry at the end of Month 2 would be this:

```
Dr.  Allowance for Market Decline . . . . . . . . . . . . . . . . . . . . . . . .  2,000
     Cr.  Unrealized Gain . . . . . . . . . . . . . . . . . . . . . . . . . . . . . . . . . . .      2,000
     To record the increase in the market value of the individual temporary investments.
```

This adjustment leaves a $4,000 balance in the contra asset account, which represents the difference between the market values and costs of Investments 2 and 3. The market value of Investment 1 remains above its cost and is not adjusted.

Permanent Declines in Value

What happens if management deems the decline in value of a particular temporary investment to be permanent? (Notice that we are speaking of an individual security not an entire portfolio.) Such a decline perhaps results from events such as disappearing markets, adverse governmental legislation, litigation, or other similar, fundamental changes that damage the long-term earnings potential of the company that issued the security.

Accounting for a permanent decline is quite straightforward. Since the decline in value for a given security is not expected to recover — that is, it is thought to be permanent — a loss is recognized immediately even though the security has not yet been sold. For example, assume that management decides that the $3,000 ($30,000 − $27,000) decline in Month 2 for Security 2 in Exhibit 6.3 is a permanent decline. To recognize this loss, an entry is required to reduce directly the carrying value of the temporary investment (i.e., no contra asset account is used) and to record the loss:

```
Dr.  Unrealized Loss . . . . . . . . . . . . . . . . . . . . . . . . . . . . . . . . .   3,000
     Cr.  Temporary Investment 2 . . . . . . . . . . . . . . . . . . . . . . . . . . .        3,000
     To record the permanent decline in temporary Investment 2.
```

After a particular security is written down because of a permanent decline, it can never be written up above this newly established *adjusted* cost. For this example, the recorded "cost" of Security 2 is now $27,000, the figure that will be used for comparison with future months' market values. The new (adjusted) aggregate cost of the current portfolio is now $72,000, and the aggregate market value for the current portfolio at the end of Month 2 is $74,000. Thus, the portfolio market value is $2,000 above its adjusted cost. Therefore, an entry in Month 2 to adjust the contra asset allowance account established in Month 1 is necessary. The Allowance for Temporary Investments account currently has a credit balance of $4,000 from the Month 1 adjustment, and this balance must be reduced to zero to recognize the appreciation in the portfolio's aggregate market value (after adjusting for the permanent decline in value of Security 2). The entry would be as follows:

```
Dr.  Allowance for Market Decline . . . . . . . . . . . . . . . . . . . . . . .   4,000
     Cr.  Unrealized Gain . . . . . . . . . . . . . . . . . . . . . . . . . . . . . . . . .        4,000
     To record the increase in the market value of the portfolio of temporary investments.
```

Adherence to the accounting for a permanent decline in temporary investments is footnoted in the following annual reports:

Canadian Mental Health Association
The investments are recorded at cost. When the market value of the investments is lower than cost and this decline is considered to be a permanent decline, the investments are written down to market value.

Canadian National Institute For The Blind (Saskatchewan Division)
Marketable securities are stated at cost which approximates market, or at cost less amounts written off to reflect a decline in value which is other than temporary.

The Arthritis Society
Investments are recorded at cost. Should the market value of investments become lower than cost and this decline in value is considered to be other than temporary, the investments are written down to market value.

The Canadian Red Cross Society
The investment portfolio is carried at cost in the absence of any evidence of permanent impairment of value. Interest and dividend income is accrued when earned. Gains and losses on the disposition of investments are recorded on the average cost basis. Included in investments are assets of the various bequests, endowment and youth funds which are restricted as to their use.

For a moment consider the managerial task of deciding whether a particular security's decline in value is permanent or temporary. In the absence of unambiguous evidence, management may prefer to identify a decline as temporary rather than permanent because permanent declines are immediately (and adversely) reflected in both the income statement, via a recorded loss, and the balance sheet account, via an asset writedown. As noted previously, a temporary decline in value in one security may be offset by a temporary gain in value in another, thereby avoiding both an income statement and a balance sheet adjustment. Moreover, the label *temporary* conveys the optimistic impression that a future recovery is possible. Thus, there are a number of considerations that, in the absence of definitive evidence, might cause management to be biased toward the *temporary* designation for individual security declines in value.

Sale of Investments

At some point in time, a company's investment manager will decide to sell a security held in its portfolio. Such an event is likely to result in the realization of either a gain or loss that should be recognized (i.e., recorded) at the time of sale. If we assume that in Month 3 Investment 3 is sold for $26,000, the entry to record that event is:

```
Dr.  Cash .......................................... 26,000
     Cr.  Temporary Investment 3 ............................      25,000
     Cr.  Gain on Sale of Investment ...........................       1,000
     To record the sale of temporary investment 3.
```

Notice that there is *no* attempt to ascertain that part of the valuation allowance account is applicable to Investment 3. Any adjustment to the allowance account will be made at the *end* of Month 3 when the portfolio's market value and cost are again compared and the allowance adjusted accordingly. Such comparison will simply no longer involve Investment 3. If Investment 3 were sold for $20,000 instead of $26,000, the preceding entry would record a $5,000 ($25,000 − $20,000) loss on the sale.

Financial Statement Disclosure: Temporary Investments

Temporary investments are classified as current assets for financial statement disclosure purposes. "The basis of valuation should be disclosed" (CICA Handbook 3010.04). "When the market value of temporary investments has declined below the carrying value, they should be carried at market value" (CICA Handbook 3010.06). Either the individual or the aggregate approach to the lower-of-cost-or-market rule for temporary investments is an acceptable accounting method. As has been illustrated, the individual approach produces the most conservative results. In the previous illustration, temporary investments with a cost of $75,000 were valued at the lower of cost or market value, or the market value of $71,000. The lower of-cost-or-market approach makes use of an allowance account to record the declines in market values. Appropriate disclosure for temporary investments would be:

Temporary investments	$75,000
Less: Allowance for decline in market value	4,000
	$71,000

Many organizations do *not* disclose the allowance account, but disclose the basis of valuation as being the lower of cost or market, and show the temporary investments at $71,000. When the difference between cost and market value is immaterial, no adjustment would be made and a footnote may be used to describe the basis of valuation. The War Amputations of Canada uses a footnote to disclose its basis of valuation for its short-term investments: "Investments in various bonds, investment certificates and term deposits are recorded at cost which approximates market value."

"Where there are holdings of marketable securities, their quoted market value as well as their carrying value should be disclosed" (CICA Handbook 3010.05). The Hospital for Sick Children Foundation provides information on both the cost *and* market value of its investments. As well, it provides a schedule to tell users the mix of their investments:

Investments, at cost plus accrued interest (market value, $134,062)	$108,789

The percentage mix of investments at year-end is as follows:

Short-term investments	2.9%
Bonds	34.8%
Stocks	60.4%
Mortgages	1.9%
	100.0%

Analyzing Temporary Investments

The analysis of temporary investments, like that of accounts receivable, principally relates to the liquidity of a company. Because temporary investments are highly liquid, they constitute an important source of immediate cash inflows, thereby alleviating a company's need to borrow in the short term or to factor receivables. Thus, the larger a company's investment in temporary investments, the larger its available cash reserves at its disposal.

Temporary investments are valued at their recorded cost or at their net realizable value as a consequence of the application of the lower-of-cost-or-market method. Although this valuation approach ensures that the liquidity value of a portfolio is not overstated, it does not prevent the true liquidity value from being understated. That is, the net realizable value of a company's portfolio of temporary investments may actually be quite a bit greater than is reported in the company's balance sheet. "Where there are holdings of marketable securities, their quoted market value as well as their carrying value should be disclosed" (CICA Handbook 3010.06). Therefore, current GAAP require the market value of the investments to be disclosed, as illustrated for The Hospital for Sick Children Foundation. The accounting for temporary investments has an impact on the current and quick ratios, and the analysis of the firm's liquidity position.

6.3 RECEIVABLES

The management of accounts or trade receivables is an important component of the larger concern of managing a company's cash and cash flows. For most businesses, the extension of credit to customers is a normal part of generating sales. Credit sales, however, do not provide immediate cash inflows; indeed, they actually create some uncertainty regarding the timing and amount of expected future cash inflows. Conse-

quently, prior to making a credit sale, management must weigh the cost of the anticipated benefit of increased sales by extending credit to customers who would normally
not be willing to purchase goods on a strictly cash basis, against the cost associated
with the possible uncollectibility of a customer's promised payments of cash.

The accounting entry to record the receipt of a promise to be paid that is generated
by $100,000 of sales on account during the period is:

```
Accounts Receivable . . . . . . . . . . . . . . . . . . . . . . . . . . . . . . . 100,000
    Sales . . . . . . . . . . . . . . . . . . . . . . . . . . . . . . . . . . . . . . . . . . . .        100,000
    Sales on account.
```

Notice that in this transaction, even though cash is not received, the revenue is still
considered to have been earned because the earnings process is assumed to be complete, and is therefore recognized in the accounting period when the sale is made.
When cash is collected on the account receivable generated by this credit sale, the
following transaction is recorded:

```
Cash . . . . . . . . . . . . . . . . . . . . . . . . . . . . . . . . . . . . . . . . . . 83,000
    Accounts Receivable . . . . . . . . . . . . . . . . . . . . . . . . . . . . . . .        83,000
    Payment received on account.
```

The organization would have an ending balance in Accounts Receivable of $17,000
(100,000 − 83,000). Note that this cash collection event does not affect the company's
profitability in the period in which the event is recorded, nor does it change the level of
total assets as of the recording date. The cash collection event is merely an exchange of
one asset for another, and the accounting entry reflects that fact.

Management and Control of Receivables

Conventional accounting practice is to use the account title Accounts Receivable only
for those receivables arising from normal, recurring credit sales. From a manager's
perspective, this practice permits the identification of amounts still to be collected
from customers who have already received the goods purchased.

The management of receivables involves two distinct processes: the granting of
credit and the collection of accounts. If the balance to be collected increases during a
period when credit sales are relatively stable, a manager is readily able to monitor such
a change and, by investigation, to determine whether the increase is due to the collection department's ineffective job or due to more lenient credit terms having been
offered to customers. Receivables generated by other events, for example, by a cash
advance to an employee, should not be combined with the unremitted credit sales
balances still reflected in the Accounts Receivable account. Separate accounts should
be created for these *other* types of receivables to preserve the ease with which this
monitoring may be done.

The primary reason that a company extends credit to customers is to increase sales.
From a customer's point of view, credit purchases are preferable to cash purchases, in
part because they are convenient and in part because they allow the customer to retain
the use of its cash for an additional period of time. From the seller's point of view,
there is clearly a delay in obtaining the cash associated with having made a credit sale
versus having made a cash sale. The managerial issue for the seller is whether the
increase in sales as a result of offering the credit terms more than offsets the cost of
granting credit.

EXHIBIT 6.4

General Ledger (Control Account)		Subsidiary Ledger	
Accounts receivable	$17,000	Stampede Services, Calgary, Alberta	$ 4,000
		Prairie Resources, Winnipeg, Manitoba	1,500
		Central Distributors, Hamilton, Ontario	6,500
		Atlantic Enterprises, Halifax, Nova Scotia	5,000
			$17,000

credit terms
Credit terms are offered to encourage customers to pay their accounts on time.

control account
A general ledger account whose balance must equal the total of all the accounts in a related subsidiary ledger. (e.g. accounts receivable)

subsidiary ledger
An accounting data file containing detailed account information to explain the aggregate account balance contained in the general ledger.

aged trial balance
An extension of the subsidiary ledger that provides information on the age of each customer's account.

A number of costs are associated with extending credit to customers. There is the consideration of the time value of money; that is, $1 received tomorrow is not worth as much as $1 received today. Thus, future receipts from customers implicitly reflect the cost of doing without those funds for, in many cases, a significant amount of time (e.g., 30 to 60 days). In addition, regardless of the care managers take to investigate the creditworthiness of customers, some accounts receivable inevitably prove to be uncollectible. This cost of making sales on a credit basis must be weighed against the benefits of such a sale. Because of the costs of extending credit to customers, managers often offer discounts to credit customers to accelerate cash payments (i.e., to induce credit customers to pay prior to the end of the normal credit period) and to increase the probability of actually being paid (i.e., to reduce the probability that credit customers will use their limited cash for other seemingly higher priority purposes).

To see the relative attractiveness of offering discounts to credit customers, consider the typical **credit terms** of 2/10, net/30. Translated, these terms mean that if a customer pays for a credit purchase within 10 days of being invoiced, the amount due is 2 percent less than the invoice amount. If, on the other hand, payment is not remitted within the 10-day discount period, full payment is expected within 30 days. Thus, the key issue is whether the 2 percent discount will be seen as a sufficient inducement for a customer to pay 20 days early. In this case, the answer should be an emphatic yes in that the 2 percent savings, when annualized, is equivalent to an opportunity cost of 36 percent annually (i.e., $365/20 \times 0.02$). Thus, a credit customer would be well advised to borrow money from a bank, even at the rate of 30 percent annually, to take advantage of a 2 percent discount offered by a seller.

The design of the financial reporting system can assist management in its analysis and control of accounts receivable. Two common control features of a system for accounts receivable are the use of subsidiary ledgers and the use of an aged trial balance. Exhibit 6.4 provides a simplified example of a subsidiary ledger for accounts receivable.

The general ledger account is referred to as the **control account**, because its balance must equal the total of all the accounts in the subsidiary ledger. The **subsidiary ledger** provides detailed information on each individual account receivable. Each subsidiary ledger account should provide information on the customer: address, telephone number, credit rating, credit limit, and other customer data. As well, the subsidiary ledger would provide details of each customer's transactions, date of purchases, date of payments, invoice numbers, and other relevant information.

The **aged trial balance** is an extension of the subsidiary ledger that provides information on the age of each customer's account. An aged trial balance is normally divided into 30-day time periods as shown in Exhibit 6.5. Generally the older the account the less probable its collection. As a rule of thumb, any account over 90 days

EXHIBIT 6.5

Aged Trial Balance

Customer	Total Accounts Receivable	Age of Account			
		1–30 Days	31–60 Days	61–90 Days	Over 90 Days
Stampede Services, Calgary, Alberta	$ 4,000	$2,000	$1,000	$ 700	$ 300
Prairie Resources, Winnipeg, Manitoba	1,500	200	700	—	600
Central Distributors, Hamilton, Ontario	6,500	3,400	1,900	800	400
Atlantic Enterprises, Halifax, Nova Scotia	5,000	2,000	1,100	1,300	600
	$ 17,000	$7,600	$4,700	$2,800	$1,900

old has a high probability of uncollectibility. The aged trial balance is beneficial in providing management with information to evaluate the success of the organization's credit granting and collection procedures.

Net Realizable Value

net realizable value
The amount of funds expected to be received upon the sale or liquidation of an asset.

From a financial reporting perspective, accounts receivable are to be reported in the balance sheet at their **net realizable value** (i.e., net collectible amount). The use of net realizable value as a valuation basis for receivables stems from the fact that receivables are a current asset and that it is assumed that financial statement users will compare the level of current assets with the level of current liabilities to assess a company's liquidity, or short-term default risk. Hence, to ensure that statement users obtain an accurate assessment of liquidity, the current assets (except prepaid expenses) are valued at (or at an approximation of) their net realizable or cash collectible amount.

One additional financial reporting concern evolves from the matching principle. As mentioned earlier, one of the costs of selling goods on a credit basis is the cost involved in the likely event that not all customers will pay what is owed. Indeed, the experience of virtually all companies indicates that some customers will *not* pay what they owe, that their accounts will be uncollectible. In view of this reality, the matching principle dictates that an expense for the cost of doing *credit* business be recorded in the period in which the benefit (i.e., the sales revenue) from doing credit business is recorded. Of course, if at the time of a credit sale management knew which specific customer would not pay, the credit sale would *not* be made. Such a situation leads to the realization that in order to follow the matching principle and report receivables at their net collectible amount, an *estimate* of their net realizable value that is consistent with prior experience involving customer defaults must be made. In reporting this estimated net realizable amount, the gross amount of the receivables account is reduced by establishing a contra asset account for the estimated allowance for doubtful accounts. The Clearly Canadian Beverage Corporation disclosed the following information pertaining to its accounts receivable:

	1994	**1993**
Trade accounts receivable	$10,876,000	$13,370,000
Claims and taxes recoverable	484,000	790,000
Other	748,000	1,120,000
	$12,108,000	$15,280,000

Trade accounts receivable are net of allowance for doubtful accounts of $1,105,000 (1993 — $53,000).

Included in accounts receivable are $250,000 of receivables from related companies with common directors.

Bombardier Capital Group ("BCG") provided the following footnote on the provision for credit losses. The note reflects the judgment used by management to exercise its responsibility to provide meaningful financial statements to its users.

BCG maintains a provision for credit losses at an amount that it believes to be sufficient to provide adequate protection against future losses in the portfolio. The provision for credit losses is determined principally on the basis of actual experience and further provisions are also provided to reflect Management's judgment of the potential loss, including specific provisions for known troubled accounts.

To establish an appropriate allowance amount, managers may use one of two estimation approaches, both based on a historical percentage: (1) a percentage of each period's credit sales or (2) a percentage of the end-of-period balance in Accounts Receivable. It is worth repeating that neither of these approaches identifies *specific* uncollectible accounts, but rather estimates dollar amounts of possible uncollectible accounts.

Percentage-of-Credit-Sales Method: Income Statement Approach

The method to estimate the dollar value of uncollectible accounts that relies on a **percentage of credit sales** assumes that a certain proportion of a period's credit sales will never be collected. For example, if credit sales for the year are $100,000 and if 3 percent, the historic average of credit sales never collected, are estimated to be uncollectible, the following adjusting entry is recorded at period-end:

```
Dr. Bad Debt Expense . . . . . . . . . . . . . . . . . . . . . . . . . . . . . . . . . 3,000
    Cr. Allowance for Doubtful Accounts . . . . . . . . . . . . . . . . . . . . . . . .         3,000
    Adjusting entry, estimated uncollectible accounts.
```

Notice the income statement emphasis implicit in this method of estimating the net realizable value of accounts receivables. The $3,000 **bad debt expense** recorded this period is derived from a calculation based on the *same* period's credit sales and is thus a direct *matching* of expenses to related revenues. It is also important to note that a contra asset account is used for the **allowance for doubtful accounts**. The reason for the use of the contra account is that specific customer accounts have not as yet been identified as uncollectible and the Accounts Receivable account, which is an aggregation of specific customer receivables, *cannot* be reduced directly. Nor can the specific subsidiary ledger accounts be identified and adjusted. Thus, the desired goal of reporting receivables in the balance sheet at their net realizable value is achieved by creating

percentage of credit sales
A method of accounting for uncollectible accounts receivable in which an estimate of the bad debts expense is recorded on the basis of the credit sales for the period.

bad debt expense
An estimate of the dollar amount of accounts receivable that will eventually prove to be uncollectible.

allowance for doubtful accounts
A contra asset account deducted from accounts receivable; represents the portion of the outstanding receivables balance whose collection is doubtful.

a contra asset account that is netted against gross accounts receivable for financial reporting purposes. For example:

Accounts receivable	$17,000
Less: Allowance for doubtful accounts	3,000
	$14,000

The contra asset account serves to reduce the gross receivables amount reported in the balance sheet to an estimated net collectible amount. This contra asset account balance represents, as of a specific point in time, an amount believed to indicate the balance of outstanding customer accounts that will not be collected. "The allowance should be the best possible estimate of the probable loss on accounts then outstanding, in the light of current conditions and assuming the continuation of the business as a 'going concern' " (CICA Handbook 3020.12). Subsequently, if evidence is obtained regarding a *specific* customer account that will not be collected (e.g., a bankrupt customer's account), the receivables account can be directly reduced along with a similar reduction in the contra asset account (in essence, a portion of the contra asset account's estimated balance is no longer needed). In summary, under the percentage-of-sales method, the balance in the Allowance for Doubtful Accounts is *increased* each period by an amount based on a percentage of credit sales (this amount is *also* the period's bad debt expense to be recorded under this method). The balance in the Allowance for Doubtful Accounts is *decreased* by the dollar amount of specific accounts deemed uncollectible and therefore written off.

Percentage-of-Receivables Method: Balance Sheet Approach

A second and perhaps more intuitively appealing implementation of the allowance method requires an aging of the outstanding end-of-period accounts receivable. A large part of a given period's credit sales has already been collected by period-end; therefore, this approach focuses only on those accounts yet to be collected. Under the **aging method**, outstanding accounts receivable are grouped according to the number of days they are past due. Typical "age" categories for the accounts receivable are current, 1–30 days, 31–60 days, 61–90 days, and over 90 days. It is normally the case that as receivables become increasingly overdue, a larger percentage of them will prove to be uncollectible. Thus, for each of the increasingly overdue categories, a larger percentage estimate is applied to the respective receivables balance in determining an aggregate estimate of period-end uncollectible receivables.

Using the information from Exhibit 6.5, it is estimated the following accounts are uncollectible:

aging method
A method of accounting for uncollectible accounts receivable in which an estimate of the bad debts expense is determined by classifying the specific receivable balances into age categories and then applying probability estimates of noncollection.

5% of the 1–30-day accounts	$0.05 \times 7,600 = \$\ 380$
10% of the 31–60-day accounts	$0.10 \times 4,700 = \ 470$
20% of the 61–90-day accounts	$0.20 \times 2,800 = \ 560$
40% of the over 90-day accounts	$0.40 \times 1,900 = \ 760$
	$2,170

The accounts receivables are reported on the balance sheet at their net realizable value, by netting the allowance account against the gross Accounts Receivable account:

Accounts receivable	$17,000
Less: Allowance for doubtful accounts	2,170
	$14,830

The aging approach focuses on determining a targeted figure for the period-end balance in the allowance for doubtful accounts ($2,170). The *difference* between the targeted ending allowance for doubtful accounts and the beginning balance provides the adjustment to be made to the contra asset account and is *also* the amount recorded as that period's bad debt expense. The adjusting entry recorded under this method is substantially the same as that shown in the percentage-of-credit-sales example, but the amounts will be different.

Assuming the Allowance for Doubtful Accounts had a *beginning* balance of $800, if no other entries were made to the allowance account during the period, the adjusting entry for bad debt expense for the period would be:

```
Dr. Bad Debt Expense . . . . . . . . . . . . . . . . . . . . . . . . . . . . . . . . . 1,370
    Cr.   Allowance for Doubtful Accounts . . . . . . . . . . . . . . . . . . . . . . .      1,370
    Adjusting entry, estimated uncollectible accounts ($2,170 – $800).
```

Writing Off a Specific Account

Note that under either allowance method, specific uncollectible accounts receivable were not identified at the time of recording the bad debt expense and adjusting the net realizable value of the receivables. When a specific account receivable is finally identified as uncollectible, it is removed from the books. "An account or note receivable should be written off as soon as it is known to be uncollectible or should be written down to its estimated realizable value as soon as it is known that it is not collectible in full" (CICA Handbook 3020.10). Under either of the allowance methods, adjusting the books to reflect the writing off of a specific account merely involves reducing the balance in the Allowance for Doubtful Accounts contra asset account and the balance in the Accounts Receivable asset account. Such an entry has *no* income statement effect, nor does it affect either the total assets or the total current assets, or the net realizable value of accounts receivable reported in the balance sheet. The income statement and balance sheet effects were anticipated and recognized at the time management recorded the estimate of the uncollectible accounts using either the percentage-of-credit-sales approach or the aging-of-outstanding-receivables approach.

Assuming the account receivable from Prairie Resources, in Exhibit 6.5, is deemed to be uncollectible, the entry to write off the account receivable for $1,500 would be:

```
Dr. Allowance for Doubtful Accounts . . . . . . . . . . . . . . . . . . . . . . . 1,500
    Cr. Accounts Receivable (Prairie Resources) . . . . . . . . . . . . . . . . .      1,500
    Entry to write off an uncollectible account.
```

Under either of the allowance methods, if a specific account previously removed from the books (i.e., written off) subsequently turns out to be collectible, the prior entry made to reduce the receivable account and the contra asset account is simply *reversed* in the amount that is now considered to be collectible. This transaction increases the balance in both the Accounts Receivable account and the Allowance for Doubtful Accounts account by the amount now deemed to be collectible. Assuming, at a later date, it is determined the account from Prairie Resources is collectible, the reversing entry and the entry for the payment received on account would be:

```
Dr. Accounts Receivable (Prairie Resources) ................ 1,500
    Cr. Allowance for Doubtful Accounts ........................        1,500
Setting up an account previously written off.


Dr. Cash ...................................... 1,500
    Cr. Accounts Receivable (Prairie Resources) .................        1,500
Payment on account previously written off.
```

Comprehensive Illustration: Accounting for Receivables

As a comprehensive example of the financial reporting issues for accounts receivables, consider the following information for Drudge Sporting Goods, Ltd. (DSG), for the fiscal year ending January 31, 1997.

1. For the year, DSG had sales of $10,512,000, of which $3,951,000 were credit sales.
2. The beginning Accounts Receivable balance as of February 1, 1996, was $1,623,500. The beginning balance in the Allowance for Doubtful Accounts was $36,500 (credit).
3. Collections during the year were $3,953,000.
4. During the year, specific accounts receivable totalling $34,200 were deemed to be uncollectible and were written off (i.e., removed from the Accounts Receivable account).
5. Receivables totalling $2,000 that had been previously written off were subsequently deemed to be collectible.
6. As of January 31, 1997, the following aging schedule was prepared for DSG accounts receivable:

Uncollected Billings on Account	
1 to 30 days	$ 62,800
31 to 60 days	1,025,200
61 to 90 days	356,900
91 to 120 days	129,700
Over 120 days	14,700
Total accounts receivable outstanding	$1,589,300

7. In the judgment of DSG management and based on past experiences of account collections, the following amounts were estimated to be uncollectible:

¼ of 1% of 1-to-30-day accounts	0.0025 × $62,800	= $ 157
½ of 1% of all 31–60-day accounts	0.005 × $1,025,200	= 5,126
2.5% of all 61–90-day accounts	0.025 × $356,900	= 8,923
10% of all 91–120 day accounts	0.10 × $129,700	= 12,970
50% of all over-120-day accounts	0.50 × $14,700	= 7,350
		$34,526

During the year, DSG would have recorded the following sales activity:

```
Cash ............................................. 6,561,000
Accounts Receivable .............................. 3,951,000
    Sales ..........................................10,512,000
    Sales during the period.
```

In *addition* to the above sales entry, an entry would be needed to adjust the Inventory and Cost of Goods Sold accounts.

During the year, collections of the accounts receivable would be recorded as follows:

```
Cash . . . . . . . . . . . . . . . . . . . . . . . . . . . . . . . . . . . . . . .  3,953,000
    Accounts Receivable . . . . . . . . . . . . . . . . . . . . . . . . . . . . . .3,953,000
Payments received on account during the period.
```

Next, the transactions recorded during the year to report accounts that were written off, as well as to reestablish the accounts previously written off that were later deemed to be collectible, should be recorded in this way:

```
Dr. Allowance for Doubtful Accounts . . . . . . . . . . . . . . . . . . . . . .34,200
    Cr. Accounts Receivable . . . . . . . . . . . . . . . . . . . . . . . . . . . .    34,200
Accounts written off during the period.


Dr. Accounts Receivable . . . . . . . . . . . . . . . . . . . . . . . . . . . . .  2,000
    Cr. Allowance for Doubtful Accounts . . . . . . . . . . . . . . . . . . . . .     2,000
Setting up accounts previously written off.
```

At year-end, management must determine the net realizable value of the outstanding accounts receivable. In this case, DSG uses the aging method; thus, the ending balance in the Allowance for Doubtful Accounts represents what management believes to be the offset required to adjust gross accounts receivables to their net realizable value. Using the balances in the aging schedule and the percentage estimates given by management, we determine that the ending balance in the contra asset allowance account *should be* $34,526. Because the balance in the contra asset account after the previous transactions were recorded *is* $4,300, the expense amount for uncollectible accounts for this period must be $30,226. In essence, $30,230 ($34,526 − $4,300) is the amount required *to balance* the contra asset allowance account to the *targeted* ending balance of $34,530. It is also the amount of the bad debt expense to appear on the current period's income statement. The adjusting entry to record this would be as follows:

```
Dr. Bad Debt Expense . . . . . . . . . . . . . . . . . . . . . . . . . . . . . .30,226
    Cr. Allowance for Doubtful Accounts . . . . . . . . . . . . . . . . . . . . .     30,226
Adjusting entry for uncollectible accounts.
```

A reconstruction of the contra asset allowance T-account is helpful to illustrate the flow of these transactions:

Allowance for Doubtful Accounts

Accounts written off	34,200	Beginning balance	36,500
		Accounts previously written off	2,000
		Subtotal	4,300
		Bad debt expense*	30,226
		Targeted ending balance	34,526

*$34,526 − $4,300 = $30,226.

If DSG had used the percentage-of-credit-sales method *instead* of the aging method, the adjusting entry would remain the same, except the amount of the bad debt expense would change. Assuming that the percentage-of-credit-sales rate used by management was 1 percent, the estimate for uncollectible accounts would be $39,510 ($3,951,000 credit sales × 0.01). Recall that under the percentage-of-credit-sales approach, this amount *is not* the targeted ending balance for the allowance account but *is* the amount by which the allowance account is increased and is the bad debt expense for the period. Thus, in this case, the year-end balance in the allowance account is $43,810 (i.e., $4,300 + $39,510). Take a moment to verify this amount.

It must be noted that a company that uses the percentage-of-credit-sales method must also carefully evaluate the resulting year-end balance in the allowance account. If that balance continues to increase from period to period, it suggests that the percentage-of-sales factor applied in prior periods is too *high* and does not reflect the company's real uncollectible accounts experience. If, on the other hand, that balance becomes negative (i.e., a debit balance), the percentage-of-credit-sales factor used to estimate uncollectibles has been too *low*. In either event, management may decide to adjust the percentage factor to a rate more likely to result in increases to the allowance account that, over time, are similar to the amounts subsequently removed from the contra asset account as the specific receivables are deemed to be uncollectible.

This latter statement is true for *both* allowance methods. This is so because under either allowance method, managers actually anticipate that some portion of a company's promises to be paid will be broken. Consistent with the matching principle, the allowance methods attempt to match the cost of granting credit (i.e., the bad debt expense) to the period in which the benefit (i.e., the credit sale) was recorded. Thus, the increases and decreases to the contra asset allowance account indicate differences between the timing of recording an *estimate* as an anticipated uncollectible and the actual default of a specific account. Consequently, if the percentage factors used to estimate the future uncollectibles reflect the *actual* level of uncollectible accounts over a number of periods, the balance in the allowance account should achieve a steady state.

In summary, it should be noted that the percentage-of-sales method (income statement approach) focuses on the matching principle by determining the bad debt expense based on a percentage of the same period's credit sales. The net realizable value of accounts receivable may be produced without reference to the actual asset, accounts receivable. On the other hand, when the aging method (balance sheet approach) is used, a better net realizable value for accounts receivable should be determined. However, with the aging method, the resulting bad debt expense for the period may not provide the best matching. To overcome this dilemma presented by the two allowance methods, they are often used in conjunction, to provide a check or comparison as to the reasonableness of the estimated uncollectible accounts for the period.

It should be noted that with the percentage-of-credit-sales method, the allowance account is adjusted by the calculated amount, whereas with the aging method, the allowance account is adjusted to a targeted, calculated amount.

Direct Write-Off Method

direct write-off method
A method of accounting for uncollectible accounts receivable in which no bad debt expense is recorded until specific receivables prove to be uncollectible.

There is one additional method to account for bad debts. This method, the **direct write-off method,** is not acceptable under generally accepted accounting principles. Only when evidence is available by which management determines that a specific customer's account is not likely to be collected is a bad debt expense recorded and the

Accounts Receivable account balance reduced to the net amount expected to be collected. Under this method, no allowance account is created, nor is there any attempt to record the bad debt expense amount in the period when the credit sale was made. The entry would be as follows:

```
Dr. Bad Debt Expense . . . . . . . . . . . . . . . . . . . . . . . . . . . . . . . . .  1,500
    Cr. Accounts Receivable . . . . . . . . . . . . . . . . . . . . . . . . . . . . . . .        1,500
Writing off an uncollectible account.
```

From a managerial perspective, deciding to write off an account receivable, whether under one of the allowance methods or under the direct write-off method, can be problematic. Managers typically require convincing evidence that a specific account is indeed uncollectible before they delete it from their records. Indirect evidence such as a customer's declaration of bankruptcy or more direct evidence such as correspondence from the customer disputing the amount owed is generally considered to be sufficient evidence to warrant reducing the Accounts Receivable account. In spite of such evidence and despite recording the account write-off, management should continue to attempt to collect any outstanding amount.

Factoring and Pledging

factoring
A process by which a company can convert its receivables into cash by selling them at face value less a service charge.

with (without) recourse
A sale with recourse obligates the selling company to "make good" the receivable in the event that the factor is unable to collect on the receivable; a sale without recourse obligates the factor to assume all liability for noncollectibility.

Most companies consider the management of accounts receivable (i.e., the efforts undertaken to make sure that payments are promptly received) a normal part of their day-to-day operations. However, if a company decides that it does not want to expend the resources necessary to manage the accounts or finds itself short of cash, the company may factor or sell its accounts receivable. **Factoring** is a process by which a company can convert its receivables into cash by selling them at face value less a service charge for processing the transaction and for the time value of money. Typically, the service charge for factoring receivables is very expensive, from 15 percent to as much as 50 percent or more. How much will be paid to a factor (usually a financial institution) is largely a function of whether the receivables are sold with or without recourse. **With recourse** means that the factor can return a receivable to the company and collect from the company if the receivable turns out to be unpaid as of a certain date. **Without recourse** means that the factor assumes the risk of any losses on collection. In either case, the customer owing the money may or may not be notified that a factor is the ultimate recipient of its payment.

The following disclosure regarding the potential of factoring receivables appeared as a footnote to the financial statements in the annual report of Abitibi-Price, Inc.: "Under agreements entered into with major banks, the Company has the right, on an ongoing basis, to sell certain trade accounts receivable with minimal recourse and with the Company continuing to administer the collection of the receivables. The total of such receivables which remained outstanding at December 31, 1994 was $89.9 million (1993 — $122.1 million)." Beckman Instruments, Inc., disclosed the following note: "During the year, the Company received proceeds of $47.1 million from factoring trade receivables. The Company is contingently liable for the possible uncollected portion of the factored receivables, if any, which was $9.4 million at December 31." Footnotes typically disclose the extent to which each company has factored its receivables and something of the terms (limited recourse) of those sales. The Beckman footnote also discloses the remaining uncollected receivables under its agreement, an amount for which Beckman is liable to the extent that the accounts prove to be uncollectible.

pledging
When assets are used as collateral for a bank loan, the assets are said to have been pledged.

Another way a firm can use accounts receivables to expedite its cash inflows is to pledge them as collateral for a short-term bank loan that may not be obtainable without the pledge. In **pledging**, a company normally retains title to the accounts receivable but pledges that it will use the proceeds from collection of the receivables to repay the loan.

Notes Receivable

promissory note
A written promise to pay a specific sum of money at a specific date; a liability.

Businesses sometimes accept promissory notes from customers in exchange for services or merchandise sold on credit or in place of an outstanding account receivable that a customer is unable to pay according to the original credit terms. A **promissory note** is a legal document that is signed by the customer (the maker) promising to pay to the company (the payee) a fixed dollar amount (the principal) plus interest. The note may become due in total on a stated maturity date or in segments on several dates, at which time(s) the payee receives from the maker the stipulated amount(s) plus any accrued interest.

A promissory note, or note receivable, might be arranged by a seller if a customer is a high credit risk or needs a longer time than usual to pay. Companies often convert overdue accounts receivable to notes receivable so that the amount in question, the new payment date, and an interest charge for the extended payment time may all be formally and specifically stated and agreed to by the customer. Notes receivable classified as current assets are carried in the financial statements at net realizable value, that is, face value, less any allowance for doubtful accounts. The evaluation process for possible uncollectible notes is exactly the same as for accounts receivable. If, on the other hand, the notes receivable are more properly classified as non-current, they should be reported at the present value of the expected future cash flows. Later chapters will have more to say about such non-current accounts, their valuation, and the concept of present value.

Because promissory notes receivable are negotiable instruments, businesses sometimes sell or pledge notes receivable to a bank (or any other type of factor) to obtain cash prior to the due date of the note. Such transactions are similar to factoring and pledging accounts receivable in that the payee receives the face value of the note less some fee or discount.

Financial Statement Disclosure: Receivables

As mentioned earlier, trade receivables appear in the balance sheet in the current assets section and are reported at their net realizable value. The net realizable value is the original value of the asset less the allowance for doubtful accounts. For example:

Accounts receivable	$133,000
Less: Allowance for doubtful accounts	22,000
	$111,000

In the above example, the $111,000 represents the collectible portion or the net realizable value of the asset accounts receivable. According to GAAP, organizations must properly evaluate their accounts receivable. Smaller organizations often disclose their receivables as shown above, indicating both the allowance account balance and the net realizable value of the asset. Most publicly held companies use, but may *not* disclose, an allowance account, but simply disclose the net realizable value of accounts receivable. "Since it is to be assumed that adequate allowance for doubtful accounts has been made if no statement is made to the contrary, it is not necessary to refer to such allowance" (CICA Handbook 3020.01). Maple Leaf Gardens, Limited, and other public companies use this disclosure.

The annual report of Moore Corporation, Limited, illustrates another typical method of receivable presentation:

	1993	1992
Accounts receivable, less allowance for doubtful accounts of $15,305 ($17,032 in 1992)	419,805	426,215

Note that the reader learns of the amount that Moore Corporation management expects ultimately to collect ($419,805), as well as the amount of gross accounts receivable *not* expected to be collected ($15,305). The sum of these two figures is the amount of gross accounts receivable not yet collected as of year-end.

Another acceptable format for reporting accounts receivable is to present only the net realizable value of receivables, and use a footnote to disclose the balance in the Allowance for Doubtful Accounts account.

Analyzing Receivables

The level of investment a company might have in receivables at any particular time is affected by many conditions: seasonal, cyclical, or growth changes in sales; the market the company serves; the company's credit and collection policies; and inflation.

The investment in receivables is closely related to the volume of sales for the period immediately preceding a given balance sheet date. If sales during that period were low, either because of seasonal or cyclical changes or declining markets, the accounts receivable balance should, all else being equal, be lower than in periods when credit sales were high.

The market a company serves also has a bearing on its receivables balance. In some markets, business cannot be conducted without using credit. Other markets, by custom, require longer or shorter credit terms than usual to facilitate commerce. For example, Wendy's Corporation requires prompt payment of a percentage of weekly sales from its franchisees, which primarily conduct business with customers on a cash basis. In the recent past, the average receivable collection period for Wendy's, Inc., was about six days. In contrast, many of the credit sales of Northrop Corporation are to the government, which relies on numerous administrative reviews prior to authorizing payment to its suppliers. Thus, it is not surprising that Northrop's financial statements reveal collection periods from the various segments of its government contracts (representing about 90 percent of Northrop's sales) ranging from 60 days to more than two years.

A company's credit policy is an important competitive weapon. By allowing more and more potential credit customers to qualify for credit sales, a company's revenues and accounts receivable balances are likely to increase. At the same time, however, the carrying costs and potential losses from uncollectible accounts may also increase. Periods of high interest rates and periods of uncertain business conditions obviously raise the cost of carrying receivables. Thus, a company must weigh the costs of additional sales (increased interest expense and bad debts) against the benefits (increased revenues and increased cash inflows).

Inflation is another factor to be considered in managing a company's investment in receivables. During periods of inflation, the purchasing power of the dollar diminishes. Consequently, future collections of receivables represent collections of cheaper dollars. The lost purchasing power of those cheaper dollars is a cost of making credit sales.

Many procedures may be used to evaluate the quality of a company's accounts receivable management. Most methods deal with ratio analysis, and the most common ratio is the **average receivable collection period**. This ratio is an extension of the receivable turnover ratio discussed in Chapter 2. It simply converts the turnover value to a days outstanding or collection period by dividing the turnover ratio by 365 days. The average collection period is computed as:

average receivable collection period
A measure of the effectiveness of accounts receivable management.

$$\text{Average receivable collection period} = \frac{365 \times \text{Accounts receivable}}{\text{Total credit sales}}$$

The receivable collection period gives a rough measure of the length of time that a company's accounts receivable have been outstanding. A comparison of this measure with a company's credit terms, with the measure for other firms in the same industry, and with the figures for prior periods indicates a company's efficiency in collecting receivables and its trends in credit management.

Other receivable-related ratios may also be of interest to managers, creditors, and investors. These include (1) the ratio of accounts receivable that are actually written off divided by credit sales or by total receivables and (2) the ratio of credit sales to total sales, which reveals how dependent a company is on credit sales. Ratios involving the written-off accounts receivable reveal how correct management has been in determining those customers to which to grant credit, as well as management's effectiveness in collecting those credit sales. In a similar vein, the aging schedule is a good indicator of the quality of the accounts receivables at a particular point in time. (Such information is usually not available to the public but it is useful to management.) Frequent preparation of an aging schedule may be crucial to the timely management of credit.

Managers must use such analytical tools to manage their investment in accounts receivable throughout the credit cycle. This cycle, starting with the approval of a credit sale and ending with the receipt of cash, is important to a company's continuing operations. Inattention to the details involved throughout the cycle often results in incurring an opportunity cost because of cash being needlessly tied up in accounts receivable and, in the worst case, may cause a firm to be critically short of cash. The mismanagement of accounts receivable prevents the organization from investing in revenue-producing assets such as inventory or capital assets.

As we have just seen, the management of accounts receivable involves managerial attention to the collection of the promises to pay that a company has received from its customers.

Ethics in Accounting

Harry and Louise formed a partnership and have just completed their first year of operations. You have been asked to prepare their first annual financial statements. The accounting records indicate accounts receivable of $47,500 owing from customers and temporary investments purchased at a cost of $23,000. The two partners are trying to measure the value of these two assets for financial statement purposes. Harry thinks accounts receivable are overvalued, because of careless credit-granting policies and poor collection during their first few months of operation. "I would speculate we might collect only $45,000 from our accounts receivable." Louise isn't sure she agrees with Harry's observation on their accounting for accounts receivable, and suggests they adopt a "wait and see" policy, and hopefully collections will be better in the new year. The temporary investments have a current market value at year-end of $21,300. Both partners believe the decline in the market value of investments is only temporary. The partnership agreement calls for partners to share net income equally during the first year. In subsequent years, net income will be shared as follows: Harry 40 percent and Louise 60 percent. The net income for the first year is $23,000. Discuss how the two assets should be valued for financial statement purposes. What are the ethical issues for the accountant?

6.4 SUMMARY

Cash, temporary investments, and receivables are key current assets. Although not considered to be cash equivalents, temporary investments and receivables are nonetheless both readily convertible into cash. All three assets strongly influence the financial strength of the organization, particularly its liquidity position.

The management and control of cash involves cash budgeting to avoid cash deficiencies and ensure any excess cash is invested wisely. Since cash is the most liquid asset, an adequate system of internal control for cash is important.

Temporary investments represent the short-term investment of excess cash into corporate securities. These investments must be highly liquid to permit their easy conversion into cash when needed to support a company's operations. The lower-of-cost-or-market method and the accounting for temporary and permanent declines in market value influence the disclosure of temporary investments. In the appendix to Chapter 8, we will discuss accounting for intercorporate investments when the purpose of the investment is based on the long-run income objectives of the company.

Accounts receivable are evidence of a company's revenue production function. Although high receivable balances are not risky in and of themselves, the risk of non-collection of cash is inherent in all "promises to pay" and thus should be closely monitored. The aging method and the percentage-of-credit-sales method are generally acceptable methods of accounting for uncollectible accounts. The following table summarizes the financial statement interrelationships of cash, temporary investments, and accounts receivable:

Financial Statement Interrelationships

Financial Statement Item	Balance Sheet	Income Statement	Statement of Changes in Financial Position
Cash	Current asset	Bank reconciliation adjustments: service charges, interest expense	Analysis of change in cash during the year
Temporary investments	Current asset	Unrealized losses/gains, applying the lower-of-cost-or-market rule	Adjustment to working capital items: operating activities
Accounts receivable	Current asset	Bad debt expense	Adjustment to working capital items: operating activities

6.5 KEY CONCEPTS AND TERMS

Aged trial balance (p. 287)
Aging method (p. 290)
Allowance for doubtful accounts (p. 289)
Allowance for market decline in
    temporary investments (p. 280)
Average receivable collection
    period (p. 298)
Bad debt expense (p. 289)
Bank reconciliation (p. 275)
Cash management (p. 273)
Control account (p. 287)
Credit terms (p. 287)
Direct write-off method (p. 294)
Factoring (p. 295)
Insurance/bonding (p. 274)
Internal control (p. 273)

Lower of cost or market (p. 279)
Net realizable value (p. 288)
Outstanding cheque (p. 275)
Outstanding deposit (p. 275)
Percentage of credit sales (p. 289)
Petty cash fund (p. 275)
Pledging (p. 296)
Promissory note (p. 296)
Responsibility (p. 274)
Separation of duties (p. 274)
Subsidiary ledger (p. 287)
Temporary investments (p. 278)
Unrealized gain/loss (p. 280)
Valuation allowance (p. 280)
With (without) recourse (p. 295)

6.6 COMPREHENSIVE REVIEW QUESTION

R6.1 Cash, temporary investments, receivable. The accounting records of Purple Mountain Company, Ltd., included the following information. The bank balance in the accounting records at December 31 was $4,312.00. The petty cash balance was $100.00. On November 19 excess cash in the amount of $2,000 was invested in a 60-day guaranteed investment certificate (GIC). The GIC will be used to purchase merchandise inventory when it matures in January. On December 31, an analysis of the banking transactions indicates there are outstanding deposits of $2,700.00 and outstanding cheques totalling $2,016. The December 31 bank statement indicates a balance of $3,300 and includes unrecorded amounts for service charges of $18.00 and a loan payment of $310. The loan payment is comprised of $90.00 for interest and the balance to be applied against the principal on the loan payable.

Two purchases of temporary investments were made during the year. On July 8, a $10,000 purchase of shares in ABC, Ltd,. was made. On September 9, an $8,000 purchase of shares in XYZ, Ltd., was made. The purchase price of the temporary investments includes all relevant taxes and commission costs. On December 31, the market values of the temporary investments were as follows: ABC, Ltd., $8,200 and XYZ, Ltd., $9,000.

The aged trial balance of accounts receivable at December 31 is shown below:

Customer	Total	Age of Account (days)			
		1–30	31–60	61–90	Over 90
Acme Services	$ 2,500	$1,200	$ 800	$ 400	$100
Brandon Resources	1,200	900	300	—	—
Cathedral Arts Board	2,200	700	1,200	—	300
Devonshire Printing	4,600	2,700	1,000	900	—
	$10,500	$5,500	$3,300	$1,300	$400

The company has decided to estimate bad debt expense based on either ½ of 1 percent of sales or on a percentage of accounts receivable outstanding as of December 31. The two aging alternatives being considered are either 5 percent of the total receivables outstanding or an estimate using percentages for each aged category as follows: 2 percent of 1–30 days, 4 percent of 31–60 days, 10 percent of 61–90 days, and 20 percent of outstanding accounts over 90 days.

The company wishes to use the accounting methods that produce the most conservative results. A condensed income statement for the year ending December 31 is shown below:

PURPLE MOUNTAIN COMPANY, LTD.
Income Statement
For the Year Ending December 31

Sales	$88,000
Cost of sales	57,000
Gross profit	$31,000
Operating expenses	17,500
Net income	$13,500
Earnings per share	$1.25

Required:

a. Provide a partial balance sheet as at December 31 to include the disclosure of cash, temporary investments, and accounts receivables.

b. Record all the journal entries for cash, temporary investments, and receivables.

c. Provide a revised income statement for the year ended December 31.

6.7 REVIEW AND DISCUSSION QUESTIONS

Q6.1 How might a manager test the reasonableness of a company's bad debt expense and its allowance for doubtful accounts?

Q6.2 What are the deficiencies of the direct write-off method for determining a company's periodic bad debt expense?

Q6.3 What are the two basic allowance methods used to estimate a company's periodic bad debt expense, and what is the theoretical justification for each?

Q6.4 Distinguish between trade and non-trade receivables. Is this a useful distinction for financial reporting purposes? Explain.

Q6.5 Discuss the significance of the net realizable value concept as it applies to receivables.

Q6.6 Once a company writes off a specific account receivable, would you expect its collections effort to cease? Explain.

Q6.7 A local florist follows the policy of billing customers at the end of each month. During the past six months, sales have remained steady but the company's accounts receivable balance has increased substantially. What steps might the owner consider taking to reduce the store's accounts receivable balance?

Q6.8 Recreate the pro and con debate that most likely took place prior to the enactment of GAAP for temporary investments. Focus specifically on the question of retaining a strict historical cost perspective versus a lower-of-cost-or-market perspective for temporary investments.

Q6.9 Peruse the five latest issues of *The Financial Post*, identifying two or three companies having a 52-week low in their stock prices and report on whether such a decline in price is or is not permanent. What issues did you focus on in making the judgment as to the permanent or temporary nature of the low?

Q6.10 GAAP detail a lower-of-cost-or-market criterion for investments in temporary investments. In the approach to implementing GAAP, some securities actually are being "reported" at market values that are in excess of their cost. Explain.

Q6.11 One of the most valuable assets an organization has is its cash. Describe four internal control procedures that safeguard this valuable asset.

Q6.12 The accounts receivable for Long, Ltd., on January 1 were $60,000 and on December 31 $75,000. Cash sales during the year were $12,000 and sales on account during the year were $210,000. During the year an uncollectible account of $3,000 was written off. Determine the cash collections on accounts receivable during the year.

Q6.13 Review the Ethics in Accounting case presented at the end of the chapter. Discuss the alternative courses of action available to the accountant. How do think the situation should be handled?

Q6.14 One of the most frequent reasons for the failure of new businesses is poor cash flow management. Explain.

Q6.15 Discuss the pros and cons of evaluating division managers on a "cash provided by operations" basis.

Q6.16 If you could receive only one cash flow figure from a company, what figure would you request? Why?

6.8 PROBLEMS

P6.1 Estimating bad debt expense. The trial balance of Aha Company at the end of its fiscal year included the following account balances:

Account	Debit	Credit
Accounts receivable	$48,900	
Notes receivable	12,500	
Temporary investments	15,000	
Allowance for doubtful accounts	2,500	
Sales		$500,000

The company has not yet recorded any bad debt expense for the year.

Required:

Determine the amount of bad debt expense to be recognized by Aha Company for the year assuming the following independent situations:

a. Experience shows that 90 percent of all sales are credit sales and that an average of 1 percent of credit sales prove to be uncollectible.

b. An analysis of the aging of trade receivables indicates that probable uncollectible accounts at year-end amount to $1,500.

c. Company policy is to maintain a balance sheet provision for bad debts equal to 3 percent of outstanding trade receivables.

P6.2 Accounting for bad debts. The following data were associated with the trade receivables and bad debts of CPL, Inc.:

1. The opening balance in the Allowance for Doubtful Accounts was $710,000 at January 1.

2. The company realized that specific trade receivable accounts totalling $820,000 had actually gone bad and been written off.

3. A trade receivable of $50,000 was collected during 1996. This account had previously been written off as a bad debt.

4. The financial officer decided that, using the aging method, the Allowance for Doubtful Accounts would need a balance of $920,000 at the end of the period.

Required:

a. Prepare journal entries to show how these events would be recognized in an accounting system using:

   (1) The allowance method for bad debts.

   (2) The direct write-off method for bad debts.

b. Discuss the advantages and disadvantages of each method with respect to the following accounting conventions:

   (1) Matching

   (2) Conservatism

P6.3 Valuing long-term receivables. Ken's Sub Shoppe, Inc., is a franchiser that offers for sale an exclusive franchise agreement for $30,000. Under the terms of the agreement, the franchisee will receive a variety of services associated with the construction of a Ken's Sub Shoppe, access to various product supply services, and continuing management advice and assistance once the retail unit is up and running. The contract calls for cash payments of $10,000 per year for three years.

Required:

How should Ken's Sub Shoppe, Inc., account for the sale of a franchise contract?

P6.4 Aging accounts receivables. The following data were taken from the accounts receivable records of Cavalier Products Company as of December 31:

Receivable Age Classification	Receivable Balance Outstanding	Probability of Non-Collection	
0–10 days	$100,000	0.5%	500
11–30 days	60,000	1.0	600
31–60 days	50,000	2.5	1250
61–90 days	40,000	4.0	1600
91–120 days	30,000	6.5	1950
Over 120 days	5,000	10.0	500
			6400

A prior credit balance of $1,000 existed in the Allowance for Doubtful Accounts account.

Required:

Determine the amount of bad debt expense to be recorded at year-end by Cavalier Products Company.

P6.5 Ratio analysis. Presented below are summary financial data for Coca-Cola Enterprises, Inc., and PepsiCo, Inc. (in millions).

	19x9	19x8
Net sales		
Coca-Cola, Inc.	$ 3,882	$ 3,875
PepsiCo, Inc.	15,242	12,533
Receivables		
Coca-Cola, Inc.	297	294
PepsiCo, Inc.	1,240	979

Required:

Using the above data, calculate the accounts receivable turnover and average number of days' receivable collection period for each company. What is your evaluation of each company's credit management?

P6.6 Allowance account analysis. From inception of operations to December 31, 1996, Harris Corporation provided for uncollectible accounts receivable under the allowance for doubtful accounts method with increases to the allowance account being made monthly at 2 percent of credit sales. Harris's usual credit term is net 30 days.

The balance in the Allowance for Doubtful Accounts was $130,000 at January 1, 1996. During 1996, credit sales totalled $9,000,000, monthly estimates for doubtful accounts were made at 2 percent of credit sales, $90,000 of bad debts were written off, and recoveries of accounts previously written off amounted to $15,000. Harris installed a computer facility in November 1996 and an aging of accounts receivable was prepared for the first time as of December 31, 1996. A summary of the aging is as follows:

Classification by Month of Sale	Aged Accounts Receivable as of December 31	Estimated Percentage Uncollectible
November–December	$1,140,000	2%
July–October	600,000	10
January–June	400,000	25
Prior to January 1, 1996	120,000	75
Total receivable December 31	$2,260,000	

Based on an item-by-item review of the collectibility of the accounts in the Prior to January 1, 1996 aging category, receivables totalling $60,000 were written off on December 31, 1996 (these were included in the $120,000 and represent write-offs in addition to the $90,000 previously written off). In addition, effective with the year ended December 31, 1996, Harris adopted a new accounting method for estimating the allowance for doubtful accounts, choosing to report the amount indicated by the year-end aging analysis of accounts receivable.

Required:

a. We know that the January 1, 1996, balance in the allowance account was $130,000. Reconstruct all of the 1995 accounting transactions affecting the allowance account.

b. What is the December 31, 1996, allowance account balance?

P6.7 Accounting for temporary investments. Philpott Mining invests its excess idle cash in temporary investments. The following portfolio of shares as of December 31, 1995, were all purchased in 1995.

	As of December 31, 1995	
	Cost	Market Value
Nella Co.	$ 40,000	$ 36,000
Zen Inc.	33,000	34,000
Aldon Co.	19,000	18,500
Leslie Inc.	18,000	16,500
Diane Properties	19,000	18,800
Stillfied Co.	12,000	13,000
	$141,000	$136,800

During 1996, all Zen, Inc., shares were sold for $35,000. As of December 31, 1996, the total market value of the portfolio was $101,000.

Required:

a. Prepare all necessary 1995 transactions pertaining to Philpott Mining's temporary investments.

b. Prepare all necessary 1996 transactions pertaining to Philpott Mining's temporary investments.

c. As of December 31, 1997, the portfolio had an aggregate market value of $104,000. Assuming that there had been no partial sales of any shares during 1997, what year-end adjusting entry (if any) is required on December 31, 1997?

P6.8 Lower of cost or market. Presented below is the temporary investments footnote taken from Expo Corporation's 1996 annual report:

	1996	1995
Current assets: Temporary investments	$620,000,000	$908,000,000

Temporary investments are stated at the lower of cost or market.

Temporary investments at year-end 1995 were carried at cost, which was $1 million less than their fair market value. At year-end 1996, temporary investments were carried at their fair market value, which was $5 million below cost.

Required:

What lower-of-cost-or-market entry did Expo record at

a. Year-end 1995?

b. Year-end 1996?

P6.9 Accounting for receivables. Suppose that Tentex Company had the following balances in some of its accounts on December 31, 1996 (in thousands of dollars):

Accounts receivable	$350.0 debit balance
Allowance for doubtful accounts	10.2 credit balance

Transactions during 1997 were (in thousands of dollars)

1. Sales on account	$1,585.0
2. Collections on account — $1,549.4 less cash discounts of $27.4	1,522.0
3. Sales returns (from credit sales)	8.5
4. Accounts written off as uncollectible	5.4
5. Accounts previously written off now determined to be collectible	0.7
6. Provision for uncollectible accounts (based on percent of credit sales)	8.0

Required:

Prepare entries for the 1997 transactions.

a. At what figure will Tentex show:

(1) Net sales in its 1997 income statement?

(2) Net trade receivables in its balance sheet of December 31, 1997?

P6.10 Accounting for receivables. Moss Products, Inc., was formed in 1986. Sales have increased on the average of 5 percent per year during its first 10 years of existence, with total sales for 1996 amounting to $350,000. Since incorporation, Moss Products has used the allowance method to account for bad debts. The company's fiscal year is the calendar year.

On January 1, 1996, the company's Allowance for Doubtful Accounts had a right-hand balance of $4,000. During 1996, accounts totalling $3,300 were written off as uncollectible.

Required:

a. What does the January 1, 1996, credit balance of $4,000 in the Allowance for Doubtful Accounts represent?

b. Since Moss Products wrote off $3,300 in uncollectible accounts during 1996, was the prior year's bad debts estimate overstated?

c. Prepare the entries to record

(1) The $3,300 write-off during 1996.

(2) Moss Products' 1996 bad debts expense assuming these two independent situations: (*i*) experience indicates that 1 percent of total annual sales prove uncollectible and (*ii*) an aging of the December 31, 1996, accounts receivable indicates that potential uncollectible accounts at year-end total $4,500.

P6.11 Credit policy review. The president, sales manager, and credit manager of Hacket Corporation were discussing the company's present credit policy and possible changes. The sales manager argued that potential sales were being lost to the competition because of Hacket Corporation's tight restrictions on granting credit to consumers. He stated that if credit were extended to a new class of customer, this year's credit sales of $2,500,000 could be increased by at least 20 percent next year with only a corresponding increase in uncollectible accounts of $10,000 over this year's figure of $37,500. With a gross margin on sales of 25 percent, the sales manager continued, the company would certainly come out ahead.

The credit manager, however, believed that a better alternative to easier credit terms would be to accept consumer credit cards like VISA or MasterCard for charge sales. The credit manager said that he had been reading on this topic and he believed this alternative offered the chance to increase sales by 40 percent. The credit card finance charges to Hacket Corporation would amount to 4 percent of the additional sales.

At this point, the president interrupted by saying that he wasn't at all sure that increasing credit sales of any kind was a good thing. In fact, he thought that the $37,500 figure was altogether too high. He wondered whether or not the company should discontinue offering sales on account.

Required:

a. Determine whether Hacket Corporation would be better off under the sales manager's proposal or the credit manager's proposal.

b. Address the president's suggestion that all credit sales be abolished.

P6.12 Lower of cost or market. The chief financial officer of Plow and Mantel Co. recently heard about a proposed new accounting rule related to investments in temporary investments. The proposal is that all temporary investments be presented at market value on the balance sheet and the changes that occur in market value be reflected in income in the current period. The CFO cannot argue with the point that market value on the balance sheet is more informative, but she sees no reason why changes in market value should be reflected in income of the current year.

The controller of Plow and Mantel Company also has misgivings about the possible new rule and has recommended the following alternatives:

1. Recognize realized gains and losses from changes in market value in income and report unrealized gains and losses in a special balance sheet account on the equity side of the balance sheet.

2. Report realized and unrealized gains and losses from market value changes in a statement separate from the income statement or as direct charges and credits to a shareholders' equity account.

3. Recognize gains and losses from changes in market value in income based on long-term yield; for example, use the past performance of the enterprise over several years (a 10-year period has been suggested) to determine an average annual rate of yield because of an increase in value. To the CFO of Plow and Mantel Company, these recommendations seemed very reasonable.

Required:

a. Discuss the pros and cons of the proposed new rule. Is it preferable to the lower-of-cost-or-market rule now in effect? Why or why not?

b. Evaluate the controller's alternatives.

P6.13 Accounting for temporary investments. Geisler Company has followed the practice of reporting its temporary investments at the lower of cost or market. At December 31, 1995, its temporary investments had a balance of $50,000, and the Allowance for Decline in Market Value of Temporary Investments account had a balance of $3,000. Analysis disclosed that on December 31, 1995, the facts relating to the securities were as follows:

	Cost	Market	Allowance Required
Carraway Company	$21,000	$19,000	$2,000
Dunstan Company	12,000	9,000	3,000
Wilcox Company	19,500	20,400	–0–
	$52,500	$48,400	$5,000

During 1996, Dunstan Company stock was sold for $9,100; the difference between the $9,100 and the "new adjusted basis" of $9,000 was recorded as a gain on sale of securities. The market price of the remaining stocks on December 31, 1996, were Carraway Company, $19,900; and Wilcox Company, $20,800.

Required:

a. Did Geisler Company properly apply the lower-of-cost-or-market rule on December 31, 1995? Explain.

b. Did Geisler Company properly account for the sale of Dunstan Company stock? Explain.

c. Are there any additional entries necessary for Geisler Company at December 31, 1996, to reflect the facts on the balance sheet and income statement in accordance with generally accepted accounting principles? Explain.

P6.14 Accounting for temporary investments. Brownlee Bearings Company has the following securities in its short-term portfolio of temporary investments on December 31, 1995:

	Cost	Market
2,000 shares Miller Motors, common	$ 68,500	$ 60,250
10,000 shares of Erving, Inc., common	257,500	257,500
1,000 shares of Magic, Ltd., preferred	52,500	56,000
	$378,500	$373,750

All of the securities were purchased in 1995.

In 1996, Brownlee Bearings completed the following securities transactions:
March 1   Sold 2,000 shares of Miller Motors, common, at $30 per share less fees of $1,500.
April 1   Bought 1,000 shares of SteelCo. common, at $45 per share plus fees of $1,000.

Brownlee Bearings Company portfolio of temporary investments appeared as follows on December 31, 1996:

	Cost	Market
10,000 shares of Erving, Inc., common	$257,500	$291,000
1,000 shares of SteelCo., common	46,000	41,000
1,000 shares of Magic, Ltd., preferred	52,500	50,000
	$356,000	$382,000

Required:

Prepare the accounting entries for Brownlee Bearings Company for

a. The 1995 adjusting entry.

b. The sale of Miller Motors stock.

c. The purchase of Steelco stock.

d. The 1996 adjusting entry.

P6.15 Average receivable collection period. The financial statements of Hamilton-Wenthworth, Ltd., include total revenues of $8,335,000 for the current year and accounts receivable of $984,000. The average receivable collection period is 43.1 days.

Required:

Explain the impact each of the following transactions would have on the company's asset management:

a. **(1)** Earned additional revenues of $666,000.

(2) Issued 10,000 common shares for $30,000 cash.

(3) Collected an additional $137,000 on accounts receivable.

(4) Invested $40,000 cash in equipment.

b. As a result of the above transactions, is the organization in a better or worse financial position?

P6.16 Bad debt policy review. The controller for Franklin Corporation provides you, the credit manager, with the following list of accounts receivable written off in the current year.

Date	Customer	Amount
March 31	Smith & Robertson, Inc.	$6,400
June 30	Lanahan Associates	3,700
September 30	Cheryl's Dress Shop	5,120
December 31	Frank Corporation	5,800

Franklin Corporation follows the policy of recording bad debt expense as accounts are written off. The controller maintains that this procedure is appropriate for financial statement purposes.

All of Franklin Corporation's sales are on a 30-day credit basis. Sales for the current year total $1,800,000, and analysis has indicated that bad debt losses historically approximate 1.5 percent of sales.

Required:

a. Do you agree or disagree with Franklin Corporation's policy concerning recognition of bad debt expense? Why or why not?

b. If Franklin were to use the percent-of-credit-sales method for recording bad debt expense, net income for the current year would change by how much?

P6.17 Financial statement disclosure: temporary investments.

a. Tub Factory Corporation invested its excess cash in temporary investments during 1995. As of December 31, 1995, the portfolio of short-term temporary investments consisted of the following common shares:

Security	Quantity (in shares)	Per Share Cost	Per Share Market
Holden, Inc.	1,000	$14	$19
Coates Corp.	3,000	27	21
Carey Marine	2,000	36	31

What descriptions and amounts should be reported in Tub Factory's December 31, 1995, balance sheet relative to temporary investments?

b. On December 31, 1996, Tub Factory's portfolio of temporary investments consisted of the following common shares:

| Security | Quantity (in shares) | Per Share | |
		Cost	Market
Holden, Inc.	1,000	$14	$21
Holden, Inc.	2,000	20	21
Lakeshore Company	1,000	17	14
Carey Marine	2,000	36	20

During 1996, Tub Factory sold 3,000 shares of Coates Corp. at a loss of $10,000 and purchased 2,000 more shares of Holden, Inc., and 1,000 shares of Lakeshore Company.

(1) What descriptions and amounts should be reported in Tub Factory's December 31, 1996, balance sheet?

(2) What descriptions and amounts should be reported to reflect the data in Tub Factory's 1996 income statement?

c. On December 31, 1997, Tub Factory's portfolio of temporary investments consisted of the following common stocks:

| Security | Quantity (in shares) | Per Share | |
		Cost	Market
Carey Marine	2,000	$36	$47
Lakeshore Company	500	17	15

During 1997, Tub Factory sold 3,000 shares of Holden, Inc., at a gain of $12,000 and 500 shares of Lakeshore Company at a loss of $2,300.

(1) What descriptions and amounts should be reported in Tub Factory's December 31, 1997, balance sheet?

(2) What descriptions and amounts should be reported to reflect the above in Tub Factory's 1997 income statement?

d. Assuming that comparative financial statements for 1996 and 1997 are presented, draft the footnote necessary for full disclosure of Tub Factory's transactions and position in temporary investments.

P6.18 Accounting for receivables. Holt Company has significant amounts of trade accounts receivable outstanding at any given time. Holt uses an allowance method to estimate bad debt expense instead of the direct write-off method. During the year, some specific accounts were written off as uncollectible, and some that were previously written off as uncollectible were collected.

Besides trade accounts receivable, Holt also has some interest-bearing notes receivable for which the face amount plus interest, at the current market rate of interest, is due at maturity. The notes were received on August 1, 1990, and are due on July 31, 1996.

Required:

a. How should Holt Company account for the collection of the accounts previously written off as uncollectible?

b. How should Holt Company report the effects of the interest-bearing notes receivable on its December 31, 1995, balance sheet and its income statement for the year ended December 31, 1995? Why?

P6.19 Estimating bad debts. Bolt Company's allowance for doubtful accounts had a credit balance of $10,000 at December 31, 1995. On a monthly basis during the year, for quick and ready reference purposes, Bolt accrues bad debt expense at 4 percent of credit sales. During 1996, Bolt's credit sales amounted to $1,500,000, and uncollectible accounts totalling $44,000 were judged to be hopelessly uncollectible and thus were written off. The year-end aging of accounts receivable indicated that a $40,000 allowance for doubtful accounts was desirable at December 31, 1996.

Required:

What should Bolt's 1996 bad debt expense be? Explain.

P6.20 Accounting for receivables. Longhorn Company had the following information relating to its accounts receivable at December 31, 1995, and for the year ended December 31, 1996:

Accounts receivable at 12/31/95	$1,000,000
Allowance for doubtful accounts at 12/31/95	60,000
Credit sales for 1996	5,300,000
Collections from customers for 1996	4,650,000
Accounts written off, 9/30/96	70,000
Estimated uncollectible receivables per treasurer's aging of receivables at 12/31/96	110,000

Required:

a. At December 31, 1996, Longhorn's allowance for doubtful accounts should be how much?

b. At December 31, 1996, Longhorn's gross accounts receivable balance should be how much?

P6.21 Bank reconciliation. Information necessary for the preparation of a bank reconciliation for the Martin Company at March 31 is listed below:

1. Accompanying the bank statement was a cheque from Ross McEwan for $186.00, which was marked NSF by the bank.

2. Cheques outstanding as of March 31 were as follows: #84 for $1,841.02; #88 for $1,323.00; #89 for $16.26.

3. Also accompanying the bank statement was a debit memorandum for $44.80 for safe deposit box rent; the bank had erroneously charged this item to the account of the Martin Company. It should have been charged to Morten Company.

4. On March 29, the bank collected a non-interest-bearing note for Martin Company. The note was for $2,963; the bank charged a collection fee of $8.40.

5. A deposit of $2,008.50 was outstanding; it had been put in the night depository on March 31.

6. In recording a $160 cheque received on account from a customer, the accountant for the Martin Company erroneously listed the collection in the cash receipts journal as $16. The cheque appeared correctly among the deposits on the March bank statement.

7. The bank service charge for March amounted to $5.31.

8. The bank statement also showed that a deposit in transit totalling $1,958.14 on the February 28 bank reconciliation had been recorded by the bank in March.

9. The balance per records of the Martin Company is $12,604.02.

10. The bank statement shows a balance of $16,638.29 as of March 31.

Required:

a. Prepare a bank reconciliation at March 31.

b. Prepare the necessary adjusting journal entries.

P6.22 Accounts receivable entries. The following information from the records of Dacy Co. is provided to assist you in reconstructing the transactions during the year:

1. The opening balance in accounts receivable was $135,000 debit and the opening balance in the allowance for doubtful accounts was $5,000 credit.

2. The ending balance in the Allowance for Doubtful Accounts after all adjustments for the current year was $5,500 credit.

3. Sales were 50 percent for cash and 50 percent on credit. Dacy Co. estimates bad debt losses using the percentage-of-sales method; Dacy Co. estimates 2 percent of credit sales as uncollectible. The current year's estimate of bad debts expense was $6,000.

4. During the year, $200,000 of accounts receivable was collected.

5. A $200 account that had been written off in the prior year was collected during the current year. This $200 is not included in the $200,000 in part 4.

6. The ending account receivable balance was $229,300.

Required:

Prepare journal entries to record *all* transactions related to accounts receivable, the allowance for doubtful accounts, sales revenue, and bad debt expense. (Hint: Use of T-accounts may be helpful.)

P6.23 Allowance for doubtful accounts. The Bank of Montreal included the following information in its annual report on its allowance for doubtful accounts (credit losses):

Allowance for Credit Losses	1993	1992
Balance at beginning of year	$2,070	$2,149
Provision for credit losses	675	550
Recoveries	59	79
Write-offs	(888)	(862)
Foreign exchange adjustment	83	154
	$1,999	$2,070

Required:

Using the above information, determine the transactions that have effected the allowance for doubtful accounts (credit losses) for the Bank of Montreal for the fiscal year 1993.

P6.24 Accounts receivable (*Certified Management Accountants of British Columbia*). Athlone Industries manufactures computer software. Information from a partial trial balance for the company at their year-end, June 30, is shown below:

	Debit	Credit
Accounts receivable	$60,225	
Allowance for doubtful accounts		$ 3,500
Sales		291,475

An aging of accounts receivable has determined that $4,326 will not be collected. Historically, it has been determined that 2 percent of sales will be uncollectible. At the end of June, it was decided to write off as uncollectible the account of William Green in the amount of $875.

Required:

a. Identify from the information given two methods that might be used to record the credit losses.

b. Prepare all journal entries for each of the methods for the year-end.

c. Prepare a statement showing the net realizable value of the accounts receivable at year-end for each of the methods.

P6.25 Bank reconciliation (*Certified Management Accountants of British Columbia*). On October 13 the MC Lumber Company receives its bank statement from the City Bank. The cheques and deposits are listed as one item only to simplify the statement.

CITY BANK
MC LUMBER COMPANY
Statement of Current Account
From Aug 31 to Sept 30

	Debits	Credits
Balance forward, Sept. 1		$10,500
Cheques, Sept.	$34,000	
Deposits, Sept.		31,000
Interest Earned on Term Deposit		500
Overdraft Charge	60	
Interest Charges on Overdraft	70	
NSF Cheque Returned	1,200	
NSF Cheque Charge	5	
Balance, Sept. 30		6,665

On September 30, the cash balance of MC Lumber Company's books is $25,000. The outstanding (not cancelled) cheques total $11,000. One cheque for $6,500 was not recorded in the cheque register but is included in the bank statement. Outstanding deposits were $22,000.

The NSF cheque returned by the bank was issued by I. Champion in payment of his account. It is company policy to charge customers for NSF cheque charges.

Required:

a. Prepare a bank reconciliation.

b. Prepare all journal entries to make the necessary adjustments.

P6.26 Temporary investments (*Certified Management Accountants of British Columbia*). PP Photographic Supplies, Ltd., had extra funds available. The president asked the company's stockbroker to make the following purchases on May 1:

Name of Stock	Number of Shares Purchased	Unit Price
A	1,500	$ 10
B	2,000	20
C	500	100

These shares were expected to be sold near the end of the year, when a shortfall of cash was projected.

On June 15, Stock B paid a dividend of $1 per share.

The company's financial year ended on October 31. On that date the stock market reports gave the following values for the shares:

Name of Stock	Market Value
A	$ 9
B	21
C	95

The company records temporary investments at the lower of cost or market, but it will select either the aggregate or individual valuation depending on which method gives the highest net income.

Required:

a. Prepare all journal entries relating to these securities.

b. How would these securities be reported on the October 31 balance sheet? Show balance sheet classification and valuation.

P6.27 Uncollectible accounts receivable (*Certified Management Accountants of British Columbia*). Gardner Building Supplies, Ltd., gives you the following aged accounts receivable list at the end of the fiscal year:

Age of Account (days)	Amount	Percent of Uncollectible Accounts Receivable
0–30	$600,000	1%
31–60	200,000	3
61–90	100,000	20
Over 90 days	20,000	60

During the year, specific uncollectible accounts receivable totalled $9,000.

Total yearly credit sales for Gardner are $3,400,000. The balance in the Allowance for Doubtful Accounts at the beginning of the year was $2,000 credit.

Gardner uses the aging of accounts receivable method to determine bad debt expense.

Required:

a. Prepare the journal entry to record the write-off of the uncollectible amounts.

b. Prepare the journal entry to record bad debt expense at the end of the year.

c. Assume the same amount of bad debt expense as calculated under part *b*. What would be the percentage of uncollectible sales had the percentage-of-sales method been used to determine the bad debt expense?

d. The company is considering a proposal to loosen its credit policy. It anticipates it would realize additional credit sales of $200,000, and net 8 percent of these additional sales. Should the company proceed with this proposal? Justify your answer.

P6.28 Accounting for cash and accounts receivable (*Certified Management Accountants of British Columbia*).

a. Cash is the most vulnerable asset a firm has. List three important internal controls that should be established to safeguard this asset.

b. In preparing a bank reconciliation, list three common sources of differences between cash balances per the accounting records and cash balances per the bank statement. For each source listed, indicate whether a journal entry is necessary to adjust the books. If one is required, prepare the entry, ignoring dollar amounts.

c. Wedgewood, Ltd.'s unadjusted trial balance at year-end included the following:

Sales (75% represent credit sales)	$1,100,000 credit
Accounts receivable	250,000 debit
Allowance for doubtful accounts	2,100 credit

Prepare the journal entries to record the bad debts expense under each of the following assumptions:

(1) Percentage-of-sales method, 1.25% of credit sales.

(2) The aging of accounts receivable method determines that an allowance of $12,000 is adequate.

d. You are reviewing the loan applications for BB, Ltd., and PB, Inc. The two firms are virtually identical in size and scope of operations except that PB, Inc., is more conservative in valuing its accounts receivable. Which company will report the higher net income? Why?

P6.29 Uncollectible accounts receivable (*Certified Management Accountants of British Columbia*). The Royal Rug Co. is a manufacturer of fine hairpieces. Some information from its trial balance at December 31, is shown below:

	Debit	Credit
Accounts receivable	$500,000	
Allowance for doubtful accounts		$ 2,500
Sales		2,500,000

An aging of accounts receivable has determined that $50,000 will not be collected. Historically, 2 percent of sales have not been collected. During the year, $42,500 of accounts were determined to be uncollectible and written off.

Required:

Identify all methods of recording credit losses. Prepare, all journal entries for each method for the year ended December 31.

P6.30 Bank reconciliation (*Certified Management Accountants of British Columbia*). JP Company had a cash balance on their books of $4,091.25 on September 30. Their bank statement as of September 30 had a balance of $3,523.47.

During the month of September the following activities occurred:

1. On September 29, the bank collected a $1,000 note for JP Company less a $25 collection fee.

2. On JP Company's cheque register a cheque was recorded at $780.23 instead of the correct amount of $870.23.

3. A deposit of $1,323.47 by JP Company was too late to be included in the September bank statement.

4. The bank debited JP Company's account for $258.07 for a cheque written by SP Company.

5. During September $519.98 of customers' cheques deposited by JP company were returned NSF by the bank.

6. The regular monthly bank service charge was $17.50.

7. The following outstanding cheques had not been cashed:

#352	$450.23
#381	171.12
#375	44.89

Required:

a. Prepare a bank reconciliation for September 30.

b Prepare the necessary journal entries for September.

P6.31 Bank reconciliation (*Certified Management Accountants of British Columbia*). The following information pertains to Samoa, Ltd., for December:

1. Cash balance per Samoa's records December 31	$22,090.90
2. Cash balance per bank statement December 31	21,211.60
3. The proceeds of a bank loan on December 31, not recorded in accounting records (Interest is payable upon maturity.)	12,500.00
4. Bank service charges	22.50
5. Cheque #1575 for a payment on account was incorrectly recorded on Samoa's books at $919.90 instead of $119.90.	
6. A cheque from B. Heenan for $1071.80 has been returned by the bank marked NSF.	
7. The December 31 deposit was not recorded by the bank until January 2.	11,195.00
8. A cheque written by Sampson, Ltd., was incorrectly deducted from Samoa's bank account.	2,390.50
9. A note receivable was collected by the bank on behalf of Samoa, Ltd.	500.50

Required:

a. Prepare a bank reconciliation for Samoa Ltd. at December 31. Include any journal entries which should be made.

b. What amount of cash should be reported on the balance sheet for Samoa, Ltd., at December 31?

P6.32 Bank reconciliation (*Certified Management Accountants of British Columbia*). Below are all data necessary to prepare Finka, Ltd.'s November 30 bank reconciliation:

Balance per bank statement $7,873

Included on the bank statement are:

1. Finka's $800 note receivable collected by the bank on Finka's behalf, less a $25 collection fee.

2. Cheque of another company, Finque, Ltd., for $145 charged to Finka's account in error. Finka has notified the bank.

Balance per Finka's books	$6,028
Deposits in transit	–0–
Outstanding cheques	1,305

When the bank statement was analyzed, it was discovered that Finka's bookkeeper had recorded in error the November 17 deposit of $457 as $547. The amount was a collection of a $457 account receivable.

Required:

a. Prepare Finka's November 30 bank reconciliation.

b. Prepare a composite journal entry to adjust Finka's books.

P6.33 Bank reconciliation (*Certified Management Accountants of British Columbia*). The Western Company reconciled its book and bank balances on November 30, with four outstanding cheques: #399 for $629, #421 for $262, #424 for $161, and #425 for $31.

The following information relates to the December 31 reconciliation.

THE BANK OF SURREY, SURREY, B.C.

Date	Cheques and Other Debits	Deposits	Balance
Dec.1	Balance forward		$2,169.00
2	$172.00	$ 807.00	2,804.00
3	262.00		2,542.00
5	239.00		2,303.00
8	472.00		1,831.00
9	629.00	4,003.00	5,205.00
11	64.00	515.00 CM	5,656.00
14	181.00		5,475.00
16	946.00	2,121.00	6,650.00
17	321.00 NSF		6,329.00
20	512.00		5,817.00
23	89.00	3,046.00	8,774.00
31	21.00 SC		8,753.00

NSF = Not sufficient funds.

CM = Credit Memorandum.

SC = Service Charge.

From Cash Disbursements Journal for December		From Cash Receipts Journal for December	
Cheque	**Cash Credit**	**Date**	**Cash Debit**
426	$ 172.00	Dec. 2	$ 807.00
427	239.00	9	4,003.00
428	427.00	16	2,121.00
430	64.00	23	3,046.00
431	181.00	30	421.00
432	946.00		$10,398.00
433	512.00		
434	89.00		
435	1,020.00		
436	290.00		
	$4,569.00		

The General Ledger balance in the Cash account on December 1 was $1,715.00.Cheque #428 was correctly drawn for $472.00 in payment for office supplies. However, the Western Company accountant recorded the amount incorrectly in the cash disbursements journal.

The NSF cheque was received from customer Bill Clark in payment of his account. Its return from the bank has not been recorded.

The credit memorandum resulted from a $525.00 note collected for Western Company by the bank. The bank deducted a $10.00 collection fee. The collection has not been recorded.

Required:

a. Prepare a December 31 bank reconciliation for the Western Company.

b. Prepare the appropriate journal general entries as a result of the reconciliation.

P6.34 Uncollectible accounts receivable (*Certified Management Accountants of British Columbia*). At December 31 Pense Company's unadjusted trial balance included the following items:

	Debit	**Credit**
Cash sales		$360,000
Credit sales		585,000
Accounts receivable	$210,000	
Allowance for doubtful accounts		200

Required:

Prepare the adjusting entry on the books of Pense Company to estimate bad debts under each of the following unrelated assumptions:

a. Bad debts are estimated to be 3.5 percent of credit sales.

b. Bad debts are estimated to be 2 percent of total sales.

c. An aging of accounts receivable indicates that 7.5 percent of accounts receivable on December 31 will prove uncollectible.

P6.35 Bank reconciliation (*Certified Management Accountants of British Columbia*). Tra Na Rosson Company, a resort hotel, has hired you to keep the books of the company for the season. Among your tasks is preparation of a bank reconciliation statement. The following data are available for preparation of the August reconciliation:

> The balance shown on the bank statement at the end of August was $3,275. The Cash balance according to the records was $3,159.95. Transactions that occurred during the period were:
>
>> A note was collected by the bank from Geoff McCallom, a guest at the resort, for $223, and a $12 collection charge was made by the bank for collection of the note.
>>
>> An NSF cheque of a guest, John Jones, for $160, was returned by the bank. The bank charged a fee of $15 on the returned cheque.
>
> Included in the bank statement was a debit memo for $21 for cheque printing charges.
>
> Another debit memo was included with the bank statement for $25, representing a six-month charge for rent of a safety deposit box by Tra Na Rosson Company.
>
> An error was discovered on the books of Tra Na Rosson Company. A cheque had been recorded as $760 instead of $730. The cheque had been received from Bardon Company as payment on their account. The bank had processed the cheque for the correct amount.
>
> Outstanding cheques were as follows: #147 for $127, and #149 for $255.15.
>
> A deposit made on August 31 was not recorded by the bank until September 2. The deposit was for $227.10.

Required:

a. Prepare a bank reconciliation statement for the Tra Na Rosson Company as at August 31.

b. Prepare the journal entries to record the changes in the company's books as a result of completion of the bank reconciliation.

P6.36 Cash analysis. Jennifer opened a bank account at the beginning of the month by depositing $2,300.00. During the month she made an additional deposit of $200.00 and on the last day of the month deposited $150.00. During the month she issued some cheques and made a number of cash withdrawals totalling $1,927.50. Jennifer recorded all the deposits, cheques, and cash withdrawals in her cheque book. At the end of the month, her records indicated a balance of $722.50 ($2,300 + $200 +$150–1,927.50).

A few days later she received her bank statement and related documents in the mail. Her statement from the bank indicated an ending balance of $596.20. As well, the midmonth deposit, a cheque for $200.00 from a friend, had been returned by the bank marked Not Sufficient Funds (NSF). Service fees charged by the bank of $5.30 for the month had not been recorded by Jennifer. When Jennifer compared the entries on the bank statement to those she had recorded in her cheque book, she noticed cheques for a total of $247.00 had not yet been deducted on the bank statement. A cheque for $153.00 had been incorrectly recorded by Jennifer in her cheque book for $135.00. The deposit Jennifer made on the last day of the month did not appear on the statement from the bank.

Required:

Determine the amount of cash Jennifer has available for future use.

P6.37 Accounts receivable (*Published with permission of CGA Canada*).

a. On December 31 the end of its annual accounting period, West Company estimated it would lose as bad debts an amount equal to 1 percent of its $340,000 of credit sales for the year, and made an addition to its Allowance for Doubtful Accounts equal to that amount. On the following March 15, it decided the $50 account of Gayle Sweet was uncollectible and wrote it off as a bad debt. On June 3, Sweet unexpectedly paid the amount previously written off.

Prepare the required general journal entries to record events of these three dates.

b. On December 31 East Company had $65,000 of accounts receivable outstanding and estimated that 3 percent would be uncollectible.

(1) Prepare the entry to record the bad debt expense under the assumption that Allowance for Doubtful Accounts had a $400 credit balance before adjustment.

(2) Prepare the entry under the assumption that Allowance for Doubtful Accounts had a $500 debit balance before adjustment.

c. Two approaches (the balance sheet and the income statement) were used to determine the amount of bad debt expense.

(1) What is the focus of the balance sheet approach?

(2) What is the focus of the income statement approach?

P6.38 Accounting for cash (*Published with permission of CGA Canada*). In examining the books of Hefty Company, you find that the following items make up the "cash" balance of the company:

Cash on deposit at bank (per book record)	$6,200
Cash on hand (with petty cashier)	200
NSF cheque from J. Snell (a customer) returned by bank	600
Signed IOUs for loans to employees	800
Refundable deposit on containers	300
American Express travellers cheque	100
Cheque postdated February 1, from Fred Chui, a customer	500
Postage stamps not yet used	40
Total cash balance per general ledger	$8,740

Required:

a. Determine the amount of cash that should be reported on the December 31 balance sheet.

b. Prepare a general journal entry to properly recognize items that should not have been included by Hefty in the "cash" balance.

P6.39 Bank reconciliation (*Published with permission of CGA Canada*). Items affecting balances in a bank reconciliation are either additions or deductions to the respective balances.

Required:

a. Indicate the following items' impact (if any) on the appropriate book balance or bank balance:

(1) Notification of note and interest thereon collected by bank for the depositor was received together with the bank statement.

(2) Cheque drawn that had not cleared the bank.

(3) Notification of charge for imprinting the company's name on cheque was received together with the bank statement.

(4) Deposit placed in night depository on the last day of the month not reflected in bank statement.

(5) Cancelled cheque of a depositor with a similar name was returned with the bank statement. The cheque was deducted by the bank from the company's account.

(6) Upon checking the cash disbursements journal it was discovered that a cheque properly drawn for $929 was recorded in the journal at $992.

b. From the list provided in *a*, identify the items that require journal entries on the company's books.

P6.40 Accounts receivable (*Published with permission of CGA Canada*). The following information pertains to Bedford Company's accounts receivable for the year ended December 31, 1992:

Accounts receivable at January 1	$ 900,000
Credit sales for 1992	5,800,000
Allowance for doubtful accounts at January 1	55,000
Collections from 1992 credit sales	4,900,000
Accounts written off August 31	70,000
Previously written off accounts received September 20	6,000

An aging analysis estimates uncollectible receivables at December 31, 1992, to be $80,000.

Required:

a. Prepare all relevant journal entries.

b. What is the accounts receivable balance at December 31?

c. What effect did the accounts written off at August 31 have on the net realizable value of accounts receivable?

P6.41 Accounts receivable (*Published with permission of CGA Canada*). As an employee of Dunlop Company, you are provided with the following information:

**Account Balances
At December 31**

Accounts receivable	$659,600 Dr.
Allowance for doubtful accounts	13,000 Cr.

Sales on credit for the year amounted to $2,500,000. An aging schedule shows the following totals:

		Number of Days Past Due			
Total Balance	Current	1–30	31–60	61–90	Over 90
$659,600	$325,000	$177,000	$72,000	$65,000	$20,600

It is estimated that the following percentage of accounts receivable balances will be uncollectible:

Number of Days Past Due	Percentage Estimated Uncollectible
Current	2%
1–30	4
31–60	12
61–90	25
Over 90	50

It is assessed that 3 percent of all credit sales during the year will be uncollectible.

Required:

a. **(1)** Assuming that Dunlop Company uses the aging analysis method, determine the balance required in the Allowance for Doubtful Accounts.

   (2) Prepare a journal entry to adjust the balance in the Allowance for Doubtful Accounts.

b. Assuming that Dunlop Company uses the percentage-of-credit-sales method instead of the aging method, calculate the required addition to the Allowance for Doubtful Accounts as of December 31 and prepare the required entry.

c. Prepare the journal entry to write off the account of Titus Kanbee, who owes the company $1,200.

P6.42 Temporary investments (*Published with permission of CGA Canada*). Duffy Company has a policy of investing idle cash in temporary investments. On April 1, 1994, it invested $20,000 in the purchase of 2,000 shares of $10 Bluenose shares. At December 31, 1994, the share price dropped to $6.00. On May 15, 1995, Duffy sold 1,000 shares for $7.50 each and the market price by December 31, 1995 rose to $8.00 per share. The uptrend continued and on October 10, 1996, Duffy sold 500 shares for $5,500. The market price per share on December 31, 1996, was $14.00.

Required:

Prepare journal entries for the following dates. If no journal entry is required, write No journal entry required.

a. April 1, 1994.

b. December 31, 1994.

c. May 15, 1995.

d. December 31, 1995.

e. October 10, 1996.

f. December 31, 1996.

P6.43 Bank reconciliation (*Published with permission of CGA Canada*). The November 30 bank statement of Myers Company shows a cash balance of $12,000. The Cash account according to Myers accounting records amounts to $3,400. The following additional data are revealed during the reconciliation process:

1. A deposit of $790 dated November 30 was not received by the bank until December 1.

2. Total outstanding cheques amounted to $7,050.

3. Bank service charge was $54.

4. A customer's NSF cheque dated November 16 amounted to $80.

5. A debit memorandum accompanying the bank statement indicated that a cheque printing charge of $50 occurred in November.

6. The bank statement also revealed that the bank had collected a note receivable of $2,000 plus interest of $48 on behalf of Myers Company. The bank charged a separate collection fee of $6 for this service.

7. Cheque #117 made out to a creditor for $116 was incorrectly recorded as $161 by Myers Company.

8. The bank statement also contained a deposit by Buyers Company of $527 that was inadvertently credited to Myers Company.

Required:

a. Prepare a bank reconciliation for Myers Company.

b. Prepare any adjusting entries relating to the bank reconciliation.

c. What Cash balance would Myers disclose on a November 30 balance sheet?

P6.44 Temporary investments (*Published with permission of CGA Canada*). The temporary investment portfolio at December 31, 1995, for Simyar Company is as follows:

	Cost	Market
Burke, Ltd. (1,200 shares)	$11,000	$11,600
Scott, Ltd. (1,500 shares)	27,000	21,500
Harrison, Ltd. (600 shares)	16,200	12,900

On June 28, 1996, Simyar sold 1,000 shares of Scott Ltd. shares for $15 per share less a broker's fee of $450. On October 1 Simyar received dividends of $1.25 and $1.80 per share on the Burke and Scott shares respectively. The December 31 market values of the three temporary investments were:

Burke Ltd.	$ 9,500
Scott Ltd.	11,500
Harrison Ltd.	15,800

Required:

a. When the current market price of temporary investments falls below original cost, there is a conflict between accounting principles. Briefly elaborate on this statement and indicate which accounting principle dominates.

b. Prepare journal entries, if necessary, on the following dates:

   (1) December 31, 1995.

   (2) June 28, 1996.

   (3) October 1, 1996.

   (4) December 31, 1996.

P6.45 Turnover analysis The partial income statement of Costless Company, Limited, for the year ended June 30 is shown below:

Sales	$1,489,000
Cost of sales	961,000
Gross profit	$ 528,000

The accounts receivable turnover ratio for the period is 4.19. The inventory turnover ratio for the same period is 3.12. Determine the average accounts receivable and inventory balances for the period.

P6.46 Receivable management. Multi Corporation has two different divisions operating in central Canada. The assistant controller for Multi has determined the accounts receivable turnover ratios for each division. Division A has a receivable turnover ratio of 7.1, while Division B has a receivable turnover ratio of 7.9. Determine the average collection period for each division. Which division is doing a better job collecting their accounts receivable?

P6.47 Liquidity ratios. For the year ended December 31, Carrie Resources, Ltd., had current assets of $136,000. Included in the current assets were quick assets of $87,000. On December 31 Carrie Resources had current liabilities of $112,000. In determining the preceding balances, the accountant failed to make two adjusting entries. The entry for bad debt expense of $12,000, based on a percentage of sales, was omitted. As well, applying the lower-of-cost-or-market rule, the entry to recognize an unrealized loss on temporary investments of $7,000 was not recorded.

Required:

Determine the quick and current ratios, before and after the adjustments are considered. Do you think the omission of the adjusting entries will have a material impact on the ratio analysis?

P6.48 Liquidity ratios. For the year ended December 31, Portage La Mare Enterprises had current assets of $77,000. Included in the current assets were quick assets of $48,000. On December 31 Portage La Mare had current liabilities of $66,000. In determining the preceding balances, the accountant failed to make three adjusting entries. After reconciling the bank statement entries for NSF cheques totalling $1,550, and a second entry for service charges of $112, were omitted. As well, the entry for bad debt expense of $3,300, based on a percentage of sales, was omitted.

Required:

Determine the quick and current ratios, before and after the adjustments are considered. Do you think the omission of the adjusting entries will have a material impact on the ratio analysis?

P6.49 Ratio analysis. Presented below are summary financial data for Epic, Inc., and Damon, Inc.

	1996	1995
Net sales:		
Epic, Inc.	$22,745	$20,121
Damon, Inc.	38,966	34,895
Receivables:		
Epic, Inc.	2,033	1,738
Damon, Inc.	3,702	3,677

Required:

Using the above data, calculate the accounts receivable turnover and average number of days' receivable collection period for each company. Evaluate the companies' credit management.

6.9 CASES

C6.1 Accounting for bad debts: Omni Products Division. The following two scenarios should be analyzed independently.

Scenario A: The Period-End Analysis Model

The manager of Omni Products Division, Harry Smith, was quite satisfied with all of his section leaders and had developed a high level of trust in their day-to-day decisions. Still, he insisted that he be involved in the critical, long-range judgments. For example, his accounting and control section was efficient and largely trouble free. However, he carefully monitored the sensitive areas, including the status of collections on accounts receivable, the follow-up on slow-pay customers, and the reasonableness of the ongoing provision for estimated bad debt losses.

Smith's monitoring effort was complicated by the fact that Omni's average sale was less than $1,000 and that the division carried more than 10,000 open customer accounts. He found it difficult to put his hands around the situation because of the amount of detail in the file. To help him monitor the receivables–collections–bad debt situation, he had engaged a consultant some years ago to establish a statistical sampling system. Under the system, the Omni computer section produced a special report each quarter that analyzed the accounts receivable balances based on the dates of the unpaid invoices. This aging report was useful to Smith, helping him identify trends in the status of the receivables.

One of Smith's accounting people tracked a sample of accounts from each aging category and determined which of those sampled accounts were ultimately uncollectible. Based on a simple formula developed by the consultant, the clerk used those findings to calculate a factor for each aging category that would predict what proportion of those accounts would ultimately be uncollectible. The accounting clerk tested the results of the current studies against the numbers developed by the original study and always found that the original numbers were quite valid:

Aging Category	Amount That Will Prove to Be Uncollectible For Every Dollar on Account
Current (0–30 days)	$0.00
1 month past due (30–60 days)	0.005
2 months past due (30–60 days)	0.05
3–4 months past due (90–150 days)	0.20
5–6 months past due (150–210 days)	0.50

Smith trusted the system and always had the accounting people adjust the period-end allowance for possible bad debts to the amount indicated by the quarterly aging report — the category totals multiplied by the above factors. In the interim months, he had his people record an estimated provision for possible bad debts, but the quarterly financial statements that were sent to the home office always included a revised provision for possible bad debt losses that was simply a forced number from the updated allowance account.

At March 31, 1996, the allowance account was adjusted to $2,658,000, the amount indicated by the aging analysis process at that date. During the months of April, May, and June, accounts totalling $1,942,000 were turned over to the attorneys and written off. During April and May, Smith had his accounting people provide $500,000 a month for possible bad debt losses. The aging of the accounts at June 30, 1996, showed the following (amounts in thousands):

	Current	$158,000
1 month past due		43,200
2 months past due		8,240
3–4 months past due		3,650
5–6 months past due		1,840
Total accounts receivable balance at June 30, 1996		$214,930

Required:

Determine the amount of the provision (expense) for bad debt losses for the month of June 1996.

Scenario B: The Percent-of-Credit-Sales Model

The manager of Omni Products Division, Harry Smith, was quite satisfied with all of his section leaders and had developed a high level of trust in their day-to-day decisions. Still, he insisted that he be involved in the critical, long-range judgments. For example, his accounting and control section was efficient and largely trouble free. However, he carefully monitored the sensitive areas, including the status of collections on accounts receivable, the follow-up on slow-pay customers, and the reasonableness of the ongoing provision for estimated bad debt losses.

Smith's monitoring effort was complicated by the fact that Omni's average sale was less than $1,000 and that the division carried more than 10,000 open customer accounts. He found it difficult to put his hands around the situation because of the amount of detail in the file. To help him monitor the receivables–collections–bad debt situation, he had engaged a consultant some years ago to establish a statistical sampling system. Following the system, a clerk randomly selected a small number of credit sales each week and followed them through to their conclusion — either collection in cash after varying periods or a write-off because of the buyer's inability to pay. The system was easy to operate, and Smith had been assured that the results of the sample would give a very accurate reflection of the results to be expected from total credit sales. However, because the system required the clerk to follow each sampled credit sale to its conclusion, the results were not always available as quickly as Smith would have liked.

Over the past several years, the results of the system had tracked Smith's expectations, given the state of the economy in each period. The results of the study showed:

Report Dated	For the Year Ended	Average Collection Period	Percent of Sales Written Off
July 5, 1992	December 31, 1991	14.2 weeks	5.5%
July 8, 1993	December 31, 1992	12.4 weeks	4.8
July 7, 1994	December 31, 1993	10.5 weeks	4.6
June 28, 1995	December 31, 1994	9.3 weeks	4.5

Based on the trend through the July 1994 report, Smith had instructed his accounting people to provide for estimated losses from bad debts for the year ending December 31, 1994, at 4.6 percent of sales, and during the first half of 1995, the division had provided for possible bad debt losses using that 4.6 percent factor. When the June 1995 report came out, Smith was delighted. He had his accounting people reduce the provision for estimated bad debt losses to 4.5 percent of sales, effective with the July 1995 monthly financial statement. They continued with that estimate through the rest of 1995 and through the first six months of 1996. However, as the 1995 spring season wore on, Smith became anxious about the continued use of that low estimate because his customers were experiencing tighter times and the number of days' sales in the receivables balance was growing, suggesting that the trend was reversing itself.

The Allowance for Possible Bad Debts had a balance of $2,152,000 at December 31, 1995, and through the first six months of 1996, a provision of $3,803,040 had been added to the allowance based on six-month sales of $84,512,000. During that same period of time, accounts totalling $4,203,000 had been turned over to the attorneys for collection and written off. When the statistical study for the year ended December 31, 1995, was completed on July 15, 1996, it confirmed Smith's fears. It showed that credit sales made during the year ended December 31, 1995, took 11.2 weeks to turn cash and that 4.7 percent of those sales were never collected but were written off. He called a meeting to review this situation with his sales and credit people. He got the sense that the ship had not been run as tightly as he would have liked, and he resolved to understand how that had happened. His immediate concern was the package of financial statements he was to send to the home office the next day for the month of June and the six months ended June 30, 1995. After consulting with his staff, he resolved to add to the allowance for possible bad debts. He instructed his accounting people to increase the six-month provision for possible losses from bad debts to 4.75 percent of sales, taking the effect of the new rate of provision as a special charge against operations for June.

Required:

Calculate the revised allowance balance as of June 30, 1996.

C6.2 Accounting for temporary investments: FHAC Corporation. During 1995, FHAC Corporation invested $25 million of working capital in short-term equity securities. At year-end, the portfolio carried the following values:

	Cost	Market
AT&T common stock	$12,000,000	$ 8,000,000
General Motors common stock	8,000,000	10,000,000
Georgia Pacific preferred stock	5,000,000	5,000,000
	$25,000,000	$23,000,000

In early February 1996, FHAC decided to liquidate its position in General Motors because the company needed cash for seasonal inventory purchases; the market value of the stock was $10.4 million at the time of the sale. On March 31, 1996, FHAC's remaining portfolio carried the following values:

	Cost	Market
AT&T common stock	$12,000,000	$ 8,200,000
Georgia Pacific preferred stock	5,000,000	4,500,000
	$17,000,000	$12,700,000

By year-end 1996, the aggregate market value of FHAC's portfolio was $18.6 million; no securities were sold or added to the portfolio during the remainder of the year.

Required:

Evaluate the facts of this case and determine the income statement effects of the transactions involving FHAC's portfolio of temporary investments. Also identify the cash flow effects of the transactions.

CHAPTER 7

Inventories and Cost of Goods Sold

Objectives

After completing this chapter, you will be able to:
1. Explain the measurement and valuation of inventory and cost of goods sold.
2. Apply the lower-of-cost-or-market rule for inventory.
3. Value inventory and cost of goods sold using the different cost-flow methods.
4. Explain and apply financial statement disclosure for inventory.
5. Perform financial analysis for inventory.

Inventory is the stock of goods the organization has purchased or manufactured for resale. This chapter examines the different accounting concepts and procedures for inventory and the impact such policies have on the financial statements. Visualize the items that are on the shelves of a large supermarket. Visualize the millions of litres of oil in various stages of refinement at Petro Canada sites across Canada. Visualize a General Motors factory with various types of cars in various stages of completion. Such images are the images of these companies' inventories — their stock in trade, composed of the goods purchased and/or manufactured to sell to their customers. On the balance sheet, inventories are regarded as current assets because they are expected to be sold and to benefit a business during the next operating cycle. The inventory items sold during a period, and therefore no longer on hand at period-end, are matched against that period's sales revenue and recorded in the income statement as the cost of goods sold. It must be quickly pointed out that in determining the amount to report for the cost of goods sold, however, management is accorded considerable leeway, and the alternative inventory accounting method chosen can significantly affect both the balance sheet (i.e., the reported cost of ending inventory) and the income statement (i.e., the reported cost of goods sold attributable to that period).

How does General Motors or Petro Canada account for its vast and varied inventories? The focus of this chapter is the accounting and valuation issues involving inventories and the cost of goods sold. The inventory accounting method chosen by management depends on the nature of the industry, and a variety of other factors discussed below. The informed reader is advised to consider both the balance sheet *and* the income statement effects during the following discussion.

7.1 TYPES OF INVENTORY

Merchandise

inventory
The aggregate cost of salable goods and merchandise available to meet customer sales.

For all companies, the principal accounting concept involved in valuing inventories is that all goods available for sale during a period must, at year-end, either have been sold or remain in ending inventory. For a merchandising business like Zellers, which simply buys goods and sells them as is, this relationship is depicted in Panel A of Exhibit 7.1, and in the following equations:

$$\text{Beginning inventory} + \text{Net purchases} = \text{Cost of goods available for sale}$$

$$\text{Cost of goods available for sale} - \text{Ending inventory} = \text{Cost of goods sold}$$

Raw Materials

In accounting for a *manufacturing* company's inventory, such as that of General Motors, which transforms raw materials into a final product, the same basic principle applies, although the process is a bit more complicated and involves a larger number of costs. Manufactured inventories are usually composed of three categories: raw materials (RM), which include materials and purchased parts awaiting assembly or manufacture; work in process (WIP), which includes partially completed products still in the factory; and finished goods (FG), which include fully assembled or manufactured goods available for sale. Each of these three physical categories of inventory must be represented in the accounting process and the financial statements.

raw materials inventory
Materials and purchased parts awaiting assembly or manufacture; classified as a current asset on the balance sheet.

Accounting for the **raw materials** component of a manufacturer's inventory is similar to accounting for inventory transactions of a merchandising company. The beginning inventory plus purchases equals the raw materials available for use. These

EXHIBIT 7.1

Status of Inventory Items at Year-End

Panel A: Merchandising companies

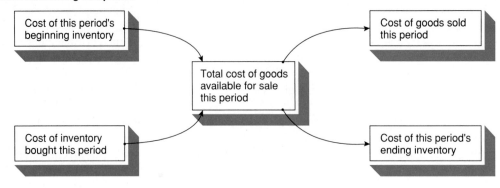

Panel B: Manufacturing companies

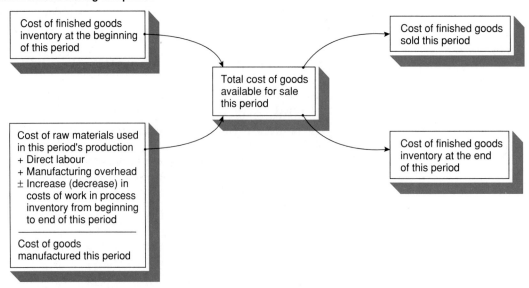

raw materials available for use either remain unused at year-end (and thus in the inventory of unused raw materials at the end of the accounting period) *or* have been placed in production. This relationship is shown in the following equations:

Beginning RM inventory + Net purchases of RM = Cost of RM available for use

Cost of RM available for use − Ending RM inventory = Cost of RM used

work in process inventory
Partially completed goods or products; classified as a current asset on the balance sheet.

Work in Process

During the **work in process** phase of production, the cost of raw materials, the cost of direct labour (i.e., the labour expended to convert raw materials to finished goods), and all manufacturing overhead costs must be assigned to the products being produced.

Thus, beginning WIP inventory plus the cost of raw materials used during the period plus direct labour costs incurred during the period plus manufacturing overhead for the period less ending work in process inventory equals the cost of goods manufactured during the period. These relationships are shown in the following equations:

$$\text{Beginning WIP inventory} + \text{Cost of RM used} + \text{Direct labour cost} +$$
$$\text{Manufacturing overhead costs} = \text{Total manufacturing costs}$$

$$\text{Total manufacturing costs} - \text{Ending WIP inventory} = \text{Cost of goods manufactured}$$

A word about the need to assign manufacturing overhead costs to work in process inventories is warranted. *Manufacturing overhead* is a phrase commonly used to describe all factory-related costs — other than raw materials and direct labour — involved in the production of a completed product: electricity, maintenance, supervision, amortization of machines, and so on.

The accounting process for manufactured inventories parallels the actual production process. When raw materials sit in a warehouse, their cost sits in the Raw Materials Inventory account. As raw materials and labour start being introduced into the manufacturing process, a Work in Process Inventory account accumulates such costs for the goods in various stages of partial production. Finally, when production is completed on an item, it is physically transferred to a finished goods warehouse or storeroom and the costs accumulated for that finished item are likewise transferred from the Work in Process Inventory account to the Finished Goods Inventory account.

Finished Goods

finished goods inventory
Fully assembled or manufactured goods available for sale and classified as a current asset on the balance sheet.

At the end of the manufacturing phase, all costs associated with a completed product are transferred to **Finished Goods Inventory**. Accounting for finished goods in a manufacturing firm is again very much like that for a merchandising company. The cost of beginning finished goods (FG) inventory plus the cost of goods manufactured (those costs transferred from work in process) equal the period's cost of goods available for sale. As of the end of a period, these costs must be attributed to *either* ending finished goods inventory (unsold goods) or to cost of goods sold. Hence, as depicted in Panel B of Exhibit 7.1, the following relationships exist:

$$\text{Beginning FG inventory} + \text{Cost of goods manufactured} = \text{Cost of goods available} \\ \text{for sale}$$

$$\text{Cost of goods available for sale} - \text{Ending FG inventory} = \text{Cost of goods sold}$$

product cost
A cost directly related to the production of a good or service, for example, the cost of goods sold.

period cost
Costs, such as administrative and selling expenses, associated with the accounting period in which they were incurred.

7.2 INVENTORY VALUATION

Product and Period Costs

Costs considered **product costs** are assigned to the cost of *inventory* rather than expensed on the income statement as incurred. Costs such as selling expenses are called **period costs** and are treated as *expenses* in the income statement in the period when they are incurred. Transportation costs related to inventory purchases may be accounted as either product or period costs. When expenditures are treated as product costs, they are deferred until the inventory is sold, whereas period costs are expensed in the period incurred. The matching principle should be the prime influence on this costing decision. If future benefits (revenues) are anticipated as a result of the expenditure, the matching principle would require deferral of the expenditure to ensure proper matching of revenues and expenses. If no future benefit is anticipated, the cost should be expensed in the current period and not deferred.

Historical Cost

The basis of accounting for inventories is historical cost, defined as the *consideration given up* to acquire an asset, including the costs incurred to bring a good to a salable condition. "In the case of inventories of merchandise purchased for resale or of raw materials, cost should be laid-down cost". (CICA Handbook 3030.05). "In the case of inventories of work in process and finished goods, cost should include the laid-down cost of material plus the cost of direct labour applied to the product and the applicable share of overhead expense chargeable to production". (CICA Handbook 3030.06). Laid-down costs include, but are not limited to, the invoice price, transportation (inbound and/or outbound, depending on the circumstances), taxes, handling fees, labour costs, and overhead costs. Any trade, cash, or special discounts should be deducted in determining the cost of inventory. Costs resulting from the marketing and selling activities of a company, even those directly related to a particular product, are normally not included as part of inventory costs.

Market Value

replacement cost
The cost to reproduce or repurchase a given asset (e.g., a unit of inventory).

net realizable value
The amount of funds expected to be received upon the sale or liquidation of an asset.   .

Certain guidelines pertain to the determination of an inventory's current market value. Specifying a market value can be quite subjective, and thus the need for guidelines exists. To avoid gross manipulations of the lower-of-cost-or-market concept, the accounting profession uses different definitions of *market value*. "In view of the lack of precision in meaning, it is desirable that the term 'market' not be used in describing the basis of valuation. A term more descriptive of the method of determining market, such as 'replacement cost,' 'net realizable value' or 'net realizable value less normal profit margin' would be preferable" (CICA Handbook 3030.11). **Replacement cost** is the cost that a company would incur today to reproduce or reacquire a *similar* item. Information pertaining to replacement cost is usually compiled from vendor catalogues, engineering estimates, and/or appraisals. The **net realizable value** of the inventory, that is, the company's selling price of the item less the costs of completing its production and of selling it, is another definition of *market value* for inventory. A CICA Research Study, yet to be adopted, has recommended that net realizable value be used as the definition of *inventory*. Once a market value is ascertained, inventories should be reported at the lower of their historical cost or market value.

Lower of Cost or Market

A departure from the historical cost basis in reporting inventories is necessary when the "market value" of the ending inventory falls below its "cost" (as determined under one of the cost-flow methods). This can occur any time during the normal course of operations because of spoilage, obsolescence, or falling market prices for the goods. For example, consider a computer leasing company. Large quantities of computers have recently been technologically superseded by a newer generation of computers and are not likely to be able to maintain their previous marketability. Thus, these computers decline in market value. This decline in market value should be recognized as an expense of the period in which the reduction in value takes place and the

Inventory account balance should be adjusted to the lower value. Most companies maintain inventory control systems to help them monitor changing market values and inventory obsolescence.

"The basis of valuation of inventories should be clearly stated in the financial statements" (CICA Handbook 3030.10). In situations where the market value of the inventory is materially below its costs, conservatism prevails, requiring the inventory to be valued at the lower of cost or market. A note from the annual report of Southam, Inc., indicates the application of the lower of cost or market and the use of all three definitions of *market value* for inventory. Southam, Inc., accounts for both merchandise and manufacturing inventories. The inventory note explains their accounting policy for inventories:

> Materials and supplies inventories are valued at the lower of cost and replacement cost. Inventories of work in progress and finished goods are valued at the lower of cost and net realizable value. Work in progress and finished goods include the cost of raw materials, direct labour and manufacturing overhead expenses. Retail merchandise is valued at the lower of cost and net realizable value less normal profit margin.

George Weston, Limited, accounts for its inventories applying the lower-of-cost-or-market rule. Its note for inventories stated: "Retail store inventories are stated at the lower of cost and net realizable value less normal profit margin. Other inventories are stated principally at the lower of cost and net realizable value."

If the market value of an organization's inventory has fallen below cost, then a write-down of the inventory's cost is required. Assuming a $1,000 write-down of the inventory's cost, the following journal entry is made:

```
Dr. Cost of Goods Sold . . . . . . . . . . . . . . . . . . . . . . . . . . . . . . 1,000
      Cr. Inventory . . . . . . . . . . . . . . . . . . . . . . . . . . . . . . . . . . . .          1,000
      To record the decline in inventory value.
```

Note that the decline in the inventory value is added to Cost of Goods Sold on the income statement, and the credit entry is a deduction to the Inventory account. Some companies may use an allowance account to credit the amount of the inventory reduction, instead of recording the entry directly against the Inventory account. The Allowance for Decline in Value of Inventory account is rarely seen on the balance sheet; most often it is netted against the balance in the Inventory account. Once inventory values have been written down, they *cannot* be written back up even if the value of the inventory recovers its previously lost value.

Current Cost

current cost
Current cost is an inventory valuation method that records inventory at its most recent cost.

Although **current costs** are not allowable for the accounting of inventory under current GAAP, the concept is worthy of consideration. The use of current cost alleviates some concerns associated with applying the lower-of-cost-or-market rule and the selection of an appropriate cost-flow assumption. Using current costs requires determining the replacement value of the inventory at the end of the accounting period and recognizing what is referred to as a *holding gain*. The prime reason current costs are not acceptable under GAAP is because they require the recognition of a gain without the earning process being completed or a transaction completed.

Assume an organization purchases 100 units of inventory in Year 1 for $5.00 each. During Year 1, 70 units are sold for $9.00 each, with the remaining 30 units being sold in Year 2. The income statements for Year 1 and Year 2, using traditional historical cost accounting, are shown below:

Historical Cost Income Statements

	Year 1 (70 units)	Year 2 (30 units)	Total (100 units)
Sales	$630	$270	$900
Cost of sales	350	150	500
Gross profit	$280	$120	$400

Assume that during Year 1 the cost of the inventory increased during the year to $6.00 a unit. Under the current cost approach, a holding gain is recognized on the ending inventory. Because the company has 30 units on hand at the end of the period, a holding gain of $30 [30 units × ($6.00 − $5.00)] is recognized in Year 1. In Year 2, when the units are sold, the cost of goods sold is recorded at the $6.00 replacement cost. Under a current cost system, a holding gain is recognized in the period the *change* in replacement cost occurs, instead of the traditional approach of deferring recognition of the gain until the units are sold. As shown in the current cost income statements presented below, only the timing of the gains/profits are affected. The total profit for the two periods remains the same.

Current Cost Income Statement

	Year 1 (70 units)	Year 2 (30 units)	Total (100 units)
Sales	$630	$270	$900
Cost of sales	350	180	530
Gross profit	$280	$ 90	$370
Holding gain	30	—	30
	$310	$ 90	$400

Standard Cost

standard cost
An inventory valuation method that uses estimated or projected costs of producing a product rather than actual costs.

A final issue involving inventory costing, but which will not be discussed at length here, involves the use of standard product costs rather than actual costs. **Standard costs** are the estimated or projected costs of producing a product. Standard costs are widely used by managers for internal reporting and control purposes, and some companies extend their use to external financial reporting. Inventory may be costed using standard cost estimates as long as the standard cost of the inventory is not materially different from actual costs. Regardless of whether or not management decides to use standard costs, decisions are still necessary regarding whether to use a periodic system or a perpetual system and what cost-flow method to adopt.

7.3 COST-FLOW METHODS

So far we have not mentioned the physical movement of inventory through a business. Clearly, purchased goods come into a company's facilities, and sold goods leave the premises. The following are pertinent questions that arise when a product is sold: Was that a sale of an item purchased or manufactured yesterday or last month? Does the answer to this question matter?

For a moment, visualize a business that makes and sells a large volume of a single model of chair. All during the year, the company incurs various costs to produce the chairs and to sell the finished product. Assume that you and another customer both arrive at the company's showroom simultaneously. You happen to walk in the west entrance, and the other customer walks in the east entrance. The showroom is full of identical chairs, and both of you select the first chair that you see. Unknown to either of you, the chair you selected was manufactured six months ago, and the one that the other customer chose was manufactured yesterday. Are the actual costs of manufacturing incurred by the company for your chair different from those of the other customer's chair? They probably are because of material cost increases or a few more minutes of labour devoted to one or the other of them. Does that fact result in the other customer paying a different price for the chair than you pay? Probably *not*. If the different costs do not result in different sales prices, there is no real need for the company even to bother keeping track of the fact that the other customer bought a chair from yesterday's production and you bought one from a prior month's production. But the company does have to record a reduction in the costs accumulated in the Finished Goods Inventory account and assign them to the Cost of Goods Sold account as a result of its sales to both of you.

Several acceptable methods are used to determine what inventory costs to identify with a particular sale. These cost-flow methods are discussed shortly, and examples of each are presented later. It first must be noted, however, that the accounting cost-flow method chosen by management to assign inventory costs to the cost of goods sold need not match the actual physical flow of inventory items into and out of a company's warehouse or showroom. As satisfying as it may be to know that inventory item no. 59, produced on June 11, was the item actually sold on August 20, and its particular cost is the cost deducted from inventory and added to the cost of goods sold, there are other considerations, providing more valued benefits, that diminish the importance of such a strict matching of *actual* inventory with *actual* items sold. These other considerations are discussed in the following sections.

Specific Identification Method

specific identification method
An inventory cost-flow method that assigns the actual cost of producing a specific unit to that unit; the only inventory method that matches exactly the cost flow and physical flow.

The **specific identification method** is usually reserved for high-value, easily distinguishable items such as automobiles and jewellery and does require individual accounting for each inventory item. However, computerization has made the specific identification method practical for relatively low cost inventory items. Under this approach, the costs associated with an inventory item are "attached" to it and remain in the Inventory account as long as the specific item is on hand. The specific identification method is the only cost-flow approach that results in the costs flowing from the balance sheet (i.e., ending inventory) to the income statement (i.e., cost of goods sold) in a sequence exactly matching the product's physical flow from store-room to customer.

Shown below is the inventory method footnote from the financial statements of Ryan Homes, Inc., a regional builder of residential dwellings in the Atlantic region. It describes the company's use of the specific identification method and how a company's inventory cost-flow method might be presented in the financial statements. The decision by Ryan Homes to adopt this method appears quite reasonable — the company builds distinctive and expensive homes, which are generally sold one at a time.

Inventories are stated at the lower of cost or market value. Cost of lots, completed and uncompleted housing units, and land in process of development represent the accumulated actual cost thereof. Field construction supervision salaries and related direct overhead expenses are included in inventory costs. Selling, general and administrative costs are expensed as incurred. Upon settlement, the cost of the units is expensed on a specific identification basis.

The main disadvantage to the specific identification method is that its use is impractical for some types of businesses (e.g., mass merchandisers and mass manufacturers of homogeneous products) because of the very detailed inventory system required to track each item or each lot of goods purchased or manufactured. On the other hand, the matching of cost of goods sold to the sales revenue of the period perfectly matches the physical flow of specific inventory items, consequently achieving a perfect income statement matching of revenue generated from the item sold and its actual cost.

Average Cost Method

average cost method
An inventory cost-flow method that assigns the average cost of available finished goods to units sold and, thus, to cost of goods sold.

The **average cost method** accounts for inventory costs in a manner that is especially useful when it is impossible (or at least impractical) to attempt to identify specifically the particular units of inventory sold, typically because large volumes of many types of similar products are sold. This is the case for such companies as food wholesalers, supermarkets, and retailers in general, and the Quaker Oats Company in particular. For example, Quaker Oats Company uses the average cost method for about 27 percent of its ending inventory. With the advent of cost-effective electronic product label scanners, retailers' ability to track the physical flow of products, and thus their costs, has greatly improved. Whether managers of companies using such tracking devices will consequently abandon the simple average cost method has yet to be determined.

The average cost method is based on the assumption that the costs of the items sold and therefore charged against revenue should be the average unit cost of all the items available for sale during the period. The average cost of a particular inventory item (e.g., Quaker Oats' instant oatmeal cartons) is determined simply by dividing the sum of the different *unit* costs incurred for the instant oatmeal cartons available for sale during the year by the number of different unit costs represented in that quantity of cartons. The resulting unit cost is used to compute both the balance sheet ending inventory cost and the income statement cost of goods sold. The advantages of this approach are that it is very easy to compute and it is very objective in its determination of profits for the period. The disadvantage is that the cost attributed to a single item is not, in reality, a cost that has ever been paid for the item (i.e., it is an average). Abitibi-Price, Inc., describes in a footnote to its financial statements how it accounts for different types of inventory, some of which are valued using the average cost method: "Inventories of finished products, work in process and materials and operating supplies are valued at the lower of average cost and net realizable value. Inventory of pulpwood is valued at average cost."

Weighted-Average Cost Method

weighted-average cost method
An inventory cost-flow method that assigns the average cost of available finished goods, weighted by the number of units available at each price, to cost of goods sold, and to ending inventory.

A variation of the average cost method is the **weighted-average cost method**. Under this method, the calculation of the cost of ending inventory (and cost of goods sold) is accomplished as under the average cost method except that each cost is *weighted* by the number of inventory units available at that cost. The weighted-average cost method is generally believed to be preferable to the average cost method because it takes into consideration the relative quantity of goods purchased at a given unit cost. Thus, if 100 units of inventory were purchased at $10 each and 1,000 at $14 each, the average cost method produces an average unit cost of only $12 [($10 + $14)/2)], which does not reflect the substantial difference in quantities purchased at the two costs. The weighted-average cost per unit, however, would be $13.64 {[(100 × $10) + (1,000 × $14)]/1,100 units)}, emphasizing the large volume of purchases at the higher cost of $14. The advantages and disadvantages of this method are the same as those for the average cost method. The accounting policy note for inventories for Silverado Mines, Ltd., is as follows: "Gold inventory is valued at the lower of weighted average cost and estimated net realizable value."

First-In, First-Out (FIFO) Method

first-in, first-out (FIFO)
An inventory cost-flow method that assigns the first cost value in finished goods inventory to the first unit sold and thus to cost of goods sold.

The **first-in, first-out cost-flow method** accounts for inventory under the assumption that the *first* product physically purchased or manufactured is the *first* product physically sold. Remember that the actual physical flow of inventory does not need to be on a FIFO basis in order for a company to elect to account for it on a FIFO basis. Thus, under the FIFO method, the costs assigned to the Cost of Goods Sold account for the products sold during the period are not the most recent costs paid, but they do represent an actual cost incurred for the item albeit at some point in the past. In times of rapid inflation, the cost of goods sold under FIFO is likely to be low relative to a product's current replacement cost and current selling price and will result in higher net income vis-à-vis other inventory cost-flow methods. On the other hand, Ending Inventory account balances will approximate the product's current replacement cost, especially if inventory turnover is frequent (i.e., if the inventory items are on hand for only a short period of time). Food stores would typically make use of the FIFO method, because of the perishable nature of the product that they sell. The Toronto Sun Publishing Corporation's note on inventory valuation states: "Inventories are valued at the lower of cost, determined on a first-in, first-out basis, and market. Market is defined as replacement cost." Similar disclosure for inventories was provided by Canadian Tire Corporation, Limited: "Merchandise inventories are valued at the lower of cost and estimated net realizable value, with cost being determined on a first-in, first-out basis."

Last-In, First-Out (LIFO) Method

last-in, first-out (LIFO)
An inventory cost-flow method that assigns the last cost value in finished goods inventory to the first unit sold and thus to cost of goods sold.

The **last-in, first-out cost-flow method** accounts for inventory under the assumption that the *last* product physically purchased or manufactured is the *first* one physically sold. Following the reasoning of the FIFO method, this approach means that under LIFO, the cost of the products sold closely approximates the current replacement cost of the product (i.e., the most recent costs incurred in acquiring the item). It is important to note that, in Canada, the LIFO method is *not* acceptable for income tax purposes. However, Canadian companies do use LIFO for financial reporting purposes, as illustrated in the financial statement notes provided in the latter part of this section.

For company management, LIFO has advantages and disadvantages just the opposite of those of FIFO. Whereas FIFO presents ending inventory in the balance sheet at an approximation of current replacement cost (i.e., the most recent cost incurred in acquiring the item), the LIFO method states the inventory balance at a mixture of costs incurred in the distant past. In times of high inflation (deflation), the reported ending balance of the inventory account under LIFO can be significantly lower (higher) than under FIFO. On the other hand, FIFO does not report cost of goods sold at the most recent costs; the LIFO method approximates current replacement cost as the cost reported on the income statement for each product sold.

The Seagram Company, Ltd., a Canadian company, conducts a large portion of its business in the United States. In the United States, the LIFO method is allowable for income tax purposes; as a result, the use of LIFO is common. The Seagram Company, Ltd., provides a footnote explaining its accounting policies for inventory:

> Inventories are stated at cost, which is not in excess of market, and consists principally of spirits, wines and fruit juices. Cost is determined by either the last-in, first-out (LIFO) method or the identified cost method. The LIFO method, used by the company in the United States, recognizes in cost of sales the current costs of producing beverages and reflects inventories in the balance sheet at production costs of prior periods.

As well, Imperial Oil, Limited, accounts for its crude using LIFO costing: "Inventories are recorded at the lower of cost or net realizable value. The cost of crude oil and products is determined using the LIFO (last-in, first-out) method."

7.4 INVENTORY SYSTEMS

Historically, the perpetual inventory system has been used only by organizations with a low volume of high-dollar-value items, such as automobile dealers. In contrast, the periodic system was mainly used by organizations with a high volume of low-dollar items, such as grocery or convenience stores. Because the perpetual system requires the maintenance of a "running balance" of items on hand, most organizations found it time consuming and near impossible to maintain. However, with the advancement of computers and electronic scanning devices, today more and more organizations are switching to the perpetual inventory system.

Periodic Inventory System

periodic inventory system
An inventory record-keeping system that determines the quantity of inventory on hand by a physical count.

Determining how much of the goods available for sale during a period are still on hand and how much should be charged against income for the period is obviously critical to measuring a company's performance during a period. In addition to the cost-flow method decision, management must also adopt either a perpetual inventory system or a periodic inventory system to record ending inventory costs and cost of goods sold. Under a **periodic system**, the quantity of inventory on hand at any given time must be determined by physically counting the inventory items (usually once a year). The physical count determines the balance sheet's ending inventory cost. The cost of goods sold for the period can then be determined from the basic relationship of beginning inventory plus purchases minus the costs attributable to ending inventory quantities. (A periodic system was assumed in the previous numerical examples.)

Perpetual Inventory System

perpetual inventory system
An inventory record-keeping system that continuously updates the quantity of inventory on hand.

When using a **perpetual system**, management maintains and regularly updates (often daily or, with computer assistance, continuously) an extensive inventory record-keeping system that is able to provide up-to-date inventory and cost of goods sold information on a moment's notice (rather than only after a physical count of items on hand). The perpetual system provides a continuous updating of both the Cost of Goods

Sold and Ending Inventory account balances. Sound business practice suggests completing an occasional physical count of the inventory on hand to verify the accuracy of a perpetual system. From a control perspective, the perpetual system is considered the superior of the two systems. The perpetual system, by maintaining a running balance of the quantity and dollar value of inventory on hand, provides valuation information to management that assists with the control and management of inventory levels. Under a periodic system, the inventory on hand and the resulting cost of goods sold is determined by a physical count, usually only once a year. Thus, the periodic system provides very little timely information to management. Section 7.6 illustrates the journal entries for the periodic and perpetual inventory methods.

Comprehensive Illustration

To assist you in understanding the calculations necessary to derive the cost of ending inventory for the balance sheet and the cost of goods sold for the income statement, we present a numerical illustration. Assume that FHAS Company begins the year with 100 units of an item in inventory and makes the following additions to inventory:

	Quantity (units)	Cost per Unit	Total Cost
Beginning inventory — January 1	100	$1.00	$100.00
Purchase — February 14	110	$1.10	$121.00
Purchase — July 31	120	$1.25	150.00
Purchase — September 9	115	$1.50	172.50
Total purchases	345		$443.50
Available	445		$543.50

The company started the period with 100 units ($100.00) and purchased an additional 345 units ($443.50) during the period. The company has 445 units available for sale, at a total cost of $543.50. During the period, there exist only two possible scenarios for the inventory available for sale: either it is *sold* or it is still *on hand* in inventory at the end of the period. Assume further that the company sells 300 units and has 145 units left in inventory at year-end. The units were sold for $2.00 each. However, what dollar value should be assigned to the cost of goods sold and the ending inventory? Were the units that cost $1.00 sold? Or are the $1.00 units still on hand?

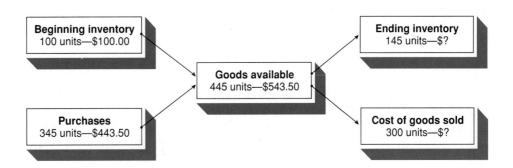

The costs allocated to each period are dependent on the inventory system used and the cost flow method used. Following is an illustration allocating costs to the reported ending inventory and cost of goods sold, using the periodic inventory system, under the FIFO, LIFO, and weighted-average cost methods:

FIFO: Periodic System

Sales (300 units at $2 per unit)			$600.00
Cost of goods available for sale		$543.50	
Less: Cost of goods sold:			
100 units at $1.00	$100.00		
110 units at $1.10	121.00		
90 units at $1.25	112.50		
Cost of goods sold		(333.50)	(333.50)
Gross profit			$266.50
Ending inventory [(145 units): (115 units at $1.50 + 30 units at $1.25) or ($543.50 − $333.50)]		$210.00	

Weighted-Average Cost: Periodic System

Sales (300 units at $2 per unit)		$600.00
Cost of goods available for sale	$543.50	
Cost of goods sold (300 units)($543.50/445=1.221)	(366.50)	(366.50)
Gross profit		$233.50
Ending inventory (145 units): 145 units at $1.221 or ($543.50 − $366.50)	$177.00	

LIFO: Periodic System

Sales (300 units at $2 per unit)			$600.00
Cost of goods available for sale		$543.50	
Less: Cost of goods sold			
115 units at $1.50	$172.50		
120 units at $1.25	150.00		
65 units at $1.10	71.50		
Cost of goods sold		(394.00)	(394.00)
Gross profit			$206.00
Ending inventory (145 units): (100 units at $1.00 + 45 units at $1.10) or ($543.50 − $394.00)		$149.50	

As these examples indicate, in times of *rising* costs, the cost of goods sold is highest using LIFO and lowest using FIFO, with the weighted-average cost method falling between them. The valuation of the units remaining in inventory is highest using FIFO and lowest using LIFO, again with weighted-average cost falling between the two. These characteristics are important when managers are contemplating what picture of their company to portray in the year-end financial statements.

This illustration assumed the use of a periodic inventory system. We will now illustrate the perpetual inventory system. Since we must now maintain a running balance of the inventory on hand, we also need to know when sales were made. It is assumed 100 units were sold on April 26, and 200 units sold on August 15. Following is an illustration allocating costs to the reported ending inventory and cost of goods sold, using the perpetual inventory system, under the FIFO, LIFO, and weighted-average cost methods:

FIFO: Perpetual System

Sales (300 units at $2 per unit)		$600.00
Cost of goods sold		(333.50)
Gross profit		$266.50

	Units	Cost per Unit	Total Cost
Inventory on hand			
January 1	100	$1.00	$100.00
February 14	110	$1.10	121.00
	210		$221.00
April 26	(100)	$1.00	(100.00)*
	110		$121.00
July 31	120	$1.25	150.00
	230		$271.00
August 15	(110)	$1.10	(121.00)*
	(90)	$1.25	(112.50)*
	30		$ 37.50
September 9	115	$1.50	172.50
Ending inventory	145		$210.00
Cost of goods sold			$333.50*

LIFO: Perpetual System

Sales (300 units at $2 per unit)		$600.00
Cost of goods sold		(341.00)
Gross profit		$259.00

	Units	Cost per Unit	Total Cost
Inventory on hand			
January 1	100	$1.00	$100.00
February 14	110	$1.10	121.00
	210		$221.00
April 26	(100)	$1.10	(110.00)*
	110		$111.00
July 31	120	$1.25	150.00
	230		$261.00
August 15	(120)	$1.25	(150.00)*
	(10)	$1.10	(11.00)*
	(70)	$1.00	(70.00)*
	30		$ 30.00
September 9	115	$1.50	172.50
Ending inventory	145		$202.50
Cost of goods sold			$341.00*

Weighted Average: Perpetual System

Sales (300 units at $2 per unit)			$600.00
Cost of goods sold			(336.40)
Gross profit			$263.60

	Units	Cost per Unit	Total Cost
Inventory on hand:			
January 1	100	$1.00	$100.00
February 14	110	$1.10	121.00
Average = $1.052 ($221.00/210)	210		$221.00
April 26	(100)	$1.052	(105.20)*
	110		$115.80
July 31	120	$1.25	150.00
Average = $1.156 ($265.80/230)	230		$265.80
August 15	(200)	$1.156	(231.20)*
	30		$ 34.60
September 9	115	$1.50	172.50
Average = $1.428 ($207.10/145)			
Ending inventory	145		$207.10
Cost of goods sold			$336.40*

Selection of an Inventory Method

With respect to inventory, "The selection of the most suitable method for determining the cost will depend upon the particular circumstances of each enterprise and the industry in which it is engaged" (CICA Handbook 3030.08). The cost of goods sold, like other costs or expenses, has a cause-and-effect relationship with revenues. Therefore, the *matching principle* should strongly influence the selection of an inventory method. "The method selected for determining cost should be one which results in the fairest matching of costs against revenues regardless of whether or not the method corresponds to the physical flow of goods" (CICA Handbook 3030.09). The choice of an inventory method does not have an impact on the cash flow of the organization. Cash flow is not affected because the cost of inventory has been incurred and the cost-flow assumption simply allocates that cost between cost of goods sold and ending inventory.

For the purpose of interperiod comparability, financial statement readers may assume the *consistent* application of cost-flow methods from period to period. "As with all accounting procedures where alternatives exist, it is presumed that, once a basis for determining cost has been selected, it will be followed consistently from one period to another unless circumstances warrant a change" (CICA Handbook 3030.01). "Any change in the basis of valuation from that used in the previous period, and the effect of such change on the net income for the period should be disclosed" (CICA Handbook 3030.13). Therefore, when a change in the inventory accounting method is adopted (e.g., from FIFO to weighted average), company management is required to disclose the nature of the change and its effect on net income, including, whenever possible, a restatement of prior years' financial statements as if the new method had been in effect during those prior years.

7.5 OTHER INVENTORY TOPICS

Estimating Inventories

Techniques for estimating the value of inventory are commonly used in two different circumstances. Firstly, management can use estimation techniques to determine the reasonableness of a physical inventory count. The volume and complexity of inventory transactions in even very small organizations can be quite overwhelming. In addition, as the volume of inventory transactions increases, the probability of inventory errors increases. Therefore, management may wish to make use of an estimation method to determine if the ending inventory value determined by physical count seems to be reasonable. Secondly, estimation methods may be needed to determine the value of inventory destroyed in a fire, a flood, or by other means. As with any estimated technique, the resulting information is only as reliable as the estimation data used. When estimating ending inventory values, the estimate is based on information from the financial reporting system of the organization. If the organization has a sound financial reporting system with proper internal controls, the estimation should be reliable. If the system lacks controls and accountability, the estimate will be less reliable.

gross margin method
A common method of estimating inventories, this method can produce good estimates if reliable gross profit margins are available.

A common method of estimating inventories is by using the **gross margin method**. This method assumes the gross margin on sales has remained relatively constant. This method can produce good estimates if reliable gross profit margins are available. Organizations with a wide variety of product lines would need to determine gross profit margins for each product and separate estimates would then be made for each different type of inventory. The gross profit method is illustrated below.

On June 17, a fire completely destroyed the merchandise inventory of Dan's Office Supply, Ltd. The accountant obtains from last year's annual report the ending inventory (this period's beginning inventory) amount of $37,500. The gross margin on sales last year was 31 percent. Fortunately the accounting records were not destroyed in the fire. For the period January 1 to June 17, the company had net sales of $177,000, and net purchases of $109,000. Using this information, an estimate of the inventory destroyed in the fire may be made. The easiest procedure is to simply prepare a partial income statement using the sales data available and the most recent gross margin percentage.

Sales — net	$177,000
Cost of goods sold	
(net sales less estimated gross profit:	
$177,000 – $54,870)	*122,130*
Estimated gross profit (31% of net sales)	$ 54,870

Using the data from the accounting records, the cost of goods available for sale can be determined. Then, the goods available for sale have either *been sold*, or were still on hand when the fire occurred.

Beginning inventory	$ 37,500
Purchases — net	109,000
Cost of goods available for sale	*$146,500*

If there were $146,500 goods available for sale, and the estimated cost of goods sold was $122,130, the difference of $24,370 ($146,500 − $122,130) is the estimated value of the ending inventory destroyed by the fire.

Cost of goods available for sale	$146,500
Estimated cost of goods sold	122,130
Estimated value of ending inventory	$ 24,370

retail method
The retail method requires the organization to price its inventory at retail and then convert to the cost price using a cost to retail percentage.

A method of estimating inventories used frequently in retail stores is the **retail method**. The retail method requires the organization to price its inventory at retail and then convert to the cost price using a cost-to-retail percentage. The procedure used is the same as the gross profit method, but the estimate is based on the ratio of cost-to-sales as compared to gross profit-to-sales. Dalmys (Canada), Limited's note on the valuation of inventory confirms their use of the retail method: "The valuation of inventory is determined by the retail inventory method which involves pricing of individual items at current selling prices and the reduction of the amounts determined to the lower of approximate cost and net realizable value less the normal profit margin by the application of departmental markup ratios."

Inventory Errors

As previously mentioned, most organizations have a high volume of inventory transactions, which makes them susceptible to mistakes or errors. An inventory error typically affects both the income statement and the balance sheet. As well, inventory errors may affect more than one accounting period. If the error is discovered before the financial statements are released, the statement can be corrected and the misstatement avoided. Quite often the inventory error may simply be a timing error with the inventory purchase or sale being recorded in the wrong accounting period. Other errors involve the misstatement or miscounting of the ending inventory, which also affects next period's beginning inventory.

Partial income statements (in thousands) for a two-year period are presented below:

	Year 1	Year 2	Total
Sales	$100	$110	$210
Cost of goods sold	70	75	145
Gross profit	$ 30	$ 35	$ 65

During Year 2 it was discovered that a $5,000 purchase that had been recorded in Year 2 should have actually been recorded in Year 1. This error had caused the Year 1 purchases and cost of goods sold to be understated and the Year 2 figures to be overstated. The correct partial income statement (in thousands) is shown below:

	Year 1	Year 2	Total
Sales	$100	$110	$210
Cost of goods sold	75	70	145
Gross profit	$ 25	$ 40	$ 65

Over the two-year period the error corrects itself, as reflected in the two-year total which shows no effect. However, the individual years are affected significantly, especially if one compares the corrected gross margin percentages (25% in Year 1, compared to 36% in Year 2). Such an error, if undetected, distorts any trend analysis.

Other inventory errors may involve the ending inventory. Once again, because of the large volume of transactions involving inventory, errors may be difficult to avoid. When ending inventory errors occur, current assets on the balance sheet are over- or understated. As well, since one period's ending inventory becomes the next period's beginning inventory, any misstatements affect both periods. As a result, the cost of goods sold for both periods is misstated.

Consignment Inventory

Some organizations (consignors) distribute inventory to other organizations (consignees) without recording a sale until the consignee sells the inventory to a third party. Once a sale is made to the third party, an exchange or sale is recognized between the consignor and the consignee. Inventory sent out on consignment does not constitute a sale, but simply a change in location. The consignor retains legal title to the inventory, and as such would continue to recognize such as a current asset on its balance sheet. The consignee, although they have physical possession of the inventory, does not recognize the asset in their accounting records. During year-end physical inventory counts, care must be taken to ensure any **consignment inventory** is accounted for properly.

consignment inventory
Inventory placed with a retailer for sale to a final consumer but not sold to the retailer; title to the inventory is retained by the manufacturer until a final sale occurs.

single-step income statement
With a single-step statement, cost of goods sold and all the expenses are combined and deducted from revenues. Gross profit on sales is often not disclosed, as cost of goods sold and other expenses are combined as a single line item.

7.6 FINANCIAL STATEMENT DISCLOSURE

Single-step Income Statement

A **single-step income statement** is commonly found in published annual reports. With a single-step statement, cost of goods sold and all the expenses are combined and deducted from revenues. Gross profit on sales is often not disclosed, as cost of goods sold and other expenses are combined as a single line item. Current GAAP require the disclosure of such items as discontinued operations and extraordinary items. Otherwise, most published income statements provide limited information to the user. Throughout this text a number of published statements are illustrated. It should be noted most are a variation of the basic single-step model illustrated below:

Revenues		$350,000
Expenses:		
Cost of goods sold	$178,000	
Marketing expenses	80,000	
Administrative expenses	45,000	
Income taxes expense	27,000	
Total expenses		330,000
Net income		$ 20,000

Multiple-Step Income Statement

multiple-step income statement
A multiple-step income statement is also referred to as a classified income statement. A multiple-step income statement provides detailed information, in particular with reference to the sales and cost of goods sold section of the income statement.

A **multiple-step income statement** is also referred to as a *classified income statement*. Multiple-step income statements are used by smaller organizations, and also by many organizations for internal reporting purposes. A multiple-step income statement provides more detailed information, in particular with reference to the sales and cost of goods sold section of the income statement. As well, operating expenses may be subdivided into additional subcategories, such as administrative or marketing expenses. These subcategories vary greatly in practice, depending on an organization's industry and the information objectives of management. A multiple-step income statement is illustrated below:

Gross sales			$368,000
Less: *Sales returns*		$ 11,000	
Sales discounts		7,000	18,000
Net sales			$350,000
Cost of goods sold:			
Beginning inventory		$ 47,000	
Purchases	$237,000		
Less: *Purchase returns*	$9,000		
Purchase discounts	3,000	12,000	
Net purchases		$225,000	
Add: *Freight-in*		7,000	
Cost of goods purchased		232,000	
Cost of goods available		$279,000	
Ending inventory		42,000	
Cost of goods sold			237,000
Gross profit			$113,000
Operating expenses:			
Wage expense		$ 33,000	
Utility expense		12,000	
Interest expense		13,000	
Advertizing expense		21,000	
Amortization expense		16,000	95,000
Income before taxes			$ 18,000
Income tax expense			6,000
Net income			$ 12,000

sales returns
When customers return merchandise that was previously recorded as a sale, the amount of the return is recorded in a sales returns account.

purchase returns
Purchase returns is an account to be deducted from purchases to determine the net cost of merchandise purchases, when merchandise is returned to the supplier.

sales discounts
Sales discounts are discounts given for prompt payment of an account.

purchase discount
A cash discount given to a buyer if the buyer pays for the purchases within the discount period.

freight-in
Freight costs associated with the purchase and receipt of inventory.

Returns and Discounts

The multiple-step income statement discloses use of the periodic inventory system, where inventory purchases are recorded in a Purchases account and beginning and ending inventory balances are disclosed. As well, returns, discounts, and freight-in classifications appear on the statement. When merchandise is defective or the wrong colour or size, it is often returned by the customer. The original entry could simply be reversed. However, for control purposes, and to provide additional information, a separate account has been used for **sales returns** and also **purchase returns**. **Sales discounts** and **purchase discounts** are actually discounts given for prompt payment of an account. Discounts were discussed previously in Chapter 6 under accounts receivable. Organizations often provide their customers a discount as an incentive to pay their accounts on time. For example, the credit terms may be 2/10, n/30, which means if the account is paid within 10 days a 2 percent discount may be taken, otherwise the full balance is due in 30 days. **Freight-in** has been added to the cost of goods sold section as the transportation costs relate directly to the inventory purchases.

The following table summarizes the transactions disclosed on the multiple-step income statement. The transactions for a perpetual system are illustrated as well. It should be noted that with the perpetual system when merchandise is bought, sold, or returned, the Inventory account must be updated. With the periodic system, the Inventory account is only updated at year-end.

Periodic Inventory System			Perpetual Inventory System		
Accounts Receivable	1,100		Accounts Receivable	1,100	
Sales		1,100	Sales		1,100
No entry.			Cost of sales	660	
			Inventory		660
Sales returns	100		Sales Returns	100	
Accounts Receivable		100	Accounts Receivable		100
No entry.			Inventory	60	
			Cost of Sales		60
Cash	980		Cash	980	
Sales Discounts	20		Sales Discounts	20	
Accounts Receivable		1,000	Accounts Receivable		1,000
Purchases	800		Inventory	800	
Accounts Payable		800	Accounts Payable		800
Accounts Payable	100		Accounts Payable	100	
Purchase Returns		100	Inventory		100
Accounts Payable	700		Accounts Payable	700	
Purchase Discount		14	Inventory		14
Cash		686	Cash		686
Freight-In	150		Freight-In	150	
Cash		150	Cash		150

net purchase method
The net method records merchandise purchases net of any purchase discounts.

The previous illustration used the gross method of recording purchases. An alternative approach is to use the **net purchase method** of recording purchases. The net method is generally considered the superior method from an internal control perspective, because it highlights any discounts that are *lost*. The gross method identifies only discounts received and ignores any discounts that have been missed or lost. The net and gross methods of accounting for purchases are now illustrated, assuming a $100 purchase, with credit terms of 2/10, n/30. If the account is paid within the discount period, a payment of only $98 is required. If the payment is delayed and the discount is lost, the gross method records no information on discounts. However, the net method highlights the missed discount in the *Discounts Lost Expense* account.

Gross Method			Net Method		
Purchases	100		Purchases	98	
Accounts Payable		100	Accounts Payable		98
Accounts Payable	100		Accounts Payable	98	
Purchase Discount		2	Cash		98
Cash		98			
Accounts Payable	100		Accounts Payable	98	
Cash		100	Cash		100
			Discount Lost Expense.	2	

Financial statement disclosure: Inventory

In general, the requirements for financial statement disclosure for inventories include the following:

1. A description of the accounting principles a company used in determining reported inventory costs.
2. Reference to any accounting principles or methods of accounting peculiar to the industry in which a company operates.
3. Major categories of inventories.

The inventory disclosure from the annual report of the Quaker Oats Company reveals the costs attributable to three categories of inventory: finished goods, grains and materials, and supplies. Quaker Oats would not be expected to have a large work in process inventory category given the relatively short production time for its products. What amounts the company does have are probably included in the grains and materials category. Also note that the disclosures make explicit mention of the lower-of-cost-or-market valuation issue and that the LIFO method is utilized for the largest percentage of inventory items. With regard to LIFO, the disclosures reveal what the value of the LIFO-accounted inventories would have been if LIFO had not been used.

QUAKER OATS COMPANY
Inventory Disclosure

Inventories:	
Finished goods	$309.1
Grain and materials	86.7
Supplies	26.5
	$422.3

Inventories are valued at the lower of cost or market, using various cost methods, and include the cost of raw materials, labour, and overhead. The percentage of year-end inventories valued using each of the methods is as follows:

Last-in, first-out (LIFO)	61%
Average quarterly cost	27%
First-in, first-out (FIFO)	12%

If the LIFO method of valuing certain inventories were not used, total inventories would have been $18.9 million higher.

7.7 ANALYZING INVENTORIES

Analyzing a company's investment in inventories typically focuses on two questions: Is the investment in inventory likely to produce an adequate return to the company? Is the level of investment in inventory appropriate for anticipated future sales? With respect to the first question, a widely used financial indicator is the gross profit margin ratio:

gross profit margin ratio
A percentage of each period's sales dollar that is available to cover the period's expenses.

$$\text{Gross profit margin ratio} = \frac{\text{Gross profit}}{\text{Sales (net)}}$$

The **gross profit margin ratio** indicates the percentage of each sales dollar that is available to cover a company's period expenses and to provide a return to its owners after the cost of goods sold has been deducted. Clearly, the higher this ratio, the more profitable a company's sales of inventory will be. A low ratio may indicate several concerns: (1) the company is underpricing its products or (2) when a product is competitively priced, the cost to manufacture it is too high, perhaps due to inefficiencies in the manufacturing process or in the purchase of raw materials or to the payment of excessively high wages to production employees. The gross profit margin ratio is important to managers because it allows them to determine whether the root of low earnings is attributable to the company's period costs or to its product costs. Likewise, this ratio is important to investors and creditors by enabling them to identify well-managed companies.

With respect to the second question above, two financial ratios are often reviewed: (1) the inventory turnover ratio and (2) the average days' inventory on hand. As discussed in Chapter 5, the inventory turnover ratio measures the number of times that the average level (or dollar investment) in inventory was sold, or "turned over" during a given accounting period:

$$\text{Inventory turnover} = \frac{\text{Cost of sales}}{\text{Inventory}}$$

In general, the higher the inventory turnover ratio, the better. Excessively high turnover ratios, however, may be problematic if the cause is an insufficient investment in inventory. For example, when a company fails to maintain an adequate supply of inventory to meet its customers' needs, it may create order backlogs and customer dissatisfaction, not to mention the possibility of lost sales. On the other hand, a low ratio not warranted by the nature of the company's business may indicate excessive inventory that may not be saleable.

average days'-inventory-on-hand ratio
A measure of the effectiveness of inventory management. A measure of the appropriateness of current inventory levels given current sales volume.

The **average number of days'-inventory-on-hand ratio** indicates the average number of days of inventory supplies on hand to meet customer needs, based on recent sales data. It simply converts the turnover value to an average days' inventory on hand by dividing the turnover ratio by 365 days:

$$\text{Average days' inventory on hand} = \frac{365 \times \text{Inventory}}{\text{Cost of sales}}$$

This ratio is important because it reveals whether there is an adequate quantity of inventory on hand or whether there is an excessive quantity; the latter indicates the need to slow or halt production. Unfortunately, there is no ideal target for the average number of days' inventory on hand or for the inventory turnover ratio. In fact, these indicators vary substantially among industries and often within the same industry. As a general rule, potential investors, lenders, and managers are well advised to compare these indicators for a given company against the leading firm in that industry.

Exhibit 7.2 provides a sample of the comparative gross profit margin ratios and inventory turnover ratios available from Dun & Bradstreet Canada. Industries with perishable goods like food stores must have a higher inventory turnover ratio than a firm selling durable goods such as a farm machinery business.

Earlier in the chapter the different inventory systems and cost-flow methods were illustrated. These methods are summarized in Exhibit 7.3 to facilitate analysis and comparison of the different inventory methods. The exhibit illustrates the impact on the income statement the different methods have during a period of rising prices (inventory costs increased from $1.00 per unit to $1.50 per unit). During periods of rising prices, LIFO matches the most recent costs against current revenues. As indicated in the exhibit, the result is LIFO produces the lowest gross profit and ending inventory values. The perpetual inventory system, since rising costs are absorbed

EXHIBIT 7.2

Ratio Guides

Industry	Gross Profit Margin Ratio	Inventor Turnover
Women's clothing	43.0%	5.6
Gas/service stations	18.6	27.3
Food stores	22.3	15.4
Farm machinery	15.5	2.6
Gold mining	49.4	13.1
Building contractors	14.5	6.3

Source: Dun & Bradstreet Canada.

EXHIBIT 7.3

	Periodic System			Perpetual System	
	FIFO Method	Weighted-Average Method	LIFO Method	Weighted-Average Method	LIFO Method
Sales	$600.00	$600.00	$600.00	$600.00	$600.00
Cost of sales	333.50	366.50	394.00	336.40	341.00
Gross profit	$266.50	$233.50	$206.00	$263.60	$259.00
Ending inventory	$210.00	$177.00	$149.50	$207.10	$202.50
Gross profit margin	44.4%	38.9%	34.3%	43.9%	43.2%
Inventory turnover	1.6	2.1	2.6	1.6	1.7

during the period, reduces the impact LIFO has on the financial statement. FIFO matches old costs on the income statement, producing a higher gross profit. The more recent costs are applied to the ending inventory using FIFO, and therefore results in the highest inventory value for balance sheet purposes. The impact of the weighted-average method falls between the LIFO and FIFO methods.

The firm's investments in inventory will also impact the firm's working capital and cash position. Overinvestment in inventory may cause cash flow problems for the organization. Possibly, working capital may be more wisely invested in other assets, other than inventory. The inventory turnover ratio, the current ratio, and the impact on working capital should all be evaluated carefully on a comparative basis, to ensure the firm's investment in inventory is well managed.

In conclusion, it is important to note that all of the financial indicators are closely tied to the specific inventory cost-flow assumption utilized by a company. Thus, during a period of rising costs, it would be quite reasonable to expect that a FIFO-accounted company would have a higher gross profit margin ratio but lower inventory turnover ratio than would a LIFO-accounted company. In addition, for cross-company comparisons in which the companies use different cost-flow assumptions, the ending inventory and current period earnings amounts should be adjusted for the LIFO company so that it may be compared more appropriately to the FIFO company. As demonstrated in

Exhibit 7.3 the use of different inventory methods may have a significant impact on the financial statements and on the related ratios. Thus, inventory-related financial indicators should be investigated with caution and with an eye toward determining the likely impact of the inventory accounting method on the ratios themselves.

Ethics in Accounting

Becker Company is a medium-sized retail distributer of computer equipment. Becker has three stores in Toronto and two in Hamilton. Economic conditions have been unfavourable the last several months and the financial position of the company has weakened. The replacement cost of computer equipment has been decreasing for the past 18 months. One of Becker's biggest assets from a total dollar perspective is its inventory of computer equipment and computer software. The president of the company has instructed Becker's accountant, Jon McLeod, to select the inventory costing methods that will disclose the most favourable financial position for the company. Jon realizes the president's motivation for disclosing a favourable position is influenced by the unstable condition of the company's short-term financing of inventory. Jon is torn between the responsibility to his employer and the users of the financial statements. Discuss the impact different inventory methods have on an organization's financial position. What are the ethical issues for the accountant?

7.8 SUMMARY

For most non-service companies, inventories represent a significant current asset. For merchandising companies, inventories may represent the largest single asset category. Manufacturing firms must account for three different types of inventory: raw materials, work in process, and finished goods.

Inventories (and cost of goods sold) are usually valued using one of several common cost-flow methods: FIFO, LIFO, average cost, weighted-average cost, or specific costs. In addition, the ending inventory must always be evaluated relative to its market (or replacement) value to ensure that the value reported on the balance sheet is not overstated and approximates its net realizable value. As well, management must consider using either a perpetual or periodic inventory system.

The financial disclosure of inventories varies depending on the industry and size of the organization. Organizations produce either single-step or multiple-step income statements. The footnote section of the firm's annual report will provide valuable information on the firms accounting policies for inventories.

The effective management and utilization of inventory is a hallmark of a well-run company. Thus, analyzing the nature of and investment in inventories is important to investors, creditors, and managers. In addition to reviewing the financial statement disclosure relating to inventories, the financial statement user would be wise to calculate such asset management ratios as the inventory turnover ratio and the average number of days' inventory on hand ratio. These ratios are useful indicators of the quality of a given company's inventory management. The following table summarizes the financial statement interrelationships for inventory:

Financial Statement Interrelationships

Financial Statement Item	Balance Sheet	Income Statement	Statement of Changes in Financial Position
Inventory	Current asset	Cost of goods sold	Adjustment to working capital items: operating activities

7.9 KEY CONCEPTS AND TERMS

Average cost method (p. 336)

Average number of days'-inventory-on-
hand ratio (p. 349)

Consignment inventory (p. 345)

Current cost (p. 333)

Finished goods inventory (p. 331)

First-in, first-out method
(FIFO) (p. 337)

Freight-in (p. 346)

Gross margin method (p. 343)

Gross profit margin ratio (p. 348)

Inventory (p. 329)

Last-in, first-out method (LIFO) (p. 337)

Multiple-step income statement (p. 346)

Net purchase method (p. 347)

Net realizable value (p. 332)

Period cost (p. 331)

Periodic inventory system (p. 338)

Perpetual inventory system (p. 338)

Product cost (p. 331)

Purchase discounts (p. 346)

Purchase returns (p. 346)

Raw materials inventory (p. 329)

Replacement cost (p. 332)

Retail method (p. 344)

Sales discounts (p. 346)

Sales returns (p. 346)

Single-step income statement (p. 345)

Specific identification method (p. 335)

Standard cost (p. 334)

Weighted-average cost method (p. 336)

Work in process inventory (p. 330)

7.10 COMPREHENSIVE REVIEW QUESTION

R7.1 Accounting for inventories. Shown below is information on the inventory of Thomas Company for the year ending December 31.

	Quantity (units)	Cost per Unit	Total Cost
Beginning inventory — January 1	100	$5.00	$ 500.00
Purchase — April 26	100	$5.10	$ 510.00
Purchase — July 31	200	$5.20	1,040.00
Purchase — October 3	100	$5.30	530.00
Total purchases	400		$2,080.00
Available	500		$2,580.00

During the year 330 units were sold for $9.00 each, leaving 170 units in ending inventory on December 31.

Required:

Answer the following *independent* questions:

a. Using a periodic inventory system and the FIFO, LIFO, and weighted-average cost-flow methods, determine the value of the ending inventory and the cost of goods sold.

b. Using a perpetual inventory system and the FIFO, LIFO, and weighted-average cost-flow methods, determine the value of the ending inventory and the cost of goods sold. On May 3 150 units were sold. The remaining units were sold on September 27.

c. On October 27, inventory on hand was destroyed by fire. Ignoring the sales information given above, assuming sales to October 27 were $2,900 and the gross profit on sales was 40 percent, determine the dollar value of the inventory destroyed in the fire.

d. Assume Thomas Company uses the weighted-average cost-flow method. Also assume an error had been made in the ending inventory count, whereby the correct number of units on hand is 150 units. Assuming the use of the periodic inventory system, describe the impact this error would have on the financial statements of Thomas Company for the year ending December 31.

e. Assume Thomas Company uses current costs for the accounting of inventory. Determine the impact on the financial statements, assuming the replacement cost of the ending inventory is $6.00 per unit. Use the FIFO cost-flow method.

f. For the year ending December 31, Thomas Company has decided to treat all transportation costs as product costs. If transportation costs for the year were $500, determine the impact on the financial statements of Thomas Company for the year ending December 31. Assume Thomas Company uses the weighted-average cost-flow method, with a periodic inventory system.

g. Using the information from part *a*, apply the lower-of-cost-or-market rule, assuming the ending inventory has a net realizable value of $880.

h. Using the information from part *a*, determine the gross profit ratio and the average days' inventory on hand.

7.11 REVIEW AND DISCUSSION QUESTIONS

Q7.1 In general, what criteria should be used to determine which costs should be included in inventory?

Q7.2 In general, why is the lower-of-cost-or-market rule used to report inventory?

Q7.3 During periods of rising prices, a perpetual inventory system would result in the same dollar amount of ending inventory as a periodic inventory system under which inventory cost-flow methods? Explain your answer.

Q7.4 Identify and discuss three or four factors contributing to the particular investment in inventory that a company might have.

Q7.5 A company records inventory at the gross invoice price. Theoretically, how should ware-housing costs and cash discounts available affect the costs in inventory? Explain.

Q7.6 Theoretically, how should insurance on raw materials while in transit and cash discounts taken on purchased raw materials affect the costs to be included in a manufacturer's inventory?

Q7.7 Distinguish between product costs and period costs.

Q7.8 Which inventory system, perpetual or periodic, is considered the best from the perspective of internal control? Explain.

Q7.9 For each of the companies listed below, state whether you think that the company would have more dollar value in raw materials, work in process, or finished goods inventory. Explain your reasons.

a. Printing plant.

b. Paper manufacturing company.

c. Specialty machine shop.

d. Toy company.

e. Tire manufacturer.

Q7.10 Which of the companies listed below would you expect to have the highest inventory turnover ratio? The lowest inventory turnover ratio? Why?

a. Supermarket.

b. Department store.

c. Automobile manufacturer.

d. Jewellery store.

Q7.11 For the year ended August 31, Acme, Limited, reported a net income of $37,000. After the financial statements had been prepared and the net income determined, the following inventory errors were discovered: beginning inventory was overstated by $1,000, ending inventory was understated by $2,000, and purchases for the year were understated by $5,000. Determine the corrected net income figure for the year.

Q7.12 Southland Books, Inc., marks up all inventory 50 percent over cost. In November, a water main broke, destroying the entire inventory. From the records of Southland, beginning inventory was $265,000 and purchases during the year totaled $148,000. Sales for the year were $180,000. Determine the value of the inventory destroyed by the flood.

Q7.13 Review the Ethics in Accounting case presented on page 351. Discuss the alternative courses of action available to the accountant. How do you think the situation should be handled?

7.12 PROBLEMS

P7.1 Calculating inventory values. The following information was taken from the accounting records of Read-for-Knowledge, Inc., a national supplier of comic books to retail outlets throughout North America:

	"Batman vs the Scum of the Slum"	"King Kong Meets T-Rex"
Inventory, January 1	1,500,000 copies at $0.10	1,000,000 copies at $0.30
Purchases: May 12	600,000 copies at 0.15	1,000,000 copies at 0.20
Aug. 20	600,000 copies at 0.20	500,000 copies at 0.15
Sales: March 3	1,200,000 copies at 0.25	900,000 copies at 0.35
July 8	300,000 copies at 0.30	300,000 copies at 0.35
September 21	900,000 copies at 0.25	200,000 copies at 0.35

Required:

Using the above information, calculate the following:

a. The cost of goods sold for each product for the year assuming that the FIFO method is used in a perpetual inventory system.

b. The value of the ending inventory for each product assuming that the LIFO method is used in a periodic inventory system.

c. The value of ending inventory for each product assuming that the FIFO method is used in a periodic inventory system.

P7.2 Cost-flow identification. Listed below are three methods of inventory costing and six numbered descriptive statements. Indicate the method that is referred to in the following descriptive statements. If none of the methods listed below apply to a statement, then so indicate.

a. LIFO.

b. FIFO.

c. Weighted average.

d. None of the above.

1. Cost of goods sold is highest in a period of steadily rising prices.

2. The ending inventory is priced at the cost of the most recently acquired goods.

3. Requires that records be maintained at both cost and selling price for goods placed in stock.

4. Most appropriately matches current costs with current revenues.

5. Produces highest ending inventory figure after a period of steadily falling prices.

P7.3 Calculating inventory values. The following data were taken from the records of The Bakery for the year:

Beginning inventory:	
100 lbs. at $10	$1,000
Purchases:	
100 lbs. at $12	$1,200
50 lbs. at $10	500
200 lbs. at $14	2,800
300 lbs. at $13	3,900
50 lbs. at $12	600
700 lbs.	$9,000

Sales were $8,000 (500 lbs. at $16.00 per lb.) and operating expenses were $1,500. Compute each of the following under LIFO, FIFO, and the lower-of-cost-or-market methods. Assume that the year-end market price is $12 per pound.

a. Cost of goods sold.

b. Ending inventory.

c. Income before taxes.

P7.4 Evaluating inventory errors. The following errors were made by Gunnison Corporation during 1996. Indicate the effect of each of these errors on the financial statements for 1996 and 1997 by completing the chart below. Use the following codes for your answers: O = overstated, U = understated, and N = no effect. (Gunnison Corporation uses the periodic inventory system.)

Error 1. The company failed to record a $500 sale on account at the end of 1996. The merchandise had been shipped and was not included in the ending inventory. The sale was recorded in 1997 when cash was collected from the customer.

Error 2. The company failed to record a $700 purchase on account at the end of 1996 and also failed to include the goods purchased in the ending inventory. The purchase was recorded in 1997 when payment was made to the creditor.

Error 3. The company failed to make an entry for a $200 purchase on account at the end of 1996, although it included this merchandise in the inventory count. The purchase was recorded when payment was made to the creditor in 1997.

Error 4. The company failed to count goods costing $400 in the physical count of goods at the end of 1996.

	Total Revenue	Total Expense	Net Income	Total Assets	Total Liabilities	Total Owners' Equity
1996:						
Error 1						
Error 2						
Error 3						
Error 4						
1997:						
Error 1						
Error 2						
Error 3						
Error 4						

P7.5 Inventory value calculation. Use the following information to answer parts *a* through *e*:

Raw materials inventory — June 1	$ 75
Raw materials purchased during June	650
Raw materials inventory — June 30	40
Other manufacturing costs, variable	150
Other manufacturing costs, nonvariable	220
Direct labour	400
Work in process — June 1	60
Work in process — June 30	25
Finished goods inventory — June 1	90
Finished goods inventory — June 30	150
Gross margin	125
Selling and administrative expenses, variable	10
Selling and administrative expenses, nonvariable	25

Required:

Calculate the following:

a. The cost of materials used for June.

b. Without adjusting your answer to part *a*, assume that the cost of materials used to be $660 during June. Use this figure for the remainder of this question. This will eliminate carry-through errors. What was the cost of goods manufactured for June?

c. Without adjusting your answer to part *b*, assume that the cost of goods manufactured for June was $1,500. What was the cost of goods sold for June?

d. Without adjusting your answer to part *c*, assume that the cost of goods sold for June was $1,400. What was the sales revenue for June?

e. Assume that the cost of goods sold for June was $1,400. What were the earnings for June?

P7.6 Calculating cost of goods sold. The following information is available concerning the Halsey Manufacturing Corporation:

Beginning inventories:	
Raw materials	$ 10,000
Goods in process	4,500
Ending inventories:	
Raw materials	15,000
Goods in process	6,000
Raw materials used	70,000
Direct labour	50,000
Total manufacturing costs	152,000
Cost of goods available for sale	155,000
Cost of goods sold	148,000
Gross profit	127,000
Income	102,000

Required:

Compute the following:

a. Raw materials purchased.

b. Raw materials available for use.

c. Manufacturing overhead.

d. Cost of goods manufactured.

e. Sales revenue.

f. Finished goods inventory, beginning.

g. Finished goods inventory, ending.

h. Operating expenses.

P7.7 Financial analysis: inventory errors. The year-end financial statements of Windsor, Ltd., included the following:

Sales	$ 225,000
Cost of sales	(135,000)
Operating expenses	(38,000)
Income tax expense	(22,000)
Net income	$ 30,000
Accounts receivable — December 31	$ 22,000
Inventory — December 31	$ 43,000

a. Determine the following ratios for Windsor, Ltd.:

(1) Gross profit margin.

(2) Inventory turnover.

(3) Receivable turnover.

b. After the above financial statements had been prepared, it was determined the December 31 inventory was overstated by $5,000. Recalculate the ratios for part *a*.

c. Do you consider the inventory error to be material?

P7.8 Average company versus FIFO company. Presented below are the financial statements of two companies that are identical in every respect except the method of valuing their inventories. The method of valuing inventory is weighted average for Average Company and FIFO for FIFO Company.

Comparative Income Statements

	FIFO Company	Average Company
Sales	$20,000,000	$20,000,000
Less: Cost of sales	9,200,000	11,280,000
Gross profit	$10,800,000	$ 8,720,000
Less: Operating expenses	5,000,000	5,000,000
Net income	$ 5,800,000	$ 3,720,000

Comparative Balance Sheets

	FIFO Company	Average Company
Assets		
Cash	$ 3,000,000	$ 3,000,000
Receivables	6,000,000	6,000,000
Inventory	3,800,000	1,720,000
Total current assets	$12,800,000	$10,720,000
Non-current (net)	20,000,000	20,000,000
Total assets	$32,800,000	$30,720,000
Liabilities and Owners' Equity		
Current liabilities	$ 4,200,000	$ 4,200,000
Non-current liabilities	9,000,000	9,000,000
Total liabilities	$13,200,000	$13,200,000
Owners' equity	19,600,000	17,520,000
Total liabilities and owners' equity	$32,800,000	$30,720,000

Required:

Using the two sets of financial statements, calculate the following ratios or financial indicators for each firm.

a. Current ratio.

b. Inventory turnover ratio.

c. Average days' inventory on hand.

d. Return on total assets.

e. Total debt to total assets.

f. Long-term debt to owners' equity.

g. Gross margin ratio.

h. Return on sales.

i. Return on equity.

j. Earnings per share (assume 2 million shares outstanding).

Based on the above ratios in parts *a–j*, explain which company represents the following:

k. The best investment opportunity?

l. The best acquisition opportunity?

m. The best lending opportunity?

P7.9 Ratio analysis. Presented below are summary financial data for Coca-Cola Enterprises, Inc., and PepsiCo, Inc.

	19x9	19x8
Cost of goods sold (in millions):		
Coca-Cola Enterprises, Inc.	$2,313	$2,268
PepsiCo, Inc.	7,468	5,957
Year-end inventory (in millions):		
Coca-Cola Enterprises, Inc.	128	125
PepsiCo, Inc.	546	442

Required:

Using the above data, calculate the inventory turnover and the average number of days' inventory on hand for 19x9 for each company. Consider using average inventory values. What is your evaluation of each company's inventory management policy?

P7.10 Lower of cost or market. Joan Sack was the proprietor of a bookstore in Charlottesville. In 1996, she decided to relocate her store to a new shopping mall and to expand her inventory as well. To finance the new facility and the increased inventory, she decided to approach the bank for a loan. In preparation for a meeting with her accountant to prepare the financial statements that she knew the bank would require as part of her loan application, she collected the following information about her book inventory for the prior three years:

	Cost	Replacement Cost
December 31, 1993	$100,000	$ 100,000
December 31, 1994	130,000	110,000
December 31, 1995	150,000	140,000

Joan also carried a very small collection of videotapes of movies based on books sold in the store. Because of the limited number of tapes on hand, she made a detailed analysis of her inventory.

	Videotapes				
	1	2	3	4	5
Cost	$5.00	$5.00	$5.00	$5.00	$5.00
Net realizable value	$5.10	$5.50	$4.80	$4.20	$4.70
Number on hand	5	4	8	10	8

She realized that carrying the videotapes had not been very profitable and decided that if the loan were approved, she would discontinue selling them.

Required:

Based on the above information, determine the value of Joan's book inventory at the end of each year. Also, what value should she assign to her videotape inventory?

P7.11 Estimating inventory values. Kahn Sporting Goods Shops' accounting records indicated the following information:

Beginning inventory	$ 400,000
Purchases	2,500,000
Sales	3,400,000

A physical inventory taken on December 31 resulted in an ending inventory of $325,000. Kahn's gross profit on sales has remained constant at 25 percent in recent years. Kahn suspects some inventory may have been taken by a new employee. Kahn uses a periodic inventory system.

Required:

At December 31 what is the estimated cost of missing inventory?

P7.12 Estimating destroyed inventory. Weiss Company sells its merchandise at a gross profit of 30 percent. Weiss uses a periodic inventory system. The following figures are among those pertaining to Weiss's operations for the six months ended June 30:

Sales	$220,000
Beginning inventory	48,000
Purchases	130,000

Required:

On June 30 all of Weiss's inventory was destroyed by fire. What is the estimated cost of this destroyed inventory?

P7.13 Calculating cost of goods sold. The following information was taken from Martin Company's accounting records for the year ended December 31:

Decrease in raw materials inventory	$ 13,000
Increase in finished goods inventory	35,000
Raw materials purchased	330,000
Direct labour payroll	200,000
Factory overhead	320,000
Freight-out	35,000

There was no work in process inventory at the beginning or end of the year.

Required:

Calculate Martin's cost of goods sold.

P7.14 Inventory valuation. Powell, Inc., purchased a significant amount of raw materials inventory for a new product that it's manufacturing. Powell purchased insurance on these raw materials while they were in transit from the supplier.

Powell applies the lower-of-cost-or-market method to these raw material inventory items. The realizable value is below the original cost of the inventory.

Powell uses the average cost inventory method for these raw materials. In the last two years, each purchase has been at a lower price than the previous purchase, and the ending inventory quantity for each period has been higher than the beginning inventory quantity for that period.

Required:

a. What is the theoretically preferable method that Powell should use to account for the insurance costs on the raw materials while they were in transit from the supplier? Why?

b. (1) At which amount should Powell's raw materials inventory be reported on the balance sheet? Why?

   (2) In general, why is the lower-of-cost-or-market method used to report inventory?

c. What would have been the effect on ending inventory and cost of goods sold had Powell used the LIFO inventory method instead of the average cost inventory method for the raw materials? Why?

P7.15 Inventory decisions. Oliver Company sells chemical compounds made from fasbium and uses LIFO inventory. The inventory on January 1, 1994, consisted of 3,000 lbs. at $45 per pound. Purchases and ending inventories in the subsequent years were as follows:

Year	Average Purchase Price per Pound during Year	Cost of Units Purchased	December 31 Inventory
1994	50	$384,000	3,600 lbs.
1995	51	352,000	2,600 lbs.
1996	52	448,000	4,000 lbs.

Because of temporary scarcities, fasbium is expected to cost $62 per pound in 1997. Sales for 1997 are expected to require 7,000 pounds of fasbium. The purchasing agent suggests that the inventory be allowed to decrease to 600 pounds by the end of 1997 and be replenished to 4,000 pounds in early 1998. The controller thinks that such a policy is foolish, and suggests that the company maintain a 1997 year-end inventory of 4,000 pounds.

Required:

a. Calculate the cost of goods sold and the dollar value of ending inventory for 1997, assuming (1) the purchasing agent's advice is followed and (2) the controller's advice is followed.

b. If you were making the decision, what other information might you consider in choosing whose advice to follow? Please list.

P7.16 Inventory Management. Missey Manufacturing, Ltd., has two different divisions operating in western Canada. The accountant for Missey has determined the inventory turnover ratios for each division. Division A has an inventory turnover of 6.2, while Division B has a turnover ratio of 5.4. Determine the average days' inventory on hand for each division. Which division is doing a better job managing their inventory?

P7.17 Liquidity ratios. For the year ended April 30, Gordon-McKay, Limited, had current assets of $179,000. Included in the current assets were quick assets of $72,000. On April 30

Gordon-McKay had current liabilities of $78,000. In determining the preceding balances, the accountant failed to make two adjusting entries. The entry for bad debt expense of $9,000, based on a percentage of sales, was omitted. As well, applying the lower-of-cost-or-market rule, the entry to recognize loss on inventory of $11,000 was not recorded. Determine the quick and current ratios before and after the adjustments are considered. Do you think the omission of the adjusting entries will have a material impact on the ratio analysis?

P7.18 Calculating net sales. Harbor Company's usual sales terms are net 30 days. Sales, net of returns and allowances, totaled $2,600,000 for the year ended December 31, 1995, before year-end adjustments. Additional data are as follows:

On December 27, 1995, Harbor authorized a customer to return, for full credit, goods shipped and billed at $40,000 on December 15, 1995. The returned goods were received by Harbor on January 4, 1996, and a $40,000 credit memo was issued and recorded on the same date.

Goods with an invoice amount of $75,000 were billed and recorded on January 3, 1996. The goods were shipped on December 30, 1995.

Goods with an invoice amount of $90,000 were billed and recorded on December 30, 1995. The goods were shipped on January 3, 1996.

Required:

Harbor's adjusted net sales for 1995 should be reported at what amount?

P7.19 Lower of cost or market. Dewey Distribution Company has determined its December 31 inventory on a FIFO basis at $201,000. Information pertaining to that inventory follows:

Estimated selling price	$210,000
Estimated cost of disposal	15,000
Current replacement cost	175,000

Dewey records losses that result from applying the lower-of-cost-or-market method. Dewey defines *market value* as net realizable value.

Required:

At December 31 calculate the loss that Dewey should recognize.

P7.20 Inventory Cost Flow Methods. Ottawa Valley Industries, Ltd., made two purchases of merchandise inventory during the most recent accounting period. The first purchase was for 500 units of inventory at a cost of $7.50 per unit. The second purchase was for 300 units at a cost of $8.00 per unit. At the beginning of the period, 200 units at a cost of $7.00 per unit were on hand. During the period, 450 units were sold for $12.00 each. The accounting department is undecided as to which inventory method would be most appropriate. The methods being considered are: LIFO, FIFO, and weighted average. Select the most appropriate inventory method assuming:

1. The company objective of financial reporting is to maximize profits.

2. The company wishes to publish conservative financial statements.

P7.21 Inventory Cost-Flow Methods. Autoparts, Inc., had the following information for its parts inventory:

Date	Units	Cost per Unit	Total Cost
January 1	50	$7.00	$ 350.00
May 17	80	8.00	640.00
October 3	40	9.00	360.00
	170		$1,350.00

During the year 110 units were sold for $20.00 each.

a. Assuming Autoparts, Inc., uses a periodic inventory system and LIFO costing, the value of the ending inventory would be:

(1) $430.00.

(2) $920.00.

(3) $830.00.

(4) $520.00.

(5) None of the above.

b. Assuming Autoparts, Inc., uses a periodic inventory system and FIFO costing, the value of the cost of goods sold would be:

(1) $430.00.

(2) $920.00.

(3) $830.00.

(4) $520.00.

(5) None of the above.

c. Assuming Autoparts, Inc., uses a periodic inventory system and weighted-average costing, the gross profit on sales would be:

(1) $1,280.00.

(2) $476.00.

(3) $874.00.

(4) $1,326.00.

(5) $1,370.00.

d. Assuming Autoparts, Inc., uses a perpetual inventory system with LIFO costing and 110 units were sold on September 27, the value of the cost of goods sold would be:

(1) $430.00.

(2) $830.00.

(3) $520.00

(4) $850.00.

(5) $1,280.00.

P7.22 Inventory Errors. Guy and Marie LaPointe operate a small retail shoe store in Gravelbourg, Saskatchewan. The LaPointes use a periodic inventory system and have a December 31 year-end. On December 30, 1994, LaPointe, Limited, received a $3,500 shipment of merchandise inventory. The merchandise was correctly included in the December 31, 1994, ending inventory, but was incorrectly omitted from the 1994 purchases. The invoice for the merchandise was received and processed on January 15, 1995, and the merchandise was incorrectly included in the 1995 purchases. A second inventory error subsequently discovered was the fact that $1,000 of merchandise had inadvertently been omitted and not included in the December 31, 1995, ending inventory.

Indicate the impact the two errors will have on the following financial statement items for the years 1994 and 1995. Indicate whether the errors have no effect, or the amount of over- or understatement.

	1994	1995
Accounts payable — December 31	_____	_____
Cost of goods sold	_____	_____
Retained earnings — December 31	_____	_____
Current assets — December 31	_____	_____
Net income	_____	_____

P7.23 Cost of goods sold (*Published with permission of CGA Canada*). The following data pertain to Howard Huntz Medical Supplies Co.:

Accounts payable, January 1	$35,000
Accounts payable, December 31	40,000
Cash payments on account	43,000
Cash discounts taken on purchases	650
Cash purchases	4,000
Inventory, January 1	7,000
Inventory, December 31	8,500
Sales returns	1,200
Purchase returns	1,500

Required:

Calculate cost of goods sold for the year.

P7.24 Analysis of an inventory error. The partial income statement of Grand Prairie Landscaping, Ltd., for the year ended December 31 is shown below:

Sales		$127,000
Cost of sales		
Beginning inventory	$ 26,000	
Purchases	88,000	
Cost of goods available	$114,000	
Ending inventory	33,000	81,000
Gross profit		$ 46,000

A few days after the financial statements of Grand Prairie Landscaping, Ltd., had been prepared and distributed to the shareholders and other users, an inventory error was discovered. It was determined that inventory in a secluded part of the warehouse had not been included in the ending inventory count. The correct value of ending inventory should be $36,000.

Required:

a. Determine the impact of this error on gross profit, the gross profit ratio, and the inventory turnover ratio.

b. Explain the impact of the error on the statement of changes in financial position.

c. Would you consider the error to have a material impact on the financial statements of Grand Prairie Landscaping, Ltd.?

P7.25 Financial analysis. Information from the year-end financial statements of Nippy Company included the following:

Sales	$ 120,000
Cost of sales	(70,000)
Operating expenses	(20,000)
Income tax expense	(12,000)
Net income	$ 18,000
Accounts receivable — December 31	$ 20,000
Inventory — December 31	$ 14,000

Required:

Determine the following ratios for Nippy Company:

a. Gross profit margin.

b. Inventory turnover.

c. Receivable turnover.

d. Prepare a brief comment on the significance of the ratios you calculated for Nippy Company.

P7.26 Inventory valuation (*Certified Management Accountants of British Columbia*). You have just taken over as accountant for a small dealership in lawn mowers. The company only sells one kind of mower: Grass Plus. The inventory reported at the beginning of the financial year was $10,000. From the records given to you, it is clear that the following purchases were made during the fiscal year:

	Number of Units	Cost per Unit
May 31	500	$200
June 30	700	210
July 31	600	250

The company uses the periodic inventory method. The ending inventory consists of 200 units of Grass Plus Machines. The cost of goods sold is $367,000.

Management prefers to change to the weighted-average method. This change of accounting policy is acceptable.

Required:

a. What inventory valuation method was used before? Show the calculation to support your conclusion. (The beginning inventory consisted of 50 units.)

b. What would be the cost of goods sold under the weighted-average method? Show your calculations.

c. What will be the difference in operating income with the new method for inventory valuation, compared to the income under the old method?

P7.27 Inventory valuation (*Certified Management Accountants of British Columbia*). Marvel Tool Company gives you the following record of the purchases of two of its products during the fiscal year ending November 30.

HD Drills			HD Saws		
	Number of Units Purchased	Unit Price		Number of Units Purchased	Unit Price
Jan. 15	200	$150	March 3	300	$300
March 15	150	170	April 2	350	310
June 15	60	170	July 30	200	320
Oct. 30	300	200	Sept. 3	200	320

There were no beginning inventories. The periodic inventory method is used. The ending inventory for HD Drills is 50 units; and for HD Saws it is 100 units. It is company policy to value the ending inventory so that the cost of goods sold reflects current replacement value of items sold. The controller of Marvel Tool argues that the cost of goods sold should be based on the oldest items in inventory that were for sale.

Required:

a. What inventory valuation method does the company policy prescribe? What is the cost of goods sold under this method?

b. What method of inventory valuation does the controller want to follow? What would be the cost of goods sold under this method?

c. What is the difference in operating income between the two methods of inventory valuation?

P7.28 Cost-flow methods (*Certified Management Accountants of British Columbia*).

Part A

The records of Royal Blue Business, Inc., an office supplies retailer, showed the following purchases of a popular calculator, the Wizard:

	Units Ordered	Unit Price
January 16	20	$33
February 9	50	30
May 31	15	34
August 15	60	32

Beginning inventory, January 1, of the Wizard was five units at $31.

In November, the supplier introduced a new model, the SuperWiz, and discontinued production of the Wizard. Royal Blue purchased 50 of these new calculators in November in anticipation of the Christmas season. Unit cost was $40. Sales were brisk and 20 additional units were purchased at $42 in December. At fiscal year-end, December 31, an inventory count determined there were 15 units of the Wizard and 10 units of the SuperWiz on hand.

Required:

a. Determine the value of the ending inventory of Wizard under each of the following inventory valuation assumptions:

(1) FIFO method.

(2) Weighted-average method.

b. Determine the value of the ending inventory of SuperWiz under each of the following inventory valuation assumptions:

(1) FIFO method.

(2) LIFO method.

Part B
Assume the cost of the Wizard is $30 per unit, the cost of the SuperWiz is $40 per unit, and Royal Blue stocks no other calculators. Because of the superiority of the SuperWiz calculator, the market value of the Wizard at December 31 was only $25 per unit. The market value of the SuperWiz is $50 per unit. Ending inventories of the Wizard and the SuperWiz are 15 and 10 units, respectively.

Required:

a. Determine the total inventory value that would appear on Royal Blue's balance sheet under the lower-of-cost-or-market rule under each of the following assumptions:

(1) The rule is applied on an individual item basis.

(2) The rule is applied to the whole inventory.

b. Prepare any necessary journal entries under each assumption.

P7.29 Inventory valuation (*Certified Management Accountants of British Columbia*). Harry and Sally are partners in a wholesale business. Neither of them is an accountant but Harry has read an accounting book and Sally purchased a software package for daily inventory records. During January the following activities occurred in their inventory account:

January	1	Beginning balance 0.00
	4	Bought 220 units @ $1.00
	8	Sold 190 units
	9	Bought 250 units @ $1.25
	14	Sold 150 units
	16	Bought 200 units @ $1.50
	25	Sold 160 units

Harry uses FIFO for inventory records and Sally's software package uses the weighted-average method of valuing inventory.

Required:

a. Calculate the ending inventory balance that would appear for each method discussed above. Round to two decimal points for weighted average. Show your work.

b. Generally, is there a difference in profits when using FIFO as compared to using weighted average?

P7.30 Inventory errors (*Certified Management Accountants of British Columbia*). The following information is for Jake the Snake, Ltd., a plumbing company, for four consecutive periods:

	1	2	3	4
Sales	$190,000	$120,000	$140,000	$150,000
Beginning inventory	$ 23,000	$ 17,000	$ 24,000	$ 25,000
Purchases	89,000	64,000	69,000	57,000
Goods available for sale	$112,000	$ 81,000	$ 93,000	$ 82,000
Ending inventory	17,000	24,000	25,000	14,000
Cost of goods sold	$ 95,000	$ 57,000	$ 68,000	$ 68,000
Gross profit	$ 95,000	$ 63,000	$ 72,000	$ 82,000

The company made the following errors:

Period	Error in Ending Inventory
1	Overstated $5,000
2	Overstated $4,000
3	Understated $3,000

Required:

Calculate the revised gross profit for each period.

P7.31 Inventory and accounts receivable (*Certified Management Accountants of British Columbia*). Fabulous Fabricators, Ltd., is a company in its first year of business. The accounts receivable person, I. M. Greedy (who is paid $1,400 per month), has just come back from a month's holiday in Tahiti. There have been rumours that Greedy is about to buy a Ferrari. It has been decided to test the accuracy of the Accounts Receivable balance.

Information from current financial records show:

Inventory purchased	$365,000
Inventory returned to supplier	12,000
Inventory ending balance	62,750
Collections from customers	247,120
Accounts receivable ending balance	45,010

All sales are made on credit. Goods are sold at 55 percent above cost.

Required:

Calculate the correct Accounts Receivable balance from the information above. Is there any money missing?

P7.32 Inventory valuation (*Certified Management Accountants of British Columbia*). Bali Company uses a periodic inventory system. The information shown below pertains to one item in the company's inventory records for the month of November.

		Units	Unit Cost
Nov. 1	Balance	125	$1.10
2	Purchase	150	1.25
10	Sale	75	
12	Purchase	125	1.35
17	Sale	150	
29	Purchase	75	1.30

Required:

a. Calculate the cost of goods sold and ending inventory for the month of November for Bali Company using the following methods:

(1) First-in, first-out.

(2) Last-in, first-out.

(3) Weighted-average.

b. There are two systems of maintaining inventory records: the periodic inventory system and the perpetual inventory system. How does each work and what are the basic differences?

P7.33 Classified income statement (*Certified Management Accountants of British Columbia*). Below are selected items (in alphabetical order) for the first year of operations of Trans-Continental Air Packaging, Ltd. The company specializes in packaging air freight items, using popcorn instead of plastic foam chips. All balances below are normal balances from the November 30 trial balance.

Accounts receivable	$ 26,000
Accumulated amortization	14,000
Administrative expenses	33,000
Amortization expense	14,000
Corporation income tax expense	8,000
Cost of goods sold	140,000
Dividend revenue on a temporary investment	6,000
Dividends declared	15,000
Dividends payable	5,000
Sales discounts and allowances	20,000
Sales revenue	280,000
Selling expenses	30,000
Unearned revenue	68,000

Required:

Prepare a classified income statement in good form for the year ended November 30.

P7.34 Partial income statements (*Certified Management Accountants of British Columbia*). Buxus Bonsai uses the periodic inventory system. They sold 1,000 plants for $200 each in their first year of operations. They made four purchases:

Date	Units Bought	Unit Price	Total Cost
Jan. 10	100	$ 75	$ 7,500
Mar. 31	500	105	52,500
June 30	200	120	24,000
Oct. 20	400	150	60,000
Total	1,200		$144,000

Required:

Prepare three income statements (you could do it by way of three columns) down to gross profit, showing details of cost of goods sold in the statements, using the following cost-flow assumptions:

a. First-in, first-out.

b. Last-in, first-out.

c. Weighted average.

P7.35 Estimating inventories (*Certified Management Accountants of British Columbia*). The Prudent Company follows the practice of taking a physical inventory at the end of each calendar year accounting period to establish the ending inventory amount for financial statement purposes. The Prudent Company has consistently shown a gross profit of 30 percent.

On Friday, November 13 a flood destroyed the entire inventory stored in the basement of the building. The records remained intact and on this date show:

Merchandise inventory, January 1	$ 29,000
Merchandise purchases	625,000
Purchase returns and allowances	7,500
Transportation-in	25,000
Sales	873,000
Sales returns and allowances	23,000
Selling expenses	50,000

The company was fully covered by insurance.

Required:

a. Determine the amount of its insurance claim for the loss of the merchandise by means of the gross profit method.

b. Under what operating conditions will the gross profit method of computing an inventory balance produce approximately correct amounts?

P7.36 Cost-flow methods (*Certified Management Accountants of British Columbia*). The inventory records for the Jippy Juice Company for raspberry juice cans shows the following for the month of December:

		Number of units	Cost per Unit	Total Cost
Dec. 1	Beginning inventory	200	$2.025	$ 405.00
5	Purchase	500	2.03	1,015.00
8	Purchase	1,000	2.10	2,100.00
13	Sale	300		
23	Purchase	400	2.12	848.00
30	Sale	600		

Required:

Assuming a periodic inventory system, determine the cost of the ending inventory using:

a. Last-in, first-out valuation method.

b. Weighted-average valuation method.

c. First-in, first-out valuation method.

d. Explain briefly how the inventory method used by the Jippy Juice Company may affect their gross profit.

P7.37 Inventory valuation (*Certified Management Accountants of British Columbia*). Joe and Sean are partners in a wholesale business, Rostrevor Products, Ltd. Neither of them is an accountant; however, Joe has read an accounting text and Sean has a software package that he used for inventory records. Together they employed a college student to record their inventory. Joe asked the student to use the FIFO method to calculate the inventory, while Sean asked the student to use the weighted-average method of recording the inventory, since his software package used that method. The student began work on May 1. Both partners agreed to compare the results of the student's calculations. The following information appeared on their books at the end of May.

May	1	Beginning inventory	25 units @ $120 each
	4	Purchase	75 units @ $125 each
	9	Purchase	60 units @ $130 each
	17	Purchase	36 units @ $132 each
	27	Purchase	44 units @ $138 each

Following an inventory count at May 31 it was determined that 57 units were left in inventory.

Required:

a. Calculate the ending inventory value using both Joe's and Sean's methods. Show all of your calculations for each of the methods.

b. If both partners had agreed to use the LIFO method of inventory valuation, would the value of the ending inventory have any effect upon the net income on the income statement, and upon the total assets on the balance sheet? Give an explanation of your responses.

c. Which of the methods of inventory valuation used in this problem is disallowed by Revenue Canada? Explain briefly why Revenue Canada does not allow this inventory valuation to be used.

P7.38 Estimating inventory. Duncan Draperies had a fire on November 11 that completely destroyed all of the company's merchandise inventory. Fortunately, the firm's accounting records were stored in a fireproof vault and they were not destroyed. An analysis of financial statements available indicates the inventory at December 31 of the previous year was valued at $37,000. As well, the statements indicate the average gross profit on sales to be 30 percent for the last several years. The accounting records for the current year include the following information for the period January 1 to November 11: sales $140,000, purchases $111,000, and purchase returns $6,000.

Required:

a. Determine the estimated dollar value of the inventory destroyed in the fire.

b. Assume that instead of an average gross profit of 30 percent on sales, Duncan Draperies used a markup over the cost of inventory of 40 percent to determine the sales price of its product. Determine the estimated dollar value of the inventory destroyed in the fire.

P7.39 Inventory errors. On December 30, 1995, Ellis Equipment, Ltd., received a $3,000 shipment of merchandise inventory. The merchandise was correctly included in the December 31, 1995, inventory. Unfortunately, the invoice was not received and processed until January 21, 1996, and the merchandise was incorrectly included in the 1996 purchases. Ellis Equipment, Ltd., uses a periodic inventory system and has a December 31 year-end. Determine the impact of this inventory error on the items listed below. Indicate for each item whether the error has no effect, or the dollar amount of the over- or understatement.

a. 1995 net income.

b. January 1, 1996, beginning inventory.

c. December 31, 1996, retained earnings.

P7.40 Gross margin (*Published with permission of CGA Canada*). Sue Company had $180,000 of sales during each of three consecutive years, and it purchased merchandise costing $140,000 during each of the years. It also maintained a $40,000 inventory from the beginning to the end of the three-year period. In accounting under the periodic inventory system, it made an error at the end of Year 1 that caused its ending inventory to appear on its statements at $50,000, rather than the correct $40,000. There were no other inventory errors.

Required:

a. Determine the gross margin reported by Sue Company in each of the three years (the error was not discovered until the beginning of the fourth year).

b. Determine the gross margin that would have been reported if the error was not made.

c. Is the total of the three-year gross margins in part *a* and part *b* the same or different? Explain.

P7.41 Net and gross purchase methods (*Published with permission of CGA Canada*). Grant Company purchased merchandise on credit for $60,000, terms 3/10, n/30. Payment was made within the discount period. At the end of the period, 25 percent of the merchandise was unsold. This is Grant's first accounting period.

Required:

Determine the following:

a. Gross method used:

   (1) Cost of goods sold.

   (2) Ending inventory.

b. Net method used:

   (1) Cost of goods sold.

   (2) Ending inventory.

c. Repeat part *a* on the assumption that payment was made after the discount period had passed.

d. Repeat part *b* on the assumption that payment was made after the discount period had passed.

e. Which method is preferable conceptually? Why?

P7.42 Cost of goods sold and inventory (*Published with permission of CGA Canada*). The following data were taken from Karen Morgan's (a proprietorship) income statement for the year ended December 31.

360

Sales	$360,000
Sales returns	2,400
Sales discounts	4,800
Inventory January 1	96,000
Purchases	228,000
Purchases returns	1,200
Purchase discounts	3,600
Transportation-in	7,200
Gross profit (gross margin)	112,800
Net loss	9,600

Required:

a. Calculate the cost of goods sold. Show all calculations.

b. Calculate the total operating expenses. Show all calculations.

c. Calculate the inventory on December 31. Show all calculations.

d. Did Karen Morgan use a perpetual or periodic inventory system? Explain.

P7.43 Income statement (*Published with permission of CGA Canada*). The following information pertains to McGraw Co.:

Cash received from customers during the year	$75,300
Cash paid for merchandise during the year	50,400
Inventory, December 31, 1995	12,000
Inventory, December 31, 1996	9,000
Inventory taken for personal use	1,500
Amortization expense	4,000
Accounts payable, December 31, 1995	14,400
Accounts payable, December 31, 1996	11,100
Accounts receivable, December 31, 1995	9,200
Accounts receivable, December 31, 1996	9,600
Other expenses	16,000

Required:

Prepare a partial income statement up to the gross profit.

P7.44 Inventory transactions (*Published with permission of CGA Canada*). The following transactions relate to the records of Xiaofei Company. The company uses the periodic inventory system and the net method for recording merchandise purchases but records sales at gross. The purchase terms are 2/10, net/30.

Nov. 1 Sold merchandise for $1,200 to Brent, Ltd., of Kitchener.   *Cost 600*
3 Purchased merchandise listed at $1,000 from Riddle Co.
7 Returned merchandise listed at $100 to Riddle Co.
13 Paid amount due to Riddle Co.
15 Purchased merchandise from Rosson Co. listed at $600.
17 Purchased office equipment from Riddle Co. for $1,500, no discount terms.
18 Paid $75 transportation charges on purchase of November 17.
30 Paid amount due to Rosson Co.

Required:

Record the transactions for Xiaofei Company.

P7.45 Accounting for inventory (*Published with permission of CGA Canada*). Grude Company began the year with a merchandise inventory of $60,000 ($6 × 10,000 units). The company purchased another 150,000 units of merchandise and had sales totalling $995,000. Merchandise purchases consisted of three separate acquisitions of the same quantity at approximately four-month intervals. This merchandise was in great demand and Grude was faced with a 5 percent rise in costs with each purchase. The ending merchandise inventory consisted of 14,000 units.

Required:

Note: Round all calculations to two decimal places.

a. Calculate the cost of the ending inventory using FIFO.

b. Calculate the cost of the ending inventory using LIFO.

c. Calculate the cost of the ending inventory using the weighted-average costing method.

d. Suppose that it was discovered that there was an error in the calculation of the beginning inventory. The correct figure was $60,000 but it was shown on the books as $66,000. How would this error have affected income before taxes in the current year and the previous year.

e. Prepare a journal entry for December 31 that would correct the error referred to in part *d*. Assume that the adjusting entries and closing entries have not been made. Briefly explain how your journal entry accomplishes the correction.

P7.46 Accounting for inventory (*Published with permission of CGA Canada*). Spruce, Ltd., began operation on January 1, 1994. Merchandise purchases and alternative inventory valuation for the first three years of operations are summarized below:

	1994	1995	1996
Purchases	$150,000	$175,000	$190,000
Ending inventory:			
LIFO	55,000	48,000	51,000
FIFO	53,000	46,500	54,000
Lower of cost or market	49,000	44,000	54,000

Required:

a. Under which inventory method would the highest net income be reported in 1994? Explain.

b. Under which inventory method would the highest net income be reported in 1995? Explain.

c. Under which inventory method would the highest net income be reported in 1996? Explain.

d. Were prices stable in 1994? Explain.

e. Were prices stable in 1996? Explain.

f. Under the periodic inventory method, what journal entry would be recorded in 1996 for the merchandise purchases?

g. Under the perpetual inventory method, what journal entry would be recorded in 1996 for the merchandise purchases?

h. Under the perpetual inventory method, show how a $300 sale of merchandise, which had cost the company $180, would be recorded.

P7.47 Inventory errors (*Published with permission of CGA Canada*). Mealiea Company reported a net income for 1995 of $75,000 and an ending retained earnings balance of $210,000. The ending merchandise balance on December 31, 1995, for Mealiea Company was $34,700. As the company accountant you discover the following additional information:

1. Merchandise on consignment to Rica Company amounting to $4,500 was excluded from the ending inventory in error.

2. Merchandise on consignment from Duffy Company of $8,000 was included in the ending inventory in error.

3. Purchases in transit of $3,000 were included in the ending inventory. They were shipped on December 31, the last day of Mealiea's fiscal year.

4. Purchases in transit of $1,400 from Brooks, Ltd., were included in the ending inventory.

Required:

a. Determine the correct ending inventory balance at December 31, 1995.

b. Determine the correct net income for 1995.

c. If no errors had been discovered, state whether the net income and retained earnings balances for 1995 and 1996 would be overstated (O), understated (U), or would have no effect (NE).

P7.48 Inventory transactions, income statement (*Published with permission of CGA Canada*). James Company uses the periodic inventory method and records purchases of merchandise at net but records sales at gross. The company began with an opening inventory balance of $33,000 and ended with an inventory of $50,000. The net realizable value of accounts receivable was $32,000 and the allowance for doubtful accounts amounted to $1,200 as of December 31. The following transactions relate to January.

1. Cash sales of merchandise were $180,000.

2. Credit sales were $410,000, terms 2/10, net 30.

3. Cash collections amounted to $339,000 of which $45,000 had been collected after the discount period.

4. Returns granted to customers amounted to $2,000.

5. The $1,500 accounts receivable of I. V. Leeg, the vice-president of a local university, was written off.

6. James Company purchased merchandise listed at $260,000. Terms were 2/10, net 30.

7. Merchandise listed at $2,500 was returned to suppliers during the discount period.

8. Wrote cheques totalling $210,000 to merchandise creditors. Of this amount, $27,000 was paid for after the discount period.

9. An aging analysis on January 31 estimated bad debts to be $3,800.

Required:

a. Prepare journal entries for the above transactions.

b. Prepare a partial income statement.

P7.49 Ratio analysis, ethical issues.

a. Using the financial information from Exhibit 7.3, determine average days' inventory on hand using the different cost-flow assumptions.

b. Discuss the ethical issues of selecting an appropriate inventory method.

P7.50 Average days' inventory on hand. The financial statements of Kamloops Kamping, Ltd., include total sales of $765,000 and cost of goods sold of $441,000 for the current year and an average inventory for the year of $97,000.

a. Explain the impact each of the following transactions would have on the company's average days' inventory on hand:

(**1**) Earned additional sales revenue of $379,000 at a gross profit margin of 40 percent.

(**2**) Average inventory increased by $11,000.

(**3**) Made payments on account of $39,000.

b. As a result of the above transactions, is the organization in a better or worse financial position?

P7.51 Turnover analysis. The partial income statement of Rider Company, Ltd., for the year ended July 31 is shown below:

Sales	$7,732,000
Cost of sales	4,581,000
Gross profit	$3,151,000

The accounts receivable turnover ratio for the period is 5.88. The inventory turnover ratio for the same period is 4.62. Determine the average Accounts Receivable and Inventory balances for the period.

7.13 CASES

C7.1 Inventory disclosures. Presented below is the inventory footnote taken from a recent Merck & Co., Inc., annual report. When necessary, assume a 40 percent corporate income tax rate.

Merck & Co., Inc. and Subsidiaries Notes to Financial Statements
Substantially all domestic inventories are valued using the last-in, first-out method (LIFO). Remaining inventories are valued at the lower of first-in, first-out (FIFO) cost or market.

(in millions)

	1996	1995
Inventories at December 31 consisted of:		
Finished goods	$359.6	$299.5
Raw materials and work in process	343.0	335.1
Supplies	46.4	41.5
Total (approximate current cost)	749.0	676.1
Reduction to LIFO cost	89.4	96.3
	$659.6	$579.8

Inventories valued at LIFO composed approximately 46 percent and 42 percent of inventories at December 31, 1996, and 1995, respectively.

Required:

a. What dollar amount for inventories appears in Merck's December 31, 1996, balance sheet?

b. If Merck had used current costs for ending inventory valuation rather than those generated by LIFO:

    (1) What dollar amount would have appeared for inventories in its December 31, 1996, balance sheet?

    (2) To what extent would its December 31, 1996, Retained Earnings balance be different? Higher or lower?

    (3) To what extent would its 1996 net income be different? Higher or lower?

C7.2 Inventory disclosures. The Reynolds Metals annual report contained the following footnote description of its accounting policies with respect to inventories:

Note A — Significant Accounting Policies
Inventories

    Inventories are stated at the lower of cost or market. Cost of inventories of approximately $283 million in 19x2 and $321 million in 19x1 is determined by the last-in, first-out method (LIFO). Remaining inventories of approximately $422 million in 19x2 and $385 million in 19x1 are determined by the average or first-in, first-out (FIFO) methods. If the FIFO method was applied to LIFO inventories, the amount for inventories would increase by approximately $576 million at December 31, 19x2, and $498 million at December 31, 19x1. As a result of LIFO, costs and expenses increased by $78 million in 19x2 and $29 million in 19x1 and decreased by $60 million in 19x0. Included in the total LIFO effect are liquidations of prior year inventories of $26 million in 19x0.

    Since certain inventories of the Company may be sold at various stages of processing, no practical distinction can be made between finished products, in-process products, and other materials, and therefore inventories are presented as a single classification.

Required:

a. What would the balance sheet inventory amounts have been in 19x2 and 19x1 if all inventories had been reported on a FIFO basis?

b. Please explain the significance of using LIFO for some inventories and FIFO for others. Why do you think Reynolds Metals does this?

c. Explain what happened to Reynolds' inventories in 19x0.

d. Suppose Reynolds had always used FIFO for all inventories and assume the company's 19x2 income tax rate was 34 percent. What difference would it have made in its 19x2 income statement? The balance sheet as of December 31, 19x2? The 19x2 statement of changes in financial position?

CHAPTER 8

Capital Assets: Property, Plant, and Equipment; Intangible Assets; and Natural Resources

Objectives

After completing this chapter you will be able to:
1. Describe the measurement and valuation of capital assets.
2. Explain and apply different amortization methods.
3. Record complex transactions for property, plant, and equipment.
4. Apply accounting concepts for intangibles and natural resources.
5. Explain and apply financial statement disclosure for capital assets.

Non-current assets represent the principal long-term revenue-producing assets of most companies. In the case of a manufacturing company, the property, plant, and equipment are used to manufacture the products that are ultimately sold to customers. In the case of a computer software development company, an intangible asset such as a copyright on a computer software package provides the company with the right to the earnings stream associated with the sale of the package. In the case of an oil and gas company, the oil and gas properties or leaseholds the company owns provide it with access to new saleable reserves.

The focus of this chapter is on the analysis and financial reporting issues pertaining to these three types of non-current assets. Two important financial reporting questions characterize the financial management of these assets: What cost should be assigned to the asset (i.e., capitalized to the balance sheet)? How should the asset's cost systematically be expensed (i.e., matched) against the revenues produced by the asset?

8.1 CAPITAL ASSETS AND ALLOCATING COSTS

capital assets
Capital assets are long-lived assets acquired to benefit the organization in the long term.

Capital assets are long-lived assets acquired with the intention of deriving a benefit from their use in an organization rather than from their resale. Capital assets include such property, plant, and equipment as buildings; land used or held as factory and office locations; land improvements such as landscaping, and parking lots; machinery and equipment; office furniture and fixtures; and vehicles.

The primary financial reporting issues associated with capital assets that must be addressed by managers are the following:

1. Determining the cost to be recorded in the balance sheet at the time of acquisition (i.e., the capitalization issue).
2. Determining the annual income statement amortization expense to be reported (i.e., the allocation issue). In this regard, decisions must be made regarding the preferred amortization method, the estimated useful life of the asset, and its estimated residual value.
3. Distinguishing between those capital asset–related expenditures made subsequent to the initial acquisition (e.g., repairs and improvements) that should be expensed when incurred and those that should be capitalized (i.e., added to the asset's reported balance sheet value) and subsequently amortized over future periods.
4. Accounting for the sale or other disposition of the capital asset.

Determining Original Cost: The Capitalization Issue

Capital assets are initially reported in the balance sheet at their original cost (i.e., the outlay of cash or cash equivalents at the date of purchase). "Cost is the amount of consideration given up to acquire, construct, develop, or better a capital asset and includes all costs directly attributable to the acquisition, construction, development or betterment of the capital asset including installing it at the location and in the condition necessary for its intended use" (CICA Handbook 3060.07). Generally, the original acquisition cost of a capital asset includes *all* costs incurred in getting the asset ready for its intended use. For example, surveying costs incurred in obtaining title to a tract of land are a part of the land's acquisition cost. If a tract of land has a building on it that is not needed by the purchaser, the cost of demolishing the building is also a part of the purchaser's cost of the land. In addition, when a company contracts with another party to construct a new building, all costs incurred up to the time the building is turned over to the company are part of its acquisition cost. Such costs are likely to include architect's fees, payments to the contractor, and interest on the funds borrowed to complete the construction of the property. On its financial statements, Cameco Corporation disclosed a note on the capitalization of interest: "Interest is capitalized on expenditures related to construction or development projects actively being prepared for their intended use. Capitalization is discontinued when the asset enters commercial operation or development ceases." The above note follows the recommendations of the CICA Handbook. "The cost of a capital asset that is acquired, constructed, or developed over time includes carrying costs directly attributable to the acquisition, construction, or development activity such as interest costs when the enterprise's accounting policy is to capitalize interest costs" (CICA Handbook 3060.26). "The cost of carrying costs ceases when a capital asset is substantially complete and ready for productive use" (CICA Handbook 3060.27).

In the case of machinery and equipment, the original cost may include the purchase price, freight-in, and the cost of initial installation. "The cost of each capital asset acquired as part of a basket purchase (i.e., when a group of assets is acquired for a single amount), is determined by allocating the price paid for the basket to each item on the basis of its relative fair value at the time of acquisition" (CICA Handbook 3060.20). Basket purchases are common with the acquisition of land and buildings.

An illustration that shows the determination of the cost of capital assets follows. Assume Omar Corporation paid $200,000 for a tract of land that had an old gas station on it. The gas station was demolished at a cost of $10,000, and a new warehouse was constructed at a cost of $250,000. In addition, several other costs were incurred:

Legal fees (for the purchase of the land) $5,000

Architect's fees $18,000

Interest on construction loan $22,000

The value of the land would include the $200,000 cost, the legal fees of $5,000, and the $10,000 cost to demolish the gas station. Assuming all transactions were for cash, Omar Corporation would record the following entry for the acquisition of the land:

```
Land . . . . . . . . . . . . . . . . . . . . . . . . . . . . . . . . . . . . . . . . . . . . . . . 215,000
    Cash . . . . . . . . . . . . . . . . . . . . . . . . . . . . . . . . . . . . . . . . . . . . . . . . . 215,000
    To record purchase of land.
```

(The value of the land is determined as follows: $200,000 + $10,000 + $5,000 = $215,000.)

The entry to acquire the building would include the construction cost of $250,000, plus the architect's fees of $18,000 and the interest on the construction loan of $22,000. Omar Corporation would record the following entry for the building:

```
Building . . . . . . . . . . . . . . . . . . . . . . . . . . . . . . . . . . . . . . . . . . . 290,000
    Cash . . . . . . . . . . . . . . . . . . . . . . . . . . . . . . . . . . . . . . . . . . . . . . . . . 290,000
    To record purchase of building.
```

(The value of the building is determined as follows: $250,000 + $18,000 + $22,000 = $290,000.) It is important to distinguish between the land and the building because only the building will be amortized. The land will not be amortized but will continue to be reported at its original cost until sold.

As an incentive to purchase a particular piece of equipment, sellers often offer discounts to potential purchasers. When a cash discount is received on the purchase of

present value
The value today of a future stream of cash flows calculated by discounting the cash flows at a given rate of interest.

equipment (or any other asset, for that matter), the equipment's cost should be reported net of the discount. Another means to attract potential buyers involves various seller-sponsored financing plans. For example, a buyer's recorded cost when capital assets are bought on an instalment payment basis is not the sum of the total payments to be made but is the **present value** of the instalment obligation (i.e., today's cash-equivalent purchase price) as of the date of purchase. Present value will be discussed in Chapter 9. Capital assets also may be acquired by issuing a company's share capital. In this case, the cash-equivalent value of the issued shares as of the date of the transaction should be used to measure the cost of acquiring the assets. Sometimes an old asset is traded in on a new one (e.g., a used truck for a new one). In such an arrangement, the carrying value of the old asset plus the cash paid for the new one becomes the acquisition cost of the new asset to be reported on the balance sheet.

It is important to note that a popular means by which corporate managers obtain property is to lease it under a long-term, non-cancellable lease. If the lease meets certain criteria, generally accepted accounting principles stipulate the recording of a leasehold right as an asset and a lease obligation as a liability. Under these circumstances, the leased asset would be amortized in the same way as any other capital asset owned by the company, except that the amortization period may be limited by the lease term. A more detailed description of lease accounting is provided in Chapter 10.

The Cost Allocation Issue

The purpose of allocating the cost of a capital asset is to reflect the "using up" of the productive capacity of a company's capital assets and to *match* this cost with the revenues that the capital assets helped generate. The process is nothing more than allocating the cost (i.e., recorded cost less estimated residual value) of a company's capital assets to the accounting periods during which the capital assets are used. This cost allocation or amortizing of capital assets is, however, *not* intended to establish a market valuation process for the capital assets.

The periodic amount of capital asset cost allocated to the income statement is called *amortization expense* and serves to reduce the net income of the period. In determining a given period's amortization expense, corporate financial managers must assess the useful lives and residual values of the capital assets, as well as select a rational and systematic method to allocate the costs of the capital assets over their respective estimated useful lives. These three management decisions (i.e., useful life, residual value, and amortization method) involve considerable discretion and judgment and may frequently have a significant financial effect on a company's reported earnings. Each of these decisions is discussed at length in the following sections. Sometimes the business use of the term *property, plant, and equipment* is meant to include the land owned by a company on which its plant, offices, loading terminals, and so forth are built. In such circumstances, even though the gross dollar amount reported for capital assets on the balance sheet may include the cost of land, such costs are *not* amortizable. In such circumstances, land is not viewed as being "used up" and therefore is not amortized.)

Throughout the ensuing discussion, it is important to remember that it is possible that a capital asset that has been fully amortized in the accounting records may still be an integral part of a company's operations and/or may be sold to another company at a significant price. It is also important to note that the value in the accounting records does *not* approximate an asset's fair market value, nor is it intended to.

The focus of this chapter is on the three types of capital assets: property, plant, and equipment; intangible assets; and natural resources. The cost allocation for each of these assets is conceptually the same. However, the terminology for the cost allocation process varies as summarized in the following table. Although the recommended terminology is **amortization**, the terms *depreciation* and *amortization* are frequently used interchangeably. *Depletion* is a term commonly used to describe the cost allocation of natural resources.

amortization
The cost allocation of a capital asset.

Cost Allocation Terminology

Capital Assets	Term
Property, plant, and equipment	Depreciation
Intangible assets	Amortization
Natural resources	Depletion

Useful Life

useful life
The estimated productive life of a noncurrent asset.

"**Useful life** is the estimate of either the period over which a capital asset, or component thereof, is expected to be used by an enterprise; or the number of production or similar units that can be obtained from the capital asset by the enterprise" (CICA Handbook 3060.17). In estimating the useful lives of various capital assets, managers must consider the manner in which the assets are expected to be used and maintained. Generally, useful lives are established based on the assumption that normal repairs and maintenance will be made to keep the assets in good operating condition. In situations in which maintenance programs deviate from what is considered normal, estimated useful lives should be adjusted accordingly.

physical life
Length of time an asset can reasonably be expected to last before it physically wears out.

The two primary factors that managers should consider when estimating useful lives of their capital assets are physical life and technological life. **Physical life** refers to the length of time an asset can reasonably be expected to last before it physically wears out. When physical life is influenced more by the passage of time than by use (e.g., for a building) or when it is difficult to assess the level of usage, useful life is usually expressed in terms of years. When physical life is influenced more by use (e.g., for a machine or a vehicle) than by the passage of time, useful life is often expressed in terms of expected output (e.g., units produced or kilometres driven).

technological life
Length of time an asset can reasonably be expected to generate economic benefits before it becomes obsolete.

For a great many capital assets, the concept of technological life has a greater relevance to managers in estimating useful life than does physical life. **Technological life** refers to the length of time an asset can reasonably be expected to generate economic benefits before it becomes obsolete. Two types of obsolescence must be considered: product obsolescence and process obsolescence. Product obsolescence pertains to the market lives of the products that are produced by the capital assets. For example, auto manufacturers normally amortize tooling costs over two or three years because of the product obsolescence brought about by frequent model changes even though the physical life of the tooling equipment may be many more years. Process obsolescence pertains to the capital asset item itself becoming obsolete because of subsequent technological improvements. For example, the useful lives of computer equipment have generally been set with the expectation that process obsolescence would occur prior to the time the equipment was physically worn out.

It is important to note that this discussion of estimating useful lives of capital assets pertains solely to financial reporting. As discussed in a later section of this chapter, Revenue Canada specifies its own useful life rules for federal income tax purposes.

Residual Value

residual value
The expected value
of the asset at the
end of its estimated
useful life.

salvage value
The amount that is
expected to be
recovered from the
sale of an asset at
the end of its total
life.

Once the useful life of the capital asset has been estimated, the next step is to estimate the asset's residual value. "**Residual value** is the estimated net realizable value of a capital asset at the end of its estimated useful life to an enterprise" (CICA Handbook 3060.14). An asset's residual value should not be confused with an asset's salvage value. "**Salvage value** is the estimated net realizable value of a capital asset at the end of its life. Salvage value is normally negligible" (CICA Handbook 3060.15). For example, an organization may purchase an automobile for $30,000. A decision is made to use the vehicle for three years and then trade it in on a new vehicle. Assume the vehicle's residual value is estimated at $17,000 at the end of its useful life of three years. Another organization may acquire the *same* $30,000 automobile and decide to use the vehicle for *10* years. The residual value of the vehicle to the second organization may be estimated at only $4,000 at the end of its useful life of 10 years. In either case, the salvage value of the automobile at the end of its total life would probably be only a few hundred dollars.

8.2 AMORTIZATION METHODS

For financial reporting purposes, management has a choice of several generally accepted methods for allocating the depreciable cost of capital assets over an asset's estimated useful life. The common element among these alternatives is that they each result in a rational, systematic process of cost allocation.

Straight-Line Method

straight-line method
A method to
amortize the cost of
a capital asset, in
which the cost
allocation is constant
over the life of the
asset.

When the **straight-line method** is used, the annual amortization expense is determined by dividing the depreciable cost of an asset by its estimated life. The depreciable cost is the original cost less the estimated residual value.

$$\text{Straight-line method: Amortization} = \frac{\text{Cost} - \text{Residual value}}{\text{Estimated useful life}}$$

For example, consider an asset with an original cost of $10,000, an estimated residual value of $400 (and thus a depreciable cost of $9,600), and an estimated useful life of five years. Under straight-line amortization, the depreciable cost of $9,600 is divided by 5 to give an annual amortization figure of $1,920 for *each* of the five years of the asset's estimated useful life.

Declining-Balance Method

declining balance
method
A method to
amortize the cost of
a tangible asset in
which the allocated
cost is greater in the
early periods of the
asset's life (i.e., an
accelerated method).

net book value.
The net book value
is the total cost of an
asset less the
accumulated
amortization.

The **declining-balance method** is a cost allocation method that applies a fixed percentage to the net book value of the asset. The **net book value** is the total cost of the asset less the accumulated amortization. The declining-balance method may be referred to as an *accelerated method* of cost allocation, because it allocates larger portions of cost during the early periods of the asset's life. Each year, as more amortization is accumulated, the net book value of the asset declines, and each period's cost allocation becomes smaller. A fixed allocation rate of 45 percent will be used to illustrate the declining-balance method. In the first year, amortization would be $4,500 (.45 × 10,000). The net book value of the asset at the end of the first year would be $5,500, the cost of the asset, $10,000, less accumulated amortization of $4,500. In Year 2, amortization would be 45 percent of the net book value of $5,500, or $2,475.

This process would continue until $9,600 has been accumulated in amortization and the net book value of the asset equals its estimated residual value of $400. As indicated in Exhibit 8.1. The allocation for the final year would normally need to be adjusted to ensure the net book value equals the residual value of $400.

Declining-balance method: Amortization = Fixed rate (%) × Net book value

The *double*-declining-balance method determines amortization in a manner very similar to the declining-balance method. The only difference is the allocation rate that is used. The **double-declining-balance method** requires the calculation of the straight-line percentage rate (i.e., $1/n$), which is then doubled, and applied each year to the capital assets's decreasing **net book value** (i.e., recorded cost less amortization taken to date). The amount of amortization taken to date for a particular asset is often referred to as the asset's *accumulated amortization*. Residual value is ignored in determining net book value, but the recording of amortization expense should *stop* when the asset's net book value *equals* its residual value.

double-declining-balance amortization
A method of calculating amortization by which a percentage equal to twice the straight-line percentage is multiplied by the declining book value to determine the amortization expense for the period.

$$\text{Double-declining-balance method: Amortization} = \frac{1}{\text{Estimated useful Life}} \times 2 \times \text{Net book value}$$

Consider again an asset with an original cost of $10,000, residual value of $400, and an estimated life of five years. The straight-line percentage rate is 20 percent (i.e., 1/5 years) and the double-declining-balance rate is 40 percent (i.e., 2/5). Thus, under the double-declining-balance method, amortization is 40 percent of $10,000, or $4,000 for the first year; 40 percent of $6,000 (i.e., $10,000 less $4,000), or $2,400, for the second year; 40 percent of $3,600 (i.e., $10,000 less $6,400), or $1,440, for the third year, and so on. When the accumulated amortization recorded for this asset reaches $9,600, its amortization expensing stops. As indicated in Exhibit 8.1, only $9,222 of amortization has been accumulated by the end of Year 5. The allocation for the final year would need to be adjusted to ensure the net book value equals the residual value of $400. Therefore Year 5 amortization should be increased by $378 ($9,600 − $9,222) to $896 ($518 + $378).

Sum-of-the-Years'-Digits Method

Just as the double-declining-balance method results in the recording of larger amortization expense amounts in the early years of an asset's life (referred to as an *acceleration method of amortization*), so also does the **sum-of-the-years'-digits (SYD) method**. Under this method, declining fractions are applied to the asset's depreciable cost. The denominator of the fraction is the sum of the digits of the years of useful life [i.e., SYD = $n(n +1)/2$]. The numerator is the number of years of useful life remaining, including the present year. The only rationale behind the mechanics of the SYD method is that it is systematic and results in higher amortization expense amounts earlier in an asset's life than under the straight-line method.

sum-of-the-years'-digits method
A method to amortize the cost of a capital asset in which the allocated cost is greater in the early periods of the asset's life (i.e., an accelerated method).

$$\text{Sum-of-the-Years'-Digits Method: Amortization} = \frac{(\text{Cost} - \text{Residual value}) \times \text{number of useful years remaining}}{\text{Sum of the digits of the useful life}}$$

Consider again an asset costing $10,000 with an estimated residual value of $400, a depreciable cost of $9,600, and an estimated life of five years. The sum of the years' digits (1, 2, 3, 4, and 5) is 15. Hence, amortization expense for the first year is 5/15 of

$9,600, or $3,200; for the second year, it is 4/15 of $9,600, or $2,560; for the third year it is 3/15 of $9,600, or $1,920, and so on.

accelerated amortization
A cost allocation method in which amortization deductions are largest in an asset's earlier years, but decrease over time.

The declining-balance method, and the sum-of-the-years'-digits methods are generally referred to as **accelerated methods** of amortization. The phenomenon captured by accelerated amortization methods is that more amortization expense is recorded in the early years of an asset's life as compared to the amount that would be recorded under the straight-line method. Two reasons frequently given for using accelerated methods are (1) that the asset is more useful in its earlier years because it is more efficient and less subject to obsolescence then, and (2) that repairs and maintenance complement the accelerated amortization over the useful life of the asset because repair and maintenance expenses are normally greater in later years. This latter notion may be more clearly understood through the following graphic representation:

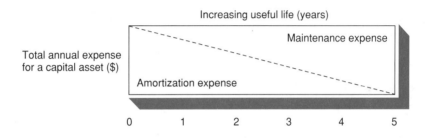

Physical-Unit Methods

machine-hour method
A cost allocation method based on the number of hours a machine is used each period.

Machine-hour method. The number of hours a machine is to be used during its useful life is often a better basis for determining amortization expense than the mere passage of time (years). Under the machine-hour method, amortization expense is determined according to the number of hours the asset is actually used during an accounting period relative to the total estimated number of hours it can ultimately be used (i.e., the usage or productivity rate):

Machine-hour method:
Amortization = (Cost − Residual value) $\times \dfrac{\text{Actual machine hours used}}{\text{Estimated total machine hours}}$

Referring again to the asset with a cost of $10,000, an estimated residual of $400, and a depreciable cost of $9,600, its estimated lifetime hours are 19,200, and the hours actually used during the first year are 1,800. The depreciable cost of $9,600 divided by the total hours of 19,200 yields $.50 to be allocated to each hour of use. Amortization expense for the first year on this machine is therefore $900 (1,800 times $.50 per hour of use).

units-of-production method
A cost allocation method based on the number of units produced each period.

units-of-production method. This method is conceptually similar to the machine-hour method except that an estimate is made of the number of units to be produced by a machine during its useful life. Amortization expense for a period is then determined according to the number of units actually produced during the period relative to the estimated lifetime potential of the machine.

Units-of-production method
Amortization = (Cost − Residual value) $\times \dfrac{\text{Actual unit produced}}{\text{Estimated total units to be produced}}$

EXHIBIT 8.1

Amortization Methods

Year	Straight-Line Method	Declining-Balance Method	Double-Declining-Balance Method	Sum-of-the-Years'-Digits Method	Machine-Hour Method	Units-of-Production Method
1	$1,920	$4,500	$4,000	$3,200	$ 900	$1,000
2	1,920	2,475	2,400	2,560	2,700	3,200
3	1,920	1,361	1,440	1,920	2,050	2,200
4	1,920	749	864	1,280	2,050	1,800
5	1,920	315*	896*	640	1,900	1,400
	$9,600	$9,600	$9,600	$9,600	$9,600	$9,600

Assumptions: A machine with an original cost of $10,000 is estimated to have a useful life of five years and an estimated residual value of $400; the machine is assumed to be operated for the following number of hours, producing the following number of units:

Year	Hours Operated	Units Produced
1	1,800	5,000
2	5,400	16,000
3	4,100	11,000
4	4,100	9,000
5	3,800	7,000
	19,200	48,000

*Amortization is adjusted in the final year to ensure accumulated amortization does not exceed $9,600.

Again using the example of an asset with a cost of $10,000 and an estimated residual value of $400, assume that its projected units of production are 48,000. The asset's depreciable cost of $9,600 divided by 48,000 units yields $.20 amortization expense per unit produced. Thus, if in its first year of use, 5,000 units are produced, the amortization expense for that year is $1,000.

Exhibit 8.1 summarizes the results of the six amortization method examples. Note the variability across the different methods for any given year. In spite of this variability, however, the *total* amortization expense reported over the life of an asset must be the same under each of the methods. Thus, it can be seen that the financial reporting of amortization is fundamentally a decision concerning the *timing* as to when an asset's cost is systematically allocated to the income statement in the form of amortization expense to reflect the cost of using the asset.

The accounting entry to record the annual amortization expense on an asset appears as follows:

```
Amortization Expense. . . . . . . . . . . . . . . . . . . . . . . . . . . . . . . . .  4,000
     Accumulated Amortization . . . . . . . . . . . . . . . . . . . . . . . . . . . .        4,000
     To record the adjusting entry for amortization.
```

Capital Cost Allowance

capital cost allowance
Amortization for income tax purposes is called capital cost allowance (CCA).

Amortization for income tax purposes is not even called *amortization*, but referred to as **capital cost allowance** (CCA). Capital cost allowance is similar to the declining-balance method previously described. Capital cost allowance is calculated using preset rates established by Revenue Canada, applied to the net book value of a class or group of assets. Depreciable assets are grouped into particular classes using guidelines set by Revenue Canada. Each class is assigned a CCA rate to be applied each tax year. Only capital cost allowance is allowable for income tax purposes. Straight-line amortization and the other methods previously illustrated are *not* allowed for income tax purposes. Amortization and capital cost allowances are discussed in further detail in Chapter 10.

Selection of an Amortization Method

The selection of an amortization method is similar to the selection of other accounting policy alternatives. Amortization is an expense, and like other expenses has a cause-and-effect relationship with revenues. Therefore, the *matching principle* should strongly influence the selection of an amortization method.

> Different methods of amortizing a capital asset result in different patterns of charges to income. The objective is to provide a rational and systematic basis for allocating the amortizable amount of a capital asset over its estimated and useful life. A straight line method reflects a constant charge for the service as a function of usage. Other methods may be appropriate in certain circumstances. For example, . . . a decreasing charge method may be appropriate when the operating efficiency of the capital asset declines over time. (CICA Handbook 3060.35)

The selection of accounting policies may have a smoothing or window-dressing effect in the short term. However, over the long term, there is no effect on income or asset values.

8.3 ACCOUNTING FOR AMORTIZATION

Amortization as a Product Cost

The amortization allocated to each accounting period may be charged, in part, against net income as a period expense (as has already been discussed) and, in part, as a product cost to work in process inventory as manufacturing overhead (see Chapter 7). To the extent that the amortization costs are incurred "under the factory roof" (i.e., are a part of the costs of manufacturing a product), management should capitalize them as a product cost by increasing the Work in Process Inventory account instead of recording amortization expense on the income statement. If added to Work in Process Inventory, the amortization will become a deduction in the income statement only when the finished goods with which it is associated are sold and an accounting entry for the cost of goods sold is made.

Changes in Accounting Policy

> Accounting policies encompass the specific principles and the methods used in their application that are selected by an enterprise in preparing financial statements. There is a general assumption that the accounting policies followed by an enterprise are consistent within each accounting period and from one accounting period to the next. A change in an accounting policy may be made, however, . . . if it is considered that the change would result in a more appropriate presentation of events or transactions in the financial statements of the enterprise. (CICA Handbook 1506.02)

change in accounting policy
A change in accounting policy may be made if it is considered that the change would result in a more appropriate presentation of events or transactions in the financial statements of the enterprise. (CICA Handbook 1506.02).

Changes in accounting policy may involve changes in inventory costing methods, for example, from LIFO to FIFO, or changes in amortization methods. During the course of amortizing either a particular asset or an entire array of capital assets, corporate financial managers may decide to modify or adjust their initial estimates and decisions underlying the calculation of amortization. For example, a change in the amortization method from the double-declining-balance method to the straight-line method might be undertaken because other similar companies are predominantly using the straight-line method. In this case, the decision to change amortization methods is probably motivated by management's desire to appear to be using the industry-preferred method, as well as a desire to improve the firm's within-industry comparative financial standing. When such a change in accounting method is made, its cumulative effect is recorded in the current financial statements, and all subsequent financial statements reflect the use of the new method.

To illustrate such a change, consider again the data presented in Exhibit 8.1. Assume, for example, that in Year 3 a change from the double-declining-balance (DDB) method to the straight-line method is to be made. Through the end of Year 2, amortization totalling $6,400 ($4,000 + $2,400) has been taken under the DDB method, whereas if the straight-line method had been used, only $3,840 ($1,920 × 2) in amortization deductions would have been recorded. Thus, at the beginning of Year 3, an entry to restate the Accumulated Amortization account balance would be needed as follows:

```
Accumulated Amortization ($6,400 – $3,840) . . . . . . . . . . . . . . . .   2,560
    Retained Earnings . . . . . . . . . . . . . . . . . . . . . . . . . . . . . . . . . . .        2,560
    To restate prior periods' amortization for the change in amortization methods.
```

Changes in accounting policy should be applied retroactively when possible. Therefore, as illustrated in the above entry, the adjustment is made to prior years' amortization by adjusting the Retained Earnings account. In other circumstances, the information necessary to properly adjust prior years may not be available. In such cases, it is permissible to adjust only future years. In all cases a footnote should be provided to explain the basis of the change in accounting policy. In addition to the above entry to reflect the change in amortization method, the regular Year 3 amortization expense under the new method also needs to be recorded:

```
Amortization Expense . . . . . . . . . . . . . . . . . . . . . . . . . . . . . . . .   1,920
    Accumulated Amortization . . . . . . . . . . . . . . . . . . . . . . . . . . . . .        1,920
    To record amortization for the period.
```

accumulated amortization
A contra account used to accumulate the cost allocation of a capital asset.

A T-account for **accumulated amortization** is provided to illustrate the changes in amortization over the first three

Accumulated Amortization

		Year 1	4,000
		Year 2	2,400
Adjustment	2,560	Balance	6,400
		Adjusted balance	3,840
		Year 3	1,920
		Balance	5,760

"For each change in accounting policy in the current period, the following information should be disclosed:
(a) a description of the change; and

(b) the effect of the change on the financial statements of the current period" (CICA Handbook 1506.16). The Ford Motor Company of Canada, Limited, disclosed a change in accounting policy in a footnote in its annual report:

Fixed assets

The method of determining amortization was changed from declining balance to straight-line for assets acquired after December 31, 1992. For assets acquired prior to January 1, 1993, amortization continues to be determined on the declining balance method until these assets are completely amortized. The impact of adopting straight-line for assets acquired in 1993 reduced amortization by approximately $4 million compared to using the declining balance method.

Change in Accounting Estimate

Changes in estimates used in accounting are the necessary consequences of the periodic preparation of financial statements. Estimating, of course, requires the exercise of judgement and reappraisal as new events occur, as more experience is acquired, or as additional information is obtained. Examples of items for which estimates are necessary include doubtful accounts receivable, inventory obsolescence, the service lives and residual values of depreciable assets. (CICA Handbook 1506.22)

change in accounting estimate
An amortization-related change involves the estimated useful life of an asset or a group of assets.

An amortization-related change often made by financial managers involves the estimated useful life of an asset or a group of assets. This is referred to as a **change in accounting estimate**. This type of change involves a change in the *estimate* rather than in the *method* and is dealt with on a prospective, or future, basis.

Using the amortization data from Exhibit 8.1, again, if in Year 3 management decided that the expected *total* useful life of the asset being amortized was really eight years instead of five, *no* accounting entry would be required to restate the previous amortization deductions. Instead, all future amortization deductions would be based on an estimated total life of eight, not five years. Therefore, at the end of Year 2, the asset would have a *remaining* life of six years (8 −2), and not three years (5 −2) as based on the original estimated life of five years. Thus, an estimated change such as this does not affect prior published financial statements but only *future* reported results. Using the information from Exhibit 8.1, the asset had an original cost of $10,000 with a residual value of $400. Assuming use of the straight-line method, at the end of the second year, $3,840 would have been accumulated in the Amortization account (2 × $1,920). If the useful life of the asset is revised, it will normally cause the residual value of the asset to be changed as well. If the asset's life is now estimated at eight years, it is assumed its *new* residual value is only $160. The amortization for Year 3 would be calculated as follows:

$$\text{Amortization} = \frac{\text{Net book value} - \textit{New} \text{ residual value}}{\text{Number of years remaining}}$$

The net book value of the asset $6,160 ($10,000 − $3,840), less the new residual value of $160, provides a *new* cost to be allocated of $6,000. When the $6,000 cost is allocated over the remaining life of six years, amortization of $1,000 per year is determined using the straight-line method.

Amortization = $10,000 − $3,840
= $6,160 − $160
= $6,000 (new cost to be allocated)/ Remaining life of 6 years
= $1,000 per year.

Since the life of the asset has been extended, the annual amortization rate has decreased from $1,920 to $1,000 per year. A T-account for accumulated amortization is provided to illustrate the changes in amortization over the life of the asset, as a result of the change in accounting estimate:

Accumulated Amortization

Year 1	1,920
Year 2	1,920
Balance	3,840
Year 3	1,000
Year 4	1,000
Year 5	1,000
Year 6	1,000
Year 7	1,000
Year 8	1,000
Balance	9,840

At the end of Year 8, a total of $9,840 has been recorded in the Accumulated Amortization account. This achieves the desired result: The net book value of the asset of $160 ($10,000 – $9,840) is equal to the residual value of the asset at the end of its estimated useful life.

When accounting method or estimate changes are undertaken by management, the effect of the change on the current financial statements must be described in the company's footnotes. Presented below are such note disclosures:

ABC Company:

Accounting Change
Effective January 1, 1996 for certain network equipment, ABC changed its method of amortization from straight-line to sum-of-the-years' digits, shortened the estimated depreciable lives and decreased the estimated net residual. These changes were implemented to better match revenues and expenses because of rapid technological changes occurring in response to customer requirements and competition. The new amortization method was applied retroactively to all digital circuit, digital operator services and radio equipment. Other network equipment, principally light guide cable and central office buildings, continues to be amortized on a straight-line basis. The changes in estimates of depreciable lives and net residual were made prospectively. The effect of these changes on 1996 results was to decrease net income by approximately $393 million or $.36 per share. The cumulative prior years' effect of the change in amortization method was not material.

Québec-Telephone:

Depreciation
Depreciation of telecommunications property is mainly calculated according to the straight-line method using rates based on the estimated service life of the assets. Estimates as to the service life of telecommunications properties are revised periodically on the basis of studies conducted for that purpose by the company.

XYZ Company:

Depreciation and Amortization
In the third quarter of 1996, the Company revised the estimated service lives of its plants and equipment and special tools retroactive to January 1, 1996. These revisions, which were based on 1996 studies of actual useful lives and periods of use, recognized current estimates of service lives of the assets and had the effect of reducing 1996 amortization charges by $1,236 million or $1.28 per share.

The accounting for changes in accounting policy and estimates can become technically quite involved. An intermediate accounting text should be consulted for additional clarification. The basic concepts have been illustrated to emphasize the impact such changes may have on the financial statements. It is important users carefully examine the notes accompanying annual reports to gain a better understanding of the firm's operations during the accounting period.

8.4 ACCOUNTING FOR CAPITAL ASSETS

Repairs, Maintenance, and Betterments

betterment
An expenditure that extends the useful life or productive capability of an asset and that is capitalized to the balance sheet as an asset.

Costs incurred for the purpose of maintaining the *existing* service level of capital assets are classified as repairs and maintenance and should be treated by managers as expenses of the period in which they are incurred. Costs incurred to improve an asset beyond its original service potential are viewed as betterments and should be capitalized rather than expensed in the period incurred. "The cost incurred to enhance the service potential of a capital asset is a **betterment**. Service potential may be enhanced when there is an increase in the previously assessed physical output or service capacity, associated operating costs lowered, the life or useful life is extended, or the quality of output improved" (CICA Handbook 3060.29). Capitalizing betterments increases an asset's book value because their costs are added to the asset's original recorded cost. The capitalized cost is subsequently expensed over future periods as an additional component of amortization.

To illustrate the accounting for repairs and betterments, we will again make use of the asset and amortization amounts from Exhibit 8.1. Each year the company performs regular maintenance inspections on all its assets. The cost of these inspections is $900 per year. Such costs are *expensed* annually as illustrated in the following journal entry:

```
Repairs Expense . . . . . . . . . . . . . . . . . . . . . . . . . . . . . . . . . . . . 900
    Cash, Accounts Payable, etc. . . . . . . . . . . . . . . . . . . . . . . . . . .        900
    To record maintenance costs for the period.
```

The asset is used, maintained, and amortized for the first three years. At the start of the fourth year, an expenditure of $3,000 is incurred, which improves the service potential of the asset. As a result of the improved service potential, the estimated useful life of the asset is *increased by two years*, for a total useful life of seven years. The expenditure should be treated as a betterment, with the $3,000 *added to the original cost* of the asset. The following journal entry would be recorded:

```
Asset . . . . . . . . . . . . . . . . . . . . . . . . . . . . . . . . . . . . . . . . . . . . . 3,000
    Cash . . . . . . . . . . . . . . . . . . . . . . . . . . . . . . . . . . . . . . . . . . . .        3,000
    To record the betterment.
```

The betterment increases the net book value of the asset and the cost to be allocated over its remaining life. The accounting for betterments frequently involves the change in estimated life of the capital asset. To determine the new amortization rate, a calculation similar to the one previously illustrated for changes in accounting estimates is required:

$$\text{Amortization} = \frac{\text{Net book value} - \text{New residual value}}{\text{Number of years remaining}}$$

The asset had been amortized three years at $1,920 per year, assuming use of the straight-line method. The *adjusted* cost of $13,000 ($10,000 + $3,000), less three years accumulated amortization of \$5,760 (\$1,920 × 3), determines the new book value of the asset to be \$7,240. Assuming the residual value remains *unchanged* at \$400, the new cost to be allocated is \$6,840 (\$7,240 − \$400). The cost to be allocated is allocated over the *new* remaining life of four years (5 + 2 −3). The new remaining life consists of the original five years, plus the two years added by the betterment, less the three years *prior* to the betterment. Therefore, the new amortization rate would be \$1,710 per year. (\$6,840/4 years). The entry for Year 4's amortization is shown below:

```
Amortization Expense. . . . . . . . . . . . . . . . . . . . . . . . . . . . . . . . .  1,710
     Accumulated Amortization . . . . . . . . . . . . . . . . . . . . . . . . . . . . .        1,710
   To record amortization for Year 4.
```

A T-account for accumulated amortization and the asset is provided to illustrate the changes in amortization and the asset account as a result of the betterment.

Asset			Accumulated Amortization		
Year 1	10,000			Year 1	1,920
				Year 2	1,920
				Year 3	1,920
				Balance	5,760
Year 4	3,000			Year 4	1,710
	13,000			Balance	7,470

Distinguishing between an ordinary repair or maintenance expenditure and an asset betterment expenditure is difficult in many instances. For both financial accounting and income tax purposes, management's rationale for a particular expenditure and the nature of the asset alteration itself are important factors in determining whether the expenditure is properly recorded as a repair/maintenance expense item or as a betterment item. For example, servicing the engines of a fleet of trucks every 5,000 kilometres represents a normal maintenance expense, but rebuilding the engines after 100,000 kilometres of use represents a betterment expenditure because the life of the asset has been extended.

The reporting of these asset-related expenditures should attempt to reflect the intended purpose of the expenditure. For financial reporting purposes, managers generally argue for capitalizing such expenditures in order to keep current reported profits as high as possible (by reducing the current level of deductions against net income). For tax purposes, however, the greatest benefit is achieved by expensing as many of these capital asset–related expenditures in the current period as is permitted. Once again, this situation presents another instance about which there may be disagreements between corporate management and Revenue Canada as to what constitutes a repair/maintenance and what constitutes a betterment. It does stand to reason, however, that the logic applied to a particular expenditure would lead to a single classification that should be used for both tax and financial reporting purposes.

Partial Years' Amortization

The acquisition and disposal of capital assets take place throughout the year. To facilitate the recording of these transactions for *financial reporting purposes*, organizations may use the half-year convention required for income tax purposes. As a result, only one-half of the normal amortization is allocated for financial reporting purposes during the *first* and *last* year of the capital asset's useful life.

Organizations producing quarterly or monthly financial statements may wish to amortize capital assets on a monthly basis. Assume the acquisition of equipment for

$135,000 and a residual value of $15,000. On a straight-line basis, assuming a useful life of 10 years, annual amortization would be $12,000 [($135,000 − $15,000)/10 years]. On a monthly basis amortization would be $1,000 (12,000/12 months). The general practice is to assume acquisitions or disposals that occur on the 1st through 15th days of the month are recorded as if they had occurred on the first day of the month. Capital asset transactions occurring on the 16th through 31st of the month are recorded as if they occurred on the first day of the *next* month, for amortization purposes. For example, equipment acquired on March 12, would be assumed to be acquired for amortization purposes on March 1st, and 10 months' amortization would be recorded during the first calendar year. Similarly, a capital asset sold on May 22, would be assumed to be sold on June 1 for amortization purposes. Five months' amortization must be recorded prior to recording the disposal transaction.

Disposition of a Capital Asset: Cash

When a capital asset is sold or otherwise disposed of, both the original cost *and* the associated accumulated amortization must be removed from the accounting records. If the organization has been 100 percent *accurate* in estimating the asset's useful life and its residual value, the proceeds from the disposition would equal the asset's net book value. Using the data from Exhibit 8.1 again, the disposition entry at the end of Year 5 would be:

```
Cash . . . . . . . . . . . . . . . . . . . . . . . . . . . . . . . . . . . . . . . . . . . . . 400
Accumulated Amortization . . . . . . . . . . . . . . . . . . . . . . . . . . . . . 9,600
    Asset . . . . . . . . . . . . . . . . . . . . . . . . . . . . . . . . . . . . . . . . . . .        10,000
        To record the disposal of the capital asset.
```

It is important to note that the Accumulated Amortization account must be brought up to date *prior to* the recording of the disposal entry. Often the disposal of a capital asset occurs at a time other than the end of the accounting period. When this is the case, an adjusting entry must be recorded to recognize the amortization expense up to the disposal date, and to update the Accumulated Amortization account. If this entry is omitted, amortization expense for the period is understated and any gain or loss on disposal of the capital asset is misstated.

If the proceeds from the disposal exceed the asset's net book value (i.e., original cost less accumulated amortization), a gain is recognized. If the asset is sold for an amount *below* its net book value, a *loss on disposal* would be recorded. For example, if the capital asset is sold for $300 cash, the entry to record the sale is as follows:

```
Cash . . . . . . . . . . . . . . . . . . . . . . . . . . . . . . . . . . . . . . . . . . . . . 300
Accumulated Amortization . . . . . . . . . . . . . . . . . . . . . . . . . . . . . 9,600
    Asset . . . . . . . . . . . . . . . . . . . . . . . . . . . . . . . . . . . . . . . . . . .        10,000
Loss on Disposal . . . . . . . . . . . . . . . . . . . . . . . . . . . . . . . . . . . . 100
        To record the disposal of the capital asset.
```

If the capital asset is sold for $1,000 cash, an amount in excess of the asset's net book value, a gain on disposal would be recognized. The entry to record the sale is as follows:

```
Cash . . . . . . . . . . . . . . . . . . . . . . . . . . . . . . . . . . . . . . . . . . . . . 1,000
Accumulated Amortization . . . . . . . . . . . . . . . . . . . . . . . . . . . . . 9,600
    Asset . . . . . . . . . . . . . . . . . . . . . . . . . . . . . . . . . . . . . . . . . . .        10,000
    Gain on Disposal . . . . . . . . . . . . . . . . . . . . . . . . . . . . . . . . . .             600
        To record the disposal of the capital asset.
```

The $600 gain on sale appears on the income statement covering the period in which the sale was made. Consistent with the reporting of gains from the sale of inventory, the gain on the sale of capital assets is reported in the period in which the sales event takes place rather than in the period in which the asset's market value appreciated above its net book value. This latter possibility, as discussed in Chapter 6, is the approach followed for temporary investments. The principal difference between these two approaches relates to the degree of objectivity present when trying to assess when the appreciation in asset value occurred. In the absence of a market mechanism, like the stock market, to establish appreciated value objectively, GAAP rely on the occurrence of an actual sale transaction as a signal to record value appreciation (i.e., a gain on sale).

In contrast to a gain on the sale of inventory, which is considered to be operations related, the gain (or loss) on the sale of capital assets is considered to be a non-operating event because it is assumed that the company is not in the business of selling its capital assets. Thus, in the statement of changes in financial position and in the income statement, capital asset sales are reported, but not as part of continuing operations. Moreover, in order to report the total proceeds from such sales, which would include amounts recognized as gains, the operating activity section shows an adjustment for the gains and losses, and the total proceeds are then shown in the investing activity section.

Disposition of a Capital Asset: Trade-Ins

Frequently, when organizations acquire new capital assets, old assets are traded in on the new asset. As with other transactions involving non-cash assets, care must be taken to determine the value of the assets exchanged. The value of the new asset should be determined based on the *consideration given* up by the purchaser. The consideration given consists of two components: the old asset to be traded in and an amount of cash. It may be possible to determine a fair market value of the old asset. If the fair market value of the old asset cannot be determined, the fair market value of the newly acquired asset may be used. The new asset may have a suggested list price provided by the seller. In almost all cases the *list price* is merely a nominal value assigned to the asset, which does *not* correspond to the fair market value of the asset. The seller of the new asset will give the purchaser a *trade in allowance* on the old asset. The trade-in allowance is a discount given when trading in one asset on another. Unfortunately, sellers manipulate their list prices and trade-in allowances to facilitate the sale of their products. Therefore, neither the list price nor the trade-in allowance provide very useful information when trying to determine the fair market value of assets being traded. Generally the fair market value of the disposed asset may be reasonably estimated. To illustrate the accounting for trade-ins, an asset originally costing $40,000, with accumulated amortization of $8,000, is traded in on a new asset. To acquire the new asset a cash payment of $3,000 is also required. An independent appraisal determines the fair market value of the old asset is $30,000. The seller provides a trade-in allowance of $34,000 on the old asset, to be exchanged for a new asset with a list price of $37,000. A journal entry illustrating a trade-in is shown below.

```
Asset (new) .........................................33,000
Accumulated Amortization ..............................  8,000
   Asset (old) ......................................           40,000
   Cash ............................................            3,000
Loss on Disposal ....................................  2,000
   Traded in an old asset on a new asset.
```

The old asset has a book value of $32,000 ($40,000 –$8,000) and a fair market value of $30,000. As well, $3,000 is paid in cash. Therefore, the new asset is recorded at a value based on the consideration given by the buyer, $33,000. The consideration given is the cash of $3,000 and fair market value of $30,000 for the old asset given in trade. Since the fair market value of the old asset was $2,000 less than its book value ($30,000 versus $32,000), a loss on disposal of the capital asset of $2,000 is recognized. If the fair market value of the old asset was $35,000, a gain on disposal of $3,000 would be recognized. However, gains on disposal of capital assets can only be recognized when *dissimilar assets* are traded. The entry is shown below:

```
Asset (new) . . . . . . . . . . . . . . . . . . . . . . . . . . . . . . . . . . . . . . . 38,000
Accumulated Amortization . . . . . . . . . . . . . . . . . . . . . . . . . . . . . 8,000
      Asset (old) . . . . . . . . . . . . . . . . . . . . . . . . . . . . . . . . . . . .            40,000
      Cash . . . . . . . . . . . . . . . . . . . . . . . . . . . . . . . . . . . . . . . . .            3,000
      Gain on Disposal . . . . . . . . . . . . . . . . . . . . . . . . . . . . . . . .            3,000
Traded in an old asset on a new asset (dissimilar).
```

The new asset is recorded at a value based on the consideration given by the buyer, $38,000. The consideration given is the cash of $3,000 and fair market value of $35,000 for the old asset given in trade. Since the fair market value of the old asset was $3,000 more than its book value ($35,000 versus $32,000), a gain on disposal of the capital asset of $3,000 is recognized. Only when dissimilar assets are traded may a gain on disposal be recognized, since it is deemed one asset's life has ended and a new asset's life begun. When similar assets are traded, the transaction is considered to be just a continuation of the original asset's life and no gain is recognized. This is another example of the principle of conservatism.

In the preceding example, a fair market value of $35,000 was assumed for the old asset. No gain would have been recognized if similar assets were being exchanged. The following entry would have been recorded:

```
Asset (new) . . . . . . . . . . . . . . . . . . . . . . . . . . . . . . . . . . . . . . . 35,000
Accumulated Amortization . . . . . . . . . . . . . . . . . . . . . . . . . . . . . 8,000
      Asset (old) . . . . . . . . . . . . . . . . . . . . . . . . . . . . . . . . . . . .            40,000
      Cash . . . . . . . . . . . . . . . . . . . . . . . . . . . . . . . . . . . . . . . . .            3,000
Traded in an old asset on a new asset (similar).
```

The new asset is valued at $35,000: the book value of the old asset of $32,000 ($40,000 – $8,000) plus the cash given of $3,000. As mentioned earlier, when similar assets are traded, the transaction is considered to be just a continuation of the original asset's life and no gain is recognized. Whenever assets are sold at an amount below their net book value, a loss on disposal should be recognized, whether similar *or* dissimilar assets are being exchanged.

Comprehensive Illustration

To facilitate your understanding of the complexities of accounting for capital assets, we now consider a numerical example covering several accounting periods. This illustration includes the use of the double-declining-balance and straight-line methods of amortization, betterments, a change in accounting policy and a change in accounting estimate, and the acquisition and disposal of a capital asset. Consider the following information. An enterprise acquires new equipment with an invoice price of $375,000 on January 7, 1991. Additional costs of $10,000 for taxes and duty are incurred. Installation costs of $15,000 are incurred to prepare the equipment ready for use.

Management estimates the equipment will have a useful life of 10 years, with a residual value of $30,000. After amortization had been allocated for two years using the double-declining-balance method, management determines the straight-line method would be more appropriate. After the equipment has been amortized for five years, a betterment of $40,000 is incurred on January 3, 1996. The betterment extends the estimated life of the equipment by 2 years, or to a total of 12 years. The betterment also changes the residual value of the equipment to $45,000. The equipment is sold on September 8, 1998, for $181,000 cash. The organization has a December 31 year-end. To account for the life of the equipment the following journal entries are required:

```
Jan. 7, 1991  Equipment . . . . . . . . . . . . . . . . . . . . . . . . . . . . . 400,000
              Cash . . . . . . . . . . . . . . . . . . . . . . . . . . . . . . . .    400,000
              To record the acquisition of equipment.
```

The cost of the equipment includes the invoice price of $375,000, the taxes and duty of $10,000, and the installation costs of $15,000. The equipment is amortized using the double-declining-balance method. Management originally estimated the asset to have a useful life of 10 years, or on a straight-line basis an amortization rate of 10 percent per year. Double the straight-line rate would therefore be 20 percent. Amortization for 1991 would be $80,000 (.20 × $400,000). The second year's amortization would be $64,000 or 20 percent of the net book value of the asset [.20 × ($400,000 − $80,000)]. The entries to record amortization for 1991 and 1992 would be:

```
Dec. 31, 1991  Amortization Expense . . . . . . . . . . . . . . . . . . . . . 80,000
               Accumulated Amortization . . . . . . . . . . . . . . . . . . .    80,000
               To record amortization for 1991.
Dec. 31, 1992  Amortization Expense . . . . . . . . . . . . . . . . . . . . . 64,000
               Accumulated Amortization . . . . . . . . . . . . . . . . . . .    64,000
               To record amortization for 1992.
```

After amortization had been allocated for 1991 and 1992 using the double-declining-balance method, management determines the straight-line method would be more appropriate. Straight-line amortization is $37,000 per year, based on the total cost of the equipment of $400,000, less the residual value of $30,000, allocated over 10 years. Through the end of 1992, amortization totalling $144,000 ($80,000 + $64,000) had been taken under the double-declining-balance method, whereas if the straight-line method had been used, only $74,000 ($37,000 × 2) in amortization deductions would have been recorded. Thus, at the beginning of 1993, an entry for $70,000 ($144,000 − $74,000) to restate the Accumulated Amortization account balance would be needed as follows:

```
Jan. 1993  Accumulated Amortization . . . . . . . . . . . . . . . . . . . . 70,000
           Retained Earnings . . . . . . . . . . . . . . . . . . . . . . . . .    70,000
           To restate prior periods (1991 & 1992) for the change in amortization
           methods.
```

Changes in accounting policy should be applied retroactively when possible. Therefore, as illustrated in the above entry the adjustment is made to prior years by adjusting the Retained Earnings account. For the next three years, 1993, 1994 and 1995, amortization of $37,000 per year is recorded on a straight-line basis.

```
Dec. 31, 1993  Amortization Expense . . . . . . . . . . . . . . . . . . . . . 37,000
               Accumulated Amortization . . . . . . . . . . . . . . . . . . .    37,000
               To record amortization for 1993.
```

```
Dec. 31, 1994   Amortization Expense  . . . . . . . . . . . . . . . . . . . . 37,000
                      Accumulated Amortization  . . . . . . . . . . . . . . . . . .      37,000
                To record amortization for 1994.
Dec. 31, 1995   Amortization Expense  . . . . . . . . . . . . . . . . . . . . 37,000
                      Accumulated Amortization  . . . . . . . . . . . . . . . . . .      37,000
                To record amortization for 1995.
```

After the equipment has been amortized for five years, a betterment of $40,000 is incurred on January 3, 1996. The betterment extends the estimated life of the equipment by 2 years, or to a total of 12 years. The following journal entry to account for the betterment is required:

```
Jan. 3, 1996   Equipment . . . . . . . . . . . . . . . . . . . . . . . . . . . . . . 40,000
                     Cash . . . . . . . . . . . . . . . . . . . . . . . . . . . . . . . . .      40,000
               To record the betterment.
```

The betterment increases the total cost of the equipment to $440,000 ($400,000 + $40,000). For the first five years, accumulated amortization on December 31, 1995, would be $185,000 ($37,000 × 5 years). The revised residual value is now $45,000. Amortization for 1996 is determined as follows:

$$\text{Amortization} = \frac{\text{Net book value} - \textit{New} \text{ residual value}}{\text{Number of years remaining}}$$

The net book value is $255,000 ($440,000 − $185,000). The new residual value is $45,000. The new cost to be allocated is $210,000 ($255,000 − $45,000). The cost to be allocated of $210,000 is allocated over the *new* remaining life of seven years (10 + 2 − 5). The new remaining life consists of the original 10 years, plus the 2 years added by the betterment, less the 5 years *prior* to the betterment. Therefore, the new amortization rate would be $30,000 per year ($210,000/7 years). The entries for amortization for 1996 and 1997 are shown below:

```
Dec. 31, 1996   Amortization Expense  . . . . . . . . . . . . . . . . . . . . 30,000
                      Accumulated Amortization  . . . . . . . . . . . . . . . . . .      30,000
                To record amortization for 1996.
Dec. 31, 1997   Amortization Expense  . . . . . . . . . . . . . . . . . . . . 30,000
                      Accumulated Amortization  . . . . . . . . . . . . . . . . . .      30,000
                To record amortization for 1997.
```

The equipment is sold on September 8, 1998, for $181,000 cash. Before the entry to record the disposal of the equipment is recorded, an entry for the 1998 amortization must be made. Since the disposal is made on September 8, for amortization purposes, the date is pushed back to August 31. This requires eight months' amortization to be recorded in 1998 or $20,000 (8/12 of $30,000). The following journal entry is made to account for the partial years' amortization:

```
Sep. 8, 1998   Amortization Expense  . . . . . . . . . . . . . . . . . . . . 30,000
                     Accumulated Amortization  . . . . . . . . . . . . . . . . . .      30,000
               To record amortization for 1998.
```

The T-account for accumulated amortization shown below summarizes the amortization transactions for the useful life of the equipment to September 8, 1998:

Accumulated Amortization

		1991	80,000
		1992	64,000
Adjustment	70,000	Balance	144,000
			74,000
		1993	37,000
		1994	37,000
		1995	37,000
		Balance	185,000
		1996	30,000
		1997	30,000
		1998	20,000
		Balance	265,000

The entry to record the disposal of the equipment on September 8, 1998, for $181,000 cash is shown below:

```
Sept. 8, 1998   Cash . . . . . . . . . . . . . . . . . . . . . . . . . . . . . . . . 181,000
                Accumulated Amortization . . . . . . . . . . . . . . . . . . 265,000
                    Equipment  . . . . . . . . . . . . . . . . . . . . . . . . . . . . . .      440,000
                    Gain on disposal . . . . . . . . . . . . . . . . . . . . . . . . .          6,000
                To record the disposal of the equipment.
```

On the disposal date the net book value of the asset is $175,000 ($440,000 − $265,000). Since the asset is sold for $181,000, an amount greater than the net book value, a $6,000 gain on disposal is recognized.

8.5 INTANGIBLE ASSETS

Accounting for Intangible Assets

intangible assets
Those resources of an enterprise, such as goodwill, trademarks, or trade names, that lack an identifiable physical presence.

Accounting for assets such as inventories and property, plant, and equipment seems relatively straightforward because these items are tangible in nature and their revenue-producing potential as assets is readily apparent. In contrast, the accounting for an intangible asset may not be so readily apparent because such assets do not physically produce goods or services. The term **intangible asset** refers to "capital assets that lack physical substance. Examples of intangible properties include brand names, copyrights, franchises, licences, patents, software, subscription lists, and trademarks" (CICA Handbook 3060.06). In the following section, we focus on such questions as: What cost figure should be assigned to an intangible asset on the balance sheet? Should an intangible be amortized? If so, what is its useful life?

In fact, the financial reporting for most intangible assets is similar to that for tangible assets such as property, plant, and equipment. At the date of acquisition, an intangible asset's cost must be determined and recorded at the fair market value of (1) the consideration given or (2) the item acquired, whichever is more clearly determinable. When payment is non-cash, every effort should be made to determine the market value of the non-cash payment. If that is not possible, then the corporate financial manager should attempt to determine the market value of the intangible asset received. The consideration given (or the value of the asset received) becomes the basis for recording the asset — in effect, its recorded cost.

Consider, for example, the purchase of a franchise agreement for cash of $300,000; hence, the accounting entry to record the acquisition of the franchise appears as follows:

```
Franchise . . . . . . . . . . . . . . . . . . . . . . . . . . . . . . . . . . . . 300,000
    Cash . . . . . . . . . . . . . . . . . . . . . . . . . . . . . . . . . . . . . . . .        300,000
    Acquired franchise for cash and capital stock.
```

Over its useful economic life, the intangible asset's recorded cost must be allocated to the periods benefited. GAAP assume that the economic utility (i.e., the useful potential) of an intangible asset declines (is used up) over its life, and therefore the total cost should be systematically allocated as a period expense against the income of the company. This process, which is similar to the amortization of capital assets, is also referred to as *amortization*. The period of time over which the recording of amortization takes place depends on the estimated economic life of the asset and varies from case to case. The period of amortization generally should not, however, exceed 40 years.

Amortization of an intangible asset normally relies on the straight-line method over the estimated economic life of the asset unless an alternative method can be shown to comply more closely with the "using up" of the asset. By convention, amortization expense usually results in a direct reduction to the intangible asset account rather than an increase to a contra asset account as is done for amortization charges related to property, plant, and equipment. In the previous franchise example, if the contractual term of the franchise agreement was 10 years, the accounting entry to record each year's amortization expense is as follows:

```
Franchise Amortization Expense  . . . . . . . . . . . . . . . . . . . . . . 30,000
    Franchise . . . . . . . . . . . . . . . . . . . . . . . . . . . . . . . . . . . . .        30,000
    Amortization of the franchise for the period.
```

As with any asset, when intangible assets are disposed of, sold, or exchanged, they must be removed from the accounts, and any gain or loss recorded at that time. Continuing with the previous example, assume that after *eight* years the franchise is sold for a cash payment of $80,000. The entry appears as follows:

```
Cash . . . . . . . . . . . . . . . . . . . . . . . . . . . . . . . . . . . . . . . . 80,000
    Franchise [$300,000 − 8($30,000)] . . . . . . . . . . . . . . . . . . . . .        60,000
    Gain on Sale of Franchise  . . . . . . . . . . . . . . . . . . . . . . . . . . .        20,000
    Franchise is sold for cash.
```

Intangible assets may differ from one another in several key ways. Depending on these key dimensions, the accounting for the intangible asset under consideration may differ from that described above for the franchises.

From a financial reporting perspective, managers must consider three key characteristics of intangibles. The first characteristic is identifiability and separability: Can the intangible asset be considered separately and distinctly from the other assets of the company? The usual test for separate identity is to determine whether the asset can be sold individually (e.g., a patent) or is so intertwined with the company that it cannot be separated (e.g., customer goodwill). The second issue pertains to the manner of acquisition: Was the intangible asset developed internally (e.g., a proprietary manufacturing process) or was it purchased externally (e.g., a franchise or an exclusive licence)? A final issue pertains to the expected period of benefit: What is the economic life of the intangible asset? For some intangible assets, such as patents and franchises, the maximum economic life is legally or contractually determined. For others, such as trademarks, the economic life is not easily determined because of the potential for continual legal renewals and extensions. Moreover, the useful life of an intangible asset, like a trademark or patent, may be affected by product or process obsolescence, competitors' actions, and changes in technology. The only guidelines available to managers in choosing an appropriate useful life is that the period selected should not be longer than the intangible's legal life, if it has one, and it cannot exceed 40 years in any case.

Internally Developed Intangibles

The costs associated with internally developed intangible assets that are not specific-ally identifiable and separable are expensed against income in the period incurred. Costs associated with maintaining and developing customer relations should be de-ducted from income when incurred. On the other hand, those internally incurred costs associated with identifiable and separable intangible assets are expensed unless it can be determined the expenditure will produce future benefit, that is, revenue. A classic example is research and development costs. Generally research costs are expensed as incurred. Because of practical realities (less than 1 in 10 new product ideas ever go to market and the ability to predict which one will be successful is highly uncertain), capitalizing research expenditures seldom achieved the ultimate matching of revenues and expenses it sought to achieve. "**Research costs** should be charged as an expense of the period in which they are incurred" (CICA Handbook 3450.16). The CICA Handbook provides very *strict* criteria for development costs that restrict their frequent use. Only when an economically viable product is reasonably assured, should develop-ment costs be capitalized and amortized to future periods. However, the CICA Hand-book recommends that **development costs** that *can be* traced to an identifiable marketable product should be capitalized as an inventory-type item (i.e., one held for sale), and amortized over a reasonable period not to exceed 40 years. "Amortization of development costs deferred to future periods should commence with the commercial production or use of the product or process and should be charged as an expense on a systematic and rational basis by reference, where possible, to the sale or use of the product or process" (CICA Handbook 33450.28).

Rogers Cantel Mobile Communications, Inc., disclosed the following note on the accounting for its research and development costs:

> Research costs are expensed in the year incurred. Development costs are capitalized and amortized on a straight line basis over three to five years. Development costs are charged to expense in total where projects are deemed unfeasible, or in part, when projects are deemed excessive in amount.

A recent case in point highlights the issue of accounting for research and develop-ment (R&D) expenditures. During the 1980s, Burroughs Welcome spent and expensed more than $80 million on R&D that ultimately led to the AIDS drug AZT. As the R&D was being incurred, management did not know whether the outcome would result in an effective, marketable AIDS drug. All expenditures therefore were expensed, as were another $700 million of R&D on other diseases that produced nothing of significance. On the day that the Food and Drug Agency approved AZT, it became a valuable asset that was not and could not be reported on the balance sheet. In setting the retail price for AZT, however, Welcome managers asked this question: What is the cost of the product? Various stakeholders in the pricing decision argued for quite different points of view — some argued that only the $80 million specifically associated with the AZT product development should be considered; others argued that AZT pricing had to be

research costs
Generally research costs are expensed as incurred, because capitalizing research expenditures seldom achieves the matching of revenues and expenses desired.

development costs
Development costs that can be traced to an identifiable marketable product should be capitalized as an inventory-type item and amortized over a reasonable period not to exceed 40 years.

sufficient to recover the entire R&D budget of $780 million. Still others argued that the price should be merely the cost involved in manufacturing the drug. This debate illustrates the divergent views that exist as to whether R&D should be considered part of a product's cost, and, if so, whether only direct R&D costs or both direct and indirect costs be considered. In so doing, GAAP emphasize objectivity over subjectivity, conservatism over optimism, and results in a decoupling of accounting policy from strategic management decisions.

Externally Developed Intangibles

patents
Exclusive legal rights to products registered with the Patent Office.

copyrights
are legal rights of protection given to the creators of published materials.

franchises
The rights granted by one company to another to use a specific designation in their business.

trademarks
Registered claims of ownership to names, symbols, slogans, or other devices providing distinctive identity of a product.

The consideration paid to external parties for control of specifically identifiable and separable intangible assets should be capitalized and systematically amortized over the economic life of the asset (but not to exceed 40 years). **Patents**, for example, are exclusive legal rights to products registered with the Patent Office; they recognize the holder's right to use, manufacture, dispose of, and control in every way the patented product or process without hindrance from others. Patents have a legal life of 17 years, but their economic life may be much shorter because of technological obsolescence. Similarly, **copyrights** are legal rights of protection given to the creators of published materials. Copyright law has recently been changed so that copyrights now extend protection for the life of the creator plus 50 years, or if the copyright is held by a corporation (deemed to have an indeterminate life), 75 years from the date of first publication. **Franchises** are the rights granted by one company to another to use a specific designation in their business; use can be limited in term by contract or be renewable indefinitely to create essentially an indeterminate life. If a franchise is renewable indefinitely, it should be amortized over a period not to exceed 40 years. **Trademarks** are registered claims of ownership to names, symbols, slogans, or other devices providing distinctive identity of a product. Although they have no legally limited life, trademarks often have limited economic life. If an estimate of the economic life can be made, it should be used as the term for amortization of the asset. If no estimate of economic life can be made, the asset should be amortized over a period not to exceed 40 years. The costs of obtaining a patent, copyright, franchise, or trademark should be capitalized as intangible assets. It is important to note that the costs of producing an asset (e.g., a feature motion picture) should be reported as an asset separate from the costs incurred in obtaining the copyright on the film. Maple Leaf Gardens, Limited's largest intangible asset noted in its footnote is for its NHL franchise. The Molson Companies, Limited, has a similar footnote on its intangible assets:

	1993	1992
Goodwill	$372,300	$338,303
Brand names(i)	63,029	81,059
Hockey franchises(ii)	11,400	11,700
	$446,729	$431,062

(i) The cost and accumulated amortization of brand names at March 31, 1993 amounted to $66,353 (1992 — $83,137) and $3,324 (1992 — $2,078), respectively.
(ii) The cost and accumulated amortization of hockey franchises at March 31, 1993 amounted to $12,000 (1992 — $12,000) and $600 (1992 — $300), respectively.

Goodwill

Costs associated with *internally* created goodwill (e.g., public service expenditures, employee development, charitable contributions, customer-service expenses) are *not* capitalized. They are expensed in the period in which they are incurred. As discussed in the appendix to this chapter, the acquisition of another business, however, often creates the need to identify and record a goodwill intangible asset pertaining to the acquired company. Consider for a moment the fact that the only reason an investing company would pay in excess of the fair market value of the net assets would be because of the customer loyalty, managerial talent, sound reputation, and so on, already built up by the company to be purchased. Although the company was never permitted to record an intangible asset for such goodwill-related factors, the external acquisition was an event that justified the recording of goodwill. In essence, a marketplace valuation of that goodwill had been made and confirmed via the payment of a price for the excess of the net assets' appraised fair market value. This premium paid was recorded as goodwill on the purchasing company's books on the acquisition date.

> Goodwill existing at the acquisition gradually disappears and may, or may not, be replaced by new goodwill. Furthermore goodwill is a cost incurred in anticipation of future earnings, and should be amortized by systematic charges to income over the periods of those future earnings to produce a proper matching of costs against revenue. The straight-line method of amortization should be applied. An analysis of all pertinent factors should normally enable the company to assess a reasonable estimated life of such goodwill. However, the period of amortization should not exceed forty years." (CICA Handbook 1580.57)

8.6 NATURAL RESOURCES

Natural resources include such assets as timber, oil, gas, iron ore, coal, and uranium. Like intangible assets, natural resources may be either internally or externally developed. When these assets are externally developed, they are reported on the balance sheet at their acquisition cost less any depletion taken subsequent to acquisition. "Mining properties are capital assets represented by the capitalized costs of acquired mineral rights and the costs associated with exploration for the development of mineral reserves" (CICA Handbook 3060.08). "Oil and gas properties are capital assets represented by capitalized costs of acquired oil and gas rights and the costs associated with the exploration and development of oil, gas and related reserves" (CICA Handbook 3060.11).

Full Cost Method

full cost method
Under the full cost method, all costs associated with the exploration for and development of natural resources are capitalized to the natural resource accounts on the balance sheet.

The two principal valuation alternatives that exist for companies in the extractive industries are the full cost method and the successful efforts method. Under the **full cost method,** all costs associated with the exploration for and development of natural resources are capitalized to the natural resource accounts on the balance sheet. There is little disagreement over this method except when unsuccessful exploration activities are involved. Under the full cost method, the costs of unsuccessful exploration activities are also capitalized on the balance sheet under the philosophy that the development of new resource reserves is a speculative activity involving some inherent failure. Home Oil Company, Limited, uses the full cost method:

The full cost method of accounting is followed for oil and gas operations, whereby all exploration and development costs are capitalized. Capitalized costs include land acquisition costs, geological and geophysical cists, lease rentals and related charges applicable to nonproducing properties, costs of drilling both productive and nonproductive wells and administrative costs related to exploration and development activities. Oil and gas costs are depleted using the units of production method based upon estimated proved reserves as determined by Company engineers.

Successful Efforts Method

successful efforts method
Under the successful efforts method, only the costs associated with successful exploration and development activity are capitalized to the balance sheet accounts.

In contrast, under the **successful efforts method**, only the costs associated with successful exploration and development activity are capitalized to the balance sheet accounts. The costs of any unsuccessful activity are expensed against net income. Shell Canada, Limited, uses the successful efforts method: "The Corporation follows the successful efforts method of accounting for exploration and development activities. Under this method, acquisition costs of resource properties are capitalized. Exploratory drilling costs are initially capitalized and costs relating to wells subsequently determined to be unsuccessful are charged to earnings." Cominco Resources International, Limited, disclosed the following note on the accounting for mineral properties and development:

> Exploration expenditures are charged to earnings in the year they are incurred except for expenditures on specific properties having indicated the presence of a mineral resource with the potential of being developed into a mine, in which case the expenditures are deferred until commencement of production, at which time they will be charged to operations on a units-of-production basis. If a property with potential for development is subsequently abandoned or if there is a permanent impairment in value, the unrecoverable portion of such investment is charged to earnings in the year such determination is made.

Brascan, Limited, had the following note on its accounting for mining and metals: "Mineral exploration costs pertaining to individual metal prospects are charged to income as incurred until an economic orebody is defined. Other mineral exploration, development and start-up costs are capitalized until commercial production commences and are then amortized using the unit of production method over the estimated life of the reserves."

Both the full cost and the successful efforts methods are generally accepted, and thus both are available for use by managers of natural resource companies in the extractive industries. Under both methods, the costs capitalized to the balance sheet are subject to certain constraints in a manner similar to the effect that the lower-of-cost-or-market method has on inventory. In the event that the current market value of a company's reserves of natural resources declines substantially, it may become necessary to write down the value of the capitalized balance sheet values. Thus, just as the lower-of-cost-or-market method prevents the overstatement of inventories and temporary investments, this "ceiling test" similarly constrains the value of natural resources on the balance sheet.

Natural resource companies not involved in the extractive industries, such as a timber company, usually capitalize all of their initial expenditures while expensing their ongoing maintenance and development costs. Except in those cases involving forest fires, which destroy substantial portions of a company's timber reserves, the initial capitalized cost is carried on the balance sheet until the reserves are harvested.

Depletion and Amortization

Depletion refers to the periodic expensing of the capitalized resource cost. Unlike amortization, there is only one generally accepted depletion approach, the units-of-production method, which is conceptually similar to the units-of-production method of amortization for machinery and equipment. First, an estimate is made of the number of units — barrels of oil, tons of coal, or board feet of timber — in an oil well, mine, or tract of timberland. Second, this estimate is divided into the original cost of acquiring the oil well, mine, or timber tract (less its estimated residual value) to determine the depletion per unit. For example, if the estimated number of tons of coal in a mine were 200,000 and the mine's original cost (less estimated residual value) was $820,000, the depletion rate per ton would be $4.10 per ton. If during the first year, 25,000 tons were taken out, the depletion expense for the year would be 25,000 times $4.10, or $102,500. The accounting entry follows:

```
Depletion Expense . . . . . . . . . . . . . . . . . . . . . . . . . . . . . . . . 102,500
    Allowance for Depletion  . . . . . . . . . . . . . . . . . . . . . . . . . . . . .   102,500
Depletion for the year.
```

The Allowance for Depletion account is conceptually similar to the Accumulated Amortization account. Some organizations may *not* use a contra account for depletion and may simply deduct the depletion directly from the asset account.

8.7 FINANCIAL STATEMENT DISCLOSURE: CAPITAL ASSETS

On the balance sheet, capital assets are shown in the non-current asset section. Land is reported at its original cost, whereas buildings, machinery, vehicles, and equipment are shown at original cost less the portion of that cost previously allocated as amortization.

Financial statement disclosure requirements for capital assets include: "For each major category of capital assets there should be disclosure of:

(a) cost;

(b) accumulated amortization, including the amount of any write downs; and

(c) the amortization method used, including the amortization period or rate" (CICA Handbook 3060.58).

"The amount of amortization of a capital asset charged to income for the period should be disclosed" [CICA Handbook 3060.60]. Users should examine the notes and schedules to the financial statements as they include substantial information regarding a company's capital assets, amortization policies, and related expenditures.

Note that the cost of the asset is preserved in the capital asset account because the credit entry is to the contra asset account, Accumulated Amortization. Using this approach, the balance sheet will reveal not only the original cost basis of the asset but also its total amortization taken to date and its remaining unamortized cost:

Machinery	$ 10,000
Accumulated amortization	(4,000)
	$ 6,000

From this information, it is also possible to make rough estimates of the age of a company's assets — the larger the net book value (i.e., cost minus accumulated amortization) relative to the original cost of the capital assets, the newer (on average) are the company's assets.

Presented below are the financial statement disclosures for capital assets for different companies pertaining to their choices of asset lives and amortization methods. In reviewing these examples, consider the impact of the different lives and amortization methods on the companies' reported amortization expense and amortizable capital assets. Note that the organizations use a variety of amortization methods. Such variations between companies highlight some of the latitude left to management as they decide how "best" to amortize their assets.

Weldwood of Canada, Limited, disclosed the following note on its accounting for capital assets:

depreciation
A term used to refer to the amortization or cost allocation of capital assets.

depletion
A term used to refer to the amortization or cost allocation of natural resources.

Depreciation, Depletion and Road Amortization
Depreciation is calculated using the straight-line method at the following rates applied to costs less estimated residual value:

Building and land improvements	2.5 to 20.0%
Machinery and equipment, other than logging	4.2 to 33.3%
Logging equipment, other than major units	10.0 to 33.3%
Automotive equipment and aircraft	10.0 to 33.3%

Major units of logging equipment are amortized on a usage basis. Timber holdings are depleted on a production basis over the volume of timber to be harvested. Capitalized logging roads are amortized on a production basis, at rates based on the volume of timber developed.

K-mart Corporation disclosed the following note on its accounting for depreciation:

Depreciation: The company computes depreciation on owned property principally on the straight-line method for financial statement purposes and on accelerated methods for income tax purposes. Most store properties are leased and improvements are amortized over the term of the lease but not more than 25 years. Other annual rates used in computing depreciation for financial statement purposes are 2% to 4% for buildings, 10% to 14% for store fixtures, and 5% to 33% for other fixtures and equipment.

Noranda, Inc., disclosed the following note on its accounting for depreciation and amortization:

Depreciation on property, plant and equipment is based on the estimated service lives of the assets calculated primarily on the straight-line basis; the unit of production method is applied to forest manufacturing assets. Preproduction and mine development expenditures are amortized over the estimated life of the mine on the unit of production method.

Stone Container Corp. disclosed the following note:

Property, plant and equipment is stated at cost. Expenditures for maintenance and repairs are charged to income as incurred. Additions, improvements and major replacements are capitalized. The cost and accumulated amortization related to assets sold or retired are removed from the accounts and any gain or loss is credited or charged to income.

For financial reporting purposes, depreciation is provided on the straight-line method over the estimated useful lives of depreciable assets, or over the duration of the leases for capitalized leases, based on the following annual rates:

Type of Asset	Rates
Machinery and equipment	5% to 33%
Buildings and leasehold improvements	2% to 7%
Land improvements	4% to 7%

Effective January 1, the Company changed its estimates of the useful lives of certain machinery and equipment at its paper mills. Mill asset depreciation lives that previously averaged 16 years were increased to an average of 20 years, while mill asset depreciation lives that previously averaged 10–12 years were increased to an average of 14–16 years. These changes were made to better reflect the estimated periods during which such assets will remain in service. The change had the effect of reducing depreciation expense by $39.8 million and increasing net income by $20.2 million, or $.34 per common share, in 1990.

Phelps Dodge Corp. disclosed the following:

Property, plant and equipment are carried at cost. Cost of significant assets includes capitalized interest incurred during the construction and development period. Expenditures for replacements and betterments are capitalized; maintenance and repair expenditures are charged to operations as incurred.

The principal depreciation methods used are the units of production method for mining, smelting and refining operations and, for other operations, the straight-line method based upon the estimated lives of specific classes or groups of depreciable assets.

Values for mining properties represent mainly acquisition costs or pre-1932 engineering valuations. Depletion of mines is computed on the basis of an overall unit rate applied to the pounds of principal products sold from mine production.

Mine exploration costs and development costs to maintain production of operating mines are charged to operations as incurred. Mine development expenditures at new mines and major development expenditures at operating mines which are expected to benefit future production are capitalized and amortized on the units of production method over the estimated commercially recoverable minerals.

8.8 ANALYZING CAPITAL ASSETS

As was illustrated in Exhibit 8.1, the different amortization methods produce different amortization expense for each period. The total cost allocation or amortization expense in the long term is the same for all methods. However, in the short term, the different methods produce different amortization expense for each period, which impacts on net income, earnings per share, return on equity, and other profitability ratios.

Capital assets have a material impact on most organizations balance sheets, and may be the most significant asset held by many organizations. As well, capital assets impact significantly on a firm's statement of changes in financial position. Capital assets, although an investing activity increasing or decreasing non-current assets, also have material impact on the financing activities of the firm.

Managerial Issues

The capital asset purchase decision is one of the most important decisions a manager makes because of the size of the investment and the long-term nature of the asset and related financing. A number of financial considerations that parallel some of this chapter's earlier discussions are involved in such purchase decisions. If the decision to buy a piece of equipment is based, in part, on the asset's estimated net present value or internal rate of return (two very common capital budgeting techniques), then the asset's estimated useful life, periodic tax amortization amount, residual value, initial cost, and gains or losses on disposal of the assets being replaced are important factors to be considered. These factors are important because they influence the amount and timing of the cash flows generated by the particular asset under consideration and, thus, are an integral part in calculating the asset's net present value.

Some observers of corporate financial reporting have sarcastically observed that corporate accounting departments have become the best performing profit centres for many companies — a comment that reflects the bottom-line impact attributable to the various financial reporting alternatives available under GAAP. Recall from Chapter 7, for example, the discussion of how net income could be significantly influenced by management's choice of LIFO versus FIFO for purposes of valuing ending inventory and the cost of goods sold. A similar concern exists with regard to capital assets: Management's choice of amortization method, expected useful life, and anticipated residual value can have a material, direct effect on the company's bottom line. Although managers do have this flexibility available to them under GAAP, changes in accounting methods and estimates must be documented in the published financial statements. Such changes should be infrequent to avoid the appearance of overt earnings management.

Other, less critical management concerns include reducing the clerical costs associated with the accounting for capital assets. In this regard, most companies, as a matter of policy, set a lower limit (e.g., $500) for capitalizing assets. The purchase of any item costing less than this amount is expensed. This policy reduces the number of items that must be amortized on a periodic basis even though many of those assets expensed will be used for more than one year. Because of the *immateriality* of these small dollar items, they do not affect the overall accuracy of the financial statements. The Kidney Foundation of Canada follows a policy of capitalizing acquisitions over $1,000: "Capital asset additions having a cost of more than $1,000 are capitalized and amortized on the straight-line basis over five years."

Another clerical-saving policy involves depreciating assets for a half-year in the year of acquisition and in the final year of their planned life rather than using the actual fractional parts of the year. Many companies adopt a half-year amortization convention for the year of acquisition. Under this convention, capitalized property is amortized on a six-month basis for the first year regardless of when it was acquired. A similar convention is normally adopted for the year of disposition if the asset is not fully amortized at the time of disposition. Fortunately, Revenue Canada recognizes the validity of this convention.

Time and money also can be saved by using similar policies for both accounting and tax purposes when possible. Adopting the same amortization method for general accounting as that used for tax purposes, for example, minimizes the amount of work required to maintain the accounting records. Managers still must ensure, however, that capital asset costs are allocated for accounting purposes in a rational and systematic manner. Managers also should be concerned with preserving cash flows to the company through well-planned tax amortization policies.

Some Misconceptions about Amortization

A number of common misconceptions exist concerning amortization accounting. One misconception states that for financial reporting purposes, amortization expense reflects the decline in the market value of the depreciable asset; in other words, original cost less accumulated amortization should approximate an asset's current fair market value. The recording of amortization is a process of *cost allocation, not of valuation.* Accordingly, amortization expense is *not* intended to equal the change in the asset's market value or to indicate the market value of the unallocated cost of assets at the end of any period.

A second amortization myth is that the purpose of amortization is to provide for the replacement of assets at the end of their useful lives. The costs allocated to amortization expense are costs *already* incurred without reference to the costs to be incurred when, and if, an asset is replaced. Moreover, the recording of amortization does not assume that assets are to be replaced at the end of their useful lives by similar assets.

Another misconception is that amortization provides cash. As discussed previously, the statement of changes in financial position usually lists net income first among the sources of operating cash flows. To adjust this figure to a cash-based net income approximation, amortization is added back. The sum of net income plus amortization and other similar items is then labelled cash flow from operations. As a consequence of this separate listing of amortization in the statement of changes, some financial statement readers have been led to the false conclusion that amortization provides cash. This is *not* so! Amortization is a non-cash expense that is recognized under the accrual basis of accounting but in no way constitutes a cash inflow. Amortization does, however, reduce the taxable net income amount reported on a company's tax return and thus lowers the amount of taxes to be paid. So, to the extent that amortization reduces the cash outflow for taxes otherwise due, it can be thought of as having an *indirect* cash flow benefit.

Ethics in Accounting

William Lawsen is the controller of a large automobile dealership in downtown Edmonton. William is responsible for the preparation of the dealership's financial reports. All department managers, including William, receive a bonus based on the annual net income of the dealership. Every Friday, the department managers, the president, and William have a management meeting. This week, Mr. Adam, the president, is out of town and William will be chairperson for the meeting. As year-end is quickly approaching, the managers have a keen interest in the results disclosed in the annual report, and in particular the annual net income figure. When William arrives at the management meeting, all the managers are present and actively discussing the annual bonus plan. They immediately start quizzing William on the different accounting policies used by the dealership in determining net income. They have a particular concern about the dealership's amortization policies. The managers believe it is unfair for amortization to be deducted when determining net income for bonus purposes, as they have no control over the amount of amortization charged each period. One manager, who was reading his daughter's accounting text, suggests there could be a change in accounting policy or a change in accounting estimate to benefit the managers' position. What would your response be to the managers' concerns? What are the ethical issues for the accountant?

8.9 SUMMARY

Capital assets are the principal long-term revenue-producing assets of most companies. Because of the significant dollar investment in these assets, the accounting methods adopted for them may have a material impact on both the balance sheet and the income statement of a company. A number of amortization methods are available to management. Although the initial cash outflow to acquire these assets affects the statement of changes in financial position, the periodic amortization of intangibles, the amortization of capital assets, and the depletion of natural resources do not affect it; amortization, depreciation, and depletion expenses are added back to net income to adjust the accrual operating results for these non-cash expenses to arrive at the cash flows from operations. This chapter examined the different amortization methods used for capital assets. Changes in accounting policy and accounting estimates were examined. Complex transactions for property, plant, and equipment were illustrated. The accounting for intangible assets and natural resources was discussed. The following table summarizes the financial statement interrelationships of capital assets:

Financial Statement Interrelationships

Financial Statement Item	Balance Sheet	Income Statement	Statement of Changes in Financial Position
Capital assets, including property, plant, and equipment, intangibles, and natural resources	Non-current asset	Amortization expense; Gain or loss on disposal	Amortization expense added back to net income as a non-cash item, operating activity. Purchases are an investing activity using cash. Disposals are an investing activity, providing cash. Gains/losses on disposal are noncash adjustment, to net income, operating activity.

8.10 KEY CONCEPTS AND TERMS

Accelerated methods of amortization (p. 385)
Accumulated amortization (p. 388)
Amortization (p. 382)
Betterment (p. 391)
Capital assets (p. 379)
Capital cost allowance (p. 386)
Change in accounting estimate (p. 389)
Change in accounting policy (p. 388)
Copyrights (p. 401)
Declining-balance method (p. 383)
Depletion (p. 405)
Depreciation (p. 405)
Development costs (p. 400)
Double-declining-balance method (p. 384)
Franchises (p. 401)

Full cost method (p. 402)
Intangible assets (p. 398)
Machine-hour method (p. 386)
Net book value (p. 384)
Patents (p. 401)
Physical life (p. 382)
Present value (p. 381)
Research costs (p. 400)
Residual value (p. 383)
Salvage value (p. 383)
Straight-line method (p. 383)
Successful efforts method (p. 403)
Sum-of-the-years'-digits method (p. 384)
Technological life (p. 382)
Trademarks (p. 401)
Units-of-production method (p. 386)
Useful life (p. 382)

8.11 COMPREHENSIVE REVIEW PROBLEM

R8.1 Accounting for capital assets. Doug's Delivery Service purchased a delivery van for $25,000 on January 2, 1991. The van is estimated to have a five-year useful life and a residual value of $3,400. The company has a December 31 year-end. Use the above information to answer the following *independent* questions:

a. Assuming straight-line amortization is used, what is the balance in the Accumulated Amortization account on December 31, 1993?

b. On January 1, 1994, it is determined the van will last for an additional two years or seven years in total, and have a revised residual value of $2,040. Assuming the use of straight-line amortization, determine the amortization expense for the year ending December 31, 1994.

c. Assuming the declining-balance method with amortization at twice the straight-line rate had been used, what is the amortization expense for the year ending December 31, 1992?

d. Assume the van was sold for $18,000 on December 30, 1992. Compute the gain or loss on sale of the van. Use straight-line amortization.

e. If Doug's Delivery Service had estimated the van would be driven 100,000 kilometres during its useful life and the actual usage the first year was 17,000 kilometres, determine the amortization expense using the units of production amortization method.

f. Assume on December 29, 1995, the old van was traded in on a new van. As well, the seller required a cash payment of $7,500 on purchase of the new van. Record the entry to acquire the new vehicle assuming the old vehicle is exchanged for the new van. Assume the straight-line method of amortization has been used and the fair market value of the old van is $13,000.

Accounting for Long-Term Investments

In today's complex business community, it is quite common to find companies investing in each other. These intercorporate investments may involve both debt and equity securities and may be for either a short or long duration. In Chapter 6, we considered the accounting associated with temporary investments. The focus of this appendix is on long-term intercorporate investments.

Long-term intercorporate investments may be undertaken for a variety of reasons, for example, to gain control of a major customer, to provide capital to a struggling supplier, or simply to provide additional sources of income for the investor company. As a way to organize our discussion of the accounting issues surrounding long-term intercorporate investments, we focus on the extent of ownership represented by the investment. When a company (the investor) owns a relatively small proportion of the outstanding voting shares of another company (the investee), the investment is most commonly accounted for using the cost method. When the investor company owns sufficient voting shares in the investee to be able to influence the activities of the investee, the equity method will most likely be used. When an investor owns sufficient voting shares to control the activities of the investee company, the financial results of the two companies must be reported on a consolidated basis. In this appendix, we focus on the accounting and analytical issues associated with the cost method, the equity method, and consolidation accounting.

8.1A TYPES OF LONG-TERM INVESTMENTS

Long-Term versus Temporary Investments

Temporary investments are normally created as the result of the efficient management of cash. In lieu of having excess cash sitting idly and not earning a return, management may invest such resources for the short term in different forms of liquid short-term investments. Intercorporate or long-term investments are acquired by organizations primarily with the intent of gaining some degree of control over another organization. Intercorporate investments may be acquired for expansion or diversification purposes. Temporary investments and intercorporate investments are valued on the same basis. The cost of either should include the purchase price of the shares or bonds acquired, including the cost of brokerage fees or taxes. The lower-of-cost-or-market rule should be used for both types of investments, with the investment being written down when the loss in value that has occurred is other than a temporary decline. Income recognition for temporary investments is based on any dividend or interest income earned in the current period. Income recognition for intercorporate investments is dependent on the degree of control the investor is able to exercise over the investee.

Degree of Control

The accounting for intercorporate investments is dependent on the degree of control the investor is able to exercise over the investee. Control may vary from very little to complete control. The following table illustrates the different levels of control an investor may have over an investee and the most commonly used accounting methods:

Degree of Control	No Control	Some Control	Complete Control
	Portfolio Investment	Significant Influence	Subsidiary
Accounting method	Cost method	Equity method	Consolidation

Depending on the relationship between the investor and the investee, the general recommendations presented above may vary. The general rule is one of conservatism. If doubt as to the relationship between the two companies is in question, the cost method may be deemed to provide the most meaningful information to the users of financial statements.

When an investor company acquires bonds or preferred shares issued by another company, those investments are, by definition, **passive investments** in that they give the investor no authority or control over the investee's activities. Similarly, when a company acquires a relatively small portion of the voting common shares issued by another company, that investment also is considered passive so long as the investor has no intent to influence or control the investee's business activities. As a general rule, when an investment involves less than 20 percent of the outstanding voting shares of a company, it is assumed that the investor company is unable to influence significantly the activities of the investee company. All long-term passive investments, whether passive because of their terms or because of the extent of the investor's ownership, are understood to be investments solely for the purpose of income and are therefore treated in much the same way as temporary investments. Such long-term intercorporate investments are referred to as *portfolio investments* and are to be accounted for using the cost method.

When an investor company acquires a sufficiently large voting interest to influence or control the business activities of an investee company, the investment is considered to be an **active investment**. Typically, investments involving ownership interests of 20 to 50 percent are evidence of significant influence, whereas investments involving more than 50 percent of a company's voting shares represent *control* situations. A closer look at different potential relationships follows.

Portfolio Investments

Portfolio investments are long-term investments over which the investor has little or no control. They are not investments in companies that are subject to significant influence by the investor. The cost method must be used.

passive investment An intercorporate investment in which the investor cannot (or does not) attempt to influence the operations of the investee-company.

active investment An intercorporate investment by an investor-company that allows the investor to exercise influence or control over the operations of the investee-company.

portfolio investments Long-term intercorporate investments over which the investor has little or no control.

Investments Subject to Significant Influence

significant influence
An investor is said to have significant influence over an investee when the investor owns about 20 percent of the investee's voting shares and has some other form of influence.

Significant influence is said to exist when the investor holds *about 20 percent* of the voting interest in the investee *and* has some other form of influence. The other forms of influence may include representation on the board of directors, participation in the policy-making process, material intercompany transactions, and interchange of managerial personnel or technical information. A substantial or majority ownership by another investor would not necessarily preclude an investor from exercising significant influence. The equity method should be used to account for significant influence situations. If significant influence ceases to exist, the cost method should be used.

Subsidiaries

subsidiary
A company in which an investor-company (the parent) holds an equity investment in excess of 50 percent of the voting shares of the investee-company.

When an investor has complete control (greater than 50 percent of the voting shares) over an investee, the investee is referred to as a **subsidiary** and the investor is called the *parent*. "Control of an enterprise is the continuing power to determine its strategic operating, investing and financing policies without the co-operation of others" (CICA Handbook 1590.03). A subsidiary is an enterprise controlled by another enterprise (the parent) that has the right and ability to obtain future economic benefits from the resources of the enterprises and is exposed to the related risks. Current practice calls for the consolidation of *all* of a parent's subsidiaries. When non-consolidated statements are thought to be more meaningful to the users, they may be prepared in addition to consolidated statements. In situations where the company is itself a wholly owned subsidiary or there are no external shareholders, non-consolidated statements may be prepared.

When one company has complete control over another company, they in effect operate as a single economic entity and should be accounted for as such. Single entity financial statements will be prepared, but it is generally assumed that consolidated statements for the two companies present the users with the most meaningful information. Consolidated statements, supplemented by segmented information, are generally thought to be more informative than *separate* financial statements for the parent and each of its subsidiaries.

8.2A ACCOUNTING METHODS

Cost Method

cost method
An accounting method for intercorporate investments that recognizes investment income on the basis of dividends paid by the investee.

The **cost method** is required when the investor has little or no control over the investee. Lack of control is generally defined as less than 20 percent of the voting shares of the investee. Assuming an investor acquires a 10 percent interest (e.g., 10,000 shares of 100,000 shares outstanding) in an investee for $400,000, the following entry would be made:

```
Investment in Investee Co. . . . . . . . . . . . . . . . . . . . . . . . . . . . . 400,000
     Cash . . . . . . . . . . . . . . . . . . . . . . . . . . . . . . . . . . . . . . . . . .        400,000
  Acquired 10% interest in Investee Co.
```

The investee declares and pays a $3.00 per share dividend. The investor's entry to record its share of that income is as follows:

```
Cash . . . . . . . . . . . . . . . . . . . . . . . . . . . . . . . . . . . . . . . . . . . . 30,000
     Investment Income . . . . . . . . . . . . . . . . . . . . . . . . . . . . . . . .        30,000
  Received dividend from Investee Co.
```

Equity Method

When an investor's ownership of an investee's voting shares is of such a size that the investor is able to influence the way the investee conducts its business (e.g., to pressure the investee to make a larger dividend payout), the investor is required to adopt the **equity method** of accounting. Under the equity method, the investor records its initial investment at the cost it paid to acquire the shares. Then, on an ongoing basis, the investor adds to its income its pro rata share of the investee's income (or subtracts its pro rata share of the investee's losses). For example, assume that an investor acquires 30 percent of the voting shares of Investee Corporation for $1,200,000 (e.g., 30,000 shares of 100,000 shares outstanding). The journal entry to record this investment is as follows:

```
Investment in Investee Co. . . . . . . . . . . . . . . . . . . . . . . . . . . .  1,200,000
     Cash . . . . . . . . . . . . . . . . . . . . . . . . . . . . . . . . . . . . . . . . . . .1,200,000
     Acquired 30% interest in Investee Co.
```

The investee's net earnings were $360,000; the investor's entry to record its share of that income is as follows:

```
Investment in Investee Co. . . . . . . . . . . . . . . . . . . . . . . . . . . . .108,000
     Investment Income  . . . . . . . . . . . . . . . . . . . . . . . . . . . . . . . . . . .  108,000
        (.30 × $360,000)
     Accrued income from the Investee Co.
```

Notice that the income recognized by the investor is added to the original cost of the investment. When an investee pays a dividend, the investor treats that cash receipt as a liquidation of part of its investment. Assuming that the investee pays a dividend of $3.00 a share, the accounting entry by the investor follows:

```
Cash . . . . . . . . . . . . . . . . . . . . . . . . . . . . . . . . . . . . . . . . . . .90,000
     Investment in Investee Co. . . . . . . . . . . . . . . . . . . . . . . . . . . . .  90,000
     Received dividend from Investee Co.
```

In effect, the equity method puts the investor/investee relationship on an accrual basis so that the investor recognizes income from the investment when it is earned rather than when it is paid out in cash.

An assumption of the above example is that Investee Corporation had income for the year. The same accounting is required if the investee incurs a loss; the investor is obligated to recognize its pro rata share of the investee's loss, reducing its income and its investment in the investee. This proration explains, at least in part, the rationale for equity accounting: There was a concern that a company could sell off a controlling share of the part of its business that was losing money and, under the cost method, avoid the recognition of those losses. The provisions of equity method accounting created a middle ground between a fully controlled investment and an investment in which the investor has no control. In that middle ground, an investor is required to recognize its pro rata share of its investee's net income or its investee's net losses.

The equity method must be used when an investor has the ability to exercise significant influence over an investee. Evidence of "ability to influence" includes, for example, the ability to elect individuals to an investee's board of directors or to force dividend increases. Official guidelines suggest that ownership of more than 20 percent of an investee's outstanding voting shares is presumptive evidence of the ability to influence. Very few companies have justified the equity method for an investment without a 20 percent holding of voting shares, and, conversely, very few companies have been able to avoid the equity method if they own more than 20 percent of an investee's voting shares. An investor may not select the cost method or the equity method; the use of one method over another is mandatory, based on voting-share ownership, unless evidence to the contrary exists.

The Interprovincial Pipe Line System, Inc.'s note on its principles of consolidation includes a comment on the use of the equity method: "The consolidated financial statements include the accounts of the Corporation and all of its subsidiaries. Investments in entities which are not subsidiaries, but over which the Corporation exercises significant influence, are accounted for using the equity method."

Under the equity method of accounting, at any point in time an investor's investment account (i.e., its investment in the investee) equals its original cost, plus its share of the investee's earnings since the date of acquisition, less any dividends received. If the investor's original cost for the investment was more (or less) than its pro rata share of the investee's net book value, under equity method accounting, any such excess (or deficiency) is amortized against (to) income in a like manner to goodwill over a period of years. The investment account balance is reported as a single line item on the investor's balance sheet. Similarly, the investor's share of an investee's earnings for a period is reported as a single line item on the investor's income statement. The equity method is sometimes referred to as a *one-line* consolidation. Note that the income recognized is the investor's share of the investee's reported net earnings without regard to whether those earnings were distributed in cash.

Consolidation

consolidated financial statements
Financial statements prepared to reflect the operations and financial condition of a parent company and its wholly or majority-owned subsidiaries.

When an investor owns enough of an investee's voting shares to be in a position to *control* the investee, rather than simply exert "significant influence" over it, the investor must include all of the investee's assets and liabilities and revenue and expenses in its financial statements as though it owned those assets and liabilities and incurred those revenues and expenses directly. Since the investee is a controlled company (rather than simply an "influenced" one), it is no longer appropriate for the investor to report its investment in its balance sheet as a single line item, nor does it report income from the investment as a single item in its income statement, that is, use the equity method. Instead, when the investor reports to its shareholders, it replaces those single investment asset and investment income numbers with all the details they represent (i.e., the investor includes in its **consolidated financial statements** all the assets, liabilities, revenues, and expenses it controls by virtue of its ownership of the investee).

For example, consider the following set of balance sheets, which assumes that Investor Corporation paid $550 in cash for 100 percent of the outstanding shares of Investee Corporation on January 1:

INVESTOR CORPORATION
Balance Sheets
At January 1

	Preinvestment	Adjustments	Postinvestment
Cash	$1,550	(550)	$1,000
Accounts receivable	1,500		1,500
Inventory	1,800		1,800
Property and plant	2,200		2,200
Investment in Investee		550	550
	$7,050	–0–	$7,050
Accounts payable	$ 900		$ 900
Long-term debt	3,500		3,500
Shareholders' equity	2,650		2,650
	$7,050	–0–	$7,050

Note that immediately following the investment, the aggregate value of the corporation's total assets is unchanged — only the mix of those assets is changed.

If Investor Corporation desires to prepare a consolidated balance sheet, as would be required of a publicly held corporation, it is a simple matter to replace the Investment in Investee Corporation account with Investee's assets and liabilities. In the following consolidated balance sheet, we assume that the total owners' equity of Investee Corporation was $550 on January 1:

INVESTOR CORPORATION
Balance Sheets
At January 1

	Investor	Investee	Adjustments	Consolidated
Cash	$1,000	$ 500		$1,500
Accounts receivable	1,500	800		2,300
Inventory	1,800	600		2,400
Property and plant	2,200	1,200		3,400
Investment in Investee	550		(550)	—
	$7,050	$3,100	(550)	$9,600
Accounts payable	$ 900	$ 300		$1,200
Long-term debt	3,500	2,250		5,750
Shareholders' equity	2,650	550	(550)	2,650
	$7,050	$3,100	(550)	$9,600

Note that the consolidated financial statements that are sent to Investor Corporation's shareholders include all of its assets and liabilities, as well as the assets and liabilities of Investee Corporation. The process of combining those two financial statements (the "consolidation") substitutes Investee's assets and liabilities (in effect, its owners' equity or net assets) for Investor's investment account. That process can also be described by the following equation:

Investor's aggregate investment = Investee's total net worth
= Investee's individual assets –Investee's
individual liabilities

The three factors in the above equation are equal, and so consolidation accounting simply substitutes Investee's individual assets and its individual liabilities for the aggregate Investor's investment.

After a year's operations, the consolidation of the two companies' income statements would appear as follows:

INVESTOR CORPORATION
Income Statement
For the Year Ended December 31

	Investor	Investee	Adjustments	Consolidated
Sales	$ 5,000	$ 2,000		$ 7,000
Cost of goods sold	(2,000)	(1,100)		(3,100)
Operating expenses	(2,000)	(400)		(2,400)
Amortization expense	(500)	(200)		(700)
Investment income	300		$ (300)	—
	$ 800	$ 300	$ (300)	$ 800

Note that in the preparation of the consolidated income statement, Investor's single line item "Investment income" is expanded to reflect all the sales and expenses it controls by virtue of that investment.

Most often, the investor and the investee continue to maintain their own accounting records as though they were stand-alone, unaffiliated entities. However, because the investor's ownership interest is 100 percent, the only external financial statements that will be prepared reflect a full consolidation of the two parties (i.e., combining investor and investee). The preparation of those consolidated balance sheets, income statements, and statement of changes in financial position occurs only when a financial report is prepared for distribution to the directors, shareholders, or other external users of the financial statements. The "adjustments" illustrated here exist only on worksheets (or on a floppy disk) as part of the process of putting the two companies' records together for the consolidated financial statement presentation.

This example is grossly oversimplified because Investor owns all the shares of Investee and because the cost of Investor's investment is exactly equal to Investee's net assets. You should study these simplified illustrations and be sure that you understand the basic concepts of consolidation accounting: Consolidated financial statements combine two (or more) companies' activities as though they conducted business as *one* entity. Consolidated financial statements substitute full details of the investee's assets and liabilities for the investor's single investment number, and the full details of the investee's operations for the investor's single investment income number. Finally, note that net income reported in the consolidated income statement is the same as for Investor — only the details are different.

Generally accepted accounting principles require that the investor present consolidated financial statements when it has the ability to control the activities of an investee. An investor's ability to elect a majority of the members of an investee's board of directors is presumed to be evidence of such control. Accounting guidelines also suggest that ownership of more than 50 percent of the outstanding voting shares is presumptive evidence of the ability to control. That quantitative measure is followed almost without exception in practice. Few companies are able to justify the preparation of consolidated financial statements with their investees without ownership of more than 50 percent of an investee's outstanding shares. Few companies are able to avoid such a consolidation when they own more than 50 percent of an investee's outstanding stock.

These three approaches — cost method with single line item presentation, equity method accounting with single line item presentation, and equity method accounting with full consolidation — are not alternatives — selection of one is required by the particular circumstances faced by an investor. The approach to be used is almost always dictated by the degree of ownership of an investor in an investee.

Non-Controlling Interest

noncontrolling interest
The percentage ownership in the net assets of a subsidiary held by investors other than the parent company.

A **non-controlling interest** exists when shares in a subsidiary company are held by other than the parent company. Since the purchase transaction does not involve the non-controlling interest in the subsidiary's assets and liabilities, it is appropriate to reflect this interest in terms of the carrying values (book values) recorded in the accounting records of the subsidiary company. Non-controlling interest is frequently referred to as *minority interest*.

Occasionally, an investor is unable to acquire all of the outstanding voting shares of an investee, and a minority shareholder position remains outstanding. So long as the investor owns more than 50 percent of the investee's outstanding voting shares, full consolidation is required. The minority shareholders' ownership of the investee's net worth is carried into the consolidated financial statements just above the investor's shareholders' equity and just below its long-term debt. (For ratio purposes, it is either considered part of long-term debt or ignored.) In a published income statement, the earnings of the investee company attributable to the minority shareholders' interest are reported just after income after taxes, just before the net earnings line.

8.13 REVIEW AND DISCUSSION QUESTIONS

Q8.1 Point: Research and development expenditures should be expensed when incurred. Counterpoint: Research and development expenditures should be capitalized until it is known whether or not a commercially viable product will result. If none results, then R&D should be expensed.

Evaluate the two viewpoints. Which one do you agree with, and why?

Q8.2 Is the purpose of amortization to provide for the replacement of a capital asset once its useful life is over? If not, what is the purpose of amortization?

Q8.3 Is amortization a source of cash? If not, why is amortization added back to net income in the statement of changes in financial position?

Q8.4 What items should be included in determining the original cost of a new machine? Explain.

Q8.5 Amos Company decides to build its own machine rather than to purchase a similar one from a machine manufacturer. Should the company capitalize the cost of its own labourers who work on building the machine? Explain.

Q8.6 Once it has fully amortized a capital asset, can a company continue to use the asset? If so, can the company continue to record amortization? If not, will net income be overstated?

Q8.7 If a company originally estimates that a machine will last six years but after two years decides that the total useful life is more likely to be eight years, how should this change in estimate be treated for financial accounting and reporting purposes?

Q8.8 How should a company account for normal repairs and maintenance for a building? For a replacement of the roof? For a general renovation of the building including air conditioning? Why?

Q8.9 What factors must management consider as they deliberate between the use of the cost method and the equity method?

Q8.10 The equity method is occasionally referred to as a *one-line* consolidation. What does that expression mean? Is it a fair description of equity accounting?

Q8.11 Digital Computer Company recently purchased a special machine that was made to the company's specifications. This machine has a physical life of 15 years at the proposed rate of production. The company's tax department reported that, for machines of this type, Revenue Canada normally specifies 12 years as the period over which the machines are written off. What factors should the company consider in estimating the useful life of this machine?

Q8.12 Thrifty Company has just completed it first year of operations and wishes to maximize its reported net income for the current year. To achieve this objective the company has a number of decisions to be made with regard to the appropriate selection of accounting polices/methods. The current year has been one of constantly rising prices. During the year the company has purchased inventory, new equipment, and a patent for a manufacturing process. Prepare a brief report recommending generally accepted accounting methods that will assist the company in achieving its objective of maximizing profits in its first year.

8.14 PROBLEMS

P8.1 Estimating amortization and book value. Equipment costing $19,000, with a residual value of $4,000, was purchased on January 1, 1995, by Yellow Creek Electrical Company. The estimated useful life of the equipment was five years or 75,000 units of production. Units produced were 12,000 in 1995 and 16,000 in 1996.

Required:

Using the straight-line, sum-of-the-years'-digits, double-declining-balance, and the units-of-production methods

a. Determine the amortization expense for 1995 and 1996.

b. Determine the book value of the capital asset on December 31, 1995, and 1996.

P8.2 Income statement preparation. Randolph Mining Corporation paid $3,040,000 for a tract of land containing valuable ore and spent $280,000 in developing the property during 1995 preparatory to beginning mining activities on January 1, 1996. Company geologists estimated that the mineral deposit would produce 6 million tons of ore, and it is assumed that the land will have a residual value of $20,000 after the ore deposit is exhausted. It is expected that it will take 12 to 14 years to extract all of the ore.

A record of capital investment during the last half of 1995, exclusive of the development costs previously mentioned, is as follows:

Asset	Estimated Service Life	Cost
Mine buildings	30 years	$300,000
Railroad and hoisting equipment	20 years	600,000
Miscellaneous mine equipment	10 years	120,000

The building, railroad, and hoisting equipment cannot be economically removed from the mine location, but other miscellaneous equipment is readily movable and has alternative uses.

Operations during 1996 are summarized below:

Tons of ore mined and sold at $4 per ton	500,000
Mining labour and other operating costs	$950,000
(exclusive of amortization and depletion)	
Selling and administrative expenses	$140,000

Required:

Prepare an income statement for 1996. (Ignore income taxes.)

P8.3 Accounting for the sale of an asset. On January 1, 1992, Home Construction Corporation purchased a number of pieces of new equipment, including a new dump truck. The truck cost $25,000 and was expected to last 10 years. Home always used double-declining-balance amortization for its financial reports, and its amortization calculations assume no residual values. By December 1996, the construction business had begun to slow down. Home found itself with idle equipment on its hands. One of the employees who was laid off as a result of the slowdown asked to buy the truck for use in a landscaping business he planned to start. On December 30, 1996, the company agreed to sell him the truck in exchange for $10,000 cash.

Required:

a. What entry(ies) should Home make regarding the truck for the year ended December 31, 1996?

b. What entry(ies) should Home make regarding the truck for the year ended December 31, 1996, if the transaction with the employee is not consummated until January 4, 1997?

P8.4 Capitalization and amortization policy decisions. Keeler Company purchased a new machine to use in its operations. The new machine was delivered by the supplier, installed by Keeler, and placed into operation. It was purchased under a long-term payment plan with interest to be charged at the current market rate. The estimated useful life of the new machine is 10 years, and its estimated residual value is significant. Normal maintenance was performed to keep the new machine in usable condition. Keeler also added a wing to its factory building in order to provide much needed manufacturing floor space. In addition, Keeler made significant leasehold improvements to office space used as corporate headquarters.

Required:

a. What costs should Keeler capitalize for the new machine? Without focusing on specific amortization methods, how should the machine be amortized?

b. How should Keeler account for the normal maintenance performed on the new machine? Why?

c. How should Keeler account for the wing added to the factory building? How should the added wing be reported on Keeler's financial statements?

d. How should Keeler account for the leasehold improvements made to its office space? How should the leasehold improvements be reported on Keeler's financial statements?

P8.5 Capital asset accounting policy. At the beginning of the year, Constance Dado acquired a computer to be used in her company's operations. The computer was delivered by the supplier, installed by Dado Corporation personnel, and placed into operation. The estimated useful life of the computer is five years, and its estimated residual value is significant.

During the year, Dado also sold one of her executive limos purchased in a prior year for cash.

Required:

a. What costs should Dado capitalize for the computer?

b. Without discussing specific amortization methods, what is the objective of amortization accounting?

c. What is the rationale for using accelerated amortization methods?

d. How should Dado account for and report the disposal of the limo?

P8.6 Accounting for capital assets. The Capital asset and Accumulated Amortization accounts of Marietta Corporation had the following balances at December 31, 1995:

	Cost Basis	Accumulated Amortization
Land	$ 250,000	—
Land improvements	160,000	$ 40,000
Building	1,500,000	350,000
Machinery and equipment	1,158,000	405,000
Automobiles	150,000	112,000

The financial reporting policies of Marietta Corporation pertaining to amortization of capital assets follow: land improvements — straight line, 15 years; building — 7.50 percent declining balance; machinery and equipment — straight line, 10 years; automobiles — 50 percent declining balance. Amortization is computed to the nearest month. All residual values are assumed to be zero.

The following transactions occurred during 1996:

On January 2, 1996, machinery and equipment were purchased at a total invoice cost of $240,000, which included a $5,500 charge for freight. Installation costs of $17,000 were incurred.

On March 31, 1996, a machine purchased for $68,000 on January 2, 1992, was sold for $46,500.

On June 1, 1996, expenditures of $40,000 were made to repave parking lots at Marietta's plant location. Damage caused by severe winter weather necessitated the work.

On November 1, 1996, Marietta acquired a tract of land with an existing building in exchange for 9,000 shares of Marietta's share capital that had a market price of $39 per share on this date. Marietta paid legal fees and title insurance totalling $24,000. The last property tax bill indicated assessed values of $250,000 for land and $50,000 for building. Shortly after acquisition, the building was demolished at a cost of $35,000 in anticipation of new building construction in 1997.

On December 31, 1996, Marietta purchased a new automobile for $15,000 cash and trade-in of an automobile purchased for $18,000 on January 2, 1995. The new automobile has a cash value of $19,000.

Required:

a. Prepare a schedule analyzing the changes in each of the plant assets during 1996 with detailed supporting computations. Disregard the related accumulated amortization accounts.

b. For each asset classification, prepare a schedule showing amortization expense for the year ended December 31, 1996.

c. Prepare a schedule showing the gain or loss from each asset disposal that would be recognized in Marietta's income statement for the year ended December 31, 1996.

P8.7 Amortization policy. Allan Corporation provided the following footnote in a recent set of financial statements detailing its amortization policies.

Property, plant, and equipment — Except for oil and gas producing properties, amortization is generally computed by the straight-line method based upon the estimated lives of the assets. The Corporation's method of computing amortization of steel assets modifies straight-line amortization based on the level of production. The modification ranges from a minimum of 80% at a production level of 50% of capacity and below, to a maximum of 130% for a 100% production level. No modification is made at the 85% production level, considered the normal long-range level.

Depletion of the cost of mineral properties, other than oil and gas, is based on rates which are expected to amortize the cost over the estimated tonnage of minerals to be removed. Amortization and depletion of oil and gas producing properties are computed at rates applied to the units of production on the basis of proved oil and gas reserves as determined by the Corporation's geologists and engineers.

When a plant or major facility within a plant is sold or otherwise disposed of by the Corporation, any gain or loss is reflected in income. Proceeds from the sale of other facilities amortized on a group basis are credited to the amortization reserve. When facilities amortized on an individual basis are sold, the difference between the selling price and the remaining unamortized value is reflected in income.

Required:

a. In your own words, explain Allan's amortization policy for steel assets.

b. What rationale would support Allan's amortization policy?

P8.8 Repair and maintenance expense. During 1996, Steamboat Company made the following expenditures relating to plant machinery and equipment:

Renovation of a group of machines at a cost of $60,000 to secure greater efficiency in production over their remaining five-year useful lives. The project was completed on December 31, 1996.

Continuing, frequent, and low-cost repairs at a cost of $45,000.

A broken gear on a machine was replaced at a cost of $6,000.

Required:

What total amount should be charged to repairs and maintenance expense in 1996?

P8.9 Cost capitalization. On June 30, 1996, Belpre, Inc., completed the rearrangement of a group of factory machines to secure greater efficiency in production. Belpre estimated that benefits from the rearrangement would extend over the remaining five-year useful lives of the machines. The following costs were incurred:

Moving	$42,000
Reinstallation	64,000
Actual maintenance (performed at this time for convenience)	9,000

Required:

How much of the costs incurred should be capitalized on June 30, 1996?

P8.10 Estimating depletion expense. In January 1996, Craig Mining Corporation purchased a mineral mine for $4 million with removable ore estimated by geological surveys at 2,300,000 tons. The property has an estimated residual value of $400,000 after the ore has been extracted. Craig incurred $1 million of development costs preparing the property for the extraction of ore. During 1996, 270,000 tons were removed and 240,000 tons were sold.

Required:

For the year ended December 31, 1996, Craig should include what amount of depletion in its cost of goods sold? Explain.

P8.11 Estimating amortization expense. Curtis Company bought a trademark from Kent Corporation on January 1, 1996, for $122,000. An independent consultant retained by Curtis estimated that the remaining useful life is 50 years. Its unamortized cost on Kent's accounting records was $61,000. Curtis decided to write off the trademark over the maximum period allowed.

Required:

How much should be amortized for the year ended December 31, 1996? Explain.

P8.12 Accounting for intangible assets. Robertson, Inc., seemed to have a balance sheet full of intangible assets. During 1996, four additional decisions were required regarding various intangible asset–related expenditures. Each is presented below.

Required:

a. Which of the following legal fees should be capitalized?

   (1) Legal fees to obtain a franchise.

   (2) Legal fees to successfully defend a trademark.

b. Which of the following costs of goodwill should be capitalized and amortized over their estimated useful lives?

   (1) Cost of goodwill from a business combination accounted for as a purchase.

   (2) Cost of developing goodwill internally.

c. Which of the following costs of goodwill should be capitalized and amortized?

   (1) Developing goodwill.

   (2) Restoring goodwill.

d. Legal fees incurred by a company in defending its patent rights should be capitalized when the outcome of the litigation is: successful or unsuccessful?

P8.13 Accounting for intangible assets. Belle Corporation incurred $140,000 of costs to develop a product for which a patent was granted on January 2, 1996. Legal fees and other costs associated with registration of the patent totalled $40,000. On March 31, 1996, Belle paid $55,000 for legal fees in a successful defence of the patent.

Required:

What is the balance in the Patent account on March 31, 1996?

P8.14 Capital asset disposals (*Published with permission of CGA Canada*). The following transactions relate to Alex Company.

1993

Jan. 3   Paid $15,000 to replace a major component of Machine No. A100. The machine originally cost $300,000 and accumulated amortization to date amounts to $225,000. The residual value is estimated at $10,000 and is not expected to be affected by the component replacement. This component will extend the life of the machine from a previous estimate of five years remaining to a new estimate of 10 years. Amortization is calculated using the double-declining-balance method.

Apr. 2   Machine No. A101, which originally cost $1,750 and was fully amortized, was discarded. A scrap company was paid $100 to haul it away.

June 28   Machine No. A105, which originally cost $2,000 and had an accumulated amortization balance of $1,300, was traded in for Machine No. B105, which has an expected useful life of five years. The new machine has a list price of $4,000 and will be amortized using the double-declining-balance method. Alex Company received a trade-in allowance of $900 on the old machine. The book value of Machine No. A105 approximates its fair value.

Oct. 1   Machine No. A110 was damaged in an accident beyond repair. This machine had been purchased one year ago at $3,000 plus installation charges of $500 and was expected to last four years. This machine had an estimated residual value of $700, was amortized using the straight-line method, and was insured for 70 percent of its cost. Assume the entry to bring Accumulated Amortization up to date for this year has already been recorded.

Required:

a. Prepare journal entries to record each of the above events. Assume that amortization is generally taken annually on December 31 and that a separate amortization account is kept for each machine.

b. Assume that a new Machine No. A115 was acquired on November 1, 1995, and is correctly recorded at $4,600. Calculate amortization for 1995 and 1996 for this machine using the CCA method. The capital cost allowance rate is assumed to be 30 percent.

P8.15 Accounting for asset exchanges. On June 30, Clay, Inc., exchanged 3,000 shares of North Corp. common shares for a patent owned by South Co. The North shares were acquired at a cost of $40,000. At the exchange date, North common shares had a fair value of $35 per share, and the patent had a net carrying amount of $90,000 on South's books.

Required:

Clay should record the patent at what amount? Explain.

P8.16 Capitalization policy. In starting a new warehousing business, Hires Partnership purchased 10 acres of land to be used as the site for a new warehouse. A building on the property was sold and removed by the buyer so that construction on the warehouse could begin.

Required:

How should the proceeds from the sale of the building be treated?

P8.17 Accounting for asset exchanges. On September 1, Ruane, Inc., exchanged a delivery truck for a parcel of land. Ruane bought this truck for $12,000. As of September 1, the truck had a book value of $7,500 and a fair market value of $5,000. Ruane gave $7,000 in cash in addition to the truck as part of this transaction. The previous owner of the land had listed the land for sale at $14,000.

Required:

At what amount should Ruane record the land?

P8.18 Amortization methods. Canadian Toy Industries Ltd. purchased equipment at the beginning of the year for $173,000. The equipment will be used by the company for an estimated useful life of eight years or 200,000 hours. It is estimated the equipment will have a residual value of $13,000. The accounting department is undecided as to which amortization method would be most appropriate for this asset. The methods being considered are: straight-line, units of production, and declining balance at twice the straight-line rate. The equipment was used for 11,000 hours during the first year of operation. Determine the amortization expense for the first year assuming:

(a) The company objective of financial reporting is to maximize profits.

(b) The company wishes to publish conservative financial statements.

P8.19 Estimating book values. Kaiser Aluminum and Chemical Corporation provided the following footnote, regarding its property, plant, and equipment, in one of its recent financial statements:

December 31	1996	1995
Land and improvements	$ 171.5	$ 157.8
Buildings	386.8	359.0
Machinery and equipment	2,342.3	2,206.1
Construction in progress	52.9	62.7
Total property — at cost (includes idle facilities: $215.8 in 1996 and $215.9 in 1995)	2,953.5	2,785.6
Accumulated amortization (includes idle facilities: $130.8 in 1996 and $126.1 in 1995)	1,467.7	1,253.9
Property, plant, and equipment — net	$1,485.8	$1,531.7

The idle facilities shown above consist of the corporation's aluminum smelter which is temporarily closed because of high energy and other costs and the market conditions for primary aluminum. In addition, production of alumina at Alumina Partners of Jamaica (ALPART) was temporarily suspended in August 1995 due to the continuing adverse economic conditions impacting the aluminum industry. ALPART, a 50%-owned partnership, has an alumina plant in Nain, Jamaica. At December 31, 1996 and 1995, investments and advances include $32.5 and $32.0 for ALPART, which is accounted for by the equity method. The corporation is obligated to pay $72.4 and $79.0 of ALPART's debt at December 31, 1996 and 1995, as discussed in Note 12.

Management believes that market conditions will improve and that operating costs of the idle facilities can be reduced sufficiently to permit economic operation of these facilities in the future. The corporation's policy is to continue normal amortization for temporarily closed facilities.

Required:

a. What is the net book value (NBV) of Kaiser's idle facilities at 12/31/96?

b. If, as of 12/31/96, an independent appraiser determined that the fair market value of the idle facilities was $50 million less than Kaiser's NBV, should the NBV be adjusted? Why or why not?

c. If the appraisal were $50 million more than NBV, should it be adjusted? Why or why not?

d. Why is Kaiser amortizing its idle facilities?

e. What rationale would support a decision not to continue amortizing facilities?

P8.20 Capitalization policy. On January 2, 1996, Keystone Corporation replaced its conveyor line with a more efficient one. The following information was available on that date:

Purchase price of new conveyor	$50,000
Carrying amount of old conveyor	5,000
Fair value of old conveyor	2,000
Installation cost of new conveyor	8,000
The old conveyor was sold for	2,000

Required:

What amount should Keystone capitalize as the cost of the new conveyor?

P8.21 Financial statement disclosure. Describe how the following items would be disclosed on a properly classified financial statement:

a. Significant accounting policies.

b. Research & development costs.

c. Sales returns.

d. Allowance for decline in market value of temporary investments.

P8.22 Capital assets. During the year amortization expense on equipment of $175,000 was recorded by Sainty Limited. New equipment at a cost of $85,000 was purchased on account. Assume the beginning balances were $825,000 for Equipment and $550,000 for Accumulated Amortization and the ending balances were $760,000 for Equipment and $615,000 for Accumulated Amortization. Determine the original cost of equipment sold and the related balance of the Accumulated Amortization account for equipment that has been sold during the accounting period.

P8.23 Accounting for capital assets (*Certified Management Accountants of British Columbia*). The Conform Metal Co. produces steel bumpers for a major car manufacturer. The demand for bumpers depends on motor car production. Conform has purchased a new press to mould bumpers. The machine cost $1,000,000 cash. The installation costs are $50,000. To install the machine a new power supply had to be installed at a cost of $10,000. The machine is expected to produce 100,000 bumpers. After that it is estimated to be worth $10,000 as scrap. Removal costs are estimated at $5,000. The machine has the following production:

Year 1	50,000 units
Year 2	20,000 units
Year 3	20,000 units

Required:

a. Give the journal entry for the purchase of the equipment.

b. What should be the amortization charges in Years 1, 2, and 3?

c. Suppose the machine is sold at the end of Year 3 for $20,000, with a $5,000 removal cost. Give the appropriate journal entry.

P8.24 Accounting for capital assets (*Certified Management Accountants of British Columbia*). George's Garage owned a wheel balancing machine, originally purchased on January 1,

Year 1, for $20,000. It was estimated to have a useful life of five years, with no residual value. At the end of Year 3, the equipment was reconditioned so that it would have another four years of useful life. The residual value was still expected to be zero. The reconditioning process cost $4,000. The straight-line method of amortization was used.

Required:

a. Prepare the journal entry to record the amortization expense for Year 5.

b. What was the book value of the equipment at the end of Year 6?

c. At the end of Year 6, the wheel balancing machine was sold for $1,000. Give the journal entry to record this sale.

P8.25 Amortization methods (*Certified Management Accountants of British Columbia*). The Western Company purchased a machine for $100,000 cash at the beginning of Year 1. The estimated useful life of the machine was 10 years with a residual value of $10,000. The machine was expected to produce 300,000 units of output during its life. Actual output for years 1 and 2 was 25,000 and 35,000 units, respectively.

Required:

Prepare a schedule like the one shown below. Make the necessary calculations.

	Amortization Expense		Book Value End of	
Amortization Method	**Year 1**	**Year 2**	**Year 1**	**Year 2**
Straight line				
Units of production				
Declining balance, using double the straight-line rate				

P8.26 Accounting for capital assets (*Certified Management Accountants of British Columbia*). On July 1, 1990, Slowtec Company purchased a word processing machine for $12,000. Expected life was 10 years with an expected residual value of $3,000. The asset was amortized on a straight-line basis. On March 1, 1995, Slowtec revised the residual value downward to $1,000. Finally, on September 30, 1996, Slowtec traded in the old machine plus $3,000 cash for a new computer that had a list price of $3,900. The old machine had a fair market value of $300 on the trade-in date. The company's fiscal year-end is June 30.

Required:

Prepare the journal entry for September 30, 1996. Show your supporting calculations.

P8.27 Amortization methods (*Certified Management Accountants of British Columbia*). Fuji, Ltd., purchased a machine for $29,500 on January 1, 1995. An additional $2,500 was spent on delivery costs, installation, and testing. Expected residual value was $2,000. It is expected that the machine will be used for 15,000 hours before being retired. Hours used for 1995 and 1996 were 3,200 and 2,400, respectively. In 1997 the machine is expected to be used 3,500 hours. The amortization expense for 1995 and 1996 using three alternative amortization methods is:

Year	Method A	Method B	Method C
1995	$ 9,600	$ 6,400	$ 6,000
1996	6,720	4,800	6,000

Required:

a. Identify the three amortization methods used.

b. When would it be appropriate to use each of the amortization methods?

c. Calculate the amortization expense for 1997 for each of the three methods.

d. Assume the machine was sold on January 31, 1997, for $18,000. Using Method C, make the appropriate journal entry.

P8.28 Accounting for capital assets (*Certified Management Accountants of British Columbia*). Treck Explorations bought their first truck for $10,000 on January 1, 1994, when they commenced business. They amortized it at a rate of 30 percent per year on the declining balance for 1994 and 1995. On July 1, 1996, they traded it in for a new truck. The list price on the new truck was $15,000 but the dealer gave them a trade-in allowance of $5,000 for the old truck. They knew that the list price was unrealistically high, but so was the trade-in allowance (they had a cash offer from someone else of $3,000 for the old truck), and it was the best deal they could make with any dealer. In addition to trading in the old truck, they paid $6,000 cash and signed a two-year 10 percent note for the difference they owed. Since the truck was used mostly in summertime they decided on a different amortization method starting July 1, 1996, based on actual use. The new truck should last for 200,000 kilometres and then they should be able to get $2,000 for it. On December 31, 1996, the odometer reads 60,000 kilometres. Treck's controller has decided to not recognize any gain or loss on the exchange transaction.

Required:

a. Prepare 1996 journal entries assuming that no journal entries have been made for 1995 yet. Use dates and brief explanations.

b. If Treck had decided to recognize any gain or loss resulting from buying the new truck and trading in the old one, what would have been the amount of the gain or loss, and what would have been the cost of the new truck?

P8.29 Amortization accounting (*Certified Management Accountants of British Columbia*). On September 30, 1996, the Pasqua Company purchased a truck for $54,000 with a cash down payment of $4,000 and signed a note for the balance. The truck's estimated life is four years with an estimated residual value of $6,000.

On December 31, 1997, after all adjustments have been made, the following account appears on the ledger:

Accumulated amortization — Truck $30,375

Required:

a. What method is the company using to amortize the truck?

b. What was the amortization expense for 1996 and 1997?

c. What other method could the company use to amortize the truck?

P8.30 Amortization methods and ratio analysis.

a. Acme Company purchased a new automobile on January 3, 1995. The automobile cost $23,000 and is estimated to have a useful life of five years and a residual value of $7,000. Acme Company uses the declining-balance method of amortization at an annual rate of 20 percent. Determine the amortization expense for the second year of use of the asset, the year ending December 31, 1996.

b. Acme Company purchased a machine for $125,000 on January 2, 1996. The machine has an estimated useful life of 100,000 hours and a residual value of $15,000. Acme uses the production method of amortization. If the machine was used 8,800 hours during the year, determine the amortization expense for the year.

c. For the year ending December 31, 1996, Acme reported a net income before amortization expenses of $47,400. The December 31 total shareholders' equity of $382,000 includes common shares, of which 33,000 shares have been outstanding for several years. Net income has not been closed to Retained Earnings. Determine the earnings per share and return on equity for Acme Company.

P8.31 Accounting for market values. Mrs. Rosewood recently approached her bank manager and requested a loan for her business, Flowers, Ltd. After reviewing Flowers' financial information, the bank manager made the following estimates concerning Flowers, Ltd.:

1. Unrecorded goodwill $300,000.

2. The market value of inventories, capital assets, and temporary investments is $125,000 higher than the book value.

Mrs. Rosewood always likes to maintain a positive outlook and thought it would be desirable to include these estimates in Flowers' financial statements. When Mrs. Rosewood asked her accountant to make the appropriate changes, he refused claiming, "I can't possibly do that. Generally accepted accounting principles do not allow me to record all assets and I certainly can't record goodwill. Furthermore, those assets you mention shouldn't be valued at market value."

Mrs. Rosewood was concerned about these remarks and discussed them with a friend. Her friend added to the confusion by stating that he had seen goodwill on balance sheets and had seen temporary investments carried at market value.

Required:

Prepare an explanation of the accountant's comments for Mrs. Rosewood. Be sure to discuss any accounting conventions or assumptions that support the accountant's position. You may also use examples to help explain the situation to Mrs. Rosewood. Include an explanation of Mrs. Rosewood's friend's comments.

P8.32 Adjusting entries and amortization methods (*Certified Management Accountants of British Columbia*). William Low started an importing business on March 1, 1996. The business, named Pacific Rim Distributors, prepares monthly financial statements. The following information is available on March 31, 1996.

1. Salaries and wages are paid to employees each Friday. Salaries and wages earned but not paid total $24,000.

2. Office space is leased on an annual basis, and the rent is payable quarterly in advance. On March 31, 1996, the company paid a quarterly installment on the annual rent, which was $36,000.

3. The company owned land valued at $125,000 on the date of purchase four years ago. A recent appraisal valued the land at a current market value of $185,000.

4. The company erected a warehouse on their land at a cost of $375,000. The warehouse building is amortized over 30 years on a straight-line basis. The estimated residual value of the building is $25,000.

5. Pacific Rim Distributors owns machinery that cost $78,500 with an estimated residual value of $5,500. It is estimated that the machinery will have a useful life of 65,000 machine hours. Machinery usage records show 12,250 hours of use to March 31, 1996.

6. The company had purchased a computer, with appropriate software, worth $27,350. It was estimated that the computer and software would have a life of five years. The company decided to use the double-declining-balance method of amortization.

Required:

a. Prepare all necessary adjusting journal entries for March 31, 1996, assuming that the company policy is to make adjustments at each month-end. If an adjustment is not required, state the reason. Show all your calculations.

b. Assume that the company had been in business for three years. Calculate the book value of the computer at the end of Year 3.

P8.33 Capital asset disposal (*Published with permission of CGA Canada*). A machine with an expected service life of five years and a residual value of $5,000 was purchased on January 2, 1994, by Sandy Company for $80,000. After taking straight-line amortization for three years, the machine was sold on December 31, 1996.

Required:

a. Present a general journal entry dated December 31, 1996, to record the sale assuming the cash proceeds from the sale were:

(1) $15,000

(2) $38,500

b. Repeat entries (1) and (2) from part *a* on the assumption that Sandy used double-declining-balance amortization for the three years.

P8.34 Capital asset cost and amortization methods (*Published with permission of CGA Canada*). A machine with an estimated useful life of five years was acquired on October 1, 1996, by Yao Company. This machinery had a list price of $180,000, but Yao Company received a trade discount of 15 percent and paid transportation costs on October 1 of $5,100. The machine was installed on October 2 at a cost of $4,000. The estimated residual value is expected to be $20,000. The machine was expected to produce 500,000 units of product. During 1996 and 1997, 70,000 and 170,000 units of product were produced, respectively. Yao Company's tax rate is 42 percent.

Required:

a. Record the journal entries for October 1 and October 2, 1996.

b. Assume that the machine acquired in part *a* has been recorded at $140,000. Record amortization for 1996 and 1997 under each of the following methods:

(1) Straight-line method.

(2) Double-declining-balance method.

(3) CCA method (the asset class is 20 percent).

(4) Units-of-output method.

P8.35 Capital assets (*Published with permission of CGA Canada*). Mary Tou, controller of Tou Trucking Company, has presented you with the following information regarding some heavy equipment:

	Equipment	Accumulated Amortization
Balance, January 1	$422,500	$ 212,000
Balance, December 31	390,000	230,000

Company records also indicate that amortization expense of $32,000 was recorded during the year, and that there were additions amounting to $80,000.

Required:

a. Prepare journal entries for the following:

(**1**) The disposal of equipment during the year at $65,000.

(**2**) Amortization expense for the period.

b. "The purpose of amortization is to provide for the replacement of equipment." Comment on this statement, indicating how, if at all, the entry for amortization expense helps the company to accumulate funds for asset replacement.

P8.36 Capital asset errors (*Published with permission of CGA Canada*). Macleod Equipment Co. purchased a new lathe on September 30. The list price of the lathe was $8,000. Transportation costs amounted to $400. Macleod took advantage of a 20 percent trade discount. The machine has an estimated useful life of five years and an expected residual value of $600. On December 31 the following adjusting entry was made using straight-line amortization:

```
Amortization Expense — Machinery  . . . . . . . . . . . . . . . . . . . . . . . .  1,600
      Accumulated Amortization — Machinery  . . . . . . . . . . . . . . . . . . . . . .        1,600
```

Required:

a. Identify and describe any errors in the above adjusting entry.

b. Prepare an entry that would correct any error(s) you found and that would generate the correct account balances.

c. If left uncorrected, by how much would the following items be affected.

(**1**) Total assets

(**2**) Total liabilities

(**3**) Shareholders' equity

(**4**) Total revenue

P8.37 Capital assets (*Published with permission of CGA Canada*). On January 1, 1995, Parsons, Ltd., bought a machine that for $90,000 by paying $20,000 down and issuing a 10 percent note for the balance. The machine has an estimated useful life of 10 years and an estimated residual value of $10,000. Parsons uses the straight-line method of amortization, which is recorded on December 31 of each year. On April 30, 1998, the machine was sold for $55,000.

Required:

a. Prepare the journal entry to record the acquisition of the machinery.

b. Prepare the journal entry(ies) to record the sale.

c. Prepare the entry(ies) to record the sale if Parsons, Ltd., had been using the double-declining-balance method to amortize the cost of the machine.

P8.38 Ratio analysis and amortization methods. Kamloops Manufacturing purchased a machine on January 3, 1995, for $95,000. The estimated residual value was expected to be $15,000. The machine was estimated to have a useful life of 10 years. The machine was also expected to produce 100,000 units of product during its useful life. During 1995, 17,000 units of product were produced. Kamloops Manufacturing reported a net income before amortization expense of $46,000 for the year ending December 31, 1995. Shareholders' equity on December 31, 1995, not including the net income for 1995, was $217,000. Kamloops has 22,000 common shares outstanding as at December 31, 1995.

Required:

a. Using the straight-line amortization method, determine the return on equity and the earnings per share figures for 1995.

b. Using the units-of-production amortization method, determine the return on equity and the earnings per share figures for 1995.

c. What are the ethical implications of selecting an amortization method for Kamloops Manufacturing?

P8.39 Change in accounting policy and ratio analysis. Montreal Services, Ltd., purchased equipment on January 1, 1995, for $187,000. Management estimated the equipment would have a useful life of 10 years, with a residual value of $10,000. After amortization had been allocated for two years using the double-declining-balance method, management determines the straight-line method would be more appropriate. Net income (before amortization expense) for 1995 and 1996 was $37,000 and $56,000, respectively. Montreal Services had 22,000 common shares outstanding during this period.

Required:

a. Determine the earnings per share for 1995 and 1996. Assume the use of the double-declining-balance method.

b. Determine the earnings per share for 1995 and 1996. Assume the use of the straight-line method.

P8.40 Change in accounting estimate and ratio analysis. Kantor Enterprises, Ltd., purchased machinery on January 1, 1995, for $760,000. Management estimated the equipment would have a useful life of 10 years, with a residual value of $60,000. The straight-line amortization method has been used. On January 1, 1996, management estimated the *total* useful life of the asset to be 20 years instead of 10 years, and a revised residual value of $44,000. Net income (before amortization expense) for 1995 and 1996 was $122,000 and $79,000, respectively. Kantor paid dividends of $15,000 in each year and had 10,000 common shares outstanding during this period. On January 1, 1995, the shareholders' equity of Kantor totalled $812,000.

Required:

a. Determine the earnings per share for 1995 and 1996.

b. Determine the return of equity for 1995 and 1996.

c. What are the implications of using average shareholders' equity versus year end shareholders' equity, to determine the return on equity each year?

P8.41 Applying the equity method. On January 5, 1996, Westover Corporation purchased 30 percent of the outstanding common stock of Graydon Corporation at a total cost of $600,000. During 1996, Graydon Corporation declared and paid quarterly dividends totalling $120,000. For its fiscal year ended December 31, 1996, Graydon Corporation reported net income of $290,000.

Required:

a. Prepare the entries required for Westover Corporation with respect to its investment in Graydon Corporation for the 1996 fiscal year.

b. Answer part *a* assuming this new set of facts: (1) only 10 percent of Graydon Corporation's outstanding common stock was purchased on January 5, 1996; (2) the cost was $200,000.

P8.42 Contrasting the equity method and cost method. The balance sheet of DAE Corporation at December 31, Year 4, shows a long-term investment in the common shares of Wallace Corporation of $350,000. The investment was purchased by DAE in January, Year 1. The following information pertaining to Wallace Corporation is available:

Year	Income (loss)	Dividend Paid
1	$ (30,000)	–0–
2	120,000	$50,000
3	150,000	60,000
4	200,000	80,000

Required:

a. Assuming that DAE Corporation's investment represents a 10 percent interest in Wallace, determine how much DAE paid for Wallace's shares in January, Year 1.

b. Assuming that DAE Corporation's investment represents a 25 percent interest in Wallace Corporation, determine how much DAE paid for Wallace's shares in January, Year 1.

P8.43 Significant influence (*Certified Management Accountants of British Columbia*). On January 2, Raratonga Company purchased 20 percent of the outstanding common shares of South Pacific, Ltd., for $100,000. During the year, South Pacific, Ltd., reported a net income of $200,000 and paid dividends of $50,000.

Required:

Prepare all journal entries without narratives for Raratonga's investment assuming:

a. Significant influence does not exist.

b. Significant influence exists.

P8.44 Cost and equity methods (*Certified Management Accountants of British Columbia*). Bear, Inc., uses the account Investment Revenue to record all revenue on long-term investment in shares, whether they be accounted for by the cost method or the equity method. If there is any goodwill to be amortized (the company rule is straight-line amortization over 10 years), such amortization is debited to the same Investment Revenue account. Early in the last financial year ended November 30, Bear made cash investments in the common shares of two companies accounted for in separate general ledger accounts, namely Investment in Shrew, Ltd. and Investment in Fish, Ltd. Details follow:

	Shrew, Ltd.	Fish, Ltd.
Percent bought of total common shares	15%	30%
Current year's net income (each company has the same year-end as Bear, Ltd.)	$ 200,000	$ 300,000
Dividends declared and paid	100,000	150,000
Fair value of net assets at Bear's time of purchase	3,500,000	4,000,000
Bear's purchase cost	600,000	1,250,000

Note: Bear is considered to have significant influence over Fish.

Required:

Prepare all journal entries made by Bear for the financial year ended November 30 (date each journal entry):

a. Regarding Shrew, Ltd.

b. Regarding Fish, Ltd.

8.15 CASE

C8.1 Capital assets and natural resources: Salem Coal Company. Near the end of 1994, Andrew and Michael Miller formed the Salem Coal Company. According to the charter of incorporation, the purpose of the new business was to "locate, develop, extract, and transport" coal reserves. The company remained closely held until January 1996, at which time a small public offering of common shares was held. According to the prospectus, the funds raised through the public offering would be used to acquire coal reserves and removal and transportation equipment and to construct miscellaneous facilities for the administration of the company's coal operations.

Approximately $4 million was raised through the offering and was dispersed during 1995 as follows:

1. In February, the Salem Coal Company paid $2.35 million for a tract of land containing estimated coal reserves of 3.5 million tons. Following extraction and reclamation, it was anticipated that the land would have a resale value of $280,000 for agricultural purposes. In addition, the purchase price included a $50,000 reclamation bond that would be refunded if the reclamation work met certain standards established by the Department of Natural Resources.

2. The following equipment was purchased:

Quantity	Item	Useful life	Price per Unit
1	Bulldozer	15 years	$195,000
1	Earthmover	10 years	425,000
3	Dump trucks	5 years	75,000

The residual value of the equipment at retirement was anticipated to be nominal. Signed checks for the equipment were delivered to the vendors on March 1.

3. A storage facility was constructed on the site at a cost of $150,000. It was anticipated that it would not be economically feasible to remove the building from the land after coal operations had terminated. In addition, it was uncertain whether the facilities might have alternative uses to subsequent landowners. Construction was completed by mid-May.

During May and June 1996, the company spent an additional $200,000 to prepare the site for operations. Finally, by mid-June, extraction operations began. By the end of 1996, 700,000 tons of coal had been mined and sold to the Monongahela Power Company at an average price of $15 per delivered ton.

Operating expenses (exclusive of amortization and depletion) and selling and administrative expenses incurred in connection with the mining operations totalled $550,000.

Required:

a. Before financial statements can be prepared for the year ended December 31, 1996, a number of accounting policy decisions must be made. Prepare a list of those policy decisions and describe what accounting methods you would adopt and why. Assume that these decisions are to be made for financial reporting purposes only.

b. On the basis of your policy selections in part *a*, prepare an income statement and a partial balance sheet as of December 31, 1996. Assume an average tax rate of 34 percent.

c. Assume that (1) coal producers are eligible for a 10 percent "statutory percentage depletion allowance" and (2) a firm may choose to deplete its natural resources for tax purposes using either a unit-of-production approach or the statutory percentage depletion approach. Which method should the Salem Coal Company use and why?

CHAPTER 9

Accounting for Liabilities

Objectives

After completing this chapter, you will be able to:
1. Explain the measurement and valuation of liabilities.
2. Apply the concept of present value to liabilities.
3. Describe and apply different amortization methods for bond discounts and premiums.
4. Record complex transactions for bonds.
5. Describe and apply financial statement disclosure for long-term liabilities.

As discussed in previous chapters, assets are tangible and intangible resources owned or controlled by an organization. When one looks at the assets on the balance sheet and wonders where the money for these assets came from, the answer is that part came from the owners — the owners' equity — and the rest came from creditors — the liabilities. Creditors are any parties to which an entity owes money or other consideration and may include lenders, suppliers, employees, or governmental agencies. For many corporations, creditors are the largest source of funding. For example, about 40 percent of Maple Leaf Garden's assets were funded by creditors.

Liabilities present a number of accounting and valuation problems. Some liabilities are current and must be paid within a few days; others may extend 25 years or more. Some are for definite amounts that can be established from invoices, employment agreements, tax filings, and other documents; others, such as the provisions for anticipated warranty expenses, pensions, lawsuits, and deferred taxes, can only be estimated.

The purpose of this chapter is to consider the questions What liabilities does an organization have? and How should these liabilities be valued? The three types of liabilities that present the most difficult valuation issues are saved for Chapter 10; these include leases, pensions, and deferred income taxes. As we will see in this chapter, in theory, all liabilities are to be reported at the present value of their related cash outflows. In reality, however, only some obligations are valued in this way. Students *unfamiliar* with the concept of present value, or the calculation of discounted cash flows, are urged to review the appendix to this chapter *before* proceeding.

9.1 CONCEPTUAL OVERVIEW

Every entity has a variety of obligations, only some of which are recognized in the financial statements as liabilities.

Liabilities have three essential characteristics:
(a) they embody a duty or responsibility to others that entails settlement by future transfer or use of assets, provision of services or other yielding of economic benefits, at a specified or determinable date, on occurrence of a specified event, or on demand;
(b) the duty or responsibility obligates the entity leaving it little or no discretion to avoid it; and
(c) the transaction or event obligating the entity has already occurred. (CICA Handbook 1000.33)

Therefore, obligations are recognized as liabilities when they can be determined with reasonable precision, cannot be avoided, and are created by an event that has already occurred. Obligations that do not meet these three tests include, for example, a signed, binding contract to purchase certain products when the goods have not been received and a lawsuit for which damages have not yet been assessed.

As a rule, short-term liabilities are recorded at their face amount, the amount printed on a bank note or an invoice. Long-term liabilities are recorded at their present value, the value today of receiving — or paying — a given sum of money. Although the conventional practice is to ignore present values on short-term items, such as accounts payable and accrued expenses payable (because the difference between the present value and face value of such a claim is usually insignificant), some current liabilities (e.g., the current portion of a mortgage payable) are nevertheless reported at their present values. Conversely, most long-term liabilities are carried at their present values, but a few are not, as shown in Exhibit 9.1.

EXHIBIT 9.1

A Taxonomy of Liabilities

	Current liabilities	Noncurrent liabilities
Valued at face amounts	Accounts payable Accrued expenses Income taxes payable Dividends payable Unearned revenue Warranty obligations	Unearned revenue Warranty obligations

Valued at present value	Loans payable
	Current portion:
	    Notes payable
	    Bonds payable
	    Leases payable
		Loans payable
		Notes payable
		Bonds payable
		Leases payable
		Pension obligations

Shown at some other value	Deferred taxes	Deferred taxes Other liablilties

current liability
An obligation whose settlement requires the use of current assets or the creation of other current liabilities and occurs within one year.

9.2 CURRENT LIABILITIES: PAYABLES AND ACCRUALS

Current liabilities are those obligations to be repaid during the next year or during the next operating cycle (if longer than a year in length). All other liabilities are non-current.

accounts payable
Amounts owed to suppliers for merchandise purchased on credit but not yet paid for.

   Accounts payable are the normally recurring obligations of a business for the purchase of materials, parts, fuel, and other items used in manufacturing or for purchases of merchandise to be resold, as in retailing. These liabilities are the easiest to value because an invoice or electronic transmission from the supplier provides the exchange price, and a receiving report from within the company shows proper receipt of the item(s). The primary accounting policy issue a business entity faces is whether to record the payable at its *gross* or *net* value.

Purchases

gross method
Purchases are recorded at full invoice or the gross amount. Discounts are recorded in a purchase discount account.

The gross and net purchase methods were previously illustrated in Chapter 7 with the discussion on inventory control. If the merchandise purchased is for $10,000 and the payment terms are 2/10, net 30, the firm may pay the net amount ($9,800) within 10 days (net of the 2 percent discount). It must pay the gross amount of $10,000 within 30 days. The transaction to record the cash disbursement is straightforward, but how should the company record the liability originally? Companies typically choose one accounting policy and follow it for all such purchases, even if they sometimes take the discount but do not at other times. When a company chooses to use the **gross method** (i.e., all purchases are initially recorded at the gross amount), when a discount is taken, the amount is recorded in the Purchase Discount account. Purchase discounts appear on the income statement as miscellaneous revenue or as a reduction to the cost of sales. If, on the other hand, the **net method** is used (i.e., all purchases are initially recorded at the net amount), when a discount is missed because the entity did not pay on time, an

net method
The net method records merchandise purchases net of any purchase discounts.

expense entry to an account such as Discounts Lost Expense is made. The latter method is the most common policy in large firms. It is typically called the "sore thumb" choice because any discounts lost are highlighted.

Using the above example, assuming the use of a periodic inventory system, the transactions would be recorded as follows:

Gross Method			Net Method		
Purchases	10,000		Purchases	9,800	
Accounts Payable		10,000	Accounts Payable		9,800
Accounts Payable	10,000		Accounts Payable	9,800	
Purchase Discount		200	Cash		9,800
Cash		9,800			
Accounts Payable	10,000		Accounts Payable	9,800	
Cash		10,000	Cash		10,000
			Discounts Lost Expense	200	

If the discount is taken, as is assumed by the net method, the liability is satisfied by a payment of $9,800. If the discount is not taken, the liability is satisfied by a cash payment of $10,000. The net method is considered the best of the two methods for internal control purposes.

Taxes

Many organizations, especially retail firms, are required to collect and remit provincial sales tax, and the Goods and Service Tax (GST). As the organization recognizes the earned revenue, the tax is collected from the customer and the liability to the government is created. Most sales taxes must be remitted monthly or quarterly and therefore are classified as current liabilities. Assuming a provincial sales tax rate of 5 percent and a GST rate of 7 percent, the following entry would be made for merchandise with a sales price of $1,000:

```
Dr. Cash/Accounts Receivable . . . . . . . . . . . . . . . . . . . . . . . . . . . . . 1,120
        Cr. Sales . . . . . . . . . . . . . . . . . . . . . . . . . . . . . . . . . . . . . . . .     1,000
        Cr. Sales Tax Payable . . . . . . . . . . . . . . . . . . . . . . . . . . . . . .        50
        Cr. GST Payable . . . . . . . . . . . . . . . . . . . . . . . . . . . . . . . . . .        70
    To record the sale and applicable taxes.
```

Each taxing body sets strict rules with respect to the collection and remittance of its taxes. On the remittance date the tax payable accounts are cleared and the cash remitted to the appropriate government agency.

Accrued Expenses

accrued expense
An accrued expense is an expense that has been incurred, but the cash payment has not been made for the goods or services received.

Accrued expenses are expenses incurred, but not yet paid. Accrued expenses include obligations such as employees' wages earned but not paid, the employer's portion of any salary or wage taxes due the government, and any amounts accrued for interest or rent expense. For example, if a company owes $15,000 for computer rental charges but payment is not due for another 10 days, the amount would be accrued by the following entry:

```
Dr. Rental Expense . . . . . . . . . . . . . . . . . . . . . . . . . . . . . . . . . . . . 15,000
     Cr. Accrued Expenses Payable . . . . . . . . . . . . . . . . . . . . . . . . . . . .      15,000
     To record the accrued rental expenses for the period.
```

Payables and accruals, including current income taxes payable and dividends payable, are valued at their face amounts and are not discounted. The time and trouble to discount are generally not worth the effort for such a slight difference in value (and it would be needlessly confusing to many readers of financial statements). For example, the present value of the $15,000 of accrued computer rentals due in 10 days is $14,959.02, assuming a discount rate of 10 percent. The purist might argue that this amount should be recorded as the liability, with the difference of $40.98 recorded as interest expense. Fortunately, for both the readers of financial statements and the preparers, this practice is not followed unless the amounts are *material*.

Unearned revenue

unearned revenue
(deferred income)
Revenue that is
received as cash but
that has not yet been
earned.

Unearned revenue (or deferred income) is another current liability not usually reported at its present value; it is shown at the amount received less whatever has been taken into income (i.e., earned) to date. For example, an airline sells a ticket for $1,000 cash, 30 days before a scheduled flight. The transaction is recorded as follows:

```
Dr. Cash . . . . . . . . . . . . . . . . . . . . . . . . . . . . . . . . . . . . . . . . . . 1,000
     Cr. Unearned Revenue . . . . . . . . . . . . . . . . . . . . . . . . . . . . . . . . . .      1,000
     To record the payment received in advance as unearned revenue.
```

Since the service has not been rendered, a liability to provide the service later, unearned revenue, is recognized. The revenue has not been earned and thus cannot be recognized. When the passenger takes the flight and the airline receives the flight coupon, the liability is fulfilled and the revenue is earned. The transaction then is recorded as:

```
Dr. Unearned Revenue . . . . . . . . . . . . . . . . . . . . . . . . . . . . . . . . . 1,000
     Cr. Revenue . . . . . . . . . . . . . . . . . . . . . . . . . . . . . . . . . . . . . . .      1,000
     To record the adjusting entry to recognize revenue when services have been
     provided.
```

Warranties

**estimated warranty
liability**
Warranty expense is
recorded and offset
with an entry to an
estimated warranty
liability account.

Warranty obligations arise when a company sells a product and agrees to repair it and/ or provide certain other services if the product fails. An automobile manufacturer, for example, may guarantee free repairs for four years or 100,000 kilometres, whichever comes first. The accounting challenge for such obligations is one of *matching*. The sale is recorded when the buyer takes delivery of the car, but the repairs may not occur until some time in the future. To match expenses with related revenues and avoid overstating income at the time of sale, the expected warranty costs associated with each car sale are estimated and recorded in an **estimated warranty liability** account. These estimates are based on historical analysis, engineering assessments, and management judgment. At the time of sale or at the end of the sale's accounting period, an entry to record the expected warranty obligation is made:

```
Dr. Warranty Expense . . . . . . . . . . . . . . . . . . . . . . . . . . . . . . . . . 500
     Cr. Estimated Warranty Liability . . . . . . . . . . . . . . . . . . . . . . . . . . . .      500
     To record the entry for estimated warranty expenses.
```

E X H I B I T   9 . 2

Maple Leaf Gardens, Limited

	1994	1993
Current Liabilities		
Accounts payable	$7,036,834	$12,315,755
Deferred compensation payable	246,718	87,616
Income and other taxes payable	110,148	330,163
Deferred income	1,045,337	1,608,055
	$8,439,037	$14,341,589

When a cash payment is made for *actual* warranty services provided to a customer, the following entry is made:

```
Dr. Estimated Warranty Liability . . . . . . . . . . . . . . . . . . . . . . . . . . . . 487
    Cr. Cash  . . . . . . . . . . . . . . . . . . . . . . . . . . . . . . . . . . . . . . . .          487
    To record the entry for actual warranty costs incurred.
```

Note that this accrual-oriented method to account for warranties reflects the total estimated warranty liability and the total estimated warranty costs at the time of the sale. There will be no income statement impact in future periods for this particular car when warranty repairs are *actually* made. From time to time, the estimating procedures need to be adjusted to ensure that the total outstanding warranty obligation is a reasonable approximation of the total warranty costs yet to be incurred.

Exhibit 9.2, taken from Maple Leaf Gardens, Limited's annual report, illustrates a typical format for reporting current liabilities. Each of the current liabilities is shown at its actual or face amount without considering its present value. Footnotes may provide further information about these current obligations, for example, the composition of the deferred compensation and the income taxes payable to federal, provincial, or foreign taxation authorities.

The Maritime Telegraph and Telephone Company, Limited, disclosed in a note its policy of accounting for long-term debt. The note indicates part of the long-term debt is due within the current year.

Debt due within one year is normally refinanced out of the proceeds of longer-term financing.

Current Liabilities	1993	1992
Short-term debt	$ 84,070	$97,571
Current portion of longer-term debt	34,743	2,000
	$118,813	$99,571

Loans and Notes

Loans and securities are basic types of interest-bearing debt. Loans are monetary agreements between two parties. The parties negotiate and sign an agreement that sets forth the terms and conditions of the loan. Loans may be of a short duration or may extend for many years. Although almost anyone can borrow or lend money, commercial banks are typically the primary source of business loans for short- and intermediate-term borrowing (i.e., up to five years). Life insurance companies, on the other hand, have been the traditional source of business loans with maturities of 10 or more years.

Debt in the form of securities includes bills, certificates, notes, and bonds. For these obligations, the borrower formalizes the terms and conditions of the loan in a document, which is then sold. The most common type of bill is a T-bill, or Treasury bill — a short-term government debt obligation. The most common type of certificate is the guaranteed investment certificate, or GIC — an obligation of a commercial bank. Notes and bonds are the most common form of intermediate and long-term debt securities issued by corporations. Bills, certificates, and, in some cases, notes are short-term obligations with maturities of less than a year. The maturity period for notes is usually 1 to 10 years, and for bonds, usually more than 10 years.

Loans, notes, certificates, bills, and other current interest-bearing debt are recorded at their present value. For example, suppose a company borrows $100,000 for six months at 10 percent with interest payable monthly. Essentially, the company receives $100,000 upon signing the loan agreement and agrees to pay a total of $5,000 ($833.33 per month) in interest over six months and a lump sum of $100,000 in six months. Thus, the cash flows for this loan appear as follows:

	Cash Flow Now	Cash Flow at End of Month						Total
		1	2	3	4	5	6	
Loan proceeds	100,000							
Interest payments		(833)	(833)	(833)	(833)	(833)	(833)	(5,000)
Principal payment							(100,000)	(100,000)

This agreement calls for the company to repay $105,000 in total, $100,000 principal and $5,000 interest. The entry to record the loan at its inception is:

```
Dr. Cash .......................................... 100,000
    Cr. Loan Payable ...................................    100,000
    To record the cash received from the loan.
```

Each month an entry for the accrued interest is also necessary:

```
Dr. Interest Expense ................................. 833
    Cr. Loan Interest Payable/Cash ...........................    833
    To record the monthly interest on the loan.
```

On the maturity date the following entry is made:

```
Dr. Loan payable .................................... 100,000
    Cr. Cash ...........................................    100,000
    To record the loan payment on maturity.
```

Sometimes a company may sign a note when it does not know the implicit interest rate; perhaps it knows only the actual payments to be made over time. (For example, the notes could be in exchange for a special, one-of-a-kind machine for which the buyer does not know the market value.) Conventional practice is to discount the payments at a rate that matches the risk characteristics of the note. For example, if the note is non-cancellable, a low-risk debt rate such as the prime rate or the company's incremental borrowing rate may be used.

9.3 ACCOUNTING FOR MORTGAGES AND OTHER LONG-TERM LOANS

mortgage
An agreement in which a lender (the mortgagee) agrees to loan money to a borrower (the mortgagor) to be repaid over a specified period of time and at a specified rate of interest.

Many organizations use mortgages for financing capital asset acquisitions. A **mortgage** is a long-term loan in which property is used as collateral by the borrower. If the borrower defaults on the mortgage payments, the lender has the option of foreclosing on the property, that is arranging to have the property sold. The lender places a lien on the property, which is not removed until the loan is paid in full. Most mortgages feature a *fixed* payment each period (month or year). The amount of the mortgage of $300,000 is based on the present value of an annuity of $32,864 for 20 periods discounted at 9 percent. The fixed payment or annuity can be determined using present value techniques. The annuity payment is determined by dividing the present value of the mortgage ($300,000) by the present value factor (9.12855). The present value factor can be found in Exhibit 9A.2 in the appendix.

$$\text{Annuity payment} = \frac{\text{Present value of the mortgage}}{\text{Present value factor}}$$

$$= \frac{\$300,000}{9.12855} = \$32,864$$

Exhibit 9.3 presents an amortization table for a $300,000 mortgage, amortized at 9 percent over 20 years (periods). The exhibit shows the annuity or fixed payment of $32,864. This is the cash payment made on the mortgage at the end of each period. The payment is comprised of two components, principal and interest. The interest expense is based on 9 percent of the outstanding mortgage balance, $27,000 for the first period ($.09 \times 300,000$). The principal portion of the cash payment is the difference between the total payment of $32,864 and the amount of the interest expense each period. For the first period, the principal or mortgage reduction is $5,864 ($32,854 − $27,000). Therefore, the mortgage balance is reduced to $294,136 ($300,000 − $5,864). The table shows that as the mortgage balance decreases each period, interest expense must also decrease, resulting in an increase in the mortgage reduction column for each period. At the end of 20 periods, the mortgage liability has been paid in full (see Exhibit 9.3). When the mortgage is obtained, it is recorded at its present value. The following entry would be made:

```
Dr. Cash  . . . . . . . . . . . . . . . . . . . . . . . . . . . . . . . . . . . . . 300,000
    Cr. Mortgage Payable  . . . . . . . . . . . . . . . . . . . . . . . . . . . . . . . .     300,000
    To record the cash received on the mortgage.
```

The annual mortgage payment made at the end of the year is allocated between principal and interest as shown in the mortgage amortization table. Each year the payment remains fixed at $32,864 with the interest expense decreasing and the mortgage reduction increasing each period. The entry for the annual payment for the first year follows:

```
Dr. Interest Expense  . . . . . . . . . . . . . . . . . . . . . . . . . . . . . . . 27,000
Dr. Mortgage Payable . . . . . . . . . . . . . . . . . . . . . . . . . . . . . . . .  5,864
    Cr. Cash  . . . . . . . . . . . . . . . . . . . . . . . . . . . . . . . . . . . . . . . . . .     32,864
    To record the annual payment on the mortgage for Period 1.
```

The cash proceeds from the mortgage would be included as a source of financing on the statement of changes in financial position. The annual reduction of the Mortgage Payable would be disclosed as a use of funds under the financing section

EXHIBIT 9.3

Mortgage Amortization Table

Period	Interest Expense (9%)	Annual Payment	Mortgage Reduction	Mortgage Balance
0				$300,000
1	$27,000	$32,864	$ 5,864	294,136
2	26,472	32,864	6,392	287,744
3	25,897	32,864	6,967	280,777
4	25,270	32,864	7,594	273,183
5	24,586	32,864	8,278	264,906
6	23,842	32,864	9,022	255,883
7	23,029	32,864	9,835	246,049
8	22,144	32,864	10,720	235,329
9	21,180	32,864	11,684	223,645
10	20,128	32,864	12,736	210,909
11	18,982	32,864	13,882	197,026
12	17,732	32,864	15,132	181,895
13	16,371	32,864	16,493	165,401
14	14,886	32,864	17,978	147,423
15	13,268	32,864	19,596	127,828
16	11,504	32,864	21,360	106,468
17	9,582	32,864	23,282	83,186
18	7,487	32,864	25,377	57,809
19	5,203	32,864	27,661	30,148
20	2,713	32,864	30,148	0

of the statement of changes in financial position. Mortgages payable would be disclosed on the balance sheet as a long-term liability, less the current portion. The annual interest expense would be included with other expenses on the income statement.

9.4 ACCOUNTING FOR BONDS

bond
An interest-bearing obligation issued by a company to various creditors, usually in amounts of $1,000 or $5,000 and payable at some future maturity date.

The term **bond** refers to a variety of long-term obligations evidenced by a document that may be sold or traded. The bond issue is given a **face value** or par value. Interest is paid on the face value at a rate called the **coupon rate**. The **maturity value** of a bond is the amount to be paid out when the bond matures. The entity issuing a bond is the borrower, and the buyer of those bonds is the lender. Debentures, for example, are general obligation bonds issued by a company. Mortgage bonds and revenue bonds are examples of bonds in which particular corporate assets are pledged as security for the debt.

face value
(maturity value) The value of a security as stated on the instrument itself.

Bond liabilities are recorded at their present value. The present value of the combined interest and principal payments on a bond is the same as the principal outstanding on the bond when discounting is done at the *effective* interest rate on the bond. (If this concept is not clear, refer to the appendix for examples and an explanation.)

coupon interest rate
(face rate) The rate of interest stated on the face of a debt instrument.

Cash Proceeds

maturity value
(face amount) The amount of cash required to satisfy an obligation at the date of its maturity.

From the bond buyer's perspective, money is lent when the bonds are purchased. In exchange for cash the buyer receives a promise of a stream of cash flows (the annuity interest payments) over the life of the bond plus a terminal cash flow payment (the

maturity date
The principal repayment date for a bond or debenture.

lump-sum principal repayment) at the **maturity date**. The value of these cash flows depends upon the effective rate, or yield rate, used to discount them. Interest (yield) rates change continually due to *market* forces such as world political conditions, the general health of the economy, inflation, and investor expectations, to name just a few. The amount of the cash proceeds is directly related to the spread between the *coupon rate* of interest and the *effective rate* of interest when the bond is issued. The **effective rate** is the market rate of interest when the bond is issued. The following table shows the cash flows for a $100,000 bond maturing in five years, with *coupon interest payments of 10 percent or $10,000* at the end of each period.

effective rate
The real rate of interest paid (or earned) on a debt instrument.

	Cash Flow Now	Cash Flow at End of Period					Total
		1	2	3	4	5	
Cash proceeds	?						
Interest payments		(10,000)	(10,000)	(10,000)	(10,000)	(10,000)	(50,000)
Principal payment						(100,000)	(100,000)

cash proceeds
The amount at which the bonds are sold.

The amount of the **cash proceeds** or the amount at which the bonds are sold depends on the effective rate of interest at the date of issue. The cash proceeds may be an amount greater than or less than the face value of the bonds.

Bonds often sell at a **premium** or **discount** when first issued because of interest rate changes in the bond market between the time the bonds are priced (and the certificates printed) and the time customers actually buy them. When the coupon rate exceeds the effective rate, the bonds will be issued at a premium, that is, the cash proceeds will be greater than the face value of the bond. If the coupon rate is less than the effective rate, the cash proceeds will be less than the face value of the bonds, that is, the bonds will be issued at a discount.

premium
An amount paid in excess of the face value of a security or debt instrument.

discount
A reduction in the price paid for a security or a debt instrument below the security's face value.

Interest Rates	Bond Will be Issued at
Coupon rate = Effective rate	Face value
Coupon rate > Effective rate	Premium (an amount greater than face value)
Coupon rate < Effective rate	Discount (an amount less than face value)

The cash proceeds from a bond issue are determined by *discounting at the effective interest rate* the cash flows associated with the bonds, that is, the interest payments and the lump-sum principal repayment:

Cash proceeds = Present value of the principal (lump sum)
                   + Present value of the coupon interest payments (annuity)

A financial calculator may be used to determine the cash proceeds of the bond issue. As well, present value tables may be used. Present value tables are provided in the appendix to this chapter. Exhibit 9A.1 is used to determine the present value of lump-sum payments received at the end of the period indicated. Exhibit 9A.2 is used to determine the present value of annuity payments received at the end of the period for *N* periods.

For example, if the $100,000 bond with the coupon rate of 10 percent is discounted at an *effective rate* of 10 percent over five periods, the cash proceeds would be

$100,000. The bonds are issued at their face value, as the coupon rate and effective interest rate are equal (10%). The cash proceeds are determined as follows:

Present value of the principal (lump sum):	
$100,000 discounted @ 10% over 5 periods (Exhibit 9A.1)	$100,000 × .62092 = $ 62,092
Present value of the coupon interest payments (annuity):	
$10,000 annuity discounted @ 10% over 5 periods	
(Exhibit 9A.2)	$10,000 × 3.79079 = $ 37,908
Cash proceeds	$100,000

When bonds are issued or sold at their face value, the accounting is straightforward. The entry to record the initial borrowing is:

```
Dr. Cash  . . . . . . . . . . . . . . . . . . . . . . . . . . . . . . . . . . . . . . . . 100,000
    Cr. Bonds Payable . . . . . . . . . . . . . . . . . . . . . . . . . . . . . . . .    100,000
    To record the issuing of the bonds at face value.
```

This entry assumes that the company sold the bonds itself, and thus incurred no transaction costs. In reality, most companies hire a bond underwriter to place or sell their debt securities and thus incur certain transaction fees when debt securities are sold.

When the annual interest payment is made, the following entry is recorded:

```
Dr. Interest Expense  . . . . . . . . . . . . . . . . . . . . . . . . . . . . . . . 10,000
    Cr. Cash  . . . . . . . . . . . . . . . . . . . . . . . . . . . . . . . . . . . . . . .    10,000
        (0.10 × $100,000)
    To record the annual interest payment.
```

The above entry for the interest payment is made each period for five periods, until the bond matures. When the bonds are retired on the maturity date, the following entry is made:

```
Dr. Bonds Payable . . . . . . . . . . . . . . . . . . . . . . . . . . . . . . . . . 100,000
    Cr. Cash  . . . . . . . . . . . . . . . . . . . . . . . . . . . . . . . . . . . . . . .    100,000
    To record the payment of the maturity of the bonds.
```

Bond Discounts

Suppose a $1,000, five-year, 10 percent, annual interest payment bond may come to market when the yield rate for the class and risk of the bond has just increased to 12 percent. This large spread in interest rates is not realistic but is used for illustration purposes. The spread between the coupon interest rate and the effective interest rate is typically only a fraction of 1 percent. Because of the rise in interest rates, the bond will actually sell for only $927.91, or a discount of $72.09. Suppose an entire issue of these bonds with a face value of $100,000 were sold in the market and brought the issuing firm $92,791. Note that 10 percent bonds pay $10,000 per year in interest (the coupon amount), and $100,000 (the maturity value) is to be repaid at the end of the fifth year. The present value of these payments at 10 percent is, of course, $100,000. Whereas at 12 percent, the effective rate, the present value is only $92,791, which is the amount of cash that the bond-issuing company can expect to receive if the bonds are sold to yield 12 percent. The difference between the face amount of $100,000 and the selling price of $92,791 is the bond discount, which must be amortized over the five-year life of the debt.

If the $100,000 bond with the coupon rate of 10 percent is discounted at an *effective rate* of 12 percent over five periods, the cash proceeds would be $92,791. The bonds are issued at a discount, as the coupon rate is less than the effective rate of interest (10 % < 12%). The cash proceeds are determined as follows:

Present value of the principal (lump sum):
  $100,000 discounted @ 12% over 5 periods (Exhibit 9A.1) $100,000 × .56743 = $56,743
Present value of the coupon interest payments (annuity):
  $10,000 annuity discounted @ 12% over 5 periods
  (Exhibit 9A.2): $10,000 × 3.60478 = $36,048
Cash proceeds   = $92,791

The entry to record the bond issue is:

```
Dr. Cash  . . . . . . . . . . . . . . . . . . . . . . . . . . . . . . . . . . . . . . .92,791
Dr. Bond Discount . . . . . . . . . . . . . . . . . . . . . . . . . . . . . . . . . . 7,209
    Cr. Bonds Payable . . . . . . . . . . . . . . . . . . . . . . . . . . . . . . . . . . .   100,000
    To record the issuing of the bonds at a discount.
```

The Bond Discount is a contra liability account to be deducted from Bonds Payable to determine the net book value of the bond issue.

The following is the accounting challenge in a situation like this:

- To show the bond liability at its present value, not its face amount.
- To show the annual interest expense at the effective rate (12 percent), not the stated or coupon rate (10 percent).

The bonds would be recorded initially on the balance sheet at $92,791, or at the *present value at the time of issuance*. At the end of each year, two transactions are required: one to record the interest paid on the bonds and the second to amortize the bond discount. Two amortization methods: straight line and the effective interest method are discussed and illustrated later in this chapter.

Bond Premiums

Although rare, bonds are also sometimes sold at a premium. When market interest rates are lower than a bond's coupon (stated) rate, a bond premium results. Conceptually, accounting for bond premiums is the reverse of accounting for bond discounts. Suppose, for example, that the $100,000 in bonds actually sell for $107,985, resulting in an effective yield of only 8 percent. The cash proceeds are determined as follows:

If the $100,000 bond, with the coupon rate of 10 percent is discounted at an *effective rate* of 8 percent over five periods, the cash proceeds would be $107,785. The bonds are issued at a premium, as the coupon rate is more than the effective rate of interest (10% > 8%). The cash proceeds are determined as follows:

Present value of the principal (lump sum):
  $100,000 discounted @ 8% over 5 periods (Exhibit 9A.1) $100,000 × .68058 = $ 68,058
Present value of the coupon interest payments (annuity):
  $10,000 annuity discounted @ 8% over 5 periods (Exhibit 9A.2) $10,000 × 3.99271 = $ 39,927
Cash proceeds $107,985

The entry to record the bond issue is:

```
Dr. Cash  . . . . . . . . . . . . . . . . . . . . . . . . . . . . . . . . . . . . . . 107,985
        Cr. Bond Premium . . . . . . . . . . . . . . . . . . . . . . . . . . . . . . . .      7,985
        Cr. Bonds Payable . . . . . . . . . . . . . . . . . . . . . . . . . . . . . . . .   100,000
        To record the issuing of the bonds at a premium.
```

The Bond Premium account should be added to the Bond Payable account to determine the net book value of the bond issue. As with bond discounts, the accounting challenge is to show the bond liability at its present value, not its face amount. As well, the annual interest expense should be shown at the effective rate (8 percent), not the stated or coupon rate (10 percent). The bonds would be recorded initially on the balance sheet at $107,985, or at the present value at the time of issuance. At the end of each year, two transactions are required: one to record the interest paid on the bonds and the second to amortize the bond premium. The two amortization methods: straight line and the effective interest method are now discussed.

Straight-Line Method of Amortization

We first illustrate the straight-line method of amortization for bond discounts (premiums) to facilitate the understanding of the basic concepts and accounting entries required. The advantage of the straight-line method, as mentioned previously in Chapter 8 in the discussion on capital assets, is its simplicity. An equal amount of amortization is taken in each period, with the same entry required each period over the life of the bond. A straight-line amortization table for a bond discount follows:

Straight-Line Amortization: Bond Discount

Period	Interest Expense	Cash Payment	Discount Amortization	Bond Discount	Net Book Value*
0				$7,209	$ 92,791
1	$11,442	$10,000	$1,442	5,767	94,233
2	11,442	10,000	1,442	4,326	95,674
3	11,442	10,000	1,442	2,884	97,116
4	11,442	10,000	1,442	1,442	98,558
5	11,442	10,000	1,442	0	100,000

*Net book value of the bond is the face value of $100,000, less the unamortized bond discount.

Straight-line amortization tables are somewhat redundant because the payments and amortizations are the same each period. However, they do illustrate the full amortization of the discount or premium and the adjustment of the book value of the bond issue to equal the face value on the maturity date.

The entries for Period 1 for this bond would be recorded as:

```
Dr. Interest Expense  . . . . . . . . . . . . . . . . . . . . . . . . . . . . . . . 10,000
        Cr. Cash  . . . . . . . . . . . . . . . . . . . . . . . . . . . . . . . . . . . . .   10,000
        To record the payment of interest on the bond.
```

and

```
Dr. Interest Expense  . . . . . . . . . . . . . . . . . . . . . . . . . . . . . . .  1,442
        Cr. Bond Discount . . . . . . . . . . . . . . . . . . . . . . . . . . . . . . . . .    1,442
        To amortize the bond discount and adjust the interest expense.
```

The two separate entries may also be combined as follows:

```
Dr. Interest Expense  . . . . . . . . . . . . . . . . . . . . . . . . . . . . . . . . .11,442
      Cr. Bond Discount . . . . . . . . . . . . . . . . . . . . . . . . . . . . . . .      1,442
      Cr. Cash  . . . . . . . . . . . . . . . . . . . . . . . . . . . . . . . . . . . .     10,000
      To record the cash payment of the bond interest and the amortization of the bond
      discount.
```

The income statement reflects total interest expense of $11,442 for Year 1. Note that this expense is not 12 percent (effective interest) of the outstanding bond liability. The straight-line method provides only a rough approximation of the effective interest expense. This concept will be better explained in the next section on amortization using the effective interest method. The accounting for bond premiums using the straight-line method is similar to the amortization of bond discounts. A straight-line amortization table for a bond premium follows:

Straight-Line Amortization: Bond Premium

Period	Interest Expense	Cash Payment	Premium Amortization	Bond Premium	Net Book Value*
0				$7,985	$107,985
1	$8,403	$10,000	$(1,597)	6,388	106,388
2	8,403	10,000	(1,597)	4,791	104,791
3	8,403	10,000	(1,597)	3,197	103,194
4	8,403	10,000	(1,597)	1,597	101,597
5	8,403	10,000	(1,597)	0	100,000

*Net book value of the bond is the face value of $100,000, plus the unamortized bond premium.

When the first interest payment is made at the end of Period 1, the two transactions necessary to record the interest payment and the amortization of the premium are as follows:

```
Dr. Interest Expense  . . . . . . . . . . . . . . . . . . . . . . . . . . . . . . . .10,000
      Cr. Cash  . . . . . . . . . . . . . . . . . . . . . . . . . . . . . . . . . . . .     10,000
      To record the payment of interest on the bond.
```

and

```
Dr. Bond Premium . . . . . . . . . . . . . . . . . . . . . . . . . . . . . . . . . . 1,597
      Cr. Interest Expense  . . . . . . . . . . . . . . . . . . . . . . . . . . . . . .      1,597
      To amortize the bond premium and adjust the interest expense.
```

The two separate entries may also be combined into one entry as follows:

```
Dr. Interest Expense  . . . . . . . . . . . . . . . . . . . . . . . . . . . . . . . .  8,403
Dr. Bond Premium . . . . . . . . . . . . . . . . . . . . . . . . . . . . . . . . . . 1,597
      Cr. Cash  . . . . . . . . . . . . . . . . . . . . . . . . . . . . . . . . . . . .     10,000
      To record the cash payment of the bond interest and the amortization of the bond
      premium.
```

Note that the premium is amortized in a manner similar to that for bond discounts, except that the effect is to reduce the effective interest expense, not to raise it.

Effective Interest Method of Amortization

effective interest method
A method to amortize a discount or a premium on a debt instrument based on the time value of money.

Bond discounts (or premiums) are typically amortized over the life of a bond using the **effective interest method**, rather than straight-line amortization. Although the straight-line method is easy to use, it does not present the best interest expense for income statement purposes. The effective interest method uses the effective rate based on the net book value of the bond issue and therefore the interest expense reflects the effective rate each period. To simplify the preparation of the two transactions, the borrower usually prepares a bond amortization schedule. This schedule adjusts the actual interest expense by amortizing the bond discount. In the previous example, the actual interest expense is based on 12 percent of $92,791 in the first period, and the bond discount to be amortized is $7,209. The key to the amortization table is that the interest expense is always 12 percent (the effective rate) of the outstanding net book value of the liability. Of course, the net book value of the liability is also equivalent to the present value of the future payments (cash interest to be paid plus the principal) at 12 percent. The amortization table for the effective interest method of amortization of bond discounts is shown below:

Effective Interest Method of Amortization: Bond Discount

Period	Interest Expense	Cash Payment	Discount Amortization	Bond Discount	Net Book Value*
0				$7,209	$ 92,791
1	$11,135	$10,000	$1,135	6,074	93,926
2	11,271	10,000	1,271	4,803	95,197
3	11,424	10,000	1,424	3,380	96,620
4	11,594	10,000	1,594	1,785	98,215
5	11,785	10,000	1,785	0	100,000

*Net book value of the bond is the face value of $100,000, less the unamortized bond discount.

Another way to think about this is that, in terms of face amounts, $100,000 is being borrowed for five years on which $10,000 per year (or $50,000 in total) of interest will be paid in cash. In fact, however, only $92,791 is borrowed, although a full $100,000 will be repaid on maturity in five years. The difference of $7,209 represents *additional interest,* and, thus, the total interest expense paid over the life of the debt is $57,209. By spreading the $7,209 over five years, the borrower's income statement shows an interest expense equal to 12 percent of the bond value as reported on the company's balance sheet (not 10 percent of $100,000).

The entry to record the interest payment and the amortization of the bond discount would be:

```
Dr. Interest Expense ................................... 11,135
    Cr. Bond Discount .......................................    1,135
    Cr. Cash ...............................................   10,000
    To record the cash payment of the bond interest and the amortization of the bond
    discount.
```

The income statement reflects interest expense of $11,135 for Year 1. Note that this expense is exactly 12 percent (the effective rate) of the outstanding bond liability (12 percent × $92,791 = $11,135).

The effective interest method of amortization is similar for bond premiums, except the interest expense is reduced instead of increased, as with a bond discount. The interest expense is always 12 percent (the effective rate) of the outstanding net book value of the liability. The income statement reflects interest expense of $8,639 for Year 1. The expense is 12 percent (effective rate) of the outstanding bond liability (12 percent × $107,985 = $8,639). The amortization table and accounting entries follow:

Effective Interest Method of Amortization: Bond Premium

Period	Interest Expense	Cash Payment	Premium Amortization	Bond Premium	Net Book Value*
0				$7,985	$107,985
1	$8,639	$10,000	$(1,361)	6,624	106,624
2	8,530	10,000	(1,470)	5,154	105,154
3	8,412	10,000	(1,588)	3,566	103,566
4	8,285	10,000	(1,715)	1,851	101,851
5	8,148	10,000	(1,852)	0	100,000

*Net book value of the bond is the face value of $100,000, plus the unamortized bond premium.

```
Dr. Interest Expense  . . . . . . . . . . . . . . . . . . . . . . . . . . . . . . . . .  8,639
Dr. Bond Premium . . . . . . . . . . . . . . . . . . . . . . . . . . . . . . . . . . .  1,361
     Cr. Cash  . . . . . . . . . . . . . . . . . . . . . . . . . . . . . . . . . . . . . . .     10,000
     To record the cash payment of the bond interest and the amortization of the bond
     premium.
```

Note that the premium is amortized in a manner similar to that for bond discounts, except that the effect is to reduce the effective interest expense, not to raise it.

The table below compares interest expense using the straight-line and effective interest amortization methods for a bond discount. With the straight-line method, the expense is the *same dollar value* for each period, but the percent rate decreases over the term of the bond. The effective interest method more accurately reflects the interest expense. As can be seen from the table, the interest expense in dollars increases for each period in direct relation to the increase in the net book value of the bond issue. Under the effective interest method, the percent rate remains constant at 12 percent. The *total* interest expense ($57,210) is the same under either method. When the spread between the coupon and market rates of interest are relatively small, the impact of using one method over another is often immaterial.

Straight-Line Method			Effective Interest Method		
Interest Expense	Interest Rate (percent net book value)	Net Book Value	Interest Expense	Interest Rate (percent net book value)	Net Book Value
$11,442	12.33	$ 92,791	$11,135	12.00	$ 92,791
11,442	12.14	94,223	11,271	12.00	93,926
11,442	11.96	95,674	11,424	12.00	95,197
11,442	11.78	97,116	11,594	12.00	96,620
11,442	11.61	98,588	11,786	12.00	98,215
$57,210		$100,000	$57,210		$100,000

Accruing Interest between Interest Dates

Assume the previously illustrated $100,000 face value bond was issued on October 1 and the issuing organization has a December 31 year-end. An adjusting entry to accrue the interest and amortize the bond discount (premium) is required. The adjusting entry is necessary to accrue interest and amortize the discount for three months (October, November, and December). Assuming the bond was issued at a discount and the effective interest method of amortization is used, the adjusting entry on December 31 is:

```
December 31, Year 1   Dr. Interest Expense . . . . . . . . . . . . . . .   2,784
                          ($11,135 × 3/12)
                          Cr. Bond Discount
                              ($1,135 × 3/12) . . . . . . . . . . . . . . . . . . .    284
                          Cr. Interest Payable
                              [(0.10 × $100,000) × 3/12] . . . . . . . . . . . . .  2,500
                          To record the accrued interest at year-end.
```

The adjusting entry is necessary to accurately determine the net book value of the bond issue, by amortizing the bond discount. As well, the interest expense must be allocated to the appropriate accounting period. When the annual interest is paid on the anniversary date of October 1, Year 2, part of the entry pertains to last year's accrual (3/12) and part of the entry relates to the current year (9/12). The following entry is made on the interest payment date:

```
October 1, Year 2   Dr. Interest Expense . . . . . . . . . . . . . . . . . . .   8,351
                        ($11,135 × 9/12)
                        Cr. Bond Discount
                            ($1,135 − $284) . . . . . . . . . . . . . . . . . . .    851
                        Dr. Interest Payable . . . . . . . . . . . . . . . . . . .  2,500
                        Cr. Cash . . . . . . . . . . . . . . . . . . . . . . . . . . .  10,000
                        To record the annual interest payment.
```

Accounting for Semiannual Interest

The preceding illustrations of the accounting for bonds have assumed interest is paid on an annual basis. Some organizations may issue bonds that pay interest on a semiannual basis. When interest is paid semiannually, the coupon and effective interest rates and the number of interest periods need to be adjusted accordingly. The annual interest rates must be halved and the number of interest periods doubled. For the $100,000 bond, with an annual coupon rate of 10 percent and an annual effective rate of 12 percent, the semiannual rates would be a 5 percent coupon rate and a 6 percent effective rate. Similarly, the number of interest periods would increase from 5 annual periods to 10 semiannual periods. The revised cash flows on a semiannual basis are shown below:

	Cash Flow Now	Cash Flow at End of Period										
		1	2	3	4	5	6	7	8	9	10	Total
Cash proceeds	?											
Interest payments		(5,000)	(5,000)	(5,000)	(5,000)	(5,000)	(5,000)	(5,000)	(5,000)	(5,000)	(5,000)	(50,000)
Principal payment												(100,000)	(100,000)

Since the interest is paid semiannually over 10 periods, the cash flow is different from that previously calculated. Therefore, the amount of the cash proceeds of the bond issue will also change. The new cash proceeds are determined using the semiannual coupon and effective interest rates. If the $100,000 bond, with a semiannual coupon rate of 5 percent, is discounted at an *effective rate* of 6 percent over 10 periods, the cash proceeds would be $92,639. The cash proceeds are determined as follows:

Present value of the principal (lump sum):
   $100,000 discounted @ 6% over 10 periods (Exhibit 9A.1) $100,000 × .55839 = $55,839
Present value of the coupon interest payments (annuity):
   $5,000 annuity discounted @ 6% over 10 periods (Exhibit 9A.2) $5,000 × 7.36009 = $36,800
Cash proceeds   = $92,639

The entry to record the bond issue is:

```
    Dr. Cash ........................................ 92,639
    Dr. Bond Discount ...................................  7,361
        Cr. Bonds Payable......................................... 100,000
            To record the issuing of the bonds at a discount.
```

Interest payments would be recorded on a semiannual basis and the bond discount would be amortized over 10 periods. The comprehensive illustration at the end of this section examines these concepts.

Bond Redemptions

If a company chooses to retire its debt early (i.e., prior to its scheduled maturity date printed on the bond certificate) by exercising call provisions or purchasing its debt securities in the open market, accounting practice requires that any gain or loss from the redemption of debt be recognized in the current income statement. For example, suppose that the $100,000 in 10 percent bonds, sold at a premium, were retired after one year by repurchasing the bonds for an aggregate price of $108,000. Since the net book value of the bonds after one year is $106,624, the seller records a loss of $1,376:

```
End of Period 1    Dr. Loss on Redemption of Bond ............. 1,376
                   Dr. Bond Premium........................  6,624
                   Dr. Bond Payable ..................... 100,000
                       Cr. Cash .............................. 108,000
                          To record the redemption of the bond.
```

When bonds are originally issued, the issuing organization must specify their intentions to possibly redeem the bonds before their maturity date. Therefore, should the organization eventually call or redeem the bonds, the bondholders are not surprised by this action. If and when the early redemption occurs, the bondholders must be notified before the redemption date. The loss on redemption may, at first glance, appear to represent a poor financial decision. However, the firm may be redeeming the bond because interest rates have fallen and the bond can be reissued at a lower interest rate, providing the firm with significant cost savings.

Investment in Bonds

Purchasers of bonds sold at a premium or discount simply record the securities at their cost. They are carried at cost, and the premium or discount is amortized over the lifetime of the bonds. For example, suppose that a company purchased the entire issue of $100,000 at a cost of $92,791. (This could happen only if the underwriter received no commission and there were no other transaction fees or expenses.) *No premium or discount account* is used. The transaction for the *purchase* of the bond is:

```
Dr. Investment in Bonds . . . . . . . . . . . . . . . . . . . . . . . . . . . . . . . . . 92,791
     Cr. Cash  . . . . . . . . . . . . . . . . . . . . . . . . . . . . . . . . . . . . . . . . . . . .      92,791
     To record the purchase of the bonds.
```

At the end of the first year, assuming interest is paid *annually,* the entry on the purchaser's books to record the receipt of interest income appears as follows:

```
Dr. Cash  . . . . . . . . . . . . . . . . . . . . . . . . . . . . . . . . . . . . . . . . . . . . 10,000
Dr. Investment in Bonds . . . . . . . . . . . . . . . . . . . . . . . . . . . . . . . . .  1,135
     Cr. Interest Income  . . . . . . . . . . . . . . . . . . . . . . . . . . . . . . . . . . .      11,135
     To record the receipt of interest income.
```

The result of this entry is that total interest income for the year is 12 percent of the bond asset. The cash received is only $10,000, or 10 percent of the bond asset, but the effective interest income becomes 12 percent once the bond discount is amortized. The amortization portion of the entry adds $1,135 to the Investment in Bonds account. The purpose of this portion of the entry is to amortize the discount over the five periods until the Investment in Bonds account reaches a value of $100,000 on the maturity date.

Comprehensive Illustration

Hardy Corporation issued a $1,000,000 20-year, 10 percent bond on April 1, Year 1. Interest is paid semiannually on April 1 and October 1. The bonds were issued to yield an effective interest rate of 12 percent. Hardy has a December 31 year-end.

1. Determine the cash proceeds from the bond issue using present value tables.
2. Prepare all journal entries for the bond issue to April 1, Year 2. Use straight-line amortization.
3. Prepare an amortization schedule for the first three interest dates for the Hardy Corporation bond issue, using the effective interest method.
4. Prepare all journal entries for the bond issue to April 1, Year 2, using the effective interest method.
5. For both amortization methods, illustrate the December 31, Year 1 balance sheet disclosure with respect to the bond issue.

1. Cash proceeds. The $1,000,000 bond, with the annual coupon rate of 10 percent is discounted at the semiannual rate of 6 percent ($\frac{1}{2}$ of 12%) over 40 (2×20) periods. The cash proceeds would be $849,535. The bonds are issued at a discount, as the coupon rate is less than the effective rate of interest (10% < 12%). The cash proceeds are determined as follows:

Present value of the principal (lump sum):	
$1,000,000 discounted @ 6% over 40 periods (Exhibit 9A.1)	$1,000,000 × .09722 = $ 97,220
Present value of the coupon interest payments (annuity):	
$50,000 annuity discounted @ 6% over 40 periods	
(Exhibit 9A.2)	$50,000 × 15.04630 = $752,315
Cash proceeds	$849,535

2. Journal entries — straight-line amortization. The entry to record the bond issue is:

```
April 1, Year 1   Dr. Cash ............................... 849,535
                  Dr. Bond Discount ...................... 150,465
                      Cr. Bonds Payable ......................... 1,000,000
                      To record the issuing of the bonds at a discount.
```

When the semiannual interest payment is made, the following entry is recorded:

```
October 1, Year 1   Dr. Interest Expense ................... 53,761
                        Cr. Bond Discount
                        ($150,465/40) ........................   3,761
                        Cr. Cash
                        (0.05 × $100,000) ...................  50,000
                        To record the semiannual interest payment.
```

At year-end , the following adjusting entry is made to accrue the interest on the bonds:

```
December 31, Year 1   Dr. Interest Expense ................ 26,880
                          Cr. Bond Discount
                          [($150,465/40) × 3/6] ...............   1,880
                          Cr. Interest Payable
                          [(0.05 × $100,000) × 3/6] ..............  25,000
                          To record the accrued interest at year-end.
```

Three months' interest must be accrued and three months' amortization of the bond discount should be recorded. The interest expense must be allocated to the appropriate accounting period. When the semiannual interest is paid on April 1, Year 2, part of the entry pertains to last year's accrual (3/6) and part of the entry relates to the current year (3/6).

```
April 1, Year 2   Dr. Interest Expense ..................... 26,881
                      Cr. Bond Discount .........................   1,881
                  Dr. Interest Payable ..................... 25,000
                      Cr. Cash ................................  50,000
                      To record the semiannual interest payment.
```

3. Amortization schedule — effective interest method.

Date	Interest Expense Dr.	Cash Payment Cr.	Discount Amortization Cr.	Bond Discount Dr.	Net Book Value*
Apr. Year 1				150,465	849,535
Oct. Year 1	50,972	50,000	972	149,493	850,507
Apr. Year 2	51,030	50,000	1,030	148,462	851,538
Oct. Year 2	51,092	50,000	1,092	147,370	852,630

*Net book value of the bond is the face value of $1,000,000 less the unamortized bond discount.

4. Journal entries — effective interest method. The entry to record the bond issue is:

```
April 1, Year 1   Dr. Cash ............................... 849,535
                  Dr. Bond Discount ...................... 150,465
                      Cr. Bonds Payable ......................... 1,000,000
                      To record the issuing of the bonds at a discount.
```

When the semiannual interest payment is made, the following entry is recorded:

```
October 1, Year 1   Dr. Interest Expense . . . . . . . . . . . . . . . . . . . 50,972
                         Cr. Bond Discount . . . . . . . . . . . . . . . . . . . . . .        972
                         Cr. Cash . . . . . . . . . . . . . . . . . . . . . . . . . . . . .   50,000
                         (0.05 × $100,000)
                    To record the semiannual interest payment.
```

At year-end, the following adjusting entry is made to accrue the interest on the bonds:

```
December 31, Year 1   Dr. Interest Expense . . . . . . . . . . . . . . . . 25,515
                           Cr. Bond Discount
                              ($1,030 × 3/6) . . . . . . . . . . . . . . . . . . . .      515
                           Cr. Interest Payable
                              [(0.05 × $100,000) × 3/6] . . . . . . . . . . . . . .   25,000
                      To record the accrued interest at year-end.
```

When the semiannual interest is paid on April 1, 19x9, part of the entry pertains to last year's accrual (3/6) and part of the entry relates to the current year (3/6).

```
April 1, Year 2   Dr. Interest Expense . . . . . . . . . . . . . . . . . . . . . 25,515
                       Cr. Bond Discount . . . . . . . . . . . . . . . . . . . . . . . .      515
                  Dr. Interest Payable . . . . . . . . . . . . . . . . . . . . . . . 25,000
                       Cr. Cash . . . . . . . . . . . . . . . . . . . . . . . . . . . . .   50,000
                  To record the semiannual interest payment.
```

5. Financial statement disclosure on the December 31, Year 1, balance sheet.
Using the straight-line method of amortization:

Current Liabilities

Interest payable	$ 25,000

Long-term Liabilities

Bonds payable	$1,000,000
Less: Bond discount (150,465 − 3,761 − 1,880)	144,824
	$ 855,176

Using the effective interest method of amortization:

Current Liabilities

Interest payable	$ 25,000

Long-term Liabilities

Bonds payable	$1,000,000
Less: Bond discount (150,465 − 972 − 515)	148,978
	$ 851,022

9.5 OTHER LIABILITIES

Most organizations incur obligations that do not completely follow the criteria for recognition as a liability in the financial statements. However, such commitments may be material and influence the users of financial statements. Therefore, the accounting profession requires disclosure of such obligations through footnotes.

Contingencies

contingencies
Contingencies are existing situations involving uncertainty as to a possible gain or loss that will be resolved when one or more future events occur or fail to occur.

Contingencies are existing situations involving *uncertainty* as to a possible gain or loss that will be resolved when one or more future events occur or fail to occur.

> The amount of a contingent loss should be accrued in the financial statements by a charge to income when both of the following conditions are met:
>
> (a) it is likely that a future event will confirm that an asset had been impaired or a liability incurred at the date of the financial statements; and
>
> (b) the amount of the loss can be reasonably estimated.
>
> Disclosure of the nature of an accrual and, in some circumstances, the amount accrued may be desirable. (CICA 3290.12)

In other words, when a liability can be determined to exist it should be *recorded and disclosed* in the financial statements.

> The existence of a contingent loss at the date of the financial statements should be disclosed in notes to the financial statements when:
>
> (a) the occurrence of the confirming future event is likely but the amount of the loss cannot be reasonably estimated; or
>
> (b) the occurrence of the confirming future event is likely and an accrual has been made but there exists an exposure to loss in excess of the amount accrued; or the occurrence of the confirming future event is not determinable. (CICA 3290.15)

When uncertainty exists with respect to a loss/liability situation, it should *not be recorded* in the accounts, but disclosed through a *note* to the financial statements. "Contingent gains should not be accrued in financial statements. When it is likely that a future event will confirm that an asset had been acquired or a liability reduced at the date of the financial statements, the existence of a contingent gain should be disclosed in notes to the financial statements" (CICA 3290.20,21).

Common contingencies arise from pending or threatening litigation, threat of expropriation of assets, or from the guarantee of the indebtedness of others. If the amount of the loss from a future event can be reasonably estimated, the loss should be accrued and recognized in the financial statements. Because of the uncertainty associated with future events, many organizations are only able to disclose their contingencies via a footnote. Acklands, Limited, included the following footnote on a contingency in its annual report:

> The company is being sued for $15,000,000 by Uni-Select Inc. for allegedly breaking a five year non-competition agreement signed on December 1, 1989 when part of the company's automotive business was sold. The alleged breach involves the acquisition of McKerlie-Merkin Inc. and the assets of Atlas Supply Company of Canada Limited. Management believes the ultimate resolution of this matter will not materially impact the financial position of the company.

A similar footnote was included in the annual report of the Clearly Canadian Beverage Company:

> The company is subject to legal proceedings and claims that arose in the ordinary course of business, and three class action suits on behalf of persons who acquired shares between August 1991 and July 1993 that have been consolidated before a U.S. district court in California. The company is defending these actions, and in the opinion of management, the amount of the ultimate liability with respect to these actions, if any, will not materially affect the financial position or results of operations of the company.

Notes very similar to the two presented above are commonly found in the annual reports of Canadian corporations. The note disclosure for contingencies and commitments reflects the importance of users carefully examining the notes to the financial statements. The impact of this information could influence the decisions of financial statement users.

Commitments

commitment
A type of contingent liability in which the value of the future obligation is known but that is not currently an obligation because various future events have not transpired.

Many organizations make **commitments** for expenditures that will impact on future periods. Although the related assets and liabilities have not been recognized in the financial statements, such contractual obligations should be disclosed in the notes to the financial statements if they are material. The Kidney Foundation of Canada included the following note on its commitments:

As at December 31, 1993, the Foundation has commitments for medical research expenses amounting to $3,171,034 as follows:

1994	$2,488,167
1995	682,867
	$3,171,034

John Labatt Limited described a number of different commitments in its footnote:

Lease commitments
The company has entered into long-term leases, all of which will be discharged within 10 years. Fixed rental expense for 1994 was $16 ($13 in 1993). Future annual fixed rental payments for the years 1995 through 1999 are: $17, $16, $14, $10 and $10, respectively. In aggregate, fixed rental payments for the years subsequent to 1999 amount to $49.

Contractual commitments
A subsidiary of the Company has commitments for employment contracts totalling U.S.$59 to 1996.

Purchase commitment
As at April 30, 1994 the Company had a commitment to purchase 168 pubs in the United Kingdom for $68.

The Canadian Rehabilitation Council for The Disabled also had a footnote on commitments:

The Council is committed for rental payments under a lease for premises expiring July 31, 1999. Minimum annual rental payments in each of the next five fiscal years, as shown below are based on a rental reduction agreement with the landlord which is subject to annual rental based on the Council's financial results.

1995	$56,667
1996 to 1998	65,000
1999	21,667

As many organizations are involved in lease agreements, the above footnote is commonly found in annual reports. The accounting for leases is discussed in detail in the next chapter.

9.6 FINANCIAL STATEMENT DISCLOSURE: LONG-TERM LIABILITIES

For financial statement purposes, the details of each bond issue should be disclosed in the footnotes. The note should reveal the aggregate present value of all bond liabilities and the aggregate principal payments to be made for each over the next five years. Bond liabilities are shown in the balance sheet net of any premium or discount. On the balance sheet, the current principal obligation is classified as a current liability; the remainder is included under non-current liabilities. The CICA Handbook requires:

> For bonds, debentures and similar securities, the title of the issue, the interest rate, maturity date, amount outstanding and the existence of sinking fund, redemption and conversion provisions should be disclosed. For mortgages and other long-term debt, similar particulars should be provided to the extent practical. The aggregate amount of payments estimated to be required in each of the next five years to meet sinking fund or retirement provisions should be disclosed. Any portion of long-term debt obligation payable within a year out of current funds should be included in current liabilities. (CICA Handbook 3210.01-03)

For the bonds under discussion here, at the end of Year 1, the balance sheet shows nothing related to these bonds under current liabilities (because *no* principal repayments are to be made in Year 2). However, any accrued interest at the end of the period would be disclosed as a current liability. The balance sheet reports $93,926 under *long-term liabilities* reflecting the net bond liability:

Long-Term Liabilities

Bonds payable	$100,000
Less: Bond discount	6,074
	$ 93,926

The mortgage liability illustrated in Exhibit 9.3 would be classified as a long-term liability, with the principal to be paid within the next year, deducted, and disclosed under current liabilities. At the end of Year 1, the mortgage balance was $294,136. During Year 2, the mortgage reduction of $6,392 would be classified as a current liability:

Current Liabilities

Current portion of the mortgage payable	$ 6,392

Long-Term Liabilities

Mortgage payable	$294,136
Less: current portion	6,392
	$287,744

A note would be used to provide additional information on the particulars of the long-term mortgage and bond payable.

9.7 ANALYZING LIABILITIES

In earlier chapters, we discussed the need to manage the components of working capital to minimize the amount of idle cash. We also observed that an important aspect of management's job was to balance:

- The need to maintain an adequate working capital position (to be able to pay bills when they come due) against the cost of maintaining that liquid position.
- The need for inventory (to be able to fill orders promptly) against the cost of carrying that inventory.
- The need to extend credit (to be able to expand sales) against the cost of carrying those receivables.

In Chapter 2, ratios were introduced as a means of analyzing an organization's financial strength. Financial strength may be viewed from a short-term or long-term perspective. *Liquidity* refers to the likelihood or ability of a company to satisfy its short-term liabilities; *solvency* refers to a company's ability to satisfy its long-term liabilities. The financial strength ratios are summarized in Exhibit 9.4

This chapter's discussion of the liability side of the balance sheet has noted the source of some of the costs involved in maintaining too liquid a position, namely tying up funds in cash, in inventory, or in receivables that could alternatively be used to reduce interest-carrying debt. To the extent that management can reduce the cost of that debt, it also reduces the cost of carrying working capital and thereby makes the balancing job easier and less critical.

Management can reduce some of the cost of carrying inventory by slowing payments to suppliers. But suppliers are important stakeholders in the company, and an extended payment program is likely to cost the company in the long run. For example, suppliers may decide to cover their own costs of carrying a receivable due from a company by raising their prices. Or they may simply decide not to do business with the company at any price. Worse, an extended payout program may force the supplier into an illiquid position, or even cause bankruptcy, resulting in the loss of a critical resource for the company. Clearly, the management of payables requires delicate balancing.

The other liability accounts can be managed in a similar fashion to provide a certain amount of low financing. Employees are occasionally content to defer their compensation because they can also defer their own personal income taxes. Those deferred compensation plans can also fund the company's operations. This is the case with Maple Leaf Gardens, Limited. As displayed earlier in this chapter, Maple Leaf Gardens disclosed a current liability for deferred compensation. In addition, Maple Leaf Gardens disclosed a long-term liability for deferred compensation:

E X H I B I T 9 . 4

Financial Strength Ratios

Liquidity	Solvency
Quick ratio	Total debt-to-equity ratio
Current ratio	Long-term debt-to-invested capital ratio

Maple Leaf Gardens, Limited	1994	1993
Long-term Liabilities		
Deferred compensation payable	3,786,959	2,248,783

Income tax regulations allow for the deferral of some income taxes, sometimes only from one year to the next, in other situations for the life of the company (e.g., when the company continues to add to its capital asset base such that the tax effects of accelerated amortization never does roll over — a topic discussed in the next chapter).

Liabilities need to be managed in much the same way as a company's assets to produce the greatest return on the shareholders' funds as is practical and consistent with the company's long-term goals and ethical values. Even the interest-bearing liabilities need to be managed for the benefit of shareholders. A company could borrow all of its funds and provide an infinite rate of return to its shareholders. It stands to reason, however, that no creditor would lend on that basis. Lenders require some equity protection for their risk, and as that protection decreases, their risk rises; and accordingly, they will charge more for their lendings. Most managements today carefully manage their company's financing to operate with the least amount of shareholder capital, consistent with the most cost advantageous credit rating from their borrowers. Managing that relationship requires careful attention to the credit markets and to the attitudes of the company's credit suppliers.

Ethics in Accounting

Vanessa Johnson is an accountant for a local retail company. Vanessa's friend Robert McDonald has been operating a manufacturing plant for about a year. The business has been moderately successful, but Robert needs long-term financing to help expand plant facilities. He has asked Vanessa to prepare financial statements that the banker will use to help decide whether to grant a loan to his company. Robert has proposed that the fee he will pay for Vanessa's accounting work should be contingent on the business receiving the loan. What factors should Vanessa consider when deciding whether to prepare financial statements for Robert?

9.8 SUMMARY

Liabilities are the short- and long-term obligations of a company, usually involving the repayment of cash. Most current liabilities are valued at their face value, whereas most long-term liabilities are valued at their present value. The present value of a liability represents the amount of cash (or other assets) necessary to satisfy a liability today, as opposed to at its maturity date in the future.

This chapter examined the accounting for current liabilities, mortgages and bonds. The complexities of the accounting for bonds was presented to illustrate the accounting for long-term liabilities. Bond discounts and premiums and the straight-line and effective interest methods of amortization were illustrated.

Understanding the extent of obligations present in a company is important. If a company has borrowed too much, it may face a high degree of default risk for non-payment of its obligations. On the other hand, for most companies, borrowing some level of funds is usually advantageous so long as the company is able to produce a return on the borrowed funds that exceeds the cost of borrowing. The following table summarizes the financial statement interrelationships of liabilities:

Financial Statement Interrelationships

Financial Statement Item	Balance Sheet	Income Statement	Statement of Changes in Financial Position
Accounts payable and other short-term payables	Current liability	N/A	Adjustment to working capital items: operating activity
Mortgage and bond payables	Long-term liability	Interest expense. Amortization of bond discounts and premiums	Amortization expense adjusted to net income as a non-cash item, operating activity. Issuing debt is a financing activity providing cash. Redemptions of debt are a financing activity, using cash

N/A = Not applicable.

9.9 KEY CONCEPTS AND TERMS

Accounts payable (p. 440)

Accrued expenses (p. 441)

Bond (p. 446)

Bond discount (p. 447)

Bond premium (p. 447)

Cash proceeds (p. 447)

Commitments (p. 460)

Compound interest (p. 467)

Contingencies (p. 459)

Coupon rate (p. 446)

Current liabilities (p. 440)

Discount (p. 447)

Effective interest method (p. 452)

Effective rate (p. 447)

Estimated warranty liability (p. 442)

Face value (p. 446)

Gross method (p. 440)

Maturity date (p. 447)

Maturity value (p. 446)

Mortgage (p. 445)

Net method (p. 440)

Premium (p. 447)

Present value (p. 466)

Time value of money (p. 465)

Unearned revenue (p. 442)

9.10 COMPREHENSIVE REVIEW PROBLEM

R9.1 Accounting for a bond. Hamilton Corporation issued a $1,000,000 10-year, 10 percent bond on November 1, Year 1. Interest is paid semiannually on November 1 and May 1. The bonds were issued to yield an effective interest rate of 9 percent. Hamilton has a December 31 year-end.

Required:

a. Determine the cash proceeds from the bond issue using present value tables.

b. Prepare all journal entries for the bond issue to May 1, Year 2. Use straight-line amortization.

c. Prepare an amortization schedule for the first three interest dates for the Hamilton Corporation bond issue, using the effective interest method.

d. Prepare all journal entries for the bond issue to May 1, Year 2, using the effective interest method.

e. For both amortization methods, illustrate the December 31, Year 1, balance sheet disclosure with respect to the bond issue.

The Time Value of Money

One of the most important and pervasive concepts in business is the **time value of money**. We take it for granted, for example, that when we deposit a sum of money in a bank or savings institution, we will receive interest on those deposited funds. In effect, the deposited funds have an income-producing feature — the time value of money. By allowing a bank or savings institution to use the funds, perhaps to loan them to someone else, we receive a fee (i.e., interest income).

Even when funds are not deposited in a financial institution, they are assumed to have a time value of money. For example, some automobile manufacturers advertise that a customer may buy their product, pay for the purchase over 48 months, but incur no interest charges. Realistically, it is improbable that any manufacturer can finance its customers' purchases over extended periods without charging some interest costs; in any case, such practice makes very little business sense. In most cases in which zero interest is advertised, the manufacturer has added an implicit cost of financing the purchase over time into the consumer's purchase price. When this occurs, the consumer is faced with an accounting dilemma, namely to determine the true cost of the item versus the implicit cost of paying for the purchase over 36, 48, or 60 months.

To illustrate, suppose that on December 31, Cavalier Company purchased a new delivery van from a local truck dealer, Keller Auto & Truck Company. According to the agreement between the two companies, Cavalier will pay Keller $20,000 on December 31, — two years hence — and issues a non-interest-bearing note in that amount. On the basis of recent conversations with a loan officer at a bank, executives at Cavalier are aware that they could have borrowed the $20,000 for the two-year period at 10 percent interest. Thus, the accounting dilemma is to answer the following questions: What amount did Cavalier pay for the van? At what value should Cavalier's note be shown on the company's December 31 balance sheet?

Both questions can be answered by determining the cash-equivalent value of the Cavalier note on December 31. Obviously, this figure is less than the $20,000 to be paid on December 31, in two years, because of the time value of money. If Cavalier had borrowed $1 from its banker at 10 percent, the $1 would become $1.10 at the end of one year, and this $1.10 would become $1.21 at the end of a second year (if interest is compounded annually)[1]. Thus, the problem is to determine the value of the Cavalier

---

[1]The concept of compound interest is based on the assumption that interest earned on a savings deposit in the current period will be left on deposit so that in subsequent periods, interest will be earned not only on the original deposit but also on the interest on deposit from prior periods.

465

note exclusive of the time value of money. And, to accomplish this, we must look to present value concepts for help.

Present value refers to today's value of receiving (or paying) a given sum of money. For example, if we are able to deposit $1 in a bank today and interest is compounded annually at 10 percent, the value of our deposit will be $1.10 at the end of one year. The value to be received at the end of one year is known as the *future value*, and, computationally, is given by the following equation:

$$F_{n,i} = (1 + i)^n$$

where $F_{n,i}$ is the future (compounded) value of $1 at interest rate i for n periods. Thus,

$$F_{1,.10} = (1 + .10)^1 = 1.10$$

To understand the concept of present value, it is a simple matter to consider merely the reverse (or inverse) of the concept of future value. For example, if we are to receive $1.10 in one year, and if interest is calculated at 10 percent annually, what is the value of that payment today? Using the equation for present value computations,

$$P_{n,i} = 1/(1 + i)^n$$

we can readily determine that the present value of receiving $1 in one year at 10 percent interest is 0.90909. To determine the present value (PV) of receiving $1.10 in one year, it is a simple matter to multiply the two figures together:

$$PV = \$1.10 \, (0.09090) = \$1$$

Thus, the present value of receiving $1.10 in one year at 10 percent interest is $1.

With these concepts in mind, we can now approach the problem of determining the cash-equivalent value of the Cavalier note. The present value of Cavalier's $20,000 so-called non-interest-bearing two-year note should bear the same relationship to $20,000 as $1 does to $1.21. Hence,

$$PV/\$20,000 = \$1.00/\$1.21$$

$$PV = \$20,000 \times (\$1.00/\$1.21)$$

$$PV = \$20,000 \times 0.82645$$

Thus, the present value factor for 10 percent compounded annually for two years is 0.82645. Therefore, $20,000 times 0.82645 is $16,529, the figure at which the note payable (and the van) should be shown on Cavalier's December 31 balance sheet.

To verify this figure, consider the perspective of Cavalier's banker. If the bank lent Cavalier the $16,529.00 on December 31 at 10 percent interest, the compounded amount owed one year later, at December 31, would become $18,181.90 ($16,529 × 1.10) and two years later, at December 31, would become $20,000 ($18,181.90 × 1.10). Thus, $16,529.00 at December 31, is equivalent, at 10 percent compounded annually, to $20,000 two years later. Stated alternatively, $16,529.00 is the present value of $20,000 in two years at 10 percent interest compounded annually.

Present Value Calculations and Inflation

The calculations just made illustrate the fact that, given a choice, one would prefer to have $1 today than $1 two years from now. As the figures revealed, at 10 percent interest, $1 today is really worth $1.10 in one year, not just $1.

Another reason to prefer $1 now compared with $1 two years from now is that, with inflation, the purchasing power of the dollar will decline. The present value techniques explained in this appendix are based on compound-interest factors and their reciprocal present value factors. These techniques do not perfectly account for inflation, but some acknowledgment of inflation effects may be made through the choice of interest factors. Although the choice of an interest factor is only a rough tool, more refined adjustments for inflation effects are beyond the scope of this appendix. Here the present value calculations deal with dollars with no discrimination as to possible differences in their purchasing power.[2]

Present Value Is the Reciprocal of Compound Interest

compound interest
A method of calculating interest by which interest is figured on both the principal of a loan and any interest previously earned but not distributed.

The calculations above also reveal that a present value factor for a specified rate and number of periods is the reciprocal of a **compound-interest** factor.[3] In the Cavalier Company example, the compound-interest factors, at 10 percent, are 1.10 for one year and 1.21 for two years, whereas the corresponding present value factors are 0.90909 (1/1.10) for one year and 0.82645 (1/1.21) for two years.

Factors for determining the present value of a single future amount based on the equation $PV = 1/(1 + i)^n$ are given in Exhibit 9A.1.

Present Value of an Annuity

The Cavalier Company illustration is an example of determining the present value of a future lump sum to be paid (or received). Now suppose that it is necessary to know the present value, at 8 percent annually, of $5,000 payable at the end of one year, another $5,000 payable at the end of two years, and another $5,000 payable at the end of three years. A uniform amount payable (or receivable) each period for a stated number of periods is called an *annuity*. To find the present value of an annuity of $5,000 for three years, compute the present value of each instalment and then sum the three present value amounts:

End of Period	Present Value Factor (Exhibit 9A.1)	Present Value of $5,000 Payable
1	.92593	$ 4,630
2	.85734	4,287
3	.79383	3,969
	2.57710	$12,886

---

[2]In the Cavalier Company example, the company promised only to pay $20,000 on December 31 with no adjustment for the difference in purchasing power of the dollar that might occur over the two-year period.

[3]The compound-interest factor, s, is determined by:

$$s = (1 + i)^n$$

where i is the interest rate and n is the number of periods. Compounding an amount is how savings accounts grow; that is, interest earned in Year 2 is based on the original investment and the amount of interest earned in Year 1.

EXHIBIT 9A.1

Present Value of $1 Received at End of Period Indicated: $PV = 1/(1 + i)^n$

Periods (n)	2%	2.5%	3%	3.5%	4%	4.5%	5%	5.5%	6%	7%	7.5%	8%	9%	10%	11%	12%	15%
1	.98039	.97561	.97087	.96618	.96154	.95694	.95238	.94787	.94340	.93458	.93023	.92593	.91743	.90909	.90090	.89286	.86957
2	.96117	.95181	.94260	.93351	.92456	.91573	.90703	.89845	.89000	.87344	.86533	.85734	.84168	.82645	.81162	.79719	.75614
3	.94232	.92860	.91514	.90194	.88900	.87630	.86384	.85161	.83962	.81630	.80496	.79383	.77218	.75131	.73119	.71178	.65752
4	.92385	.90595	.88849	.87144	.85480	.83856	.82270	.80722	.79209	.76290	.74880	.73503	.70843	.68301	.65873	.63552	.57175
5	.90573	.88385	.86261	.84197	.82193	.80245	.78353	.76513	.74726	.71299	.69656	.68058	.64993	.62092	.59345	.56743	.49718
6	.88797	.86230	.83748	.81350	.79031	.76790	.74622	.72525	.70496	.66634	.64796	.63017	.59627	.56447	.53464	.50663	.43233
7	.87056	.84127	.81309	.78599	.75992	.73483	.71068	.68744	.66506	.62275	.60275	.58349	.54703	.51316	.48166	.45235	.37594
8	.85349	.82075	.78941	.75941	.73069	.70319	.67684	.65160	.62741	.58201	.56070	.54027	.50187	.46651	.43393	.40388	.32690
9	.83676	.80073	.76642	.73373	.70259	.67290	.64461	.61763	.59190	.54393	.52158	.50025	.46043	.42410	.39092	.36061	.28426
10	.82035	.78120	.74409	.70892	.67556	.64393	.61391	.58543	.55839	.50835	.48519	.46319	.42241	.38554	.35218	.32197	.24718
11	.80426	.76214	.72242	.68495	.64958	.61620	.58468	.55491	.52679	.47509	.45134	.42888	.38753	.35049	.31728	.28748	.21494
12	.78849	.74356	.70138	.66178	.62460	.58966	.55684	.52598	.49697	.44401	.41985	.39711	.35553	.31863	.28584	.25668	.18691
13	.77303	.72542	.68095	.63940	.60057	.56427	.53032	.49856	.46884	.41496	.39056	.36770	.32618	.28966	.25751	.22917	.16253
14	.75788	.70773	.66112	.61778	.57748	.53997	.50507	.47257	.44230	.38782	.36331	.34046	.29925	.26333	.23199	.20462	.14133
15	.74301	.69047	.64186	.59689	.55526	.51672	.48102	.44793	.41727	.36245	.33797	.31524	.27454	.23939	.20900	.18270	.12289
16	.72845	.67362	.62317	.57671	.53391	.49447	.45811	.42458	.39365	.33873	.31439	.29189	.25187	.21763	.18829	.16312	.10686
17	.71416	.65720	.60502	.55720	.51337	.47318	.43630	.40245	.37136	.31657	.29245	.27027	.23107	.19784	.16963	.14564	.09293
18	.70016	.64117	.58739	.53836	.49363	.45280	.41552	.38147	.35034	.29586	.27205	.25025	.21199	.17986	.15282	.13004	.08081
19	.68643	.62553	.57029	.52016	.47464	.43330	.39573	.36158	.33051	.27651	.25307	.23171	.19449	.16351	.13768	.11611	.07027
20	.67297	.61027	.55368	.50257	.45639	.41464	.37689	.34273	.31180	.25842	.23541	.21455	.17843	.14864	.12403	.10367	.06110
25	.60953	.53939	.47761	.42315	.37512	.33273	.29530	.26223	.23300	.18425	.16398	.14602	.11597	.09230	.07361	.05882	.03038
30	.55207	.47674	.41199	.35628	.30832	.26700	.23138	.20064	.17411	.13137	.11422	.09938	.07537	.05731	.04368	.03338	.01510
40	.45289	.37243	.30656	.25257	.20829	.17193	.14205	.11746	.09722	.06678	.05542	.04603	.03184	.02209	.01538	.01075	.00373
50	.37153	.29094	.22811	.17905	.14071	.11071	.08720	.06877	.05429	.03395	.02689	.02132	.01345	.00852	.00542	.00346	.00092

A shorter way to figure the present value of such an annuity would be to go to an annuity present value table, which shows successive sums of present value factors, find the appropriate factor, and apply it to the constant annual annuity amount. Exhibit 9A.2 shows a factor of 2.57710 for three years at 8 percent; this factor multiplied by the $5,000 annuity amount results in the present value figure of $12,886.

To verify this calculation, let us again assume the perspective of a lender. If a financial institution lent $12,886 repayable in three annual instalments of $5,000 each, the debtor would record the receipt of $12,886 in cash and the associated liability for the same amount. At the end of each year, however, a $5,000 cash disbursement must be made to the bank, for a total outflow of $15,000 over the life of the loan. Clearly, each of the $5,000 payments contains amounts applicable to (1) the interest income required by the bank in exchange for forgoing the use of the $12,886 loaned to the debtor and (2) the repayment of the loan principal. The following table depicts the annual parts of each payment attributable to interest and principal:

Year	Loan Principal at Beginning of Year	Portion of $5,000 Applied to	
		Interest at 8 percent	Principal Repayment
1	$12,886	$1,031	$ 3,969
2	8,917	713	4,287
3	4,630	370	4,630
		$2,114	$12,886

Present value factors for uniform amounts payable at the end of each period, for a series of periods, are shown in Exhibit 9A.2 for specified rates and periods. Note that Exhibit 9A.2 presents merely the successive sums of the factors from Exhibit 9A.1.

An Illustration

Suppose that Cavalier Company wanted to raise $20 million by issuing bonds payable five years from the date of issue, with 10 percent interest payable annually. Suppose further that the net proceeds the company receives from the issuance of the bonds are $20 million. What liability should Cavalier report on its balance sheet?

The company will pay $30 million over the five-year period, but the present value, at 10 percent, is only $20 million. The present value calculation is comprised of two distinct cash flows (principal and interest). The principal is to be repaid at the end of five years, and the interest is paid *annually* for each of the five years. Exhibit 9A.1 may be used to determine the present value of the principal repayment and Exhibit 9A.2 may be used to determine the present value of the annual interest payments (annuity) as follows:

Principal (PV @10%, 5 periods) = $20,000,000 × 0.62092 = $12,418,400

Interest (PV annuity @10%, 5 periods) = $2,000,000 × 3.79079 =   7,581,600
                                                                 $20,000,000

EXHIBIT 9A.2

Present Value of $1 Received at End of Period for N Periods: $PV = 1/i\,[1 - 1/(1 + i)^n]$

Periods (n)	2%	2.5%	3%	3.5%	4%	4.5%	5%	5.5%	6%	7%	7.5%	8%	9%	10%	11%	12%	15%
1	.98039	.97561	.97087	.96618	.96154	.95694	.95238	.94787	.94340	.93458	.93023	.92593	.91743	.90909	.90090	.89286	.86957
2	1.94156	1.92742	1.91347	1.89969	1.88609	1.87267	1.85941	1.84632	1.83339	1.80802	1.79557	1.78326	1.75911	1.73554	1.71252	1.69005	1.62571
3	2.88388	2.85602	2.82861	2.80164	2.77509	2.74896	2.72325	2.69793	2.67301	2.62432	2.60053	2.57710	2.53129	2.48685	2.44371	2.40183	2.28323
4	3.80773	3.76197	3.71710	3.67308	3.62990	3.58753	3.54595	3.50515	3.46511	3.38721	3.34933	3.31213	3.23972	3.16987	3.10245	3.03735	2.85498
5	4.71346	4.64583	4.57971	4.51505	4.45182	4.38998	4.32948	4.27028	4.21236	4.10020	4.04588	3.99271	3.88965	3.79079	3.69590	3.60478	3.35216
6	5.60143	5.50813	5.41719	5.32855	5.24214	5.15787	5.07569	4.99553	4.91732	4.76654	4.69385	4.62286	4.48592	4.35526	4.23054	4.11141	3.78448
7	6.47199	6.34939	6.23028	6.11454	6.00205	5.89270	5.78637	5.68297	5.58238	5.38929	5.29660	5.20637	5.03295	4.86842	4.71220	4.56376	4.16042
8	7.32548	7.17014	7.01969	6.87396	6.73274	6.59589	6.46321	6.33457	6.20979	5.97130	5.85730	5.74664	5.53482	5.33493	5.14612	4.96764	4.48732
9	8.16224	7.97087	7.78611	7.60769	7.43533	7.26879	7.10782	6.95220	6.80169	6.51523	6.37889	6.24689	5.99525	5.75902	5.53705	5.32825	4.77158
10	8.98259	8.75206	8.53020	8.31661	8.11090	7.91272	7.72173	7.53763	7.36009	7.02358	6.86408	6.71008	6.41766	6.14457	5.88923	5.65022	5.01877
11	9.78685	9.51421	9.25262	9.00155	8.76048	8.52892	8.30641	8.09254	7.88687	7.49867	7.31542	7.13896	6.80519	6.49506	6.20652	5.93770	5.23371
12	10.57534	10.25776	9.95400	9.66333	9.38507	9.11858	8.86325	8.61852	8.38384	7.94269	7.73528	7.53608	7.16073	6.81369	6.49236	6.19437	5.42062
13	11.34837	10.98318	10.63496	10.30274	9.98565	9.68285	9.39357	9.11708	8.85268	8.35765	8.12584	7.90378	7.48690	7.10336	6.74987	6.42355	5.58315
14	12.10625	11.69091	11.29607	10.92052	10.56312	10.22283	9.89864	9.58965	9.29498	8.74547	8.48915	8.24424	7.78615	7.36669	6.98187	6.62817	5.72448
15	12.84926	12.38138	11.93794	11.51741	11.11839	10.73955	10.37966	10.03758	9.71225	9.10791	8.82712	8.55948	8.06069	7.60608	7.19087	6.81086	5.84737
16	13.57771	13.05500	12.56110	12.09412	11.65230	11.23402	10.83777	10.46216	10.10590	9.44665	9.14151	8.85137	8.31256	7.82371	7.37916	6.97399	5.95423
17	14.29187	13.71220	13.16612	12.65132	12.16567	11.70719	11.27407	10.86461	10.47726	9.76322	9.43396	9.12164	8.54363	8.02155	7.54879	7.11963	6.04716
18	14.99203	14.35336	13.75351	13.18968	12.65930	12.15999	11.68959	11.24607	10.82760	10.05909	9.70601	9.37189	8.75563	8.20141	7.70162	7.24967	6.12797
19	15.67846	14.97889	14.32380	13.70984	13.13394	12.59329	12.08532	11.60765	11.15812	10.33560	9.95908	9.60360	8.95011	8.36492	7.83929	7.36578	6.19823
20	16.35143	15.58916	14.87747	14.21240	13.59033	13.00794	12.46221	11.95038	11.46992	10.59401	10.19449	9.81815	9.12855	8.51356	7.96333	7.46944	6.25933
25	19.52346	18.42438	17.41315	16.48151	15.62208	14.82821	14.09394	13.41393	12.78336	11.65358	11.14695	10.67478	9.82258	9.07704	8.42174	7.84314	6.46415
30	22.39646	20.93029	19.60044	18.39205	17.29203	16.28889	15.37245	14.53375	13.76483	12.40904	11.81039	11.25778	10.27365	9.42691	8.69379	8.05518	6.56598
40	27.35548	25.10278	23.11477	21.35507	19.79277	18.40158	17.15909	16.04612	15.04630	13.33171	12.59441	11.92461	10.75736	9.77905	8.95105	8.24378	6.64178
50	31.42361	28.36231	25.72976	23.45562	21.48218	19.76201	18.25593	16.93152	15.76186	13.80075	12.97481	12.23348	10.96168	9.91481	9.04165	8.30450	6.66051

Using the Exhibit 9A.2 factor of 3.79079 (10 percent, 5 years) times $2 million annual interest cash outflows, which equals $7,581,600, plus $12,418,400, the present value of the single $20 million principal amount ($20 million times Exhibit 9A.1 factor of 0.62092), gives $20,000,000.

Note that the present value of any interest-bearing obligation, discounted at its stated interest rate, is the same as the principal amount of the obligation. Stated alternatively, debt issued at a yield rate equal to its coupon rate will be sold at an amount equal to its face value.

Now suppose that two years after the above bonds were issued (three years remaining life), an investor wished to buy $10,000 of the bonds at a price that would yield a 12 percent return. How much should the investor pay?

Graphically, the cash flows of such an investment involve an annuity stream of $1,000 in annual interest inflows (or 10 percent of $10,000) and a one-time principal receipt of $10,000. Using an effective interest rate of 12 percent, the investor should pay $9,519.63.

| Cash Flows at End of Year | | | Exhibit 9A.1 | Present Value |
1	2	3	Factors at 12 percent	Amount
$1,000			0.89286	$ 892.86
	$1,000		0.79719	797.19
		$ 1,000	0.71178	711.78
		10,000	0.71178	7,117.80
				$9,519.63

Note that the appropriate present value interest factors were selected using the real (or effective) rate of interest (i.e., 12 percent) on the bonds, not the coupon or stated rate of interest (i.e., 10 percent). Even though the bonds carry a stated rate of 10 percent, the price at which the bonds may be bought (or sold) will fluctuate to enable the investor to earn a fair (market) rate of return.

9.12 REVIEW AND DISCUSSION QUESTIONS

Q9.1 Compare and contrast the following transactions:

a. Tom Barry borrows $3,000 from his local bank, agreeing to repay a total of $3,600 in principal and interest over the coming year.

b. Dana Howard signs a non-cancellable, non-transferable lease on an apartment for one year, agreeing to pay $3,600 in rent payments over the coming 12 months.

How would you account for each of these transactions?

Q9.2 National Airlines recently introduced its frequent flyer program, the National Points Program, as a means to attract new customers and retain old ones. According to a study, the potential revenue loss from the free tickets earned by the National Airlines passengers totalled $190 million by year-end. How should National Airlines account for the unused (and unordered) tickets earned by its frequent flyer club members?

Q9.3 What is the effect of purchase discounts on the manufactured costs of a product? What circumstances are possible in this situation? What is the impact of each on a product's cost?

Q9.4 The following appeared in Centel Corporation's annual report: "In December, an investor in The Argo Group, Inc. (TAGI) filed suit against a subsidiary of the company for damages from alleged breach of fiduciary duty and negligence related to the bankruptcy of a subsidiary of TAGI. The company cannot predict the ultimate outcome of this action but believes it will not have a material effect on the company's financial position." Is this a liability? How should it be reported? Why?

Q9.5 The following footnote appeared in the annual report of Bausch & Lomb, Inc.:

> The terms of a revolving credit and term loan agreement provide for a 364-day revolving credit line with a six-month term loan provision thereafter, under which the company may borrow up to $100,000,000. A commitment fee at a rate of .05% is charged on the unused portion. For any six-month period during the year the agreement includes a provision which allows the company to increase its borrowings up to an additional $150,000,000. A commitment fee of $62,500 per year is paid under this provision. The interest rate for total borrowings under the agreement is the prime rate or, at the company's option, a mutually acceptable market rate. At December 29, this revolving credit and term loan agreement supported $100,000,000 of unsecured promissory notes which have been classified as long-term debt. While the company intends to refinance these obligations, the level of the outstanding debt may fluctuate from time to time.

What business event has occurred? Bausch & Lomb's fiscal year ended December 29. What would you expect on its balance sheet and on the income statement related to this footnote?

Q9.6 The Financial Post recently included an ad placed by ABC Securities Corporation announcing a new issue. The details were:

$150,000,000
Family Products Corporation
11 ½% Senior Secured Notes Due 1999
Price 99.50%

Explain what happened. What are the accounting issues?

Q9.7 In accounting, a distinction is made between the concept of an obligation and a liability. Prepare a list of the different types of non-liability obligations that a company might have. What prevents each type from being a liability?

Q9.8 What is the difference between accounts payable and accrued expenses? If an accrued item is not yet due, how can it be considered a liability?

Q9.9 Consider the accounting for a deposit or prepayment. Why is this receipt of cash a liability? Does such an event leave the business better off or worse off than it was before?

Q9.10 In the bond market, bonds are traded freely. Bond prices, representing actual trades, are published in daily newspapers. Why not value bonds, notes, and other marketable liabilities at market for purposes of financial statement preparation? How would such a concept work? (What are the entries one would make each period?) Would this be better than using current GAAP?

Q9.11 Ellie Corporation is issuing a $1,000,000 bond issue with a coupon rate of 8%. If the yield rate is 7 percent, will the proceeds of the bond issue be greater than or less than the face value of the bond? If the effective rate is 9 percent, will the bond be issued at a discount or with a premium?

Q9.12 Garfunkel, Limited, is planning a major acquisition of capital assets. The company is considering either issuing bonds or obtaining a mortgage. Either method of financing can be obtained with an interest rate of 10 percent. The firm's management is concerned about the impact the financing will have on the firm's financial ratios. Discuss the impact the mortgage or bond issue would have on the company's liquidity and solvency ratios.

9.13 PROBLEMS

P9.1 Bond valuation. MTF, Inc., is a manufacturer of electronic components for facsimile equipment. The company financed the expansion of its production facilities by issuing $10 million, 10-year bonds carrying a coupon rate of 8 percent, with interest payable annually on December 31. The bonds had been issued on January 1, and at the time of the issuance, the market rate of interest on similar risk-rated instruments was 6 percent. Hence, the bonds were sold into the market at a price reflecting an effective yield of 6 percent.

Two years later, the market rate of interest on comparable debt instruments had climbed to a record high level of 12 percent. The CEO of MTF, Inc., realized that this might be an opportune time to repurchase the bonds, particularly since an unexpected surplus of cash made the outstanding debt no longer necessary.

	Present Value of $1 to Be Received at the End of Year n			Present Value of $1 to Be Received at the End of Each Year for n Years		
n	6%	8%	12%	6%	8%	12%
1	0.9434	0.9259	0.8930	0.9434	0.9259	0.8930
2	0.8900	0.8573	0.7970	1.8334	1.7833	1.6900
3	0.8396	0.7938	0.7120	2.6730	2.5771	2.4020
8	0.6274	0.5403	0.4040	6.2098	5.7466	4.9680
9	0.5919	0.5002	0.3610	6.8017	6.2469	5.3280
10	0.5584	0.4632	0.3220	7.3601	6.7101	5.6500

Required:

Using the present value data above,

a. Calculate the proceeds received by the company at initial issuance.

b. Calculate the interest expense to be reported in each of the two years that the bonds were outstanding.

c. Calculate the amount of cash needed to retire the debt after two years, assuming a yield rate of 12 percent.

d. Evaluate the merits of retiring the bonds early. Do you agree with the CEO?

P9.2 Debt retirement. In March 1987, Continental Airlines sold $350 million of aircraft bonds. The bonds took their name from the fact that Continental had secured the debt with a pool of 53 airplanes and 55 engines, initially valued at $467 million. By 1990, however, Continental was experiencing serious financial difficulties and lacked sufficient cash flows to continue operations. Consequently, with bondholder approval, Continental removed some of the planes from the pool and sold them to raise cash to support operations. After taking the airplanes from the asset pool, Continental was required (within a reasonable period of time) either to replenish the pool or to retire some of the bonds. Continental chose the latter option, and in late 1990, went into the market and repurchased $167 million (face value) of its aircraft bonds at a price of $.58 on the dollar.

Required:

a. Assuming that Continental initially issued the aircraft bonds at face value, how would the company account for the debt repurchase?

b. Was the decision to retire the debt a good one?

P9.3 Accounting for long-term bonds. On April 1, 1991, Nash Company sold to a group of underwriters $5,000,000 principal amount of its 8 percent bonds. The principal is due 20 years from the date and interest is due semiannually on October 1 and April 1. Nash received $5,200,000 for the bonds.

Required:

a. Why should the underwriters pay the company more than the face amount of the bonds?

b. What items concerning the bonds would appear on the company's balance sheet at December 31, 2000, and on its 2000 income statement, and at what amounts?

c. If the bonds are outstanding for the 20 years, as scheduled, what will be the net interest cost to the company for the 20 years? How much per year?

P9.4 Issuing bonds at a discount. On January 1, 1996, Jerry, Inc., issued $10,000,000 principal amount of its 14 percent bonds. The bonds were to be repaid at the end of 10 years, and interest was payable June 30 and December 31 of each year. Jerry, Inc., received $9,600,000 for the bonds.

Required:

Using straight-line amortization:

a. Prepare an entry for the bonds at their issue date, January 1, 1996.

b. Prepare the entries relating to the bonds for June 30 and December 31, 1996.

c. Prepare an entry for the repayment of the bonds on December 31, 2005.

P9.5 Issuing bonds at a discount. On November 1, 1995, James Transfer Corporation issued $10,000,000 of 14 percent bonds due November 1, 2005. Interest is payable quarterly. Proceeds to the company were $9,760,000.

Required:

a. What entry(ies) would James Transfer make on its books on November 1, 1995, to record the issuance of the bonds?

b. How much cash will James Transfer pay the bondholders for interest during 1995?

c. How much bond interest expense will James Transfer show on its income statement for the fiscal year ended December 31, 1995?

d. How much bond interest payable will James Transfer show on its balance sheet as of December 31, 1995?

e. How much cash will James Transfer pay the bondholders on February 1, 1996?

f. What is the total amount of bond interest expense that James Transfer will report on its income statement over the life of the bond?

P9.6 Accounting for purchase discounts. Suppose two companies were similar except that the first, NetCo, usually takes all purchase discounts available from its vendors and thus records all purchases at net. NetCo uses a periodic inventory system. The second company, GrossCo, does not usually take such discounts and, accordingly, records all purchases at invoice cost. GrossCo uses a perpetual inventory system.

Required:

a. What entries would the two companies make if they purchase $10,000 of materials under the conditions of 2/10, net 30?

b. What entries would the two companies make on Day 9 if they both decided to take the discount?

c. What entries would the two companies make if they pay the bill on Day 29?

d. What is the income statement impact of parts *b* and *c* on NetCo and GrossCo? What should these income statement items be called?

P9.7 Amortization of debt discount. In October 1989, Sun Microsystems, Inc., sold $135 million of 6⅜ percent convertible subordinated debentures due October 15, 1999. They were sold at 84.85767 percent of face value, an effective annual yield to maturity of 8.67 percent. Interest is to be paid semiannually beginning April 1990. As of June 30, 1991, the debentures were valued at $117,013 on Sun's balance sheet.

Required:

Assuming no early retirements or conversions, what will these debentures be valued at June 30, 1992?

P9.8 Accounting for warranties. Signal Communications provides certain warranties for its products. As of January 1, 1994, the Estimated Warranty Liability account stood at $72,500. Warranty costs were estimated to be 0.5 percent of sales.

	Sales (millions)	Actual Warranty Costs
1994	$6.5	$53,200
1995	7.9	49,800
1996	5.8	61,100

Required:

a. What will appear on the income statements for each of these three years relating to warranties?

b. What will be the amount in the Estimated Warranty Liability account at December 31, 1996?

P9.9 Mortgages. A mortgage is a type of loan that is secured by property. Suppose a company acquired a building financed with a 20-year, 9.5 percent mortgage with level payments to be made monthly. An amount of $20 million was to be borrowed under this mortgage.

Required:

a. What would the payments be (using a financial calculator)?

b. How would the mortgage appear in the company's balance sheet after the third month?

Suppose that after three months, the building is refinanced with a new 20-year mortgage; this time the rate is 8 percent. The amount of the new loan is to be the exact principal amount of the loan it replaces.

c. What difference would it make in the monthly payments?

d. What transactions would be made to repay the old loan and consummate the new one? Explain.

P9.10 Accounting for mortgages in the United Kingdom. Most home mortgages in the United Kingdom are of a variable-rate type. At the time the mortgage is issued, a monthly payment is determined by the bank or building society holding the mortgage. As interest rates change, the monthly payment typically remains constant (at least during the early years) while the principal is adjusted to account for the change in interest rates. The following is an example to show how this might work.

Suppose one had a 100,000 pound, 20-year mortgage established when interest rates were 10 percent. Monthly payments would be 965 pounds. Now suppose the following:

Month	Interest Rate Percentage
1	10
2	11
3	12
4	11
5	10
6	9

Required:

At the end of six months, what is the outstanding principal on this mortgage? How much interest has been paid?

P9.11 Analyzing debt securities. On January 16, 1996, Dayton-Hudson announced its intent to sell $200 million of debentures due January 15, 2016, with a coupon of 8.6 percent, priced at 99 ⅞ percent.

Required:

What does this mean? (Explain the business event.) What will such an investment yield? (Assume the debentures paid interest semiannually.)

P9.12 Accounting for debt securities. In the Dayton-Hudson debentures described above (the $200 million at 8.6 percent, due January 15, 2016), what would the yield be if the debentures sold for only $199 million? What entry would be made at the time of sale? What entry at December 31, 1996?

P9.13 Accounting for debt securities. Again with respect to the Dayton-Hudson debentures, interest rates had been falling rapidly in January 1996. Suppose that the 8.6 percent debentures due January 15, 2016, actually sold at a price yielding 8.495 percent.

Required:

How much would Dayton-Hudson receive? What accounting entry would be made when the bonds were sold? What entry would be made on December 31, 1996? On January 15, 1997?

P9.14 Contingencies. "At December 31, certain lawsuits and other claims arising in the ordinary course of business were pending against the Corporation. While the outcome of these matters is not determinable, management believes that the ultimate resolution of these matters will not have a material effect on the Corporation's financial position or results in operations."

Required:

The above information was provided in the annual report of Moore Corporation, Limited. Explain how such information should be disclosed in the annual financial reports of the corporation.

P9.15 Accounting for mortgages (*Certified Management Accountants of British Columbia*). Edwards Welding, Ltd., has a mortgage on its workshop. The mortgage dates from September 1, Year 5. The principal amount was $100,000 borrowed at 14 percent. Interest is payable every six months, for 10 years.

On March 1, Year 7, Edwards has the opportunity to engage in a new mortgage for 10 years at an annual interest rate of 12 percent. They can pay off the first mortgage without any penalty.

Required:

(Round off to the nearest dollar figure.)

a. How much capital should be borrowed under the new mortgage to pay off the old one?

b. Give the journal entry to record the new mortgage and the cancellation of the old one.

c. Give the journal entry to record the payment of the new mortgage on September 1, Year 8.

P9.16 Accounting for bonds (*Certified Management Accountants of British Columbia*). Peterson and Company, Ltd., a large road paving contractor, issued 10-year bonds on January 31 at a stated rate of 12 percent per annum, with interest paid semiannually on July 31 and January 31. Ten thousand (10,000) bonds with a face value of $1,000 each were sold at 89.4 to Jerome, Ltd.

Required:

Prepare the January 31 journal entry to record the issuing of the bond by Peterson, Ltd.

P9.17 Accounting for liabilities (*Certified Management Accountants of British Columbia*).

a. According to the CICA Handbook, what criteria are used to determine whether an estimated loss from a contingency should be recognized in the accounts?

b. Powder Retailers made sales of $127,200 during the month of July. It calculates its liability for provincial sales tax at the end of the month (July 31) and remits the tax on the first day of the subsequent month (August 1). Assume all sales are subject to tax, and the provincial sales tax rate is 6 percent. Prepare Powder's month-end adjusting entry to record its liability. Prepare the August 1 entry to record the payment.

P9.18 Accounting for bonds (*Certified Management Accountants of British Columbia*). ABC Company issued $1,000,000 of 10 percent 15-year bonds on July 1, Year 1. Interest is payable semiannually on January 1 and July 1. The amount amortized every six months on a straight-line basis is $4,588. The market rate of interest on July 1, Year 1 was 12 percent. ABC Company has a financial year-end of April 1. On January 1, Year 2, ABC Company sold some assets and retired the bonds at 92.

Required:

Prepare, without explanation, all journal entries relating to the $1,000,000 bond for ABC Company using straight-line amortization.

P9.19 Accounting for bonds (*Certified Management Accountants of British Columbia*). On February 1, Year 4, the Hawaii Company sold $5,000,000 14 percent, 20-year bonds at 96. The bonds, which were dated February 1, Year 4, pay interest semiannually on August 1 and February 1. The Hawaii Company uses the straight-line method to recognize interest expense. Any premium or discount is amortized on a straight-line basis semiannually.

On August 1, Year 9, Hawaii Company purchased and retired 20 percent of its own bonds on the open market for $1,100,000. The company uses October 31 for its financial year-end.

Required:

Prepare journal entries relating to the bonds for Year 4 and Year 9.

P9.20 Accounting for bonds (*Certified Management Accountants of British Columbia*). Minimus Corp. sold a $100,000 9 percent three-year bond issue due on March 31, Year 1, at a price to yield the investors 10 percent. These interest rates are per annum, compounded semiannually. The bond interest is payable each September 30 and March 31, with the first payment due September 30, Year 1. Any premium or discount is to be amortized by the straight-line method. Minimus Corp.'s year-end is each December 31.

Below are some present value interest table factors:

Periods	Present Value of $1				Annuity of $1 (arrears)			
	10%	9%	5%	4.5%	10%	9%	5%	4.5%
1	.909	.917	.952	.957	.909	.917	.952	.957
2	.826	.842	.907	.916	1.736	1.759	1.589	1.873
3	.751	.772	.864	.876	2.487	2.531	2.723	2.749
4	.683	.708	.823	.839	3.170	3.240	3.546	3.588
5	.621	.650	.784	.802	3.791	3.890	4.329	4.390
6	.564	.596	.746	.768	4.355	4.486	5.076	5.158

Required:

Use cents where applicable. If you have a financial calculator you may use it instead of the tables given, or you may use a formula if you know one. In any case, show your computations.

a. Calculate the price the bond sold for.

b. Prepare all Year 1 journal entries regarding these bonds, plus the journal entry needed March 31, Year 2. Use dates.

P9.21 Contingencies (*Certified Management Accountants of British Columbia*). You are the controller for The InnoTech Group, Inc., and just before the fiscal year-end, November 30, your company gets sued by a competitor for patent infringement. The claim is for $20 million. You phone the company solicitor who says, "What can I say? I will defend you as best I can when the case comes up in court in January next year. At any rate, the amount of the claim is ridiculously high."

When the case came to trial in January of the following year, InnoTech did not admit guilt, but the judgment against InnoTech was for $50,000 to be paid to the claimant. InnoTech decided not to appeal the verdict and paid the money.

Required:

a. For purposes of the financial statements for the year ended November 30, what, if anything, would you do? Explain.

b. When you record the $50,000 payment, which account will you debit, and why? Explain.

P9.22 Capital assets and mortgages (*Certified Management Accountants of British Columbia*). On March 31, Year 2, the Pacific Manufacturing Co., Ltd., purchased land and a building for $320,000, paying $40,000 and assumed a 12 percent, $280,000 mortgage. Based on an appraisal report, the building is valued at $260,000 and the land at $60,000. Each semiannual payment on the mortgage is $20,000, principal and interest included. Payments are due on March 31 and September 30 of each year. The company closes its books once a year on December 31.

Required:

For each of the following dates prepare journal entries reflecting the above transaction for the Pacific Manufacturing Co., Ltd. Do not record the amortization.

a. March 31, Year 2.

b. September 30, Year 2.

c. December 31, Year 2.

d. March 31, Year 3.

P9.23 Accounting for bonds, semiannual interest. Trickle, Ltd., issued a $10,000,000 20-year, 10 percent bond on February 1, Year 7. Interest is paid semiannually on February 1 and August 1. The bonds were issued to yield an effective interest rate of 9 percent. Trickle has a December 31 year-end.

Required:

a. Determine the cash proceeds from the bond issue.

b. Prepare an amortization schedule for the first five interest dates for the Trickle, Ltd., bond issue. Use the effective interest method of amortization.

c. Prepare all journal entries for the bond issue to August 1, Year 8, using the effective interest method.

d. Prepare all journal entries for the bond issue to August 1, Year 8, using the straight-line method.

P9.24 Accounting for bonds, semiannual interest. Buffalo Hill Company issued a $5,000,000 five-year, 8 percent bond on February 1, Year 3. Interest is paid semiannually on February 1 and August 1. The bonds were issued to yield an effective interest rate of 10 percent. The company has an October 31 year-end.

Required:

a. Determine the cash proceeds from the bond issue.

b. Prepare an amortization schedule for the first three interest dates for the bond issue. Use the effective interest method of amortization.

c. Prepare all journal entries for the bond issue to October 31, Year 4.

P9.25 Accounting for bonds, semiannual interest. On May 1, Year 1, Merdock, Ltd., issued $500,000 par value 20-year bonds for $585,800. The bond pays interest semiannually on May 1 and November 1 at an annual rate of 12 percent. The bonds were priced to yield 10 percent on the date of issue. Merdock's year-end is December 31.

Required:

a. Prepare an amortization table for Years 1 and 2. Round to the nearest whole dollar.

b. Record any necessary journal entries for Years 1 and 2.

P9.26 Accounting for bonds (*Published with permission of CGA Canada*). T. Q. Hopps, controller of the Toronto Brewers has given you responsibility for recording the company's bond transactions. On October 1, 1995, the company issued $1,000,000 of 12 percent 10-year bonds, dated October 1, when the market rate was 14 percent. Interest is paid each March 31 and September 30 and the company operates on the calendar year. Hopps uses the effective method for recording interest.

Required:

a. Calculate the price of the bond.

b. Prepare the journal entry at the date of sale.

c. Prepare the journal entry on December 31, 1995.

d. Prepare the journal entry on March 31, 1996.

e. Prepare the journal entry on September 30, 1996.

f. Show how the bond would be reported one year after issue and after all interest has been paid.

P9.27 Accounting for bonds (*Published with permission of CGA Canada*). On December 31, 1995, Brady Corporation issued $100,000 par value 12 percent, five-year bonds (interest payable annually on December 31) to yield 10%. Thus, the corporation received $107,580 for the bonds.

Required:

a. Record the issuance of the bonds.

b. Determine the amount of interest expense to be recorded on December 31, 1996, assuming Brady uses the effective interest method.

c. Determine the amount of interest expense to be recorded on December 31, 1996, assuming Brady uses the straight-line method.

d. Which method is the more theoretically correct? Why?

P9.28 Accounting for bonds (*Published with permission of CGA Canada*). Black Company has issued 10-year, 6 percent bonds dated January 1, 1995. These bonds pay interest every June 30 and December 31. On June 30, 1996, Black retired bonds with a face value of $10,000 at 104. A partial amortization table is as follows:

Date	Cash Interest	Interest Expense	Net Change	Net Liability
January 1, 1995				$43,205.00
June 30, 1995	$1,500	$1,728.20	$228.20	43,433.20
December 31, 1995				

Required:

a. Complete the amortization table to the end of 1996.

b. What is the annual effective rate of interest?

c. Prepare the journal entry on June 30, 1996, prior to the bonds' retirement.

d. Prepare the journal entry to record the bonds' retirement.

P9.29 Accounting for bonds (*Published with permission of CGA Canada*). Brown Company has issued 10-year, 6 percent bonds dated January 1, 1995. These bonds pay interest every June 30 and December 31. On June 30, 1996, Brown retired bonds with a face value of $5,000 at 104. A partial amortization table is as follows:

Date	Cash Interest	Interest Expense	Net Change	Net Liability
January 1, 1995				$23,270.00
June 30, 1995	$600	$465.40	$134.60	23,135.40
December 31, 1995	600			

Required:

a. Complete the amortization table to the end of 1996.

b. What is the annual effective rate of interest?

c. Prepare the journal entry on June 30, 1996, prior to the bond retirement.

d. Prepare the journal entry to record the bond retirement.

P9.30 Liquidity and solvency analysis. Simon, Limited, is planning a major acquisition of capital assets for $770,000. The company is considering a number of different financing alternatives. Simon has temporary investments of $160,000 that could be used to partially finance the acquisition. Either bonds or a mortgage can be obtained to finance the balance. As well, Simon is considering financing 100 percent of the acquisition and not selling the temporary investments. Either method of financing can be obtained with an interest rate of 9 percent. The condensed balance sheet for Simon immediately prior to the acquisition is shown below:

Current assets	$ 990,000	Current liabilities	$ 810,000	
Capital assets	2,440,000	Long-term liabilities	1,500,000	
		Shareholders' equity	1,120,000	
	$3,430,000		$3,430,000	

Required:

The firm's management is concerned about the impact the financing will have on the firm's financial ratios. Discuss the impact the financing alternatives would have on the company's liquidity and solvency ratios.

P9.31 Long-term debt-to-invested capital ratio. The financial statements of Sudbury Products, Ltd., include long-term debt of $222,000 and shareholders' equity of $177,000.

a. Explain the impact each of the following transactions would have on the company's long-term debt-to-invested capital ratio:

(1) Made a payment of $25,000 on the mortgage, including $14,000 interest and $11,000 on principal.

(2) Made a payment of $23,000 on accounts payable.

(3) Issued long-term bonds payable for $60,000.

b. As a result of the above transactions, is the organization's financial position better or worse?

P9.32 Current ratio. The financial statements of Labrador Services, Ltd., include current assets of $445,000 and current liabilities of $288,000.

a. Explain the impact each of the following transactions would have on the company's current ratio:

  (1) Made payments on account payable of $33,000.

  (2) Redeemed long-term bonds for their net book value of $96,000.

  (3) Collected payments on account receivable of $59,000.

  (5) Made a payment of $34,000 on the mortgage, including $21,000 interest and $13,000 on principal.

b. As a result of the above transactions, is the organization's financial position better or worse?

P9.33 Total debt-to-equity ratio. The financial statements of Prairie Malt Processors, Ltd., include total debt of $2,100,000 and shareholders' equity of $1,125,000.

a. Explain the impact each of the following transactions would have on the company's total debt to-equity ratio:

  (1) Redeemed long-term bonds for their net book value of $217,000.

  (2) Issued share capital for $70,000 cash.

  (3) Accrued interest of $14,000 on a mortgage.

b. As a result of the above transactions, is the organization's financial position better or worse?

P9.34 Accruals and ratio analysis. Broadwick, Ltd., disclosed the following information in its annual report:

Total current liabilities	$80,000
Net income	$65,000
Earnings per share	$ 3.25
Current ratio	1.5:1.0

After the statements had been prepared, it was determined the following transactions were not included in the above information:

1. Sales on account of $27,000 were not recorded. As well, provincial sales tax of 4 percent and the 7 percent goods and service tax was not recorded on the $27,000 sales.

2. Unpaid invoices for goods received and used total $15,000.

3. Amortization of bond discount of $1,000.

Required:

Determine the revised net income, earnings per share, and current ratio.

9.14 CASES

C9.1 Bond valuation: R. J. Miller, Inc. R. J. Miller, Inc., is a real estate development company headquartered in Charlottetown, Prince Edward Island. Since its inception in 1970, the company has been involved in the development of numerous shopping centres and apartment complexes in the Maritimes. In 1976, the company went public with an initial offering of 2.5 million shares of common stock. The public offering was quickly sold out at $10 per share. Over the next six years, the price of the common shares more than doubled.

Other than the initial public offering of shares, the company generated capital for its development projects primarily through the sale of limited partnership interests and bank borrowing. By 1979, however, interest rates had begun to climb sharply and, by 1980, the prime rate of interest (i.e., that rate charged by banks to their most preferred customers) had reached 20 percent. R. J. Miller, Inc., was not considered a preferred customer and consequently found itself facing the prospect of borrowing funds at nearly 22 percent.

To escape these high bank rates of interest, which substantially reduced profit margins, the firm decided to undertake a bond offering. On April 1, 1981, the company successfully completed the sale of 10-year, 15 percent coupon rate, first mortgage bonds having a maturity value of $40 million. The bonds required semiannual interest payments and were sold to yield 16 percent. They were callable at any time after April 1, 1986, at a price of $105 per bond, and were also convertible into R. J. Miller common stock ($1 par value) at any time after April 1, 1983, at a rate of 58.82 shares of common per $1,000 bond.

Over the next two years, interest rates fell by more than 50 percent. By April 1983, the prime rate of interest had fallen to 10 1/2 percent. The stock market, in turn, had moved into a bullish trend with the stock market indices reaching new high levels. In response to these market trends, the price of R. J. Miller common rose to $25 per share.

Required:

Calculate the following:

a. Determine the amount of the proceeds from the April 1, 1981, sale of bonds (ignore transaction costs). Illustrate the December 31, 1981, balance sheet disclosures related to the debt. (Use the effective interest method and use specific dollar amounts.)

b. Determine the amount of interest expense to be deducted during the year ended December 31, 1982. (Note: Use the effective interest method.)

c. Assume that bonds having a maturity value of $5 million are converted into common stock on April 1, 1983. Describe the balance sheet and income statement effects of the conversion. (Use specific dollar amounts.)

d. Assume that the market yield on the outstanding bonds is 12 percent per annum and that the price per share of common is $18.75. Assume also that on April 1, 1986, the firm decides to repurchase in the open market bonds having a maturity value of $20 million. Describe the balance sheet and income statement effects of this transaction. (Use specific dollar amounts.) Do you agree with this decision?

e. Assume that the company decides to force the conversion of the remaining outstanding bonds by calling the bonds as of December 31, 1988. Assume that on that date the company's common stock was trading at $28 per share. Show the journal entries needed to record (1) the calling of the bonds and (2) the conversion of the bonds. If you were a bondholder, what option would you take?

C9.2 Purchase discounts: Olympic Distributors. Olympic Distributors distributes general hardware items to more than a thousand retail customers in the Northwest. Olympic's management manages its cash flow carefully and almost always takes the purchase discounts offered by its suppliers. Recently, many manufacturers have reduced their discounts or have changed the terms and conditions. Occasionally, Olympic has lost discounts by choosing to pay later. Naomi Herring, Olympic's accounts payable supervisor, set out to bring some order to the process. The company has a long-standing revolving loan agreement with Rainier Bank whereby the effective interest rate is one point over prime; thus, Olympic is currently paying 9.5 percent on its short-term borrowing. In the past three years, that cost has been as high as 14 percent and as low as 8.5 percent.

Herring rummaged through the pile of invoices on her desk, noting the different purchase discounts, terms, and conditions given by various vendors. Most fell into one of three categories:

1. 1/10 days, net 30.

2. 2/10 days, net 30.

3. Net 30 days, 2 percent monthly finance charge on balances over 30 days.

Required:

a. Prepare a table for interest rates from 10 to 20 percent, indicating for each of the three types of conditions whether Olympic should take the discounts for prompt payment or not.

b. How would you explain to a new employee why the typical 2/10, net 30 terms and conditions are really a good deal for a company paying (or earning) 12 percent on its money?

C9.3 Estimating warranty liabilities: General Motors. Roger Smith, the chairman of General Motors, kept his promise to drive the first automobile produced at the Saturn Automobile Subsidiary. In the new, integrated manufacturing and assembly facility at Spring Hill, Tennessee, the ceremony was a brief and quiet one since GM did not wish to associate its name with the new cars; Saturn was to be a new American automobile. After eight years of planning and a total cost of more than $3 billion, the new high-tech automobiles went on sale in November 1990. The new company was steering clear of its GM ownership as much as it could. There were no corporate GM officials at the introduction of the cars, nor was there any mention of GM in any Saturn advertising. By December 1, only 2,162 cars had been built, but the 1991 plan targeted a volume of 120,000 units. Saturn's goal in its first year was to attract 55 percent of its buyers from non-GM owners.

With a base price of $7,995, the Saturn was predicted to get 27 miles a gallon in the city and 37 on the highway. To overcome the reluctance of car buyers to try a brand-new model that had not been tested in the real world, Saturns were offered with a guarantee. Initial buyers of the 1991 cars, if not completely satisfied, could return them for a full refund within 30 days or 1,500 miles. The guarantee presented a real challenge to those who had to estimate the costs of its warranty.

The 2,400-acre site of the Saturn complex is one of the most vertically integrated parts production and vehicle assembly plants ever built at a single location by the U.S. automotive industry. The equipment for the casting plant, including the metal melting systems, casting production equipment, and robots, has been designed for simplicity of operation, reliability, and durability. The plant has a modified "skillet" system, or moving sidewalk, which substantially increases manufacturing quality while reducing worker fatigue. Unlike typical auto assembly operations, major components are on site at the six-building Saturn plant.

The automobiles produced in this complex are quite different from those of other complexes. Some 35 percent of the exterior and interior components are produced in-plant at Spring Hill. They have a stylish aerodynamic design facilitated by the freedom of plastics. GM management considers the operation in Spring Hill to be the last word in auto production with plastic. Fender and rear quarter panels are injection molded of polyphenylene ethernylon alloy; door outers are of a special grade of Dow Chemicals' Pulse polycarbonate ABS alloy, and front and rear facias are of thermoplastic olefin elastomers. The vertical side panels are made of plastic to eliminate annoying parking lot dents and dings. The plastic molds can be switched quickly, making for fast styling changes. Steel is used for the horizontal panels — the hood, roof, and trunk lid.

All Saturns have aluminum engines. The sedan comes with a single overhead cam engine, and the sport coupe with a twin-cam, multivalve engine. The sedan was expected to accelerate from 0 to 60 miles per hour in less than eight seconds — good for its class. The power train plant is

Saturn's most high-tech operation. The engine block and heads, the crankshaft, and the differential housing are formed by a newly perfected method called *lost-foam casting*. Molten metal is poured into molds containing plastic foam patterns of the desired parts. The plastic vaporizes, producing more intricate parts with greater precision, which then needs less costly machining to meet exacting dimensions, which translates into 30 percent less spending on tools and machinery. Lost-foam casting has been around for years, but Saturn is the first to apply it to high-volume production of large components such as engine blocks.

In addition, Saturn machines and assembles both manual and automatic transmissions on the same line in any sequence. Doing both on the same line allows an exact match to car production, with no inventory buildup and at a lower investment. GM had never tried it before. In the past, the engineers designing automatics and those designing manuals worked for different divisions. The power train also was designed for ease of manufacturing, which reduced the number of operations required. One supplier estimated that production costs on the power train lines should be 20 to 40 percent lower than those of conventional engine plants.

The steps to world-class manufacturing in the engineering context began with an understanding of the benefits of designing the product and the process together and the need for quickly getting product concepts to market. The emphasis was not on technological solutions but on how people integrated solutions. The conventional practice of dividing product development into separate tasks to be done sequentially was not followed. Instead, the organization used simultaneous engineering so that projects were shaped by teams. Represented on these teams were finance, marketing, product design, manufacturing, engineering, and material engineering departments.

As part of its assault on rivals Toyota and Honda, Saturn's materials management operation developed a strict approach to finding the right transportation partners for the just-in-time manufacturing plant. Saturn sought carriers that were willing to enter into a long-term relationship and that had a proven performance record, a quality program in place, and a commitment to continuous improvement. GM also developed a strategy to train its 3,000-person work force at the Saturn plant. The strategy combined the theories of GM, Japanese carmakers, United Auto Workers (UAW) members, and other leading firms, such as Hewlett-Packard and IBM. The individualized training plan recognized each worker's knowledge base and learning speed. Saturn cars were to be built using the teamwork concept with teams of 7 to 15 employees. Saturn trainers adopted a needs-driven, competency-based approach: Team members learned at their own pace and advanced only after they mastered a required task. The average employee received 300 to 600 hours of training, including training on team concepts and leadership skills. Thirteen days of training per employee per year were written into the UAW contract.

Required:

How should GM go about estimating the warranty liabilities for its new and very different Saturn car?

CHAPTER 10

Leases, Pensions, and Deferred Income Taxes

——————— **Objectives** ———————

After completing this chapter, you will be able to:
1. Explain the measurement and valuation of leases, pensions, and deferred income taxes.
2. Record transactions for operating and capital leases.
3. Describe the complexities of accounting for pensions.
4. Determine deferred income tax balances.
5. Explain and apply financial statement disclosure for leases, pensions and deferred income taxes.

I n the previous chapter, we considered the valuation processes for current and non-current liabilities in general. In this chapter, we consider three unique liabilities that frequently arise in the financial statements of publicly held companies: leases, pensions, and deferred income taxes. Both leases and pensions depend on present value concepts for their measurement; deferred income taxes, on the other hand, do not. Our focus in this chapter is similar to that of Chapter 9; namely, we consider two questions: Do these obligations exist? If so, how should they be disclosed on the financial statements?

10.1 LEASES

Leasing of assets is a common activity for many corporations, governmental agencies, and not-for-profit entities. It is used by large organizations and small ones, by the financially strong as well as the weak. Some types of leases result in the reporting of both assets and liabilities on the balance sheet, but others do not.

Companies lease assets for many reasons. They use leases, for example, as a form of financing that permits a company to acquire an asset without the immediate cash consequences of purchasing it. Moreover, companies with weak credit ratings sometimes find borrowing money difficult. Thus, for these companies, leasing may be the only way that they can obtain the assets needed to carry on their business. Financially healthy companies, on the other hand, often lease simply because they have better alternatives for investing their cash. Sometimes the decision to lease an asset is driven by tax considerations. Finally, many companies lease assets because they find the ancillary services provided by leasing companies attractive. Leasing specialists often become experts at purchasing, installing, and maintaining the assets that they lease. They frequently make it easy to upgrade an asset and thereby obtain access to the latest available technology. Moreover, these leasing specialists often tailor the lease payments to the particular cash flow circumstances of the lessee. Just about any kind of asset can be leased — computers, copy machines, vehicles, aircraft, naval vessels, buildings, and manufacturing equipment, to name just a few.

As one might expect, there are some drawbacks to leasing. The interest rate implicit in the lease payments is frequently somewhat higher than long-term borrowing rates. In addition, lessees often face restrictions as to how an asset can be used. For example, if a purchased computer becomes redundant or is no longer needed, it can be sold, whereas with a leased computer, the lessee may be unable to cancel the lease without incurring a costly penalty.

operating lease
A lease agreement in which the risks and rewards of asset ownership are retained by the lessor.

lessee
An individual or company who leases an asset.

lessor
The maker of a lease agreement; an individual or company who leases an asset to another individual or company.

Operating Leases

From an accounting perspective, there are two types of leases: operating leases and capital leases. **Operating leases** are nothing more than short-term rental agreements. For example, a grocery store (the lessee) may lease a new delivery vehicle from an auto dealership (the lessor) for one year. The **lessee** is the party acquiring use of the leased asset. The **lessor** is the party who owns the asset to be leased. An operating lease is a lease in which the lessor does not transfer substantially all the benefits and risks incident to ownership of property. Accounting for such a lease is simple: Each month, an entry is made for the lease or rent expense, which is matched and deducted from revenues in the income statement. No lease asset or lease liability appears on the balance sheet. "Disclosure should be made of the future minimum lease payments, in the aggregate and for each of the five succeeding years under operating leases. The nature of other commitments under such leases should also be described'' (CICA Handbook 3065.32). Since the company has use of the asset without having to purchase it, this type of arrangement is often referred to as **off-balance sheet financing.**

off-balance sheet financing
When a company has use of the asset without having to purchase it, this type of arrangement is often referred to as off-balance sheet financing. The company does not disclose the asset or related liability on its financial statements.

capital lease
A lease agreement in which the risks and rewards of asset ownership are passed (either formally or informally) to the lessee.

Capital Leases

Other leases are simply long-term purchase agreements structured as leases; essentially, they are instalment purchases. The grocery store, for example, might sign a non-cancellable agreement to lease a delivery vehicle for four years at amounts sufficient to cover the cost of the vehicle, interest, and administrative costs and with an option to purchase the vehicle for a nominal sum at the end of the lease period. The substance of this type of lease agreement is clear: The company has acquired an asset and has incurred a liability. Except for legal distinctions, it is equivalent to borrowing the money and buying the asset outright. Leases of this type are called **capital leases** and appear as both assets and liabilities on the lessee's balance sheet. A capital lease is a lease that, from the perspective of the lessee, transfers substantially all the benefits and risks incident to ownership of property to the lessee. The periodic lease payments are discounted (see appendix to Chapter 9) at either the interest rate implicit in the lease or the lessee's borrowing rate, whichever is lower, and this present value amount is used to value *both* the leased asset and the lease liability on the balance sheet.

For many years, executives, accountants, and leasing companies have considered what lease arrangements constitute a capital lease and thus necessitate disclosure on the balance sheet. The CICA Handbook provides guidelines for the accounting of leases:

> From the point of view of a lessee, a lease would normally transfer substantially all of the benefits and risks of ownership to the lessee when, at the inception of the lease, one or more of the following conditions are present:
> (a) There is reasonable assurance that the lessee will obtain ownership of the leased property by the end of the lease term. Reasonable assurance that the lessee will obtain ownership of the leased property would be present when the terms of the lease would result in ownership being transferred to the lessee by the end of the lease term or when the lease provides for a bargain purchase option.
> (b) The lease term is of such a duration that the lessee will receive substantially all of the economic benefits expected to be derived from the use of the leased property over its life span. Although the lease term may not be equal to the economic life of the leased property in terms of years, the lessee would normally be expected to receive substantially all of the economic benefits to be derived from the leased property when the lease term is equal to a major portion (usually 75% or more) of the economic life of the leased property. This is due to the fact that new equipment, reflecting later technology and in prime condition, may be assumed to be more efficient than old equipment which has been subject to obsolescence and wear.
> (c) The lessor would be assured of recovering the investment in the leased property and of earning a return on the investment as a result of the lease agreement. This condition would exist if the present value, at the beginning of the lease term, of the minimum lease payments, excluding any portion thereof relating to executory costs, is equal to substantially all (usually 90% or more) of the fair value of the leased property, at the inception of the lease. (CICA Handbook 3065.06)

''A lease that transfers substantially all of the benefits and risks of ownership related to the leased property from the lessor to the lessee should be accounted for as a capital lease by the lessee and as a sales type or direct financing lease by the lessor'' (CICA

Handbook 3065.09). "A lease where the benefits and risks of ownership related to the leased property are substantially retained by the lessor should be accounted for as an operating lease by the lessee and lessor" (CICA Handbook 3065.10).

The Arthritis Society disclosed the following note on leases in its annual report:

Leased automobiles and equipment:
Automobiles and equipment leased on terms which transfer substantially all of the benefits and risks of ownership to the Society are accounted for as "capital assets", and are therefore accounted for as though an asset had been purchased and a liability incurred. All other leased items are accounted for as operating leases.

Accounting for Capital Leases

Terminology is critical to any discussion of leases. There are capital-lease *assets* and capital-lease *liabilities* and, of course, lease interest *expense* for lessees and lease *revenues* for lessors. The agreement itself is called the *lease*. From a lessee's perspective, the accounting issues related to capital leases involve measuring the lease liability and asset, the cost of financing (*interest* expense), and the cost of the use of the asset (*amortization* expense).

The related accounting issues for a lessor, the owner of the asset, pertain to the valuation of the lease asset and the amount of lease revenue.

The following example will be used in this chapter to illustrate lease accounting for a lessee. Suppose PWA Corporation decides to acquire the use of a new Boeing 747 valued at $125 million. Because of its current cash position, the airline does not want to purchase the aircraft outright at this time. Instead, it decides to approach several insurance companies that might be interested in purchasing the aircraft and then leasing it to them. The best terms available are from Prudential Insurance Co. for a 10-year, quarterly instalment, level payment, full-payout lease, with a quarterly payment of $5,250,000. Assume further that the airline's bank borrowing rate is 14 percent, that the lease transfers ownership to the airline after the last payment, and that the airline is to perform all maintenance and repairs and is responsible for insuring the aircraft.

From the lessee's point of view, the agreement should be considered a capital lease. It meets both the ownership and the valuation tests of the capital-lease decision rules. The interest rate implicit in the lease is 12 percent (3 percent per quarter), which can be derived by simple present value techniques.[1] Because the implicit rate is lower than the company's incremental borrowing rate (i.e., 14 percent), the lease payments are discounted at the 3 percent quarterly rate. The present value of the capital-lease liability and the capital-lease asset is $125 million; hence, PWA Corporation would record the lease signing as:

---

[1] Using a financial calculator, this can be easily derived. Since lease payments are made at the beginning of a period, set the calculator to begin. (The default option on many popular financial calculators assumes that cash flows occur at the end of a period.) Then, enter PV = 125,00,000, $I = 3$, $N = 40$ to obtain PMT = −5,250,288 — or a quarterly payment of $5.25 million.

EXHIBIT 10.1

Lease Amortization Schedule:
Aircraft Financing Example
(in millions)

Quarter	Payment	Interest Portion	Principal Reduction	Ending Principal
				$125.000
1	$ 5.250		$ 5.250	119.750
2	5.250	$ 3.592	1.658	118.092
3	5.250	3.543	1.708	116.384
4	5.250	3.492	1.759	114.626
5	5.250	3.439	1.812	112.814
6	5.250	3.384	1.866	110.948
7	5.250	3.328	1.922	109.026
8	5.250	3.271	1.979	107.047
9	5.250	3.211	2.039	105.008
10	5.250	3.150	2.100	102.908
11	5.250	3.087	2.163	100.745
12	5.250	3.022	2.228	98.517
13	5.250	2.956	2.295	96.222
14	5.250	2.887	2.364	93.859
15	5.250	2.816	2.435	91.424
16	5.250	2.743	2.508	88.916
17	5.250	2.667	2.583	86.334
18	5.250	2.590	2.660	83.673
19	5.250	2.510	2.740	80.933
20	5.250	2.428	2.822	78.111
21	5.250	2.343	2.907	75.204
22	5.250	2.256	2.994	72.210
23	5.250	2.166	3.084	69.126
24	5.250	2.074	3.177	65.949
25	5.250	1.978	3.272	62.678
26	5.250	1.880	3.370	59.308
27	5.250	1.779	3.471	55.837
28	5.250	1.675	3.575	52.561
29	5.250	1.568	3.682	48.579
30	5.250	1.457	3.793	44.786
31	5.250	1.344	3.907	40.879
32	5.250	1.226	4.024	36.855
33	5.250	1.106	4.145	32.711
34	5.250	0.981	4.269	28.442
35	5.250	0.853	4.397	24.045
36	5.250	0.721	4.529	19.516
37	5.250	0.585	4.665	14.851
38	5.250	0.446	4.805	10.046
39	5.250	0.301	4.949	5.097
40	5.250	0.153	5.097	(0.000)
Totals	$210.012	$85.012	$125.000	

```
Dr. Leased Aircraft . . . . . . . . . . . . . . . . . . . . . . . . . . . . 125,000,000
     Cr. Lease Obligation  . . . . . . . . . . . . . . . . . . . . . . . . . . . . 125,000,000
     To capitalize the lease asset and liability.
```

The lease obligation or liability will be amortized using an interest amortization schedule similar to a mortgage payment table that separates the lease payments into two parts, principal repayment and interest expense. The interest amortization schedule for the PWA Corporation/Prudential lease is shown in Exhibit 10.1. Column 2 is the quarterly payment due at the *beginning* of each quarter, and columns 3 and 4 identify the interest expense portion and the principal reduction portion of this payment. Thus, the first quarter's payment is all principal reduction. After this payment, the principal is then $119,750,000. The following entry illustrates how the quarterly lease payment at the beginning of the second quarter would be recorded:

```
Dr. Lease Obligation  . . . . . . . . . . . . . . . . . . . . . . . . . . . . .   1,658,000
Dr. Interest Expense  . . . . . . . . . . . . . . . . . . . . . . . . . . . . .   3,592,000
    Cr. Cash  . . . . . . . . . . . . . . . . . . . . . . . . . . . . . . . . . . . . . . .5,250,000
    To record the lease payment.
```

Note that the payment of $5.25 million is divided into principal repayment and interest payment.

The key to Exhibit 10.1 is the way that the interest expense and principal recovery portions of the payment are separated. We know that the interest rate per quarter is 3 percent. Thus, for the second payment, the interest expense portion must be 0.03 × $119,750,000, or $3,592,000. Since the payment is always $5,250,000 per quarter for this lease, the remainder is the principal recovery, or $1,658,000 ($5,250,000 − $3,592,000). Since the principal balance is reduced by this amount, the ending principal balance for Quarter 2 is $118,092,000 ($119,750,000 − $1,658,000). Each quarter's payment is separated in this manner. Note that the last payment's principal recovery is $5,097,000, just exactly the outstanding principal balance at the beginning of the last quarter.[2]

Note one more thing about Exhibit 10.1: The total payments are $210,012,000, of which $85,012,000 is interest and the rest principal. Thus, in PWA Corporation's footnotes, the lease would be disclosed as follows:

Future minimum lease payments	$210,012,000
Less: Amount representing interest	85,012,000
Present value of minimum lease payments	$125,000,000

The lease asset also must be amortized following the asset amortization policies that PWA Corporation uses for similar assets. Assuming that PWA Corporation amortized the leased asset over 12 years (or 48 quarters) using the straight-line method, the quarterly amortization expense would be $2,604,167 ($125,000,000/48), and the accounting entry would be:

```
Dr. Amortization Expense  . . . . . . . . . . . . . . . . . . . . . . . . . . .   2,604,167
    Cr. Accumulated Amortization  . . . . . . . . . . . . . . . . . . . . . . . . . . .2,604,167
    To record amortization on the leased asset.
```

Capitalized leases for buildings and equipment are ordinarily included with other capital assets, net of the accumulated amortization, in the balance sheet. In classified balance sheets, the next year's principal reduction is shown as a current liability, and the long-term liabilities section includes the capital-lease liabilities less any current portion.

As can be seen in Exhibit 10.2, in its annual report footnotes, PWA Corporation listed its flight equipment acquired with capital leases separately from its other capital

---

[2] One might ask why there is any interest portion at all in the last payment since the payment is made at the beginning of the period. The explanation is that annuities such as this lease with 40 payments, with payments made at the beginning of the period, are really liabilities that extend over only 39 periods. It is as if one borrowed $119,750,000 and repaid it at $5,250,000 per quarter for 39 quarters, with payments made at the end of the period — when the interest expense for that period had been accrued.

E X H I B I T 1 0 . 2

PWA CORPORATION

Property and Equipment
The following assets under capital lease have been included in property and equipment:

	19x3	19x2
Flight equipment	$142.7	$171.8
Buildings and equipment	.8	.8
	$143.5	$172.6
Less: accumulated amortization	65.4	76.6
	$ 78.1	$ 96.0

Amortization is provided at straight-line rates to estimated residual values based on the following estimated useful lives:

Asset	Basis
Flight equipment	12–20 years
Buildings	10–40 years
Ground equipment	5–10 years

Future minimum lease payments at December 31, 19x3 under capital leases for aircraft and operating leases for aircraft, airport terminal facilities and other assets are as follows:

		Operating Leases	
	Capital Leases	Aircraft	Other
19x4	$ 14.1	$ 237.5	$ 57.0
19x5	16.2	228.8	48.1
19x6	15.7	208.5	40.6
19x7	15.2	186.3	39.8
19x8	15.0	178.8	37.6
Thereafter	100.5	1,019.5	318.3
Total minimum lease payments	$176.7	$2,059.4	$541.4
Less: amount representing interest	71.8		
Present value of obligations	$104.9		

The amount representing interest has been calculated at the rates (8.6% to 11.9%) implied by the terms of the leases.

assets. The lease obligations are described in the note. As of December 31, PWA Corporation valued its equipment and property under capital leases at $78.1 million. The present value of lease obligations was $104.9 million. Note that it appears that the capital-lease liability exceeds the capital base asset, no doubt because the asset was amortized on a straight-line basis while the effective interest method is used to amortize the capital-lease liability. Additional details of these leases and other flight equipment under operating leases are described in the note.

In summary, at the inception of a capital lease, the present value of the future lease payments is the value assigned to the capital-lease liability (net of any executory costs). Lease payments are discounted at the lessee's incremental borrowing rate unless the rate implicit in a lease is at a lower rate; then the implicit rate is used. The capital-lease asset is also valued at the present value of the lease payments. From that moment, the two figures are rarely the same. Assets acquired under capital leases are amortized using the straight-line (or some accelerated) method as if the assets were owned. Capital-lease liabilities are amortized using the effective interest method as if they were bonds.

Financial Statement Disclosure: Leases

To distinguish between the resources owned by the organization and the assets leased by the organization, leased assets should be disclosed separately from owned assets. As well, the related lease obligations should be disclosed separately. The CICA Handbook recommends the following disclosure requirements:

> The gross amount of assets under capital leases and related accumulated amortization should be disclosed. Disclosure of leased property and accumulated amortization by major category, e.g., land, buildings, machinery, may be desirable.
>
> Obligations related to leased assets should be shown separately from other long-term obligations. Particulars of obligations related to leased assets, including interest rates and expiry dates, should be shown separately from other long-term obligations. Significant restrictions imposed on the lessee as a result of the lease agreement should be disclosed. It may be desirable to disclose the existence and terms of renewal or purchase options that are not included in the computation of minimum lease payments.
>
> Any portion of lease obligations payable within a year out of current funds should be included in current liabilities.
>
> Disclosure should be made of the future minimum lease payments in aggregate and for each of the five succeeding years. A separate deduction should be made from the aggregate figure for amounts included in the minimum lease payments representing executory costs and imputed interest. The resultant net amount would be the balance of the unpaid obligation.
>
> The amount of amortization of leased property included in the determination of net income should be disclosed separately or as part of amortization expense for capital assets. Disclosure should also be made of methods and rates of amortization.
>
> Interest expense related to lease obligations should be disclosed separately, or as part of interest on long-term indebtedness. (CICA Handbook 3065.21–.26)

For example, Exhibit 10.2 contains the PWA Corporation annual report footnote pertaining to its leases. The gross amount of these capital leases was $143.5 million. The present value of these lease obligations, $104.9 million, is included on the balance sheet as long-term debt; the rest is interest and executory costs. The Maritime Telegraph and Telephone Company, Limited, also included a note on capital leases in its annual report:

Capital leases
Telecommunications property includes equipment of $27,650,000 (1992, $21,851,000) held under capital leases. Accumulated amortization as at December 31, 1993, related to this equipment is $2,100,000 (1992, $670,000). The related obligations of $27,574,000 (1992, $21,851,000) are included in long-term debt.

Lessors follow rules similar to those for lease capitalization so long as there are no uncertainties as to the amounts to be received or any question as to their collectibility. Lease assets and liabilities for lessors must be shown separately on the balance sheet, and there are substantial footnote disclosure requirements as well.

Lease Illustration

The following information will be used to compare the accounting for operating and capital leases. It should be noted that whether the lease is structured as a capital or operating lease does not affect the *total* cost of the lease. The lessor is not concerned about how the lease is disclosed in the financial statements of the lessee. The lessor is only concerned about receipt of the periodic lease payments. Assume on January 2, 1996, Waterton Enterprises, Ltd., the lessee, leases a new automobile from Rocky Mountain Motors, a local auto dealer. The lease calls for annual payments of $5,000 at the end of each year, for four years. Waterton's incremental borrowing rate is 12 percent.

Assuming the lease agreement is structured as an operating lease, the lessee will simply record the lease payment as rent expense each year:

```
December 31, 1996, 1997, 1998, 1999:
Dr. Rent Expense  . . . . . . . . . . . . . . . . . . . . . . . . . . . . . . . . . .  5,000
    Cr. Cash  . . . . . . . . . . . . . . . . . . . . . . . . . . . . . . . . . . . . .         5,000
    To record the rent expense on the operating lease.
```

No additional entries are required for operating leases.

However, assuming the lease agreement is structured as a capital lease, where substantially all the benefits and risks of ownership have been transferred to the lessee, the lessee would capitalize the asset and the related liability at a value of $15,186. The present value of an annuity of $5,000 for four years, discounted at 12 percent is $15,186. The lessee would capitalize and amortize the lease asset. As well, the lease liability would be recognized and a payment amortization schedule prepared. The accounting entries for a capital lease follow:

```
January 2, 1996:
Dr. Leased Asset . . . . . . . . . . . . . . . . . . . . . . . . . . . . . . . . . . 15,186
    Cr. Lease Liability  . . . . . . . . . . . . . . . . . . . . . . . . . . . . . . .        15,186
    To capitalize the lease asset and liability.
```

Assuming the lessee amortizes the asset using the straight-line method, with an estimated useful life of four years, and no residual value [($15,186 − 0)/4], the adjusting entry each year would be:

```
December 31, 1996, 1997, 1998, 1999:
Dr. Amortization Expense  . . . . . . . . . . . . . . . . . . . . . . . . . . . .  3,796.50
    Cr. Accumulated Amortization  . . . . . . . . . . . . . . . . . . . . . . . . .       3,796.50
    To record amortization on the leased asset.
```

In addition, when the $5,000 lease payment is made each year, the payment must be broken down into two components: principal and interest. The following lease amortization schedule provides this information:

Lease Amortization Schedule

Date	Interest Expense (12%) Dr.	Lease Liability Dr.	Cash Cr.	Lease Liability Balance
Jan. 2, 1996	—	—	—	$15,186
Dec. 31, 1996	$1,823	$ 3,177	$ 5,000	12,009
Dec. 31, 1997	1,441	3,559	5,000	8,450
Dec. 31, 1998	1,014	3,986	5,000	4,464
Dec. 31, 1999	536	4,464	5,000	0
	$4,814	$15,186	$20,000	

The lease amortization schedule provides the information for the entries for the annual lease payments:

```
December 31, 1996:
Dr. Interest Expense  ................................. 1,823
Dr. Lease Liability  .................................. 3,177
    Cr. Cash  .......................................          5,000
    To record the annual lease payment.

December 31, 1997:
Dr. Interest Expense  ................................. 1,441
Dr. Lease Liability  .................................. 3,559
    Cr. Cash  .......................................          5,000
    To record the annual lease payment.

December 31, 1998:
Dr. Interest Expense  ................................. 1,014
Dr. Lease Liability  .................................. 3,986
    Cr. Cash  .......................................          5,000
    To record the annual lease payment.

December 31, 1999:
Dr. Interest Expense  .................................  536
Dr. Lease Liability  .................................. 4,464
    Cr. Cash  .......................................          5,000
    To record the annual lease payment.
```

Whether the lease is classified as a capital lease or an operating lease, the total cash outflow and the total expenses are the same: $20,000. Under an operating lease total costs are the four years' rent expense of $5,000 per year. With a capital lease, total costs include interest expense of $4,814 and amortization expense of $15,186. The following table presents the cost comparison.

Total Cost Comparison: Operating and Capital Lease

Total Costs:

```
Operating lease:
  Rent expense              4 × 5,000 = $20,000

Capital lease:
  Interest expense                      $ 4,814
  Amortization expense 4 × $3,756.50 =   15,186
                                        $20,000
```

The financial statement disclosure of the operating lease would only include the rent expense on the income statement and a note to the financial statements detailing any future commitments associated with the lease. Disclosure of the capital lease would include amortization and interest expense on the income statement. As well, on the balance sheet, the leased asset and liability would be disclosed. A portion of the liability would be current, and a portion would be classified as long term. The financial statement disclosure of the capital lease on the December 31, 1997, financial statements is shown below:

WATERTON ENTERPRISES, LTD.
Balance Sheet
December 31, 1997

Capital Assets

Lease asset	$15,186	
Less: accumulated amortization	7,593	$7,593

Current Liabilities

Current portion of long-term liabilities		3,986

Long-Term Liabilities

Lease obligation	$ 8,450	
Less: current portion	3,986	4,464

WATERTON ENTERPRISES, LTD.
Income Statement
For the Year Ended December 31, 1997

Amortization expense	$ 3,796.50
Interest expense	1,441.00

Footnote:
    At December 31, 1997, the future minimum lease payments under capital leases (or operating leases) are:

1998	$5,000
1999	5,000

10.2 PENSIONS

Of all the obligations of a corporation (or a government), pensions probably present the most complex accounting issues. The size of the private pension system is enormous. Perhaps one-half of the full-time work force is covered by private pension plans, with thousands of billions of dollars being managed by pension fund administrators. Some major corporations today have more pensioners than employees! Almost everyone has a stake in the pension system: current employees and retirees, corporate executives, investment managers and advisors, unions, government officials, Revenue Canada, accountants, actuaries, shareholders, and lenders.

The employer's objective in accounting for pension costs is distinctly different from the objective in funding a pension plan. The objective of accounting is to provide a proper allocation of the cost of the plan to the years in which the related employee services are rendered. This objective is achieved by allocating that cost in a rational and systematic manner to the employees' pre-retirement years. The objective of funding a pension plan is to provide cash or other consideration to discharge pension

EXHIBIT 10.3

Pension Considerations

Expense	Funding
Current provision + adjustments	Cash flow position

obligations and to provide for pension security. Funding is a financing procedure that considers cash requirements and other matters such as pension or income tax legislation. Accordingly, the amount contributed to a pension fund in a period is not necessarily the appropriate amount to be recognized as pension expense of the period. (CICA Handbook 3460.07)

Exhibit 10.3 displays the two principal considerations for pensions: expense recognition and funding. The extent to which a firm funds its pension plan is dependent on its short-term and long-term cash flow position. Growth firms, looking for funds to expand or diversify operations, may fund their pension plans over an extended period. The pension expense relates to the benefits earned by employees in a given accounting period. Since employees will not be retiring and receiving their pension benefits until sometime in the future, various adjustments for future benefits must be made over the life of the pension plan. As additional insights into the retirement status of employees become known, the pension expense is adjusted. The matching principle is predominate in determining the pension expense for each accounting period.

In periods where the pension expense is greater than the funding, an accrual or liability is created. When the pension expense is less than the funding, a deferred charge results. "For defined benefit pension plans, there may be a difference between the cumulative amounts expensed and the funding contributions. This difference would be reflected in the balance sheet as either a deferred charge or an accrual for pension costs"(CICA Handbook 3460.57)

As one might expect, one must learn a unique vocabulary before understanding the subject of pensions. In simple terms, a **pension** is a promise to pay certain benefits to employees as specified in an agreement (the *plan*). The terms *contribution* and its derivatives appear frequently in any discussion of pensions. Unfortunately, *contribution* can refer either to the amounts paid *into* the plan or to the amount of benefits paid out of the plan to the pensioner. In regard to payments to a plan, **contributory pension plans** are those to which employees may be required to contribute. **Non-contributory pension plans** are plans where the employer makes *all* the payments to such plans. On the payout side, regardless of who makes the actual contributions, defined-contribution and defined-benefit plans are the two broad types of pension plans.

Defined-Contribution Plans

Under a defined-contribution plan, an employer promises to pay a specific amount per month (or quarter or year) to an employee's pension fund trustee on behalf of an employee. As well, the employee generally makes monthly contributions to the pension. "A **defined contribution pension plan** is one in which the employer's contributions are fixed, usually as a percentage of compensation, and allocated to specific individuals. The pension benefit for each employee is the amount that can be provided at retirement based on the accumulated contributions made on that individual's behalf and investment earnings on those contributions"(CICA Handbook 3460.03).

pension
A retirement plan for employees that will provide income to the employee upon retirement.

contributory pension plans
Contributory pension plans are those to which employees may be required to make contributions, in addition to the contributions made by the employer.

non-contributory pension plans
Non-contributory pension plans are plans where the employer makes all the payments to such plans.

defined contribution plan
A pension plan in which an employer promises to make periodic payments to the plan on behalf of its employees.

When an enterprise establishes a defined contribution pension plan, it does not assume the economic risks inherent in a defined benefit pension plan. The employer agrees to contribute a certain amount to the pension fund in each period in exchange for services rendered by the employees and has no responsibility to make any further contributions. It is the employees who are at risk because the amount of the pension benefit that will be payable to an individual employee is entirely dependent upon the amount of funds accumulated for the employee's account and the economic conditions prevailing at the retirement date. (CICA Handbook 3460.09)

Many organizations pay a set percentage of an employee's salary each month to a pension plan founded just for this purpose. The pension trustee invests the money and keeps track of the contributions made on behalf of each employee and the related earnings on those contributions. Upon retirement, the employee then begins receiving a monthly pension cheque based on his or her accumulated pension account balance. The organization really has no pension liability to the employees beyond making those monthly payments. An employee's retirement benefits are purely a function of the total contributions (both employer and employee), plus the earnings on those funds (and his or her retirement age, gender, and certain choices made as to payout options). Thus, the more contributions made and the better the earnings record of the invested contributions, the larger the employee's retirement income.

Accounting for defined-contribution pension funds is a simple task. Each month, the employer makes an entry to record the pension expense and the accrued pension liability. Within a few days or weeks, the liability is settled by a cheque written to the pension fund.

Defined-Benefit Plans

defined benefit plan
A pension plan in which an employer promises to pay certain levels of future benefits to employees on their retirement from the company.

"A **defined benefit pension plan** specifies either the benefits to be received by employees after retirement or the method for determining those benefits" (CICA Handbook 3460.03). "When an enterprise establishes a defined benefit pension plan, it assumes economic risks. The enterprise is at risk with respect to the amount of the benefit that each employee will receive because the amount is not known with certainty until the benefits related to the employee's retirement cease. The enterprise is also at risk with respect to the returns on amounts invested in the pension fund, because any shortfall from expected returns must be funded by the employer and any excess reduces required funding"(CICA Handbook 3460.08).

As the term suggests, *defined-benefit plans* specify the *future* amount an employee will receive on retirement. The amount is usually a function of age, years of service, and salary level; other factors may also affect the amount. Organizations must estimate the current cost of these future pension benefits and record this cost as the pension expense for the year. The offsetting entry is a current pension liability. Ordinarily, the organization then eliminates this pension liability by paying cash (called *funding*) to an independent, third-party trustee. The trustee invests these funds and pays the retirees when they become eligible.

The assets of a pension fund appear in the accounting records of the pension trust, *not* in the records of the employer. It is important to understand that the trustee is only the agent of the employer. The employer's obligation remains even after it has made the payments to the trustee. If the trustee makes poor investments and runs out of money, the employer is still obligated to pay the pensions for the committed retirement benefits.

Ideally, the trustee should have just enough funds to satisfy the terms of the pension agreement. Occasionally, however, a fund becomes overfunded and an employer may either stop contributing to the fund or may request that the trustee return the excess funds.

It is important to note that organizations are not required to provide pensions to their employees. However, if they choose to do so, there are laws that prescribe how pensions are to be administered. As well, income tax regulations prescribe how much pension cost can be deducted for income tax purposes. And, of course, generally accepted accounting practices specify how such costs are to be expensed, how liabilities are to be valued, and what supplemental information is to be disclosed in the footnotes to the financial statements.

Pension Expense

GAAP for defined-benefit pension plans require that the cost of pension benefits be recognized during the period in which those benefits are earned. For example, suppose that a particular pension plan promised an employee a monthly pension of 2.5 percent of her salary at retirement for each year of service to a company. Consequently, if the employee worked 30 years prior to retirement, she would receive a monthly pension equal to 75 percent of her monthly salary at retirement. Assuming that she worked from 1990 to 2020, she would begin receiving her pension payments in 2021. Clearly, however, some portion of the payments received in 2021 were earned in 1990. Consequently, the cost of that portion of her expected pension benefit, adjusted for various estimates, including the present value, must be recognized as **pension expense** in 1990.

pension expense
The cost of expected pension benefits, adjusted for various estimates, including the present value, must be recognized as pension expense in the current accounting period.

A typical pension expense entry would appear as follows:

```
Dr. Pension Expense . . . . . . . . . . . . . . . . . . . . . . . . . . . . . . 100,000
      Cr. Accrued Pension Liability . . . . . . . . . . . . . . . . . . . . . . . . . . .   100,000
      To accrue the pension expense for the year.
```

The liability account is offset when the year's pension expense is funded (i.e., when cash is paid to the pension trust):

```
Dr. Accrued Pension Liability . . . . . . . . . . . . . . . . . . . . . . . . . 100,000
      Cr. Cash  . . . . . . . . . . . . . . . . . . . . . . . . . . . . . . . . . . . .   100,000
      To record the payment on the pension liability.
```

If the pension liability is not funded, the accrued pension liability remains. If it is funded at an amount higher than the accrued pension liability, the account Prepaid Pension Cost becomes an asset.

As you might expect, the accounting for defined-benefit pension plans requires considerable *estimating:*

How many employees will qualify for pensions?

How long will they work?

How many will live to retirement age?

What salaries will they be receiving?

How long will they live while retired?

How much will the trustee earn on the funds?

What must the company pay now to satisfy all of its future obligations?

Is the pension fund currently overfunded or underfunded?

If underfunded, how should the company "catch up"?

For defined-benefit pension plans, the pension expense for a period includes the cost of pension benefits provided in exchange for employees' services rendered in the period. In addition, the pension expense includes adjustments arising from changes in the pension plan and any actuarial adjustments related to future estimated benefits of the employees.

For many years, defined-benefit pension plans were considered to be economic obligations but *not* accounting liabilities. It was argued that an employer did not legally have a liability to an employee until that employee actually reached retirement age — and then the only liability was to make one month's benefit payment! If the retiree lived another month, another month's benefit payment was due, and so on. How could pension promises made to employees with many years still to work be considered accounting liabilities when no one could know even what future salary levels would be?

In view of the history of this issue, today's accounting represents a compromise. Employers must record as expense the current cost of pension benefits earned by employees, but the estimate of the overall pension obligation is relegated to the footnotes and the emphasis is on the projected benefits at current salary levels.

postretirement benefits
Benefits such as medical or dental coverage, or discounts on merchandise purchases.

In addition to pension costs, many organizations incur additional postretirement costs. Many employees are provided a retirement package that includes various postretirement benefits in addition to their pension plan. **Postretirement benefits** may include such items as medical and dental insurance coverage, or employee discounts on merchandise purchases. Employees earn these benefits during their working years, but receive the benefits upon retirement. Current GAAP do not provide specific guidelines for the accounting of postretirement benefits. However, the costs of these benefits should be treated similarly to pension costs. That is, the matching principle should be followed and the expense should be recognized before the employee's retirement.

Financial Statement Disclosure: Pensions

accrued actuarial pension benefits
The present value of all pension benefits earned by employees as of a particular date.

pension fund assets
The market value of the investment portfolio held by the pension trustee as of the balance sheet date.

Because of the importance of pensions and the complexity presented by their accounting, GAAP require footnote disclosure. Two items, the actuarial present value of accrued pension benefits and the pension fund assets at fair value, deserve special attention in these disclosures. The **accrued actuarial pension benefits** is the present value of all pension benefits earned by employees as of a particular date. Of course, it must reflect expected mortality, future wage levels, and some of the other assumptions we have already mentioned. The term **pension fund assets** at fair value refers to the market value of the investment portfolio held by the pension trustee as of the balance sheet date. "For defined benefit pension plans, an enterprise should disclose separately the actuarial present value of accrued pension benefits attributed to services rendered up to the reporting date and the value of pension fund assets" (CICA Handbook 3460.60). "Market related values should be used for valuing pension fund assets" (CICA Handbook 3460.34). Other pension information, such as the pension expense for the period, may be shown, but is not a required disclosure. The Canadian Cancer Society included the following note on pensions in its annual report:

> The Society maintains a defined benefit pension plan which covers substantially all of its employees. The plan provides pensions based on length of service and final average earnings.
>
> During the year, the Society made cash contributions to the defined benefit pension plan of $473,000 (1992 — $436,000).
>
> As of September 30, 1993, the defined benefit pension plan is fully funded with the market value of pension fund assets of $15,428,000 (1992 — $13,486,000) exceeding the actuarial present value for accounting purposes of accrued pension benefits of $9,401,000 (1992 — $8,741,000).

Xerox Canada, Inc., explained its accounting for pensions in a note as follows: "As at December 31, 1993 the estimated actuarial present value of accrued pension obligations was $243,066,000 and the estimated adjusted market value of pension fund assets was $242,720,000. The pension expense for 1993 was $12,753,000 (1992 — $11,900,000)." The Salvation Army in Canada disclosed the following information on its pensions: "The Salvation Army maintains a defined benefit pension plan covering all eligible officers. The actuarial present value of the accrued pension benefits attributed to services rendered up to December 31, 1993 was $73,317 (1992 — $70,365). The market value of assets in the pension fund at December 31, 1993, was $97,674 (1992 — $79,567).

10.3 DEFERRED INCOME TAXES

Income taxes represent one of the larger obligations arising from operations that a company must satisfy. Some of these taxes must be paid currently; others may be postponed for many years. This section focuses on those income taxes that, because of the particular provisions of Revenue Canada, may be postponed until some future date.

Because of differences between GAAP and rules used by Revenue Canada, the amounts due to the taxation authorities for a given period are not necessarily the accounting income tax *expense* of that period. The accounting issue behind deferred taxes is one of *matching:* Income tax expense is the periodic cost associated with particular revenue and expense items recognized in that accounting period. This cost, however, is independent of *when* those particular revenue and expense items are recognized for tax purposes. If revenues and expenses are recorded in this year's income statement, the related income tax expense *should* also appear in this year's income statement even if the recognition of those revenues and expenses (and their associated income tax liability) can be *deferred* until some later date for income tax purposes. This process is called **interperiod tax allocation;** it is really just another form of accrual accounting. It recognizes business events (in this case, the income tax expense) at some more appropriate moment than simply when the tax bill appears or must be paid in cash. Without interperiod tax accounting, a company's operating results can fluctuate wildly because of tax accounting conventions, even if the basic operations of the business are stable.

Almost all business events have the potential to be recognized at different times for tax purposes than for accounting purposes, but the most common accounting-tax differences leading to deferred income taxes are those listed in Exhibit 10.4.

interperiod tax allocation
The process of allocating the actual taxes paid by a company over the periods in which the taxes are recognized for accounting purposes.

E X H I B I T   1 0 . 4

Common Events Associated with Deferred Income Taxes

Event	Common Accounting Treatment	Treatment for Income Tax Purposes
Amortization of capital assets	Straight-line method	Capital cost allowance
Instalment sales	Estimated and recognized in the period corresponding with the actual credit sale	Recognized when cash is received
Warranty expense	Estimated and recognized in the period of product sale	Recognized when paid

Accounting for Deferred Taxes

Ideally, in published financial statements, the cost of an asset is assigned to various years in whatever manner best reflects the use of the asset over its lifetime. Tax accounting also expenses that same cost over the asset's life but often with different amounts being charged to different years. One often hears the expression "companies keep two sets of books;" what this means is simply that tax rules are often different from GAAP. Moreover, companies have different objectives when reporting income to Revenue Canada than when reporting income to owners and potential shareholders. Thus, in the case of amortization, although both tax and accounting statements reflect the same *total* amortization expense over the life of an asset, the capital cost allowance or tax amortization is accelerated or "front loaded" while the accounting amortization is usually flat or straight line.

Imagine that Sample Company purchases an asset costing $1,000 that, because of special tax incentives, can be amortized over only two years (50 percent each year), and that, for accounting purposes, can be amortized over four years (25 percent per year). For simplicity, assume that the company is subject to a 40 percent tax rate. The differences between the accounting amortization and tax amortization deductions are as follows:

	Year 1	Year 2	Year 3	Year 4
Accounting amortization	$ 250	$ 250	$250	$250
Tax amortization (CCA)*	500	500	–0–	–0–
Difference	$(250)	$(250)	$250	$250
Tax impact of difference at 40% tax rate	$(100)	$(100)	$100	$100

*Revenue Canada applies a half-year rule for capital cost allowance. The half-year rule has not been used in this illustration.

In essence, $250 more tax amortization will be taken in Years 1 and 2 and $250 less tax amortization taken in Years 3 and 4. Take a moment and consider the implications of these differences. The taxes actually due in Years 1 and 2 will be $100 lower and, in Years 3 and 4, the actual taxes due will be $100 higher than will be reflected in the accounting income statements. In total, however, over the four-year period, the amount of taxes will be the same under either system. If this were the only accounting-tax difference that the company had, the accounting income tax expense in Years 1 and 2 would simply be the taxes actually due plus $100. In Years 3 and 4, this process would be reversed — the accounting income tax expense would be the taxes actually due minus $100.

In Exhibit 10.5, the effect of these accounting-tax differences, as well as the use of interperiod tax allocation to account for these differences, is illustrated. In this example, we assume that revenues for each period are $1,000 and that all other expenses other than amortization total $400 per year. Note that the income tax liability (per the tax return) for each of the first two years would be only $40 and then would increase to $240 per year for the next two years. On the accounting income statement, the total income tax expense is adjusted to eliminate what would otherwise be a distortion caused by the special tax amortization allowances. The additional $100 of income tax expense in Years 1 and 2 increases the Deferred Income Taxes account. Note that this account builds up in Years 1 and 2 and then reverses in Years 3 and 4 when the total income tax liability is higher than the total income tax expense. Also note that the

E X H I B I T 1 0 . 5

EXHIBIT 10.5

Deferred Income Taxes for Sample Company

Income Tax Returns of Sample Company

	Year				
	1	**2**	**3**	**4**	**Total**
Sales	$1,000	$1,000	$1,000	$1,000	
Capital cost allowance	500	500			
All other expenses	400	400	400	400	
Taxable income	100	100	600	600	
Income tax @ 40%	40	40	240	240	$560

On the Balance Sheets of Sample Company

	Year			
	1	**2**	**3**	**4**
Deferred income taxes	$100	$200	$100	$0

Deferred taxes

	Balance 0
	Year 1 100
	Balance 100
	Year 2 100
	Balance 200
Year 3 100	
	Balance 100
Year 4 100	
	Balance 0

Income Statement of Sample Company

	Year				
	1	**2**	**3**	**4**	**Total**
Sales	$1,000	$1,000	$1,000	$1,000	
Amortization	250	250	250	250	
All other expenses	400	400	400	400	
Income before taxes	350	350	350	350	
Current income tax expense	40	40	240	240	
Deferred income tax expense	100	100	−100	−100	
Total income tax expense	140	140	140	140	$560
Net income	210	210	210	210	

events that gave rise to this situation was the purchase of an asset and the decision to use different accounting and tax amortization schedules.

The use of a Deferred Income Taxes account on the balance sheet eliminates the distortion that would otherwise occur if the current tax liability (per the tax return) were considered to be the income tax expense for the year. Deferred tax accounting adheres to the *matching* principle and makes the total income tax expense in the income statement conform to the accounting treatment used for amortization in that statement.

The Deferred Income Taxes account at the end of Years 1, 2, and 3 is a liability in the sense that someday income taxes will be payable in excess of what the accounting statements would otherwise suggest. In simple terms, Sample Company temporarily avoided $100 of income tax payments in Year 1 because it used a more rapid method of amortization for tax reporting than was used for accounting purposes. Someday that advantage will reverse; the fast amortization write-offs will run out with straight-line amortization continuing on the accounting records. Like a buffer, the Deferred Income Taxes account is used to prevent such distortions. Expenses are credited to this account when temporary tax advantages lower taxable income, and when the differences reverse, the buffer is drawn down.

Using the data for Sample Company, at the end of Year 1 there should be a $100 deferred tax liability associated with this asset (i.e., $0.40 \times \$250$). In Year 2, the difference in the two cost bases continues, so the deferred tax liability must be increased another $100, to a balance of $200. In Years 3 and 4 the differences reverse and the deferred tax liability is removed. The accounting entries for income taxes each year would be:

```
Years 1 and 2:
Dr. Income Tax Expense . . . . . . . . . . . . . . . . . . . . . . . . . . . . . . . . . 140
    Cr. Deferred Income Taxes . . . . . . . . . . . . . . . . . . . . . . . . . . . . .        100
    Cr. Income Taxes Payable  . . . . . . . . . . . . . . . . . . . . . . . . . . . . .         40
    To record deferred taxes for the year.


Years 3 and 4:
Dr. Income Tax Expense . . . . . . . . . . . . . . . . . . . . . . . . . . . . . . . . . 140
Dr. Deferred Income Taxes . . . . . . . . . . . . . . . . . . . . . . . . . . . . . . . 100
    Cr. Income Tax Payable . . . . . . . . . . . . . . . . . . . . . . . . . . . . . .        240
    To record deferred taxes for the year.
```

Note that at the end of Year 1, it was determined that the ending balance for deferred tax liability should be $100. It was assumed there was no beginning balance for deferred taxes. In reviewing the above data, it is important to recall the purpose of deferred tax accounting: Deferred tax liabilities (and assets) measure the future tax expenditures (or benefits) that a company faces due only to the differences between tax accounting and financial statement accounting.

Timing and Permanent Differences

timing differences
Differences in accounting policies for income tax reporting and financial reporting that reverse themselves at some point in time.

Timing differences. Interperiod tax allocation is used when tax returns and the accounting reports reflect timing differences, as with amortization. By definition, timing differences for individual assets *always reverse* themselves at some point. Tax amortization may exceed accounting amortization for a while for any particular asset, but eventually the reverse will occur and by the end of the life of the asset, the sum of the differences (positives and negatives) will always be zero. Accordingly, the deferred tax liability associated with this asset may increase for a few years on the balance sheet, but then it will decline and eventually become zero.

Even though the timing difference that triggered the deferred tax liability (or asset if the account has a debit balance) will always reverse itself for any particular item having a timing difference, it is possible for an account such as Deferred Income Taxes to keep increasing in *total,* for example, if a business is growing and more assets are being acquired. Companies that follow a policy of expansion, by acquiring amortizable assets, accumulate large deferred tax balances. In such circumstances, the deferred balances will take several years to reverse, and may appear to *never* be completely reversed, if the companies continue to grow and acquire additional amortizable assets.

Events that lead to timing differences. Timing differences may arise as a result of four types of events:

1. Expenses (or losses) become tax deductible *before* being expensed for accounting purposes. The most frequent example of this is amortization.
2. Revenues (or gains) become taxable *after* they are recognized in the accounting income statement. For example, certain types of instalment sales are recognized as sales immediately but are treated as taxable income only as payments are received.
3. Expenses (or losses) become tax deductible *after* the recognition of the expense. This happens when a company provides warranties or guarantees on a product or service. Generally accepted accounting principles require such a company to estimate the expense and to record it when the revenue is recognized; tax rules permit warranty deductions only when the repairs or adjustments are actually made (essentially the cash basis).
4. Revenue (or gains) become taxable *before* being recognized as accounting income; rent collected in advance is such an item.

It should be noted that in the first two instances, accounting income exceeds taxable income, thus giving rise to a deferred tax liability; in the latter two examples, the reverse is true: There is a deferred tax asset that, in simple terms, is like a prepaid income tax. (To be precise, it is the income tax benefit of future deductions.) Many companies have both — perhaps a deferred tax liability because of different amortization policies and a deferred tax asset because of the alternative treatment of warranty expenses.

The accounting for some items, such as warranties, is the reverse of that for amortization. For example, the balance sheet may show a reserve for future warranty claims or some such liability. This represents a liability with an accounting-tax difference the other way: Expensing on the accounting statements has preceded its tax deduction. A deferred tax asset must be created to reflect this accounting-tax difference. The following example illustrates how the accounting for warranties might lead to the creation of a deferred tax asset:

	End of Year		
	1	**2**	**3**
Accounting basis of warranty liability	$(500)	$(400)	$(200)
Tax basis of warranty liability	–0–	–0–	–0–
Difference	$(500)	$(400)	$(200)
Tax rate	0.4	0.4	0.4
Deferred tax asset	$ 200	$ 160	$ 80
Deferred tax expense (benefit)	$(200)	$ 40	$ 80

Suppose that during Year 1, an allowance for future warranty expense was established for the first time at $500. Since estimated warranty expenses cannot be deducted for tax purposes, at the end of Year 1 there is a warranty liability with an accounting-tax difference, in this case $500. The deferred tax asset related to this liability is $200 (0.40 × $500). The difference between the beginning and ending deferred tax assets is thus $200. As a consequence, a $200 deferred tax adjustment (or negative expense) exists. At the end of Year 2, the warranty is $400. Obviously, the actual warranty cost recognized on the tax return exceeded the warranty expense reflected in the accounting statements. Since this accounting-tax difference is $400, the deferred tax asset is $160 (0.40 × $400). To reduce the deferred tax asset from its opening balance of $200, a deferred tax expense of $40 will be recorded. A similar situation occurs in Year 3.

permanent differences
Absolute difference in accounting policies for income tax reporting and financial reporting that do not reverse.

Permanent differences. Amortization differences between tax and accounting statements illustrate a timing difference because for any given asset, the total difference over time is zero. Permanent differences, on the other hand, arise when an item is included for accounting purposes but will never appear in the determination of taxable income (or vice versa). For example, dividends from Canadian corporations are a revenue item for accounting purposes but are not taxable — they represent a permanent difference in the income reported to Revenue Canada versus the income reported to shareholders. Amortization of goodwill is another example — it is an accounting expense but is only partially deductible for income tax purposes. Deferred taxes are never calculated for permanent differences; they are simply ignored in the interperiod tax allocation process.

Financial Statement Disclosure: Deferred Income Taxes

The classification of deferred tax assets and liabilities in the balance sheet must reflect the classification of the liabilities or assets with which they are associated. Thus, deferred tax liabilities resulting from accounting-tax amortization differences are always classified as non-current because the assets associated with them, capital assets, are always classified as non-current. It is possible to have four deferred tax items in a balance sheet: current and non-current liabilities, and current and non-current assets. However, current deferred tax assets should be netted against current deferred tax liabilities; and non-current deferred tax assets should be netted against non-current deferred liabilities. As a result, only two deferred tax items appear in a balance sheet: current and non-current.

Algoma Steel, Inc., provides an example of the accounting for income taxes in a note in its annual report: "The corporation follows the tax allocation method of providing for income taxes. Under this method, timing differences between reported and taxable incomes result in deferred income taxes."

Northern Canadian Oils, Limited's note on income taxes explains that its deferred taxes are the result of claiming capital cost allowance for income tax purposes: "The Company follows the tax allocation method of accounting under which the income tax provision is based on the earnings reported in the accounts. Under this method, the Company provides for deferred income taxes to the extent that income taxes otherwise payable are eliminated by claiming capital cost allowance in the accounts."

Deferred Income Tax Illustration

The following information will be used to illustrate the accounting for deferred taxes. Osoyoos Mountain Recreation, Ltd., reported a net income of $77,000 before income taxes. Included in the determination of the reported net income were the following items:

Amortization expense of $22,000.

Dividend income of $6,000.

Estimated warranty expense of $11,000.

For income tax purposes Osoyoos claimed capital cost allowance of $29,000 and actual warranty costs of $13,000. The accounting for the amortization/capital cost allowance and warranty costs are timing differences. Since dividends from Canadian corporations are not taxable, the dividend income is a permanent difference. These differences between accounting for tax purposes and GAAP will affect the determination of the income tax expense for the period, the current taxes payable, and the deferred income taxes. The following formula may be used to simplify these concepts and the determination of the income tax components:

Reported income
± Permanent differences
Accounting income   × Tax rate = Income tax expense
± Timing differences   × Tax rate = *Deferred income taxes*
Taxable income   × Tax rate = Income tax payable

Assuming a tax rate of 35 percent, the above format may be used to determine the income disclosures for Osoyoos Mountain Recreation, Ltd.:

Reported income	$77,000	
Permanent differences:		
Less: Dividends from		
Canadian corporations	(6,000)	
Accounting income	$71,000	× .35 = $24,850 income tax expense
+/– Timing differences:		
Add back: Amortization	22,000	
Less: Capital cost allowance	(29,000)	
Add back: Warranty expense	11,000	
Less: Actual warranty costs	(13,000) $ (9,000)	× .35 = $3,150 deferred income taxes
Taxable income	$62,000	× .35 = $21,700 income tax payable

The entry to accrue income taxes is:

```
Dr. Income Tax Expense . . . . . . . . . . . . . . . . . . . . . . . . . . . . . 24,850
      Cr. Deferred Income Taxes . . . . . . . . . . . . . . . . . . . . . . . .      3,150
      Cr. Income Taxes Payable  . . . . . . . . . . . . . . . . . . . . . . . .     21,700
   To record deferred income taxes.
```

The financial statement disclosure on the December 31 financial statements is shown below:

OSOYOOS MOUNTAIN RECREATION, LTD.
Balance Sheet
December 31

Current Liabilities

Income tax payable	$21,700
Deferred income taxes	700

Long-Term Liabilities

Deferred income taxes	2,450

The income tax payable to Revenue Canada of $21,700 is disclosed as a current liability. Deferred income taxes total $3,150. "Accumulated tax allocation credits and/or debits should be segregated in the balance sheet as between current and non-current according to the classification of the assets and liabilities to which they relate" (CICA Handbook 3470.23). The deferred taxes for warranties will reverse in the short term and are therefore classified as a current liability of $700 [.35 × ($11,000 − $13,000)]. The deferred taxes related to amortization expense will reverse over the long term and are therefore classified as a long-term liability of $2,450 [.35 × ($22,000 − $29,000)].

OSOYOOS MOUNTAIN RECREATION, LTD.
Partial Income Statement
For the Year Ended December 31

Net income — before taxes		$77,000
Less:		
Income taxes:		
Current	$21,700	
Deferred	3,150	24,850
Net income — after taxes		$52,150

On the income statement, income tax expense of $24,850 is allocated to current income taxes of $21,700 and deferred income taxes of $3,150. On the statement of changes in financial position, the deferred income taxes are an adjustment of non-cash items, under operating activities.

10.4 FINANCIAL STATEMENT ANALYSIS

When an organization invests in a capital asset such as a building, and finances the purchase with a mortgage, the event is disclosed in the financial statements. The building is disclosed as a capital asset on the balance sheet. The mortgage is classified as a long-term liability on the balance sheet. However, when an organization leases an asset, the investing/financing activity may not be disclosed on the balance sheet. Users of financial reports should realize only capital leases are fully disclosed on the financial statements. The disclosure of capital assets produces financial statement elements similar to the building/mortgage transaction previously mentioned. A capital lease requires the disclosure of the lease asset and the lease liability. With operating leases, no lease asset or liability appears on the balance sheet.

The off-balance-sheet financing of operating leases may significantly impact on the financial position of the organization and not be reflected in the user's ratio analysis. The exclusion of liabilities related to operating leases may significantly impact on a firm's liquidity and solvency ratios. As note disclosure is required for all leases, operating and capital, financial statement users should carefully review the notes accompanying the financial statements.

The disclosure requirement of pensions provides minimal information to the user. Users should realize the estimates necessary for organizations to determine the pension expense associated with defined-benefit pension plans. However, the main concern of the user should be whether the pension liability has been fully disclosed. Current GAAP require footnote disclosure of the actuarial present value of accrued pension benefits, and the pension fund assets at fair value. When the fair value of the pension assets exceeds the pension benefits, the organization has no unrecorded pension liability. However, when the opposite is true, that is, when the fair value of the pension assets is less than the pension benefits, the organization has a potential pension liability. This information is only disclosed via notes to the financial statements. No liability is disclosed on the balance sheet. As with operating leases, there may be a significant impact on the financial position of the organization that is not reflected in the user's ratio analysis.

The accounting for deferred income taxes is a controversial subject. The controversy revolves around the existence of large deferred tax liabilities disclosed on the balance sheet. Many argue that deferred taxes are not really a liability. The argument is based on the fact that many organizations continue to expand their operations. This expansion activity, in effect, eliminates the possible reversal of the deferred tax account in the foreseeable future. As long as the firm continues to acquire amortizable assets, the complete reversal of amortization and capital cost allowance is delayed indefinitely. A related question is, should deferred income taxes be classified as a liability for ratio purposes? If the reversal is probable, a liability exists. Others would argue against including deferred income taxes as a liability. The CICA in a recent exposure draft has supported the liability approach to deferred taxes. As well, the exposure draft suggests a change in terminology to *future income taxes*. If the exposure draft is recommended for inclusion in the CICA Handbook, the accounting for deferred income taxes will be clearer.

10.5 SUMMARY

Leases, pensions, and deferred income taxes are significant obligations that present unique valuation issues. Capital leases are reported in the balance sheet at their present value and pension obligations are disclosed in the footnotes at their present value. Deferred income taxes, on the other hand, are not reported at their present value but are reported in the balance sheet.

Many types of leases exist, but only those that meet one or more of the three tests (i.e., ownership, economic life, and value) are considered to be capital leases. Capital leases are recorded on the books of the lessee, as both an asset and a liability at their present value at the time the lease is signed. Lease assets are amortized in a manner similar to other capital assets as if the asset were owned. Lease liabilities, on the other hand, are amortized using the effective interest method as one would amortize a bond.

Pensions are important because of the sheer magnitude of the dollars involved. They are complex because of the variety of estimates one must make to value an entity's pension obligation. No matter how a pension is to be funded, whether by contributions from the employer, the employee, or both, the two basic types are defined-contribution and defined-benefit plans. The latter is more complex because accountants, actuaries, and management must estimate future benefits, employee mortality and retirement ages, and the future earnings rate of pension assets.

Differences between the accounting procedures adopted for tax purposes and for financial reporting purposes may result in deferred tax liabilities and/or assets and deferred tax expenses and/or benefits. Some items, such as dividends from Canadian corporations, result in permanent accounting-tax differences and are not subject to deferred tax accounting. Only timing differences, such as those created by differences in amortization, result in interperiod income tax allocations. The following table summarizes the financial statement interrelationships of different financial statement items:

Financial Statement Interrelationships

Financial Statement Item	Balance Sheet	Income Statement	Statement of Changes in Financial Position
Leases — operating	N/A	Rent expense	N/A
Leases — capital	Long-term liability and non-current asset	Interest expense and amortization expense	Amortization expense added back to net income as a non-cash item, operating activity.
Pensions	Footnote	Pension expense	N/A
Deferred income taxes	Current and/or long-term asset/liability	Income tax expense, current and deferred	An adjustment to non-cash items, operating activity

N/A = Not applicable.

10.6 KEY CONCEPTS AND TERMS

Accrued actuarial pension benefits (p. 500)
Capital leases (p. 488)
Contributory pension plans (p. 497)
Defined-benefit pension plan (p. 498)
Defined-contribution pension plan (p. 497)
Interperiod tax allocation (p. 501)
Lessee (p. 487)
Lessor (p. 487)

Non-contributory pension plans (p. 497)
Off-balance-sheet financing (p. 488)
Operating leases (p. 487)
Pension (p. 497)
Pension expense (p. 499)
Pension fund assets (p. 500)
Permanent differences (p. 505)
Postretirement benefits (p. 500)
Timing differences (p. 504)

10.7 COMPREHENSIVE REVIEW PROBLEM

R10.1 Deferred taxes, pensions, and leases. Cavendish Resorts, Limited, reported a net income of $133,000, before income taxes. Included in the determination of the reported net income were the following items:

Estimated warranty expense of $19,000.

Amortization expense of $35,000.

Dividends income from Canadian corporations of $9,000.

Instalment sales income of $27,000.

Expenses of $6,000 not allowable for tax purposes.

For income tax purposes Cavendish claims capital cost allowance of $48,000, actual warranty costs of $28,000, and instalment sales income of $32,000. Cavendish has a 40 percent income tax rate.

Required:

a. Determine the deferred tax liability/asset.

b. Describe the disclosure of income tax items on Cavendish's financial statements.

c. Cavendish signed a three-year lease agreement on January 2, 1996. The lease calls for annual payments of $8,000 to be made at the end of each calender year. The interest rate implicit to the lease is 10 percent. Determine the impact on the December 31, 1996, financial statements assuming the lease is to be accounted for as a: (1) capital lease and (2) an operating lease.

d. Describe the disclosure of pension data on Cavendish's financial statements, if Cavendish has a defined-benefit plan for most of its employees. The pension plan is fully funded with pension assets having an estimated market value of $538,000 and estimated actuarial pensions obligations of $422,000.

10.8 REVIEW AND DISCUSSION QUESTIONS

Q10.1 Explain timing and permanent differences as they relate to deferred tax accounting

Q10.2 Explain the difference between contributory and non-contributory pension plans.

Q10.3 Explain the impact the accounting for an operating lease as compared to a capital lease would have on the ratio analysis of an organization.

Q10.4 Why do some organizations use capital cost allowance rates to determine their annual amortization expense for financial reporting purposes?

Q10.5 If an organization is concerned about its profitability and liquidity, would it prefer to account for its leases as operating or capital leases?

Q10.6 Point: All leases should be capitalized on the balance sheet as liabilities. Counterpoint: Only capital leases should be treated as liabilities. Evaluate the two viewpoints. Which one do you agree with, and why?

Q10.7 Point: Deferred income taxes represent a liability. Counterpoint: Deferred income taxes represent owners' equity. Evaluate the two viewpoints. Which one do you agree with, and why?

Q10.8 Suppose you are the chief financial officer of a corporation and a director has some questions about your annual report. The director notes that accounts called Deferred Taxes appear both on the asset and the liability sides of the balance sheet, and asks, "What are those things supposed to be?" How would you explain them to the director?

Q10.9 Who benefits from a company-sponsored pension plan? When do those benefits happen? If there is a benefit, there is no doubt a cost somewhere. What are the costs of those benefits just identified? When are those costs paid?

Q10.10 As an employee, would you prefer to receive a defined-benefit pension or a defined-contribution pension, assuming the pension benefits appeared to be about the same during that important first year of retirement?

Q10.11 Describe the disclosure of pension data on the financial statements for a defined-benefit plan. The pension plan is fully funded with pension assets having an estimated market value of $1,222,000 and estimated actuarial pension obligations of $1,009,000.

Q10.12 An analysis of the financial statements of Pasto, Limited, produced a long-term debt-to-invested capital ratio for the current year of approximately 2:1. Comment on the significance of this ratio.

Q10.13 The Maritime Telegraph and Telephone Company, Limited, included a note on capital leases in its annual report:

> **Capital leases**
> Telecommunications property includes equipment of $27,650,000 (1992, $21,851,000) held under capital leases. Accumulated amortization as at December 31, 1993, related to this equipment is $2,100,000 (1992, $670,000). The related obligations of $27,574,000 (1992, $21,851,000) are included in long-term debt.

Discuss the meaning of this note, explaining the impact the leases have on the company's balance sheet and income statement.

10.9 PROBLEMS

P10.1 Accounting for leases: the lessee. SC Company leases an asset with a market value of $200,000 under conditions by which the company agrees to pay $47,479.28 each year for five years (assume annual payments at year-end, and an interest rate of 6%). The agreement is non-cancellable; five years is the expected economic life of the asset; there is no expected residual value to the asset. (Thus, the lease is to be capitalized.) The lease is executed on January 1, 1991.

Required:

a. What entry does the lessee make on January 1, 1991?

b. What entry does it make at the end of 1991 to record the cash payment of $47,479.28?

c. For 1991, what expenses will be reflected on the income statement with respect to the lease?

d. How will the lease asset and liability items appear on the books as of January 1, 1991? 1992? 1993? 1994? 1995? 1996?

e. How much of the lease liability will appear as a current item in the balance sheet as of December 31, 1991? How much of the leased asset will appear as a current item on that date?

P10.2 Accounting for leases. Burlington, Ltd., signed a three-year lease agreement on January 2, 1996. The lease calls for annual payments of $112,590 to be made at the end of each calender year. The interest rate implicit to the lease is 10 percent. Determine the impact on the December 31, 1996, financial statements assuming the lease is to be accounted for as: (*a*) a capital lease and (*b*) an operating lease.

P10.3 Accounting for leases. Kenyon Auto Company owns land on which it can build a new showroom at a cost of $60,000. As an alternative, Kenyon can have Robbin Leasing Company build the showroom and Kenyon can lease it for $7,010 a year for 15 years, which is the estimated useful life of the building. Kenyon would pay all maintenance and insurance costs. The $7,010 a year will give Robbin an 8 percent return on its investment of $60,000. Lease payments would be made at the end of each year.

If Kenyon decides to lease the property, the following accounts will be used:

Lease Asset
Lease Obligations.
Interest Expense.
Amortization of Lease Asset.

Required:

a. According to present GAAP, how should a lease of this type be classified and why?

b. If Kenyon decides to lease the showroom from Robbin, what entry(ies) will Kenyon make in its books on January 2, 1996, the date the lease would begin?

c. If Kenyon decides to lease the showroom from Robbin, what entry(ies) will Kenyon make in its books on December 31, 1996, the end of the lease year and the company's fiscal year?

P10.4 Deferred income taxes. The consolidated balance sheet of Wendy's International, Inc., contains an item listed in the liabilities and shareholders' equity section titled Deferred Income Taxes in the amount of $53,008,000. What does this represent? If Wendy's had the opportunity either to increase or decrease the amount of this item, which would it prefer to do? Why?

P10.5 Deferred income taxes. Ottawa Office Services, Ltd., reported a net income for the year ending December 31 of $122,000, before income taxes. The income tax rate is 30 percent for the current year. Included in the determination of the reported net income were the following items:

Amortization expense of $31,000.

Dividend income of $4,000.

Estimated warranty expense of $7,000.

For income tax purposes, capital cost allowance of $42,000 and actual warranty costs of $10,000 were allowable as deductible expenses.

Required:

a. Determine the income tax expense for the year.

b. Prepare the journal entry to record income taxes.

P10.6 Deferred income taxes. Concorde, Ltd., prepared the following income statement, before income taxes:

CONCORDE, LTD.
Income Statement
For the Year Ended December 31

Revenue		$2,420,000
Cost of goods sold		1,460,000
Gross profit		$ 960,000
Amortization expense	115,000	
Advertising	85,000	
Other	60,000	260,000
Net income before taxes		$ 700,000

Concorde is uncertain as to how to proceed regarding income tax. You have discovered the following information:

1. Capital cost allowance for the year is $169,400.

2. Revenue includes tax-free dividends of $52,000 that will never be included in Concorde's taxable income.

3. Concorde's tax rate is 45 percent.

Required:

a. Determine the income tax expense.

b. Prepare the journal entry to record income taxes.

P10.7 Leases and ratio analysis. Janvier, Ltd., needs to replace some capital equipment in its largest manufacturing plant. It has decided to lease the equipment. The leased assets are valued at $150,000, using an implicit rate of 9 percent. The annual minium lease payments over the five-year lease term are $38,563. A partial balance sheet for Janvier, Ltd., is shown below:

Current assets	$187,000
Current liabilities	139,000
Long-term liabilities	370,000
Shareholders equity	222,000

Assume the lease agreement may be structured as either a capital lease or an operating lease.

Required:

Determine the impact the lease agreement will have on the liquidity and solvency ratios of Janvier, Ltd.

P10.8 Estimating pensions. Barsack Corporation on January 1, 1991, adopted a pension plan providing for the retirement of its employees at age 65. The company will "fund" its pension costs each year on December 31 when it will deposit the required cash with the pension fund trustee.

For the purpose of simplifying calculations, assume the following:

1. The company obligates itself to provide monthly payments to each employee who reaches age 65 while still employed.

2. The monthly payments will be made for a 10-year period — either to the employee (if he lives 10 years beyond age 65) or to his named beneficiary (for such portion of the 10-year period that the employee does not live).

3. The amount of the monthly payment will be $10 for each year of service — for example, for 15 years of service, the payments will be $150 a month, or $1,800 a year.

4. The company had 600 male employees at January 1, 1973, and these 600 worked all 1991 and were the same 600 employees the company had on December 31, 1991.

5. Data concerning the 600 employees at December 31, 1991, follow:

   a. 100 40-year-old employees had been with the company 16 years (15 years prior to January 1 1991).

   b. 500 25-year-old employees had joined the company just before January 1, 1991.

Let us suppose the standard ordinary table that shows for 1,000 males at birth (that is, age 0), there would be living: 958 at age 25, 924 at age 40, and 680 at age 65. Thus, for our purposes, we can say that for 100 living at age 40 on December 31, 1991, 73.6 [(680/924) × 100] should be living at age 65. Let us say that 13.6 of this 73.6 would have left the company because of turnover (18.5 percent rate). You may assume further that the comparable turnover rate for the 25-year-olds over the next 40 years will be 25 percent [(680/958) × 500 = 355] living at December 31, 2031, of which 75 percent (266) would still be with the company. Note: Please use a calculator in preparing your answers.

Required:

a. For the 100 40-year-old employees at December 31, 1991, what is the present value, as of December 31, 2016, of the 10-year annuity of $108,000 a year ($120 × 15 years × 60 surviving employees): (Calculate using monthly payments.)

   (1) At a 4 percent rate?

   (2) At a 6 percent rate?

b. What is the present value at December 31, 1991, and at January 1, 1991, of the above amounts:

   (1) At a 4 percent rate?

   (2) At a 6 percent rate?

c. What is the present value as of December 31, 2016, and December 31, 2031, respectively, of the $120 for current service for 1991:

(1) To be provided for:

(i) The survivors of the 100 employees aged 40 at December 31, 1991?

(ii) The survivors of the 500 employees aged 25 at December 31, 1991?

(2) At a 6 percent rate to be provided for:

(i) The survivors of the 100 emplyees aged 40 at December 31, 1991?

(ii) The survivors of the 500 employees aged 25 at December 31, 1991?

d. What is the present value at December 31, 1991, of the amounts in part *c* above

(1) At a 4 percent rate to be provided for:

(i) Employees aged 40 at December 31, 1991?

(ii) Employees aged 25 at December 31, 1991?

(2) At a 6 percent rate to be provided for:

(i) Employees aged 40 at December 31, 1991?

(ii) Employees aged 25 at December 31, 1991?

e. As of January 1, 1991, how much cash would Barsack Corporation have to pay the trustee to satisfy the pension obligation? At December 31, 1991? Explain.

P10.9 Deferred income taxes. Early in 1992, Strafford Corporation acquired a $100,000 asset that was to be amortized on a straight-line basis for accounting purposes and using capital cost allowance for taxes according to the following schedules:

	Straight Line	Capital Cost Allowance
1992	$ 8,333	$ 16,667
1993	16,666	27,778
1994	16,667	18,519
1995	16,667	12,347
1996	16,667	8,230
1997	16,667	8,230
1998	8,333	8,229
	$100,000	$100,000

Required:

Prepare a schedule illustrating the annual effect on deferred taxes for each year associated with this asset. Use a 34 percent tax rate. When will the deferred income tax liability begin to reverse?

P10.10 Leases and ratio analysis. Atlantic Services, Ltd., is considering leasing equipment from a local supplier. The terms of the lease agreement have not been finalized. The lease may be established as either an operating lease or a capital lease. Discuss the impact the two different accounting methods for leases would have on the following financial statement elements:

a. Statement of changes in financial statement.

b. The long-term debt-to-equity ratio.

c. The current ratio.

P10.11 Financial statement disclosure. Describe how the following items would be disclosed on a properly classified financial statement:

a. Ending merchandise inventory.

b. Future commitments on an operating lease.

c. Current income taxes payable.

d. Deferred income tax asset.

P10.12 Accounting for leases. Grande Prairie Services, Ltd., is considering signing a five-year lease for the rental of office equipment. The lease requires five annual payments of $39,567. The lease payments are such that they have a present value of $150,000 on the starting date, when discounted at 10 percent per year. The lease agreement may be structured as either an operating lease or as a capital lease. It is undecided as to which lease method would be most appropriate.

a. Select the most appropriate method assuming:

(1) The company objective of financial reporting is to maximize reported profits during the first year of the lease.

(2) The company objective of financial reporting is to minimize reported profits during the first year of the lease.

b. Which lease method would result in a higher total profit over the five-year life of the lease?

P10.13 Accounting for deferred taxes. During the first five years of operations, Hamilton Enterprises, Ltd., made the following capital asset purchases:

19x1	$ 80,000
19x2	60,000
19x3	90,000
19x4	120,000
19x5	125,000

All capital assets are amortized on a straight-line basis over 10 years, with no residual value. For income tax purposes, a capital cost allowance rate of 30 percent is allowable. Apply the half-year rule for income tax purposes. Assume a full year's amortization is taken in the year of acquisition for accounting purposes. The income tax rate is 45 percent.

Required:

a. Determine the deferred income taxes for 19x1 and 19x2.

b. If Hamilton continues to increase its acquisition of capital assets each year, what would be the effect on the deferred tax liability?

c. What are the arguments against deferred tax accounting?

P10.14 Long-term debt-to-invested capital ratio. The financial statements of Ponds Point, Limited, include long-term debt of $1,377,000 and shareholders' equity of $981,000.

a. Explain the impact each of the following transactions would have on the company's long-term debt-to-invested capital ratio:

(1) Made a payment of $300,000 on the mortgage, including $227,000 interest and $73,000 on principal.

(2) Made a payment of $23,000 on current income taxes payable.

(3) Redeemed long-term bonds payable at their face value of $50,000.

b. As a result of the above transactions, is the organization's financial position better or worse?

P10.15 Current ratio. The financial statements of Athabasca Supplies, Ltd., include current assets of $337,000 and current liabilities of $297,000.

a. Explain the impact each of the following transactions would have on the company's current ratio:

(1) Collected payments on accounts receivable of $47,000.

(2) Redeemed long-term bonds for their net book value of $99,000.

(3) Omitted making an adjusting entry for accrued interest of $29,000.

(4) Made a payment of $57,000 on the mortgage, including $42,000 interest and $15,000 on principal.

b. As a result of the above transactions, is the organization's financial position better or worse?

P10.16 Total debt-to-equity ratio. The financial statements of Valley View Manufacturing, Ltd., include total debt of $2,100,000 and shareholders' equity of $1,125,000.

a. Explain the impact each of the following transactions would have on the company's total debt-to-equity ratio:

(1) Redeemed long-term bonds for their net book value of $217,000.

(2) Issued share capital for $70,000 cash.

(3) Accrued interest of $14,000 on a mortgage.

b. As a result of the above transactions, is the organization's financial position better or worse?

P10.17 Accounting for leases. On January 1, 1996, Sandiego Data, Ltd., leased equipment with a fair value of $1,000,000 for five years with an annual payment of $277,778, due at the end of each year. Sandiego's borrowing rate is normally 12 percent. At the end of the lease term, the equipment will belong to Sandiego.

Sandiego amortizes its buildings on a straight-line basis over 20 years, and its equipment on a declining-balance basis at twice the straight-line rate. The leased equipment is expected to have a useful life of 10 years.

The following factors apply:

The factor for the present value of a lump sum in five years at 10 percent is 0.62092.
The factor for the present value of a lump sum in five years at 12 percent is 0.56743.
The factor for the present value of an annuity for five years at 10 percent is 3.790879.
The factor for the present value of an annuity for five years at 12 percent is 3.60478.

Required:

a. Prepare the journal entries for the lease for 1996 assuming it is to be classified as a *capital* lease.

b. Prepare the journal entries for the lease for 1996 assuming it is to be classified as an *operating* lease.

P10.18 Long-term debt-to-invested capital ratio. The financial statements of Humming Canada, Ltd., include total long-term liabilities of $665,000 and total shareholders' equity of $488,000. Explain the impact *each* of the following transactions would have on the company's long-term debt-to-invested capital ratio:

a. Issued long-term bonds for $150,000.

b. Signed an operating lease with annual payments of $30,000 for each of the next four years.

c. Declared and paid common share dividends for $25,000

P10.19 Deferred income taxes. Edmonton Stereo Supply House, Ltd., reported a net income of $371,000, before income taxes. Included in the determination of the reported net income were the following items:

Instalment sales revenue of $44,000.
Amortization expense of $27,000.
Dividend income of $4,000.
Estimated warranty expense of $7,000.

Capital cost allowance of $22,000, instalment sales revenue of $33,000, and actual warranty costs of $10,000 were recognized for income tax purposes. Assume a 40 percent income tax rate.

Required:

a. Determine the income tax expense for the year.

b. Prepare the journal entry to record income taxes for the year.

P10.20 Deferred income taxes. The condensed income statement of Rambler, Limited, is shown below:

Income statement

	Year 1	Year 2	Year 3
Revenues	$234,000	$299,000	$321,000
Expenses	201,000	252,000	287,000
Net income before taxes	$ 33,000	$ 47,000	$ 34,000

Included in the expenses is amortization on equipment purchased for $90,000 at the beginning of Year 1. The equipment has a 10-year estimated useful life and a residual value of $10,000. Straight-line amortization is used for accounting purposes. A capital cost allowance rate of 40 percent is allowable for income taxes. The income tax rate is 30 percent.

Required:

a. For each year determine the income taxes payable and the income tax expense.

b. Prepare the journal entry for income taxes for each year.

c. Indicate the financial statement disclosure for income taxes on the Year 1 income statement and balance sheet.

P10.21 Deferred income taxes and financial analysis. Shown below is the shareholders' equity of Rambler, Limited, for the year ended December 31, Year 1.

Common shares — 100 shares issued	$ 50,000
Retained earnings	117,000
Total equity	$167,000

The retained earnings includes the net income for the year.

Required:

Using the above information and the financial information from P10.20, determine the return on equity and the earnings per share for Rambler, Limited, assuming:

a. Deferred income tax accounting is used.

b. Deferred income tax accounting is not used.

P10.22 Accounting for leases. Montreal Computer Warehouse, Ltd., needs to acquire new equipment for its distribution department to improve the delivery of merchandise to its customers. The equipment that is required is available from a number of different suppliers. The company is considering different financing opportunities. It is considering signing a four-year lease for the rental of the equipment. The lease requires four annual payments at the end of each year. The lease payments are such that they have a present value of $225,000 on the starting date, when discounted at 8 percent per year. The lease agreement may be structured as either an operating lease or a capital lease. The company may also borrow the funds at 8 percent and purchase the equipment for $225,000. It is undecided which method of financing would be most appropriate. Advise the company on the most appropriate financing method, considering the impact each method will have on the following financial statements of the company:

a. Statement of changes in financial position.

b. Balance sheet.

c. Income statement.

P10.23 Accounting for income taxes. Fundy, Limited, reported the following information for the year ended December 31.

Financial statement pretax income	$106,000
Income tax expense	52,000
Income taxes payable	16,000
Income tax rate	30 percent

Required:

a. What is the amount of the timing differences for the year?

b. What is the amount of the permanent differences for the year?

10.10 CASES

C10.1 Lessee accounting: FHAC Corporation. FHAC Corporation was considering the purchase of a minisupercomputer. Under a proposal from Convex Computer Co., FHAC could acquire the computer under a 10-year lease agreement. The lease proposal called for quarterly lease payments of $3,655.57 and carried an implicit interest rate of 8 percent. At the end of the lease, FHAC would be entitled to purchase the computer for its expected residual value, currently estimated to be $10,000. Alternatively, FHAC could purchase the computer outright at a price of $115,000, inclusive of installation costs.

Required:

Evaluate the above proposals. Should FHAC lease or buy? How would each option (i.e., lease or buy) affect FHAC's financial statements?

C10.2 Lessee accounting: Sybra, Inc. Sybra, Inc., a newly incorporated research and development company, decided to lease additional laboratory space. The lease commenced on January 1, 1990, and was to extend for a 20-year period ending December 31, 2009. The annual rental rate on the new facility was $115,200 (exclusive of property taxes, maintenance, and insurance costs, which were also to be paid by Sybra). Because of the length of the lease and the generally poor rental market, Sybra had negotiated so that rent payments would be made only once a year on December 31.

The facility's original construction cost had been approximately $480,000, but its current market value was now in excess of $1 million. On the basis of conversations with the lessor, Sybra's chief financial officer determined that the lease payments included implicit interest at the rate of 10 percent per annum. Further, as of 1990, the facility was estimated to have a remaining useful life of 25 years. At the end of the initial 20-year-lease period, Sybra would have the option of renewing for another 10 years at a rate equal to one-half of the annual lease rate during the initial lease period.

Required:

a. What accounting treatment should be adopted for the above lease? Why?

b. Illustrate the balance sheet and income statement effects in 1990 for the lease agreement assuming that it is to be accounted for as (1) an operating lease and (2) a capital lease.

C10.3 Leases: Lion Metal Forming, Inc. On January 2, Lion Metal Forming, Inc., entered a lease for a new 50-ton hydraulic press costing $75,000 and having an estimated life of eight years. The management of Lion Metal believes the new press will be much more efficient than equipment presently in use and that it will allow Lion Metal to manufacture certain items that it previously had to subcontract out. The non-cancellable term of the lease is seven years, at which time the press is returned to the lessor. The residual value is expected to be minimal. Rental payments of $16,433 are due at the end of each year. All executory costs are to be paid directly by Lion Metal, which amortizes its fixed assets on the straight-line basis. Its incremental borrowing rate is 15 percent.

Required:

a. Calculate the lessor's implicit interest rate in the lease.

b. Why does this lease qualify as a capital lease to Lion Metal for financial reporting purposes? For *c* and *d*, assume the implicit rate is 12 percent.

c. Prepare the entry that Lion Metal should make to record the lease on January 2.

d. What amounts (properly labelled) related to the lease would appear in Lion Metal's:

(1) Balance sheet as of December 31?

(2) Income statement for the year ending December 31?

CHAPTER 11

Accounting for Equity

―――――――― Objectives ――――――――

After completing this chapter, you will be able to:
1. Describe the different elements of equity.
2. Record entries for different equity transactions.
3. Prepare the shareholders' equity section of a financial report.
4. Explain and apply the financial statement disclosure of equity.
5. Analyze shareholders' equity.

According to the basic accounting equation (A = L + E), equity is simply the difference between a company's assets and its liabilities. It is the amount that would be left over if the assets were liquidated at their book values and the liabilities were then paid. Equity is also sometimes referred to as the *net worth* or the *net book value* of a company. However, equity can also be considered on its own terms — as one of the three elements of the accounting equation — rather than only the residual of assets minus liabilities.

Equity usually takes two principal forms: **contributed capital**, as represented by the capital shares of a company, and **earned capital**, as represented by the cumulative retained earnings of a company. For many organizations, transactions involving equity accounts are simple and straightforward. In fact, some publicly held companies bypass the presentation of a formal statement of shareholders' equity and provide what little detail might be of interest to financial statement users as a part of a footnote or as part of the income statement. To a very large degree, the equity accounts are of more interest to lawyers than to management or accountants because the lawyers are responsible for a company's legal status and because many of the transactions in the equity accounts have to do with a company's legal life. However, the equity accounts are always of interest to a company's shareholders because these accounts measure the shareholders' residual interest in the net assets of the company.

In the first section of this chapter, we consider the various ways in which an organization can be legally organized and explore some of the activities common to the corporate form of organization. Next, we examine some of the most common transactions affecting the equity accounts, and the financial statement presentation that is conventionally followed. Finally, we illustrate the typical equity disclosures using data from annual reports, and discuss the analysis of equity.

11.1 ACCOUNTING ENTITIES

contributed capital
The sum of the share capital accounts of a corporation.

earned capital
The cumulative earnings of an organization.

Entities can be organized in different ways, and the differences are important. An entity can be a proprietorship, a partnership, a corporation, a consolidated corporate group, a non-profit organization, or a government unit depending on its objectives and legal structure. These different economic units were first described in Chapter 1. Exhibit 11.1 summarizes the different types of accounting entities. For the purposes of describing the accounting for equity, the above economic units can be combined into three basic entities: partnerships, corporations, and non-profit organizations.

Proprietorships and Partnerships

proprietorship
A business enterprise owned by one person.

partnership
A business enterprise jointly owned by two or more persons.

Many small businesses are organized as proprietorships or partnerships because both of these types are relatively simple and inexpensive to form. To establish a **proprietorship**, one simply obtains the required permits to do business from a local or provincial governmental agency. The same is true for a **partnership** except that, in addition, the partners typically execute a written contract among themselves detailing the terms of their financial arrangements. The desirability of having a written agreement is as great for a two-person partnership as it is for partnerships composed of several partners. Some of the items usually detailed in a partnership agreement include the amount of each partner's investment, the rights of partners to withdraw funds, the manner in which profits and losses are to be divided, and the procedure to be followed in admitting a new partner.

We can make some general statements about partnerships (and proprietorships) that follow in part from the legal characteristics accorded to partnerships and in part from the way managers have applied these legal forms in practice:

Types of Accounting Entities

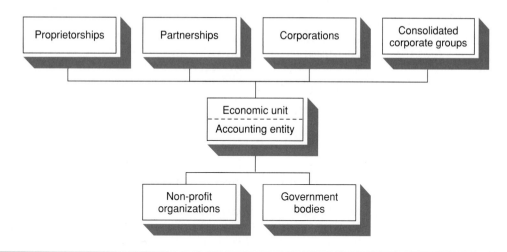

Limited ownership: As a practical matter, most partnerships have relatively few partners.

Owners as managers: The partners frequently manage the business.

Mutual agency: Each partner, acting within the scope of reasonable partnership activities, acts as an agent for the business entity, and any single partner may act on behalf of all the other partners.

Unlimited liability: Ordinarily, each partner is personally liable for all of the debts of the partnership.

Division of profit and loss: Partnership profits and losses may be divided in whatever manner the individual partners agree.

Withdrawal of resources: Unless the partners agree otherwise, they may withdraw resources from the business in an amount equal to their total investment in the partnership any time they wish to do so.

Limited life: Unless the partners agree otherwise, the death or withdrawal of a partner automatically dissolves the partnership.

Taxes: The partnership itself is not subject to income tax. Income earned (or a loss incurred) by the partnership is taxable income for the individual partners, whether or not it is distributed. This requirement is sometimes an advantage (as in the early years of a partnership when amortization throws off large tax losses) and sometimes a disadvantage (as in the early years of a growing company that generates earnings but must retain the operating cash flow for reinvestment).

The accounting for the equity of a partnership (or a proprietorship) is accumulated in a single account, Capital. The Capital account accumulates the net income/losses of the organizations and any distributions to the owners, that is, withdrawals or drawings deducted from the Capital account. For a partnership, a distinct capital account is used for each individual partner. Often a separate schedule is provided in the notes to the financial statements providing the details of the organization's equity. The balance sheet may only disclose the total equity for the organization. A statement of partnership equity is shown below:

Statement of Partnership Equity

	Alex	Barb	Casey	Total
January 1, Capital	$37,000	$41,000	$21,000	$ 99,000
Net income	19,000	22,000	12,000	53,000
Withdrawals	(8,000)	(13,000)	(9,000)	(30,000)
December 31, Capital	$48,000	$50,000	$24,000	$122,000

Corporations

The creation of a corporation is a more complex, legal procedure than the creation of partnerships and proprietorships. The incorporators (the initial shareholders) must first apply to a provincial or federal agency, requesting permission to form a corporation. When the agency grants that permission, a new entity comes into being. The newly incorporated entity's charter of incorporation thereby creates a legal entity that can sell shares to shareholders, own property, borrow money and incur obligations, and sue and be sued, all in its own name independently of its owners.

Again, we can make some general statements about the operations of corporations, in part because of their legal characteristics and in part because of the way corporate life has evolved in practice:

Diverse ownership: The owners of a corporation are called *shareholders*, and ownership in a corporation is evidenced by shares of capital. The number of shareholders a corporation may have is not limited. A corporation can be formed with as few as two shareholders. On the other hand, a corporation may be owned by a very large number of shareholders (General Motors' shares are owned by more than 925,000 investors) and the shares may be traded in a public market. The shares of a corporation may be held by individuals, mutual funds, or other corporations.

Separation of ownership and management: The management of public corporations generally owns only a small percentage (or none) of the company's outstanding share capital.

Limited liability: As a separate legal entity, a corporation is responsible for its own debts. Shareholders are not personally liable for a corporation's debts, and the maximum financial loss that shareholders can incur is limited to the amount of their investment in the corporation. With a small corporation, the advantage of limited liability is often lost, as the owners may be required to *personally* guarantee any debts of the corporation.

Withdrawal of resources: Shareholders are entitled to withdraw resources from a corporation only in the form of dividends and only after the board of directors has authorized a dividend payment. Dividends are paid to all shareholders in proportion to their ownership of the corporation, unless otherwise provided in the share agreement.

Transferability of ownership: Shareholders may buy and sell shares in a corporation without interfering with the activities or the life of a corporation. Most of the millions of shares that are traded daily on the stock exchanges represent private transactions between independent buyers and sellers. The activities of the corporations themselves are unaffected by such transactions.

Government regulation: Corporations exist as a result of a charter granted by a government agency. Many organizations are incorporated federally under the **Canada Business Corporations Act**. Organizations may also be incorporated under provincial legislation. The applicable rules vary according to the chartering process.

Taxes: As separate legal entities, corporations pay federal and provincial income taxes on their earnings. When any part of these earnings is subsequently distributed to shareholders in the form of dividends, the shareholders also pay income taxes on the amount of dividends received. This separation of entity and ownership provides the owners of a privately held corporation with an opportunity to plan their personal income. However, it also results in double taxation.

Canada Business Corporations Act Corporations exist as a result of a charter granted by a government agency. Many organizations are incorporated federally under the Canada Business Corporations Act.

Typically, individual shareholders have very little say in the management of the company they own. Small shareholders "vote with their feet," selling their shares if they conclude that the company is not going forward. Major shareholders can be more assertive and use their voting rights to elect a board of directors to represent them (and all shareholders). In most companies, the board of directors is responsible for the corporation's overall direction. The board of directors elects and oversees the corporate officers who are directly responsible for the day-to-day management of the corporation. The officers usually include a president, vice president, secretary, and treasurer.

The officers report periodically to the board of directors and at least once a year to the shareholders. The officers (management) usually present a business plan for the board's approval and request the board's advice and concurrence regarding major decisions. The board members, on the other hand, prepare employment agreements for the officers, and generally monitor their progress in moving the company forward according to the approved business plan. Board members and officers have significant legal obligations, as fiduciaries, to always work in the best interests of a company's shareholders.

Corporations typically hold an annual meeting of shareholders subsequent to the end of each fiscal year. A fiscal year is the 12-month period a corporation selects as its accounting year, and it may or may not be the calendar year. The annual meeting is held for purposes such as reviewing the past year's financial performance; discussing business, economic, and political issues of importance to the corporation; selecting an accounting firm to audit the corporation's financial statements; electing directors; and voting on any other business that requires shareholders' ratification. The board of directors also decides, depending on the corporation's earnings' history, expectations for the future, cash position and expected cash needs, and (last but not least) expectations of the stock market — how much of the corporation's earnings should be paid out to shareholders as dividends. Such information is also presented in the corporation's annual report under Management, Discussion, and Analysis.

Even though corporate shares can be bought and sold without affecting the company, corporations must keep track of shareholder transactions to know who is entitled to receive dividends and who is entitled to vote at shareholder meetings. A small corporation can keep track of its shareholders relatively easily because it has few transactions involving shares. For a large, publicly held company, however, keeping track of its shareholders is very difficult because its shares trade in large volumes every day on the public stock exchanges. In fact, many corporations engage the services of a transfer agent and registrar to record shareholder transactions, cancel old share certificates, issue new ones, and maintain a current record of shareholder names and addresses and the number of shares each owns. Transfer agents and registrars are usually banks or trust companies.

Publicly held companies must publish quarterly and annual reports for use by shareholders and other interested parties. These reports generally include status reports on a company's progress, from both the chairperson of the board and the president, and financial statements for the period. The financial statements in the annual report are accompanied by an audit report from an independent accounting firm, stating the accountants' opinion as to whether the financial statements are presented fairly, in all material respects, in conformity with generally accepted accounting principles.

Non-Profit Organizations

appropriations
Appropriations of retained earnings are created when management wants to indicate to the users of the financial statements that a portion of retained earnings is not available for distribution for dividends or other purposes.

The accounting for equity for non-profits and government bodies may be less involved than for profit-oriented organizations. Non-profits do *not* have any owners and therefore do not use capital or share capital accounts. Equity for non-profits is often simply referred to as surplus. In many cases the equity of non-profits and government bodies may be restricted or **appropriated** for specific purposes. The most common way of managing equity for non-profits is simply to split equity into components — that is, restricted equity and equity that is unrestricted or unappropriated and available for any purpose.

To illustrate the accounting for equity in non-profit organizations, the equity for the Girl Guides of Canada is shown below:

Surplus	1993	1992
Unappropriated	$5,061,100	$5,240,100
Appropriated (Note 3)	408,400	175,000
	$5,469,500	$5,415,100

The Girl Guides of Canada have total equity or surplus of $5,469,500 in 1993. Of the total surplus, $5,061,100 is unappropriated or unrestricted. Note 3 indicates equity appropriations or restrictions at December 31, 1993, and 1992, in respect of the following:

	1993	1992
1993 Girls' event	—	$ 75,000
Building renovations	$100,000	100,000
Leadership recruitment	308,400	—
	$408,400	$175,000

11.2 TYPES OF SHARES

Depending on the size, the objectives, and financing requirements of the corporation, a number of different types of shares may be issued. A corporation may issue shares with or without par value, common shares and/or preferred shares, and shares with different dividend rates and preferences. This section describes the different characteristics of share capital.

Authorized, Issued, and Outstanding Share Capital

authorized capital
The total number of shares that are authorized to be sold under a company's charter of incorporation.

When a corporation obtains its charter of incorporation, it must specify the number of shares it intends to distribute to its shareholders. The charter must specify the authorized capital of the corporation. **Authorized capital** is the maximum number of shares the corporation has been authorized to issue under its charter of incorporation. Some corporations select the option of specifying *unlimited* authorized capital to prevent any restrictions on share issues over the long term. **Issued capital** is the number of shares distributed or issued to the corporation's shareholders. Outstanding capital is the number of shares issued and currently in the hands of the shareholders. **Outstanding capital** is the number of shares issued less the number of shares reacquired and held in treasury by the corporation.

issued capital
The number of authorized shares of share capital sold to shareholders.

outstanding capital
The number of authorized shares that have been sold to shareholders; the number of issued shares less the shares held in treasury.

Par Value and Non-Par Value

par value
A legal value assigned to a share.

Par value is a legal value of a share of capital required by some provincial incorporation agencies. Originally, it was meant to be the minimum capital required to be contributed to, and maintained in, a company by the shareholders. That concept has eroded in practice, however, and today the concept of par value has very little practical significance. Par value is a nominal value assigned to the shares that may over time have *no* relation to the market value of the shares. The Canada Business Corporations Act *requires* corporations to issue only **non-par-value** shares. It is generally thought the use of par values may be misleading to the users of financial statements.

non-par value
The Canada Business Corporations Act requires corporations to issue only non-par value shares.

Common Shares

common shares
A form of share capital that usually carries the right to vote on corporate issues.

The **common shares** of a corporation are generally the *voting* shares of the corporation. The common shareholders are able to elect the board of directors, who hire the senior management of the corporation. Thus, the common shareholders are able to *control* the corporation.

Class B common shares usually have the same provisions as a company's regular common shares regarding liquidation and dividend rights, but they may have disproportionate (usually lower) voting rights. For example, in some companies, the class B shares carry only one-tenth the voting power of a company's class A common shares. In many cases, the class B shares are traded publicly, but the class A shares can only be exchanged between members of the company's founding family. Class B shares have become popular in recent years as a defence against hostile takeovers.

Preferred Shares

preferred shares
A (usually) nonvoting form of share capital whose claims to the dividends and assets of a company precede those of common shareholders.

Every corporation issues common shares as its basic equity security. But it is also possible to raise capital by selling other equity securities with special terms. A preferred share, for example, is an equity security with some of the characteristics of a bond. Preferred shares usually carry a specific dividend rate, stated as an amount per share or as a percentage of its par value. Preferred shares are usually non-voting. A **preferred share** is "preferred" in that its dividend requirements have a first claim on a company's earnings before any claims of the common shareholders. Thus, in the event that earnings are limited, the preferred shareholders must receive their full dividend before common shareholders receive any. Should a company be liquidated, the preferred shareholders are entitled to any distributions before the common shareholders. Preferred shares may also be *convertible* into a stated number of common shares. They also may be *callable* in that a company may have the right to call the security for redemption, usually at a premium above the stated or par value of the shares.

The accounting for preferred shares and class B common shares is straightforward, following the legal terms of the security. The footnotes to the financial statements detail any special provisions of these securities and describe any preference entitlement that might burden the common shares.

11.3 ISSUING SHARES

The most common transactions affecting the equity accounts include the recognition of revenue and expenses for the year (which result in a net income/loss), the payment of dividends, and the sale or repurchase of share capital. This section examines the process of issuing shares of share capital.

Cash Transactions

A corporation may sell shares to new shareholders or to its existing shareholders. The shares may be issued for cash or non-cash assets or on a subscription basis. Those share sales are recorded in the equity account at the net cash (or other consideration) that the company receives for the shares issued. The journal entry to record the issuing of 5,000 non-par-value common shares for $72,000 cash follows:

```
Dr. Cash  . . . . . . . . . . . . . . . . . . . . . . . . . . . . . . . . . . . . . . . 72,000
    Cr. Common Shares  . . . . . . . . . . . . . . . . . . . . . . . . . . . . . . . . .   72,000
    To record the issuing of non-par-value common shares for cash.
```

When a corporation issues non-par-value shares, the *total* proceeds received from the shareholders is recorded in the Common Shares account. When par value shares are issued, only the par value amount is entered in the Common Shares account and the additional proceeds are recorded in a Contributed Surplus in Excess of Par Value account. The journal entry to record the issuing of 5,000 $10 *par value* common shares for $72,000 cash follows:

```
Dr. Cash  . . . . . . . . . . . . . . . . . . . . . . . . . . . . . . . . . . . . . . . 72,000
    Cr. Common Shares ($10 par value)  . . . . . . . . . . . . . . . . . . . . . . .   50,000
    Cr. Contributed Surplus in Excess of Par Value  . . . . . . . . . . . . . . . .   22,000
    To record the issuing of $10 par value common shares for cash.
```

Note that if the sale price of the shares exceeds the par (or stated) value of the purchased shares, the excess is recorded in the contributed surplus in excess of par value account. Thus, the sum of the Common Shares account and the Contributed Surplus in Excess of Par Value account represents the aggregate *contributed surplus* of a company, and both accounts are disclosed in the shareholders' equity section of the financial statement. Par value shares are generally not allowed in Canada.

Non-Cash Transactions

Most often, shares are issued for cash and so the value of the capital received in the exchange is easy to determine. However, companies sometimes exchange their shares for other forms of assets. In these exchanges, the total capital issued (and, in turn, the assets received) are valued at the market value of the shares issued or the asset received, whichever provides the most reliable measure of value. When shares are actively traded on a public stock exchange, the per share market price from those trades is usually considered the most reliable measure of the value involved in a swap of shares for other forms of assets. When the shares are not actively traded, the transaction may have to be valued at the value of the assets exchanged. Suppose a corporation whose shares are *not* actively traded issues 10,000 non-par-value shares in exchange for land with a market value of $110,000 and a building with a market value of $375,000:

```
Dr. Land . . . . . . . . . . . . . . . . . . . . . . . . . . . . . . . . . . . . . . . . 110,000
Dr. Building . . . . . . . . . . . . . . . . . . . . . . . . . . . . . . . . . . . . . . 375,000
    Cr. Common Shares . . . . . . . . . . . . . . . . . . . . . . . . . . . . .    485,000
    To record the issuing of non-par-value common shares for non-cash assets.
```

When a corporation is first organized, various start-up costs will be incurred, such as legal costs, registration fees, and other costs associated with incorporation. In practice, such costs are frequently deducted from the proceeds of shares issued. As the corporation will benefit from such costs for several years, a less common practice is to create an intangible asset called **organization costs**. Organization costs should be amortized over a period not to exceed 40 years. When a corporation is first established, it may issue shares in exchange for various organization costs:

organization costs The expenditures associated with starting a new business venture, including legal fees and incorporation fees; frequently accounted for as an intangible asset of a company.

```
Dr. Organization Costs . . . . . . . . . . . . . . . . . . . . . . . . . . . . . 25,000
    Cr. Common Shares . . . . . . . . . . . . . . . . . . . . . . . . . . . . . .    25,000
    To record the issuing of non-par-value common shares for organization costs.
```

Subscriptions

When corporations are first created, it may be difficult to raise capital by issuing shares. To attract potential investors, corporations may issue shares on a subscription basis. **Share subscriptions** involve a contract between the corporation and the shareholders to purchase the shares of the corporation on an instalment basis. The subscription contract would normally call for a down payment, followed by subsequent payments on account. When the final payment is received by the corporation, the shares are *issued* to the shareholder. Assume a corporation offers 1,000 shares of non-par-value common shares under a subscription contract for $10 per share. The subscription contract calls for a initial payment of 30 percent and the balance payable in 90 days. When the subscription contract is signed and the initial payment received, the following entry is made:

share subscription A contract between the corporation and shareholders to purchase shares of the corporation on an instalment basis.

```
Dr. Cash . . . . . . . . . . . . . . . . . . . . . . . . . . . . . . . . . . . . . . . .  3,000
Dr. Subscriptions Receivable . . . . . . . . . . . . . . . . . . . . . . . . . .  7,000
    Cr. Common Shares — Subscribed . . . . . . . . . . . . . . . . . . . . . .    10,000
    To record the subscription contract for common shares with a 30% initial payment.
```

The Subscriptions Receivable account is a current asset. The Common Shares — Subscribed account would be classified under shareholders' equity. When the final subscription payment is received, the common shares are issued. The entry removes the Common Shares — Subscribed account and replaces it with the Common Shares account used for standard share issues. The cash collection and share issuance entries follow:

```
Dr. Cash . . . . . . . . . . . . . . . . . . . . . . . . . . . . . . . . . . . . . . . .  7,000
    Cr. Subscriptions Receivable . . . . . . . . . . . . . . . . . . . . . . . . .    7,000
    To record the payment received on the share subscriptions.
```

```
Dr. Common Shares — Subscribed . . . . . . . . . . . . . . . . . . . . . . 10,000
    Cr. Common Shares  . . . . . . . . . . . . . . . . . . . . . . . . . . . . . . . . .    10,000
    To record the issuing of the common shares.
```

This section has illustrated the issuing of share capital using the Common Shares account in the examples provided. It should be noted the concepts and procedures would be identical for preferred shares.

11.4 DIVIDENDS

Dividend Policy

dividend policy
The dividend policy
of a corporation is
dependent on its
financial strength, its
financial objectives,
and the type of
investors its wishes
to attract.

The **dividend policy** of a corporation is dependent on its financial strength, its financial objectives, and the type of investors it wishes to attract. Some investors are not interested in receiving a flow of dividend payments, but are more interested in seeing the corporation grow and the market value of their share investments increase, while other investors rely on a steady stream of cash dividends from the corporations as a source of income. Most investors are looking for stability and consistency in a corporation's dividend policy, whether it is in the form of a high return each year or no dividend at all.

The board of directors decides the amount and timing of dividends. Legal restrictions generally require the corporation to declare dividends only if retained earnings exist. To protect the firm's creditors, corporations may not declare dividends if share capital or contributed surplus is the only form of shareholders' equity. The other consideration to be made by the board of directors is the impact the dividends will have on the corporation's cash flow position. If the corporation is experiencing cash flow problems, a share dividend may be declared to satisfy the shareholders and maintain a consistent stream of dividend payments.

Dividend Dates

After net income, the second most common entry to the Retained Earnings account is the declaration of dividends. We have said several times, but it is worth repeating — dividends are a distribution of a company's income to its shareholders but are not an expense of the organization. The accounting entry to record the declaration of a $5,000 cash dividend is as follows:

```
Dr. Dividends Declared (R.E.) . . . . . . . . . . . . . . . . . . . . . . . . . . 5,000
    Cr. Dividends Payable . . . . . . . . . . . . . . . . . . . . . . . . . . . . . . . .    5,000
    To record the declaration of the cash dividend.
```

date of declaration
The date on which
the dividend is
officially declared by
a company's board
of directors.

The **date of declaration** is the date on which the board of directors declares the dividend. At that point in time, a legal liability for payment of the dividend exists and the above entry is required to recognize the liability, dividends payable. The debit portion of the entry may be made directly to Retained Earnings, or to the temporary account Dividends Declared, as shown above. On the **date of payment** the following entry is made:

date of payment
The date on which a
cash or share
dividend is actually
paid or distributed.

```
Dr. Dividends Payable . . . . . . . . . . . . . . . . . . . . . . . . . . . . . . . . 5,000
    Cr. Cash . . . . . . . . . . . . . . . . . . . . . . . . . . . . . . . . . . . . . . . . . . . .    5,000
    To record the cash payment of the dividends.
```

date of record
The date on which a shareholder must own a company's shares to be entitled to receive a declared dividend.

To be entitled to receive a dividend, a shareholder must own the shares on the **date of record** . At the end of the accounting period, the Dividends Declared account is netted against the Retained Earnings account (see these closing entries in Chapter 4).

Dividends on Preferred Shares

Preferred shares normally have a fixed dividend rate expressed in terms of dollars per share or a fixed percentage of par value. As well, preferred shareholders must receive their dividend before any dividends are paid to common shareholders. Preferred shares are normally **cumulative**; that is, dividend preferences accumulate year to year even if the company has *not* earned enough to pay the dividend in any one year. Unpaid accumulated dividends are called **dividends in arrears**, and although not representing a liability of a company until the dividends are declared, they must be disclosed in the footnotes to the financial statements.

cumulative preferred shares
A preferred share in which any unpaid prior dividends accumulate year to year (called dividends in arrears).

Preferred shares may be *participating* in that they may share in a company's earnings in excess of its stated dividend requirements, along with the common shares.

Assume a corporation has 10,000 non-par-value common shares outstanding and 1,000 preferred shares outstanding. The preferred shares are non-par, cumulative, with a dividend rate of $5.00 per share. During the first three years of the corporation's life, the board of directors declared the following *total* dividends:

dividends in arrears
The dividends on cumulative preferred shares that have been neither declared nor paid.

Year	Total Dividends
1	$ 3,000
2	11,000
3	20,000

The preferred shareholders should receive a total of $5,000 each year. However, in Year 1, only $3,000 in dividends were declared. The preferred shareholders would receive the $3,000 and the common shareholders would not receive a dividend in Year 1. As well, the common shareholders would have no claim for any years in which dividends are not declared and paid. However, because the preferred shares are *cumulative*, and there are $2,000 dividends in arrears on preferred shares, the next time a dividend is paid the dividends in arrears must be paid *first*. Therefore, in Year 2, $2,000 must first be paid to the preferred shareholders, plus the $5,000 annual dividend. The remainder of $4,000 is allocated to the common shareholders. In Year 3, the preferred shareholders receive their annual dividend of $5,000 and the balance of $15,000 is paid to the common shareholders. The dividend allocation to preferred and common shareholders is summarized below:

Year	Preferred Dividends	Common Dividends
1	$3,000*	–0–
2	7,000	$ 4,000
3	5,000	15,000

*The Year 1 annual report would include a footnote indicating there were $2,000 dividends in arrears on cumulative preferred shares.

Share Dividends

Typically, dividends are paid in cash. Growth-oriented companies that have profitable places to invest their cash, however, may pay a **share dividend** instead. The shareholders — who *now* own a few more shares than they did before the share dividend — can then ride along with a company's expected growth, or they can liquidate part of their share holdings by selling the share dividend and converting it to cash. The accounting entry for a share dividend is conceptually the same as for a cash dividend, except that the credit portion of the entry is an increase in common shares rather than a decrease in cash. The dollar value of the entry is measured by the fair market price of the shares issued at the date the dividend was declared.

Assume a corporation has 10,000 non-par-value common shares outstanding. The shares have a fair market value of $5.00 per share. Further assume the corporation declares a 10 percent share dividend. The entry on the date of declaration to record the declaration of the 10 percent share dividend would be:

```
Dr. Dividends Declared (R.E.) . . . . . . . . . . . . . . . . . . . . . . . . . . .  5,000
    Cr. Share Dividend Distributable  . . . . . . . . . . . . . . . . . . . . . . . . .     5,000
    To record the declaration of the 10% share dividend (1,000 shares).
```

When the share dividend is issued, the following entry is made:

```
Dr. Share Dividend Distributable  . . . . . . . . . . . . . . . . . . . . . . . .  5,000
    Cr. Common Shares . . . . . . . . . . . . . . . . . . . . . . . . . . . . . . . . .     5,000
    To record the issuing of common shares as a share dividend.
```

If financial statements are prepared after the share dividend has been declared, but *before* the share dividend has been issued, the Share Dividend Distributable account appears in the shareholders' equity section. As with a cash dividend, the Dividend Declared account must be closed to Retained Earnings at the end of the accounting period and thus has the effect of transferring a portion of retained earnings to the share capital accounts.

Share Splits

A company may "split" its share for any number of reasons, but most often it is to reduce the market value of each share. The theory supporting a **share split** is that investors will be more interested in a share with a current market value of $25 than in one with a current market value of $100. Ordinarily, no journal entry is required for a share split, although the number of shares outstanding increases and the par value (or stated value) of each share decreases proportionately. In a two-for-one share split, for example, the number of shares outstanding doubles and the par value is halved, leaving the aggregate value of shareholders' equity *unchanged*. A share split is, quite simply, a pro rata issuance of new shares to all existing shareholders.

The economic substance of a share split is not very different from that of a share dividend; however, the accounting implications are very different. Note that a share dividend transfers some part of a company's retained earnings to the capital accounts, whereas (usually) the accounting for a split simply reallocates the contributed surplus in capital over a larger number of shares. That theoretical accounting difference is perhaps justifiable when a split is large — two for one or four for one. That difference is less justifiable, however, with a smaller split. The general rule for reporting share dividends and share splits is based on 25 percent of the shares outstanding. A share split is any distribution of share in *excess* of 25 percent of the previously outstanding shares, whereas a distribution of *less* than 25 percent is always considered a share dividend. Thus, for example, a share distribution equal to 10 percent of the previously existing shares must be accounted for as a share dividend even if it is legally described as a share split. In that situation, the fair market value of the newly distributed shares is transferred from Retained Earnings to the capital accounts.

11.5 EQUITY TRANSACTIONS

Treasury Shares

Corporations may, at the discretion of management, buy back a proportion of their own outstanding shares. A company may, for example, repurchase its own shares because it has commitments for future issuances of shares to satisfy various share options, share warrants, or convertible securities (to be discussed shortly). Or a company may reacquire some of its own shares because it has excess cash and because the board of directors believes that the company's own shares represent the best investment opportunity for that cash. A company also may buy some of its outstanding shares because management believes that the current market price of the share is too low, and it hopes to raise that price by reducing the supply of available shares. Corporations incorporated under the Canada Business Corporations Act are allowed to reacquire their own shares, but must cancel any reacquired shares. Therefore, companies incorporated under the Canada Business Corporations Act do not disclose any treasury shares on their financial statements. Companies incorporated under provincial agencies in jurisdictions still allowing treasury holdings must disclose treasury shares as a deduction from shareholders' equity.

treasury shares
Outstanding share capital that has been repurchased but not retired and is usually held to be reissued at some future date.

If the reacquired shares are to be held and reissued sometime in the future, they are accounted for in a *contra* shareholders' equity account entitled **Treasury Shares**. The reacquired shares are recorded in the Treasury Shares account at the cost paid to repurchase the shares. For example, suppose that Smith Company purchased 100 of its *own* shares at $12 a share. The entry to record that purchase records an increase in the Treasury Shares account (a contra shareholders' equity account) for $1,200 and a decrease in the Cash account of like amount. It is as follows:

```
Dr. Treasury Shares . . . . . . . . . . . . . . . . . . . . . . . . . . . . . . . . . . . . .   1,200
     Cr. Cash  . . . . . . . . . . . . . . . . . . . . . . . . . . . . . . . . . . . . . . . . .           1,200
        To record the acquisition of shares previously issued.
```

Note that a company's investment in its own shares is *not* considered to be an asset; instead, it is treated as a reduction in shareholders' equity. "Where a company acquires its own shares, the shares should be carried at cost and shown as a deduction from shareholders' equity until cancelled or resold" (CICA Handbook 3240.11).

When treasury shares are reissued at a later date, the cost of the reissued shares is removed from the Treasury Shares account. If the proceeds related to that reissue differ from the cost of the treasury shares issued, that difference is added to (or subtracted from) the Contributed Surplus account. Assuming that 100 shares are issued for $1,300, the following accounting entry is made:

```
Dr. Cash  . . . . . . . . . . . . . . . . . . . . . . . . . . . . . . . . . . . . . . . . . .   1,300
     Cr. Treasury Shares . . . . . . . . . . . . . . . . . . . . . . . . . . . . . . . . . .           1,200
     Cr. Contributed Surplus  . . . . . . . . . . . . . . . . . . . . . . . . . . . . . . .            100
        To record the issuing of the shares at $13 each.
```

If we change the assumption, and assume the 100 shares are issued for *only* $1,000, the following entry is made:

```
Dr. Cash  . . . . . . . . . . . . . . . . . . . . . . . . . . . . . . . . . . . . . 1,000
Dr. Contributed Surplus  . . . . . . . . . . . . . . . . . . . . . . . . . . . . 200
      Cr. Treasury Shares . . . . . . . . . . . . . . . . . . . . . . . . . . . . . . . . . .  1,200
         To record the issuing of the shares at $10 each.
```

If no contributed surplus exists, the debit entry for $200 must be made to *Retained Earnings*. "Where a company resells shares that it has acquired, any excess of the proceeds over cost should be credited to contributed surplus; any deficiency should be charged to contributed surplus to the extent that a previous net excess from resale or cancellation of shares of the same class is included therein, otherwise to retained earnings" (CICA Handbook 3240.20).

If a company reacquires its own shares with *no* intention of reissuing them, it formally, legally, retires them. Instead of a debit entry to the Treasury Shares account, the company makes debit entries for the cost of the shares acquired to the Common Shares (at Par) account and the Contributed Surplus account for any difference. If the spread between the par value and the per share cost of the reacquired shares is more than the average per share contributed surplus in capital from prior issuances of shares, that excess may have to be charged against Retained Earnings.

Share Options and Share Warrants

share option plan
A right issued by a company to its employees entitling an employee to buy a set quantity of capital shares in the future at a prespecified price.

Many companies maintain **share option plans** for their employees, and issuance of shares in satisfaction of those commitments are frequent shareholders' equity transactions. A share option plan might work this way: Assume that Smith Company is on the verge of a new business cycle and that its board of directors concludes that management motivation will be a major factor in the company's success. At the present time, the company's shares are selling at $10 a share. The board might agree to grant options to key management people to purchase the company's shares at $10 a share any time after five years from today, thereby creating a financial incentive for the executives.

Under most share option plans, no accounting entry is necessary when such an option is granted. However, disclosure of the details of any share options plans via a footnote is recommended. The entry to record the issuance of 1,000 of those shares when the employees exercise their options assumes that the transaction is simply a sale of shares at $10 a share — even if the stock market value is $20 a share on the exercise date. Assuming non-par-value shares, the entry would be:

```
Dr. Cash  . . . . . . . . . . . . . . . . . . . . . . . . . . . . . . . . . . . . . . . . 10,000
      Cr. Common Shares  . . . . . . . . . . . . . . . . . . . . . . . . . . . . . . . . .  10,000
         To record the issuing of common shares under the share option plan.
```

In recent years, a great variety of option plans has come into use, some of which do require the company to recognize an option expense over the option period and do require the employee to recognize taxable income. Companies establish one plan or another (sometimes combinations of plans) depending on the impact of the plans on their earnings and their tax position, and the needs of their employees.

Pennington's Stores, Limited, disclosed a footnote on its employees' share option plan. The note indicates the exercise price and the expiry date of a series of share options:

As at January 29, 1994, options to purchase 185,000 common shares were outstanding with the following attributes:

Number of shares	Exercise price	Expiry date
165,000	$12.00	May 2, 1999
5,000	$12.00	June 26, 1999
5,000	$11.75	Sept. 21, 1999
5,000	$ 5.00	June 24, 2001
5,000	$ 2.40	May 4, 2003

share warrant
A certificate issued by a company that carries the right or privilege to buy a set quantity of share capital in the future at a prespecified price.

A cash-short firm that is going through a difficult period may find that it is unable to sell new shares at a price it believes is reasonable. In lieu of a share sale, a company may sell **share warrants**, which enable the holder to purchase shares at a fixed price at some time in the future. The proceeds from the sale of warrants is simply added to the Share Warrants account, which is disclosed as part of shareholders' equity.

```
Dr. Cash  . . . . . . . . . . . . . . . . . . . . . . . . . . . . . . . . . . . . .  4,000
    Cr. Share Warrants  . . . . . . . . . . . . . . . . . . . . . . . . . . . . . . .     4,000
    To record the issuing of share warrants.
```

When a warrant is exercised, the proceeds are added to the Common Shares account. However, unlike share options, the share warrant calls for an additional payment of cash when the warrant is exercised. For example the warrants may have sold for $4.00 each, with each warrant giving the holder the option to purchase non-par-value, common shares for $9.00 a share, anytime within the next three years. The entry to record the exercising of the 1,000 share warrants would be:

```
Dr. Cash  . . . . . . . . . . . . . . . . . . . . . . . . . . . . . . . . . . . . .  9,000
Dr. Share Warrants  . . . . . . . . . . . . . . . . . . . . . . . . . . . . . . . .  4,000
    Cr. Common Shares  . . . . . . . . . . . . . . . . . . . . . . . . . . . . . . .    13,000
    To record the issuing of common shares, when the share warrants are exercised.
```

Therefore, the total cost of each share is $13.00. If the market value of the actual shares does not equal or exceed the exercise price ($9.00), plus the warrant price ($4.00), the warrant will most likely not be exercised. The entry to record the expired warrants would be:

```
Dr. Share Warrants  . . . . . . . . . . . . . . . . . . . . . . . . . . . . . . . .  4,000
    Cr. Contributed Surplus  . . . . . . . . . . . . . . . . . . . . . . . . . . . .     4,000
```

Convertibles

convertible debt (bond)
An obligation or debt security exchangeable, or convertible, into the common shares of a company at a prespecified conversion (or exchange) rate.

Many companies sell convertible bonds that enable the holder to exchange a bond for common shares at a predetermined ratio (the conversion ratio). **Convertible bonds** are usually less expensive for the issuing corporation because they can be sold with a *lower* interest rate than would otherwise be required (i.e., because the conversion feature itself has value). Convertible bonds are attractive to the holder because they ensure a steady stream of interest income for a certain number of years, as well as the possibility of sharing in any potential appreciation of the common shares. The proceeds from the sale of a convertible bond increase the Cash account and increase the Bond Payable account.

```
Dr. Cash  . . . . . . . . . . . . . . . . . . . . . . . . . . . . . . . . . . . 97,300
Dr. Bond Discount . . . . . . . . . . . . . . . . . . . . . . . . . . . . . . .  2,700
    Cr. Bond Payable (convertible)  . . . . . . . . . . . . . . . . . . . . . . . .   100,000
    To record the issuing of convertible bonds at a discount.
```

If some of the bonds are subsequently converted, a pro rata share of the bond's carrying value is transferred from the Bond Payable and Bond Discount accounts (a decrease) to the Common Shares and Contributed Surplus accounts (increases). In theory, there are two methods that may be used for bond conversions.

market value method
The market value method records the common shares at their market value and any difference between the market value and the book value of the bonds is treated as a gain or loss on conversion of the bonds.

The book value method or the market value method may be used. The **market value method** records the common shares at their market value and any difference between the market value and the book value of the bonds is treated as a gain or loss on conversion of the bonds. Assume $100,000 face value bonds, with unamortized bond discount of $1,800 are converted into common shares with a market value of $105,000. The following entry would be made:

```
Market value method:
Dr. Bonds Payable . . . . . . . . . . . . . . . . . . . . . . . . . . . . . . . . . . . 100,000
      Cr. Bond Discount . . . . . . . . . . . . . . . . . . . . . . . . . . . . . . . . . .     1,800
Dr. Loss on Conversion of Bonds . . . . . . . . . . . . . . . . . . . . . . . .   6,800
      Cr. Common Shares . . . . . . . . . . . . . . . . . . . . . . . . . . . . . . . . . 105,000
   To record the conversion of bonds.
```

book value method
The book value method removes the bond issue at its book value and charges the book value to the common share account.

Under GAAP, when bonds are redeemed a gain or loss is recognized. However, when shares are issued or cancelled, GAAP state *no gain or loss* should be recognized. In other words, any transaction involving equity is treated as an adjustment to equity. Thus, bond conversions create a dilemma when trying to adhere to GAAP. The CICA Handbook section on financial instruments is unclear on the accounting for such conversions. Use of the **book value method** may be the easiest way to solve this problem. The book value method removes the bond issue at its book value and charges the book value to the Common Shares account, as illustrated in the following entry. By using the book value method, no residual value is created, and *no gain or loss* is recognized.

```
Book value method:
Dr. Bonds Payable . . . . . . . . . . . . . . . . . . . . . . . . . . . . . . . . . . . 100,000
      Cr. Bond Discount . . . . . . . . . . . . . . . . . . . . . . . . . . . . . . . . . .     1,800
      Cr. Common Shares . . . . . . . . . . . . . . . . . . . . . . . . . . . . . . . . . 98,200
   To record the conversion of bonds.
```

Organizations may also issue convertible preferred shares. Similar accounting is followed for convertible preferred shares.

11.6 RETAINED EARNINGS

Net Income and Dividends

As we saw in Chapter 3, revenue- and expense-producing transactions affect many balance sheet accounts — Cash, Accounts Receivable, Inventory, Capital Assets, Liabilities — but ultimately, the effects of these transactions are recorded in the Retained Earnings account. It may be useful at this point to recall the relationship between the balance sheet and the income statement. As the diagram below depicts, these two statements are linked by the Retained Earnings account:

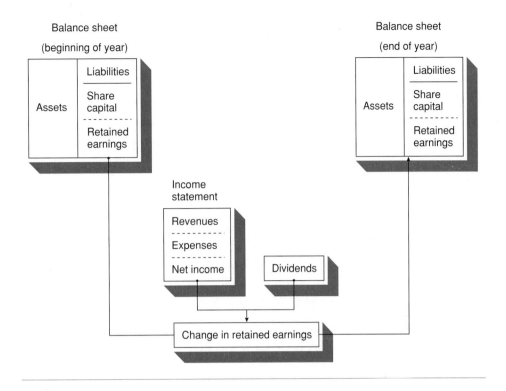

The net income for the period, less any dividends declared, is added to the beginning Retained Earnings and the ending balance is disclosed on the balance sheet. This addition reflects the shareholders' increasing ownership interest in the net worth of the company. This information is disclosed in a statement of retained earnings or in a schedule in the notes accompanying the financial statements:

Retained earnings — beginning	$78,000
Add: net income	33,000
Less: dividends	20,000
Retained earnings — ending	$91,000

Appropriations

Appropriations of retained earnings are created when management wants to indicate to the users of the financial statements that a portion of retained earnings is not available for distribution for dividends or other purposes, but has been appropriated or restricted for a specific purpose. Appropriations are used frequently by non-profit organizations, as much of their funding is designated for specific purposes. To convey this message, a restriction is placed on the equity or surplus of the non-profit organization. As well, a footnote should be provided to further explain the restriction and the impact on the financial statements.

The Council on Drug Abuse included a total of $68,030 for equity on its March 31, 1994, balance sheet. Of this total equity, $9,212 was restricted for specific purposes:

Restricted (note)	$ 9,212
General	58,818
	$68,030

Note: During the year $56,270 was received from the Masonic Foundation of Ontario specifically for the cost of Peer Education Programs in Ontario schools. At year-end, the balance of the funds was $9,212.

IPSCO, Inc., included a note to its financial statements pertaining to a dividend restriction: "Covenants in the company's financing agreements require a minimum of $190,000 of both consolidated and unconsolidated shareholders' equity to remain after the distribution of dividends. As of December 31, 1992, $130,759 are available for dividends."

Changes in Accounting Policy

change in accounting policy
A change in accounting policy may be made "if it is considered that the change would result in a more appropriate presentation of events or transactions in the financial statements of the enterprise."

Although organizations attempt to prepare their financial statements on a *consistent* basis, due to changing economic conditions, organizations may wish to change their accounting policies. **Changes in accounting policy** involve retroactive application and the restatement of prior period financial statements. Thus, a change in accounting policy will normally include an adjustment to the *beginning* Retained Earnings for the period. As well, a footnote is recommended further to explain the impact on the financial statements of the change in accounting policy. "For each change in accounting policy in the current period, the following information should be disclosed:

(a) a description of the change; and

(b) the effect of the change on the financial statements of the current period" (CICA Handbook 1506.16). The Ford Motor Company of Canada, Limited, disclosed a change in accounting policy in a footnote in its annual report:

Fixed assets

The method of determining amortization was changed from declining balance to straight-line for assets acquired after December 31, 1992. For assets acquired prior to January 1, 1993, amortization continues to be determined on the declining balance method until these assets are completely amortized. The impact of adopting straight-line for assets acquired in 1993 reduced amortization by approximately $4 million compared to using the declining balance method.

Changes in accounting policy have been discussed previously. For additional information on the accounting for changes in accounting policy, review the discussion of the impact of a change in amortization methods presented in Chapter 8.

11.7 FINANCIAL STATEMENT DISCLOSURE: EQUITY

Disclosure should be made of authorized share capital, including:

(a) the number of shares for each class, giving a brief description and the par value, if any;

(b) dividend rates on preference shares and whether or not they are cumulative;

(c) the redemption price of redeemable shares;

(d) the existence of conversion provisions;

(e) details of changes during the year. (CICA Handbook 3240.01)

Disclosure should be made of issued share capital including:

(a) the number of shares and the amount received or receivable that is attributable to capital for each class. Where any shares have not been fully paid, disclosure should be made of the amounts which have not been called and the unpaid amounts which have been called or are otherwise due as well as the number of shares in each of these categories;

(b) arrears of dividends for cumulative preference shares. (CICA Handbook 3240.02)

To illustrate the typical annual report disclosures involving equity, we again refer to the annual reports of Canadian organizations. A statement of retained earnings is normally provided to disclose the information on earned capital. The retained earnings statement of Maple Leaf Gardens, Limited, is shown below:

MAPLE LEAF GARDENS, LIMITED
Statement of Retained Earnings
For the Year Ended June 30

	1994	1993
Retained earnings, as previously reported	$14,808,800	$15,098,021
Net income	6,211,265	5,253,099
Dividends	(2,942,330)	(2,942,330)
Redemption of common shares	(16,895)	—
Retained Earnings — June 30	$18,060,850	$14,808,800

The Maple Leaf Gardens statement of retained earnings indicated a beginning balance of $14,808,800. Net income of $6,211,265 was added to the account, and dividends of $2,942,330 and an adjustment of $16,895 for the redemption of common shares at a price in excess of the original issue price was deducted, to determine the ending balance of $18,060,850.

Kerr Addison Mines, Limited, included a footnote in its annual report on its share capital:

In 1993 and 1992, preferred and common shares without par value are authorized for issuance in an unlimited number. There are no preferred shares issued. The changes in common shares issued for the years 1993 and 1992 are set out below:

	1993		1992	
Issued, beginning of year	17,592,927	$185,107	17,589,852	$185,061
Issued under share option plan	—	—	3,075	46
Purchased for cancellation	(61)	(1)	—	—
Issued, end of year	17,592,866	$185,106	17,592,927	$185,107

At December 31, 1993 and 1992, there were no options outstanding.

11.8 ANALYZING EQUITY

Ratio Analysis

Because the absolute level of net income is often difficult to compare between periods and among different companies, it is an accepted practice for companies to report a standardized measure of their performance. Under GAAP, net income is divided by the number of shares of a company's share capital, and the resulting standardized measure of performance is called *earnings per share (EPS)*.

The rules followed in calculating earnings per share (EPS) are quite complex. At the end of each quarter and the end of each year, publicly held companies release earnings information for the period, in total and on a per share basis. The quarterly and annual reports are summarized in the financial press and then are used on an ongoing basis in calculating various stock market performance indicators. As a result, the determination of the earnings per share figure is an important aspect of financial statement disclosure. The earnings per share figures may be disclosed in a footnote to the financial statements. Frequently, the earnings per share figure is disclosed as part of the income statement, as is the case with Maple Leaf Gardens, Limited. Maple Leaf Gardens discloses earnings per share of $1.69 for 1994, and $1.43 for 1993. The absolute level of net income increased to $6,211,265 in 1994, from $5,253,099 in 1993.

For publicly held companies, the return to investors is one of the most frequently evaluated areas of company performance. Since investors are often the largest group of stakeholders in a company, how well they are rewarded for their investment is of considerable interest and importance. Most indicators of the return to investors are based on current income statement data. Perhaps the most often cited measure of shareholder return is a company's earnings per share, or EPS. Earnings per share represent only those earnings of a company accruing to its voting, or *common, shareholders*. Thus, in the calculation of EPS, a company's earnings are first reduced for any dividends paid to the preferred shareholders. The calculation of EPS can be quite complex, depending on whether a company has other securities outstanding that are convertible into, or exchangeable for, additional common shares. In the simplest case in which a company has only common and preferred shares outstanding, the computation of EPS is straightforward:

$$\text{Basic earnings per share} = \frac{\text{Net income} - \text{Preferred dividends}}{\text{Number of common shares outstanding}^1}$$

basic earnings per share
A standardized measure of performance calculated as net income applicable to common shares.

Note that in the calculation of **basic EPS**, the divisor is not merely the number of shares outstanding at year-end but rather is an average of the shares outstanding, weighted by the proportion of a given year (or quarter) that the shares were actually in the hands of shareholders. "Basic earnings per share figures should be shown either on the face of the income statement or in a note to the financial statements cross-referenced to the income statement. Ordinarily disclosure by note would be the more effective method where fully diluted or pro-forma earnings per share figures are also included"(CICA Handbook 3500.09).

For a company with securities outstanding that are *convertible* (e.g., convertible bonds or convertible preferred shares) or exchangeable (e.g., share options or warrants) for common shares, the calculation of EPS can be surprisingly difficult. Under these conditions, two calculations may be required — one for basic EPS and one for fully diluted EPS.

fully diluted earnings per share
A standardized measure of performance calculated as net income applicable to common shares, plus common share equivalents and any other potentially dilutive securities.

Fully diluted EPS is calculated by including in the divisor all potentially dilutive securities. "Where the effect of potential conversions of senior shares or debt, exercises of rights, warrants and options and contingent issuances on earnings per share

---

[1]Earnings per share should be calculated using the weighted-average number of common shares outstanding. However, this information is not always readily available to the user. Therefore, the end-of-period number of shares outstanding may have to be used. In practice, this is generally not a problem, because according to GAAP, the earnings per share figure should be disclosed as part of the organization's financial report.

would be materially dilutive, fully diluted earnings per share figures for 'income before discontinued operations and extraordinary items' and 'net income for the period' should be disclosed, for the current period, in a note to the financial statements, cross-referenced to the income statement. Such figures should be described as fully diluted" (CICA Handbook 3500.30). Fully diluted EPS is calculated as follows:

$$\text{Fully diluted earnings per share} = \frac{\text{Net income} - \text{Preferred dividends}}{\text{Number of common shares outstanding} + \text{Other potentially dilutive securities}}$$

For an example, consider the following EPS data:

$$\text{Basic EPS} = \frac{\text{Net income} - \text{Preferred dividends}}{\text{Weighted average of common shares outstanding}}$$

$$= \frac{\$12,000,000 - \$1,500,000}{3,500,000} = \$3.00$$

If outstanding convertible preferred shares are *assumed* to be converted at the beginning of the year into 1 million common shares, the following would be the new EPS:

$$\text{Fully diluted EPS} = \frac{\$12,000,000}{(3,500,000 + 1,000,000)} = \$2.67$$

As this example demonstrates, the earnings applicable to common shareholders for each convertible security included in the EPS denominator requires an adjustment. For example, if the number of common shares attributable to a convertible preferred share is used to increase the EPS denominator, the numerator should be increased by the amount of preferred dividends that would *no longer* be required if the conversion took place. The one exception to this involves the exercising of share options or warrants, which affects only the number of shares outstanding.

The principle of conservatism is the premise for the fully diluted earnings per share calculation. A worst-case scenario is depicted, assuming all potential conversions occur in the current year. The result is the most conservative or lowest earnings per share figure.

The return-on-equity ratio is one of most commonly used profitability measures. The **return on equity** (ROE) measures a company's profitability relative to the resources provided by its owners. ROE measures the adequacy of the return on capital invested by the owners. The ROE is calculated as follows:

return on equity (ROE) A measure of the relative effectiveness of a company in using the assets provided by the owners to generate net income.

$$\text{Return on equity} = \frac{\text{Net income}}{\text{Equity}}$$

In general, the higher the ROE, the more profitable a company is thought to be. As illustrated in this chapter, the determination of equity is comprised of several different elements. These complexities do not significantly change this ratio, as it remains basically the same calculation as discussed in Chapter 3.

Issuing Shares versus Bonds

An organization must consider many alternatives when faced with a need for financing. Financing may be obtained by issuing share capital or long-term debt. Some of the questions to be considered include:

Are the current financial markets more receptive to a share or bond issue from the corporation?

If common shares are issued, will control of the corporation change hands?

What will be the impact on earnings per share if additional common shares are issued? If preferred shares are issued? If long-term bonds are issued?

What is the impact on the return-on-equity ratio if share capital is issued? If long-term bonds are issued?

What is the impact on the debt-to-equity ratio if share capital is issued? If long-term bonds are issued?

What is the future impact on cash flow if interest is to be paid annually on bonds or if dividends are to be paid on share capital?

If long-term bonds are issued, will there be an opportunity to refinance the bond issue upon maturity?

What are the income tax considerations since interest on bonds is tax-*deductible*, but dividends on share capital are not?

Consider the following illustration. The shareholders' equity of a corporation at December 31 is as follows:

Statement of Shareholders' Equity
At December 31

Common shares — authorized		
100,000 shares, issued 10,000 shares		$100,000
Retained earnings, January 1	$55,000	
Net income for the year	50,000	
Less: common dividends	(5,000)	
Retained earnings, December 31		100,000
Total shareholders' equity		$200,000

Basic earnings per share is $5.00. The net income allocable to common shareholders is $50,000. There are 10,000 common shares outstanding.

$$\text{Basic EPS} = \frac{\$50,000}{10,000} = \$5.00$$

The return on equity is 25.0 percent (net income of $50,000 for the year divided by the total shareholders' equity of $200,000).

$$\text{Return on equity} = \frac{\$50,000}{\$200,000} = 25.0\%$$

The company requires an additional $100,000 financing to diversify its operations. It is considering issuing either 8 percent preferred shares or an 8 percent bond issue. As-suming the financing for $100,000 had been in place at the beginning of the past year, the impact on the financial statement and ratios would be as follows.

8 percent bonds are issued. In exchange for the $100,000 received from issuing the bonds, the company would annually pay 8 percent or $8,000 in interest. Since interest expense is tax deductible, assuming a 50 percent tax rate, the cost is reduced to $4,000 [$8,000 × (1 − .50)]. The additional interest expense, net of tax, of $4,000 would reduce the net income for the year to $46,000 ($50,000 − $4,000). As well, the reduc-tion in net income would reduce the shareholders' equity by $4,000 to $196,000 ($200,000 − $4,000).

The revised basic earnings per share would be $4.60. The net income allocable to common shareholders is $46,000. There are 10,000 common shares outstanding.

$$\text{Basic EPS} = \frac{\$46,000}{10,000} = \$4.60$$

The return on equity is 23.47 percent (net income of $46,000 for the year divided by the total shareholders' equity of $196,000).

$$\text{Return on equity} = \frac{\$46,000}{\$196,000} = 23.47\%$$

The solvency ratios would be significantly affected by these transactions. Assume that prior to the issuing of the bonds, there is no other long-term debt outstanding. The long-term debt-to-invested capital ratio would be zero. The long-term debt-to-invested capital ratio would increase dramatically to .34 after the bonds are issued:

$$\frac{\$100,000}{(\$100,000 + \$196,000)} = .34$$

8 percent preferred shares are issued. In exchange for the $100,000 received from issuing the preferred shares, the company would annually pay 8 percent or $8,000 in preferred dividends. The dividends are *not* tax deductible. The net income for the year remains the same, $50,000. The shareholders' equity would be reduced by the preferred dividends of $8,000 and increased by $100,000 by the issuing of preferred shares. The revised shareholders' equity would be $292,000 ($200,000 + $100,000 − $8,000).

The revised basic earnings per share would be $4.20. The net income allocable to *common* shareholders is $42,000 — the net income of $50,000 less the preferred dividends of $8,000. There are 10,000 common shares outstanding.

$$\text{Basic EPS} = \frac{\$42,000}{10,000} = \$4.20$$

The return on equity is 17.12 percent (net income of $50,000 for the year divided by the total shareholders' equity of $292,000).

$$\text{Return on equity} = \frac{\$50,000}{\$292,000} = 17.12\%$$

The long-term debt-to-invested capital ratio would not change but remain at zero, as no long-term debt has been issued.

Ratio	Before Financing	Bonds Issued	Preferred Shares Issued
Earnings per share	$5.00	$4.60	$4.20
Return on equity	25.00%	23.47%	17.12%
Long-term debt to invested capital	–0–	.34	–0–

As can be seen by comparing the above ratios, the financing decision has a significant impact on the financial statements and the ratios. The preceding illustration shows some of the basic concepts that influence financing decisions. This is a complex issue, and as stated at the start of this section, several additional factors may ultimately influence the financing decisions made by management.

11.9 COMPREHENSIVE ILLUSTRATION

Cando, Ltd., was incorporated under provincial legislation. Cando is authorized to issue 100,000 non-par-value common shares, and 50,000 cumulative, non-par-value preferred shares, with an annual dividend rate of $1.00 per share. Cando has a December 31 year-end. The following transactions occurred during the first year of operations:

a. Issued 1,000 common shares at $115 per share cash.

b. Issued 2,000 preferred shares in exchange for equipment. The equipment is determined to have a fair market value of $40,000.

c. Issued 1,000 preferred shares at $20 per share cash.

d. Declared a cash dividend on preferred shares of $1.00 per share.

e. Issued 1,500 common shares at $120 per share cash.

f. Paid the preferred dividend.

g. Declared and issued a 10 percent share dividend on common shares. Market value of the common shares is $122.

h. Convertible bonds with a face value of $50,000 and a book value of $53,000 were converted into 500 common shares. The convertible bonds were issued earlier in the year.

i. Closed the Income Summary account. Net income for the year was $64,000.

Required:

a. Prepare general journal entries for the above transactions.

b. Prepare a retained earnings statement.

c. Prepare a statement of shareholders' equity.

d. Calculate the basic earnings per share and the return on equity.

The general journal entries for the equity transactions of Cando, Ltd., follow. The journal entry to record the issuing of 1,000 non-par-value common shares for $115,000 cash is:

```
a.  Dr. Cash . . . . . . . . . . . . . . . . . . . . . . . . . . . . . . . . . . . . . 115,000
        Cr. Common Shares . . . . . . . . . . . . . . . . . . . . . . . . . . . . . . .     115,000
            To record the issuing of 1,000 non-par-value common shares for $115,000 cash.
```

When a corporation issues non-par-value shares, the *total* proceeds received from the shareholders is recorded in the Common Shares account. Entry *b* records the issuing of non-par-value preferred shares for a non-cash asset.

```
b.  Dr. Equipment . . . . . . . . . . . . . . . . . . . . . . . . . . . . . . . . . 40,000
        Cr. Preferred Shares  . . . . . . . . . . . . . . . . . . . . . . . . . . . .      40,000
            To record the issuing of 2,000 non-par-value preferred shares.
```

Entry *c* records the issuing of 1,000 non-par-value preferred shares, for cash.

```
c.  Dr. Cash . . . . . . . . . . . . . . . . . . . . . . . . . . . . . . . . . . . . . 20,000
        Cr. Preferred Shares . . . . . . . . . . . . . . . . . . . . . . . . . . . . . .     20,000
            To record the issuing of 1,000 non-par-value preferred shares.
```

Entry *d* records the declaration of a $1.00 per share cash dividend on preferred shares. There are 3,000 preferred shares issued and outstanding when the dividend is declared.

    d.   Dr. Dividends Declared (R.E.) 3,000
            Cr. Preferred Dividends Payable   3,000
            To record the declaration of the cash dividend.

Entry *e* records the issuing of 1,500 non-par-value common shares for $180,000 cash.

    e.   Dr. Cash 180,000
            Cr. Common Shares   180,000
            To record the issuing of 1,500 non-par-value common shares for $180,000 cash.

Entry *f* records the payment of the dividends declared in entry *d*.

    f.   Dr. Preferred Dividends Payable 3,000
            Cr. Cash   3,000
            To record the cash payment of the dividends.

Entry *g* records the declaration and issuing of the share dividend. When the 10 percent share dividend on common shares is declared, there are 2,500 common shares outstanding. Therefore, 10 percent or 250 common shares are issued as a share dividend. The share dividend is valued at the market value of the shares, $122, for a total value of $30,500 (250 × $122). Entry *g* records the declaration and issuing of the share dividend.

    g.   Dr. Share Dividends Declared (R.E.) 30,500
            Cr. Common Shares Distributable   30,500
            To record the declaration of the 10 percent share dividend.

The Share Dividends Declared account records a reduction to Retained Earnings, similar to the declaration of a cash dividend. The Common Shares Distributable account is an equity account, and would be disclosed as part of shareholders' equity, if a statement was prepared at this point. The following entry is made when the common shares are issued:

    g.   Dr. Common Shares Distributable 30,500
            Cr. Common Shares   30,500
            To record the issuing of 250 non-par-value common shares.

    The book value method will be used to record the conversion of the bonds into common shares. Convertible bonds with a face value of $50,000 and a book value of $53,000 were converted into 500 common shares.

    h.   Dr. Bonds Payable 50,000
        Dr. Bond Premium 3,000
            Cr. Common Shares   53,000
            To record the conversion of bonds into 500 non-par-value common shares.

When the bonds are converted to shares, the $53,000 book value for the bonds must be allocated to equity. Entry *i* is the closing entry to transfer the net income for the year to Retained Earnings.

    i.   Dr. Income Summary 64,000
            Cr. Retained Earnings   64,000
            To record the closing entry, to transfer net income to retained earnings.

The equity transactions are summarized in a statement of retained earnings and a statement of shareholders' equity.

CANDO, LTD.
Statement of Retained Earnings
For the Year Ended December 31

Retained earnings, January 1		$ 0
Add: net income		64,000
Less: Preferred dividends	$ 3,000	
Common share dividend	30,500	33,500
Retained earnings, December 31		$30,500

CANDO, LTD.
Statement of Shareholders' Equity
December 31

Common shares, non-par value — authorized 100,000 shares, issued 3,250 shares.	$378,500
Preferred shares, non-par value, cumulative — authorized 50,000 shares, issued 3,000 shares	60,000
Retained earnings	30,500
	$469,000

Basic earnings per share is $18.77. The net income allocable to common shareholders is $61,000 — the net income of $64,000 less the preferred dividends of $3,000 for the year. There are 3,250 common shares outstanding.

$$\text{Basic EPS} = \frac{(\$64,000 - \$3,000)}{3,250} = \$18.77$$

The return on equity is 13.64 percent (net income of $64,000 for the year divided by the total shareholders' equity of $469,000).

$$\text{Return on equity} = \frac{\$64,000}{\$469,000} = 13.64\%$$

11.10 SUMMARY

The shareholders' equity represents the residual value of a company, or its assets minus its liabilities. The transactions affecting the shareholders' equity accounts are summarized in the statement of equity. The principal equity transactions include the sale of share capital, the results of operations (i.e., the net income or net loss resulting from a company's principal business activity), the payment of dividends (either cash or shares), the exercise of share options or warrants, the conversion of convertible preferred shares or convertible bonds, and the purchase or reissue of treasury shares.

The equity of a company is also referred to as its *net worth* or *book value*. In many cases, the market value of a company, as defined by the market price of its share capital, far exceeds the company's net worth or book value. The following table summaries the financial statement interrelationships:

Financial Statement Interrelationships

Financial Statement Item	Balance Sheet	Income Statement	Statement of Changes in Financial Position
Share capital	Shareholders' equity	Capital transactions do not affect net income.	Issuing shares is a financing activity, providing cash. Redemptions of shares are a financing activity, using cash.
Dividends	Deducted from retained earnings	Dividends do not affect net income.	A financing activity, using cash.

11.11 KEY CONCEPTS AND TERMS

Appropriations (p. 526)

Authorized capital (p. 527)

Basic EPS (p. 540)

Book value method (p. 536)

Canada Business Corporations
Act (p. 525)

Change in accounting policy (p. 538)

Common shares (p. 527)

Contributed capital (p. 522)

Convertible bonds (p. 535)

Cumulative preferred shares (p. 531)

Date of declaration (p. 530)

Date of payment (p. 530)

Date of record (p. 531)

Dividends in arrears (p. 531)

Dividend policy (p. 530)

Earned capital (p. 522)

Fully diluted EPS (p. 540)

Issued capital (p. 527)

Market value method (p. 536)

Non-par value (p. 527)

Organization costs (p. 529)

Outstanding capital (p. 527)

Par value (p. 527)

Partnership (p. 522)

Preferred shares (p. 527)

Proprietorship (p. 522)

Return on equity (p. 541)

Share dividend (p. 532)

Share option plans (p. 534)

Share split (p. 532)

Share subscriptions (p. 529)

Share warrants (p. 535)

Treasury shares (p. 533)

11.12 COMPREHENSIVE REVIEW PROBLEM

R11.1 Shareholders' equity. White Eagle Corporation, Ltd., is authorized to issue 50,000 non-par-value common shares, and 20,000 $.80, non-par-value preferred shares. The following transactions occurred during the first year of operations:

1. Issued 15,000 common shares at $6 per share cash.

2. Issued 2,000 common shares to the corporation's lawyers for their services in getting the corporation organized. The directors placed a $10,000 value on the services.

3. Issued 5,000 preferred shares at $12 per share cash.

4. Declared the semiannual dividend on preferred shares.

5. Declared a $.50 per share cash dividend on common shares.

6. Declared and issued a 10 percent share dividend on common shares. Market value of the common shares is $6.

7. Closed the Income Summary account. Net income for the year was $27,000.

8. Paid the dividends previously declared.

Required:

a. Prepare general journal entries for the above transactions.

b. Prepare a statement of shareholders' equity.

c. Calculate the basic earnings per share and the return on equity.

11.13 REVIEW AND DISCUSSION QUESTIONS

Q11.1 Assume that you and two of your friends are about to form a business. Anticipating a meeting with your lawyer, what factors should you consider in deciding between establishing a partnership or forming a corporation? Why might these factors be important to your planning?

Q11.2 Point: Treasury shares should be accounted for as an asset; after all, a company's resources must be expended to repurchase the shares.

Counterpoint: Treasury shares should be accounted for as a contra shareholders' equity account in that the shares held in the treasury represent a reduction in the total shares outstanding.

Comment on the two viewpoints. Which one makes most sense to you and why?

Q11.3 Point: Investors who have agreed to buy shares in a growing company and who have signed notes for their share subscriptions represent real shareholders, and their notes should be counted as assets and equity, even though they have not yet been paid in cash. That, after all, is what accrual accounting is all about.

Counterpoint: Share subscriptions should not be recorded as assets because the funds are not available for the company's use until the notes are paid. We should treat notes receivables from shareholders differently than we treat notes from customers or creditors because the notes do not arise in the ordinary course of business. More importantly, the users of the financial statements are entitled to assume that shareholders' equity is really in place and is fully ready to absorb the deepest layer of business risk facing the company. Comment on the two viewpoints. Which one makes the most sense to you and why?

Q11.4 What does the expression "vote with their feet" mean to you? Why should it be necessary for shareholders to vote with their feet? What message might management look for from such a voting process?

Q11.5 Brown-Foreman Corporation has class A and class B non-par-value common shares outstanding. Both the A and B shares are paid the exact same dividend. The shares appear to be the same in every respect, except that the class A shares have a vote, whereas the class B shares do not. There are 12 million class A shares outstanding and 26.6 million class B shares outstanding. In the last quarter of 1996, the class A shares traded in a range between $75 and $57½ a share; the class B shares traded in a range between $78⅞ and $58⅜ per share. Why would the company have these two classes of common shares outstanding? Would you expect the two classes to trade in the market at the same or at different prices? How would you interpret the price data in this case? What are the implications of that data for other companies that might be contemplating a two-class share program?

Q11.6 In 1988, the directors of Schuchardt Software Systems, Inc., declared a 2,000-for-1 share split. SSS, Inc., a publisher of business software, was organized in 1983 and each founding shareholder paid $5,000 per share. At that time, 84 individuals purchased shares in the company. Since then, the founding shareholders have sold a few shares between themselves at prices ranging from $5,800 to $6,800 a share. The company is preparing itself for its initial offering of shares to the public.

Required:

a. Why would the directors decide on a 2,000-for-1 split?

b. Assume that the company declared a 2,000 percent share dividend instead of a share split. How would you account for the share dividend?

Q11.7 Pacific Corporation made the comment below in its 1990 annual report to shareholders:

Dividends and Share Repurchases
In the past five years, we have distributed approximately $1.7 billion to our shareholders through a combination of dividends and share repurchases. Our policy is to pay dividends at a rate of approximately one-third of sustainable earnings, recognizing the cyclical nature of our business. Following four consecutive years with fourth-quarter dividend increases, we left our quarterly dividend unchanged in 1990. We view the dividend payout in conjunction with our share repurchase program. Our board of directors authorized a share repurchase program that began in

1987 as a means of distributing excess cash to our shareholders and maintaining our ratio of debt to capital within a target range, currently set at 40 to 45 percent. In 1989, for example, cash provided by operations exceeded our capital expenditures and dividend payments by $729 million. Of this free cash flow, $468 million was used to repurchase 9.7 million shares of common shares. This brought total share repurchases since 1987 to 26.2 million at a cost of $1.1 billion.

In October 1989, we suspended our share repurchase program, anticipating the higher leverage that resulted from the Great Northern acquisition. Our board's authorization to repurchase shares remains in effect, however, and we expect to resume our share repurchase program after we reduce debt to an appropriate level.

Required:

a. Is the company justified in its position that dividends and share repurchases should be considered in the same way? Why or why not?

b. How are they the same and how are they different in their impact on the company?

c. How are they the same and how are they different in their impact on the shareholders?

Q11.8 Quick Start, Inc., had a public offering of shares in 1991, and as a result, it has 250,000 common shares outstanding. Because of its need for cash, the company has never paid a dividend. Quick Start has been moderately successful, but it was subject to the seasonality that affected the automobile industry. Results for the last five years were as follows (in thousands):

Year	Net Income	Cash from Operations
1991	$20,000	$32,000
1992	8,000	14,000
1993	12,000	15,000
1994	16,000	20,000
1995	19,000	22,000

The company has debt and lease commitments that require about $18,000,000 a year. Its capital expansion plans are now at a level at which they could be met by additional borrowing, and the company has open credit lines of $75,000,000 available. Retained earnings are $90,000,000. Because of pressure from the public shareholders, Quick Start's board of directors is considering making a dividend payment in 1996.

Required:

a. Outline all of the factors you might want the board to address as it considers the possibility of making a dividend payment. How much should the 1996 dividend be?

b. Suggest and justify a range of per share amounts that the board might consider.

11.14 PROBLEMS

P11.1 Share issuances and dividend payments. CRS Corporation was incorporated on January 1, 1996, and issued the following shares, for cash:

1,000,000 non-par common shares were authorized; 100,000 shares were issued on January 1, at $24 per share.

200,000 non-par-value, $1.00, cumulative preferred shares were authorized, and 50,000 shares were issued on January 1, 1996, at $12 per share.

The year went relatively well. Net income was $525,000, and the board of directors declared dividends of $175,000.

Required:

Prepare the entries required to record the issuances of the shares and the declaration of the dividends.

P11.2 Issuing shares to the founders. Three entrepreneurs have come together to exploit an invention that one of them recently patented. The inventor has very little cash, but he is willing to put his patent into the venture. Similarly, the second entrepreneur has very little cash, but he has a manufacturing plant he can contribute to the venture. (The plant is presently vacant but can be used to manufacture the inventor's product. The plant was recently appraised as having a value of between $180,000 and $225,000.) The third entrepreneur has plenty of cash, and she is willing to put $200,000 into the new venture. They agree to form a corporation and that each will receive 2,000 common shares for the contributions of cash, the building, and the patent.

Required:

Prepare the entries required to record the issuance of the shares. Explain your rationale for the entries you made and the numbers you used.

P11.3 Treasury share transactions. Smith Company has sold, issued, and given shares to its employees and to outsiders at various times during its life as follows:

1990   100,000 shares originally sold for $100,000 cash.
1991   25,000 shares sold to an independent investor for $50,000 cash.
1992   100,000 shares sold to a group of 25 investors at $30 a share.
1993   A two-for-one share split declared.
1994   500,000 shares sold in a public offering at $25 a share.
1995   100,000 shares given to the top management as a bonus. The market price was then $20.

In 1996, the company purchased 50,000 shares on the open market at $12 a share.

Required:

a. Prepare the entry required to record the 50,000 share purchase, assuming the company plans to reissue the shares as a bonus to employees at a future date.

b. Prepare the entry required to record the share purchase, assuming the company plans to retire the reacquired shares.

P11.4 Convertible preferred shares. Clever Corp. raised $1,000,000 in capital by the sale of 10,000 shares of convertible, non-par-value preferred shares. The preferred shares required an annual dividend of only $4 a share even though the prime rate at the time was 10 percent. Each share of preferred was convertible into five shares of Clever common shares, which had a market value of $10 at the time of the preferred shares' issuance.

Required:

a. Prepare the entry to record the sale of the preferred shares. How would you propose to recognize the value of the conversion feature in the financial statements? Please provide the rationale for your answer.

b. Why would Clever want to issue convertible preferred instead of regular preferred or additional common shares?

c. Why would an investor buy the Clever convertible preferred when it pays only a $4 dividend?

P11.5 Convertible preferred. All of the holders of Clever Corp. convertible preferred shares (discussed in P11.4) turned in their shares for conversion and were given five shares of common for each share of preferred.

Required:

a. Why would the holders of the preferred shares turn their shares in for redemption at this time?

b. What entry would Clever Corp. make at the time of the conversion?

P11.6 Share options. Aggressive Corporation was doing very well with its new product line, and it seemed as though the company could double in size over the next three years. It was a tense time for the management people, however, and good fortune brought its own questions. Do we have enough inventory to meet demand? Should we expand the plant to accommodate one more assembly line? If we encourage sales by granting extended credit terms, how will we pay our own bills? Nonetheless, management had worked very hard for a long time with very little reward and members were delighted to bask in the prospects of the future. The board of directors was pleased, too, and at the end of the year awarded the top five people share options, which would enable each of them to buy 10,000 of the company's shares at $9 each, the current market price. It was indeed a happy new year.

Required:

a. Why might Aggressive's board of directors have believed it appropriate to issue the share options to the top management people at this time at $9 a share?

b. How might you feel about the share options if you were one of the top management people? Why? How might you feel if you were a non-management shareholder in the company?

c. Prepare the entry required to recognize the issuance of the options at the issue date. Explain the reasons for your entry.

P11.7 Share options exercised. Three years after Aggressive's board of directors issued the share options to its top five employees (see P11.6) the company's sales had grown nearly three times and profits were up 250 percent. The share market had recognized the company's success, and the shares regularly traded at $32. Three of the top five employees exercised their options in full, but the other two had not as yet done so.

Required:

a. Prepare the entry required to recognize the exercise of the options for 30,000 shares. Explain the rationale for your entry and then explain the source of your numbers.

b. What factors might have motivated the three management people to exercise their share options? What factors might have motivated the other two to hold on to the options, at least for the time being?

P11.8 Accounting for share warrants. Poorboy Limited had been through difficult years, but management was hopeful that the recent financial restructuring and product reorganization would turn things around. The company needed cash to carry out its new strategy, but the banks had refused any further credit extension. Shares were trading at an all-time low, around $2.50 per share. An investment adviser suggested that the company consider selling warrants. After some negotiation, the adviser helped the company sell 1,000,000 warrants, each good for the purchase of a common share at $5 in eight years. The warrant sale raised $500,000.

Required:

a. Why might the market pay $500,000 for warrants to purchase Poorboy's shares at $5 a share eight years from now when the company has been through such difficult times and when that same market has concluded that the company's common shares are worth only $2.50 each?

b. Prepare the entry required to record the sale of the warrants. Explain the rationale for your entry and your numbers.

P11.9 Share warrant redemptions. Five years after Poorboy's emotional reorganization (and its sale of warrants), things were finally looking up (see P11.8). Sales were growing, earnings were up very nicely, and cash flow was finally looking strong. The common shares were trading at about $10 a share. Management looked for a place to put the excess cash flow and decided to buy some of the company's shares back. An investment adviser suggested buying the warrants back because the same impact on the outstanding common shares could be had with a little less cash outflow. (The warrants were then trading at about $6.25.) Poorboy published an offer to buy and subsequently did purchase all of the outstanding warrants at $7.50 each.

Required:

a. Prepare the entry to record the purchase of the warrants, assuming they will be retired after acquisition.

b. Prepare the entries that would have been required had the company purchased $7,500,000 of common shares instead of the warrants and had all warrant holders tendered their warrants for conversion.

c. What do you think of the company's warrant buyback?

P11.10 Share for debt exchange. In 1989, RJR Nabisco, Inc., was taken private by Kohlberg Kravis Roberts & Co. (KKR & Co.) in a leveraged buyout. As part of the buyout, RJR Nabisco issued large amounts of high-yield bonds. For example, one part of the leveraged buyout involved the issuance of $2.86 billion of 17 percent bonds due in 2007.

Beginning in late 1990, KKR & Co. began efforts to reduce the level of debt carried on the books of RJR Nabisco. One such proposal involved the issuance of 82.8 million RJR shares and $350 million of cash in exchange for $753 million (face value) of the 17 percent bonds.

Assume that the RJR Nabisco shares are non-par value. The shares, being privately held, have no readily determined market value; and the bonds are trading at their face value.

Required:

a. Why would the company make that exchange at this time?

b. What entry would the company make at the time of the exchange?

c. What entry would be made if the bonds were trading at $830 rather than the $1,000 face value?

P11.11 Paying share dividends. On November 21, 1996, the board of directors of Eastman Kodak Company declared a share dividend of 1 share of common shares for each 20 shares outstanding, payable February 10, 1997, to holders of common shares of record on January 3, 1997. In a message to shareholders, the company explained:

The purpose of this share dividend is to place in the hands of each shareholder tangible evidence of his share in the portion of the earnings of the Company which have been retained for use in the business and which are being capitalized by the share dividend . . . The receipt by you of this share dividend does not increase your proportionate equity in the Company. However, a disposal of such dividend will reduce your equity in the Company by $4.7619.

Common shares of 38,382,246 were outstanding prior to the declaration of the share dividend. The market value of the common shares was $106.00. The company's retained earnings at September 8, 1996 (the end of its third quarter), were $397,727,028.

Required:

a. What entry should the company make for the share dividend? When?

P11.12 Convertible preferred shares. On August 16, The Business Journal carried an advertisement concerning Baker Hughes. The following is from that advertisement: "Baker Hughes Incorporated has called for redemption of all its $3.50 Convertible Preferred shares." According to the advertisement, Baker Hughes had decided to exercise the redemption feature on its outstanding preferred shares and to redeem the share at a price of $52.45 per share plus accrued dividends of $.16, for a total of $52.61, on August 31. The preferred shares also carried a conversion feature that would permit the owner to convert a preferred share into 1.9608 common shares. The market price of the common shares on August 13, was $32.625 per share. The advertisement emphasized that the conversion feature of the preferred shares expired on August 27.

Required:

a. Assume that Baker Hughes has 1 million preferred shares outstanding, and that its par value is $5. How would the company account for (1) the redemption of all shares and (2) the conversion of all shares?

b. If you held 100 preferred shares of Baker Hughes, which alternative (conversion or redemption) would you choose, and why?

c. If you were the CEO of Baker Hughes, which alternative would you prefer, and why?

P11.13 Share transactions (*Certified Management Accountants of British Columbia*). The New Cold Storage Company decides to issue new shares. 100,000 new shares will be sold by an investment dealer. The dealer charges a 5 percent commission on the value of the shares sold. These common shares with no par value sell for $50.00 each. The issue is complete at June 1, 1994, and is then recorded. The company then has 1,100,000 shares outstanding.

On June 1, 1995, New Cold Storage has extra funds available and uses them to buy 10,000 of its own shares. At that time the market value of the shares is $45.00. On June 1, 1996, New Cold Storage sells all of its treasury shares for $55.00 per share.

Required:

a. Give the journal entries required on June 1, 1994, June 1, 1995, and June 1, 1996.

b. On May 31, 1994, the book value of the shares of New Cold Storage is $40.00 per share. How much is the book value on June 2, 1994? No other transactions took place than are considered here.

P11.14 Accounting for equity (*Certified Management Accountants of British Columbia*). Sapphire Corporation was formed January 1, and 50,000 no-par-value common shares were issued to investors at a price of $18 per share. Pre-tax accounting income for the year ending December 31, was $160,000. Dividends of $0.45 per share were declared on September 15, but remain unpaid. Sapphire's income tax rate for 1989 was 42 percent.

Required:

a. Prepare the journal entries to record the issuance of shares on January 1, and the declaration of dividends on September 15.

b. Prepare a statement of retained earnings for Sapphire's first year.

c. What earnings per share figure should be reported for the year?

P11.15 Shareholders' equity (*Certified Management Accountants of British Columbia*). Northern, Ltd., started business January 15. Northern was authorized to issue unlimited no-par common shares.

The transactions following occurred:

Feb. 7	Sold 75,000 common shares at $3.25 each.
14	Exchanged 40,000 common shares for equipment that had a fair market value of $100,000.
June 1	Declared and issued a 5 percent share dividend. Northern common shares were selling for $15 on June 1.
Oct. 15	Declared and issued a two-for-one share split. Selling price of Northern common shares that day was $18.
Nov. 1	Purchased 10,000 of its own common shares on the open market at $2.25 per share.
Dec. 1	Declared a $.10 per share cash dividend on common shares payable January 15, next year.
Dec. 31	Net income for the year was $250,000.

Required:

a. Prepare journal entries for the above transactions.

b. Prepare in good form the shareholders' equity section of Northern, Ltd., at December 31.

P11.16 Financial statement disclosure (*Certified Management Accountants of British Columbia*). Each part is independent of the others.

a. The Vancouver Canucks are considering building a new arena to meet the ever-increasing popularity of their team. The stadium will require an investment of $100,000,000. To raise the money the Canucks are considering either borrowing the money at 10 percent or selling no-par common shares. List any advantages and disadvantages of raising money by:

(1) borrowing

(2) selling shares

b. Your friend, Hulk Hogan, has asked you to tell him about amortization. Explain to him what amortization is and tell him about different methods of amortization.

c. The president of Worrywart, Ltd., a retail store, has just heard that a customer injured himself while shopping at the store. The customer says that he has severe injuries and is going to sue the store for thousands of dollars. Sales staff of the store said that the customer tripped over his own feet while shopping. The store's lawyer said that in the event of a lawsuit, the store would face little or no damages. Nevertheless, the president of the store, Mr. Worry, has instructed the accounting department to account for the customer's claim by making the following entry:

```
Loss on Injury Claim  . . . . . . . . . . . . . . . . . . . . . . . . . . . . . . . 50,000
    Estimated liability for injury  . . . . . . . . . . . . . . . . . . . . . . . . . . . .    50,000
```

Required:

Comment on Mr. Worry's instructions. Is this the generally accepted treatment for accident claims such as this?

P11.17 Equity transactions (*Certified Management Accountants of British Columbia*). Victoria Company, Ltd., is a recently incorporated provincial company. It was authorized to issue unlimited no-par common shares. The information below relates to their first year of business:

Jan. 3	Sold 5,000 common shares at $25 each.
5	Sold 10,000 common shares on a subscription basis at $25 per share. A 50 percent down payment accompanied the subscriptions.
Feb. 14	Exchanged 12,500 shares for land that had a fair market value of $350,000.
April 1	Collected the balance of the subscription price on common shares and issued them.
July 4	Declared and paid a 10 percent share dividend. Selling price for Victoria common shares on July 4 was $30 per share.
Sept. 15	Declared a two-for-one share split. The selling price of Victoria common on that day was $31 per share.
Oct. 7	Reacquired 2,000 of its own common shares at $16 per share.
Dec. 15	Declared a $.12 per share cash dividend on common shares payable January 10, next year.
20	Sold 500 of the treasury shares at $18 per share.

Required:

Record the journal entries for the transactions listed above.

P11.18 Equity transactions (*Certified Management Accountants of British Columbia*). Share dividends, share splits, and share subscriptions are used on occasion by corporations.

Required:

Explain what these three items are and what the appropriate accounting treatment is in each case.

P11.19 Financial statement disclosure. Describe how the following items would be disclosed on a properly classified financial statement:

a. Accounts receivable.

b. Convertible bonds payable.

c. Mortgage payable.

d. Patents.

P11.20 Financial statement disclosure. Describe how the following items would be disclosed on a properly classified financial statement:

a. Writeoff of obsolete inventory.

b. Premium on preferred shares.

c. Deferred income tax.

d. Partner's withdrawals.

P11.21 Dividends and Earnings per Share (*Certified Management Accountants of British Columbia*). Below is the shareholders' equity section of Quercus, Ltd., at March 31.

Common shares, non-par value, 20,000 shares authorized, 10,000 shares issued and outstanding	$120,000
Preferred shares, non-par value, $.20, cumulative and non-participating, 10,000 shares authorized, issued, and outstanding	10,000
Retained earnings (before dividends)	70,000
	$200,000

Note: There are two years' dividends in arrears on preferred shares.

Net income for the year ended March 31 of $30,000 is included in the above retained earnings. The board of directors wants to declare a $40,000 cash dividend dated March 31.

Required:

a. Determine the distribution of the dividends between preferred and common shareholders.

b. Calculate earnings per common share for the year ended March 31, 1991.

P11.22 Equity transactions (*Certified Management Accountants of British Columbia*). The shareholders' equity section at the beginning of a business year (January 1) was as follows:

Common shares non-par value, 20,000 shares issued and outstanding	$300,000
Retained earnings	300,000
	$600,000

During the year, the following transactions took place:

Feb. 1 The company bought back 10,000 of its shares in the market for $25 cash per share.

March 1 The company resold 5,000 of its treasury shares at $35 cash per share. The remaining treasury shares still belonged to the company on December 31.

July 1 The company split its shares two-for-one. (No journal entry necessary.)

Dec. 1 The company declared and distributed a 10 percent share dividend when the market price per share was $16.

Net income for the year was $70,000, and no cash dividends were declared.

Required:

Use dates for the journal entries, and show calculations by way of explanations.

a. Prepare the February 1 journal entry.

b. Prepare the March 1 journal entry.

c. Prepare the December 1 journal entry.

d. Prepare the shareholders' equity section at December 31.

e. Calculate the book value per share.

P11.23 Earnings per share. Royal Charters Canada, Inc., discloses earnings per share figures as part of the company's financial report. During the past few years the company has performed very well and has experienced an increase in earnings per share each year.

Required:

Describe the impact the following events would have on the company's earnings per share figure:

a. The company issued additional common shares during the year.

b. The company redeemed a long-term loan that had matured during the year.

c. During the year, the company introduced a new share option plan for its employees.

d. The company issued additional preferred shares during the year.

e. The company has convertible bonds outstanding.

P11.24 Equity transactions (*Certified Management Accountants of British Columbia*). John Pak and several of his friends organized the Pitman Company and it was authorized to issue 50,000 shares of non-par-value, $10 cumulative preferred shares and an unlimited number of non-par-value common shares. The following are some of the transactions that occurred over the past year.

Jan. 8   Issued for cash 20,000 common shares at $14 per share to Pak and some other investors.

     10   Issued an additional 600 shares of common shares to Pak in exchange for his services in organizing the company. The shareholders agreed that these services were valued at $8,400.

Feb. 1   Issued 2,000 preferred shares for cash of $256,000.

March 10   Acquired land for a building site in exchange for 16,000 common shares. The directors, after due consideration of all relevant factors, agreed that the common shares were to be valued, for purposes of this transaction, at $15 per share.

June 1   The first dividend of $10 per share was declared on the preferred shares, to be paid July 12.

July 12   Paid the cash dividend declared on June 1.

Dec. 31   After revenue and expenses (except income taxes) were closed to the Income Summary account, that account showed a before-tax net income of $160,000. Income taxes were calculated to be $48,000. There are no permanent or timing differences.

Required:

Prepare journal entries in the general journal to record the above transactions. Include December 31 entries to (1) record the income tax liability; (2) close the Income Tax expense account to the Income Summary account, and (3) close the Income Summary account.

P11.25 Shareholders' equity (*Certified Management Accountants of British Columbia*). The shareholders' equity of Mossbank Company at January 1st is as follows:

Shareholders' equity:

Common shares, no par value, unlimited shares authorized, 260,000 issued and outstanding	$5,365,000
Retained earnings	1,610,000
Total shareholders' equity	$6,975,000

During the year the following transactions relating to shareholders' equity occurred:

June 10   Declared a 5 percent share dividend to shareholders of record on June 30, to be distributed on July 15. At June 10 the market price was $35 per share.

July 15   Distributed the share dividend declared June 10.

Aug. 4   Purchased 5,000 treasury shares at a price of $30 per share.

Oct. 15   Reissued 3,000 treasury shares at a price of $32 per share.

Dec. 10   Reissued 1,000 treasury shares at a price of $28.50 per share.

Required:

a. Prepare journal entries in general journal form to record these transactions.

b. How many shares were outstanding at December 31?

c. How many shares were issued at December 31?

P11.26 Accounting for equity (*Published with permission of CGA Canada*). The records of Gassman Corp. reveal the following information:

Year 1

Jan.	2	Gassman Corp. was established in Halifax, N.S., with authorized capital of 10,000 shares of non-par-value, cumulative, $12.00, preferred shares and 100,000 shares of non-par-value common shares.
	3	Issued 30,000 shares of common and 3,000 shares of preferred shares at $60 and $102, respectively.
	7	The city of Halifax donated a plant site, which had a market value of $130,000.
Dec.	31	After closing all temporary accounts, the Income Summary account had a credit balance of $250,000. No dividends were declared in 1991.

Year 2

Jan.	3	Gassman Corp. declared cash dividends totalling $100,000.
	30	Cash dividends were paid.
Feb.	4	Issued 1,200 shares of common shares for machinery with a market value of $70,000.
March	31	Declared and issued a 5 percent share dividend when common shares had a market price of $78.00.
May	1	Issued 10-year 6 percent bonds with a face value of $50,000 dated May 1 at 103. Interest is paid annually on April 30.
June	2	A lawsuit has been launched against Gassman for a patent infringement. Although the lawsuit is unlikely to be successful, Gassman decided to restrict $75,000 of retained earnings for possible loss.
Dec.	31	Net income is $310,000.
	31	Any bond discount or premium was amortized.

Required:

Prepare all required journal entries. If no journal entry is required, state No journal entry required.

P11.27 Accounting for equity (*Published with permission of CGA Canada*). Natasha Designs, Ltd., was incorporated in Vancouver, B.C., in January 1993, during which the company issued 80,000 of its 500,000 authorized non-par-value common shares for $4 each. On January 10, 1994, Natasha received authorization and issued 20,000 shares of 10 percent $20 par, cumulative preferred shares at $40 each. On February 5, 1995, Natasha issued 10,000 shares of $3, non-par cumulative preferred shares for $420,000. The company was authorized to issue 70,000 of this class of shares. Natasha incurred a net loss in 1993 of $130,000. In 1994, Natasha again incurred a loss. This time, however, it was reduced to $20,000. In 1995 the company prospered and its net income reached $300,000 and by 1996 net income had actually reached $500,000. The company paid cash dividends in 1995 of $.60 per common share, and on December 22, 1996, it paid common shareholders $1.20 per share. In September of 1996, the city of Vancouver donated land valued at $200,000 to the company. On December 10, 1996, Natasha acquired 8,000 of its own common shares at a total cost of $40,000.

Required:

a. Calculate the balance in the Retained Earnings account as at December 31, 1996.

b. Prepare the shareholders' equity section of the December 31, 1996, balance sheet.

P11.28 Accounting for equity (*Published with permission of CGA Canada*).

a. On September 21, Export Corporation accepted subscriptions to 10,000 shares of its non-par-value common shares at $20 per share. The subscription contracts called for one-quarter of the subscription price to accompany each contract as a down payment and the balance to be paid October 31.

Required:

Prepare general journal entries for:

(1) The subscriptions with the down payment.

(2) Receipt of amounts due on the subscriptions.

(3) Issuance of the shares.

b. Superior Company, Limited, has outstanding 1,000 shares of $8, cumulative non-participating preferred shares and 20,000 shares of non-par-value common shares. During the first two years of its life, the corporation paid out the following amounts in dividends:

Year 1 $0
Year 2 $20,000

Required:

Determine the total dividends paid to each class of shareholders each year.

P11.29 Accounting for equity (*Published with permission of CGA Canada*). Comparative shareholders' equity for the past two years is shown below for Curtis, Limited. Additional common shares were issued in 1996 as a result of the exercise of convertible preferred shares. In addition to the preferred share conversion, common shares were issued for $100,000.

	1996	**1995**
6% preferred shares, $10 par	$ 150,000	$ 200,000
Common shares, non-par	1,190,000	1,000,000
Contributed surplus	60,000	100,000
Retained earnings	2,000,000	1,500,000
Total shareholders' equity	$3,400,000	$2,800,000

Each preferred share was convertible to three common shares. Curtis, Limited, reported a net income of $650,000 for the fiscal year ending December 31, 1996, amounting to $2.00 for each common share outstanding.

Required:

a. How many common shares were outstanding throughout 1996?

b. What was the average issue price for the preferred shares outstanding at the end of 1996?

c. How many preferred shares were actually converted into common shares in 1996?

d. What journal entry was made to record the preferred share conversion?

P11.30 Financial statement disclosure and long-term debt-to-invested capital ratio. Describe how the following items would be disclosed on the financial statements and the impact each would have on the long-term debt-to-invested capital ratio:

a. During the year the company sold common share warrants.

b. The company issued convertible bonds during the year.

c. The company acquired a mortgage during the year.

d. The company issued additional preferred shares during the year.

e. The company acquired treasury shares.

P11.31 Accounting for equity (*Published with permission of CGA Canada*). Primrose Company was organized on January 2. It was authorized to issue 300,000, $10 par value common shares and 150,000 shares of $1.50 non-par-value cumulative preferred. During the year, 100,000 common and 50,000 preferred shares were issued but no dividends were declared. The following account balances were extracted from the company's December 31 year-end financial statements:

Common shares	$1,000,000
Contributed surplus	70,000
Discount on bonds issued	5,000
Investment in Purvis Company	15,000
Organization costs	7,000
Preferred shares	200,000
Retained earnings	175,000

Required:

a. **(1)** On the basis of the above information, prepare a statement of shareholders' equity.

   (2) What was the net income?

   (3) Was Primrose incorporated federally or provincially? Explain.

b. Prepare journal entries relating to the following transactions that occurred during the second year:

   (1) On January 2, the company issued 20,000 preferred shares in exchange for land acquired from Paradise Company. This land was carried on the books of Paradise Company at $80,000. The appraised value of the land was $105,000, but the president of Primrose feels that it is worth at least $120,000.

   (2) On February 3, Primrose issued 50,000 common shares at $13.00 per share.

   (3) On November 30, a 5 percent common shares dividend was declared and distributed. On this date, the market price of the common shares was $16 per share.

   (4) Cash dividends for the year were declared on December 30. For the common shareholders, this amounted to $.80 per share.

   (5) Net income for the year amounted to $550,000.

c. Prepare a statement of retained earnings to reflect the information contained in part *a* and part *b*.

P11.32 Accounting for equity (*Published with permission of CGA Canada*). Parker Co. was legally incorporated on January 2, 1990. Its articles of incorporation granted it the right to issue an unlimited number of common shares at no par and 100,000 shares of $4, non-par, cumulative preferred shares. Several key transactions that occurred during the first three years of operations are presented below.

Year 1

Feb. 15   Issued 30,000 common shares at $2 each.

20   Issued 5,000 common shares to promoters who provided legal services that got the company up and running. These services had a fair value of $15,000.

28   Issued 80,000 common shares in exchange for land, building, and equipment, which have fair market values of $100,000, $160,000, and $20,000 respectively.

Apr. 3   Purchased a minicomputer at a cost of $1,400. This was a special bargain price. It was felt that this computer would normally be sold for at least $2,000.

Dec. 31   Parker Co. incurred a net loss of $30,000. Closed the Income Summary account.

Year 2

Jan. 3   Issued 5,000 preferred shares at $35 per share.

Nov. 16   Reacquired 10,000 previously issued common shares at $5 per share. These shares were immediately cancelled upon purchase.

Dec. 31   The Income Summary account was closed. Net income was $130,000.

Year 3

Dec. 20   Declared a 10 percent share dividend to be issued on January 3, 1993. Parker Co. common shares had a market value of $6 per share on this date.

28   The company declared a cash dividend of $.09 on each of the common shares payable on January 17, 1993.

31   Net income for the year was $80,000.

Required:

a. Journalize the above transactions.

b. Prepare the shareholders' equity section as of December 31, Year 3.

P11.33 Accounting for equity and ratio analysis. Empress Ltd. is authorized to issue 100,000 non-par-value common shares, and 50,000, $.70, preferred shares of non-par value. The following transactions occurred during the first year of operations:

1. Issued 10,000 common shares at $12 per share cash.

2. Issued 5,000 common shares in exchange for equipment. The directors placed a $60,000 value on the equipment.

3. Issued 5,000 preferred shares at $11 per share cash.

4. Declared the annual dividend on preferred shares.

5. Declared a $.20 per share cash dividend on common shares.

6. Closed the Income Summary account. Net income for the year was $44,000.

7. Paid the dividends previously declared.

Required:

a. Prepare general journal entries for the above transactions.

b. Prepare a statement of shareholders' equity, in good format.

c. Determine the return on equity and the basic earnings per share.

P11.34 Ratio analysis. The shareholders' equity of Christensen Corporation at December 31 is as follows:

Statement of Shareholders' Equity
December 31

Common shares, authorized 10,000 shares, issued 5,000 shares		$50,000
Retained earnings, January 1	$25,000	
Net income for the year	20,000	
Less: common dividends	(3,000)	
Retained earnings, December 31		42,000
Total shareholders' equity		$92,000

Required:

a. Determine the return on equity and the basic earnings per share.

b. If $40,000 of 10 percent preferred shares had been issued at the beginning of the year, determine the return on equity and the basic earnings per share.

c. If $40,000 of 10 percent bonds had been issued at the beginning of the year, determine the return on equity and the basic earnings per share. Assume a 50 percent income tax rate.

P11.35 Financial statement disclosure and return on equity. Describe how the following items would be disclosed on the financial statements and the impact each would have the company's return on equity:

a. The company issued convertible bonds during the year.

b. The company redeemed a long-term loan that had matured during the year.

c. The company purchased capital assets during the year.

d. The company issued additional preferred shares during the year.

P11.36 Financial statement disclosure and fully diluted earnings per share. Describe how the following items would be disclosed on the financial statements and the impact each would have on the fully diluted earnings per share ratio:

a. During the year, the company sold additional common shares.

b. The company issued convertible bonds during the year.

c. During the year, the company introduced a new share option plan for its employees.

d. The company issued additional preferred shares during the year.

e. The company declared preferred dividends during the year.

11.15 CASE

C11.1 Trading shares with another corporation: Candu Mining Corporation.
Candu Mining Corporation (CMC) owned the mineral rights to a silver claim. The mine itself had been inactive for some time, although the rights had been bought and sold several times in the last five years. CMC had purchased the rights most recently from a group of lawyers, paying $50,000 in cash and giving two notes totalling $250,000. One note, for $100,000, bore interest at 10 percent and was due in 12 months; the other, for $150,000, carried a 5 percent interest rate and was due in five years.

Immediately on taking possession of the claim, CMC regraded the access roads and cleared the accumulated debris from the property. It hired a maintenance worker who began to pump water from the mine so that it could be worked. He brought out a few samples and had them processed and evaluated by an independent laboratory; the results showed that the samples contained good quality ore, although in small traces. The company also sent out a photographic team who took pictures of the activity, and the president managed to get a newspaper to run a story on CMC's plans for reactivating the mine. The company spent about $15,000 on this start-up activity.

Latenight Entertainment, Inc., had once been a high-flying record and video producer, but its stars had fallen out of favour and the company was now inactive. In its glory days, its shares had an active following and had once traded as high as $12. There was no trading now, although there were still 150,000 shares outstanding, and there was a shareholder list with 350 names.

CMC purchased the shareholder list from a company called Corporate Brokers, Inc., and sent the Latenight shareholders a proposal whereby CMC would exchange its mining claim in exchange for 850,000 shares of Latenight. It also proposed that the name Latenight Entertainment, Inc., be changed to Candu Mining Corporation. In the offering document sent to the Latenight shareholders, CMC stated that the mine had the potential to produce $3,000,000 worth of silver in the next five years. On that basis, the offering document stated that the property was worth at least $1,000,000 and that the value of the Latenight shares would be worth $1 after the exchange was consummated. The exchange was approved by a majority of Latenight shareholders, and the transaction was completed as planned.

Required:

a. What accounting would be appropriate for all of the above acquisitions and exchanges in the affected companies' accounts? Please explain your proposed accounting.

b. Why would CMC want to enter into this exchange? What would you expect the next step in its plan to be? How might your accounting in part *a* help or frustrate that plan?

PART IV

Understanding Financial Reports

Analyzing and Interpreting Financial Statements

──────── **Objectives** ────────

After completing this chapter, you will be able to:
1. Describe complex statements of changes in financial position.
2. Describe the impact of alternative accounting policies on financial statements.
3. Complete detailed financial statement analysis.

In the previous 11 chapters, we focused on developing an understanding of the principal elements of financial statements. We have considered what each account means individually and, in the aggregate, and what the financial statements portray about a given organization. This last chapter is the capstone to your course in financial accounting. This chapter examines three important areas: the statement of changes in financial position, the impact of accounting policy alternatives, and financial statement analysis and interpretation.

We first return to the topic of evaluating an organization's cash flows. The statement of changes in financial position, examined earlier in Chapters 2 and 3, is revisited, with the added complexities from recent chapters. Attention then is turned to the alternative GAAP and how they impact the financial statements and ratio analysis. Finally, we attempt to broaden your understanding of accounting information and its uses by considering a number of topics in the analysis of financial statements. A comprehensive illustration is presented for review purposes at the end of the chapter.

12.1 CASH FLOW ANALYSIS

Cash flow analysis is one of the most important elements of financial statement analysis. Not only are the reported cash flows not affected by the GAAP methods used to portray accrual net income, but cash is also the only asset without which an organization cannot operate. Organizations presenting audited financial reports are required to present a statement of changes in financial position. The focus here is the analysis of those reported cash inflows and outflows.

The Importance of Cash Flows

Cash flows represent the most fundamental and prevalent economic events engaged in by businesses. In fact, talk to just about any small business owner, entrepreneur, banker, or chief financial officer and he or she will tell you that the "bottom line" of the income statement has little to do with staying solvent. It is cash planning — specifically, understanding the sources and uses of current and future cash flows — that often makes the difference between success and failure.

Organizations that manage cash effectively benefit in numerous ways. For example, they benefit by having lower financing costs. By accurately forecasting the amount and timing of cash flows, managers minimize their need to borrow, thus lessening their company's interest expense. In addition, improving the amount of cash generated from operations decreases the need to solicit external financing, thus preserving proportionate shareholder value and unused debt capacity.

Cash is also important to external users of financial statements. Shareholder and creditor interests are seldom settled by means other than cash. Therefore, cash flow information is very useful in enabling these users to assess a company's ability to (1) generate future positive cash flows from operations, (2) meet its maturing obligations, and (3) pay dividends.

Concerning this point, accrual accounting often masks a company's underlying cash flows. Under the accrual basis of accounting, revenues are recognized at the time of sale, not when cash is received. Thus, credit sales increase net income but not current cash inflows. The accrual basis of preparing an income statement also reports such non-cash expenses as amortization, and accrued warranty estimates, which reduce net income and further widen the gap between it and cash flows. From a balance sheet perspective, when an organization enters into a loan agreement, the loan is reflected as an increase in Loans Payable. As the loan is repaid, cash outflows increase and the Loans Payable balance decreases. At no time, however, does any record of the cash outflow for the loan repayment appear in the income statement; only the interest expense appears there. For reasons such as this, a business can easily find itself with an income statement that portrays an attractive net income number, but without sufficient cash for tomorrow's tax bill, payroll, dividend, or loan payment. To ensure that such payments can be made, and that operations continue in an orderly manner, managers must manage both the timing and amount of cash flows.

Statement of Changes in Financial Position

For many years, the principal focus of all financial statement users — creditors, investors, and managers alike — was the accrual-based financial statements, namely the balance sheet and the income statement. These two statements were thought to be not only necessary but also *sufficient* to present a *complete* picture of the financial condition and operations of a company. In recent years, however, financial statement user preference has shifted from a purely accrual-based information orientation to one that includes *both* accrual and cash flow information. In recognition of these changing consumer preferences, a cash flow statement or a statement of changes in financial position (SCFP) is required in all published financial statements. The purpose of this section is to expand on the material presented in Chapters 2 and 3 on the statement of changes in financial position. This section will reinforce and expand your understanding of the information conveyed by the statement of changes and you will learn how the statement is prepared and how it can be used and analyzed.

The primary objective of the statement of changes in financial position (SCFP) is to explain the change in cash and cash equivalents occurring during a given reporting period. This relationship is portrayed in Exhibit 12.1.

For purposes of the SCFP, cash includes currency on hand and demand deposits and cash equivalents, which are short-term, liquid investments that are both readily convertible to cash and so close to maturity as to be essentially risk-free. Companies must disclose which items are considered to be cash equivalents in their financial statements. Securities of terms longer than three months are not considered to be cash equivalents.

The SCFP should clearly classify cash flows into three principal areas of activity: operating, investing, and financing. Investing activities primarily affect the non-current asset accounts and include such transactions as buying and selling capital assets and other long-lived productive assets. Cash flows from financing activities are the results of transactions generally affecting the non-current liability and shareholders' equity accounts and include such transactions as obtaining resources from owners and providing them a return on and a return of their investment and borrowing and repaying amounts borrowed. Finally, **operating activities** primarily affect the income statement and working capital accounts — in essence, the cash flows from sales of goods or services and cash payments for acquisition of the inputs used to provide the goods or services sold.

operating activities
The day-to-day functions of the organizations, of earning revenues and incurring expenses.

Operating activities. In regard to the operating activities section of the SCFP, two preparation methods may be used: the direct method and the indirect method (see Exhibit 12.2). The direct method presents major classes of cash receipts and payments. The direct method involves reporting, at a minimum, the cash flows from operating

E X H I B I T   1 2 . 1

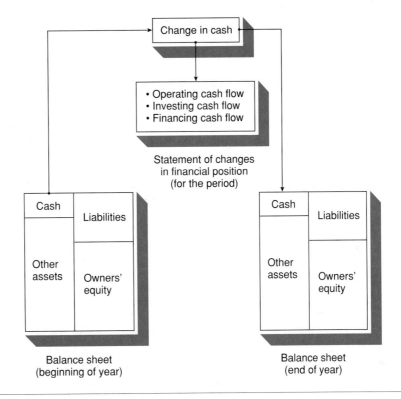

The Relationship between the Statement of Changes in
Financial Position and Consecutive Balance Sheets

activities as the difference between the receipts and payments pertaining to the following separately reported items:

Cash collected from clients and customers.

Dividends and interest received.

Other receipts of operating cash, if any, such as insurance settlements and refunds from suppliers.

Cash payments for wages and other goods and services received.

Interest paid.

Taxes paid.

Other operating cash payments, if any, such as charitable contributions.

Refunds to customers.

The direct method was illustrated for Ted's Trucking in Section 3.3 of Chapter 3. The direct method is not commonly used; the indirect method produces the format most frequently used for financial statement disclosure.

The distinctive feature of the indirect method of presenting the SCFP is that it reconciles a company's accrual net income with its cash flows from operations. Beginning with net income (see Exhibit 12.2), the reconciliation process converts net income to its cash-basis equivalent by (1) adding back the non-cash expenses (e.g., deferred

The Statement of Changes in Financial Position:
The Direct versus the Indirect Method

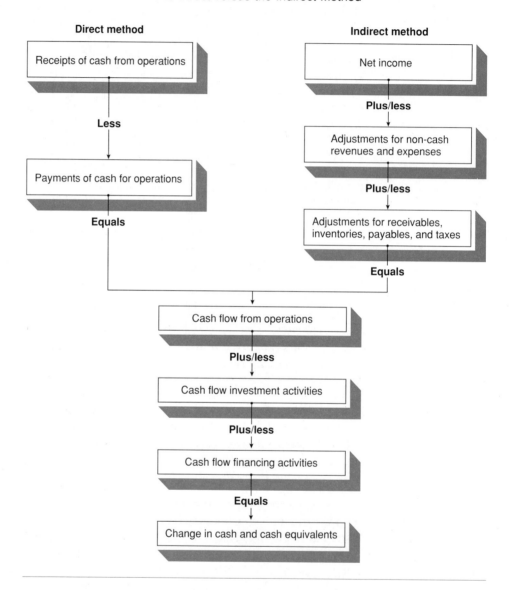

income taxes, amortization expense) deducted that period in deriving net income and subtracting the non-cash revenues (e.g., undistributed earnings of affiliates) included in the period's net income, and (2) subtracting any gains and adding back any losses incurred on various transactions (e.g., the sale of a non-current asset or the early retirement of long-term debt) that will be reported in the investing and financing sections of the SCFP. The first type of adjustment is designed to eliminate any non-cash items that are included in net income under the accrual basis of accounting, whereas the second type of adjustment is designed to avoid the double counting of certain cash flows. For example, if a long-term investment recorded on the books at $100,000 is sold for $120,000, the entire cash inflow of $120,000 should be reported on the SCFP as an investing activity. To avoid *double counting* the $20,000 cash inflow representing the gain on the sale, the $20,000 gain included in accrual net income is subtracted from net income in deriving cash flow from operations in the SCFP.

To complete the conversion of the accrual net income figure to the cash flows from operations figure under the indirect method, a final set of adjustments involving the operations-related current asset and current liability accounts is needed. Consider, for example, the fact that the sales figure in Maple Leaf Garden's income statement (most of which represents credit sales) is equal to this period's cash inflows from sales activities only if the year-end Accounts Receivable balance remains unchanged as compared to the Receivable balance at the beginning of the period. If, during the year, an organization collected less than it billed its customers for credit sales, thereby creating an increase in the ending Accounts Receivable balance, the net income figure in the SCFP needs to be reduced by the increase in receivables in order to approximate the period's true cash inflows from sales. Finally, a reduction in the ending Receivable balance as compared to the beginning balance indicates that more cash had been collected than is reflected in the current period's sales figure. Thus, the amount of the reduction in the Receivable balance should be added to the net income figure on the SCFP in order to reflect this higher cash inflow.

This final set of adjustments needed to derive the cash flow from operations may involve *more* accounts than Accounts Receivable. Consider for example, the case of inventory. Every period, service businesses accumulate billable time, merchandisers make new purchases, and manufacturers produce additional items. If reported inventory amounts have increased beyond the beginning-of-period balance (i.e., purchases have exceeded sales of inventory), an increased outflow of cash has occurred. Thus, the net increase in inventory must be subtracted from the accrual-based net income to reflect accurately the total cash spent or invested in inventory. On the other hand, if the reported ending inventory amounts have declined relative to their beginning balances, the net decline represents a part of the cost of goods sold that is deducted in the income statement but for which no cash was expended *this* period. This means that the amount of the net decline must be added back to the accrual-based net income number to accurately reflect the actual cash outflows for inventory.

Similar analyses apply to Accounts Payable and to the Accrued Expenses Payable that are a function of purchasing materials, supplies, and labour used in conducting a firm's operations. For example, an increase in Accrued Expenses Payable (e.g., Accrued Wages Payable) in effect represents a form of cash inflow because the business has not yet expended cash for some of the expenses currently deducted in the income statement. Alternatively, a decrease in Accrued Expenses Payable in effect signifies an additional cash outflow for expenses booked on the current and/or prior income statement, thus necessitating a reduction in the cash-based net income estimate on the SCFP in order to bring it into line with this period's actual cash outflows for expensed items. In this regard, Exhibit 12.3 depicts Maple Leaf Garden's adjustment of $(5,131,485) to reduce accrual net income in 1994 for a net increase in working capital items in deriving cash flow from operations, whereas in 1993 just the opposite is shown.

The statement of changes in financial position of Maple Leaf Gardens indicated operating activities provided cash of $2,776,219. The operating activities section is the most complex section of the statement, and requires additional explanation. To determine the cash provided or used in operations requires converting from the accrual basis of accounting to the cash basis. It is therefore necessary to back out or reverse any accrual or non-cash transactions. The cash from operations is most commonly comprised of three elements: net income (accrual basis), operating items not involving cash (amortization), and accrual items affecting current assets and current liabilities (working capital). These three elements are summarized below, using the figures for Maple Leaf Gardens, Limited.

Operating Activities:

Net income (loss)	$6,211,265
±Items not involving cash	1,696,439
±Change in working capital items	(5,131,485)
Cash provided (used) in operations	$2,776,219

It is important to understand fully these current asset and current liability adjustments. One way to facilitate one's understanding of the need for these adjustments is to focus on the more intuitively obvious accounts such as Accounts Receivable and Accrued Wages Payable. Once you become familiar with how the adjustments to these accounts relate to the SCFP, the remaining working capital accounts can be viewed as extensions of the same logic but applied to different balance sheet accounts. Another means to achieve a greater level of understanding of these adjustments is actually to prepare an SCFP — an opportunity that is presented in a subsequent section of this chapter.

Cash flows from operations is arguably the most important cash flow indicator for users of financial statements because it demonstrates the ability of a company's operations to generate cash for its shareholders, creditors, or future investment. It informs the financial statement reader whether the business is a net provider or a net user of cash in its core internal operations. If the operations of a business use more cash than they provide, cash must then be provided by liquidating investments, seeking further external financing, or decreasing the company's reserves of cash and cash equivalents. If, on the other hand, the operating activities provide cash, such as in the case for Maple Leaf Gardens, this additional cash will be available to invest in the business, to repay prior financing, to pay dividends, or merely to increase the cash reserves of the company. In 1994, Maple Leaf Garden's continuing operations generated $2.7 million in cash flows, which was available to finance a variety of firm-related activities.

An analysis of the comparative balance sheets of Maple Leaf Gardens, Limited, provides information on cash and equivalent balances at the end of the fiscal year. A comparison of 1994 with 1993 indicates an approximate decease in cash of $1.9 million. This may or may not be significant. But, most users of financial reports would desire more information about the cash position of the company. This is the purpose of the statement of changes in financial position. The statement of changes in financial position of Maple Leaf Gardens, Limited, discloses information on cash provided and used for operating, financing, and investing activities. Operating activities provided cash of $2,776,219. Investment activities required the use of $3,412,108 cash, including $1,716,489 for the purchase of fixed assets. Financing activities used $1,261,942 cash during the period, including cash of $2,942,330 to pay dividends. The analysis of the statement of changes in financial position provides insight into an organization's cash activities during a given period. This analysis may be completed in conjunction with a financial strength ratio analysis.

investing activities
Investing is the activity of acquiring long-lived, noncurrent assets such as property, plant, and equipment.

Investing activities. The next section of the SCFP, as shown in Maple Leaf Garden's SCFP (Exhibit 12.3), reports cash flows from **investing activities**. This section details the amounts an organization has invested in its own business, equity investments in other firms, and dispositions and purchases of other assets. From Exhibit 12.3, we can see that in 1994 Maple Leaf Gardens invested more than $1.7 million in fixed assets; and more than $1.6 million in deferred charges. Overall in 1994, Maple Leaf Garden's investing activities involved net cash outflows of $3.4 million.

EXHIBIT 12.3

MAPLE LEAF GARDENS, LIMITED
Statement of Changes in Financial Position
For the Year Ending December 31

	1994	1993
Operating Activities:		
Net income	$ 6,211,265	$ 5,253,099
Items not involving cash (depreciation)	1,696,439	1,937,663
Change in working capital items	(5,131,485)	4,366,915
Cash provided by operations	$ 2,776,219	$11,557,677
Investing Activities:		
Purchase of fixed assets	$(1,716,489)	$ (1,483,428)
Increase in deferred charges	(1,695,619)	(1,202,178)
Cash used in investing	$(3,412,108)	$ (2,685,606)
Financing Activities:		
Increase in deferred compensation	$ 1,697,278	$ 1,534,508
Dividends	(2,942,320)	(2,942,320)
Redemption of share capital	(16,900)	—
Cash used in financing	$(1,261,942)	$ (1,407,812)
Increase (Decrease) in Cash	$(1,897,831)	$ 7,464,259
Cash — January 1	12,086,374	4,622,115
Cash — December 31	$10,188,543	$12,086,374

financing activities
Financing is the activity of funding the organization by issuing long-term debt or other noncurrent liabilities or equity funding received from the owners of the organization.

Financing activities. The final section of an SCFP is the cash flow from **financing activities**. This section details the changes in the capital structure of a company and payments made to provide a return to investors on (and of) their investments in the firm. If cash flows from operations are positive, the company may wish to reduce its debt load, pay dividends, or buy back some of its outstanding shares. These choices must be considered in light of the firm's capital expenditure needs. If, on the other hand, the cash flows from operations are negative, or if they are positive but investing activities used more cash than operations provided, a firm might want to reconsider paying cash dividends; it could be argued that paying dividends under these circumstances involves a partial liquidation of the firm. The SCFP for Maple Leaf Gardens, Limited, indicates an increase in cash from the financing activity related to deferred compensation of nearly $1.7 million. Financing activities using cash include $2.9 million for dividends and $16,900 for the redemption of share capital. Overall in 1994, Maple Leaf Garden's financing activities involved net cash outflows of over $1.2 million.

Non-cash investing and financing activities. Organizations often engage in non-cash investing and financing activities. For example, the conversion of debt into shareholders' equity does not involve any cash inflows or outflows, nor does the acquisition of equipment financed entirely by the seller. To provide the users of financial statements with all relevant information, such non-cash activities should be disclosed as *both* financing and investing activities, even though cash has not been directly exchanged.

In summary, Exhibit 12.3 presents a statement of changes in financial position for Maple Leaf Gardens, Limited, for 1993 and 1994. As the exhibit reveals, Maple Leaf Garden's cash and cash equivalents decreased by nearly $1.9 million during 1994. Operating activities provided $2.7 million in cash inflows, financing activities consumed $1.2 million, and investing activities consumed $3.4 million in cash.

Preparing a Statement of Changes in Financial Position

With the preceding discussion in mind, the best way to gain a full understanding of the SCFP is to prepare one. The following example is designed to illustrate the preparation of the SCFP, using the indirect method, produced from the comparative financial statements of the Oakville Cabinet Company.

	1996	1995
Cash	$ 70,000	$ 48,000
Accounts receivable	80,000	71,000
Merchandise inventory	283,000	306,000
Prepaid insurance	21,000	22,000
Capital assets*	186,300	144,800
Accumulated amortization	(72,300)	(62,000)
	$568,000	$529,800
Accounts payable	$ 79,000	$ 75,000
Accrued liabilities	10,000	8,000
Deferred taxes liability	4,000	5,000
Bonds payable	75,000	55,000
Common shares	316,000	300,000
Retained earnings	84,000	86,800
	$568,000	$529,800
Sales	$670,000	
Cost of goods sold	360,000	
Gross profit	$310,000	
Amortization expense	22,000	
Operating expenses	253,000	
Income tax expense	17,000	
Loss — sale of equipment	1,500	
Net income	$ 16,500	

*During 1996 Oakville acquired capital assets for $60,000.

As noted earlier, the starting point for preparing an SCFP using the indirect method is the accrual net income for the period. From such a starting point, the net income number must be adjusted for the non-cash revenues and expenses that are present in the income statement — primarily amortization, deferred taxes, and the undistributed earnings of affiliate companies. The 1996 Oakville income statement reveals, for example, that $22,000 was deducted as amortization expense. Because amortization of capital assets requires no cash outlay, the $22,000 must be added back to net income in deriving an estimate of the cash flows from operations. Oakville's income statement reveals no other non-cash revenues or expenses with the exception of deferred income taxes. The balance sheet indicates there was an decrease in the Deferred Taxes Liability account of $1,000. The overall effect of this change represents an additional cash outlay this period for income taxes owed from an earlier accounting period; that is, the tax expense for this additional amount was recorded in an earlier accounting period but was not paid until this period. Thus, the decrease in deferred taxes liabilities represents a decrease in operating cash flows this period that was not revealed in the income statement where only $17,000 was deducted as income tax expense. This decrease in a liability should, therefore, be subtracted from net income in the operating activities section.

As pointed out earlier, the objective of the SCFP is to explain the change in cash and cash equivalents by reporting all of the changes in the non-cash accounts. In a sense, this is like trying to define a word without using the word in the definition. In effect, the

SCFP provides a definition of the change in cash by examining all of the other balance sheet account changes. Thus, the next step in our efforts to develop Oakville's SCFP is to focus on the adjustments to net income associated with changes in the current asset and current liability operations-related accounts.

From the balance sheet data, note that Accounts Receivable increased $9,000 from 1995 to 1996. This means that the company billed its customers for more than it collected from them, which represents sales for which collections have not yet been received. The amount is thus shown as a reduction to net income in the pursuit of converting an accrual-based net income amount to an operating cash flow estimate. With similar logic, the balance sheet data also reveal that Accounts Payable increased, indicating that the company was billed for more expenses than it paid; hence, this amount is like a provision of cash and is therefore shown as a positive cash flow. Similar adjustments must be made for *all* the working capital items including merchandise inventory and prepaid insurance. The sum of these items (i.e., net income plus/minus the non-cash revenues and expenses plus/minus the changes in working capital accounts) equals the cash flow from operating activities of $60,000.

The investment section of the SCFP shows changes in the balance sheet for investments in capital assets. The accounting for changes in capital assets is one of the most complex calculations required to complete the SCFP. When determining the investing activities for the period, the Capital Assets account *and* the contra account for accumulated amortization should be analyzed as a *single* account. The accounting for capital assets involves three basic activities: acquisitions, disposals, and amortization for the period. The information provided indicates amortization for the year was $22,000 and acquisitions were for $60,000. The balancing adjustments to the Capital Assets account and Accumulated Amortization account *must* therefore relate to the third activity, a capital asset *disposal*. This is also confirmed on the income statement, where a loss on disposal of $1,500 is disclosed. Note that the balance sheet data indicate that capital assets increased by $41,500, which includes the $60,000 acquisition. The change in the Accumulated Amortization account of $10,300 includes this period's amortization expense of $22,000, which has already been placed as an adjusting item in the operating section of Oakville's SCFP.

It is often helpful to construct a T-account for the Capital Assets and Accumulated Amortization accounts to facilitate these calculations. For this example, the T-accounts are shown below:

Capital Assets		Accumulated Amortization	
144,800			62,000
Acquisition 60,000		Amortization expense	22,000
	18,500*	11,700*	
186,300			72,300

*The cost of asset disposed must equal $18,500 to prove the ending balance of $186,300 in the asset account. Similarly, the accumulated amortization on the disposed asset must have been $11,700 to prove the ending balance in the contra account. These amounts when combined with the $1,500 loss on disposal provide $5,300 cash from investing activities.

The entry to record the disposal would have been as follows:

```
Dr. Cash ......................................... 5,300
Dr. Accumulated Amortization ........................... 11,700
Dr. Loss on Disposal ................................. 1,500
     Cr. Capital Assets ...................................    18,500
     To record the disposal of capital assets.
```

Under this scenario, the SCFP would report $1,500 added back to net income in the operations section and a line item of $5,300 for "proceeds on disposal on capital assets" in the investing section. As well, another line item of $60,000 for purchases of capital asset would be disclosed.

The final section of the SCFP, financing activities, shows the net changes in cash flows in long-term liabilities and shareholders' equity items, such as payments and proceeds from loans, share sales and share repurchases, dividends paid to shareholders, and other financing transactions. Cash was provided from two financing activities, issuing common shares for $16,000 and an additional bond issue of $20,000. Cash dividends paid to shareholders of $19,300 represent a use of cash and thus are shown as a negative cash flow.

As a vehicle to determine the dividends for the period and to verify that the entire change in the Retained Earnings balance has been accounted for in the SCFP, it is useful to reconstruct the changes in this account balance using a T-account. In the Retained Earnings T-account portrayed below, note that the net income and dividend figures, both of which now appear in the SCFP, fully explain the change in Oakville's Retained Earnings account for the period:

Retained Earnings

			86,800
Dividend	19,300	Net income	16,500
			84,000

T-accounts have been used to facilitate the analysis of the Retained Earnings and Capital Assets accounts. As previously mentioned, the analysis of the change in cash actually involves an analysis of all the non-cash accounts to determine the change in cash for the period. Therefore, a worksheet format or T-accounts for *every* balance sheet account *could be* established and the changes in each non-cash account determined. This process, although reliable, is very time consuming, and in most cases not necessary. However, to facilitate the preparation of the SCFP, most students find it beneficial to prepare a T-account for the changes in cash. The T-account for Cash should be set up with the beginning and ending cash balances and three sections to record the operating, investing, and financing activities for the period:

Cash

48,000	
Operating Activities	
Investing Activities	
Financing Activities	
70,000	

Once the T-account for Cash has been set up, the next step is to analyze the changes in the *non-cash* accounts and determine the impact each change has on cash. A T-account for Cash for the Oakville SCFP is shown below:

Cash

Beginning	48,000		

Operating Activities

Net income	16,500	Accounts receivable	9,000
Amortization	22,000	Deferred taxes	1,000
Loss on capital asset	1,500		
Inventory	23,000		
Prepaid insurance	1,000		
Accounts payable	4,000		
Accrued liabilities	2,000		
	60,000		

Investing Activities

Disposal of capital asset	5,300	Purchase of capital assets	60,000
			54,700

Financing Activities

Issued common shares	16,000	Dividends	19,300
Issued bonds	20,000		
	16,700		
Ending	70,000		

The format for reporting these results is shown in Exhibit 12.4. The sum of the three separate sections represents the increase (or decrease) in cash and cash equivalents for the period. When added to the beginning balance of cash and cash equivalents, the resulting sum should equal the ending cash and cash-equivalent balance on the latest balance sheet. If all of the balance sheet changes reflected have been included in the SCFP, it should balance to the actual change in the cash and cash-equivalent balance at the end of the period ($70,000 for Oakville), and the SCFP is then complete. The comprehensive problem in Section 12.4 provides an additional illustration of the statement of changes in financial position.

12.2 ALTERNATIVE ACCOUNTING POLICIES

Accounting Policies

Generally accepted accounting principles require organizations to disclose all significant accounting policies as part of their financial reports. As disclosed by Maple Leaf Gardens, Limited (see Chapter 1), the first footnote to the financial statements is "Significant Accounting Policies." The Maple Leaf Gardens note includes comments on its accounting for segmented reporting, fixed assets, deferred charges, foreign exchange, franchises, income taxes, and deferred income and revenue. Most organizations include such a footnote, and, as has been illustrated throughout this text, several

EXHIBIT 12.4

OAKVILLE CABINET COMPANY
Statement of Changes in Financial Position
For the Year Ending December 31, 1996

Operating Activities:		
Net income	$16,500	
Items not involving cash		
Amortization	22,000	
Deferred taxes	(1,000)	
Loss on disposal-capital asset	1,500	
Change in working capital items:		
Accounts payable	4,000	
Accounts receivable	(9,000)	
Inventory	23,000	
Accrued liabilities	2,000	
Prepaid insurance	1,000	$60,000
Investing activities:		
Disposal of capital asset	$ 5,300	
Purchase of capital assets	(60,000)	(54,700)
Financing Activities:		
Bonds issued	$20,000	
Common shares issued	16,000	
Dividends paid	(19,300)	16,700
Increase in cash:		$22,000
Cash — January 1, 1996		48,000
Cash — December 31, 1996		$70,000

additional notes explaining their accounting policies and methods. GAAP require the disclosure of accounting policies peculiar to the industry or in which acceptable alternatives exist to be disclosed. As we have seen over the previous 11 chapters, a number of different accounting policies and procedures exist. Some accounting policies require adherence to strict guidelines. GAAP provide a set of criteria to distinguish between capital and operating leases. On the other hand, organizations have far more freedom in the selection of their amortization and inventory costing methods. Exhibit 12.5 provides a summary of many of the accounting topics presented in previous chapters. This list should not by any means be considered to be all inclusive, but merely a list of important accounting policies discussed throughout the first 11 chapters.

As has been repeatedly noted throughout this text, the reporting of earnings and financial position of a company involves considerable latitude in selecting from the array of generally accepted accounting principles, and in the inevitable need for management to make numerous valuation estimates and judgments. Given the flexibility available to management in the presentation of financial results, the very human desire to portray their companies in the best light possible, and their awareness of users' concerns about the quality of reported earnings and financial position, it is important to consider the subtle and not-so-subtle items that external users should look for in financial reports as they perform their evaluations of a company.

Consider, for example, the revenue recognition method decision that managers of construction companies must make. Under GAAP, the revenues of such companies may be presented using either the completed-contract method or the percentage-of-completion method. "In the case of rendering of services and long-term contracts, performance should be determined using either the percentage of completion method or the completed contract method, whichever relates the revenue to the work accom-

EXHIBIT 12.5

Summary of Accounting Topics and Policies

Topics	Accounting Policies
Accounts receivable	Aging method
	Percentage-of-sales method
Promotion costs	Defer and amortize
	100% period expense
Inventory purchases	Specific identification method
	LIFO method
	FIFO method
	Average cost method
	Weighted-average cost method
Inventory costs	Period cost
	Product cost
Capital assets	Straight-line method
	Declining-balance methods
	Physical-units methods
	Sum-of-the-years'-digits method
Natural resources	Full cost method
	Successful efforts method
Long-term investments	Cost method
	Equity method
	Consolidation
Long-term liabilities	Straight-line method
	Effective interest method
Revenue recognition	Completed-contract method
	Percentage-of-completion method
	Completion of production method
	Point-of-sale method
	Instalment sales method
	Cost-recovery method
Leases	Operating lease
	Capital lease

plished. Such performance should be regarded as having been achieved when reasonable assurance exists regarding the measurement of the consideration that will be derived from rendering the service or performing the long-term contract'' (CICA Handbook 3400.08). Under the completed-contract method, management takes the position that no revenues should be recognized until the work to be provided under a contract is fully completed. Under the percentage-of-completion method, management takes the position that revenue recognition is a function of the amount of work actually completed.

Exhibit 12.6 provides a simple illustration contrasting the completed-contract and percentage-of-completion methods for a hypothetical firm. In May 1994, Erie Corporation signed a long-term construction contract to build a shopping centre in Toronto, Ontario. Under the terms of the three-year contract, Erie would receive a total of $12 million. During 1994, 30 percent of the project was completed at a cost of $3.2 million. In 1995, 40 percent of the project was completed at a cost of $4.3 million; in 1996, the project was completed at a cost of $2.8 million. The exhibit reveals that under the completed-contract approach, Erie Corporation would report no earnings in 1994 or 1995, and $1.7 million in earnings in 1996. Under the percentage-of-completion approach, however, a positive income stream ($.4 million, $.5 million, and $.8 million, in 1994, 1995, and 1996, respectively) is reported in each year. The first method essen-

EXHIBIT 12.6

Alternative GAAP: Completed-Contract versus Percentage-of-Completion Methods

	1994	1995	1996
Completed-Contract Method:			
Revenues	$–0–	$–0–	$12.0
Expenses	–0–	–0–	10.3
Net income	$–0–	$–0–	$ 1.7
Return on sales	–0–%	–0–%	14.2%
Percentage-of-Completion Method:			
Revenues	$3.6	$4.8	$3.6
Expenses	3.2	4.3	2.8
Net income	$ .4	$ .5	$ .8
Return on sales	11%	10.4%	22.2%

tially defers all income until 1996, whereas the second spreads the income across the three years as a function of the amount of work actually completed.

It is clear that although the aggregate results, viewed in their entirety over the three-year period, are equivalent, substantially different impressions are created in any individual year as to the relative success of Erie Corporation in performing under the contract. It is important to recognize that either the completed-contract or the percentage-of-completion method may be adopted for financial reporting purposes. Moreover, the decision to use one method or the other is exclusively a managerial decision, although the percentage-of-completion method is preferred by most accountants because it more closely reflects the accrual basis of accounting.

As we see from the data in Exhibit 12.6, the method that a company adopts to report its revenues or expenses may have a significant impact on its actual reported results. Not only will the level of revenues and expenses on the income statement be affected, but so too will be the level of reported assets and equities on the balance sheet, along with all the financial ratios calculated using those income statement and balance sheet values. Thus, when analyzing a company's reported performance and financial condition, using either absolute figures or ratios, it is important to know just which accounting methods are being used and how those methods are likely to impact the reported values and calculated ratios. For example, in Exhibit 12.6, note how the trend in the return on sales dramatically differs for the two methods of reporting revenues.

Exhibit 12.7 provides further evidence of this analytical concern. This exhibit presents the income statement and selected financial indicators for two *economically identical* companies that differ only in regard to the accounting method used to value the cost of goods sold and ending inventory. A review of these financial data reveals that since inventory costs are rising, FIFO Company appears to be financially better off than LIFO Company — earnings and working capital are higher by $7.8 million and $5.15 million, respectively, and the current ratio (liquidity), the total debt-to-equity ratio (solvency), and the earnings per share (profitability) are superior. Only the inventory turnover ratio (asset management) appears to be better for LIFO Company.

But are these financial indicators depicting the true economic reality? The answer is a resounding no. The two companies are economically identical in spite of the information revealed by the accounting data and the ratio analysis.

EXHIBIT 12.7

Alternative GAAP and Financial Statement Analysis:
FIFO versus LIFO

	FIFO Company	LIFO Company
Net sales	$75,000,000	$75,000,000
Cost of goods sold	(34,500,000)	(42,300,000)
Gross margin	$40,500,000	$32,700,000
Operating expenses	(15,000,000)	(15,000,000)
Net income	$25,500,000	$17,700,000
Ending inventory	$17,250,000	$ 9,450,000
Selected Financial Ratios:		
Earnings per share	$2.55	$1.77
Current ratio	1.67:1	1.41:1
Working capital	$10,800,000	$5,650,000
Inventory turnover	2.00:1	4.50:1
Total debt-to-equity ratio	1:5.17	1:4.91

One thing is clear from these illustrations — the use of different financial accounting methods may produce *very different* impressions about the financial performance of a company and its management. Of importance, then, is whether these different accounting impressions are also reflected, or even should be reflected, in a company's share price.

The Efficient Market Hypothesis

Although there is some disagreement over exactly what causes share prices to move upward and downward, there is little disagreement over the notion that *accounting information* is at least partially responsible for share price movements. The relationship between accounting information and share prices is largely captured by a theory of the functioning of capital markets called the **efficient market hypothesis**, or EMH. EMH is a widely accepted theory describing how share and bond prices respond to information. In fact, the theory is now so well documented that it has been relied on by the Supreme Court as a description of the behaviour of capital markets.

efficient market hypothesis
A theory to explain the functioning of capital markets in which share and bond prices always reflect all publicly available information, and any new information is quickly impounded in security prices.

Under EMH, share prices are assumed to reflect fully (in terms of price) all publicly available information. When new information is made public, share prices adjust very quickly to the new information. Evidence also exists to suggest that the capital markets are not "fooled" by the differences in reported accounting numbers caused by the use of alternative GAAP; that is, sophisticated analysts and investors are apparently able to see through the differential accounting effects created by alternative GAAP (e.g., completed contract versus percentage of completion, LIFO versus FIFO) and are able to properly adjust share prices (by buying or selling) to reflect the true underlying economic value of a company.

An important implication of this theory is that managers of publicly held companies should be unable to manipulate the value of their companies' shares merely by selecting accounting methods that result in the highest level of reported earnings. Since share prices reflect only real economic changes, they will be relatively unaffected by the cosmetic wealth changes associated with alternative GAAP.

Unfortunately, it is sometimes possible to "fool" the stock market and its many investors by disclosing fraudulent financial data. Since share prices are based on all publicly available information, misleading or fraudulent financial information will often cause share prices to adjust inappropriately. The independent public auditor, however, does investigate an organization's records to identify any material misstatements, and, although not all fraudulent acts will be identified, most major errors (be they intentional or not) are identified as part of the annual audit investigation.

12.3 FINANCIAL STATEMENT ANALYSIS

Overview of Financial Statement Analysis

Financial reports are the primary means by which organizations report their financial condition and performance to interested external parties. Financial reports should present useful, meaningful information to the users, for the purposes of making rational investment and credit decisions. Implicit in these uses of financial reports are the concerns of users pertaining to an organization's past performance, present condition, and future prospects. The first two of these are the primary focus of the financial statements, related footnotes, management discussion and analysis, and auditor's report. The latter is often the focus of management's letter to shareholders. Quite frankly, though, the assessment of future prospects is best served by users performing their *own* analysis of company performance and using supplementary third-party commentaries.

Because no one knows for certain what an organization's *future* financial results will be, a great deal of emphasis is placed on past and present performance as indicators of the future. In projecting a link between the past and the future, issues falling under the general rubric of the quality of reported earnings and financial position become significant considerations. For example, although the amount of reported earnings is important, so too are the rate of earnings generated on available resources, the stability of earnings, the specific sources of earnings, and the accounting methods used to measure the earnings. Similarly, although it is useful to know the size and variety of asset categories, it is also important to determine their liquidity, operating capacity, and flexibility.

The Canadian Institute of Chartered Accountants has issued a research report entitled "Using Ratios and Graphics in Financial Reporting." The research study provides an interesting look at many of the problems and difficulties of financial statement analysis. The framework for financial statement analysis recommended by the CICA research study has been modified to be more relevant for an introductory-level discussion of the topic. A basic framework of financial statement analysis is summarized in Exhibit 12.8.

financial strength
Financial strength is the organization's ability to meet its financial obligations.

Different forms of financial analysis may be utilized to gain an understanding of an organization's financial strength and/or its management performance. Depending on the individual users and their objectives, different analysis approaches may be appropriate. Creditors may focus on **financial strength** to evaluate the organization's ability to meet its financial obligations. Owners of the organizations may be more interested in the performance of management and the profitability of the firm. **Management performance** involves profitability and asset management. *Profitability* refers to a company's overall income-generating ability, and *asset management effectiveness* refers to the ability of a company's managers to utilize its assets effectively to produce a return for the company's creditors and owners.

management performance
Management performance involves the analysis of profitability and asset management.

EXHIBIT 12.8

Financial Statement Analysis

Financial Strength		Management Performance	
Liquidity	**Solvency**	**Profitability**	**Asset Management**
Quick ratio	Total debt to equity	Earnings per share	Total asset turnover
Current ratio	Long-term debt to invested capital	Return on equity	Receivable turnover
		Gross profit percentage	Inventory turnover

Ratio Analysis

In previous chapters, financial ratios were suggested as sources of insight regarding an organization's financial strength and the performance of management. For example, in Chapter 3, the accounts receivable turnover ratio was discussed as a means to estimate the rate at which an organization's receivables were converted into cash. Chapter 3 also included the return on owners' equity ratio as an indication of the return earned by a organization on non-creditor funds. Exhibits 12.8 and 12.9 summarize the various ratios discussed throughout this text.

The topic of financial statement analysis has been a common thread linking many of the previous 11 chapters. As Exhibit 12.8 shows, the analysis of financial statements using ratios can be organized into two categories: financial strength and management performance:

Financial Strength

Liquidity: the assessment of an organization's ability to meet current short-term obligations as they fall due.
Solvency: the assessment of an organization's long-term debt-payment ability.

Management Performance

Profitability: the assessment of an organization's ability to generate revenues in excess of expenses.
Asset management: the assessment of how effectively an organization utilizes its available resources.

Liquidity. Liquidity may be evaluated on the basis of four indicators:

1. The amount of cash on hand.
2. The level of working capital.
3. The current ratio.
4. The quick ratio.

The amount of cash and cash equivalents on hand is a precise indication of the level of highly liquid resources available for a company's debt repayment or other operating needs. Cash on hand is very measurable and therefore quite certain, but it is also a very conservative measure of liquidity. Only in the most extreme circumstances would a company have to pay all of its bills using only its cash on hand.

working capital
A measure of liquidity calculated as total current assets minus total current liabilities.

A somewhat more general indicator of liquidity that is broader in scope is the level of working capital. **Working capital** is measured as current assets minus current liabilities. Thus, working capital is a measure of the net current assets that would be available to support a company's continuing operations if all of its current assets could be converted to cash at their balance sheet values and the proceeds used to satisfy its current liabilities.

<u>E X H I B I T   1 2 . 9</u>

Financial Ratios

Liquidity

$$\text{Quick ratio} = \frac{\text{Cash + Temporary investments + Accounts receivable}}{\text{Current liabilities}}$$

$$\text{Current ratio} = \frac{\text{Current assets}}{\text{Current liabilities}}$$

Solvency

$$\text{Total-debt-to-equity ratio} = \frac{\text{Total debt}}{\text{equity}}$$

$$\text{Long-term debt-to-invested capital ratio} = \frac{\text{Long-term debt}}{\text{Invested capital}}$$

Profitability

$$\text{Basic earnings per share} = \frac{\text{Net income – Preferred dividends}}{\text{Number of common shares outstanding}}$$

$$\text{Return on equity} = \frac{\text{Net income}}{\text{Shareholders' equity}}$$

$$\text{Gross profit margin ratio} = \frac{\text{Gross profit}}{\text{Sales (net)}}$$

Asset Management

$$\text{Total asset turnover} = \frac{\text{Sales (revenue)}}{\text{Total assets}}$$

$$\text{Receivable turnover} = \frac{\text{Sales (revenues)}}{\text{Accounts receivable}}$$

$$\text{Inventory turnover} = \frac{\text{Cost of sales}}{\text{Inventory}}$$

---

current ratio
A measure of liquidity calculated as current assets divided by current liabilities.

A ratio based on the concept of working capital is the **current ratio**, which is calculated by dividing current assets by current liabilities. Both working capital and the current ratio are "coverage" indicators; the former indicates the extent to which current assets cover current liabilities in an absolute sense, and the latter indicates the extent of coverage in a relative sense. A high current ratio (i.e., a substantial amount of working capital) indicates good liquidity, suggesting that a company's currently maturing obligations are likely to be paid on time. A ratio that is too high, however, may indicate an unproductive use of resources and suggest the current assets might be used more effectively by investing them in other resources.

quick ratio
(acid test ratio) A measure of liquidity calculated as quick assets divided by current liabilities.

The **quick ratio** examines only the liability coverage provided by the quick assets. Quick assets are highly liquid current assets such as cash, cash equivalents, temporary investments, and receivables. Temporary investments may be easily sold and quickly converted to cash. Accounts and notes receivables are considered to be quick assets because they can usually be sold to a factor. A *factor* is a financial institution that buys receivables from other companies at a discount (i.e., at a price less than the amount to be collected) and earns a profit when the receivables are collected.

Solvency. Solvency may be evaluated on the basis of a number of different techniques. We have selected two common ratios to illustrate the analysis of a firm's solvency:

1. The total debt-to-equity ratio.
2. The long-term debt-to-invested capital ratio.

The concept of solvency and the thrust of these debt-level ratios suggest a negative connotation, as though debt is to be avoided and reduced whenever possible. Debt is not always bad; in fact, it is sometimes healthy. A more positive way to describe a company's debt level is to say that the shareholders' equity is leveraged; in effect, a leveraged company supplements its owners' funds with funds borrowed from other sources to "lever up" the return to the owners. The objective of the firm is to increase the return on its net assets. This may be achieved by borrowing additional funds, as long as the net interest cost of the debt is less than the interest rate earned on the net assets. The ratios that follow describe a company's debt exposure, but they should be looked at from two perspectives. Creditors obviously want to maximize their protection, but shareholders look for the best balance of debt and equity to ensure the highest return at the least level of risk. These ratios measure the relative amount of long-term debt outstanding.

total debt-to-equity ratio
The total debt to equity ratio is a measure of the extent to which a company's assets are financed by creditors as compared to the amount financed by owners.

The **total debt-to-equity ratio** is a measure of the extent to which a company's assets are financed by creditors as compared to the amount financed by owners. This ratio provides a measure of the extent to which an organization relies on borrowed funds to finance its operations. In general, the lower this ratio, the higher the proportion of long-term financing provided by the owners and the more solvent a company is thought to be. Alternatively, the higher this ratio, the more leveraged a company is and the less solvent it is thought to be. In general, creditors like a lower debt-to-equity ratio because they have a prior claim on a company's assets and prefer to have a larger equity cushion beneath them.

long-term debt-to-invested capital ratio
The long-term debt to invested capital ratio measures the relative composition of a company's long-term capital structure. Invested capital refers to the *total* of long-term debt and total shareholders equity.

The **long-term debt-to-invested capital ratio** measures the relative composition of a company's long-term capital structure, or capitalization. *Invested capital* refers to the *total* of long-term debt and shareholders' equity. The ratio measures the portion of total capital provided by long-term debt. A high ratio may indicate a difficulty in meeting interest payments during periods of low earnings. However, this ratio varies significantly from industry to industry. A careful *comparative* analysis should be used with this ratio. In general, the lower the ratio, the more solvent a company is thought to be. The higher the ratio, the less solvent and the more highly leveraged a company is considered to be.

Profitability. *Profitability* refers to a company's overall income-generating ability. Much attention is placed on the organization's operating activities and the analysis of the income statement. The principal focus of the income statement is the current operations of a company, and thus the overall profitability of those operations. An analysis of profitability may occur in many ways. The absolute level of revenues, gross margin, or net income, can be investigated over time (i.e., a trend analysis). As well, a series of profitability ratios can be calculated. A number of different ratios are available to the financial statement user when it comes to the analysis of a company's profitability. Because the absolute level of net income is often difficult to compare between periods and among different companies, it is accepted practice for companies to report a standardized measure of their performance.

Under GAAP, net income is divided by the number of shares of a company's share capital, and the resulting standardized measure of performance is called **earnings per share** (EPS). Earnings per share results from dividing the weighted-average number of common shares outstanding during the year into the net income for the year, which is available to the common shareholders. At the end of each quarter and the end of each year, publicly held companies release earnings information for the period, in total and on a per share basis. The quarterly and annual reports are summarized in the financial press and then are used on an ongoing basis in calculating various stock market performance indicators. As a result, the determination of the earnings per share figure is an important aspect of financial statement disclosure. The earnings per share figures may be disclosed in a footnote to the financial statements or as part of the income statement.

The second profitability ratio we considered was the return-on-equity ratio. The return-on-equity ratio is one of most commonly used profitability measures. The **return on equity** (ROE) measures a company's profitability versus the resources provided by its owners. ROE measures the adequacy of the return on capital invested by the owners. In general, the higher the ROE, the more profitable a company is thought to be.

One of the most commonly used profitability ratios used to measure management performance is the gross profit margin ratio. The **gross profit margin ratio** indicates the percentage of each dollar of revenue that is realized as gross profit after deducting the cost of goods or services sold. It represents the profit available to cover a company's other operating expenses, such as selling and administrative expenses, interest, and taxes. It provides an indicator of a company's pricing policies. Generally, a high gross profit margin is good. However, if the profit margin is too high it may mean the loss of potential customers to competitor firms.

Asset management.   Asset management refers to the ability of a company's managers to utilize its assets effectively to produce a return for the company's creditors and owners. The **total asset turnover ratio** is a measure of an organization's utilization of available resources to generate revenues. This ratio examines a company's utilization of its revenue-producing assets. In general, the higher the ratio the better. A high turnover ratio indicates that management is effective in generating revenues from the assets that it has at its disposal. A high turnover rate can also be problematic, however, if the reason for the high turnover is the liquidation of the company's assets. Similarly, a decreasing ratio may not necessarily indicate poor asset utilization. The total asset turnover is influenced by the turnover rate of the individual assets such as receivables and inventory. The slow collection of receivables, the buildup of inventory levels, or large capital asset purchases would adversely affect the ratio. When using this ratio, it is important to compare it to ratios of similar firms in the same industry or ratios for the same firm on a trend basis.

A second indicator of the quality or effectiveness of a company's asset management is given by the **accounts receivable turnover ratio.** The quality of receivable management is usually evaluated in the context of the accounts (notes) receivable turnover ratio. The receivable turnover ratio is a measure of the rate at which a company's accounts and notes receivable are converted to cash. In general, a high ratio indicates excellent receivables management. A low ratio, on the other hand, may indicate serious problems in the sales-receivables-collection cycle.

---

earnings per share
A standardized measure of performance calculated as net income divided by the weighted-average number of common shares outstanding during an accounting period.

return on equity
(ROE) A measure of the relative effectiveness of a company in using the assets provided by the owners to generate net income.

gross profit margin ratio
A measure of profitability that assesses the percentage of each sales dollar that is recognized as gross profit (i.e., after deducting the cost of goods sold).

total asset turnover ratio
The total asset turnover ratio is a measure of an organization's utilization of available resources to generate revenues.

accounts receivable turnover ratio
A measure of the effectiveness of receivable management calculated as net credit sales for the period divided by the average balance in accounts receivable.

EXHIBIT 12.10

Maple Leaf Gardens, Limited, Financial Ratios

	1994	1993
Liquidity		
Cash and equivalents	$10,188,543	$12,086,374
Working capital	$4,466,346	$1,391,794
Current ratio	1.53:1	1.10:1
Quick ratio	1.41:1	1.06:1
Solvency		
Total debt-to-equity ratio	.68:1	1.12:1
Long-term debt-to-invested capital ratio	.17:1	.13:1
Profitability		
Earnings per share	$1.69	$1.43
Return on equity	34.3%	35.3%
Gross profit percentage	n.a.	n.a.
Asset management		
Total asset turnover	2.07	1.76
Receivable turnover	36.1	17.7
Inventory turnover	n.a.	n.a.

n.a. = Not available.

inventory turnover ratio
A measure of the effectiveness of inventory management calculated as the cost of goods sold for a period divided by the average inventory held during that period.

The quality of a company's inventory management is often revealed by the inventory turnover ratio. The **inventory turnover ratio** measures the number of times that the average level of inventory on hand was sold, or turned over, during an accounting period. In general, the higher the inventory turnover ratio, the more profitable a company is and the more effective the inventory management is thought to be. A high turnover rate also helps to reduce the potential of loss due to product obsolescence or deterioration. If the turnover ratio is too high, however, it may indicate that the company is losing sales opportunities because inventory levels are inadequate. Unfortunately, there is no ideal turnover rate, and, to judge the effectiveness of inventory management, it is important to compare this ratio to that of prior periods, to industry averages, or to competitor ratios.

Although analysis techniques were previously discussed in the early chapters, it is instructive to review the ratios using Maple Leaf Gardens, Limited, financial statements. As Exhibit 12.10 reveals, Maple Leaf Gardens' results indicate both positive and negative trends. With respect to liquidity, the balance sheet reveals that, as of June 30, 1994, Maple Leaf Gardens had cash and cash equivalents of $10,188,543 on hand, working capital of $4,466,346, a current ratio of 1.53, and a quick ratio of 1.41. The current and quick ratios reveal that for every dollar of current liabilities, Maple Leaf Gardens held $1.53 of current assets and $1.41 of quick assets. To determine whether these measures indicate high, low, or average liquidity, one may compare the data to comparative data for 1993. A comparison indicates that Maple Leaf Gardens' liquidity in 1994 improved significantly from that in 1993. Although the level of cash and cash equivalents actually decreased by about $2 million, the level of working capital increased by more than $3 million. The increase in working capital is confirmed by the increase in both the current and quick ratios.

As compared to 1993, Maple Leaf Gardens' solvency in 1994 improved significantly. The ratio of debt to equity declined from 1.12 times to only .68 times in 1994.

(Stated alternatively, the level of debt as a percentage of equity declined from 112 percent to 68 percent.) The long-term debt to invested capital increased from .13 in 1993 to .17 on 1994. However, the portion of the business financed by long-term debt is still very low.

Maple Leaf Gardens discloses earnings per share of $1.69 for 1994, and $1.43 for 1993. The absolute level of net income has increased to $6,211,265 in 1994, from $5,253,099 in 1993. The return on equity for Maple Leaf Gardens, Limited, was 34.3% in 1994, compared to 35.3% in 1993. Although the return on equity has declined slightly from 1993 for Maple Leaf Gardens, the 1994 earnings per share and dollar value of net income has increased.

The asset management ratios may be used to measure the management performance of Maple Leaf Gardens, Limited. Maple Leaf Gardens' asset management position in 1993 and 1994 compares very favourably. The receivable turnover ratio has improved significantly from 17.7 in 1993 to 36.1 in 1994. The total asset turnover ratio improved marginally from 1.76 in 1993 to 2.07 in 1994. Both of these turnover ratios indicate Maple Leaf Gardens' sound asset management.

Limitations of Ratio Analysis

Ratio analysis is undoubtedly the most widely used analytical technique for interpreting financial statement data. In spite of its widespread use, however, ratio analysis suffers from certain limitations and is subject to certain constraining assumptions.

For example, since a ratio involves two financial statement numbers (e.g., sales divided by total assets), the reader must be cautious in interpreting its cause when a change in a ratio is observed. Ratio changes may result from a change in either the numerator, the denominator, or both. Thus, when using ratios, the reader must be prepared to look beyond the ratio itself in an effort to understand the economic event(s) causing the change.

Another concern is that, quite often, changes in financial statement data may be more cosmetic than real. Trend analysis presupposes a constant relationship underlying the financial statement numbers. Consequently, any event — be it a real economic event or a cosmetic one — that disturbs an underlying relation will impact the reported ratios. Although not an exhaustive listing, the following are examples of cosmetic events that will disturb the underlying financial statement relationships and thus must be taken into consideration by the astute reader:

1. A structural change in the accounting entity (e.g., a merger or an acquisition of another company).
2. A change in an accounting method or principle (e.g., a switch from LIFO to FIFO).
3. A change in accounting estimate (e.g., an increase in the estimated life of a capital asset).
4. A change in accounting classification (e.g., segregating the income [or loss] on a division recently sold from the income from operations).

time-series analysis
The analysis of financial statement data over multiple periods is called time-series analysis.

These concerns are particularly relevant when accounting data are investigated for trends over a number of accounting periods. The analysis of financial statement data over multiple periods is frequently called **time-series analysis**.

As noted before, ratio analysis is most effective when the resulting ratios can be *compared* against some standard. Frequently, that standard is a similar ratio from a prior period, as in a trend analysis of time-series data. Another useful standard, however, is a ratio from a leading competitor or perhaps the industry in general. Unfortunately, the use of cross-sectional analysis — that is, the comparison of a given company's ratios with other companies' data or with industry averages — involves certain restrictive assumptions, including these:

1. The individual company is assumed to be structurally similar to the competitor or the average of the industry, which is rarely the case.
2. The industry and the company under review are assumed to use a common set of accounting principles and accounting estimates. When a company under review uses one set of GAAP and the industry or comparative company uses another set, large cosmetic ratio differences tend to occur.
3. The company under review and the industry are assumed to experience a common set of external influences. A given company, however, may have undergone an unusual economic event (e.g., a labour strike) having multiple-period implications for its financial data that are not reflected in the industry standard.

Despite these concerns, ratio analysis can be a very powerful analytical tool so long as the analyst recognizes the following important maxim: *Ratios help the financial statement user identify important questions but seldom offer direct answers.* Only by a comprehensive review of the financial statements can answers be obtained.

Horizontal and Vertical Analysis

horizontal analysis
When comparative balance sheets or income statements are presented side by side, the statements can be made more meaningful if the dollar amount of increase or decrease and the percentage change is shown.

In addition to ratio analysis, two other types of financial statement analysis are frequently performed: horizontal analysis and vertical analysis. When comparative balance sheets or income statements are presented side by side, the statements can be made more meaningful if the dollar amount of increase or decrease and the percentage change is shown. This type of analysis is known as **horizontal analysis** because the data comparisons are made on a horizontal plane from left to right.

Exhibit 12.11 illustrates a horizontal analysis of Maple Leaf Gardens, Limited, income statement. In this two-year comparison, the earlier year (1993) is the base year. The percentage changes are rounded to the nearest tenth of a percent. For Maple Leaf Gardens, revenues from operations increased by 13.1 percent over 1993, expenses also increased by 18.3 percent. These increases, combined with a large increase in N.H.L. expansion fees, net a 18.2 percent increase in net income and earnings per share.

vertical analysis
In vertical analysis, three financial statement numbers—total assets, total equities, and net sales—are converted to a base of 100 percent. Each item within the assets and equities on the balance sheet, or each item on the income statement, is then expressed as a percentage of the base number.

In **vertical analysis**, three financial statement numbers — total assets, total equities, and net sales — are converted to a base of 100 percent. Each item within the assets and equities on the balance sheet, or each item on the income statement, is then expressed as a percentage of the base number. Since for any given set of financial statements the base numbers represent 100 percent, the restated financial statements are called *common-size statements*.

To illustrate vertical analysis, Exhibit 12.12 presents Maple Leaf Gardens' common-size income statements for 1994 and 1993. An interpretation of vertical statements often parallels the interpretation of horizontal statements. Note that the common-size statements permit both a within-period analysis (e.g., in 1994, total expenses were 87.8 percentage of total revenues) and across-period trend analysis (e.g., total expenses as a percentage of total revenues increased from 84.1 percent in 1993 to 87.8 percent in 1994).

EXHIBIT 12.11

— Horizontal Analysis

Maple Leaf Gardens, Limited
Statements of Income
For the Years Ending June 30

	1994	1993	Increase (Decrease)	Percentage Increase (Decrease)
Revenues from operations	$62,693,174	$55,444,270	$7,248,904	13.1
Investment and other income	850,022	754,089	95,933	12.7
	$63,543,196	$56,198,359	$7,344,837	13.1
Expenses:				
Operating expenses	$53,175,423	$44,320,930	$8,854,493	20.0
Depreciation	1,097,556	957,841	139,715	14.6
Amortization	1,545,663	1,969,962	(424,299)	(21.5)
	$55,818,642	$47,248,733	$8,569,909	18.3
Operating Income	$ 7,724,554	$ 8,949,626	$1,225,072	13.7
N.H.L. expansion fees (note 7)	3,112,931	525,333	2,587,598	492.5
Income before income taxes	$10,837,485	$ 9,474,959	$1,362,526	14.4
Income taxes — current	$ 5,573,000	$ 5,212,000	$ 361,000	6.9
Income taxes — deferred	(946,780)	(990,140)	(43,369)	(4.4)
	$ 4,626,220	$ 4,221,860	$ 404,360	9.6
Net Income	$ 6,211,265	$ 5,253,099	$ 958,166	18.2
Earnings per share	$ 1.69	$ 1.43	$ .26	18.2

EXHIBIT 12.12

— Vertical Analysis

Maple Leaf Gardens, Limited
Statements of Income
For the Years Ending June 30

	1994	Common-Size Percentage	1993	Common-Size Percentage
Revenues from operations	$62,693,174	98.7	$55,444,270	98.7
Investment and other income	850,022	1.3	754,089	1.3
Total revenues	$63,543,196	100.0	$56,198,359	100.0
Expenses:				
Operating expenses	$53,175,423	83.7	$44,320,930	78.9
Depreciation	1,097,556	1.7	957,841	1.7
Amortization	1,545,663	2.4	1,969,962	3.5
Total expenses	$55,818,642	87.8	$47,248,733	84.1
Operating income	$ 7,724,554	12.2	$ 8,949,626	15.9
N.H.L. expansion fees (note 7)	3,112,931	4.9	525,333	.9
Income before income taxes	$10,837,485	17.1	$ 9,474,959	16.8
Income taxes — current	$ 5,573,000	8.8	$ 5,212,000	9.3
Income taxes — deferred	(946,780)	(1.5)	(990,140)	(1.8)
	$ 4,626,220	7.3	$ 4,221,860	7.5
Net income	$ 6,211,265	9.8	$ 5,253,099	9.3
Earnings per share	$ 1.69		$ 1.43	

Graphics in Financial Reporting

Many organizations make use of graphics in their annual report. Graphics may be very helpful in explaining trends or changes in direction of various financial statement elements. Unfortunately, no GAAP exist for the presentation and disclosure of financial information in graphical format. The CICA research study "Using Ratios and Graphics in Financial Reporting" illustrated many potential problems with graphics in financial reporting. **Graphics in financial reporting** will not be examined in any great detail in this text. However, as graphics are used extensively by most organizations, the users of financial reports should be aware of the potential for the presentation of misleading financial information via the graphical format.

graphics in financial reporting
Many organizations make use of graphics in their annual report. Graphics may be very helpful in explaining trends or changes in direction of various financial statement elements.

The following example is presented to illustrate the possible misleading information that may be presented. Assume an organization has experienced a downward trend in sales or net income over the past five years as follows:

Year	Financial Data
1991	$100
1992	80
1993	60
1994	40
1995	20

The above chart indicates a $20 decrease in each of the last four years. This unfavourable trend may also be presented in graphical format, as shown below:

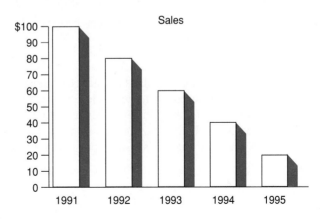

It is obvious from a quick look at the financial data or the graphics presentation that a downward trend has occurred. However, as previously mentioned no GAAP exist with respect to the graphical presentation of financial data when disclosed in the annual financial reports of organizations. An organization could chose to present the same data in the graphical format displayed below:

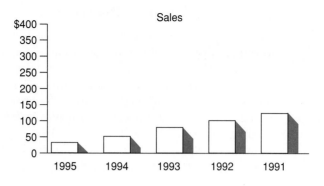

The second graph presents the identical data, but with significant modifications. The series of years has been reversed, and the y-axis of the graph greatly extended. The result is the disclosure of a flat or upward trend in financial data. If the organization wished to disguise the trend to an even greater extent, a pie graph of the same data could be used:

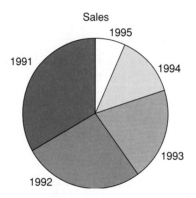

This section on graphics in financial reports has not been presented to infer organizations may purposely try to disclose misleading or confusing information. The graphs presented in this section have been used to illustrate the degree to which misstatement is possible, whether intentional or not. It is important that users of financial information carefully analyze any data presented in graphical format.

12.4 COMPREHENSIVE ILLUSTRATION

The comparative financial statements of Gatineau, Limited, for the years ending December 31 are presented below:

	1996	1995
Cash	$ 82,000	$ 53,000
Accounts receivable	80,000	66,000
Merchandise inventory	271,000	296,000
Prepaid expenses	30,000	32,000
Capital assets*	195,000	163,000
Accumulated amortization	(78,000)	(70,000)
	$580,000	$540,000
Accounts payable	$ 89,000	$ 86,000
Accrued liabilities	10,000	8,000
Long-term debt	57,000	50,000
Deferred taxes	14,000	10,000
Common shares, non-par value	214,000	200,000
Preferred shares, 9%, cumulative, non-par value	100,000	100,000
Retained earnings	96,000	86,000
	$580,000	$540,000
Sales	$710,000	$635,000
Cost of goods sold	(390,000)	(310,000)
Gross profit	$320,000	$325,000
Amortization expense	(22,000)	(24,000)
Operating expenses	(258,000)	(268,000)
Income tax expense	(17,000)	(19,000)
Gain-disposal of capital asset	3,000	—
Net income	$ 26,000	$ 14,000
Weighted-average shares outstanding:	21,400	20,000

*During 1996, Gatineau, Limited, sold capital assets with a net book value of $37,000 for $40,000.

Required:

  a. Complete a comparative ratio analysis of Gatineau, Limited, including comments on your analysis.

  b. Prepare a statement of changes in financial position for the year ending December 31, 1996.

Liquidity Analysis: Gatineau, Limited

The liquidity position of Gatineau has shown a modest improvement during the year. The increase in cash during the period has produced a significant improvement in the quick ratio. Both working capital and the current ratio show only a small change from the previous period, indicating a stable liquidity position.

	1996	1995
Cash on hand	$82,000	$53,000
Working capital	$364,000 ($463,000 − $99,000)	$353,000 ($447,000 − $94,000)
Quick ratio	1.64:1 ($162,000/$99,000)	1.27:1 ($119,000/$94,000)
Current ratio	4.68:1 ($463,000/$99,000)	4.76:1 ($447,000/$94,000)

Solvency Analysis: Gatineau, Limited

The solvency position of Gatineau has shown very little change during the year. Both debt-to-equity ratios have increased an insignificant amount during the period. The solvency position appears to be stable.

	1996	1995
Total debt-to-equity ratio	.41:1 ($170,000/$410,000)	.39:1 ($154,000/$386,000)
Long-term debt-to-invested capital ratio	.12:1 [$57,000/($57,000 + $410,000)]	.11:1 [$50,000/($50,000 + $386,000)]

Profitability Analysis: Gatineau, Limited

Gatineau, Limited, has had a profitable year. Net income nearly doubled from $14,000 to $26,000. This increase is also reflected in the improved earnings per share and return-on-equity figures. Gross profit percentage has shown a significant decrease during the period. This ratio should be watched carefully. The lower profit margins may have been a management decision that led to the increased sales volume during the period. Comparative industry data would be helpful to further analzye this ratio.

	1996	1995
Earnings per share	$1.21 ($26,000/21,400)	$.70 ($14,000/20,000)
Gross profit percentage	45.07% ($320,000/$710,000)	51.18% ($325,000/$635,000)
Return on equity	6.34% ($26,000/$410,000)	3.62% ($14,000/$386,000)

Asset Management Analysis: Gatineau, Limited

The analysis of the asset management of Gatineau indicates different results for each type of asset. The total asset turnover has shown a modest increase during the period. Inventory is turning over significantly faster than the previous period. The ending inventory for 1996 is actually less than 1995, despite the increase in sales during the period. The receivable turnover has dropped from the previous period. This could be a problem area, considering the increase in sales. This ratio should be watched closely in future periods.

	1996	1995
Total asset turnover	1.22 ($710,000/$580,000)	1.17 ($635,000/$540,000)
Receivable turnover	8.88 ($710,000/$80,000)	9.62 ($635,000/$66,000)
Inventory turnover	1.44 ($390,000/$271,000)	1.05 ($310,000/$296,000)

GATINEAU, LIMITED
Statement of Changes in Financial Position
For the Year Ending December 31

Operating activities:		
Net income	$26,000	
Non-cash items:		
Gain-on-disposal capital asset	(3,000)	
Amortization expense	22,000	
	$45,000	
Working capital items:		
Accounts receivable	(14,000)	
Prepaid expenses	2,000	
Accounts payable	3,000	
Accrued liabilities	2,000	
Inventory	25,000	
Cash provided from operations		$63,000
Investing activities:		
Sale of capital asset	$40,000	
Purchase of capital assets	(83,000)	
Cash used in investing		(43,000)
Financing activities:		
Issued common shares	$14,000	
Deferred taxes	4,000	
Issued long-term debt	7,000	
Declared and paid dividends	(16,000)	
Cash provided from financing		9,000
Increase in cash		$29,000
Cash — January 1		53,000
Cash — December 31		$82,000

12.5 SUMMARY

Accounting information is frequently analyzed by users as a basis to predict the future performance of an organization. Some of the specific indicators that may be used to evaluate current performance and to predict future company performance include ratio analysis, horizontal and vertical analysis, and graphic presentations. Analysis of an organization may be completed on the basis of its liquidity, solvency, profitability, and management performance.

When evaluating an organization's performance, users need to consider the effects of alternative accounting methods (e.g., LIFO versus FIFO, completed contract versus percentage of completion) on the ratios that they use. Failure to consider these accounting method effects may result in a misallocation of investor resources by overpaying when purchasing a company's shares.

One way to examine an organization's performance independent of the GAAP used to portray its results is to analyze its cash flows. The statement of changes in financial position provides users with information on the operating, investing, and financing activities of the organization.

By examining the financial statements in total and by considering the various trends revealed by ratio analysis, horizontal and vertical analysis, and cash flow analysis, the financial statement user should be able to develop a well-informed assessment of an organization and its potential. The following table summarizes the financial statement interrelationships of different financial statement items:

Financial Statement Interrelationships

Financial Statement Item	Chapter	Balance Sheet	Income Statement	Statement of Changes in Financial Position
Cash	6	Current asset	Bank reconciliation adjustments: service charges, interest expense	Analysis of change in cash during the year
Temporary investments	6	Current asset	Unrealized losses, applying the lower-of-cost-or-market rule	Adjustment to working capital items: operating activities
Accounts receivable	6	Current asset	Bad debt expense	Adjustment to working capital items: operating activities
Inventory	7	Current asset	Cost of goods sold	Adjustment to working capital items: operating activities
Capital assets, including property, plant, and equipment, intangibles, and natural resources	8	Non-current asset	Amortization expense. Gain or loss on disposal	Amortization expense is added back to net income as a non-cash item, operating activity. Purchases are an investing activity using cash. Disposals are an investing activity, providing cash. Gains/losses on disposal are non-cash adjustment to net income, operating activity
Accounts payable and other short-term payables	9	Current liability	Not applicable	Adjustment to working capital items: operating activities
Mortgage and bond payables	9	Long-term liability	Interest expense. Amortization of bond discounts and premiums	Amortization expense adjusted to net income as a non-cash item, operating activity. Issuing debt is a financing activity, providing cash. Redemptions of debt is a financing activity, using cash
Leases — capital	10	Long-term liability and non-current asset	Interest expense and amortization expense	Amortization expense added back to net income as a non-cash item, operating activity
Leases — operating	10	Not applicable	Rent expense	Not applicable
Pensions	10	Footnote	Pension expense	Not applicable
Deferred income taxes	10	Current and/or long-term liability	Income tax expense, current and deferred	An adjustment to non-cash items, operating activity
Share capital	11	Shareholders' equity	Capital transactions do not affect net income	Issuing shares is a financing activity, providing cash. Redemptions of shares is a financing activity, using cash
Dividends	11	Deducted from retained earnings	Dividends do not affect net income	A financing activity, using cash

12.6 KEY CONCEPTS AND TERMS

Accounts receivable turnover
 ratio (p. 587)
Current ratio (p. 584)
Earnings per share (p. 586)
Efficient market hypothesis (p. 581)
Financial strength (p. 582)
Financing activities (p. 573)
Graphics in financial reporting (p. 591)
Gross profit margin ratio (p. 586)
Horizontal analysis (p. 589)
Inventory turnover ratio (p. 587)
Investing activities (p. 572)

Long-term debt-to-invested capital
 ratio (p. 585)
Management performance (p. 582)
Operating activities (p. 568)
Quick ratio (p. 584)
Return on equity (p. 584)
Time-series analysis (p. 588)
Total asset turnover ratio (p. 586)
Total debt-to-equity ratio (p. 585)
Vertical analysis (p. 589)
Working capital (p. 583)

12.7 COMPREHENSIVE REVIEW QUESTION

R12.1 Financial statements and financial analysis. Listed below, in alphabetical order, are the account balances from the adjusted trial balance of Finale, Ltd., for the year ended December 31. You may assume that all accounts have normal debit or credit balances.

	1996	1995
Accounts payable	$ 42,000	$ 25,000
Accounts receivable	65,000	37,000
Accumulated amortization — capital assets	75,000	68,000
Accumulated amortization — capital lease assets	12,000	8,000
Allowance for doubtful accounts	3,000	2,500
Amortization expense	26,500	—
Bad debts expense	1,000	—
Bank loan due December 31, 1999	30,000	20,000
Bond discount	4,000	4,500
Bonds payable due December 31, 2004	100,000	100,000
Capital assets	240,000	190,000
Capital lease asset	40,000	40,000
Capital lease liability	32,000	35,000
Cash	46,500	80,000
Commissions payable	2,000	3,000
Common shares, non-par value, 1996 — 1,500 shares issued, 1995 — 1,000 issued	90,000	80,000
Customer deposits	3,000	4,000
Deferred income taxes	2,000	3,000
Dividends declared	8,000	—
Dividends payable	2,000	1,000
Income tax expense	4,000	—
Income taxes payable	3,000	2,000
Interest expense	2,000	—
Inventory, December 31	50,000	45,000
Loss on disposal of capital asset	4,000	—
Notes payable, due January 2, 1999	5,000	10,000
Patents — net	27,000	30,000
Pension expense	9,000	
Preferred shares, non-par value, 1996 — issued 375 shares, 1995 — 300 issued	40,000	32,000

(continued)

	1996	1995
Prepaid rent	3,000	1,000
Purchases	76,000	—
Purchases returns and allowances	10,000	—
Rent expense	24,000	—
Retained earnings	47,000	47,000
Salaries expense	13,500	—
Sales	163,000	—
Sales commissions expense	3,500	—
Sales returns and allowances	5,000	—
Temporary investments	11,000	13,000
Treasury shares — 20 common shares at cost	3,000	—

Notes:

1. Amortization expense includes the amortization of capital assets, capital lease assets, and patents.

2. The current portion of long-term liabilities is $7,000 on December 31, 1995, and 1996.

3. Capital assets purchases were made during 1996 for $77,500.

Required:

a. Prepare an income statement and a statement of retained earnings for the year ended December 31, 1996.

b. Prepare comparative balance sheets as at December 31, 1995, and December 31, 1996.

c. Prepare a statement of changes in financial position for the year ended December 31, 1996.

d. Perform an analysis of financial strength and management performance of the company. Your report should include comments as to the financial position of the company.

12.8 REVIEW AND DISCUSSION QUESTIONS

Q12.1 Point: There are too many alternative methods under GAAP — accounting should be more standardized.

Counter-point: Multiple alternative reporting approaches are necessary under GAAP to enable companies to portray the diverse circumstances that they face. Evaluate the two viewpoints. Which one do you agree with, and why?

Q12.2 Sugar, Ltd.'s annual report reveals that during the year it purchased a number of other companies at an aggregate cost of $3.4 billion. Moreover, "goodwill and other intangibles recorded in connection with the 19x9 acquisitions totalled $3.0 billion." Thus, the fair market value of the identifiable tangible assets was only $0.4 billion. Why would Sugar, Ltd., pay so much for the other companies if the fair market value was only $.4 billion? Did Sugar's management overpay?

Q12.3 Lockheed Corporation's common shares were trading on the stock exchange at approximately $25 per share. NL Industries, a company that already owned about 18 percent of Lockheed's shares, made a tender offer to buy Lockheed's remaining shares at $40 per share, or a premium of $15 per share above Lockheed's current market price per share. Why would NL Industries offer a premium of 60 percent for the Lockheed shares? If the share market is efficient, does this indicate that NL overpaid for the Lockheed shares?

Q12.4 What are the major limitations of annual reports as a source of information about a company's statement of income?

Q12.5 Obtain a copy of any corporation's annual report to shareholders and consider the following questions:

a. What are the three most significant pieces of information you observe about the company's income statement?

b. What are the three most significant pieces of information you observe about the company's balance sheet?

c. How well did the company do in the most recent year?

d. Was the company better off at the end of the most recent year as compared with the preceding year?

e. How much was the company worth at the end of the most recent year?

f. Compare the company's book value and its market value per share. Why are these values different?

g. How do you explain the difference in the company's profit or loss for the year and its change in cash?

h. How do the five basic concepts listed below affect the financial statements presented in the company's annual report?

(1) Entity concept.

(2) Historical cost principle.

(3) Use of estimates and exercise of judgment.

(4) Conservatism.

(5) Materiality.

Q12.6 For what audience are a company's annual reports prepared? Do you think this audience has a good understanding of the information presented in a "typical" annual report?

Q12.7 The text suggests that an analyst should learn as much as possible about a company and its environment.

a. Why?

b. To what sources should the analyst go?

c. Can you cite any specific instances in which knowledge of Maple Leaf Gardens and its environment contributed to your understanding of Maple Leaf Gardens' figures?

Q12.8 If the numerator in computing earnings per share is subject to all the limitations of the income statement, how does one account for the concept being so widely quoted?

Q12.9 What effect, if any, would each of the following items have on the statement of changes in financial position assuming the direct method presentation is used to present cash flows from operations?

(1) Accounts receivable.

(2) Inventory.

(3) Amortization.

(4) Deferred tax liability.

(5) Issuance of long-term debt in payment for a building.

(6) Payoff of a current portion of long-term debt.

(7) Sale of a capital asset.

12.9 PROBLEMS

P12.1 Financial analysis: The income statement. Presented below are the consolidated statements of income for Coca-Cola Enterprises, Inc., for the fiscal years ending 1988, 1989, and 1990. Evaluate Coca-Cola's operations using whatever analyses (e.g., ratio analysis, trend analysis, vertical and horizontal analysis) you believe are appropriate.

COCA-COLA ENTERPRISES, INC.
Consolidated Statements of Income
(in thousands except per share data)

	Fiscal Year		
	1990	**1989**	**1988**
Net operating revenues	$4,034,043	$3,881,947	$3,874,445
Cost of sales	2,359,267	2,313,032	2,268,038
Gross profit	1,674,776	1,568,915	1,606,407
Selling, general, and administrative expenses	1,339,928	1,258,848	1,225,238
Provision for restructuring	9,300	—	27,000
Operating income	325,548	310,067	354,169
Non-operating income (deductions):			
Interest income	6,566	6,564	8,505
Interest expense	(206,648)	(200,163)	(210,936)
Other income (deductions) — net	(519)	10,463	12,183
Gain on sale of operations	59,300	11,000	103,800
Income before income taxes	184,247	137,931	267,721
Provision for income taxes	90,834	66,207	115,120
Net income	93,413	71,724	152,601
Preferred stock dividend requirements	16,265	18,217	9,882
Net income available to common shareholders	$ 77,148	$ 53,507	$ 142,719
Average common shares outstanding	119,217	129,768	138,755
Net income per common share	$ 0.65	$ 0.41	$ 1.03

P12.2 Financial analysis: The balance sheet. Presented below are the consolidated balance sheets for Coca-Cola Enterprises, Inc., as of fiscal year-end 1989 and 1990. Evaluate Coca-Cola's financial condition using whatever analyses (e.g., ratio analysis, trend analysis, vertical and horizontal analysis) you believe are appropriate. (Use the consolidated statement of income from P12.1 if necessary.)

COCA-COLA ENTERPRISES, INC.
Consolidated Balance Sheets
(in thousands except share data)

	December 28, 1990	December 29, 1989
Assets		
Current:		
Cash and cash equivalents, at cost (approximates market)	$ 507	$ 9,674
Trade accounts receivable, less allowances of $18,754 and $13,472, respectively	296,822	297,098
Inventories	128,450	127,880
Prepaid expenses and other assets	69,562	58,735
Total current assets	495,341	493,387
Investments and other long-term assets:		
Property, plant, and equipment:	105,637	73,286
Land	157,008	129,591
Buildings and improvements	453,100	427,206
Machinery and equipment	1,302,938	1,243,969
Containers	37,238	34,830
	1,950,284	1,835,596
Less allowances for depreciation	723,856	665,999
	1,226,428	1,169,597
Construction in progress	146,319	116,748
	1,372,747	1,286,345
Goodwill and other intangible assets	3,046,871	2,878,928
	$5,020,596	$4,731,946
Liabilities and Shareholders' Equity		
Current:		
Accounts payable and accrued expenses	$ 456,765	$ 395,069
Accounts payable to The Coca-Cola Company	21,396	51,657
Loans and notes payable and current maturities of long-term debt	576,630	549,396
Total current liabilities	1,054,791	996,122
Long-term debt	1,960,164	1,755,626
Deferred income taxes	335,008	266,086
Other long-term obligations	44,154	33,975
Shareholders' equity:		
Preferred stock, $1 par value		
Authorized — 100,000,000 shares;		
Issued and outstanding — 2,500 shares	250,000	250,000
Common stock, $1 par value		
Authorized — 500,000,000 shares;		
Issued — 140,491,081 shares and 140,363,166 shares, respectively	140,471	140,363
Paid-in capital	1,262,755	1,262,288
Reinvested earnings	382,243	311,198
Common stock in treasury, at cost		
25,636,358 shares and 17,317,010 shares, respectively	(408,990)	(283,712)
	1,626,479	1,680,137
	$5,020,596	$4,731,946

P12.3 Financial analysis: The statement of changes in financial position. Using the financial statements presented in P12.1 and P12.2, prepare a consolidated statement of changes in financial position for Coca-Cola Enterprises, Inc., as of fiscal year-end 1990. Using this statement, identify the major sources and uses of cash flows by the company. How would you evaluate the company's overall cash position?

P12.4 Restating financial statements: inventories. Presented below are the condensed financial statements for Scott Furniture as of December 31, 1989, and 1990. In the company's 1990 annual report, the following statement appeared: "If first-in, first-out had been in use, inventories would have been $1,960 million, $1,654 million, and $1,388 million higher than reported at December 31, 1990, 1989, and 1988, respectively." Scott had used the LIFO method since 1960 for financial reporting purposes.

SCOTT FURNITURE
Condensed Balance Sheets
As of December 31, 1990, and 1989
(in millions)

	December 31 1990	December 31 1989
Assets		
Cash and cash equivalents	$ 404	$ 147
Receivables	912	693
Inventories	1,750	1,670
Land	81	66
Building and equipment (net)	2,928	2,572
Long-term investments	103	85
Other assets and goodwill	220	146
Total	$6,098	$5,379
Liabilities and Owners' Equity		
Payables and accruals	1,067	790
Income tax payable	198	133
Notes payable	430	404
Deferred income tax	23	(24)
Long-term debt (total)	948	1,011
Total	2,666	2,314
Owners' Equity:		
Common stock	180	177
Retained earnings	3,252	2,888
Total	6,098	5,379

SCOTT FURNITURE
Condensed Statement of Income
For the Years Ending December 31, 1990, and 1989
(in millions)

Sales	$8,598	$7,613
Cost of goods sold	6,957*	6,172
Other expenses (net)	844	715
Income taxes	232	234
Total expenses	8,033	7,121
Income	565	492
Note:		
Depreciation for year	370	312
Dividends	201	182

*This figure includes depreciation allocable to cost of goods sold.

Required:

a. Assume that Scott had adopted the FIFO method (rather than LIFO) in 1960 and continued to use FIFO through 1990. Restate Scott's balance sheets as of year-end 1989 and 1990 to reflect the use of FIFO.

b. By how much would Scott's net income change in 1989 and 1990 if FIFO were used instead of LIFO?

c. Calculate the following ratios for Scott for 1989 and 1990 under both LIFO and FIFO:

   (1) Current ratio.

   (2) Inventory turnover.

   (3) Average number of days' inventory on hand.

   (4) Total debt-to-equity ratio.

d. Under which method do the ratios look best?

P12.5 Restating financial statements: amortization. Scott Furniture's 1990 annual report included the following statement:

> Amortization is computed principally using accelerated methods . . . for both income tax and financial reporting purposes . . . If the straight-line method had always been in use, "Buildings, machinery, and equipment — net" would have been $504 million, $430 million, and $370 million higher than reported at December 31, 1990, 1989, and 1988, respectively, and amortization expense for 1990, 1989, and 1988 would have been, respectively, $74 million, $60 million, and $48 million less.

Required:

a. Using the condensed financial statements presented in P12.4 and assuming a 35 percent tax rate, restate Scott's balance sheets for 1989 and 1990 to reflect the use of straight-line (rather than accelerated) amortization. Assume that the straight-line method is used for financial reporting purposes and that accelerated amortization is used for tax purposes.

b. By how much would Scott's net income change in 1989 and 1990 as a consequence of using the straight-line method?

c. Calculate the following ratios for Scott in 1989 and 1990 under both amortization approaches:

   (1) Return on sales.

   (2) Return on total assets.

   (3) Noncurrent asset turnover.

   (4) Total asset turnover.

d. Under which method do the ratios look best?

P12.6 The statement of changes in financial position. Peter's Pond Service, Ltd., had the following transactions during the year ending December 31:

Net income for the year was $39,000.

Accounts receivable increased $21,000 during the year.

Issued common shares for $30,000 cash.

Supplies inventory decreased by $8,000.

Dividends paid during the year were $12,000.

Amortization expense for the year was $23,000

Cash balance at January 1 was $19,000.

Redeemed long-term debt for $25,000.

Purchased equipment for $22,000.

Purchased land and obtained a mortgage for $50,000.

Accounts payable decreased $14,000 during the year.

Equipment with accumulated amortization of $27,000, that originally cost $40,000 was sold for $15,000.

$ 2000

Required:

Using the above information prepare a statement of changes in financial position for the year ended December 31.

P12.7 Calculating earnings per share. Edna Lake, Inc., reported the following income data:

Income before extraordinary items	$174,000
Extraordinary loss (net of income taxes*)	(15,000)
Net income	$159,000

*Effective tax rate is 30 percent.

Throughout the year, the company had 60,000 shares of common shares outstanding. The shares had traded at an average price of $25, and closed on December 31 at $30 per share. The company also had the following securities outstanding:

Common share options for the purchase of 8,000 shares at a price of $20 per share.

10 percent convertible bonds, with a face value of $190,000. The bonds had been sold for $200,000 and yielded 9.4 percent when the average AA corporate bond yield was 15 percent. The bonds were convertible into 7,600 shares.

9.2 percent convertible bonds, with a face value of $250,000. The bonds had been sold for $237,500 and yielded 9.7 percent when the average AA corporate bond yield was 14 percent. The bonds were convertible into 10,000 shares.

Required:

a. Using the above data, calculate the basic EPS and the fully diluted EPS for Edna Lake, Inc.

b. Which of the EPS numbers most accurately reflect the company's actual performance during the year.

P12.8 Identifying industries from ratio analysis. Shown below is a comparative ratio analysis of four different retail operations. Identify retail operation A, B, C, and D as either an automobile dealership, a jewellery store, a florist, or a womens' clothing store.

Retail Industry	Gross Profit Margin	Return on Equity	Inventory Turnover	Total Debt to Equity
A	53.6%	24.0%	10.6	270.9%
B	46.0	8.3	2.2	168.0
C	12.0	−11.7	5.5	466.9
D	43.0	12.8	5.6	206.4

P12.9 Alternative GAAP: LIFO versus FIFO. The following information was taken from the 1996 financial statements of Acme Electric Company, a major conglomerate with significant product lines in both industrial and consumer markets:

Inventories are valued on a last-in, first-out basis and carry the following balances (in millions) at December 31:

	1996	1995
Ending inventory	$3,158	$3,029

If FIFO had been used to value the inventories, they would have been $2,152 million higher than reported at December 31, 1996 ($2,266 million higher at year-end 1995). During 1996, net reductions in inventory levels resulted in liquidations of LIFO bases of $114 million, and in 1995, $163 million.

Required:

Presented below are the condensed financial statements of Acme Electric Company. Using this information, answer the following questions:

a. If FIFO was used instead of LIFO in all prior years, how would the company's 1995 and 1996 financial statements differ? (Ignore any effects on income taxes.)

b. Calculate the following ratios for 1996 under both FIFO and LIFO:

(1) Current ratio.

(2) Quick ratio.

(3) Inventory turnover.

(4) Average number of days' inventory on hand.

ACME ELECTRIC COMPANY
Statement of Financial Position
For the Year Ending December 31

	1996	1995
Assets		
Quick assets	$ 7,754	$ 7,327
Inventories	3,158	3,029
Total current assets	$10,912	$10,356
Non-current assets	12,376	$11,259
Total assets	$23,288	$21,615
Equities		
Current liabilities	$ 8,688	$ 8,153
Long-term liabilities	3,162	3,099
Total liabilities	$11,850	$11,252
Owners' equity	11,438	10,363
Total equities	$23,288	$21,615

ACME ELECTRIC COMPANY
Statement of Earnings
For the Years Ended December 31, 1996, 1995, and 1994
(in millions)

	1996	1995	1994
Sales of products and services rendered	$26,797	$26,500	$27,240
Cost of goods sold	(24,248)	(24,095)	(24,793)
Other income and expenses	450	312	167
Provision for income taxes	(975)	(900)	(962)
Net earnings	$ 2,024	$ 1,817	$ 1,652

P12.10 Alternative GAAP: leases. ABC Company is a telecommunications company that leases a substantial quantity of its non-current assets. For example, as of March 31, ABC had leased more than one-third of its total non-current assets, and the obligations associated with those leases represented nearly 50 percent of the company's total long-term debt.

Presented below are condensed balance sheets for ABC as of March 31. The company's foot-notes revealed the following additional data:

Amortization of noncurrent assets is calculated using straight-line amortization, assuming an average useful life of 10 years, unless the lease life is shorter. (No residual value is assumed.) The value of capitalized leases included in noncurrent assets was as follows (in thousands):

	March 31	
	1996	1995
Total capitalized leases	$227,582	$ 250,451

At March 31, the aggregate minimum rental commitments under noncancelable leases were as follows:

Years Ending March 31	Capital Leases	Other Leases	Total
1997	$ 57,876,000	$ 16,610,000	$ 74,486,000
1998	50,753,000	15,443,000	66,196,000
1999	42,721,000	14,441,000	57,162,000
2000	35,620,000	12,669,000	48,289,000
2001	24,410,000	10,580,000	34,990,000
2002 and thereafter	17,213,000	49,220,000	66,433,000
Minimum lease payments	228,593,000	$118,963,000	$347,556,000
Less — Amount representing interest	47,388,000		
Present value of future lease payments	$181,205,000		

Interest rates on capital lease obligations on a weighted-average basis approximate 12%.

Required:

Assuming that all "other leases" should be capitalized on the balance sheet, restate ABC's balance sheet as of March 31. Calculate the following ratios both before and after restatement:

a. Long-term debt-to-equity.

b. Total debt-to-total assets.

c. Comment on how the company's bond ratings might be affected following the capitalization of all "other leases."

ABC COMPANY
Balance Sheet
As of March 31
(in thousands)

	1996	1995
Assets		
Current assets	$228,428	$ 48,946
Non-current assets	631,970	417,946
Total assets	$860,398	$466,892
Equities		
Current liabilities	$185,540	$ 73,729
Deferred income taxes	34,058	2,409
Long-term debt	400,018	242,707
Owners' equity	240,782	148,047
Total liabilities and owners' equity	$860,398	$466,892

P12.11 Alternative GAAP: Weighted average versus FIFO. Presented below are the balance sheets and income statement of Phoenix Imports, Inc., as of December 31. In the company's annual report, the following statement appeared: "Inventories are valued on a FIFO basis. If weighted average had been used, inventories would have been valued at $889,000 at January 1, and at $1,270,000 at December 31."

Required:

Calculate the following ratios under both weighted average and FIFO:

a. Current ratio.

b. Inventory turnover.

c. Average number of days' inventory on hand.

d. Total debt-to-equity ratio.

e. Which method do you think Phoenix Imports should use, and why?

PHOENIX IMPORTS
Balance Sheet
As of December 31

Assets			Equities		
Current assets:			Current liabilities:		
Cash	$ 436,000		Accounts payable	$ 820,000	
Trade receivables (net of allowance for uncollectible accounts)	828,000		Accrued expenses payable	80,000	
Inventories	1,720,000		Total current liabilities	900,000	
Prepaid expenses	30,000				
Total current assets	3,014,000				
Non-current assets:					
Property, plant, and equipment	$3,940,000				
Less: Accumulated depreciation	(1,360,000)		Non-current liabilities:		
	2,580,000		Notes payable	2,320,000	
Land	560,000		Deferred federal income taxes	800,000	
Deferred research and development cost	1,150,000		Total liabilities	4,020,000	
Total assets	$7,304,000		Owners' equity:		
			Common stock, $1 par	2,000,000	
			Retained earnings	1,284,000	
			Total equities	$7,304,000	

PHOENIX IMPORTS
Income Statement
For the Year Ended December 31

Sales revenue		$4,950,000
Less: Cost of sales		
Beginning inventory	$1,205,000	
Cost of production	3,665,000	
Goods available for sale	4,870,000	
Less: Ending inventory	1,720,000	
		(3,150,000)
Gross margin		1,800,000
Less: Research and development expenses	350,000	
Licensing fees	100,000	
Selling and administrative expenses	400,000	
Net income before taxes		(850,000)
		950,000
Less: Income taxes	475,000	
Investment and research tax credits	(60,000)	
		(415,000)
Net income after taxes		$ 535,000

P12.12 Alternative GAAP: amortization. Phoenix Imports' annual report included the following statement: "Property, plant and equipment is amortized on a straight-line basis. If an accelerated method had been used, the amortization expense would have been $230,000 higher, and the year-end balance in the accumulated amortization account $450,000 greater."

Required:

a. Using the financial statements presented in P12.11 and assuming a 50 percent tax rate, restate Phoenix Imports' financial statements to reflect the use of accelerated amortization rather than the straight-line method. Phoenix Imports reports all amortization as a component of cost of goods sold.

b. Calculate the following ratios under both accelerated and straight-line amortization:

(**1**) Return on equity.

(**2**) Return on total assets.

(**3**) Total asset turnover.

c. Which method do you think Phoenix Imports should use, and why?

P12.13 Alternative GAAP: capitalizing versus expensing R&D. Phoenix Imports' annual report included the following statement:

> The research and development expense represented one-half of the actual R&D expenditure for the year; the remaining balance had been capitalized. The company's policy is to begin amortization of these capitalized costs once a commercially productive asset has been developed. To date, no productive assets have resulted from the research program represented by the currently capitalized R&D costs.

Required:

a. Using the financial statements presented in P12.11 and assuming a 50 percent tax rate, restate Phoenix Imports' financial statements to reflect the full current expensing of all R&D costs.

b. Calculate the following ratios under the old and new policies regarding expensing R&D expenditures:

(**1**) Return on equity.

(**2**) Return on total assets.

(**3**) Total asset turnover.

c. Which method do you think Phoenix Imports should adopt, and why?

P12.14 Alternative GAAP: completed contract versus percentage of completion. Thunderbird Construction Company (TCC) was employed to construct a new office facility. The three-year project is projected to cost $100 million to complete and is expected to produce gross revenues of $150 million during the three-year period. In anticipation of the preparation of financial reports covering the project, TCC's controller collected the following financial data (in millions) relating to the project:

	Year 1	Year 2	Year 3
Construction costs incurred	$400	$300	$325
Estimated costs to complete	600	350	—
Progress billings	500	500	500
Collections on billings	—	450	900
Administrative expense	25	25	25

Required:

a. Using the above data, prepare income statements for the company under (1) the completed-contract method and (2) the percentage-of-completion method for each of the three years.

b. Which set of results do you believe most accurately depicts the performance of the company?

P12.15 Calculating earnings per share. Assume that during 1996, Erie Enterprises has the following securities outstanding:

1. 250,000 shares of common shares with an average market price of $25 per share.

2. Options granted to executives to purchase 4,000 shares of common shares during the next three years at a price of $20 per share.

3. Convertible debentures with a maturity value of $10 million, which had been sold at a yield of 12 percent. Each $1,000 face value bond is convertible into 15 shares of common shares.

4. Convertible preferred shares, which had been sold at its par value of $100 to yield 9.5 percent. The preferred shares are convertible into 3 shares of common and 3,000 shares are outstanding. During 1996, Erie Enterprises earned $3.2 million after taxes. (Assume that taxes are calculated at 33 percent.)

Required:

Calculate the basic and fully diluted earnings per share for the company.

P12.16 Alternative accounting methods. After successfully completing an introductory accounting course, Marj Smythe was asked by her uncle to prepare the financial statements for his business, Nifty Corporation. The company has a December 31 year-end and commenced operations in early 1996. Marj has reviewed the following information about her uncle's business:

1. On January 2, 1996, machinery was purchased for $1,500,000. It was estimated to have a useful life of 10 years and a residual value of $100,000. Marj is considering using either straight-line amortization or the declining-balance method at twice the straight-line rate.

2. To finance the purchase of machinery Nifty Corporation has issued $1,000,000 in bonds. The bonds payable have a five-year term effective January 1, 1996. The bonds have an annual coupon rate of 10 percent. Interest is paid annually. The bonds were sold for $927,908, an annual yield or effective rate of 12 percent. Either the straight-line or effective interest methods may be used to determine the interest expense for 1996.

3. Nifty Corporation has signed a five-year lease for the rental of printing equipment. The lease requires five annual payments of $52,760. The lease payments are such that they have a present value of $200,000 on January 1, 1996, when discounted at 10 percent per year. The lease agreement may be structured as either an operating lease or a capital lease.

4. Merchandise purchases for the year were:

Number of Units	Unit Cost	Total Cost
50,000	$6.00	$ 300,000
60,000	6.20	372,000
40,000	6.25	250,000
50,000	6.50	325,000
200,000		$1,247,000

There were 80,000 units in ending inventory, on December 31, 1996. Sales during the year totalled $2,000,000, of which 70 percent were on account and the balance were for cash. Nifty uses a periodic inventory system. Marj is considering either LIFO, FIFO, or weighted average as alternative accounting methods.

5. Marj's uncle has estimated approximately 1.5 percent of sales on account will be uncollectible. During the year, $950,000 was collected on accounts receivable. If the aging method is used, it is estimated 5 percent of the December 31, 1996, accounts receivable outstanding will be uncollectible.

6. At the end of the year, the business had the following temporary investments:

Investment	Cost	Market
IPSCO shares	$100,000	$105,000
IBM shares	50,000	40,000

7. On December 31, 1996, a $25,000 dividend on common shares was paid.

Required:

Prepare an income statement for the year ending December 31, 1996, selecting the accounting policies that will produce the lowest net income.

P12.17 Statement of changes in financial position. Wallace, Limited, had the following transactions during the year ending December 31:

Patent amortization expense for the year was $5,000.

Amortization expense for the year was $12,000.

Prepaid insurance costs increased by $1,000.

Redeemed bonds payable for $24,000.

Purchased machinery for $20,000.

Issued for $10,000 cash, non-par-value common shares.

Merchandise inventories increased by $4,000.

Obtained a long-term loan for $13,000 and used the proceeds to purchase land.

Declared and paid cash dividends of $3,000.

Cash balance at January 1 was $21,000.

Accounts payable decreased $8,000 during the year.

Equipment with accumulated amortization of $15,000 that originally cost $25,000 was sold for a gain of $2,000.

Net income for the year was $24,000.

Accounts receivable decreased $7,000 during the year.

Required:

Using the above information, prepare a classified statement of changes in financial position for the year ended December 31.

P12.18 Alternative accounting methods. On January 1, Year 1, two corporations are formed to operate merchandising businesses. The firms are alike in all respects except for their method of accounting. Ballete, Limited, chooses the accounting policies that will minimize its reported net income. Jazzet, Inc., chooses the accounting policies that will maximize its reported net income but, where different procedures are permitted, will use accounting methods that minimize its taxable income. The following events occur during Year 1.

1. Both companies issue 200,000 no-par-value common shares for $5 per share on January 2, Year 1.

2. Both firms acquire equipment on January 2, Year 1, for $800,000 cash. The equipment is estimated to have a five-year life and zero residual value.

3. Both firms engage in extensive advertising campaigns during Year 2 incurring costs of $250,000.

4. The two firms make the following purchases of merchandise inventory:

Date	Units Purchased	Unit Price	Cost of Purchase
January 21	50,000	$6.00	$ 300,000
April 26	60,000	6.20	372,000
August 15	40,000	6.25	250,000
October 30	50,000	6.50	325,000
Total	200,000		$1,247,000

5. During the year, both firms sell 120,000 units at an average price of $12 each.

6. Selling, general, and administrative expenses, other than advertising, total $85,000 during the year.

Ballete, Limited, uses the following accounting methods (for both book and tax purposes): weighted-average inventory cost-flow assumption, declining-balance amortization method, with a rate of 30 percent, and immediate expensing of the costs of sales promotion.

Jazzet, Inc., uses the following accounting methods: FIFO inventory cost-flow assumption for both book and tax purposes, the straight-line amortization method for book purposes, the declining-balance method for tax purposes with a rate of 20 percent, capitalization and amortization of the costs of the sales promotion campaign over four years for book, and immediate expensing for tax purposes.

Required:

a. Prepare comparative income statements for the two firms for Year 1. Include separate computations of income tax expense. The income tax rate is 40 percent.

b. Prepare comparative balance sheets for the two firms as of December 31, Year 1. Both firms have $45,000 of outstanding accounts receivable on this date and a single current liability for income taxes payable for the year.

c. Prepare comparative statements of changes in financial position for the two firms for Year 1, defining funds as cash.

P12.19 Income statement and a statement of retained earnings. Listed below, in alphabetical order, are the balances from the adjusted trial balance for a firm for its year ended November 30, 1996. You may assume that all accounts have normal debit or credit balances.

Accounts payable	$ 22,000
Accounts receivable	35,000
Accumulated amortization	15,000
Allowance for doubtful accounts	3,000
Bad debts expense	500
Bank loan due December 31, 1999	15,000
Cash	25,500
Commissions payable	2,000
Common shares, non-par value, 1,000 shares issued	17,500
Customer deposits liability	3,000
Amortization expense	2,500
Furniture and fixtures, at cost	25,000
Income tax expense	4,000
Income taxes payable	3,000
Interest expense	2,000
Inventory, November 30, 1995	50,000
Notes payable, due January 2, 1998	5,000
Preferred shares, non-cumulative, non-par value, authorized and issued 375 shares	37,500
Prepaid rent	500
Purchases	75,000
Purchases returns and allowances	10,000
Rent expense	2,000
Retained earnings (December 1, 1995, balance less dividends declared in year)	8,000
Salaries expense	13,500
Sales	105,000
Sales commissions expense	3,500
Sales returns and allowances	5,000
Treasury shares, 5 common shares held at cost	2,000

Note: 1. Cash dividends declared and paid during the year were $7,000.

2. Inventory (at lower of FIFO cost and market) as counted at November 30, 1995, was $55,000.

Required:

Prepare in good form an income statement and a statement of retained earnings for the year ended November 30, 1996.

P12.20 Financial statement disclosure. Describe how the following items would be disclosed on a properly classified financial statement:

a. Significant accounting policies.

b. Research and development costs.

c. Sales returns.

d. Allowance for decline in market value of temporary investments.

P12.21 Comparative analysis. Using the information provided in the earning statements of the Hudson Bay Company, prepare a vertical and horizontal analysis. Provide comments on the results of your analysis.

HUDSON BAY COMPANY
Consolidated Statement of Earnings
Year Ended January 31

	1994	1993
Sales and Revenue:		
The Bay	$2,182,570	$2,017,189
Zellers	3,159,451	3,021,171
Other	99,477	113,856
	$5,441,498	$5,152,216
Operating profit:		
The Bay	$ 121,722	$ 91,473
Zellers	256,098	229,053
Other	(13,969)	(5,477)
	$ 363,851	$ 315,049
Gain on sale of investment	—	12,266
Earnings before interest and taxes	$ 363,851	$ 327,315
Interest expense	(97,381)	(127,842)
Earnings before income taxes	$ 266,470	$ 199,473
Income taxes	(118,769)	(82,750)
Net earnings	$ 147,701	$ 116,723

P12.22 Statement of changes in financial position Montvue Corporation's transactions for the year ended December 31, 1996, included the following:

Acquired 50 percent of the common shares of Melvin Corp. for $325,000 cash, which was borrowed from a bank.

Issued 5,000 shares of its preferred shares for land having a fair value of $500,000.

Issued 500 of its 11 percent debenture bonds, due in 1997, for $590,000 cash.

Purchased a patent for $375,000 cash.

Paid $250,000 on a bank loan.

Sold investment securities for $1,095,000.

Had a net increase in customer deposits of $210,000.

Required:

a. Determine Montvue's net cash provided by investing activities for 1996.

b. Determine Montvue's net cash provided by financing activities for 1996.

P12.23 Statement of changes in financial position (*Published with permission of CGA Canada*). The following financial information refers to Mitchel Company:

	December 31, 1993	December 31, 1992
Cash	$ 15,000	$ 20,000
Accounts receivable (net)	23,000	25,000
Inventory	37,000	34,000
Prepaid expenses	6,000	8,000
Long-term investments	37,000	40,000
Operational assets	92,000	80,000
Accumulated amortization	(30,000)	(25,000)
	$180,000	$182,000
Demand loan	$ 67,000	$ 65,000
Accounts payable	38,000	30,000
Common shares	40,000	37,000
Retained earnings	35,000	50,000
	$180,000	$182,000
Sales	$250,000	
Cost of goods sold	165,000	
Gross margin	85,000	
Operating expenses	40,000	
Operating income before taxes	45,000	
Gain on sale of investments	8,000	
Income before taxes	53,000	
Less income taxes	14,800	
Net income	$ 38,200	

Required:

Prepare a statement of changes in financial position for Mitchel Company.

P12.24 Alternative accounting policies (*Published with permission of CGA Canada*). Halifax, Ltd., has reported net income of $30,000, $42,000, and $50,000, respectively, during each of the past three years. The company currently uses the straight-line method of amortization but is considering switching to the double-declining-balance method. Similarly, it plans to change from the FIFO inventory method to LIFO and from the direct write-off method of handling uncollectibles to the allowance method. The following information is extracted from the company's financial statements:

	Year 1	Year 2	Year 3
Amortization expense	$ 8,000	$ 8,400	$12,000
Bad debts expense	900	1,400	800
Ending inventory	18,000	23,000	25,000

If the proposed changes had been in effect over the last three years, the following figures would have been reported:

	Year 1	Year 2	Year 3
Amortization expense	$14,000	$13,900	$13,000
Bad debts expense	1,500	1,900	2,400
Ending inventory	16,000	21,500	22,300

Required:

Prepare revised net income figures for each of the past three years assuming the proposed changes had been in effect over that period.

P12.25 Statement of changes in financial position. The comparative financial statements of the Price-Wilson, Limited, for the years ending December 31 are presented below:

	1996	1995
Cash	$ 62,000	$ 63,000
Accounts receivable	70,000	67,000
Merchandise inventory	321,000	286,000
Supplies inventory	25,000	31,000
Capital assets*	300,000	223,000
Accumulated amortization	(93,000)	(70,000)
	$685,000	$600,000
Accounts payable	$ 71,000	$ 86,000
Accrued liabilities	13,000	8,000
Deferred taxes	11,000	20,000
Mortgage payable	65,000	15,000
Common shares, non-value†	310,000	250,000
Preferred shares, 7%, redeemable cumulative, non-par value	100,000	135,000
Retained earnings	115,000	86,000
	$685,000	$600,000
Sales	$960,000	$825,000
Cost of goods sold	(590,000)	(490,000)
Gross profit	$370,000	$335,000
Amortization expense	(35,000)	(29,000)
Operating expenses	(276,000)	(270,000)
Income tax expense	(20,000)	(15,000)
Loss — disposal of capital asset	(6,000)	—
Net income	$ 33,000	$ 21,000

*During 1996 Price-Wilson sold capital assets with a net book value of $48,000 for $42,000.

†Weighted average shares outstanding: 3,100 — 1996, 2,500 — 1995.

Required:

a. Complete a comparative ratio analysis of Price-Wilson. Include comments on your analysis.

b. Prepare a statement of changes in financial position for the year ending December 31, 1996.

P12.26 Alternative accounting policies and financial analysis. Comox, Ltd., has reported net income of $123,000, $174,000, and $156,000, respectively, during each of the past three years. The company currently uses the double-declining-balance method of amortization but is considering switching to the straight-line method. Similarly, it plans to change from the FIFO inventory method to the weighted-average method and from the aging method of handling uncollectibles to the percentage-of-sales method. As well, the company is planning on changing from the completed-contract method to the percentage-of-completion method for revenue recognition on long-term contracts. The following information is extracted from the company's financial statements.

	Year 1	Year 2	Year 3
Amortization expense	$ 22,000	$ 19,400	$ 17,000
Completed contract	0	78,000	0
Bad debts expense	1,700	1,200	1,100
Ending inventory	16,000	21,000	22,000
Total shareholders' equity (end of period)	555,000	686,000	814,000

The total shareholders' equity includes net income for current year and share capital of $25,000. If the proposed changes had been in effect over the last three years, the following figures would have been reported:

	Year 1	Year 2	Year 3
Amortization expense	$18,000	$16,000	$12,000
Percentage completion	33,000	27,000	42,000
Bad debts expense	1,400	2,300	2,800
Ending inventory	18,000	19,000	23,000

Required:

a. Prepare revised net income figures for each of the past three years assuming the proposed changes had been in effect over that period.

b. Determine the return on equity before and after the proposed changes in accounting policies.

c. If the retained earnings was $450,000 at the beginning of Year 1, determine the total dividends declared each year. (Ignore any proposed changes in accounting policy.)

P12.27 Cash provided from operations. The following information is extracted from the records of Campobello, Ltd.:

CAMPOBELLO, LTD.
Income Statement
For the Month Ended April 30

Sales		$288,000
Cost of goods sold		177,000
Gross profit		$111,000
Expenses/losses:		
Wages	$47,000	
Rent	12,000	
Loss on disposal of capital asset	4,000	
Interest	9,000	
Amortization	13,000	85,000
Net income		$ 26,000

Additional data:

1. During April, the Accounts Receivable balance increased by $17,000.

2. Accounts Payable decreased by $15,000 during the month.

3. The Wages Payable balance increased by $3,000 during the month.

4. Rent Payable decreased by $2,500 during April.

Required:
Prepare a statement to determine the cash provided by operations for Campobello, Ltd., for the month of April.

P12.28 Turnover analysis. The partial income statement of Fredericton Supplies & Services, Ltd., for the year ended March 31 is shown below:

Sales	$927,000
Cost of sales	714,000
Gross profit	$213,000

The accounts receivable turnover ratio for the period is 7.12. The inventory turnover ratio for the same period is 3.19. Determine the average Accounts Receivable and Inventory balances for the period.

P12.29 Gross profit analysis. The financial statements of the Murray River Rentals, Inc., include average Accounts Receivable and Inventory balances of $71,000 and $112,000, respectively. An analysis of the financial statements determines the accounts receivable turnover ratio for the period to be 5.61. The inventory turnover ratio for the same period is 2.71. Determine the dollar value of gross profit and the gross profit ratio for the period.

P12.30 Financial analysis and statement of changes in financial position. Presented below is St. John's Supplies, Limited's comparative financial statements for the year ended December 31.

ST. JOHN'S SUPPLIES LIMITED
Income Statement
For the Year Ended December 31

	1996	1995
Sales	$882,000	$772,000
Cost of goods sold	550,000	510,000
Gross profit	$332,000	$262,000
Expenses:		
Operating and maintenance	62,000	52,000
Selling and administrative	158,000	160,000
Amortization	21,000	16,000
	$241,000	$228,000
Income before income taxes	$ 91,000	$ 34,000
Income taxes	(19,000)	(12,000)
Net income	$ 72,000	$ 22,000

ST. JOHN'S SUPPLIES, LIMITED
Balance Sheet
As at December 31

	1996	1995
Assets		
Current assets:		
Cash	$ 23,000	$ 29,000
Accounts receivable	99,000	76,000
Inventories	83,000	60,000
Supplies	34,000	16,000
Total current assets	$239,000	$181,000
Long-term investments	38,000	23,000
Capital assets	410,000	269,000
Accumulated amortization	(58,000)	(37,000)
	$629,000	$436,000
Liabilities and Shareholders' Equity		
Current liabilities:		
Notes payable	$ 92,000	$ 61,000
Accounts payable	97,000	82,000
Current portion — long-term debt	12,000	10,000
Total current liabilities	$201,000	$153,000
Long-term debt	170,000	135,000
Total liabilities	$371,000	$288,000
Shareholders' equity:		
Share capital*	$134,000	$ 90,000
Retained earnings	124,000	58,000
Total shareholders' equity	$258,000	$148,000
	$629,000	$436,000

* Weighted-average shares outstanding: 1996: 16,000 shares; 1995: 10,000 shares.

Required:

a. Perform an analysis of financial strength and management performance of the company. Your report should include comments as to the financial position of the company.

b. Prepare a statement of changes in financial position for the year ending December 31, 1996.

P12.31 Financial analysis. A group of ratios for Oakville Productions and Hamilton Manufacturing are presented below. Both companies operate in the same industry. Prepare a report commenting on the comparative financial strength of each company.

OAKVILLE PRODUCTIONS

	1996	1995
Liquidity Analysis:		
Cash on hand	$521	$433
Working capital	$6,676	$6,482
Quick ratio	.56:1	.46:1
Current ratio	1.40:1	1.32:1
Solvency Analysis:		
Total debt-to-equity ratio	4.32:1	4.11:1
Long-term debt-to-invested capital ratio	2.72:1	2.55:1

HAMILTON MANUFACTURING

	1996	1995
Liquidity Analysis:		
Cash on hand	$339	$287
Working capital	2,123	2,987
Quick ratio	.31:1	.41:1
Current ratio	1.36:1	1.45:1
Solvency Analysis:		
Total debt-to-equity ratio	3.71:1	4.13:1
Long-term debt-to-invested capital ratio	2.36:1	2.57:1

P12.32 Financial analysis. Ratios for Lethbridge Services and Fernie Enterprises are presented below. Both companies operate in the same industry. Prepare a report commenting on the comparative strength of each company.

LETHBRIDGE SERVICES

	1996	1995
Profitability Analysis:		
Gross profit percentage	35.6%	35.3%
Earnings per share	$.69	$.52
Return on equity	8.67%	7.78%
Asset Management Analysis:		
Inventory turnover	4.18	4.52
Total asset turnover	.88	.99
Receivable turnover	9.8	9.0

FERNIE ENTERPRISES

	1996	1995
Profitability Analysis:		
Gross profit percentage	34.2%	32.7%
Earnings per share	$.42	$.49
Return on equity	9.11%	9.79%
Asset Management Analysis:		
Inventory turnover	3.57	3.11
Total asset turnover	1.11	1.23
Receivable turnover	6.3	6.9

P12.33 Ratio Analysis. Ratio corporation is a small retail business operating in northern Ontario. The accountant completed a ratio analysis of the financial statements of Ratio Corporation for the year ended December 31. The ratios for the financial statements are as follows:

Return on equity	35.0%
Earnings per share	$28.00
Gross margin	30.0%
Total asset turnover	.889
Inventory turnover	4.00
Receivable turnover	5.00
Total debt to equity	1.25:1
Long-term debt to invested capital	0.428:1
Current ratio	2.00:1
Quick ratio	1.30:1

Required:

Using the ratio information for Ratio Corporation, complete the financial statements for the year ended December 31.

RATIO CORPORATION
Income Statement
For the Year Ended December 31

Sales	$80,000
Cost of goods sold	?
Gross profit	?
Expenses	10,000
Net income	?

RATIO CORPORATION
Balance Sheet
December 31

Cash	$10,000	Accounts payable	?
Accounts receivable	?	Long-term debt	?
Inventory	?	Common shares*	14,000
Capital assets	?	Retained earnings	?
	?		?

*500 common shares have been issued.

SOLUTIONS TO COMPREHENSIVE
REVIEW PROBLEMS

R1.1 Financial statement elements.

Prepaid expenses	$ 981,915	Balance sheet
Purchase of fixed assets	1,716,489	Statement of changes
Revenue from operations	62,693,174	Income statement
Accounts payable	7,036,834	Balance sheet
Operating expenses	53,175,423	Income statement
Financing activities	1,680,378	Statement of changes
N.H.L. expansion fees	3,112,931	Income statement
Investment and other income	850,022	Income statement
Decrease in accounts receivable	1,400,746	Statement of changes
Income before income taxes	10,837,485	Income statement

R2.1 Analysis of financial strength. Financial analysis should be completed on a comparative basis whenever possible. Financial information for two comparative periods is provided for Coca-Cola Beverages, Ltd. Financial strength analysis may be completed by examining the liquidity and solvency of the organization.

The analysis of Coca-Cola Beverages, Ltd., indicates a definite weakening of the firm's financial strength over the two-year period. The liquidity or short-term ability of the firm to meet its financial obligations has weakened as reflected in the negative working capital and lower quick and current ratios in the second year. The solvency or ability to meet long-term obligations is also significantly weaker in the second year. Both solvency ratios are significantly higher in the second year, indicating a weaker financial position.

	1993	1992
Liquidity Analysis:		
Cash on hand	$13,480	$13,681
Working capital	$(36,909)	$63,896
Quick ratio	.45:1 ($13,480 + $69,277) ÷ $184,955	.66:1 ($13,681 + $77,314) ÷ $136,944
Current ratio	.80:1 ($148,046 ÷ $184,955)	1.47:1 ($200,840 ÷ $136,944)
Solvency Analysis:		
Total debt-to-equity ratio	5.37:1 [($184,955 + $411,512) ÷ $111,082]	2.12:1 [($136,944 + $386,412 + $37,005) ÷ $264,346]
Long-term debt-to-invested capital ratio	.79:1 [$411,512 ÷ ($411,512 + $111,082)]	.62:1 [($386,412 + $37,005) ÷ ($386,412 + $37,005 + $264,346)]

R2.2 Balance sheet.

WONG COMPANY
Balance Sheet
December 31, 1996

Assets		Liabilities	
Cash	$ 37,300	Accounts payable	$ 27,000
Accounts receivable	17,000	Salaries payable	11,200
Temporary investments	4,400	Loan payable	14,000
Inventory	22,000	Total current liabilities	$ 52,200
Total current assets	$ 80,700	Bonds payable	30,000
Land	$ 29,000	Mortgage payable	42,500
Building	39,000	Total liabilities	$124,700
Equipment	16,000		
Patent	17,000	**Shareholders' Equity**	
Total capital assets	$101,000	Share capital	$ 20,000
	$181,700	Retained earnings	37,000
		Total equity	$ 57,000
			$181,700

R2.3 Statement of changes in financial position.

a. Cash balance at the end of the period is $8,000 ($19 − $12 − $20 + $20 +$5 − $4).

b.

TERRA INTERIOR DESIGNS LTD.
Statement of Changes in Financial Position
For the Year Ending December 31

Investing activities:		
Sale of land	$ 5,000	
Purchase of equipment	(12,000)	
Purchase of land	(20,000)	
Cash used in investing		(27,000)
Financing activities:		
Issue common shares	$ 19,000	
Obtain long-term loan	20,000	
Payment on long-term loan	(4,000)	
Cash provided from financing		35,000
Increase in cash		$ 8,000
Cash — January 1		–0–
Cash — December 31		$ 8,000

R3.1 Analysis of financial strength and management performance. Financial analysis should be completed on a comparative basis whenever possible. Financial information for two comparative periods is provided for Cineplex Odeon Corporation. Financial strength analysis may be completed by examining the liquidity and solvency of the organization. An analysis of the financial strength of Cineplex Odeon Corporation shows the liquidity position has weakened during the second year. Working capital is a larger negative amount and both the quick and current ratios are slightly worse. The long-term or solvency position of the firm shows a small improvement over the previous year.

Although the firm is not profitable, a significant improvement is shown in the profitability ratios over the first year. The loss per share has been reduced to $(.069) from $(.482) in the first year. The asset management ratios also show an improvement over the previous year.

Because of the specialised nature of the business of Cineplex Odeon Corporation, a complete financial analysis is difficult without comparative data from similar firms in the same industry.

	1993	**1992**
Liquidity Analysis:		
Cash on hand	$1,268	$1,350
Working capital	$(110,493)	$(89,453)
Quick ratio	.15:1 [($1,268 + $19,640)/$139,669]	.19:1 [($1,350 + $21,578)/$120,106]
Current ratio	.21:1 ($29,176/$139,669)	.26:1 ($30,653/$120,106)
Solvency Analysis:		
Total debt-to-equity ratio	2.48:1 ($496,718/$200,387)	2.73:1 ($542,689/$198,966)
Long-term debt-to-invested capital ratio	.64:1 [($324,852 + $32,197)/ ($324,852 + $32,197 + $200,387)]	.68:1 [($413,500 + $9,083)/ ($413,500 + $9,083 + $198,966)]
Profitability Analysis:		
Earnings per share (Loss)	$(.069) [$(7,372)/$106,730]	$(.482) [$(41,349)/$85,823]
Return on equity	(3.68)% [$(7,372)/$200,387]	(20.78)% [$(41,349)/$198,966]
Asset Management Analysis:		
Total asset turnover	.78 ($546,230/$697,105)	.70 ($518,723/$741,652)
Receivable turnover	27.8 ($546,230/$19,640)	24.0 ($518,723/$21,578)

R3.2 Accrual versus cash basis of accounting.

MCGREGOR AND EPP
Income Statement (Accrual basis)
For the Eight Months Ending December 31

Revenues ($82,000 + $7,600)		$89,600
Expenses:		
Rent expense ($550 × 8)	$4,400	
Amortization expense		
Interest expense		
Utility expense		
Salary expense	7,500	
Interest expense		
Office supplies expense	1,760	16,952
Net income		$72,648

MCGREGOR AND EPP
Balance Sheet (Accrual basis)
December 31

Assets		**Liabilities**	
Cash [$15,000 + $15,000 + $20,000 − (9 × $550) − $4,500 + $71,000 − $1,450 − $6,800 − $1,760]	$101,540	Accounts payable ($180 + $700)	$ 880
Accounts receivable ($11,000 + $7,600)	18,600	Interest payable	1,100
Prepaid rent	550	Loan payable	20,000
Office equipment	4,500	**Equity**	
Accumulated amortization	(562)	Capital, McGregor [$15,000 + ($72,648/2)]	51,324
	$124,628	Capital, Epp [$15,000 + ($72,648/2)]	51,324
			$124,628

MCGREGOR AND EPP
Statement of Changes in Financial Position
For the Eight Months Ending December 31

Operating Activities:

Net income	$72,648	
Items not involving cash:		
Change in working capital items:		
Increase in interest payable	1,100	
Increase in accounts payable	880	
Increase in prepaid rent	(550)	
Increase in accounts receivable	(18,600)	$ 56,040
Investing activities:		
Equipment purchase	$ (4,500)	$ (4,500)
Financing activities:		
Loan payable	$20,000	
McGregor's contributed capital	15,000	
Epp's contributed capital	15,000	50,000
Increase in cash		$101,540
Cash — May 1		–0–
Cash — December 31		$101,540

MCGREGOR AND EPP
Income Statement (Cash basis)
For the Eight Months Ending December 31

Revenues ($82,000 − $11,000)		$71,000
Expenses:		
Rent expense ($550 × 9)	$4,950	
Utility expense	1,450	
Salary expense	6,800	
Office supplies expense	1,760	14,960
Net income		$56,040

R4.1 Accounting cycle.

a. and **c.** General journal

1 Cash	2,000	
Capital, Sally		2,000
2 Office Supplies	50	
Cash		50
3 Equipment	300	
Accounts Payable		300
4 Cash	100	
Revenues		100
5 Accounts Payable	200	
Cash		200
6 Accounts Receivable	300	
Revenues		300
7 Utility Expense	25	
Cash		25
8 Cash	150	
Accounts Receivable		150
9 Amortization Expense	30	
Accumulated Amortization		30
10 Office Supplies Expense	40	
Office Supplies		40
11 Revenues	20	
Unearned Revenues		20

b. and **f.** General ledger (T-accounts)

Cash			
(1) 2,000		(2) 50	
(4) 100		(5) 200	
(8) 150		(7) 25	
1,975			

Accounts Receivable	
(6) 300	(8) 150
150	

Office Supplies	
(2) 50	(10) 40
10	

Equipment	
(3) 300	
300	

Accumulated Amortization	
	(9) 30
	30

Capital, Sally	
	(1) 2,000
	(14) 285
	2,285

Unearned Revenue	
(11) 20	
	20

Accounts Payable	
(5) 200	(3) 300
	100

Utility Expense	
(7) 25	(12) 25
–0–	

Amortization Expense	
(9) 30	(12) 30
–0–	

Office Supplies Expense	
(10) 40	(12) 40
–0–	

Revenues	
(11) 20	(4) 100
	(6) 300
(13) 380	380
	–0–

d.

SALLY SMITH
Adjusted Trial Balance
December 31

Account	Debit	Credit
Cash	$1,975	
Accounts receivable	150	
Office supplies	10	
Store equipment	300	
Accumulated amortization		$ 30
Accounts payable		100
Unearned revenue		20
Capital, Sally		2,000
Revenues		380
Utility expense	25	
Amortization expense	30	
Office supplies expense	40	
Total	$2,530	$2,530

e.

SALLY SMITH
Income Statement
For the Year Ending December 31

Revenues		$380
Utility expense	$25	
Office supplies expense	40	
Amortization expense	30	95
Net income		$285

SALLY SMITH
Balance Sheet
As at December 31

Assets			**Liabilities**		
Current assets:			Current liabilities:		
Cash		$1,975	Accounts payable		$ 100
Accounts receivable		150	Unearned revenue		20
Office supplies		10	Total current liabilities		$ 120
Total current assets		$2,135	**Owner's Equity**		
Capital assets:			Capital, Sally ($2,000 + $285)		$2,285
Equipment	$ 300				$2,405
Accumulated amortization	(30)				
Total capital assets		$ 270			
Total assets		$2,405			

SALLY SMITH
Statement of Changes in Financial Position
For the Year Ending December 31

Operating activities:		
Net income		$ 285
Items not involving cash:		
Amortization		30
Change in working capital items:		
Accounts payable		100
Accounts receivable		(150)
Office supplies		(10)
Unearned revenue		20
		$ 275
Investing activities:		
Equipment purchase		(300)
Financing activities:		
Capital from Sally	2,000	2,000
Increase in cash		$1,975
Cash — January 1		–0–
Cash — December 31		$1,975

f. General journal — closing entries

12	Income Summary	95	
	Office Supplies Expense		40
	Utility Expense		25
	Amortization Expense		30
13	Revenues	380	
	Income Summary		380
14	Income Summary	285	
	Capital, Sally		285

g.

SALLY SMITH
Postclosing Trial Balance
December 31

Account	Debit	Credit
Cash	$1,975	
Accounts receivable	150	
Office supplies	10	
Store equipment	300	
Accumulated amortization		$ 30
Accounts payable		100
Unearned revenue		20
Capital, Sally		2,285
Total	$2,435	$2,435

R5.1 Financial analysis. The financial position of Alberta Natural Gas, Ltd., has remained very stable over the two-year period. Both the liquidity and solvency analysis reveal only a small change from the previous year. The most significant change is in the area of profitability where the EPS and the return on equity have improved significantly. The asset turnover ratios reflect a slightly weaker position over the previous year.

	1993	1992
Liquidity Analysis:		
Cash on hand	$13,668	$39,501
Working capital	$(6,593)	$(5,823)
Quick ratio	.65:1 [($13,668 + $115,571)/$197,839]	.74:1 [($39,501 + $86,132 + $10,876)/$184,833]
Current ratio	.97:1 ($191,246/$197,839)	.97:1 ($179,010/$184,833)
Solvency Analysis:		
Total debt-to-equity ratio	2.08:1 ($432,860/$207,756)	2.00:1 ($339,796/$169,476)
Long-term debt-to-invested capital ratio	.53:1 [($176,748 + $58,273)/ ($176,748 + $58,273 + $207,756)]	.48:1 [($111,813 + $43,150)/ ($111,813 + $43,150 + $169,476)]
Profitability Analysis:		
Earnings per share	$1.93 ($49,584/$25,697)	$.70 ($17,905/$25,654)
Return on equity	23.86% ($49,584/$207,756)	10.56% ($17,905/$169,476)
Asset Management Analysis:		
Total asset turnover	1.03 ($662,693/$640,616)	1.12 ($572,819/$509,272)
Receivable turnover	5.73 ($662,693/$115,571)	6.65 ($572,819/$86,132)

R6.1 Cash, temporary investments, and receivables. The bank reconciliation for December is shown below:

Bank Reconciliation — December 31

Accounting Records		Bank Records	
Balance per records	$4,312	Balance per bank	$3,300
Service charge	(18)	Outstanding deposit	2,700
Loan payment	(310)	Outstanding cheques	(2,016)
Adjusted cash balance	$3,984	Adjusted cash balance	$3,984

Cash disclosure for financial statement purposes:

Bank	$3,984
Petty cash	100
G.I.C.	2,000
	$6,084

Temporary Investments	Cost	Market
ABC, Ltd.	$10,000	$ 8,200
XYZ, Ltd.	8,000	9,000
	$18,000	$17,200

Lower of cost or market is $17,200.

Based on past experiences of account collections, the following amounts were anticipated to be uncollectible:

Percentage of Sales:

.005 × $88,000 = $440

Percentage of Aged Categories:

2% of all accounts 1–30 days	0.02 × $5,500 = $110
4% of all accounts 31–60 days	0.04 × $3,300 = 132
10% of all accounts 61–90 days	0.10 × $1,300 = 130
20% of all accounts over 90 days	0.20 × $ 400 = 80
	$452

Percentage of Total Receivables:

.05 × $10,500 = $525*

* The percentage-of-total-receivables method provides the most conservative (highest expense) estimate of uncollectible accounts, $525.

Balance Sheet — December 31

Current assets:		
Cash		$ 6,084
Temporary investments	$18,000	
Less: Allowance for decline in market value	800	17,200
Accounts receivable	$10,500	
Less: Allowance for doubtful accounts	525	9,975
		$33,259

Dr. Service Charge Expense	18	
Cr. Cash		18
To record bank charges.		
Dr. Interest Expense	90	
Dr. Loan Payable	210	
Cr. Cash		300
To record the loan payment.		
Dr. Unrealised Loss — Temporary Investments	800	
Cr. Allowance for Decline in Market Value		800
To record the decrease in market value of the temporary investments.		
Dr. Bad Debt Expense	525	
Cr. Allowance for Doubtful Accounts		525
Adjusting entry for uncollectible accounts.		

PURPLE MOUNTAIN COMPANY, LTD.
Revised Income Statement
For the Year Ending December 31

Sales		$88,000
Cost of sales		57,000
Gross profit		$31,000
Operating expenses	$17,500	
Service charge expense	18	
Interest expense	90	
Bad debt expense	525	
Unrealised loss — temporary investments	800	$18,933
Net income		$12,057
Earnings per share		$ 1.12

R7.1 Accounting for inventories.

a. Periodic inventory system:

	FIFO	LIFO	Weighted Average
Ending inventory	100@5.30 70@5.20	100@5.00 70@5.10	$\frac{2,580}{500 \text{ units}} = 5.16$
			170@5.16
	$ 894	$ 857	$ 877
Cost of goods sold (2,580 − Ending inventory)	$1,686	$1,723	$1,703

b. Perpetual inventory system:

FIFO — same as the periodic inventory system.

LIFO

Cost of goods sold — May 3
100 @ 5.10 = 510
50 @ 5.00 = 250 $ 760
Cost of goods sold — Sept 27
180 @ 5.20 =   936
Total cost of goods sold $1,696   Ending inventory   (2,580 − 1,696) = $884

Weighted Average

On May 3, the weighted average per unit is $1,010/200 units = $5.05
(100 @ 5.00 + 100 @ 5.10)
On September 27, the weighted average per unit is $1,292.50/250 units = $5.17
(100 @ 5.00 + 100 @ 5.10 − 150 @ 5.05 + 200 @ 5.20)
Cost of goods sold — May 3
150 @ 5.05 = 758 $ 758
Cost of goods sold — Sept 27
180 @ 5.16 =   931
Total cost of goods sold $1,689   Ending inventory   (2,580 − 1,689) = $891

c. Estimating inventories:

Sales	$2,900
Cost of sales (60%)	1,740
Gross profit (40%)	$1,160
Cost of goods available	$2,580
Cost of sales	1,740
Inventory (lost)	$ 840

d. Periodic inventory — weighted-average method: From part *a* it was determined the weighted-average cost per unit was $5.16. If the ending inventory is actually only 150 units and not 170 units as originally determined, the ending inventory would be overstated by $103.20 [(170 − 150 units) × 5.16].

If there are 20 fewer units in the ending inventory (170 − 150), using the periodic inventory method, there must have been an additional 20 units sold during the period. Therefore, sales would be understated by $180 (20 units × 9), cost of goods sold understated by $103.20 (20 units × 5.16), and gross profit understated by the difference of $76.80 (180 − 103.20).

e. Current costs: Using FIFO the ending inventory is:

100 units @ 5.30 = $530
70 units @ 5.20 =   364
$894

Using current costs

170 units @ 6.00 = $1,020

Holding gain on ending inventory is $126 ($1,020 − $894).

f. Product costs — weighted-average method:

Cost of goods available	$2,580
Transportation costs	500
	$3,080/500 units = $6.16 cost per unit
Cost of goods sold	330 units @ 6.16 = $2,033
Ending inventory	170 units @ 6.16 = $1,047

g.

	FIFO	LIFO	Weighted Average
Ending inventory	$894	$857	$877
N.R.V. (Market)	880	880	880
Lower of cost or market	$880	$857	$877

h.

	FIFO	LIFO	Weighted Average
Sales	$2,970	$2,970	$2,970
Cost of goods sold	1,686	1,723	1,703
Gross profit	$1,284	$1,247	$1,267
Gross profit percentage	43.2	42.0	42.7
Average days' inventory	193.5 [(365 × 894)/1,686]	181.5 [(365 × 857)/1,723]	188.0 [(365 × 877)/1,703]

R8.1 Accounting for capital assets.

a. $\dfrac{25{,}000 - 3{,}400}{5 \text{ years}} = \dfrac{21{,}600}{5} = 4{,}320/\text{year}$

Accumulated amortization: $3 \times 4{,}320 = 12{,}960$

b. Change in accounting estimate:

Original cost	$25,000
Accumulated amortization	(12,960)
Net book value	$12,040
Revised residual value	(2,040)
Cost to be allocated	$10,000
Revised remaining life (7 – 3 years)	4 years

$10,000/4 \text{ years} = \$2,500$

c.

1991: $1/5 \times 2 = 2/5 \times 25{,}000 = \$10{,}000$
1992: $2/5 \times 15{,}000 = \$6{,}000$

d.

Asset was sold for:	$18,000
Book value [25,000 – (2 × 4,320)]	16,360
Gain on disposal	$ 1,640

e. Amortization — units-of-production method:

$$\frac{\$25{,}000 - \$3{,}400}{100{,}000 \text{ km}} = \frac{\$21{,}600}{100{,}000 \text{ km}} = .216/\text{km} \times 17{,}000 \text{ km} = \$3{,}672$$

f.

Van (new) ($3,000 + $7,500)	10,500	
Accumulated Amortization	21,600	
Loss on Disposal	400	
Cash		7,500
Van (old)		25,000
To record the trade-in of the old van.		

R9.1 Accounting for bonds.

Present value of the principal (lump sum):	
$1,000,000 discounted @ 4.5% over 20 periods (Exhibit 9A.1)	$1,000,000 × .41464 = $ 414,640
Present value of the coupon interest payments (annuity):	
$50,000 discounted @ 4.5% over 20 periods (Exhibit 9A.2)	$50,000 × 13.00794 = $ 650,397
Cash proceeds	$1,065,037

Effective Interest Method Amortization Table

Date	Interest Expense Dr.	Cash Cr.	Bond Premium Dr.	Bond Premium Cr.	Net Book Value Cr.
Nov. 1/Year 1				$65,037	$1,065,037
May 1/Year 2	$47,927	$50,000	$2,073	62,964	1,062,964
Nov. 1/Year 2	47,833	50,000	2,167	60,797	1,060,797
May 1/Year 3	47,736	50,000	2,264	58,533	1,058,533

	Straight-Line Method		Effective Interest Method	
Nov. 1/Year 1 Dr. Cash	1,065,037		1,065,037	
Cr. Bond Premium		65,037		65,037
Cr. Bonds Payable		1,000,000		1,000,000
To record the issuing of the bonds at a premium.				

	Straight-Line Method		Effective Interest Method	
Dec. 31/Year 1 Dr. Interest Expense	15,583		15,976	
Cr. Interest Payable		16,667		16,667
Dr. Bond Premium	1,084		691	
To accrue 2 months' interest at year-end.				

	Straight-Line Method		Effective Interest Method	
May 1/Year 2 Dr. Interest Expense	31,165		31,951	
Dr. Interest Payable	16,667		16,667	
Cr. Cash		50,000		50,000
Dr. Bond Premium	2,168		1,382	
To record the semiannual interest payment.				

Balance Sheet — December 31, Year 1

	Straight-Line	Effective Interest
Long-term liabilities:		
Bond payable	$1,000,000	$1,000,000
Add: Bond premium	63,912	64,303
	$1,063,912	$1,064,303

R10.1 Leases, pensions, and deferred income taxes.

a.

Reported Income		$133,000
Permanent differences:		
Non-allowable expenses		6,000
Less: Dividends from		
Canadian corporations		(9,000)
Accounting income		$130,000 × .40 = $52,000 (income tax expense)
+/– Timing differences:		
Add back: amortization	$35,000	
Less: Capital cost allowance	(48,000)	
Accrued instalment sales	(27,000)	
Actual instalment sales	32,000	
Add back: warranty expense	19,000	
Less: actual warranty costs	(28,000)	(17,000) × .40 = $6,800 (deferred income taxes)
Taxable income		$113,000 × .40 = $45,200 (income tax payable)

The entry to accrue income taxes is:

Dr. Income Tax Expense	52,000	
Cr. Deferred Income Taxes		6,800
Cr. Income Taxes Payable		45,200
To record deferred income taxes.		

b. The financial statement disclosure on the December 31 financial statements is shown below:

Balance Sheet
December 31

Current liabilities:	
Income tax payable	$45,200
Long-term liabilities:	
Deferred income taxes	6,800

Partial Income Statement
For the Year Ended December 31

Net income — before taxes		$133,000
Less:		
Income taxes — current	$45,200	
Income taxes — deferred	6,800	52,000
Net income — after taxes		$ 52,150

The income tax payable to Revenue Canada, $45,200, is disclosed as a current liability. Deferred income taxes of $6,800 are included under long-term liabilities. On the income statement, income tax expense of $52,000 is allocated to current income taxes of $45,200 and deferred income taxes of $6,800.

c.

January 2, 1996:		
Dr. Leased Asset	19,920	
Cr. Lease Liability		19,920
To capitalize the lease asset and liability.		

The lessee amortizes the asset, using the straight-line method, with an estimated useful life of three years, and no residual value [($19,920 – 0)/3], the adjusting entry would be:

```
December 31, 1996:
Dr. Amortization Expense                        6,640
    Cr. Accumulated Amortization                          6,640
    To record amortization on the leased asset.
```

When the $8,000 lease payment is made, the following entry is made:

```
December 31, 1996:
Dr. Interest Expense                            1,992
Dr. Lease Liability                             6,008
    Cr. Cash                                              8,000
    To record the annual lease payment.
```

When the lease agreement is structured as an operating lease, the lessee will simply record the lease payment as rent expense each year:

```
December 31, 1996:
Dr. Rent Expense                                8,000
    Cr. Cash                                              8,000
    To record the rent expense on the operating lease.
```

No additional entries are required for operating leases. The only financial statement disclosure for the operating lease on the December 31, 1996, financial statements would be to show rent expense of $8,000 on the income statement. No disclosure is required on the balance sheet. A note would be included disclosing the future minimum lease payments.

The financial statement disclosure of the capital lease on the December 31, 1996, financial statements is shown below:

Balance Sheet
December 31, 1996

Current liabilities:		
Current portion of long-term liabilities		$6,609
Long-term liabilities:		
Lease obligation	$13,912	
Less: current portion	6,609	7,303

Income Statement
For the Year Ended December 31, 1996

Amortization expense	$6,640
Interest expense	1,992

*At December 31, 1996, the future minimum lease payments under capital leases (or operating leases) are:

1997	$8,000
1998	8,000

d. Note: Cavendish Resorts, Limited, maintains a defined-benefit pension plan. The actuarial present value of the accrued pension benefits attributed to services rendered up to December 31 was $422,000. The market value of assets in the pension fund at December 31 was $538,000.

R11.1 Accounting for equity.

a. Dr. Cash   90,000
    Cr. Common Shares   90,000
    To record the issuing of 15,000, non-par-value common shares for cash.

b. Dr. Organization Costs   10,000
    Cr. Common Shares   10,000
    To record the issuing of 2,000 non-par-value common shares.

c. Dr. Cash   60,000
    Cr. Preferred Shares   60,000
    To record the issuing of 5,000 non-par-value preferred shares for $12.

d. Dr. Dividends Declared (R.E.)   2,000
    Cr. Preferred Dividends Payable   2,000
    To record the declaration of the cash dividend ($.80 × ½ × 5,000).

e. Dr. Dividends Declared (R.E.)   8,500
    Cr. Common Dividends Payable   8,500
    To record the declaration of the cash dividend (.50 × 15,000 + 2,000).

f. Dr. Share Dividends Declared (R.E.)   10,200
    Cr. Common Shares Distributable   10,200
    To record the declaration of the 10% share dividend.

f. Dr. Common Shares Distributable   10,200
    Cr. Common Shares   10,200
    To record the issuing of 1,700, non-par-value common shares.

g. Dr. Income Summary   27,000
    Cr. Retained Earnings   27,000
    To record the closing entry to transfer net income to retained earnings.

h. Dr. Preferred Dividends Payable   2,000
    Dr. Common Dividends Payable   8,500
    Cr. Cash   10,500
    To record the cash payment of the dividends.

The equity transactions are summarized in a statement of retained earnings and a statement of shareholders' equity.

WHITE EAGLE CORPORATION, LTD.
Statement of Retained Earnings
For the Year Ended December 31

Retained earnings, January 1		$ 0
Add: net income		27,000
Less: Preferred dividends	$ 2,000	
Common share dividend	8,500	
Share dividend	10,200	$20,700
Retained earnings, December 31		$ 6,300

WHITE EAGLE CORPORATION, LTD.
Statement of Shareholders' Equity
December 31

Common shares, non-par value, authorized 50,000 shares, issued 18,700 shares.	$110,200
Preferred shares, 8%, non-par value, authorized 20,000 shares, issued 5,000 shares	60,000
Retained earnings	6,300
	$176,500

R12.1 Financial analysis and statement of changes in financial position. The liquidity position of Finale has weakened significantly during the year. The large decrease in cash during the period has produced a significant weakening of the firm's working capital position. Both the current and quick ratios confirm this change in liquidity.

	1996	**1995**
Liquidity Analysis:		
Cash on hand	$46,500	$80,000
Working capital	$111,500 ($172,500 − $61,000)	$128,500 ($173,500 − $45,000)
Quick ratio	1.96:1 ($119,500/$61,000)	2.83:1 ($127,500/$45,000)
Current ratio	2.83:1 ($172,500/$61,000)	3.86:1 ($173,500/$45,000)

The solvency position of Finale has shown very little change during the year. Both debt-to-equity ratios have decreased an insignificant amount during the period. The solvency position appears to be stable.

	1996	**1995**
Solvency Analysis:		
Total debt-to-equity ratio	1.24:1 ($217,000/$175,500)	1.25:1 ($198,500/$159,000)
Long-term debt-to-invested capital ratio	.47:1 [$156,000/($156,000 + $175,500)]	.49:1 [$153,500/($153,500 + $159,000)]

Finale, Limited, has had a profitable year. The profitability analysis cannot be properly completed, as comparative data for last year for Finale, Ltd., are not available. Comparative industry data would also be helpful to further analyze this ratio.

	1996	**1995**
Profitability Analysis:		
Earnings per share	$6.33 ($9,500/$1,500)	n.a.
Gross profit percentage	61.39% ($97,000/$158,000)	n.a.
Return on equity	5.41% ($9,500/$175,500)	n.a.

n.a. = Not available.

The analysis of the asset management of Finale indicates different results for each type of asset. The total asset turnover appears to be low for the period. Inventory turnover and the receivable turnover should be watched closely, as each of these items may be the cause of the firm's significant decrease in liquidity.

	1996	**1995**
Asset Management Analysis:		
Total asset turnover	.40 ($158,000/$392,500)	n.a.
Receivable turnover	2.55 [$158,000/($65,000 − $3,000)]	n.a.
Inventory turnover	1.22 ($61,000/$50,000)	n.a.

n.a. = Not available.

FINALE, LIMITED
Income Statement
For the Year Ending December 31

Gross sales			$163,000
Less: Sales discounts			5,000
Net sales			$158,000
Cost of goods sold:			
Beginning inventory		$ 45,000	
Purchases	$76,000		
Less: Purchase returns	10,000		
Net purchases		66,000	
Cost of goods available		$111,000	
Ending inventory		50,000	
Cost of goods sold			61,000
Gross profit			$ 97,000
Operating expenses:			
Interest expense		$ 2,000	
Pension expense		9,000	
Rent expense		24,000	
Salaries expense		13,500	
Sales commission expense		3,500	
Bad debt expense		1,000	
Loss on disposal		4,000	
Amortization expense		26,500	83,500
Income before taxes			$ 13,500
Income tax expense			4,000
Net income			$ 9,500

FINALE, LIMITED
Retained Earnings Statement
For the Year Ending December 31, 1996

Retained earnings — January 1	$47,000
Add: net income	9,500
Less: dividends	8,000
Retained earnings — December 31	$48,500

FINALE, LIMITED
Balance Sheet
As at December 31

	1996	1995
Assets		
Current assets:		
Cash	$ 46,500	$ 80,000
Temporary investments	11,000	13,000
Accounts receivable	65,000	37,000
Allowance for doubtful accounts	(3,000)	(2,500)
Inventory	50,000	45,000
Prepaid rent	3,000	1,000
Total current assets	$172,500	$173,500
Patents	$ 27,000	$ 30,000
Lease asset	40,000	40,000
Accumulated amortization	(12,000)	(8,000)
Capital assets	240,000	190,000
Accumulated amortization	(75,000)	(68,000)
Total capital assets	$220,000	$184,000
	$392,500	$357,500
Liabilities and Shareholders' Equity		
Current liabilities:		
Accounts payable	$ 42,000	$ 25,000
Commissions payable	2,000	3,000
Customer deposits	3,000	4,000
Deferred income taxes	2,000	3,000
Dividends payable	2,000	1,000
Income taxes payable	3,000	2,000
Current portion — long-term debt	7,000	7,000
Total current liabilities	$ 61,000	$ 45,000
Bank loan, due 1999	$ 30,000	$ 20,000
Notes payable, due 1999	5,000	10,000
Bond payable, due 2004	100,000	100,000
Bond discount	(4,000)	(4,500)
Capital lease liability	32,000	35,000
Less: current portion	(7,000)	(7,000)
Total long-term liabilities	$156,000	$153,500
Total liabilities	$217,000	$198,500
Shareholders' equity:		
Common shares	$ 90,000	$ 80,000
Preferred shares	40,000	32,000
Retained earnings	48,500	47,000
Treasury shares	(3,000)	—
Total shareholders' equity	$175,500	$159,000
	$392,500	$357,500

FINALE, LIMITED
Statement of Changes in Financial Position
For the Year Ending December 31

Operating activities:		
Net income	$ 9,500	
Non-cash items:		
Loss–disposal capital asset	4,000	
Bond discount amortization	500	
Amortization expense	26,500	
	$ 40,500	
Working capital items:		
Accounts receivable	(27,500)	
Prepaid expenses	(2,000)	
Accounts payable	17,000	
Temporary investments	2,000	
Commissions payable	(1,000)	
Customer deposits	(1,000)	
Deferred income taxes	(1,000)	
Dividends payable	1,000	
Income taxes payable	1,000	
Inventory	(5,000)	
Cash provided from operations		$ 24,000
Investing activities:		
Sale of capital asset	$ 11,000	
Purchase of capital assets	(77,500)	
Cash used in investing		(66,500)
Financing activities:		
Issued common shares	$ 10,000	
Issued preferred shares	8,000	
Bank loan	10,000	
Note payable	(5,000)	
Lease liability	(3,000)	
Treasury shares	(3,000)	
Declared dividends	(8,000)	
Cash provided from financing		9,000
Decrease in cash		$(33,500)
Cash — January 1		80,000
Cash — December 31		$ 46,500

GLOSSARY

Accounting has been described as the language used to communicate financial information about organizations. Similar to other languages, accounting follows certain conventions and concepts. Users of financial statements must understand the language of accounting to better appreciate the story conveyed by an organization's financial statements. This glossary provides an alphabetical listing or vocabulary of the key terms and concepts used in the language of accounting.

Accelerated amortization A cost allocation method in which amortization deductions are largest in an asset's earlier years, but decrease over time.

Account (T-account) An accounting information file usually associated with the general ledger.

Accounting A language to communicate the financial status of an organization to interested parties.

Accounting cycle The process of analyzing a transaction, then journalizing it, followed by posting it to the ledger accounts, and then preparing a trial balance, any necessary adjusting entries, financial statements, and closing entries.

Accounting equation Assets = Liabilities + Equity. An equation depicting the balance sheet or statement of financial position.

Accounting period The time period, usually a quarter or one year, to which accounting reports are related.

Accounting policies The specific accounting principles and practices adopted by a company to report its financial results.

Accounting Standards Board, established by the CICA, is responsible for the development of accounting standards in Canada.

Accounts payable (trade payable) Amounts owed to suppliers for merchandise purchased on credit but not yet paid for; normally classified as a current liability.

Accounts receivable (trade receivable) Amounts due to a company from customers who purchased goods or services on credit; payment is normally expected in 30, 60, or 90 days.

Accounts receivable turnover ratio A measure of the effectiveness of receivable management calculated as net credit sales for the period divided by the average balance in Accounts Receivable.

Accrual basis of accounting An accounting measurement system that records the financial effects of transactions when a business transaction occurs without regard to the timing of the cash effects of the transaction.

Accruals Accruals relate to adherence to the accrual basis of accounting. An accrued expense is an expense that has been incurred, but has not been paid for, and has not been recorded. An accrued revenue is revenue that has been earned, but no payment has been received and no entry has been recorded to recognize the revenue. Accruals also impact assets and liabilities.

Accrued actuarial pension benefits The present value of all pension benefits earned by employees as of a particular date. It must reflect the expected mortality, future wage levels, and other assumptions related to the employees.

Accrued expense An expense that has been incurred, but the cash payment has not been made for the goods or services received.

Accrued revenue Revenue that has been earned, but cash has not been collected for the goods and services provided.

Accumulated amortization A contra asset account deducted from the acquisition cost of property, plant, and equipment that represents the portion of the original cost of an asset that has been allocated to prior accounting periods.

Acquisition cost All costs incurred in bringing an asset to its intended, usable condition.

Active investment An intercorporate investment by an investor company that allows the investor to exercise influence or control over the operations of the investee company.

Adjusted trial balance A listing of the account balances from the general ledger after the adjusting entries have been recorded. The trial balance is prepared to verify that the sum of the accounts with debit balances equals the sum of the accounts with credit balances.

Adjusting entries Journal entries recorded to update or correct the accounts in the general ledger.

Administrative expense A general operating expense, such as amortization on a company's headquarters building, associated with the overall management of the company; a period expense.

Aged trial balance An extension of the subsidiary ledger that provides information on the age of each customer's account. An aged trial balance is normally divided into 30-day time periods.

Aging method A method of accounting for uncollectible accounts receivable in which an estimate of the bad debts expense is determined by classifying the specific receivable balances into age categories and then applying probability estimates of non-collection.

Allocation concept An accounting concept that permits the financial effects of business transactions to be assigned to or spread over multiple accounting periods.

Allocations Pertain to the apportionment of revenues and expenses to different accounting periods. Frequently, economic activities overlap more than one accounting period. Allocations are necessary to distribute the appropriate amount of revenue or expense to the correct accounting period. Allocations also impact on asset and liability values at the end of the accounting period in question.

Allowance for Market Decline in Temporary Investments A contra asset account deducted from the cost basis of temporary investments; represents the unrealized decline in a portfolio of securities resulting from the application of the lower-of-cost-or-market method.

Allowance for Doubtful Accounts (Allowance for Bad Debts) A contra asset account deducted from accounts or notes receivable; represents the portion of the outstanding receivables balance whose collection is doubtful.

Amortization A systematic allocation process that allocates the acquisition cost of a long-lived asset over the estimated productive life of the asset.

Annual report The report prepared by a company at year-end for its shareholders and other interested parties. It frequently includes a letter to the shareholders from the chairperson of the board, management's discussion and analysis of financial performance, and a variety of financial highlights in addition to the basic financial statements. It also includes the auditor's report in which the independent accountants express an opinion as to the fairness of the financial data presented in the financial statements.

Annuity A payment, or a receipt, occurring every period for a set number of periods (e.g., interest expense or interest income on a debt instrument).

Antidilutive security A security that, if converted or assumed to be converted into common shares, causes the level of earnings per share to increase.

Appropriations Appropriations of retained earnings are created when management wants to indicate to the users of the financial statements that a portion of retained earnings is not available for distribution for dividends or other purposes, but has been appropriated or restricted for a specific purpose. Appropriations are used frequently by non-profit organizations, as much of their funding is designated for specific purposes.

Asset management The effective utilization of a company's revenue-producing assets; a measure of management's ability to effectively utilize a company's assets to produce income.

Assets Tangible and intangible resources of an enterprise that are expected to provide it future economic benefits.

Asset's useful life The time period that is estimated for the asset to be used by the organization.

Audit A process of investigating the adequacy of a company's system of internal controls, the company's consistent use of generally accepted accounting principles, and the presence of material errors or mistakes in the company's accounting data.

Auditor's report A report to a company's shareholders and the board of directors issued by an independent auditor summarizing his or her findings with regard to the company's financial statements. The four types of opinions that may be issued are clean or unqualified, qualified, adverse, and disclaimer.

Authorized shares The total number of capital shares that are authorised to be sold under a company's charter of incorporation.

Average cost method An inventory cost-flow method that assigns the average cost of available finished goods to units sold and, thus, to cost of goods sold.

Average days'-inventory-on-hand ratio A measure of the effectiveness of inventory management calculated as 365 days divided by the inventory turnover ratio; a measure of the appropriateness of current inventory levels given current sales volume.

Average receivable collection period A measure of the effectiveness of accounts receivable management calculated by dividing the receivable turnover ratio into 365 days.

Bad debt An account receivable considered to be uncollectible.

Bad debt expense An estimate (under the allowance method) of the dollar amount of accounts receivable that will eventually prove to be uncollectible; the actual bad debts that are written off if the direct write-off method is used.

Balance The difference between the total left-hand (debit) entries and the total right-hand (credit) entries made in an account.

Balance sheet (statement of financial position) An accounting statement describing, as of a specific date, the assets, liabilities, and shareholders' equity of an enterprise.

Balance sheet equation The balance sheet or accounting equation may be used to conceptually record economic activities for any organization, large or small, profit or non-profit. The accounting equation is the basis of double entry accounting. The balance sheet equation states Assets = Liabilities + Equity.

Bank reconciliation A bank reconciliation compares the accounting for cash recorded by the bank to the accounting for cash recorded by the company. The purpose of the bank reconciliation is to help ensure no errors have been recorded by the company or the bank in the accounting for cash. As well, the bank reconciliation is necessary to determine the correct cash balance for financial reporting purposes at the end of the accounting period.

Basic earnings per share A standardized measure of performance calculated as net income applicable to common shares (i.e., net income minus preferred dividends) divided by the weighted-average number of common shares outstanding plus common share equivalents.

Betterment An expenditure that extends the useful life or productive capability of an asset and that is capitalized to the balance sheet as an asset.

Board of directors A group of individuals elected by a company's shareholders to oversee the overall management of the company (i.e., a board of advisers for the company's managers).

Bond (debenture) An interest-bearing obligation issued by a company to various creditors, usually in amounts of $1,000 or $5,000, and payable at some future maturity date.

Bond discount The amount by which the net proceeds of a bond issue are less than the amount of the principal that must be repaid at maturity date. The amount of the bond discount must be amortized over the life of the bond, thereby making the bond's effective rate of interest greater than its coupon rate of interest.

Bond indenture The document in which the details associated with a bond issue are specified.

Bond payable A financial instrument sold in the capital markets, carrying a specified rate of interest (coupon rate) and a specified repayment date (maturity date); usually classified as a long-term liability.

Bond premium The amount by which the net proceeds of a bond issue exceed the amount of the bond principal that must be repaid at maturity date. The amount of the bond premium that must be amortized over the life of the bond, thereby making its effective rate of interest less than its coupon rate of interest.

Bonding Bonding is really the same as insurance except it pertains to safeguarding the organization against losses due to theft or fraud committed by its employees. Should an employee steal from their employer, the organization would be reimbursed for any losses caused by the bonded employee.

Book value (per share) The dollar amount of the net assets of a company on a per common share basis; calculated as: (total assets minus total liabilities) divided by the number of outstanding shares of class A common stock.

Book value (of an asset) The original cost of an asset less any accumulated amortization (depletion or amortization) taken to date; also known as *carrying value*.

Book value method A method of accounting for convertible bonds. The book value method removes the bond issue at its book value and charges the book value to the common share account. By using the book value method, no residual value is created, and no gain or loss is recognized.

Business combination When one or more businesses are brought together into one accounting entity but not necessarily into one legal entity.

Callable debt Bonds or other obligations that may be legally retired before maturity at the discretion of the debtor company.

Canada Business Corporations Act Corporations exist as a result of a charter granted by a government agency. Many organizations are incorporated federally under the Canada Business Corporations Act. Organizations may also be incorporated under provincial legislation.

Capital Another term for *equity*; also used to mean the total assets of an organization.

Capital assets Capital assets are long-lived assets necessary to conduct an organization's basic operations. Capital assets include property, plant, and equipment; intangible properties; and natural resources.

Capital cost allowance amortization for income tax purposes. Capital cost allowance is similar to the declining-balance method of amortization.

Capital expenditure An expenditure for the purchase of a non-current asset, usually property, plant, or equipment.

Capitalization The process of assigning value to a balance sheet account, for example, a capitalized asset (a leased asset) or a capitalized liability (a lease liability).

Capitalization (of a company) The composition of a company's long-term financing, specifically, shareholders' equity and long-term debt.

Capital lease A non-cancellable lease obligation accounted for as an asset and liability on the balance sheet; a lease agreement in which the risks and rewards of asset ownership are passed (either formally or informally) to the lessee.

Cash A current asset account representing the amount of money on hand or in the bank.

Cash basis of accounting An accounting measurement system that records the financial effects of business transactions when the underlying event has a cash effect.

Cash discount An amount, usually 2 percent of the gross purchase price, that a buyer may deduct from the final price of an asset if cash is remitted within the discount period, usually 10 days of purchase.

Cash equivalents Bank deposits, usually in the form of certificates of deposit, whose withdrawal may be restricted but whose maturity is expected in the current accounting period.

Cash flow from operations A measure of the net cash flows from transactions involving sales of goods or services and the acquisition of inputs used to provide the goods or services sold; the excess of cash receipts over cash disbursements relating to the operations of a company for a given period; net income calculated on a cash basis.

Cash management The management of cash involves two functions: the efficient management of any excess cash and proper cash planning to avoid cash shortages.

Cash proceeds The amount at which the bonds are sold. The amount of the cash proceeds depends on the effective rate of interest at the date of issue. The cash proceeds may be an amount greater than or less than the face value of the bonds, creating a bond premium or discount.

Change in accounting estimate An amortization-related change often made by financial managers involving the estimated useful life of an asset or a group of assets. This type of change involves a change in the estimate rather than in the method and is dealt with on a prospective, or future, basis.

Change in accounting policy A change in accounting policy may be made "if it is considered that the change would result in a more appropriate presentation of events or transactions in the financial statements of the enterprise" (CICA Handbook 1506.02). When a company implements an accounting policy change, the current period's income statement is prepared using that new policy as if it had been adopted on the first day of the period. A change in accounting policy should be applied retroactively, with the statements for prior periods presented, restated for purposes of comparability.

Chartered accountant An accountant who has passed the Uniform Final Examination prepared by the Canadian Institute of Chartered Accountants and who has met prescribed practical experience requirements of the institute.

Charter of incorporation A legal document creating a corporate entity; specifies (among other things) the number and type of shares that the corporate entity can sell.

Chart of accounts A list of the general ledger accounts used by an enterprise in its accounting system.

CICA Handbook The CICA Handbook provides recommendations for the accounting of specific financial statement items. The process by which accounting recommendations are added to the CICA Handbook is a function of the standard-setting process. The Handbook is not a static document, as each year sees revisions and additions of accounting policies and procedures.

Class B common shares A form of common shares that usually carries a lower voting power and lower dividend return than Class A common shares.

Classified balance sheet A balance sheet that delineates the assets and liabilities as current and non-current.

Closing entries Accounting data entries prepared at the end of an accounting period designed to close or set equal to zero the temporary accounts.

Collateral The value of various assets used as security for various debts, usually bank borrowings, that will be transferred to a creditor if the obligation is not fully paid.

Commitment A type of contingent liability in which the value of the future obligation is known but that is not currently an obligation because various future events or conditions have not transpired or are currently satisfied.

Common shares A form of share capital that usually carries the right to vote on corporate issues.

Common-size financial statements Financial statements in which all amounts are expressed as a percentage of some base financial statement item. For example, a common-size balance sheet might express all asset accounts as a percentage of total assets and all equity accounts as a percentage of total equities.

Comparability "A characteristic of the relationship between two pieces of information rather than of a particular piece of information by itself. It enables users to identify similarities in and differences between information provided by two sets of financial statements. Comparability is important when comparing the financial statements of two different entities and when comparing the financial statements of the same entity over two periods or at two different points in time" (CICA Handbook 1000.22).

Completed contract A revenue recognition method in which project or contract revenues are unrecognized until the project or contract is substantially completed.

Completion-of-production method If upon completion of production the revenue recognition criteria have been met, it is appropriate to recognize revenue at that time. The prime criteria would be reasonable assurance that the product can be sold, at a determinable price, and that an identifiable seller exists.

Compound interest A method of calculating interest by which interest is figured on both the principal of a loan and any interest previously earned but not distributed.

Conservatism principle An accounting concept that stipulates that when there is a choice between two approaches to record an economic event, the one that produces the least favourable yet realistic effect on net income or assets should be adopted.

Consignment Inventory placed with a retailer for sale to a final consumer but not sold to the retailer; title to the inventory is retained by the manufacturer until a final sale occurs.

Consistency principle An accounting concept underlying the preparation of financial statements that stipulates that an enterprise should, when possible, use the same set of GAAP from one accounting period to the next.

Consolidated corporate group Business combinations created when one corporation gains control over another corporation. Business combinations allow organizations to diversify and expand their operations.

Consolidated financial statements Financial statements prepared to reflect the operations and financial condition of a parent company and its wholly or majority-owned subsidiaries.

Consolidated reporting A reporting approach in which the financial statements of the parent and subsidiary companies are combined to form one set of financial statements.

Contingencies Existing situations involving uncertainty as to a possible gain or loss that will be resolved when one or more future events occur or fail to occur.

Contingent asset An asset that may arise in the future if certain events occur.

Contingent liability A liability that may arise in the future if certain events occur.

Contra account (contra asset, contra liability) An account that is subtracted from a related account, for example, Accumulated Amortization is subtracted from the Building or Equipment account; other examples include the Allowance for Doubtful Accounts, the Bond Discount account.

Contributed capital (contributed surplus) The sum of the Share Capital accounts and the Capital in Excess of Par (or stated) Value accounts. Also called *paid-in capital*.

Contributory pension plans Plans to which employees may be required to make contributions, in addition to the contributions made by the employer.

Control account A general ledger account is referred to as the *control account* when its balance must equal the total of all the accounts in a related subsidiary ledger (e.g., Accounts Receivable).

Conversion The exchange of convertible bonds or convertible preferred shares for a predetermined quantity of common shares.

Conversion ratio The exchange ratio used to determine the number of common shares that will be issued on conversion of a convertible bond or a convertible preferred share.

Convertible debt (bond) An obligation or debt security exchangeable, or convertible, into the common shares of a company at a prespecified conversion (or exchange) rate.

Convertible preferred shares A preferred share that is exchangeable or convertible into the common shares of a company at a prespecified conversion (or exchange) rate.

Copyrights Legal rights of protection given to the creators of published materials. Copyright law extends protection for the life of the creator plus 50 years, or if the copyright is held by a corporation (deemed to have an indeterminate life), 75 years from the date of first publication.

Corporation A business enterprise owned by one or more owners, called *shareholders,* that has a legal identity separate and distinct from that of its owners.

Cost The total acquisition value of an asset; the value of resources given up to acquire an asset.

Cost/benefit The concept of cost/benefit states "the benefits expected to arise from providing information in the financial statements should exceed the cost of doing so. The nature and amount of benefits and costs is substantially a judgement process" (CICA Handbook 1000.16).

Cost of goods manufactured The total cost of goods manufactured in an accounting period; the sum of all product costs (e.g., direct materials, direct labour, and manufacturing overhead).

Cost of goods sold The value assigned to inventory units actually sold in a given accounting period.

Cost recovery method The cost recovery method is only used for high-risk transactions in which the realization of any profit is highly speculative. Under this method, all costs incurred must be recovered before any profit is recognized.

Coupon interest rate (face rate) The rate of interest stated on the face of a debt instrument.

Credit An entry on the right side of an account; credits increase liability, shareholders' equity, and revenue accounts but decrease asset and expense accounts.

Credit terms Terms offered to encourage customers to pay their accounts on time (e.g., 2/10, net/30).

Creditor An individual or company that loans cash or other assets to another person or company.

Cumulative preferred shares A preferred share in which any unpaid prior dividends accumulate year to year (called *dividends in arrears*) and must be paid in full before any current period dividends may be paid to either preferred or common shareholders.

Current asset Those resources of an enterprise, such as cash, inventory, or prepaid expenses, whose consumption or use is expected to occur within the current operating cycle.

Current cost An inventory valuation method that records inventory at its most recent cost.

Current liability An obligation of an enterprise whose settlement requires the use of current assets or the creation of other current liabilities and occurs within one year.

Current maturity of long-term debt That portion of a long-term obligation that is payable within the next operating cycle or one year.

Current rate method A method of restating foreign financial statements using the current exchange rate.

Current ratio A measure of liquidity and short-term solvency calculated as current assets divided by current liabilities.

Date of declaration The calendar date on which the payment of a cash or share dividend is officially declared by a company's board of directors.

Date of payment The calendar date on which a cash or share dividend is actually paid or distributed.

Date of record The calendar date on which a shareholder must own a company's shares to be entitled to receive a declared dividend.

Debenture A general obligation bond of a company.

Debit An entry on the left side of an account; debits increase asset and expense accounts but decrease liability, shareholders' equity, and revenue accounts.

Declining-balance method A method to amortize the cost of a tangible asset in which the allocated cost is greater in the early periods of the asset's life (i.e., an accelerated method).

Default risk The probability (or risk) that a company will be unable to meet its short-term or long-term obligations.

Deferral A postponement in the recognition of an expense (e.g., Prepaid Insurance) or a revenue (e.g., Unearned Rent) account.

Deferred charge An asset that represents an expenditure whose related expense will not be recognized in the income statement until a future period. Prepaid rent is an example.

Deferred income taxes The portion of a company's income tax expense not currently payable, and that is postponed because of differences in the accounting policies adopted for financial statement purposes versus those policies used for tax reporting purposes.

Deferred revenue Revenue received as cash but not yet earned.

Deficit An accumulated loss in the Retained Earnings account; a debit balance in Retained Earnings.

Defined-benefit plan A pension plan in which an employer promises to pay certain levels of future benefits to employees on their retirement from the company.

Defined-contribution plan A pension plan in which an employer promises to make periodic payments to the plan on behalf of its employees.

Demand deposit A bank account that may be drawn against on demand.

Depletion A term used to refer to the amortization or cost allocation of natural resources.

Depreciation A term used to refer to the amortization or cost allocation of capital assets.

Development costs Costs that can be traced to an identifiable marketable product should be capitalized as an inventory-type item (i.e., one held for sale), and amortized over a reasonable period not to exceed 40 years. Only when an economically viable product is reasonably assured, should development costs be capitalized and amortized to future periods.

Direct-financing-type lease A capital lease in which the lessor receives income only from financing the "purchase" of the leased asset.

Direct method A method of preparing the statement of changes in financial position whereby the changes in the Cash account resulting from the operating transactions, from the beginning to the end of the period, are analyzed.

Direct write-off method A method of accounting for uncollectible accounts receivable in which no bad debt expense is recorded until specific receivables prove to be uncollectible.

Disclosure principle The disclosure principle states financial statements must disclose all of the relevant information about the economic affairs of the entity. The objective of the disclosure principle is to provide users of financial statements sufficient information to make rational investment and credit decisions. Disclosure also implies providing understandable, comparable, timely information. Disclosure often requires the use of notes, schedules, and other supplementary presentations.

Discontinued operations "Discounted operations are the operations of a business segment that has been sold, abandoned, shut down or otherwise disposed of, or that is subject to a formal plan of disposal'' (CICA Handbook 3475.02). Discontinued operations are when a company decides to divest itself of a division, a subsidiary, or other business segment (so long as it is a separate, major line of business).

Discount A reduction in the price paid for a security or a debt instrument below the security's face value.

Discount rate The rate of interest used to discount a future cash flow stream when calculating its present value.

Discounted cash flows The present value of a future stream of cash flows.

Discounting receivables The process of selling accounts or notes receivables to a bank or other financial company at a discount from the maturity value of the account or note.

Dividend A distribution of the earned income of an enterprise to its owners.

Dividend payout A measure of the percentage of net income (or cash flows from operations) paid out to shareholders as dividends; calculated as cash dividends divided by net income (or cash dividends divided by the cash flow from operations).

Dividend policy The dividend policy of a corporation is dependent on its financial strength, its financial objectives, and the type of investors it wishes to attract. Some investors are not interested in receiving a flow of dividend payments, but are more interested in seeing the corporation grow and the market value of their share investments increase, while other investors rely on a steady stream of cash dividends from the corporations as a source of income.

Dividends in arrears The dividends on a cumulative preferred shares that have been neither declared nor paid. Dividends are not a legal liability of a company until declared.

Dividend yield A measure of the level of cash actually distributed to common shareholders calculated as the cash dividend per common share divided by the market price per common share.

Donated capital The increase in shareholders' equity resulting from a donation of an asset to a company.

Double-declining-balance amortization A method of calculating amortization by which a percentage equal to twice the straight-line per-

centage is multiplied by the declining book value to determine the amortization expense for the period. Salvage value is ignored when calculating it.

Double-entry system An accounting record-keeping system that records all financial transactions in the accounting system using (at least) two data entries.

Double taxation The taxation of income at the company level plus the taxation of dividends declared and paid to investors from the company earnings.

Doubtful account An account receivable thought to be uncollectible.

Early retirement The process of prepaying, or retiring, outstanding debt before its stated maturity.

Earned surplus Synonymous with *retained earnings*.

Earnings Income or profit.

Earnings per share A standardized measure of performance calculated as net income divided by the weighted-average number of common shares outstanding during an accounting period.

Economic income The excess or additional resources of an enterprise resulting from its primary business activity and measured relative to the beginning level of resources.

Effective interest method A method to amortize a discount or a premium on a debt instrument based on the time value of money.

Effective interest rate The real rate of interest paid (or earned) on a debt instrument.

Efficient market hypothesis A theory to explain the functioning of capital markets in which share and bond prices always reflect all publicly available information, and any new information is quickly impounded in security prices.

Emerging Issues Committee An affiliate organization of the CICA whose purpose is to address new accounting and reporting issues before divergent practice can become widely adopted.

Entity concept An accounting convention that views a corporate enterprise as separate and distinct from its owners; thus, the financial statements of the corporation describe only the financial condition of the enterprise itself, not that of its shareholders.

Equity A claim against the assets of a company by the owners.

Equity in earnings of investee An income statement account representing an investor company's percentage ownership of an investee's (or subsidiary's) net earnings.

Equity method A method to value intercorporate equity investments by adjusting the investor's cost basis for the percentage ownership in the investee's earnings (or losses) and for any dividends paid by the investee.

Estimated warranty liability To match expenses with related revenues and avoid overstating income at the time of sale, the expected warranty costs associated with each sale are estimated. The warranty expense is recorded and offset with an entry to an estimated warranty liability account.

Excess of revenues over expenses Non-profit organizations commonly use the terminology excess of revenues over expenses in lieu of net income.

Ex-dividend A condition of share capital if sold (or purchased) after the date of record; that is, the purchaser of an ex-dividend share is not entitled to receive the most recently declared dividend.

Expenditure An outflow of cash, usually representing the acquisition of an asset or the incurring of an expense.

Expense An outflow of assets, an increase in liabilities, or both, from transactions involving an enterprise's principal business activity (e.g., sales of products or services).

External reporting Financial reporting to shareholders and others outside an enterprise.

Extraordinary item A loss or gain that is both unusual in nature and infrequent in occurrence.

Face amount (maturity value) The value of a security as stated on the instrument itself.

Factor A financial corporation, bank, or other financial institution that buys accounts and notes receivables from companies; receivables may be purchased with or without recourse.

Factoring A process by which a company can convert its receivables into cash by selling them at face value less a service charge for processing the transaction and for the time value of money.

Factory overhead Manufacturing overhead. For inventory valuation purposes, it is allocated to units of production by some type of rational systematic method.

Fair value basis Fair value basis may be the replacement cost, net realizable value, or present value. The fair value or market value basis of measurement is subjective. For many assets the determination of a market value may be very difficult. Therefore, the use of fair values occurs infrequently.

Federal income tax The tax levied by the federal government on corporate and individual earnings.

Financial accounting The accounting rules and conventions used in preparing external accounting reports.

Financial Accounting Standards Board (FASB) An independent, private-sector organization responsible for establishing generally accepted accounting principles in the United States..

Financial reporting system The financial reporting system sorts all of the transactions and judgments into similar or related groupings and then aggregates that input so that the summarized financial statements can be prepared.

Financial statements The basic accounting reports issued by a company, including the balance sheet, the income statement, and the statement of cash changes in financial position.

Financial strength The organization's ability to meet its financial obligations.

Financing activities The activities of funding the organization by issuing long-term debt or other non-current liabilities or equity funding received from the owners of the organization.

Finished goods Inventory having completed the manufacturing process and ready for sale.

Finished goods inventory Fully assembled or manufactured goods available for sale and classified as a current asset on the balance sheet.

First-in, first-out (FIFO) An inventory cost-flow method that assigns the first cost value in finished goods inventory to the first unit sold and thus to cost of goods sold.

Fiscal year Any continuous 12-month period, usually beginning after a natural business peak.

Fixed assets A subcategory of non-current assets, usually represented by property, plant, and equipment. The terminology often used in practice for capital assets.

FOB Free-on-board, some location. Examples are FOB shipping point and FOB destination. The location denotes the point at which title passes from the seller to the buyer.

Footnotes Written information by management designed to supplement the numerical data presented in a company's financial statement.

Foreign Currency Translation Adjustment A shareholders' equity account measuring the change in value of a company's net assets held in a foreign country, attributable to changes in the exchange rate of a foreign currency as compared to the Canadian dollar.

Foreign exchange risk The risk associated with changes in exchange rates between the Canadian dollar and foreign currencies when a company maintains operations in a foreign country.

Franchises The rights granted by one company to another to use a specific designation in their business; use can be limited in term by contract or be renewable indefinitely to create essentially an indeterminate life. If a franchise is renewable indefinitely, it should be amortized over a period not to exceed 40 years.

Freight-in Freight costs associated with the purchase and receipt of inventory.

Freight-out Freight costs associated with the sale and delivery of inventory.

Full cost method Under the full cost method, all costs associated with the exploration for and development of natural resources are capitalized to the natural resource accounts on the balance sheet. Under the full cost method, the costs of unsuccessful exploration activities are also capitalized to the balance sheet under the philosophy that the development of new resource reserves is a speculative activity involving some inherent failure.

Fully diluted earnings per share A standardized measure of performance calculated as net income applicable to common shares divided by the weighted-average number of common shares outstanding plus common share equivalents and any other potentially dilutive securities.

Functional currency The currency of the primary business environment (i.e., country) of a company's operations.

Future-oriented financial information Projected or forecasted financial statements.

Gain An increase in asset values, usually involving a sale (realized) or revaluation (unrealized), unrelated to the principal revenue-producing activity of a business.

General journal An accounting data file containing a chronological listing of financial transactions affecting an enterprise.

General ledger An accounting data file containing aggregate account information for all accounts listed in an enterprise's chart of accounts.

Generally accepted accounting principles (GAAP) Those methods identified by authoritative bodies as being acceptable for use in the preparation of external accounting reports.

Generally accepted auditing standards (GAAS) Those auditing practices and procedures established by the CICA that are used to evaluate a company's accounting system and financial results.

Going-concern concept An accounting concept underlying the preparation of financial statements that assumes that the enterprise will continue its operations for the foreseeable future.

Goodwill An intangible asset representing the excess of the purchase price of acquired net assets over their fair market value.

Government bodies Municipal, provincial, and federal governments, including all their related subunits and departments.

Graphics in financial reporting Many organizations make use of graphics in their annual report. Graphics may be very helpful in explaining trends or changes in the direction of various financial statement elements. No GAAP exist for the presentation and disclosure of financial information in graphical format.

Gross margin method A common method of estimating inventories. This method can produce good estimates if reliable gross profit margins are available.

Gross profit (gross margin) A measure of a company's profit on sales calculated as net sales minus the cost of goods or services sold.

Gross profit margin ratio (gross profit percentage) A measure of profitability that assesses the percentage of each sales dollar recognized as gross profit (i.e., after deducting the cost of goods sold) and available to cover other operating expenses (e.g., selling, administrative, interest, and taxes).

Gross purchase method The gross method records all purchases at their gross amount. No discounts are recognized until a payment is made on account. The gross method identifies only discounts received and ignores any discounts that have been missed or lost.

Historical cost concept An accounting concept that stipulates that all economic transactions should be recorded using the dollar value incurred at the time of the transaction.

Holding company (parent company) A company that owns a majority of the voting share capital of another company.

Horizontal analysis When comparative balance sheets or income statements are presented side by side, the statements can be made more meaningful if the dollar amount of increase or decrease and the percentage change is shown. This type of analysis is known as *horizontal analysis* because the data comparisons are made on a horizontal plane from left to right.

Income A generic term that may be used to indicate revenue from miscellaneous sources (e.g., interest income or rent income) or the excess of revenue over expenses for product sales or services.

Income from continuing operations The results of a company's operations are frequently broken down into recurring and non-recurring categories. Recurring (or continuing) results are those that can reasonably be expected to reoccur in future periods and are usually included in income from continuing operations.

Income summary A temporary account used to transfer the net income or loss of an enterprise from the income statement to the Retained Earnings account on the balance sheet.

Income statement An accounting statement describing the revenues earned and expenses incurred by an enterprise for a given period.

Independent auditor A professionally trained individual whose responsibilities include the objective review of a company's financial statements prepared for external distribution.

Indirect method A method of preparing the statement of changes in financial position whereby net income determined on the accrual basis of accounting is converted to the cash basis, to determine the cash provided/used in operating activities.

Industry practices The concept of industry practices states selective exceptions to general accounting principles and practices may be made in the financial statements of specialized industries,

assuming such departure from GAAP provides more useful, meaningful information to the users.

Inflation A phenomenon of generally rising prices.

Insolvent (bankrupt) A condition in which a company is unable to pay its current obligations as they come due.

Instalment sales method A method of recognizing revenue that parallels the receipt of cash. In situations where uncertainty exists as to the collectibility of the proceeds of the transactions, revenue recognition is deferred until the proceeds are collected.

Instalment sale A credit sale in which the buyer agrees to make periodic payments, or instalments, on the amount owed.

Insurance A fundamental means of safeguarding the assets of the organization and a basic principle of internal control. With insurance coverage, any losses will be minimized or possibly totally recovered depending on the specifications of the insurance policy.

Intangible assets Those resources of an enterprise, such as goodwill, trademarks, or tradenames, that lack an identifiable physical presence.

Intercompany profit The profit resulting when one related company sells to another related company; intercompany profits are removed from the financial statements when consolidated financial statements are prepared.

Intercorporate investments Investments in the shares and bonds of one company by another.

Interest expense The cost of borrowing funds.

Interim financial statements Financial statements prepared on a monthly or quarterly basis; usually unaudited.

Internal control The policies and procedures implemented by management to safeguard a company's assets and its accounting system against misapplication or misuse.

Internal control system The internal control system assures that all transactions and all necessary judgments have been recognized and that they are classified and correctly described in the accounting records.

International Accounting Standards Committee (IASC) An association of professional accounting bodies formed in 1973 to develop and issue international accounting and reporting standards.

Interperiod tax allocation The process of allocating the actual taxes paid by a company over the periods in which the taxes are recognized for accounting purposes.

Inventory The aggregate cost of salable goods and merchandise available to meet customer sales.

Inventory turnover ratio A measure of the effectiveness of inventory management calculated as the cost of goods sold for a period divided by the average inventory held during that period.

Investing activities The activities of acquiring long-lived, non-current assets such as property, plant, and equipment.

Investment tax credit A reduction in the current income taxes payable earned through the purchase of various applicable assets.

Investor company A company that holds an equity investment in another company (the investee company).

Issued shares The number of authorized shares of share capital sold to shareholders less any shares repurchased and retired.

Journal A chronological record of events and transactions affecting the accounts of a company recorded by means of debits and credits; a financial diary of a company.

Journal entry A data entry into a company's journal system.

Journalizing The process of recording data in the journal system of a company by means of debits and credits. The recording of the financial information from the source documents to a journal.

Last-in, first-out (LIFO) An inventory cost-flow method that assigns the last cost value in finished goods inventory to the first unit sold and thus to cost of goods sold.

Lease An agreement to buy or rent an asset.

Leasehold improvement Expenditures made by a lessee to improve or change a leased asset.

Lessee An individual or company who leases an asset.

Lessor The maker of a lease agreement; an individual or company who leases an asset to another individual or company.

Leverage The extent to which a company's long-term capital structure includes debt financing; a measure of a company's dependency on debt. A company with large quantities of debt is said to be highly leveraged.

Liabilities The dollar value of an enterprise's obligations to repay monies loaned to it, to pay for goods or services received by it, or to fulfil commitments made by it.

Limited liability The concept that shareholders in a corporation are not held personally liable for its losses and debts.

Limited partnership A partnership composed of at least one general partner and at least one limited partner, in which the general partner(s) assumes responsibility for all debts and losses of the partnership.

Line of credit An agreement with a bank by which an organization obtains authorization for short-term borrowings up to a specified amount.

Liquid assets Those current assets, such as cash, cash equivalents, or short-term investments, that either are in cash form or can be readily converted to cash.

Liquidating dividend A cash dividend representing a return of invested capital and, hence, a liquidation of a previous investment.

Liquidation The process of selling off the assets of a business, paying any outstanding debts, and then distributing any remaining cash to the owners.

Liquidity The short-term debt repayment ability of a company; a measure of a company's cash position relative to currently maturing obligations.

Long-term debt (long-term liabilities) The obligations of a company payable after more than one year.

Long-term debt-to-invested capital ratio A ratio that measures the relative composition of a company's long-term capital structure. *Invested capital* refers to the total of long-term debt and shareholders' equity. The ratio measures the portion of total capital provided by long-term debt. The long-term debt-to-invested capital ratio compares long-term debt to invested capital.

Long-term investments Investments in other companies' shares or bonds that will be held for longer than 12 months. In most cases the purpose of the long-term investment is to gain a degree of control over another entity.

Loss The excess of expenses over revenues for a single transaction. Losses are decreases in equity/net assets from peripheral or incidental transactions.

Lower of cost or market A method to value inventories and temporary investments; the lower of an asset's cost basis or current market value is used to value the asset account for balance sheet purposes.

Machine-hour method A method to amortize the cost of a machine or other equipment based on its actual usage.

Maintenance expenditure An expenditure to maintain the original productive capacity of an asset; deducted as an expense.

Management performance Management performance involves profitability and asset management. *Profitability* refers to a company's overall income-generating ability, and *asset management effectiveness* refers to the ability of a company's managers to utilize its assets effectively to produce a return for the company's creditors and owners.

Management's discussion and analysis The management's discussion and analysis section of the annual report includes an overview of the company's operations and financial position for the most recent accounting period. Any special or unusual circumstances or events that may have impacted the financial statements are described. Comments on general economic conditions and the impact on the organization may be discussed.

Managerial accounting The accounting rules and conventions used in the preparation of internal accounting reports.

Manufacturing overhead The factory-related costs indirectly associated with the manufacture or production of a good; for example, the costs of production-line supervision, maintenance of the production equipment, and amortization of the factory building.

Market price The current fair value of an asset as established by an arms'-length transaction between a buyer and a seller.

Market value method A method of accounting for convertible bonds. The market value method records the common shares at their market value and any difference between the market value and the book value of the bonds is treated as a gain or loss on conversion of the bonds.

Marketable securities Temporary investments in the shares or bonds of other corporations.

Matching principle An accounting concept that stipulates that when revenues are reported, the expenses incurred to generate those revenues should be reported in the same accounting period.

Materiality principle An accounting concept underlying the preparation of financial statements; stipulates that only those transactions that might influence the decisions of a reasonable person should be disclosed in detail in the financial statements; all other information may be presented in summary format.

Maturity date The principal repayment date for a bond or debenture, specified as part of the indenture agreement.

Maturity value (face amount) The amount of cash required to satisfy an obligation at the date of its maturity.

Merger A combination of one or more companies into a single corporate entity.

Minority interest (noncontrolling interest) The percentage ownership in the net assets of a subsidiary held by investors other than the parent company.

Monetary assets Resources of an enterprise, such as cash and marketable securities, whose principal characteristic is monetary denomination.

Mortgage An agreement in which a lender (the mortgagee) agrees to loan money to a borrower (the mortgagor) to be repaid over a specified period of time and at a specified rate of interest.

Mortgage bond A bond secured or collateralized by a company's non-current assets, usually its property, plant, and equipment.

Multiple-step income statement A classified income statement. Multiple-step income statements are used by smaller organizations, and also by many organizations for internal reporting purposes. A multiple-step income statement provides more detailed information, in particular with reference to the sales and cost of goods sold section of the income statement. As well, operating expenses may be subdivided into additional subcategories.

Natural resources Non-current, non-renewable resources such as oil and gas, coal, ore, and uranium.

Negative goodwill The excess of the net book value of an acquired company over the consideration paid for it.

Negotiable instruments Receivables, payables, or securities that can be bought and sold (i.e., negotiated) between companies.

Net assets Total assets minus total liabilities; equal total shareholders' equity.

Net book value The total cost of an asset less the accumulated amortization.

Net current assets Current assets minus current liabilities; working capital.

Net income (net earnings) The difference between the aggregate revenues and aggregate expenses of an enterprise for a given accounting period; when aggregate expenses exceed aggregate revenues, the term *net loss* is used.

Net income before extraordinary items When extraordinary items are reported on the income statement, an intermediate subtotal designated net income before extraordinary items is disclosed.

Net income from discontinued operations All of the final period's sales and expenses related to discontinued operations should be netted together and reported in a single line on the income statement with the designation net income from discontinued operations.

Net loss A net loss is incurred when aggregate expenses exceed aggregate revenues.

Net purchase method The net method records merchandise purchases net of any purchase discounts. The net method assumes accounts will be paid within the discount period and all discounts will be received. The net method is generally considered the superior method from an internal control perspective because it highlights any discounts that are lost.

Net realizable value The amount of funds expected to be received upon the sale or liquidation of an asset.

Net sales Total sales less sales returns and allowances and sales discounts.

Net worth (of an enterprise) Total assets minus total liabilities, or the value of shareholders' equity; also known as the *book value* of an enterprise.

Non-classified balance sheet A balance sheet in which the assets and liabilities are not classified as current or non-current; in non-classified balance sheets, assets and liabilities are considered to be non-current.

Non-contributory pension plans Plans where the employer makes all the payments on the employees' behalf.

Non-current assets The long-lived resources of an enterprise, such as property, plant, and equipment, whose consumption or use is not expected to be completed within the current operating cycle.

Non-current liability An obligation of an enterprise whose settlement is not expected within one year.

Non-monetary assets Those resources of an enterprise, such as inventory or equipment, whose principal characteristic is other than its monetary denomination or value.

Non-par value The Canada Business Corporations Act requires corporations to issue only non-par-value shares. It is generally thought the use of par values may be misleading to the users of financial statements.

Non-profit organizations Organizations as small as a church group, to the very large government units like the federal government of Canada. To simplify the classification, non-profits may be broken down into two broad groups: government bodies and other non-profits.

Normal balance An account's normal balance is its positive or increase side of the debit/credit, accounting equation rule. Therefore, assets have normal balances of debits, and liabilities normal balances of credits. Equity and revenue accounts would normally have a credit balance and expenses a debit balance.

Notes payable An obligation to repay money or other assets in the future evidenced by a signed contractual agreement or note.

Notes receivable Amounts due a company from customers who purchased goods or services on credit; the obligation is evidenced by a legal document called a *note*.

Notes to financial statements Explanations and supporting schedules to which the financial statements are cross-referenced. The notes are an integral part of such statements.

Off-balance-sheet financing The type of financing arrangement used when a company has use of the asset without having to purchase it. The company does not disclose the asset or related liability on its financial statements.

Operating activities The day-to-day functions of the organization, of earning revenue and incurring expenses. Once an organization is established, it may commence operating activities.

Operating cycle The average length of time between the investment in inventory and the subsequent collection of cash from the sale of that inventory.

Operating expenses Expenses incurred in carrying out the operations of a business, for example, selling expenses.

Operating lease A lease agreement in which the risks and rewards of asset ownership are retained by the lessor; accounted for as rent expense by the lessee.

Operational risk The probability that unforeseen or unexpected events will occur and consequently reduce or impair the revenue, earnings, and cash flow streams of a company.

Organization costs The expenditures associated with starting a new business venture, including legal fees and incorporation fees; frequently accounted for as an intangible asset of a company.

Outstanding cheque A cheque that has been recorded in the accounting records, but not yet received or recorded by the bank.

Outstanding deposit A deposit that has been recorded in the accounting records, but not yet received or recorded by the bank.

Outstanding shares The number of authorized shares of capital that have been sold to shareholders and are currently in the possession of shareholders; the number of issued shares less the shares held in treasury.

Paid-In-Capital in Excess of Par Value (Contributed Capital in Excess of Par Value) A shareholders' equity account reflecting the proceeds from the sale of share capital in excess of the par value (or stated value) of the share capital.

Participating preferred shares Preferred shares that entitle shareholders to share in any "excess dividend payments" (i.e., after the common shareholders have received a fair dividend return).

Partnership A business enterprise jointly owned by two or more persons.

Par value A legal value assigned to a share of capital that must be considered in recording the proceeds received from the sale of the shares. See also *stated value*.

Passive investment An intercorporate investment in which the investor cannot (or does not) attempt to influence the operations of the investee company.

Past service cost The cost of committed pension benefits earned by employees for periods of work prior to the adoption of a formal pension plan.

Patents Exclusive legal rights to products registered with the Patent Office; they recognize the holder's right to use, manufacture, dispose of, and control in every way the patented product or process without hindrance from others. Patents have a legal life of 17 years, but their economic life may be much shorter because of technological obsolescence.

Pension A retirement plan for employees that will provide income to the employee upon retirement.

Pension expense The cost of expected pension benefits, adjusted for various estimates, including the present value, must be recognized as pension expense in the current accounting period, even though the pension benefits may not be paid to employees for several years.

Pension fund assets The term *pension fund assets at fair value* refers to the market value of the investment portfolio held by the pension trustee as of the balance sheet date.

Percentage of completion A revenue recognition method in which total project or contract revenues are allocated between several accounting periods on the basis of the actual work completed in those periods.

Percentage-of-credit sales method A method of accounting for uncollectible accounts receivable in which an estimate of the bad debts expense is recorded each period on the basis of the credit sales for the period.

Period cost Costs, such as administrative and selling expenses, associated with the accounting period in which they were incurred.

Periodic concept The periodic concept assumes users need financial information for decision-making purposes on a periodic basis. The periodic concept requires the accruing of revenues and expenses and the allocating of costs to the appropriate time periods. Many organizations select the calendar year as their time period for financial reporting. Other annual periods may be equally acceptable. Most organizations also prepare quarterly or monthly financial statements.

Periodic inventory system An inventory record-keeping system that determines the quantity of inventory on hand by a physical count.

Permanent accounts Those accounts, principally the balance sheet accounts, that are not closed at the end of an accounting period and that carry accounting information forward from one period to the next.

Permanent difference A difference in reported income or expenses between a company's tax return and its financial statements that will never reverse (that is, permanent).

Perpetual inventory system An inventory record-keeping system that continuously (or perpetually) updates the quantity of inventory on hand on the basis of units purchased, manufactured, and sold.

Petty cash fund A fund used for small cash expenditures. It is used for infrequent small expenditures to avoid the process of issuing a cheque for immaterial items.

Physical life The length of time an asset can reasonably be expected to last before it physically wears out.

Pledging When assets are used as collateral for a bank loan, the assets are said to have been pledged.

Point-of-sale method The most commonly used revenue recognition method. At the point of sale, goods or services are rendered in exchange for cash or a promise to pay (receivable). The risk of ownership is transferred to the buyer and the proceeds from the sale are earned by the seller.

Pooling of interests A consolidation method that combines the financial results of a parent company and its subsidiary on the basis of existing book values.

Postclosing trial balance A listing of the account balances from the general ledger after the accounts have been closed. The trial balance is prepared to verify that the sum of the accounts with debit balances equals the sum of the accounts with credit balances.

Posting An accounting process involving the transfer of financial data from the general journal to the general ledger.

Postretirement benefits Benefits including medical and dental insurance coverage, or employee discounts on merchandise purchases. Employees earn these benefits during their working years, but receive the benefits upon retirement.

Preferred shares A (usually) non-voting form of share capital whose claims to the dividends and assets of a company precede those of common shareholders.

Premium An amount paid in excess of the face value of a security or debt instrument.

Prepaid expenses A current asset that represents prior expenditures and whose consumption is expected to occur in the next accounting period.

Present value The value today of a future stream of cash flows calculated by discounting the cash flows at a given rate of interest.

Price-level-adjusted financial statements Financial statements in which the account balances have been restated to reflect changes in price levels due to inflation.

Prime rate The interest rate charged by banks on borrowings by preferred customers.

Principal The remaining balance of an outstanding obligation to be paid in the future.

Prior period adjustment An accounting event or transaction that does not affect the current period's earnings but instead is reflected as an adjustment to Retained Earnings.

Product cost A cost directly related to the production of a good or service, for example, the cost of goods sold.

Professional judgment An accountant's judgment as to the most appropriate alternative accounting approach to solve financial reporting issues.

Profit The excess of revenues over expenses for a single transaction.

Profitability The relative success of a company's operations; a measure of the extent to which accomplishment exceeded effort.

Pro forma (financial statement) A forecasted or projected financial statement for a future accounting period.

Promissory note A written promise to pay a specific sum of money at a specific date; a liability.

Property, plant, and equipment The non-current assets of a company, principally used in the revenue-producing operations of the enterprise.

Proprietorship A business enterprise owned by one person.

Prospectus A document describing the nature of a business and its recent financial history, usually prepared in conjunction with an offer to sell share capital or bonds by a company.

Proxy A legal document granting another person or company the right to vote for a shareholder on matters involving a shareholder vote.

Purchase accounting A consolidation method in which the financial results of a parent company and its subsidiary are combined using the fair market value of the subsidiary's net worth.

Purchase discount A cash discount (usually 2 percent) given to a buyer if the buyer pays for the purchases within the discount period (usually 10 days after purchase).

Purchase Discounts Lost An expense account representing the finance or interest costs incurred as a consequence of not paying for goods purchased on credit on a timely basis (e.g., 2/10, net 30).

Purchase Returns An account to be deducted from purchases to determine the net cost of merchandise purchases. When merchandise is returned to the supplier that was previously recorded as purchases, the amount of the return is recorded in the Purchase Returns account.

Purchases Goods or inventory acquired for sale or manufacture.

Qualified opinion An opinion issued by an independent auditor indicating that the financial statements of a company are fairly presented on a consistent basis and use generally accepted accounting principles, but for which some concern or exception has been noted.

Qualitative characteristics Characteristics that define and describe the attributes of information provided in financial statements that make that information useful to users. The four principal qualitative characteristics are understandability, relevance, reliability, and comparability.

Quick assets Highly liquid, short-term assets such as cash, cash equivalents, short-term investments, and receivables.

Quick ratio (acid test ratio) A measure of liquidity and short-term solvency calculated as quick assets divided by current liabilities.

Ratio A financial indicator (e.g., the current ratio) formed by comparing two account balances (e.g., current assets and current liabilities).

Ratio analysis A common financial statement analysis technique that compares financial statement elements on a ratio basis (e.g., return on equity this year compared to last year).

Raw material inventory Materials and purchased parts awaiting assembly or manufacture; classified as a current asset on the balance sheet.

Realized loss (gain) A loss (gain) that is recognized in the financial statements, usually due to the sale of an asset.

Recognition concept An accounting concept that stipulates that revenues should not be recorded in the accounting records until earned and that expenses should not be recorded until incurred.

Redeemable (callable) preferred shares Preferred shares that may be retired (i.e., redeemed or called) at the discretion of the issuing company, usually after a specified date and usually at a premium above the stated (or par) value of the preferred shares.

Redemption The retirement of preferred shares or bonds before a specified maturity date.

Registrar An independent agent, normally a bank or a trust company, that maintains a record of the number of shares of capital of a company that have been issued and to whom.

Relevance concept An accounting concept used to select which accounting information should be presented in a company's financial statements.

Reliability concept An accounting concept that stipulates that accounting information, and, hence, accounting reports, must be reliable to be useful to financial statement users.

Reorganization (quasi-reorganization) A process of changing the ownership structure of a company, usually as a direct result of a deficit in Retained Earnings.

Replacement cost The cost to reproduce or repurchase a given asset (e.g., a unit of inventory).

Research costs Generally, research costs are expensed as incurred, because capitalizing research expenditures seldom achieves the matching of revenues and expenses desired. Research costs should be charged as an expense of the period in which they are incurred.

Residual value The amount that is expected to be recovered when an asset is retired, removed from active use, and sold. The expected value of the asset at the end of its estimated useful life.

Responsibility The assigning of responsibility is a basic element of a sound internal control system. It is important all employees clearly understand what tasks they are and are not responsible for.

Retail method A method of estimating inventories used frequently in retail stores. The retail method requires the organization to price its inventory at retail and then convert to the cost price using a cost-to-retail percentage.

Retained earnings Those earnings of an enterprise that have been retained in the enterprise (i.e., have not been paid out as dividends) for future corporate use.

Retained earnings — appropriated The amount of total retained earnings that has been allocated for specific corporate objectives, such as the redemption of debt or capital shares.

Retained earnings — restricted The amount of total retained earnings that is legally restricted from being paid out as dividends to shareholders; the restriction usually results from a borrowing agreement with a bank or other financial institution.

Return on equity (ROE) A measure of profitability; a measure of the relative effectiveness of a company in using the assets provided by the owners to generate net income; calculated as net income divided by equity.

Revenue bond A bond secured or collateralized by a revenue stream from a particular group of assets.

Revenues The inflow of assets, the reduction in liabilities, or both, from transactions involving an enterprise's principal business activity (e.g., sales of products or services).

Sale A legal term suggesting that the title to an asset has passed from a seller to a buyer. Most sales transactions qualify as revenue.

Sale/leaseback An accounting transaction in which an asset is first sold and then immediately leased back by the selling entity; a financing transaction.

Sales discounts Discounts given for prompt payment of an account. (See *credit terms*.) Sales Discounts is a contra sales account to be deducted from Sales to determine net sales.

Sales Returns A contra sales account to be deducted from Sales to determine net sales. When customers return merchandise that was previously recorded as a sale, the amount of the return is recorded in a Sales Returns account.

Sales-type lease A capital lease that generates two income streams: (1) from the "sale" of the asset and (2) from financing the "purchase" of the asset.

Salvage value The amount that is expected to be recovered from the sale of an asset at the end of its total life.

Securities and Exchange Commission (SEC) A U.S. government agency responsible for the oversight of the U.S. securities markets; this agency also specifies the form and content of all financial reports by companies issuing securities to the public.

Selling expense Expense incurred directly as a consequence of selling and delivering a product to customers.

Separation of duties A basic concept of internal control. The basic premise is that the individual who has custody of an asset must be different from the person who is responsible for accounting for the asset. The purpose of this procedure is to avoid assigning complete responsibility for an activity to one person.

Share capital A certificate representing an ownership interest in an enterprise. See also *common shares* and *preferred shares*.

Share certificate A legal document evidencing the purchase of share capital in a company.

Share dividend A distribution of additional shares of capital to a company's shareholders.

Shareholders' equity The shareholders' equity of a corporation; comprises paid-in capital and retained earnings.

Share option A right issued by a company to its employees entitling employees to buy a set quantity of capital shares in the future at a prespecified price.

Share split An increase (a forward split) or a decrease (a reverse split) in the number of shares issued by a company; equivalent to a large share dividend.

Share warrant A certificate issued by a company that carries the right or privilege to buy a set quantity of share capital in the future at a prespecified price.

Single-step income statement An income statement commonly found in published annual reports. With a single-step statement, cost of goods sold and all the expenses are combined and deducted from revenues. Gross profit on sales is often not disclosed, as cost of goods sold and other expenses are combined as a single line item.

Sinking fund A trust account established in conjunction with the issuance of bonds into which funds are paid periodically to be used to retire the debt at maturity; an asset account.

Solvency The long-term debt repayment ability of a company.

Source document Any document used to record financial information related to the economic activities of the organization.

Special journal An accounting data file containing a chronological listing of special financial transactions (e.g., cash purchases or cash receipts) affecting an enterprise.

Specific identification An inventory cost-flow method that assigns the actual cost of producing a specific unit to that unit; the only inventory method that matches exactly the cost flow and physical flow.

Stakeholder Any party that has an interest in the financial operations of the organization.

Standard cost An inventory valuation method that uses estimated or projected costs of producing a product rather than actual costs.

Stated value The recorded accounting value of share capital. See also *par value.*

Statement of changes in financial position An accounting statement describing the sources and uses of cash flows for an enterprise for a given period. The statement discloses the impact on cash as a result of all three activities: investing, financing, and operating.

Statement of retained earnings An accounting statement describing the beginning and ending balances in Retained Earnings and the major changes to the Retained Earnings account (e.g., dividends and net income).

Statement of shareholders' equity An accounting statement describing the principal transactions affecting the owners' (or shareholders') interests in an enterprise for a given period.

Stewardship The management and supervision of enterprise resources.

Straight-line method A method to amortize the cost of a capital asset in which the cost allocation is constant over the life of the asset. A method of amortizing bond discounts/premiums.

Subsidiary An investee company in which an investor company (the parent) holds an equity investment in excess of 50 percent of the voting shares.

Subsidiary ledger An accounting data file containing detailed account information to supplement or explain the aggregate account balance contained in the general ledger.

Successful efforts method Under the successful efforts method, only the costs associated with successful exploration and development activity are capitalized to the balance sheet accounts. The costs of any unsuccessful activity are expensed against net income.

Sum-of-the-years'-digits method A method to amortize the cost of a tangible asset in which the allocated cost is greater in the early periods of the asset's life (i.e., an accelerated method).

Tangible asset Those resources of an enterprise, such as property, plant, and equipment, that possess physical characteristics or have a physical presence.

Technological life The length of time an asset can reasonably be expected to generate economic benefits before it becomes obsolete.

Temporary accounts Those accounts that are closed at the end of each accounting period, for example, the income statement accounts, dividends, and the income and loss summary.

Temporary investments Short-term investments in the shares or bonds of other corporations.

Time-series analysis The analysis of financial statement data over multiple periods.

Time value of money Because money can always be invested at a bank to earn interest for the period it is on deposit, money is said to have a "time value."

Timing differences Differences in the timing of the reporting of certain revenues and expenses for tax purposes and for external financial reporting purposes that will reverse out in some future period.

Total asset turnover ratio A measure of an organization's utilization of available resources to generate revenues. This ratio examines a company's utilization of its revenue-producing assets.

Total debt-to-equity ratio A measure of the extent to which a company's assets are financed by creditors as compared to the amount financed by owners. This ratio provides a measure of the extent to which an organization relies on borrowed funds to finance its operations. The total debt-to-equity ratio compares total liabilities to total shareholders' equity.

Trademarks Registered claims of ownership to names, symbols, slogans, or other devices providing distinctive identity of a product. Although they have no legally limited life, trademarks often have limited economic life. If an estimate of the economic life can be made, it should be used as the term for amortization of the asset. If no estimate of economic life can be made, the asset should be amortized over a period not to exceed 40 years.

Transaction concept A concept underlying the preparation of financial statements that requires the source of all accounting information be economic transactions affecting an enterprise and its resources.

Transfer agent An independent agent, usually a bank or a trust company, that maintains a record of, and executes all, share transfers and sales, as well as the payment of dividends on those shares.

Translation exposure A source of foreign exchange risk resulting from the restatement of foreign financial statements denominated in a foreign currency into Canadian dollar equivalents; also known as *accounting exposure.*

Treasury shares Outstanding share capital that has been repurchased but not retired and is usually held to be reissued at some future date.

Trend analysis The analysis of ratios or absolute account balances over one or more accounting periods to identify the direction or trend of a company's financial health.

Trial balance A listing of the account balances from the general ledger designed to verify that the sum of the accounts with debit balances equals the sum of the accounts with credit balances.

Uncollectible account An account receivable that a company expects not to be able to collect.

Understandability A concept that assumes information provided in financial statements must be capable of being understood by users. "For the information provided in the financial statements to be useful, it must be capable of being understood by users. Users are assumed to have a reasonable understanding of business and economic activity and accounting, together with a willing-

ness to study the information with reasonable diligence" (CICA Handbook 1000.19).

Underwriter A brokerage house or investment banker hired by a company to help sell a bond or share offering.

Unearned revenue (deferred income) Revenue that is received as cash but that has not yet been earned. Unearned revenue is a current liability; it is shown at the amount received less whatever has been taken into income (earned) to date. Since the service has not been rendered, a liability to provide the service later is recognized.

Unit of measure In Canada the unit of measure is the Canadian dollar. Therefore, the economic activities of the organization are presented on the financial reports in Canadian dollars.

Unit-of-production method A method to amortize the cost of a tangible asset or to deplete the cost of a natural resource; the allocated cost is based on the actual production by the asset.

Unrealized loss (gain) A loss (gain) that is recognized in the financial statements but is not associated with an asset sale; usually involves a revaluation of an asset value.

Unqualified opinion An auditor's positive opinion that the financial statements do present fairly the company's financial condition and results of operations in accordance with generally accepted accounting principles.

Useful life The estimated productive life of a non-current asset. "Useful life is the estimate of either the period over which a capital asset, or component thereof, is expected to be used by an enterprise; or the number of production or similar units that can be obtained from the capital asset by the enterprise" (CICA Handbook 3060.17).

Valuation allowance A contra account used to record the market decline in temporary investments.

Vendor A company selling goods or services.

Vertical analysis In vertical analysis, three financial statement numbers — total assets, total equities, and net sales — are converted to a base of 100 percent. Each item within the assets and equities on the balance sheet, or each item on the income statement, is then expressed as a percentage of the base number.

Vested benefits Pension benefits owed to employees at retirement regardless of whether they continue to be employed by the company until they reach retirement age.

Warrant A legal document enabling the holder to buy a set number of shares at a prespecified price within a set period of time.

Warranty obligation An obligation for future costs to maintain a product sold in good working condition.

Wasting assets Non-current assets, such as natural resources, that decrease in value as a result of depletion or consumption of the asset.

Weighted-average cost method An inventory cost-flow method that assigns the average cost of available finished goods, weighted by the number of units available at each price, to a unit sold and thus cost of goods sold, and to ending inventory.

Withdrawals The distribution of resources to the owners of a proprietorship or partnership. Dividends and withdrawals are the exact opposite of capital contributed by owners.

With (without) recourse Terms of the sale of an account or note receivable. A sale with recourse obligates the selling company to "make good" the receivable in the event that the factor is unable to collect on the receivable; a sale without recourse obligates the factor to assume all liability for non-collectibility.

Work in process inventory Partially completed goods or products; classified as a current asset on the balance sheet.

Working capital A measure of liquidity calculated as total current assets minus total current liabilities.

INDEX

J.T.